OUTLOOK 2000
IN A NUTSHELL

A Power User's Quick Reference

OUTLOOK 2000
IN A NUTSHELL

A Power User's Quick Reference

Tom Syroid & Bo Leuf

O'REILLY®

Beijing • Cambridge • Farnham • Köln • Paris • Sebastopol • Taipei • Tokyo

Outlook 2000 in a Nutshell
by Tom Syroid and Bo Leuf

Copyright © 2000 O'Reilly & Associates, Inc. All rights reserved.
Printed in the United States of America.

Published by O'Reilly & Associates, Inc., 101 Morris Street, Sebastopol, CA 95472.

Editor: Troy Mott

Production Editor: Colleen Gorman

Cover Designer: Hanna Dyer

Printing History:

    May 2000:   First Edition.

Library of Congress Cataloging-in-Publication Data

Syroid, Tom
    Outlook 2000 in a nutshell : a power user's quick reference/Tom Syroid and Bo
      Leuf.--1st ed. p. cm.
    ISBN 1-56592-704-4
    1. Microsoft Outlook 2. Time management--Computer programs. 3. Personal
      information management--Computer programs. I. Leuf, Bo. II. Title.

HD69.T54 S97 2000
005.369--dc21   00-038510

ISBN: 1-56592-704-4
[M]

Table of Contents

■ **Part 3: Beyond the Basics**

■ Part 4: Appendixes

Preface

Outlook is a big, complex program. We knew this at the onset of this project, and we were reminded time and time again as we scratched and prodded its underbelly looking for answers. What surprised us, however, was the passionate love/hate relationship Outlook engenders in users. They love it and they hate it. They love it enough to use it every day, and hate it enough to break into more than the occasion tirade when asked about the product. After ten months of exhaustive exploration and living with Outlook for twenty hours a day, we can relate.

Outlook has more than its share of quirks and nuances. Option dialogs reside in the strangest places. Configuration settings for one component quietly affect another. The program's engineers appear to have taken great delight in using multiple naming conventions for identical objects. (Quickly now, what's the difference between a Personal Store, a Store, an Information Store, and a Personal Folders file?)

Outlook has a steep learning curve. The good news is that as you progress along this curve, you'll discover what a powerful and flexible program it is (sometimes too flexible—but flexible nonetheless). As you read through the pages to follow, you will quickly find that Outlook can adapt to almost any style or task you throw at it, sometimes with elegance, and sometimes with a kludge or two. There is not much you cannot do with Outlook given a little patience (well, OK, sometimes a lot of patience) and a healthy dose of ingenuity.

Most users don't even begin to tap into Outlook's full potential. One of the biggest reasons for this is the lack of clear, accurate documentation on how to use its many features and components. Outlook's Help files are woefully inadequate for all but the most basic questions—and even then, the answers Clippit serves up often have no relevance whatsoever. Many of the books already written on Outlook tell you where to find something, but not why you might want to use it. We have done our very best to address these shortcomings in a tone and style that makes learning enjoyable.

The definitive guide to Outlook has yet to be written, and probably never will. The program is just too multifaceted to exhaustively cover in any one place. What we've tried to compile is an accurate and useful reference to Outlook's major components. The end result is 600 pages of densely packed, "need-to-know" material, rather than a 1500 page tome. If you want fluff, this is not the place to look.

In the immortal words of our editor, "Get in, tell it like it is, and get out." Amen, Troy.

Organization of This Book

Outlook 2000 in a Nutshell is structured in three parts.

Part 1, *The Big Picture*

The Big Picture is an overview of the tools and features of Outlook. Here we show the reader how program elements work in concert with Outlook's other components.

Chapter 1, *Outlook "in a Nutshell"*, is a quick reference to the fundamental "how-tos" of Outlook. It's organized around a Task List, which functions as a topical map of both this book and the program itself. Use this map as a guide to what Outlook can do, and where to find it in subsequent chapters. You'll want to put a bookmark at the beginning of this chapter.

Chapter 2, *Installing Outlook*, gets you up and running with Outlook. It starts at the beginning of the installation process and walks you carefully through every junction along the way. Outlook is not hard to install, but the choices you make at setup determine a great deal of the program's behavior down the road.

Chapter 3, *Program Insights*, is the seminal chapter of this book. It's organized around the building blocks of Outlook: information stores, address books, forms, views, categories, printing, and search tools. Understanding these building blocks is a prerequisite to unlocking Outlook's hidden potentials.

Chapter 4, *Outlook's Navigation Tools*, looks at Outlook's menus and toolbars—how they're arranged, how they work, and how to customize them.

Chapter 5, *Mail Editors*, is an in-depth look at the options available for creating and editing mail messages. Many of these options can be orchestrated directly from the mail editor. A message format can be selected; addresses can be resolved using the information contained in the Contacts folder; contacts can be associated with the message; flags can be set and categories assigned. In addition, most of these features can be set as a default action and overridden on a per-message basis.

Part 2, *Menu Reference*

Menu Reference is the core of the book. The chapters are organized by menu commands, with each section detailing a different topic. Each topic goes beyond what a command does—it tells you *why* you might want to use.

Chapter 6, *Mail*, details the menu commands used to create, reply to, and send email.

Chapter 7, *Calendar*, details the menu commands used to create and track Outlook's three distinct types of calendar entries: appointments, meetings, and events.

Chapter 8, *Contacts*, details the menus used to create and manage contact records for the businesses and people you associate with every day.

Chapter 9, *Tasks*, details the menu commands used to create, organize, and delegate your task list.

Chapter 10, *Notes*, details the menu commands used to create, edit, and manage your electronic sticky-notes.

Chapter 11, *Journal*, details the menu commands used to create and maintain Journal entries.

Part 3, *Beyond the Basics*

In *Beyond the Basics*, we bring all the various pieces and components discussed in previous chapters together and show you how to use Outlook with external programs and/or data sources. It's also where you'll find topics that did not fit neatly anywhere else.

Chapter 12, *Import and Export*, looks at ways to get data in and out of Outlook. Topics include supported import and export filters and how to use them effectively and safely without damaging your existing files.

Chapter 13, *File Management*, is a compilation of need-to-knows for managing your data, backing up Outlook, using multiple data stores, and working with the Folder List.

Chapter 14, *Collaborating with Outlook*, details how to configure and use Net Folders to share your data with others, and covers Free/Busy as a way of addressing the quandary of scheduling meetings with a group of people.

Chapter 15, *Security and Encryption*, provides an overview on encryption and cryptography, digital certificates, and configuring Outlook to send and receive secure mail.

Chapter 16, *Outlook and the Palm*, shows you how to set up and configure the software necessary to synchronize Outlook with a Palm handheld organizer.

Chapter 17, *Outlook and Exchange*, looks at some of the features unique to Outlook when the program is used as a client to Exchange. If you want to know how to set-up and configure Public Folders or Out of Office Rules, this is where to turn.

Chapter 18, *Working with VBA*, is a primer on how use VBA to leverage Outlook's interface and data structures.

Part 4, *Appendixes*

This section includes supplemental reference information and several quick-reference lists.

Appendix A, *Keyboard Shortcuts*, is a comprehensive reference to Outlook's keyboard shortcuts, arranged by component and task.

Appendix B, *Registry Keys*, provides an inventory of the common Registry keys used by Outlook, their paths, and what they do.

Appendix C, *Command-Line Switches*, details various ways to start Outlook from the command line, as well as several options to either reset a program default or rebuild a configuration file.

Appendix D, *Tip Reference*, is a complete list of all the tips included in the book.

On the Horizon

At the time this book went to production, several new developments relating to Outlook were either just released, or were within days of release.

Fax in Windows 2000

This year marks the release of Windows 2000. Windows 2000 passes two milestones. First, it marks the end of Windows Messaging as an operating-system component. Windows 95, Windows 98 (if you know where to look), and Windows NT 4.0 all included Windows Messaging as a way of connecting not just to Internet mail servers, but also to Microsoft Mail and other in-house servers. In Windows 2000, though, you see the completion of the migration to Internet mail.

For most users, the passing of Windows Messaging is just a blip. Much more exciting is the second milestone: the return of a supported fax service to Windows. The Microsoft Fax component included in Windows 95 has been without significant updates for years. It is substantially upgraded and included with Windows 2000 under the moniker "Outlook Express Fax."

If the Windows 2000 setup detects a fax modem, it automatically installs Outlook Express Fax, configured from the Fax icon in the Control Panel and Start → Programs → Accessories → Communications → Fax. Outlook Express Fax can deliver faxes to your Outlook Inbox if you're using Outlook in Corporate/Workgroup mode. The MSKB (Microsoft Knowledge Base) article at *http://support.microsoft.com/ support/kb/articles/q246/1/51.asp* provides details.

Microsoft Office SR-1

Just days prior to this book going into production, Microsoft posted a long-awaited Office 2000 Service Release (SR-1) to their website. We did not have time to thoroughly test the patch, but at the time of this writing, we urge caution in its deployment. While numerous well-documented bugs in Office 2000 programs have been addressed with SR-1, unfortunately, a new slew of bugs were introduced with this patch. We strongly suggest waiting for the dust to settle before updating your Office installation to SR-1.

Information regarding SR-1 can be found at: *http://officeupdate.microsoft.com/2000/ downloadDetails/O2kSR1DDL.htm*.

Several important administration tools and additional information/utilities can be found on the Office Resource Kit site at: *http://www.microsoft.com/office/ork/2000/appndx/toolbox.htm*. For a complete listing of the issues addressed by SR-1, download the file *SR1Changes.xls* from the aforementioned page.

Conventions Used in This Book

The following typographical conventions are used in this book:

`Constant width`
Indicates command-line computer output, code examples, and Registry keys.

`Constant width italic`
Indicates variables in examples and in Registry keys. It is also used to indicate variables or user-defined elements within italic text (such as path names or filenames). For instance, in the path *Windows**username*, replace username with your name.

`Constant width bold`
Indicates user input in examples.

`Constant width bold italic`
Indicates replaceable user input in examples.

Italic
Introduces new terms and indicates URLs, variables in text, user-defined files and directories, commands, file extensions, filenames, directory or folder names, and UNC pathnames.

TIP # 1

Tip Title

This is an example of a tip, which gives specific instructions on how to use a given Outlook element that the authors feel is important and beneficial to the user.

NOTE   *This is an example of a note, which signifies valuable and timesaving information.*

WARNING

This is an example of a warning, which alerts users to a potential pitfall in the program. Warnings can also refer to a procedure that might be dangerous if not carried out in a specific way.

Path Notation

We use a shorthand path notation to show you how to reach a given Outlook or Windows user interface element or option. The path notation is relative to a well-known location. For example, the following path:

Tools → Options → Calendar Options

means "Open the Tools menu (in Outlook), then choose Options, then choose the Calendar Options button."

In Part 2, *Menu Reference,* we occasionally title a section or topic without an arrow. For example:

Calendar Options

In this case, we have grouped a collection of options or features under a single header for organizational purposes.

Keyboard Shortcuts

When keyboard shortcuts are shown (such as Ctrl-Alt-Del), a hyphen means that the keys must be held down simultaneously, while a plus means that the keys should be pressed sequentially.

How to Contact Us

We have tested and verified the information in this book to the best of our ability, but you may find that features have changed (or even that we have made mistakes!). Please let us know about any errors you find, as well as your suggestions for future editions, by writing to:

O'Reilly & Associates, Inc.
101 Morris Street
Sebastopol, CA 95472
1-800-998-9938 (in the U.S. or Canada)
1-707-829-0515 (international/local)
1-707-829-0104 (fax)

You can also send us messages electronically. To be put on the mailing list or request a catalog, send email to:

info@oreilly.com

To ask technical questions or comment on the book, send email to:

bookquestions@oreilly.com

We have a web site for the book, where we'll list examples, errata, and any plans for future editions. You can access this page at:

http://www.oreilly.com/catalog/out2000ian/

For more information about this book and others, see the O'Reilly web site:

http://www.oreilly.com

Acknowledgments

Writing the acknowledgments for a book is an exciting time for any author because it means that the months of research, long hours of writing, and absence from friends and family is finally drawing to a close. It's also a time to reflect and thank all those people who helped make it happen—which, of course, is impossible. That's not going to stop us from giving it a shot, however.

This book, like all books, was not written solely by the authors listed on the cover.

First and foremost, we'd like to tip our hat to the hundreds of people who helped us toil through Outlook's nuances. This group will never be justly acknowledged in the space provided, despite the fact they were the driving force in asking the questions that led to the answers you are about to read. You know who you are—thank you.

A deep bow of respect and gratitude goes to Troy Mott, our editor at O'Reilly. He was a source of inspiration. He pushed us to get things right. He was critical when it was appropriate, and the first to offer praise when it was due. He polished our writing skills, pushed us in new directions, and pulled us from the brink of despair more than once. Troy's name belongs on the cover of this book just as much as ours. As you read the following pages, keep in mind that there were three architects of *Outlook 2000 in a Nutshell*, not two.

Next are the technical reviewers who scoured every word we wrote for errors and ways to describe a concept better, and dotting all the "i's." Many, many thanks to: Moshe Bar, Brian Bilbrey, Steve DeLassus, Helen Feddema, and Matt Beland.

We also extend a very special thanks to Robert Bruce Thompson. Without his pushing and prodding, this book would not have been written. Not only did he review our work, strike-through the "wills" (that's "display," Tom, not "will display"), and ask hard questions, he graciously offered the advice of a respected and seasoned author when we needed it most. Thank you Bob, for helping us to keep our eyes on the ball.

In addition, we'd like to express our thanks to Carrie-Anne Rombough at Environics Communications for providing us with an evaluation Palm IIIx. Chapter 16 would not have been possible without her kindness and technical insights.

On a personal note, Tom would like to thank his friends and family for their patience and support. In particular:

My dear wife, Leah, who worked twenty hours a day pacifying a teething seven-month-old and ministering after our five-year-old daughter who is at that stage in her life where she wants to do everything RIGHT NOW (except clean her room). When I needed quiet, Leah somehow managed to arrange it. When I needed food, she slipped it under the door. When I couldn't be there for my children, she filled in. And when I needed sleep, she reminded me of this fact—with mixed success.

My friends Matt, Brian, and Billy who took time the time to call and remind me not how much further I had to go, but how far I had already come.

And last but not least, my friend Moshe. There's an old saying, "If you save one life, you save the world." I want to thank Moshe for his life-saving advice, and for saving my world on more than one occasion.

We hope you get as much out of reading this book as we did writing it.

—Tom Syroid and Bo Leuf
February 2000

Part 1

The Big Picture

Chapter 1

Outlook "in a Nutshell"

Outlook 2000 is more than just a flexible, robust email client. It is a multidimensional program made up of six powerful components: Mail, Calendar, Contacts, Tasks, Notes, and Journal. These components work seamlessly to perform the following functions:

- Communicate electronically

- Schedule activities and events

- Maintain an intelligent address book

- Manage and track projects

- Save and organize notes

- Log and time various activities

To realize the full potential of Outlook 2000, you must understand that Outlook is a database that stores items (e.g., mail messages, addresses, dates, times, notes, etc.) in folders. Regardless of the component, Outlook uses forms as containers to input and display items. Outlook items have *properties*, such as date, owner, and category, that can be used as selection criteria for Outlook *views*, which allow you to display, sort, and filter items almost endlessly. You can use predefined views, sorts, and filters, create custom views based on predefined views, or create your own views from scratch. Outlook 2000 provides access to all of its commands via menus and toolbars that are customizable and adaptive, as well as via powerful context menus (launched by right-clicking an area). It provides the Outlook Bar (a container for shortcuts) and the Folder List (a tree-like folder display) to help navigate the program.

The remainder of this chapter covers the Outlook components, providing you with common uses, the command-line syntax, some keyboard shortcuts, and a task list for each component. The task list is a mini-index that points out some of the interesting features of a given component and the page where it is discussed. Think of this chapter as the jumping-off point to the rest of the book; revisit when you want an overview of a component and its capabilities.

Mail

Mail is used more often than any other component, both because email itself is a common task and because other Outlook components use Mail to extend their functionality.

Outlook Mail is very configurable. You may use the default editor or Word to send email using Plain Text, HTML, or MS-RTF. Outlook Mail has myriad other options that are covered in Chapter 5, *Mail Editors*, and Chapter 6, *Mail*. Given the feature richness of Mail, it's no surprise that we devote two chapters to it.

Uses and Functions of Mail

- Check the spelling of a mail message before sending it

- Create filters to automatically control incoming messages

- Use a read receipt to "track" a mail message

- Use stationary to jazz up outgoing mail messages

- Forward a Task request to several Contacts

Command-Line Syntax

To open Outlook with the Inbox folder displayed:

```
outlook.exe /select Outlook:Inbox
```

To open a new default mail message without starting Outlook:

```
outlook.exe /c ipm.note
```

Keyboard Shortcuts

Create a new mail message: Ctrl+Shift+M
Mark a message as read: Ctrl+Q
Reply to a message: Ctrl+R
Reply to All: Ctrl+Shift+R
Check for new mail: F5

Mail Task List

Change default mail editor to Microsoft Word: Chapter 5, page 174
Change default font for new mail messages: Chapter 5, page 175
Send a one-time read receipt: Chapter 5, page 180
Create new mail message: Chapter 6, page 226
Enable automatic name checking: Chapter 6, page 227
Override default mail editor for one message: Chapter 6, page 230
Color-code junk email: Chapter 6, page 238
Check Outbox for pending messages to send: Chapter 6, page 242

Create a new rule: Chapter 6, page 244
Assign categories based on content: Chapter 6, page 248
Permanently delete message: Chapter 6, page 255

Calendar

The most obvious function of Calendar is as a graphical, electronic Daytimer®. Calendar is much more than that, however. Calendar is a flexible time-management tool that you can use to track and manage appointments, events, and meetings. Calendar can filter, sort, and display items in various layouts (e.g., by day, week, month, etc.). To help manage this, Calendar contains the Date Navigator (a graphical mini-calendar) and the TaskPad (a miniature view of the Tasks folder). Calendar makes it easy to plan and track meetings, invite attendees, allocate resources, and reschedule activities if necessary.

Uses and Functions of Calendar

- Track and manage appointments and meetings

- Use Recurrence to create Calendar entries for events such as birthdays and anniversaries

- View appointments by day, week, or month

- Configure different time zones and holidays

- Use Free/Busy to publish your schedule to a LAN or Internet server

Command-Line Syntax

To open Outlook with the Calendar folder displayed:

```
outlook.exe /select Outlook:Calendar
```

To open a new appointment without starting Outlook:

```
outlook.exe /c ipm.appointment
```

Keyboard Shortcuts

Create a new appointment: Ctrl+Shift+A
View 1–10 days (0 to 10 for *n*): Alt+<*n*>
Move between Calendar, TaskPad, and Folder List: F6
Move selected appointment forward: Alt+Down Arrow
Select next appointment: Tab

Calendar Task List

Print one month per page: Chapter 3, page 98
Specify which days of week are "working days": Chapter 7, page 277
Add Holidays to Calendar: Chapter 7, page 281

Contacts

Contacts is a repository for important names, email addresses, locations, telephone numbers, and other information you need to interact. Think of it as an intelligent address book that does the behind-the-scenes work when you want to send out mail, verifying the correct email address and other pertinent information.

Like all Outlook components, Contacts provides many different views that allow you to choose how to find, display, and update information. You can easily drop a vCard (packaged contact information) from another Outlook user's information into Contacts to create a Contact or automatically update an existing one.

Uses and Functions of Contacts

- Generate a distribution list to send out a mass mailing.

- Store birthday dates for friends, family, and business contacts

- Display items from other components using the Activities tab

- Verify email addresses when sending Mail

- Use Categories to create custom sorts

Command-Line Syntax

To open Outlook with the Contacts folder displayed:

```
outlook.exe /select Outlook:Contacts
```

To open a new contact entry without starting Outlook:

```
outlook.exe /c ipm.contact
```

Keyboard Shortcuts

Create a new Contact: Ctrl+Shift+C
Go to last card in the folder: End
Select or unselect active card: Ctrl+Spacebar
Display last list item without selection: Ctrl+End
Open selected Contact: Enter

Contacts Task List

Set locations for saving new Contact entries (CW mode): Chapter 2, page 39

Find a Contact by phone number: Chapter 3, page 121

Create a new Contact: Chapter 8, page 330

Change default Contact options: Chapter 8, page 330

Display any Outlook item related to a contact: Chapter 8, page 344

Create a Distribution List for a group of contacts: Chapter 8, page 348

Assign a Task to a Contact: Chapter 8, page 353

Dial a Contact directly from Outlook: Chapter 8, page 355

Forward a Contact as a vCard: Chapter 8, page 359

Find a Contact without knowing the full name: Chapter 8, page 360

Customize Contact views: Chapter 8, page 368 (Also in Chapter 3)

Globally search and replace Contact text strings: Chapter 12, page 453

Field mapping for exporting Contacts: Chapter 12, page 444

Tasks

Tasks automate the traditional paper to-do list. Using Tasks, you can enter, edit, track, and display to-do items, reprioritizing and rescheduling them as necessary. Outlook supports three task types: those with no assigned dates, those with a due date, or those with both a start and due date. The real power of Tasks is most apparent in the ways you can sort, filter, and view to-do items. Delegation is another powerful Tasks feature, which allows you to assign tasks to a subordinate via a Task Request, and subsequently track the progress of that task.

Uses and Functions of Tasks

*   Link important Tasks with Contacts

*   Use table views to look at tasks in many different ways

*   Track in detail a process with multiple deadlines

*   Forward a task to a Contact and receive updates of its progress

Command-Line Syntax

To open Outlook with the Tasks folder displayed:

```
outlook.exe /select Outlook:Tasks
```

To open a new Note without starting Outlook:

```
outlook.exe /c ipm.task
```

Keyboard Shortcuts

Create a new Task: Ctrl+Shift+K

Create a Task request: Ctrl+Shift+U

Decline a Task request: Alt+D
Accept a Task request: Alt+C
Perform the action assigned to a button: Spacebar

Tasks Task List

Create a new Task: Chapter 9, page 377
Add a reminder for overdue Tasks: Chapter 9, page 379
Linking Tasks and Contacts: Chapter 9, page 381
Assign a Task: Chapter 9, page 381
Create a new Task request: Chapter 9, page 385
Accept a Task request: Chapter 9, page 389
Forwarding a Task to another Contact: Chapter 9, page 393
View active Tasks: Chapter 9, page 396
View Task timeline: Chapter 9, page 399
Auto-Archive Tasks folder: Chapter 13, page 459
Pros and cons of sharing a Task folder: Chapter 14, page 481

Notes

Notes are small text-only scratch pads that can be used on the fly to store tidbits of information that you don't have time to file properly or that are not of long-term value. A Note can store about 30 KB of text, which allows considerable room for details. Many users either disdain Notes as too simplistic or try to use Notes to do things for which they were not intended. Notes are a powerful and useful feature of Outlook, as long as you don't try to exceed their design limitations.

Uses and Functions of Notes

- Record a quick reminder or phone number

- Keep a list of interesting URLs to check next time you're surfing

- Jot down details of a phone conversation; after you're through, cut and paste the contents into a Journal item or Contact record

- Jot down an idea for a project; when time permits, flesh it out, transfer it to email, and forward it to your boss

Command-Line Syntax

To open Outlook with the Notes folder displayed:

```
outlook.exe /select Outlook:Notes
```

To open a new Note without starting Outlook:

```
outlook.exe /c ipm.sticknote
```

Keyboard Shortcuts

Create a new Note: Ctrl+Shift+N
Insert text from the Clipboard to a Note: Ctrl+V or Shift+Insert
Save a Note: Ctrl+S
Save a Note as a separate file: F12
Forward a Note: Ctrl+F

Notes Task List

Organize your Notes: Chapter 3, page 121
Find information in a Note folder: Chapter 3, page 113
Create a new Note: Chapter 10, page 402
Embed a URL in a Note: Chapter 10, page 405
Create a link between a contact and a Note: Chapter 10, page 406
Forward a Note to someone: Chapter 10, page 407
Set default Note options (size, color, and font): Chapter 10, page 407
Change the view used in Note folder: Chapter 10, page 408
Assign a category to a Note: Chapter 10, page 412
Change the color of a Note: Chapter 10, page 413
Copy a Note into an Office document: Chapter 10, page 416
Copy a Note to your desktop: Chapter 10, page 416
Notes and PalmPilot Memos: Chapter 16, page 529

Journal

For those of us not blessed with a perfect memory, Outlook's Journal component is a lifesaver. With it you can record email messages sent and received, meeting requests, responses, and cancellations, and task requests. In addition, Journal can also track the time spent working in a specific Office document (FrontPage excluded). Journal entries can be manually created, or generated automatically when a specific application is opened or Outlook item created.

Uses and Functions of Journal

• Track Activity duration

• Create a link between a Contact and a Journal Entry

• Forward a Journal entry to a co-worker

• Keep track of all email sent to an individual

• Log time spent with each client for billing purposes

Command-Line Syntax

To open Outlook with the Journal folder displayed:

```
outlook.exe /select Outlook:Journal
```

To open a new Journal entry without starting Outlook:

```
outlook.exe /c ipm.activity
```

Keyboard Shortcuts

Create a new Note: Ctrl+Shift+J
Move selected item: Ctrl+Shift+V
Open a drop-down list: Alt+Down Arrow
Organize Journal: Alt+Z
Expand a Journal group: Right Arrow

Journal Task List

Disable/enable automatic tracking: Chapter 11, page 419
Create a new Journal entry: Chapter 11, page 424
Edit the Journal Time field: Chapter 11, page 425
Track activity duration: Chapter 11, page 425
Create a link between a Contact and a Journal entry: Chapter 11, page 427
Link a document to a Journal entry: Chapter 11, page 429
Forward a Journal entry to someone: Chapter 11, page 431
Restore Default View: Chapter 11, page 432
Group related correspondence with Category View: Chapter 11, page 434
Open context menu for a single Journal item: Chapter 11, page 436

Chapter 2

Installing Outlook

Outlook's primary *raison d'être* is connectivity. Whether we're talking connectivity between Outlook's individual components, between its Office cousins, or between your friends and business associates around the world, how you install Outlook will determine the tools and options you have at your disposal, and how they work.

Outlook is not really one program—there are three separate installations to choose from. You can install Outlook as a standalone Personal Information Manager or PIM (No E-mail mode), as a PIM plus an email client for Internet-based messaging (Internet Mail Only or IMO mode), or as a PIM plus an email client for corporate-based messaging (Corporate or Workgroup or CW mode). This chapter details these three installations: how they differ, how to choose the best one for your needs, and how to configure the installation you've chosen.

Installation Overview

Installing Outlook is not necessarily difficult, but it can quickly become confusing due to the array of available options. As you can see from Figure 2-1, the installation process ranges from the simple (Install, Upgrade, Import settings), to the complex (Install, No Outlook upgrade, No other upgrade, Choose a Service Option, and Configure that option). This section provides you with a "big picture" of the various junctures you will encounter while installing Outlook, and where each of these roads leads.

The choices you make throughout this process will depend on what you start with on your hard drive, and where you want to end up when all is said and done. The four key points to take note of are:

- Installing the program files (component options)

- Upgrading options (from a previous version or another email client)

- Choosing an E-mail Service Option (No E-mail, IMO, or CW)

- Configuring your chosen service option

Before we get into these various options and what they entail, we need to take a brief side step and examine the messaging protocols and standards Outlook supports. Understanding these protocols and standards will be important when it

11

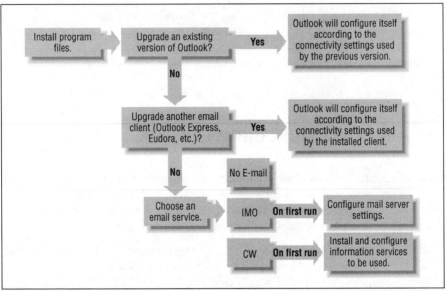

Figure 2-1: Flowchart of Outlook's installation process

comes time to choose an email service, because Outlook's functionality varies according to the service option you select, and service options are primarily formed around messaging protocols.

Messaging Protocols and Standards

Loosely defined, a *protocol* is an agreed upon bi- or multilateral form of behavior. In the world of messaging, protocols provide a framework that ensures both email clients and host servers can interpret each other's commands.

A *standard*, on the other hand, is an agreed-upon set of specifications (usually in the form of content and structure). Agreeing upon standards makes it possible for different manufacturers to create products that are compatible with each other. Standards may be set by official standards organizations, or they may be industry standards established by common use.

Perhaps an example will clarify the difference between these two terms. When you send an email message to a friend over the Internet, it travels from your computer to your mail server, and on to your friend's mail server, according to *Simple Message Transport Protocol* (*SMTP*). This protocol defines how your message is transported, and how each forwarding server knows who sent the message and how to find the recipient. *Multipurpose Internet Mail Extension* (*MIME*) on the other hand, is a standard that dictates how your message is formatted and put together (encoded) before it is sent.

A simple way to spot the difference between a protocol and a standard is: a client must negotiate a protocol with a server before data can be transmitted between the two. If they cannot agree, the data does not get exchanged—period, end of story. A standard is not so rigid. It is possible for an email client to transmit information that does not conform to a given standard (for example, a *vCard*). The recipient client, however, will not be able to translate that information into usable data.

 Messaging formats (Plain Text, HTML, RTF) are definitely considered standards as far as email clients are concerned; they are absent from the following list because we are focusing on transport protocols and standards in this chapter. Full details on message formats can be found in Chapter 5, Mail Editors.

Outlook supports the following messaging protocols and standards:

SMTP (Simple Mail Transport Protocol)
SMTP is the backbone of Internet messaging. Its sole purpose is to ensure that messages get reliably transferred from source (the client) to destination (a mail server).

POP3 (Post Office Protocol Version 3)
POP enables a mail client to check for and retrieve messages from a mail server. SMTP transfers a message *to* the server; POP retrieves messages *from* the server. POP3 supports server-based message storage, meaning a client can request the server store messages for a specified period of time.

IMAP4 (Internet Message Access Protocol Version 4)
IMAP is a protocol that expands on the functionality of POP3. It allows users to access messages on a mail server, store messages in multiple folders, read message headers without downloading the entire message, select certain messages for downloading while leaving others on the server, and post messages to a public folder. IMAP is not used for Internet mail transport (delivering messages to a mail server); this remains the job of SMTP. IMAP, like POP, is a "fetch" protocol. In order to use IMAP, both client and server must support it.

LDAP (Lightweight Directory Access Protocol)
LDAP is an Internet protocol that specifies both the structure and access methods for a directory service. Using an LDAP client, you can access a directory on a server supporting this protocol and create, view, edit, or delete objects in that directory (if the user has the necessary permissions). For example, Outlook uses LDAP to search an Exchange database for a name or email address stored there. A user who has the necessary permissions can modify or create a new entry in this database directly from their client. LDAP is also the protocol used by many Internet name-search engines, such as BigFoot.

NNTP (Network News Transport Protocol)
NNTP is the protocol used to post, distribute, and retrieve messages on Internet and intranet news groups or bulletin boards.

MAPI (Messaging Application Programming Interface)

MAPI is a messaging system layer developed by Microsoft that provides a common interface for mail-enabled applications to communicate with each other. MAPI mediates communications between a client application (like Outlook) and a server application (like Exchange). When you configure Outlook to access an Exchange server, MAPI is used as the foundation for data transfer between these two programs.

MIME (Multipurpose Internet Mail Extensions)

MIME is a specification for enhancing the capabilities of standard Internet electronic mail. It offers a simple standardized way to represent and encode a wide variety of media types for transmission via Internet mail.

When using the MIME standard, messages can contain the following types:

- Text messages in US-ASCII

- Character sets other than US-ASCII

- Multimedia: image, audio, and video messages

- Multiple objects in a single message

- Multifont messages

- Messages of unlimited length

- Binary files

MIME is open to extensions, meaning that new attachment standards can be defined and inserted as new content types and yet remain distinct from the message body itself.

S/MIME (Secure Multipurpose Internet Mail Extensions)

S/MIME helps ensure the security of email messages. Outlook's implementation of S/MIME includes digital signing, which allows users to verify the identity of the sender and integrity of messages, and digital encryption, which protects the contents of messages from being read by anyone except the intended addressee. Users can thus exchange signed and encrypted mail with any mail client that supports S/MIME.

vCard (Internet Contacts Format)

vCard is a standard devised for exchanging contact information such as telephone numbers, and addresses across a network. The information sent is not restricted to basic text, but can include photos, Internet addresses, and anniversaries.

vCalendar (Internet Free/Busy)

vCalendar is an Internet standard that defines a platform-independent format for exchanging calendar and schedule information consistently. Outlook can exchange meeting requests and scheduling information with any email client that supports vCalendar.

iCalendar (Internet Appointments)

iCalendar is an emerging standard (that is, not fully developed) for the format and storage of schedule information such as free/busy times used when inviting people to meetings and events.

With all this fine technobabble carefully stored in the back of your mind, it is time to look at the actual program installation itself.

Program Installation and Component Options

Outlook 2000 provides two setup choices: Install Now and Customize. Install Now transfers a default set of components to your hard drive. Customize opens the dialog shown in Figure 2-2. Note that the default installation settings for Customize are the same as Install Now.

 NOTE *Most of the screenshots in this section show an installation from an Office 2000 Professional CD. If you purchased Outlook as a separate product, your installation will be similar—you just won't see the other Office product choices.*

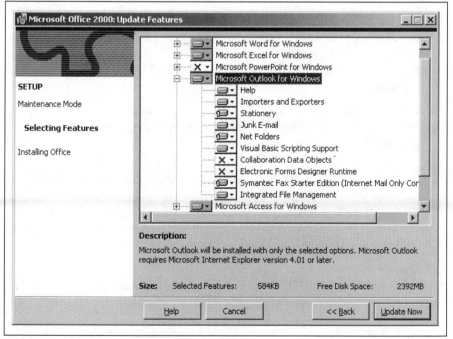

Figure 2-2: Outlook's default installation choices

The symbol next to the feature indicates how it will be installed. You can change this installation method by clicking the description of the component and selecting another from the list that appears (see Figure 2-3). If a feature has subfeatures, a symbol with a white background indicates that all of these subfeatures have the same installation method. A symbol with a gray background indicates that the feature and its subfeatures have mixed installation methods.

Figure 2-3: Component Run options

The installation options are as follows:

Run from My Computer
    The feature is installed and stored on your hard disk.

Run all from My Computer
    The feature and all of its subfeatures are installed and stored on your hard disk.

Run from Network (only available if installing from a network server)
    The files needed to use this feature remain on the network server and are not copied to the local hard disk. Features installed by this method require access to that network server.

Run all from Network
    Similar to "Run from Network" except that the feature and all its subfeatures are selected.

Run from CD
    The files needed to use this feature remain on the CD from which the feature was installed. Components installed by this method require access to that CD. For example, if you installed from the CD and try to use the feature when the CD isn't in the CD-ROM drive, you will be prompted to insert the CD in order to use the feature.

Run all from CD
    Similar to "Run from CD" except the feature and all its subfeatures are selected.

Installed on First Use

> The feature will be installed on your hard disk when used for the first time. You will need access to the CD or network server you installed from in order to activate the feature. This option is not available for all items.

Not Available

> The feature isn't installed. To install it later you will need to rerun Setup.

TIP # 1

First Use Versus Not Installed

The difference between Installed on First Use and Not Installed is how Outlook responds to the request for a feature after Setup has run. Installed on First Use prompts you for your Office CD and installs the necessary component. If a component tagged as Not Available is requested, you will have to rerun the setup program. Installed on First Use is the best option to choose when available, as it allows you to update Outlook without rerunning Setup.

Most of the component options shown in Figure 2-2 are self-explanatory. Install Importers and Exporters when you anticipate exchanging data with other programs; otherwise they are good candidates for the Installed on First Use option. Stationery is a set of custom HTML templates that allow you to send messages dressed up with a variety of backgrounds and fonts. Junk E-mail is a useful tool for screening mail arriving in your Inbox that might qualify as spam. Net Folders allows you to share a local folder with other users via an Internet connection (see Chapter 14, *Collaborating with Outlook*).

Visual Basic Scripting Support gives you debugging capabilities if you plan to create custom forms. Collaboration Data Objects is an interface that allows a programmer to link code to Outlook's information stores. If you have forms that were created with Electronic Forms Designer, you'll need the runtime module to use them in Outlook.

Symantec Fax Starter Edition is only available for an IMO installation. It allows you to send and receive faxes directly from Outlook. Integrated File Management installs support for viewing files and folders located on your hard drive (or network drives) directly from Outlook.

When you've completed your setup choices, click the Install/Update Now dialog button to begin the file copy process. On completion, the installer will place an Outlook icon on your Desktop and either force a system reboot or inform you "Office has been successfully installed."

Upgrade Options

Starting Outlook subsequent to a first-time installation will not run the program itself, but instead the *Startup Wizard*. The purpose of this wizard is to guide you

Adding or Removing Outlook Components

Once Office is installed, simply reinserting the original CD in your CD-ROM will not automatically run the setup program. The setup program checks your system, sees an existing installation, and assumes you inserted the CD because an Office program requested it. There are three ways to add or remove Outlook components after your original installation:

1. Go to Control Panel → Add/Remove Programs and select the Office 2000 entry there. The "Change" button will prompt you for your CD if it is not already in the drive, and the Office setup program will start. Choose the Add/Remove Features button to get to the "Choose Components" dialog.

2. Insert the Office CD in your CD-ROM drive and open the My Computer icon on your desktop. Highlight the Office icon displayed there, and from the right-click context menu choose Install or Configure. This will start the Office setup routine.

3. Insert your Office CD, open Windows Explorer, and double-click on Setup.exe.

through the installation choices available and configure the program's connectivity options.

Here is the logic behind the Startup Wizard:

- The wizard begins by searching for any email clients installed on your system. If it comes up empty handed, the configuration process skips forward to choosing an E-mail Service Option.

- If the wizard finds an earlier version of Outlook (not Outlook Express), it asks if you want to upgrade this existing installation. "Yes" will configure Outlook 2000 to use the same configuration your previous version used (mail settings, program options, and data files). "No" will advance you to the next dialog. Choose No if you have an existing version of Outlook on your system and you either want to start with a fresh set of data files or you want to install Outlook 2000 under a different service option (for example, your previous version is installed as CW and you want to install Outlook 2000 as IMO). To find out under which service option an existing installation is configured, go to the Help menu and choose About Microsoft Outlook.

- If the wizard does not detect a previous version of Outlook or you answer No to the first dialog, a second dialog will be displayed showing a list of recognized email clients found on your system. Selecting any one of the programs listed will import the mail settings *and data* used by that program into Outlook. Generally speaking, if Outlook lists your email program in this dialog, it has filters in place to accurately import its configuration and data. If you have any doubt at this point, choose None of the Above and, after Outlook is installed and configured, import your data manually (see Chapter 12, *Import and Export*).

TIP # 2

Manually Selecting a Service Option

If you want to manually select a service option (which we recommend), make sure you answer No to upgrading a previous Outlook installation, and None of the Above from the list of other email clients to upgrade from.

If you've bobbed and weaved your way through these choices and elected not to upgrade an existing installation, the next option dialog you see asks you to choose a service option.

Service Options

What's a service option? The term E-mail Service Option is one of those innocuous-sounding choices Microsoft likes to use that are a lot more significant than you might think. As alluded to in the introduction to this chapter, the service option* you choose (or Outlook chooses for you) actually determines a whole array of connectivity choices that go hand-in-hand with each installation. And unbeknownst to most people, service options have a direct impact on the performance of Outlook, due to the drivers and code each mode installs.

Regardless of the installation mode you choose, setup will install a base set of components with Outlook's executable and library files. These components are listed in Table 2-1 along with the name Outlook uses to reference them. The last column lists the chapter of this book where details can be found for each item.

Table 2-1: Basic Outlook Components

Feature	Outlook Component	Chapter Reference
A personal calendar	Calendar	Chapter 7
A contact manager	Contacts	Chapter 8
A to-do list	Tasks	Chapter 9
An activity journal	Journal	Chapter 11
Free-form notes	Notes	Chapter 10

Outlook also creates several *System Folders*: Inbox, Outbox, Sent Items, and Deleted Items. These folders are inherent to the program functionality. In a No E-mail installation, the Inbox, Outbox, and Sent Items folders are not necessary and will not be created.

---

* We sometimes use the term "mode" interchangeably with "service option," as in *installation mode*.

Outlook also provides an extensive range of tools that enable you to sort, view, find, and manipulate the data shown in these component views. These tools are part of Outlook's core program files:

Categories
Customized Views
Customized Forms (VB Script procedures)
Macros (VBA procedures)
Fax Capability (not available under a No E-mail installation)
Find and Organize Tools
AutoArchive
Integrated File Management

The rest of this section looks closely at Outlook's three service options and the functionality involved in each. Your choices are:

Internet Only (also referred to as Internet Mail Only or IMO)
The Internet Only service uses the same PIM structure as the No E-mail service, and adds the underlying transport mechanisms to connect to mail servers that use the Internet-standard POP3, SMTP, and IMAP4 protocols. This service does not support mail servers that use the MAPI standard.

The Internet Only service also supports sharing calendaring information by email using the vCalendar standard, and the exchange of Internet Free/Busy information using the iCalendar standard. Email addresses can be stored in the user's Contacts folder and automatic Name Checking (ensuring the email address entered is correct by comparing it to this field in a contact's record) is enforced through the Windows Address Book interface. Faxes can be sent and received directly from Outlook using Symantec's integrated WinFax Starter Edition program.

Corporate or Workgroup (CW)
The Corporate or Workgroup installation is geared toward the user who needs connectivity with corporate messaging platforms such as Microsoft Exchange, Microsoft Mail, or Lotus cc:Mail. Inherent in all of these enterprise-level platforms is a broader range of workgroup/collaboration features not available on Internet-based mail servers. For example, Exchange Server supports message recall and voting buttons, public information stores, server-based mail filters, document tracking features, and global address lists. In addition to supporting these higher-end messaging features, a CW installation also installs the services needed to interface with Internet-standard mail systems.

Under CW Outlook, user data can be stored in a variety of locations: locally in a Personal Folders file (PST), locally in an Offline Folders file (OST), remotely on a mail server, or remotely in an Exchange Server Public Folder (PF). Using Public Folders on an Exchange Server is covered in Chapter 17, *Outlook and Exchange*.

No E-mail

Under this option Outlook functions as a self-contained personal information manager, or PIM. Data is saved in a Personal Folders file (or PST). Inside this file is a hierarchy of folders where Calendar, Contact, Task, Note, and Journal entries are stored. The No E-mail service does not install any connectivity options (email, fax, or shared scheduling).

TIP # 3

Accessing Exchange with IMAP

While IMO does not support MAPI servers directly, if your Exchanger Server has the IMAP service installed you can create an IMAP mail account in Outlook and access Exchange message stores via IMAP4.

Service Options: Considerations and Caveats

So which service option should you choose? The answer is another question: How much connectivity do you need? One of the most important things to keep in mind when installing Outlook is to add the program features and functions you need—no more and no less. Configuring Outlook with components you do not use adds program overhead and leaves the door open for more things to break. The principle of *KISS* (Keep it Simple, Stupid) should be firmly entrenched in the back of your mind when installing Outlook.

For 99% of Outlook users, the mail server (or servers) determines the service option to choose (see Figure 2-4). To wit:

- If you need no connectivity between Outlook and the outside world, choose No E-Mail. If your needs change over time, mail and fax capabilities are easy enough to add. For details on how to do this, see the section "Reconfiguring an Installed Service Option" later in this chapter.

- If you only need to connect to Internet mail servers, choose Outlook's IMO installation. IMO supports all common Internet messaging protocols in a relatively stable and well-mannered way. You can configure multiple mail accounts for an IMO installation, and if your system is configured for multiple users, Outlook will keep each user's data and configuration files separate.

- If you need access to Exchange or another corporate messaging platform, CW Outlook is, in most cases, your only option. While CW provides a more diverse range of Information Service options (see the section later in the chapter on "Configuring CW Outlook"), these options come at a cost. If you do not need corporate messaging services, we recommend IMO, for the following reasons:

    Disk usage

    CW Outlook occupies significantly more disk space than IMO Outlook.

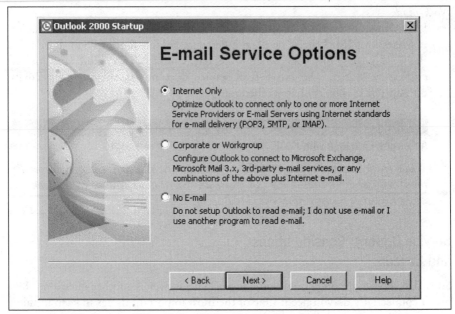

Figure 2-4: The Startup Wizard E-mail Service Options dialog

Resource usage

With CW Outlook the more Information Services you install, the slower Outlook is to open and close.

Error messages

If CW Outlook runs into errors when polling a server for mail, the messages you receive are less than informative.

Connectivity

CW Outlook has no provision for automatic mail checking through a dialup connection.

Program response

CW Outlook is painfully slow in almost every respect compared to IMO Outlook. Also be aware that, at least for this author, running CW dramatically slowed other applications as well; Word "thought" for long periods before opening a document, Internet Explorer paused before opening a URL, and Windows Explorer slowed to molasses both on opening and when reading the contents of a directory. Restoring Outlook to IMO immediately restored all the applications to their spry selves. Your mileage, of course, may vary.

To make some sense out of the maze of choices, options, and terminology discussed so far, we summarize this section with two tables. Table 2-2 shows the relationship between Outlook's three service options and the protocols and features each option supports. Table 2-3 outlines the various group scheduling and collaboration features supported by the three different installations.

Table 2-2: Protocol, Feature, and Mail Configuration Matrix

Protocol or Feature	No E-mail	IMO	CW
SMTP/POP3	No	Yes	Yes
IMAP4	No	Yes	No
LDAP	No	Yes	Yes
Exchange Server Access	No	Yes (Limited)	Yes
MS Mail and other third-party mail systems	No	No	Yes
S/MIME digital signatures and encryption	No	Yes	Yes
Store email on server	No	Yes	Yes
Offline access to messages	No	Yes	Yes
Contact look-up for mail addressing	No	Yes	Yes
Personal distribution lists	No	Yes	Yes
Stationery	No	Yes	Yes
HTML mail	No	Yes	Yes
File attachments	No	Yes	Yes
Forward and reply options	No	Yes	Yes
Name-checking for mail addressing	No	Yes	Yes
Automatic Dial-up for mail accounts	No	Yes	No
Offline mail storage	No	Yes	Yes
Multiple mail signatures	No	Yes	Yes

Table 2-3: Group Scheduling and Collaboration Features

Item	No E-mail	IMO	CW: Exchange	CW: MS Mail and Others
Send/receive meeting requests for group scheduling	No	Yes	Yes	Yes
Send/receive meeting accept/decline messages	No	Yes	Yes	Yes
Access other's Free/Busy information	No	Yes	Yes	No
See details of Free/Busy information	No	No	Yes	No
Interoperability with Microsoft Schedule+ for group scheduling	No	No	Yes	No
Delegate Access for scheduling	No	No	Yes	No
Open other's calendars	No	No	Yes	No
Access to Exchange public folders	No	No	Yes	No
Share folders	No	Yes	Yes	Yes
vCard, vCalendar, and iCalendar support	No	Yes	Yes	Yes
Participate in Internet (NNTP) newsgroups	No	Yes[a]	Yes[a]	Yes[a]

Table 2-3: Group Scheduling and Collaboration Features (continued)

Item	No E-mail	IMO	CW: Exchange	CW: MS Mail and Others
Create private discussion groups	No	Yes	Yes	Yes
Collaboration, workflow, and tracking applications	No	No	Yes	No
Task delegation	No	Yes	Yes	Yes
Save Calendar as web page	Yes	Yes	Yes	Yes
Direct booking of resources	No	No	Yes	No
Microsoft NetShow Integration	Yes	Yes	Yes	Yes
Microsoft NetMeeting Integration	Yes	Yes	Yes	Yes
Add and remove meeting attendees	Yes	Yes	Yes	Yes
Personal distribution lists	Yes	Yes	Yes	Yes

a Via Outlook Express.

Now that you have the program files on your hard disk and you've determined which service option best suits your needs, there is one final step before you can actually begin using Outlook—configuring all these various components and options to actually connect with something.

The next two sections of this chapter discuss configuring the connectivity options available for IMO and CW Outlook. Note that the No E-mail Service Option is not discussed beyond this point, as it has no connectivity options to configure.

Configuring IMO Outlook

Running an IMO installation for the first time invokes the Internet Connection Wizard, which helps you configure an email account. If you upgrade a previous Outlook installation or another email client, then Outlook already has the details it needs and will bypass this wizard. Manually creating an account is outlined in the next section, "IMO Outlook: Account Maintenance."

WARNING

If you are already using server-based message storage, read this warning before continuing unless you want to delete all the messages saved on your server. The Internet Connection Wizard automatically disables the "Leave a copy of messages on server" option for newly created accounts and does not give you access to this option when it is run. To work around this dilemma, configure an account and leave the logon password blank to ensure Outlook cannot connect to this server without your consent. Then choose Tools → Options → Accounts, select the Advanced tab, and mark the "Leave a copy..." option.

The Internet Connection Wizard requires the following information:

Your Name

> This is how your name displays on the "From" line when it arrives in a recipient's mailbox. Anything goes here (full name, nickname, initials), but we suggest that you enter something that will uniquely identify you as the sender of a message.

Internet E-mail Address

> Enter the email address assigned to you by your ISP or system administrator, typically of the form *yourname@provider.com*.

E-mail Server Names

> Choose the protocol Outlook will use when checking for new mail (POP3 or IMAP) and then enter the addresses for both your incoming and outgoing mail servers. These addresses typically take the form of *smtp.server.com* and *pop.server.com*. The IMAP protocol is not widely supported on Internet mail servers, so check with your service provider before enabling this option.

Internet Mail Logon

> Enter your mail account username (typically the *yourname* before the @ of your email address) and password. Check the box provided if you want Outlook to remember your password. If you leave this checkbox blank, you will be prompted for a password every time a Send/Receive command to this mail account is requested.

> When you log on to most Internet mail servers, username and password information is sent in clear text, leaving open the possibility of a hacker intercepting and capturing this information. Some mail servers support Secure Password Authentication, which, in effect, establishes an encrypted link between the client and server before sending username/password information for verification. Check with your ISP before enabling this option to ensure it is supported.

Mail Connection Type

> And finally, a dialog to choose how Outlook accesses your mail connection. The choices here are phone line, LAN, or manual. The first two options determine whether Outlook tries to locate your mail server through a dial-up (modem) connection, or directly through a LAN connection. The third option is available for users who either want to control the connection manually or have the choice of both dial-up and LAN. For example, you use a notebook to connect to a corporate messaging system at work via a LAN connection. At home you use a dial-up connection to access your personal mail via an ISP. Selecting this option will prompt Outlook to ask you which service to use when checking email.

TIP # 4

Multiple Choice Configurations

Another way to retain the option of manually selecting dial-up or LAN connectivity to the same mail account is to define two Outlook accounts, one for each connection choice. Make sure however that only one—or neither—is set for automatic mail checks.

IMO Outlook: Account Maintenance

To reconfigure, import, export, or add accounts to your existing configuration, use the Tools → Accounts command. The Internet Accounts dialog is shown in Figure 2-5.

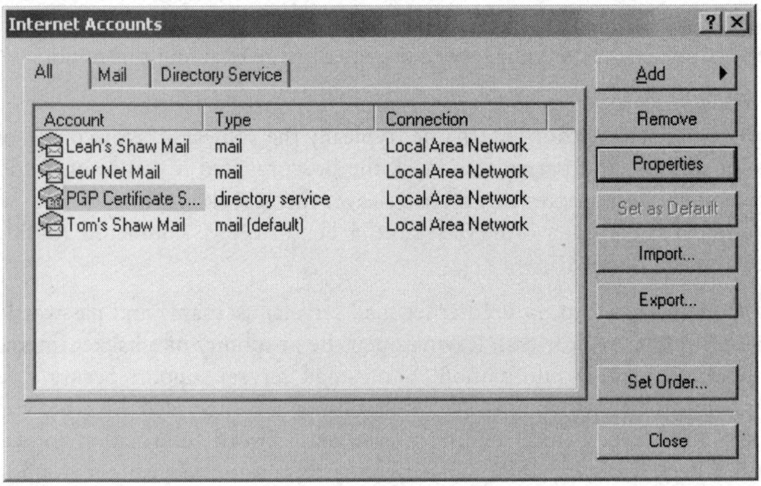

Figure 2-5: Internet Accounts (IMO) configuration dialog

TIP # 5

Opening the Internet Accounts Dialog

There are two additional ways to open the Internet Accounts dialog, neither of which requires Outlook to be running. Right-click the Outlook icon on your desktop and choose Properties from the context menu displayed, or, open the Mail icon from the Windows Control Panel. Note both approaches allow you to configure or add mail accounts only. Directory services must be added through Outlook's Tools menu.

From the buttons on the right of the Internet Accounts dialog you can:

Add a Mail or Directory Service
Selecting the Add button runs the Internet Connection Wizard.

Remove an existing account

The Remove button deletes a selected account from your configuration. This deletes configuration settings only—no messages already received from the removed account are affected.

Set the Properties of an existing account

Selecting the Properties button displays the Mail (or Directory) account properties dialog as shown in Figure 2-6 (left). The General, Servers, and Connection tabs contain the information you provided when the account was first configured with the Internet Connection Wizard.

Set the default mail account

The default mail account is where Outlook sends all outgoing mail. To override this setting, use the mail editor's File → Send Using command.

Import an account configuration

To import a configuration file, select this button and point the browse dialog displayed to the location of the backup file. If you have not yet made a backup of your accounts, do so *now*. Trust us on this one.

Export an account configuration

To save a configuration, select the account and export it to your local filesystem or a floppy disk. Outlook mail configurations have a tendency to mysteriously self-destruct on occasion. Having a backup of your accounts somewhere handy is *strongly recommended*.

There are several fields on the Mail Properties dialog that are either given default entries or left blank when the wizard is run. Those of significance on the General tab are:

- The Mail Account Name field is initially set to the SMTP name provided on the Servers tab (for example, *smtp.host.com*); you will probably want to change this to something more meaningful.

- When someone replies to an email message, that response is sent by default to the "From:" address in the original message. You can override this default behavior by entering a "Reply-To:" address in this field that differs from the "From:" address. Use the Reply To field when you have two or more email addresses and you want all responses to go to the same mailbox, or when you want replies sent from a specific mail account to go to a secretary or assistant for sorting.

- "Include this account…" determines if this account is included in a mail check (either automatically according to the settings contained on the Tools → Options → Mail Delivery tab, or manually with the Send/Receive command). All new accounts created by the Internet Connection Wizard have this option enabled.

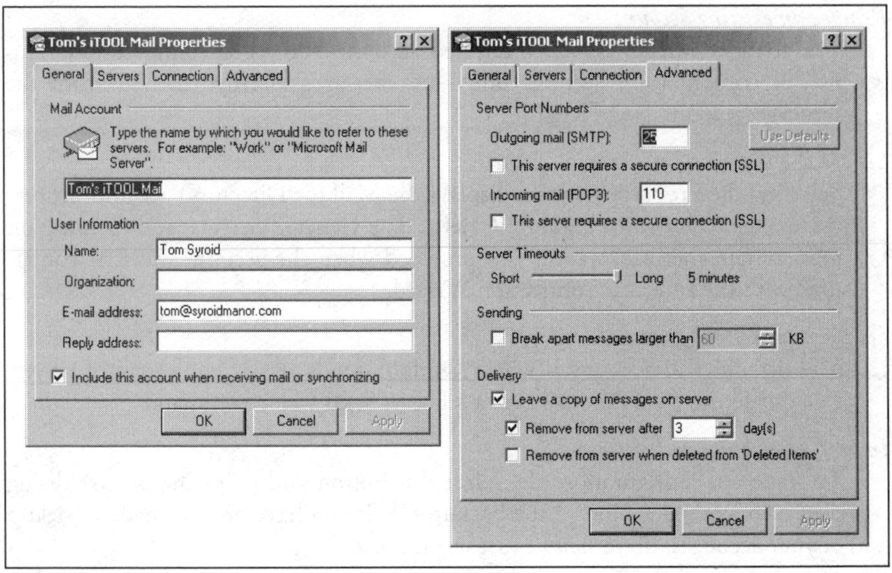

Figure 2-6: The Mail Properties dialog showing the General tab (left) and the Advanced tab (right)

The Advanced tab (Figure 2-6, right) contains settings that specify how Outlook and your mail server interact. These settings are assigned defaults when a mail account is configured with the Internet Connection Wizard, and they can only be changed from this dialog:

Server Port Numbers

Server Port Numbers designate the TCP ports that the mail servers listen on (by default, Port 25 for outbound traffic via SMTP and Port 110 for inbound traffic via POP3). Do not change these ports unless your ISP or system administrator tells you to.

Server Timeouts

The Server Timeouts option specifies how long Outlook waits for a nonresponding server before it returns a time-out error message.

Sending

The Sending option forces Outlook to break messages larger than the size specified into smaller pieces before they are sent.

Delivery

The Delivery option allows you to specify whether Outlook deletes messages from the server after reading them. This is an important option to be aware of if you use multiple systems to check the same mailbox. Typically you would configure your main system to delete messages after they are downloaded (by leaving this option unchecked) and set the rest of your systems to leave messages on the server after they are checked.

TIP # 6

Message Backup Via Your ISP's Server

Use the "Leave a copy of messages on server" option as a quasi-backup method to safeguard your email. By leaving your messages on the server, if your information store becomes damaged or corrupted for any reason, the option is there to recreate a new PST and download any saved messages to this new folder. This tip should not, of course, replace routine backups, and will not help you regain lost Contact or Calendar records.

Selecting server-based storage will further enable two options for when these messages are deleted. Removal after X days will force Outlook to check the dates of messages stored on the server against local records (stored in the user's *POP-enabled* PST file) of when the message was downloaded and delete those older than the number of days specified. You can also configure Outlook to delete messages stored on the server when the corresponding message is deleted from your local "Deleted Items" folder.

Three caveats regarding server-side message storage are in order:

– Some ISP and server administrators have a policy of periodically clearing out "old" mail from hosted mailboxes.

– The overhead Outlook requires to track and synchronize local copies and server copies is noticeable. For maximum performance, disable this option.

– Most administrators place limits on mailbox storage. If you receive a large number of messages and do not put a reasonable limit on the number of days these messages are stored before being deleted, you will soon find yourself exceeding your mailbox capacity.

Insights on Server-Side Storage

Many people misunderstand the concept of server-side message storage, and mistakenly think that the server has a role in determining what messages are retained and what messages are deleted. It is actually the mail client that holds and plays the cards on this feature.

When a mail client accesses a server message store, it sends the command RETR # to retrieve a specific message and the command DELE # to delete that message from the server. All enabling the option to leave messages on the server does is cause Outlook to issue RETR # commands, but no DELE # commands. Disabling the option to leave messages on the server simply causes Outlook to follow each RETR # command with a DELE # command.

Configuring CW Outlook

At the heart of every CW installation is a small configuration file called a *profile*. This file is so crucial to the operation of CW Outlook that without it the program simply will not run. So before we get into what a profile is and what it contains, if you are presently using CW Outlook, search (Start menu → Find → For Files or Folders) the partition containing your Windows installation for all files ending in the extension *.fav*. Now copy this file (or files, if you use more than one profile) to a floppy disk and store it somewhere safe. You will understand the importance of this step by the time you are finished reading this section.

What's so crucial about a profile? This file contains a list of the services loaded at startup. These services tell Outlook what messaging protocols the program has available, how to connect to those services, where those services can be found, your user login name and password, where mail from those services is to be sent and delivered, and most important of all, where your data is stored. Outlook requires at least one profile configured before it will start, and that profile must contain—at the very least—the location of your data files. Without an information store to open, Outlook simply refuses to run.

Profiles can be confusing because of the many configuration options they contain and how these options interrelate with each other. To help keep this layered onion in perspective, we refer you to Figure 2-7 which details the relationship between profiles, services, and service options.

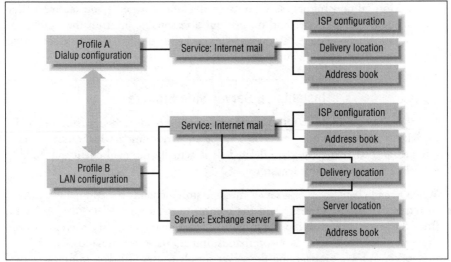

Figure 2-7: The relationships between profiles, services, and service options

The first thing to note in this figure is that while Outlook requires at least one profile, nothing keeps you from creating additional profiles, each tailored to a specific connectivity scenario. For example, if you use a notebook you might have one profile for connecting to the Exchange Server at your office, and a separate profile for dialing into your ISP from home.

The second point to note is that while the directory or tree structure analogy is often used to describe the hierarchical relationship between profiles and services and service options, this is not strictly true. Delivery options are a good example of where this linear model breaks down. A profile can have only one *incoming* delivery location (where incoming messages are stored), but you can configure Outlook to deliver *outgoing* messages to one location and, if that location is not available, to try another. All this works, of course, only if you have multiple messaging services configured, and the delivery order of those services is set correctly.

It's easy to see why profiles are confusing to the average user, and often poorly implemented. Keep in mind the following points when configuring profiles and services:

- Do not use CW Outlook if you connect only to an Internet-based mail server. CW Outlook is painfully slow at sending and receiving Internet mail compared to IMO Outlook.

- Do not configure a profile to use more services than you need. Every service Outlook loads uses memory and system resources, which degrades performance.

- Create separate profiles for unique needs. This keeps the number of services loaded to a minimum and keeps the performance hits to a minimum.

- Always keep a current backup of your profiles. Profiles are powerful, but fragile files. For some reason, they corrupt easily, and remember, without a working profile you cannot start Outlook.

The balance of this section details how to create a profile, the information services a profile can be populated with, setting delivery and addressing options, and profile maintenance.

Creating a New Profile

The Outlook Setup Wizard is invoked the first time Outlook is run and any time you create a new profile (see "Profile Maintenance" later in this section). The first dialog of this wizard is shown in Figure 2-8.

The services displayed are the *mail* connectors available (installed); if the messaging service you want to install is not on this list, select "Manually configure…" and choose Next.

You are then asked to name this profile (see Figure 2-9). This name should reflect the services you intend to add to this profile. If there will be more than one user on the same machine or you are using more than one profile, incorporate this information into your naming convention. For example: TomS: Exchange Settings, or TomS: Internet Dialup Settings.

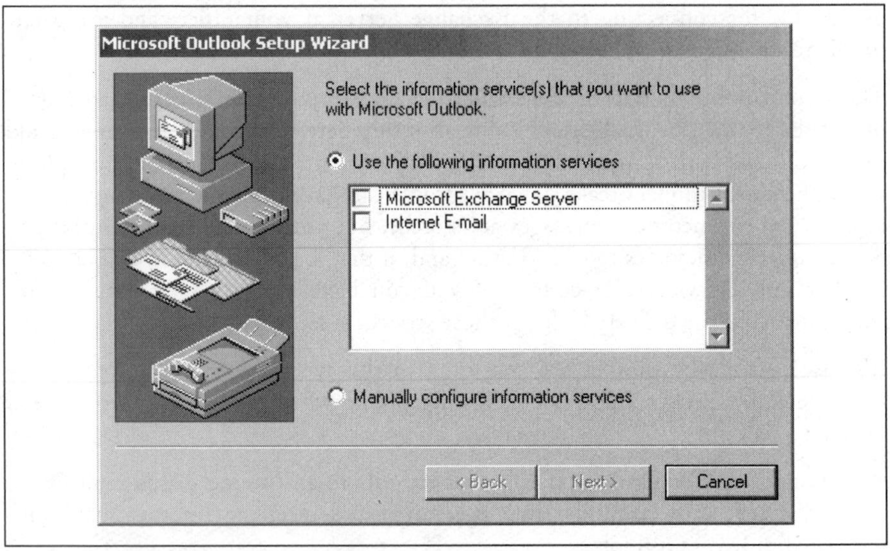

Figure 2-8: The Outlook Setup Wizard—Information Services dialog

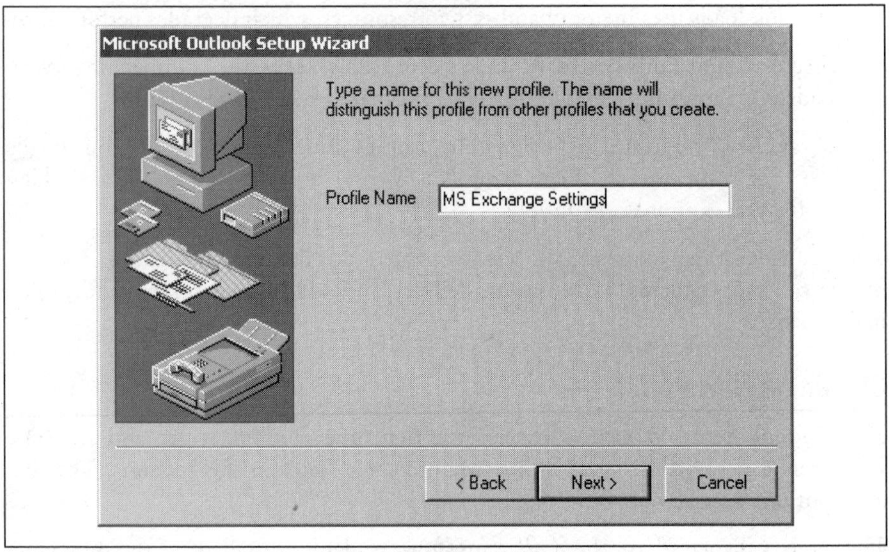

Figure 2-9: The Outlook Setup Wizard—Profile Name dialog

TIP # 7

Choose Meaningful Filenames

We do not recommend accepting the default filenames Outlook provides for profiles, .ost, .pab, or .pst files. Always change the suggested name to some combination of username/profile. This eliminates any danger of overwriting existing files when you create new profiles, and it makes it much easier to find a specific file later if you need to edit it.

From here you are going to be led down one of three garden paths depending on the choices made in the first Setup Wizard dialog shown in Figure 2-8.

If you choose Internet E-mail as the only service to install, you will see the dialog shown in Figure 2-10. Choose the "Setup Mail Account" button to run the Internet Connection Wizard discussed earlier in this chapter under "Configuring IMO Outlook." If you do not want to configure a mail account at this time, simply choose Next and the Setup Wizard will continue.

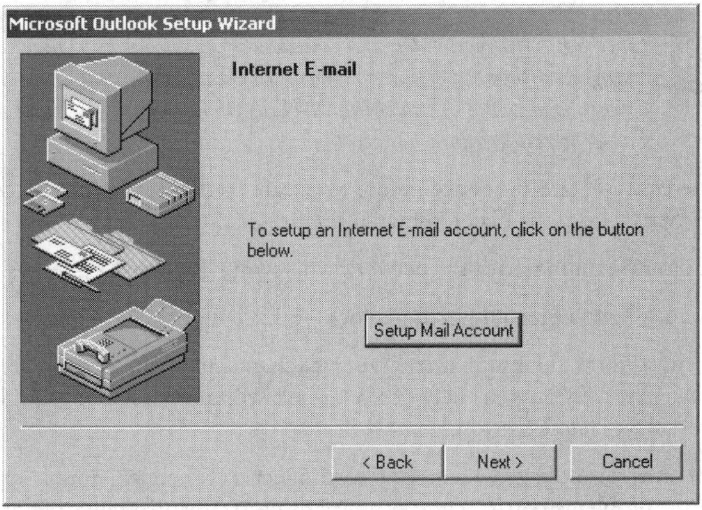

Figure 2-10: The Outlook Setup Wizard—Setup Mail Account dialog

If you choose to install the Microsoft Exchange service, you will see the dialog shown in Figure 2-11 (left). Pay attention to the question "Do you travel with this computer?" if you own a notebook or you do not have a dedicated LAN connection to Exchange.

While it is not explicitly stated anywhere on this dialog, selecting Yes here instructs Outlook to create an *Offline Folder* file for this profile. An Offline Folder file is similar in structure to a Personal Folder file with one key difference—it's designed to synchronize its contents with the user's Exchange-based mailbox. This allows you

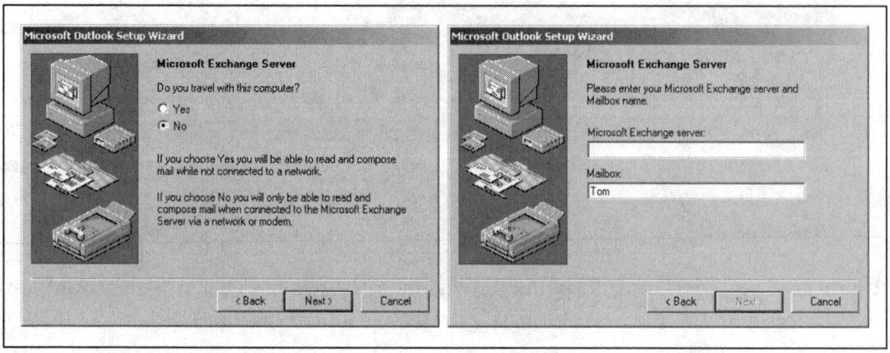

Figure 2-11: The Outlook Setup Wizard—Exchange Server identification

to work off-line, and when a connection to Exchange is re-established, the contents of both information stores are automatically synchronized. Offline Folders are discussed in Chapter 3, *Program Insights*, and instructions for synchronizing and creating Offline Folders after-the-fact are covered in Chapter 17, *Outlook and Exchange.*

NOTE *Once an Offline Folder is created, the filename and path cannot be changed without deleting the local file and recreating a new one. Pay attention to Tip # 7 and think carefully about where you want an Offline Folder to reside before you create it.*

Three prerequisites are necessary before you can configure the connection to an Exchange Server from the dialog shown in Figure 2-11:

- You must be online with the network where your Exchange server resides.

- You must have a preconfigured mailbox on Exchange.

- You must know the user name of your Exchange mailbox. If there are multiple Exchange servers on your network, Outlook will query each one and locate the correct server name for you.

If you get an error message while trying to connect to Exchange, double-check these steps, and if problems persist, contact your administrator. If the entries are correct, there could be a problem with either name resolution to the server or with your mailbox.

Finally, if you choose to manually configure information services, you will see a blank profile Properties dialog as shown in Figure 2-12.

Choose the Add button, and select the information services you wish to add from the list provided in the next section.

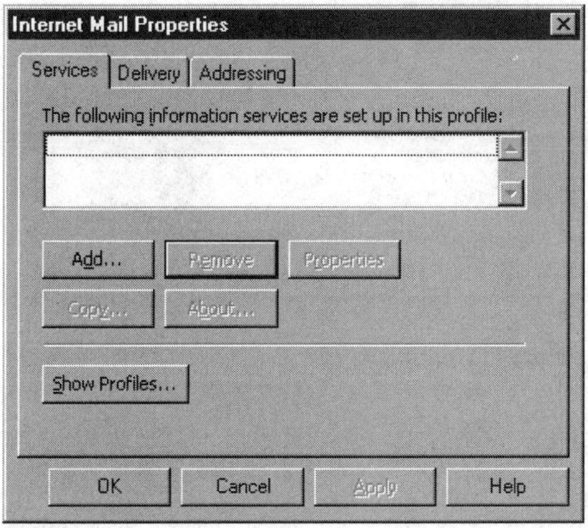

Figure 2-12: Blank profile Properties dialog

Information Services

An *information service* is the driver Outlook installs (typically in the form of a *Dynamic Link Library*, or DLL) that enables it to connect to a database. These databases take two general forms: messaging platforms (like Exchange or an Internet mail server) or address books (like the Outlook Address Book).

 It is beyond the scope of this book to detail the setup procedures and options for all possible information services. If you do not find the information you need here, check with your system administrator or the distributor of your messaging platform.

Keep in mind that some services described in this section may have multiple instances per profile (for example, Personal Folders), while others may have only one (for example, Microsoft Exchange Server). Outlook will give you an error message if you try to install a single instance service more than once.

If the information services you require appeared in the dialog described in Figure 2-8, the Setup Wizard takes you directly to the necessary dialogs to complete the configuration of the services selected. If, on the other hand, you opted to manually select the information services Outlook installs, you will see the dialog shown in Figure 2-13.

The following is a list of the services Microsoft provides for installation under Outlook 2000, what they do, and the instances supported.

 If you do not see the service you require listed here, check the Web for a third-party driver.

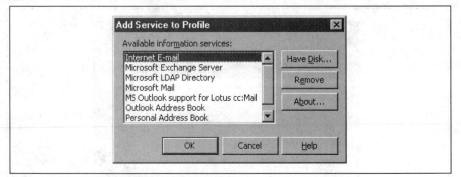

Figure 2-13: Add Service to Profile dialog

Exchange Server

This is the service Outlook uses to connect (using MAPI) to an Exchange Server. Creating a connection to Exchange automatically sets Outlook's mail delivery locations to this location. (For details on changing these locations, see the "Delivery Locations" section, next.) You can install only one instance of the Exchange Server service per profile.

Personal Folders (PST)

Selecting this option opens a dialog allowing you to Open/Create a Personal Folders file. This file can reside locally or on a shared network drive. You can have multiple instances of PSTs installed, but be advised that the more Personal Folders you load, the slower Outlook is to start and shutdown.

Personal Address Book (PAB)

The Personal Address Book is a holdover from earlier versions of Outlook. Microsoft recommends adding contact entries through either the Outlook Address Book or the Contacts folder of a PST. The PAB service supports multiple instances.

Outlook Address Book (OAB)

The OAB service allows Outlook to use the contents of the Contacts folder contained in a PST for name lookups and/or mail merges with Word. While it is possible to install multiple instances of this service, a better approach is to create one OAB entry and display multiple Contact folders from one source. This procedure is outlined under the "Addressing Options" section later in this chapter.

Microsoft Mail

This service provides the connectivity to a MS Mail post office. Like Exchange, you can have only one instance of Microsoft Mail running per profile.

Microsoft LDAP Directory

The LDAP service allows Outlook to connect to an LDAP server and search its database; this entry also allows Outlook to search an Exchange Server Global

Address List (GAL). Multiple instances are supported, and in fact necessary for each unique LDAP server being queried.

Internet E-mail

This option configures Outlook to connect to an Internet-based SMTP/POP3 server. Do *not* select this option if you are connecting to an Exchange Server and it is configured to handle Internet mail. Users installing both Internet E-mail and Exchange Server are advised to create separate profiles for each option. Outlook supports multiple instances of this service.

MS Support for Lotus cc:Mail

Configures Outlook to connect to a cc:Mail post office. The cc:Mail service supports one instance per profile.

Delivery Locations

The Delivery tab shown in Figure 2-14 defines the folder where incoming messages from your mail server (or servers) are delivered, and which mail server will process outgoing messages.

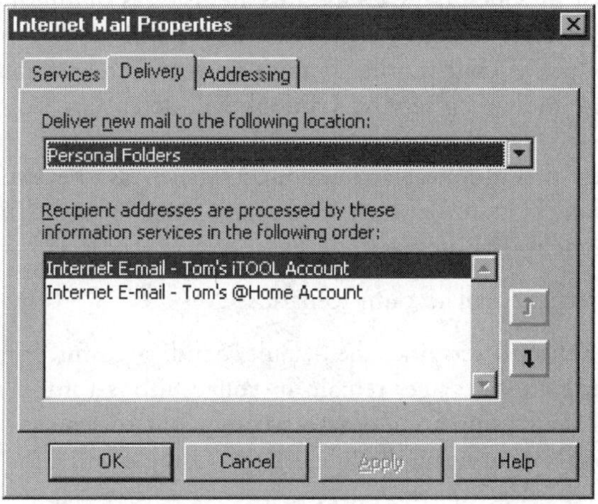

Figure 2-14: The Delivery tab of the CW Internet Mail Properties dialog

Incoming mail

Under CW Outlook, new messages can be delivered to one of three locations:

* An Exchange Server mailbox

* A Personal Folder

* An Offline Folder

The "Deliver new mail to the following location" field lets you choose where incoming messages from *all* messaging services configured for a given profile are delivered. This means that if you have services set up for both an ISP's mail server and an Exchange Server, all messages sent to you from either source will go to this folder.

Before Outlook can deliver new messages to a local information store (PST or OST), it must be a *valid delivery location*. This simply means that the information store contains the necessary system folders to support message handling (Inbox, Outbox, and Sent Items). If you move your delivery location from a remote source (for example, an Exchange mailbox) to a newly created local PST, Outlook will automatically add these system files to this new store.

 Many Exchange administrators frown on using a local PST as a delivery location for messages. To understand why, see the section "PSTs: An Exchange Administrator's Perspective" in Chapter 17, Outlook and Exchange .

Outgoing mail

The lower section of the Delivery tab lists the mail services configured for a given profile. The order in which these connectors are listed is significant *only* when there is a duplication of services across entries, or, as we will see in a moment, *within* a service. For example, if your profile contains both an Internet email service and an internal corporate messaging service, Outlook will determine from the address you enter which server to send a message to. On the other hand, if there is more than one service listed that duplicates functionality (such as the two Internet E-mail services shown in Figure 2-14), their display order directly impacts Outlook's behavior when it delivers a message.

In a multiple Internet email account scenario:

- The first list entry determines the default "Send" account. If this account is not available, outgoing messages remain in your Outbox until it is available. Messages can be sent using an alternate account, but this must be done manually from the email editor using the File → Send Using command.

- All accounts listed are then checked for new messages in the order shown.

A slightly different scenario unfolds when one messaging connector provides more than one service. This is a common source of confusion for both the user and Outlook, and arises when the Exchange Server you connect to supports both corporate mail handling and a gateway for Internet email.

Let's say you have two services configured on your system: one is a dialup connection for Internet email, the other is a LAN connection to your company's Exchange Server. This Exchange Server is set up to provide *both* internal messaging services *and* Internet mail connectivity. Using Outlook, you dash off a message to a recipient with an Internet-based mail address. Which service will Outlook use to send the message? Here is where the ordering of the services listed in the lower half of the Delivery tab comes into play:

- If the dialup connection for Internet email is the first entry on the list, Outlook will attempt to send the message through this connection. If this connection fails (because you forgot to plug the phone cord in), the message is not sent and remains in your Outbox until such time as you establish a dialup connection.

- If your Exchange Server is the first entry on the list, Outlook will first attempt to send the message through this service. If this connection is not available (because you are working at home), Outlook will then try the dialup connection.

To set the order Outlook uses to deliver messages, select an information service and use the arrow buttons to the right of the list pane.

TIP # 8

Just Because Outlook Says It's Sent...

Despite your careful attention to service orders, Outlook still gets befuddled at times when it has a choice of accounts to send Internet email through. If your profile matches this scenario, make it a habit to check your Outbox every now and then to ensure that Internet destined messages are being delivered as advertised.

Addressing Options

The Addressing tab (see Figure 2-15) sets three parameters: the address list displayed when you select the "To" button on a new message form, where new contact records are saved, and how Outlook *resolves* an address entry (see the section "Addressing a Message" in Chapter 5).

 NOTE *A full discussion of Address Books and their roles can be found in Chapter 3.*

Show this address list first

Your choice here determines which address book is displayed when you select the "To" button on a new message form. Common choices include a contact folder contained either in a local PST file, a local OST file, an Exchange mailbox, or the Global Address List.

Keep in mind that the Outlook Address Book is not a discrete object, per se—it is an interface that displays all the records from a contact folder selected as an E-mail Address Book.

Keep personal addresses in

This entry determines where Outlook saves new contact entries when you:

- Open a received message, right-click any address field, and choose Add to Contacts from the context menu displayed.

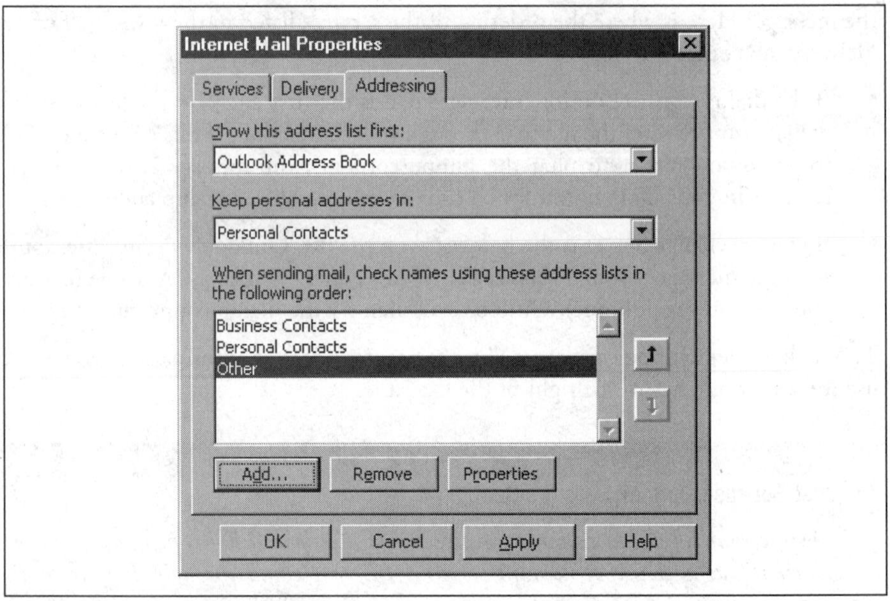

Figure 2-15: The Addressing tab of the CW Services dialog

- Address a new message to a recipient not listed in your contacts database; again, right-click the entry and choose Add to Contacts from the context menu.

- Select To → New Contact from an open message form.

A Contacts folder must be designated as an Outlook Address Book before it will be shown on this list.

TIP # 9

Enabling a Contacts Folder

Adding a new Contacts folder to your Personal Folders file or Exchange Mailbox does not automatically add it to the address list displayed. To have it displayed on this list, go to the folder's properties dialog (File → Folders → Properties) and on the Outlook Address Book tab select "Show this folder as an email Address Book."

Check names using

Under "When sending mail, check names using these address lists in the following order:" is a list of the address books Outlook recognizes and the order in which they will be used when resolving a name or displaying an address list:

Add button

Selecting this will include an address book on the list. Contact folders selected as email address books are not automatically displayed here; they need to be specifically added.

Remove button

> Selecting this excludes an address book from the list. This does not delete the address book or the data it contains, it simply prevents it from being displayed by the Outlook Address Book or used for name resolution.

Properties button

> Selecting this displays an information dialog detailing where the address book is located (i.e., which information store), and what folder in that store contains the contact information.

Outlook resolves addresses according to the order in which an Address Book appears in the lower pane of the Addressing tab. Place the Address Book you use most frequently at the top of the list.

The following illustrates the interrelatedness of the three options on the Addressing tab. Referring back to Figure 2-15:

- The first option, "Show this address list first," is set to use the Outlook Address Book. Remember that any contact folder can be (and in fact, *must* be, if it is to show on this list) designated as an Outlook Address Book (OAB). In this case, we have chosen to include all three folders listed in the lower order pane (Business, Personal, and Other). By choosing to include all folders, and selecting the Outlook Address Book as a first display choice, we have corralled all our addresses into a single (virtual) list. Alternatively, we could have chosen any one of the three aforementioned folders as a "first list."

> **NOTE** *The choice of which address list to display first does not prevent you from selecting another address list to display once the OAB is open. Simply use the drop-down list provided on the OAB form.*

- For the option "Keep personal addresses in" we have chosen the folder Personal Contacts. New contact records will automatically be added to this folder.

- Finally, the "When sending mail, check name…" list has been set to resolve addresses in the following order: Business Contacts, Personal Contacts, Other. We have elected to save new contact records in the Personal Contacts folder, Business Contacts ordered first, because this is where the majority of our addresses are kept and the folder most likely to contain the address for new messages being sent. When you use multiple folders to organize contact records, consider both frequency of access and the number of records a folder contains in determining the best order to use.

Profile Maintenance

Connectivity needs and configurations change, which means at some point in time you are probably going to be faced with the task of adding a new profile, deleting a profile, or modifying an existing profile.

At the risk of sounding repetitious, we remind you again—*always* ensure you have a current backup of your profiles. This is especially important when all your connectivity options are contained in a single profile, and doubly so if that profile consists of multiple services that are *currently working as advertised*. It may take all of two minutes to back up your profile; on the other hand, you may end up spending two hours reconfiguring a complex profile that you accidentally deleted.

There are several ways to get to the profile dialog shown in Figure 2-16:

- Right-click on the Outlook icon on your desktop. Select Properties from the context menu displayed, and click the "Show Profiles" button.

- If you have Outlook configured to prompt for a profile to start with (configured from the Outlook menu bar Tools → Options → Mail Services tab), select New from the Choose Profile dialog.

- From the Windows Control Panel, double-click the Mail icon and choose Show Profile.

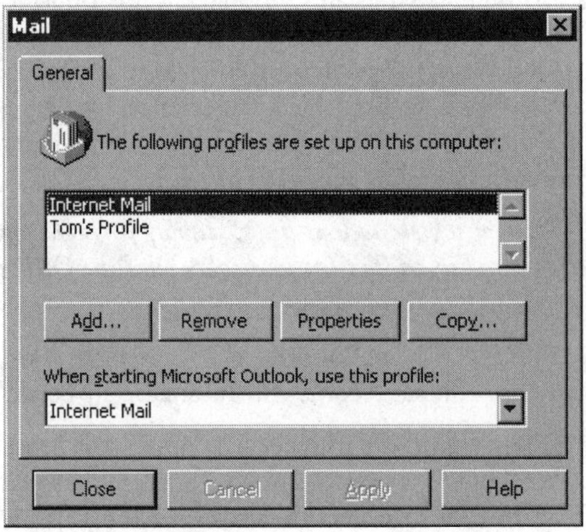

Figure 2-16: CW Mail Profiles dialog

From this dialog, you can:

Add a profile
    Runs the Outlook Startup Wizard discussed earlier in this section.

Remove a profile
    Be careful—one warning dialog and it's gone, with no way to recover it.

View the Properties of a profile
    Opens the dialog shown in Figure 2-17.

Copy a profile
Allows you to create a duplicate of an existing profile and either modify the original or the copy.

TIP # 10

Renaming Profiles

Outlook has no direct provision for renaming a profile. You can, however, copy a profile, give this copy a new name, and then delete your old profile.

Information Service management

Keep in mind that information services are profile-specific, so before you start modifying or reconfiguring a service, make sure you are working with the desired profile. The Properties dialog title always refers to the active profile. In the example shown in Figure 2-17, the services listed belong to the Internet Mail profile. To change the open profile, use the Show Profiles button located on the Services tab.

 When you configure information services from within Outlook (Tools → Options → Services tab), you can only set up those services associated with the profile you are running. To configure services associated with a different profile, either log in under that profile or do your tweaking from the Outlook icon on the Windows desktop.

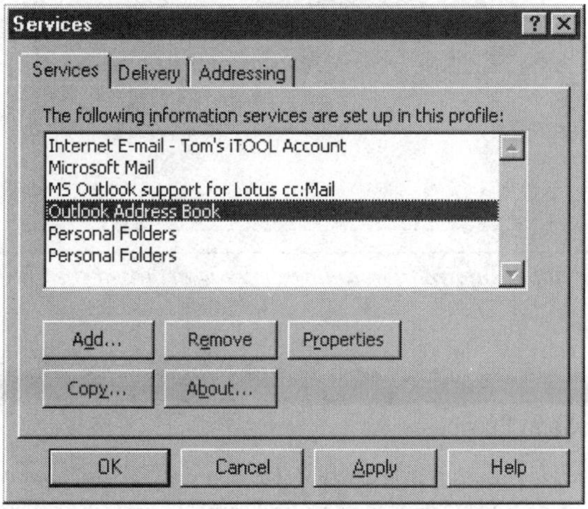

Figure 2-17: The Profile Properties dialog showing the Services tab

Add button
Use the Add button to select and configure a new or additional information service to the active profile.

Remove button

Use the Remove button to delete an information service from a profile. Be careful not to remove a service being used. Outlook will gladly comply with your request, and unless you made a copy of the profile you are modifying or have a current backup, reconfiguring an information service can be a time-consuming process.

Properties button

The Properties button displays the selected service's properties dialog, allowing you to view or modify configuration settings.

Copy button

Choose the Copy button if you have an information service already configured and you want to create a duplicate entry to modify rather than reconfiguring a new service from scratch.

About button

Use the About button to display an information dialog similar to that shown in Figure 2-18.

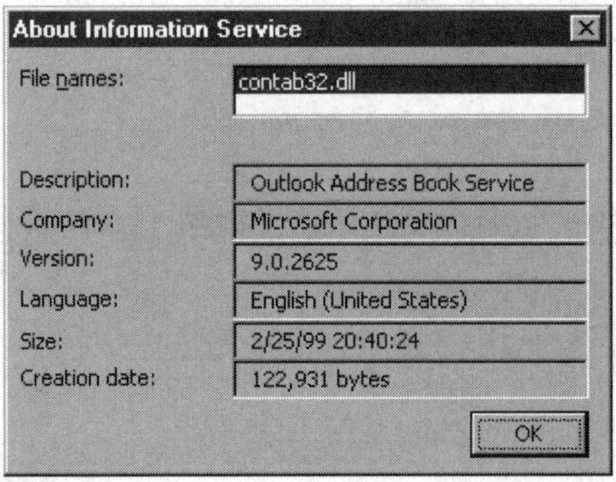

About Information Service

File names:	contab32.dll
Description:	Outlook Address Book Service
Company:	Microsoft Corporation
Version:	9.0.2625
Language:	English (United States)
Size:	2/25/99 20:40:24
Creation date:	122,931 bytes

OK

Figure 2-18: The About information dialog showing details of the Outlook Address Book Service

---

TIP # 11

About Information Services

The About dialog shown in Figure 2-18 is a very useful tool for troubleshooting badly behaved drivers. If you are having problems with a particular service, use the information here to ascertain the date and version number of the driver being used, and then check the vendor's web site for possible updates.

Changing the Profile Used at Startup

By default, CW Outlook will prompt you for a startup profile every time you open the program. To change this behavior and remove the Choose Profile prompt, go to Tools → Options → Mail Services, toggle the "Always use this profile" option, and select a profile from the list provided (see Figure 2-19).

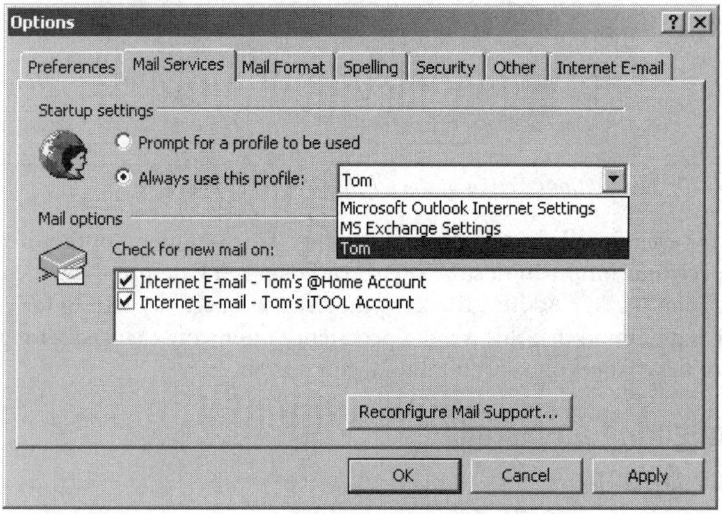

Figure 2-19: Startup settings on the CW Options dialog—Mail Service tab

The second startup option you have is which profile will be displayed as the default (given you have more than one).

NOTE *Selecting a default profile will not suppress the Choose Profile dialog when you start Outlook; it simply allows you to select which profile is listed first when the prompt is displayed.*

There are three ways to change this option:

- Under the Windows Control Panel, open the Mail icon. Choose a profile from the drop-down list under "When starting Microsoft Outlook…" and close the dialog.

- From the Choose Profile dialog presented when you start Outlook, select the Options button and check the "Set as default profile" option (see Figure 2-20).

- Right-click on the Microsoft Outlook icon on your desktop. From the properties dialog displayed, choose Show Profiles and follow the instructions given at the beginning of this list.

Below the default profile setting is an option to "Show Logon screens for all information services." Placing a checkmark here forces Outlook to display the configuration

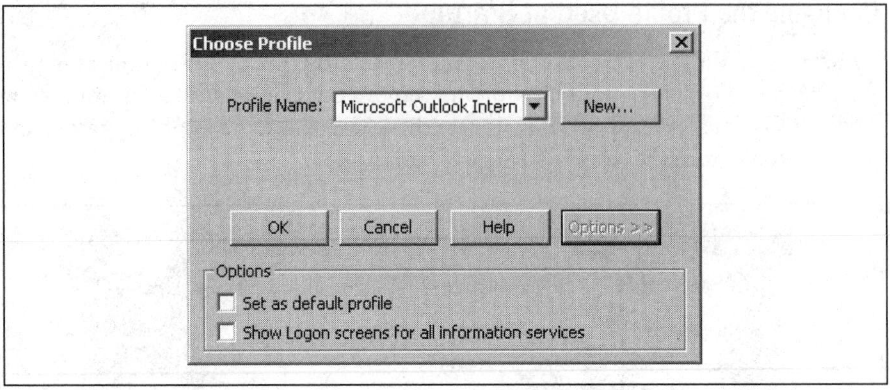

Figure 2-20: The Options section of the Choose Profile dialog

dialogs for each installed service before starting. This is a useful option if you want to compact your information store (Personal Folders → Compact Now), change the configuration of your Address Book, or modify a connectivity setting for your mail server. Keep in mind that this is not a persistent option; any changed settings will be saved but the changes only last for one Logon session.

Reconfiguring an Installed Service Option

A long overdue and welcome addition to Outlook 2000 is the ability to reconfigure mail support after installation. Changing an installed service option reruns Outlook's Startup Wizard, and reconfigures the program to work with a different messaging system.

WARNING

We strongly recommend closing all other running programs and backing up your Outlook files before reconfiguring a service option.

The following sections describe how to reconfigure a service option.

No E-mail to IMO

To switch your existing No E-mail service to an IMO service simply go to the Internet Accounts dialog (Tools → Accounts) and add a mail account as described in the section earlier in this chapter, "Configuring IMO Outlook."

NOTE *You cannot change your service option directly from No E-mail to CW. You can, however, reconfigure your installation to IMO, and then go from IMO to CW.*

IMO to CW

To change your service option from IMO to CW, go to Tools → Options and select the Mail Delivery tab. At the bottom of the dialog is a button labeled Reconfigure Mail Support. This displays the option dialog shown in Figure 2-21.

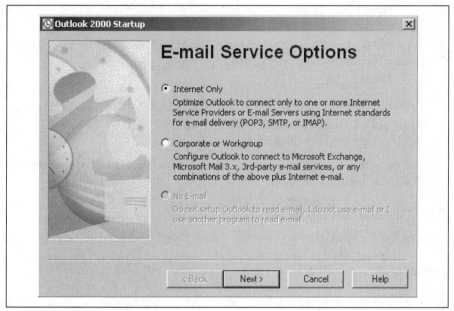

Figure 2-21: Reconfiguring an E-mail Service Options dialog

CW to IMO

To switch from CW to IMO, follow the same steps outlined in the previous section. The only difference here is a cosmetic one: the option tab (Tools → Options) in a CW installation is labeled Mail Services instead of Mail Delivery.

CW or IMO to No E-mail

There is no automatic reconfiguration option to go from a CW or IMO service to a No E-mail service; you must uninstall Outlook completely, and then reinstall the program again.

WARNING

While the ability to dynamically switch mail options is a welcome addition to Outlook's feature-set, it did not arrive without a few rough edges. In particular, mail and Personal Folder settings do not always transfer cleanly from one service option to the next. Always make sure you have your configuration settings written down somewhere before reconfiguring your mail support. Better yet, use a screen capture program and take screenshots of all pertinent configuration dialogs.

Outlook's Startup Options

The following section outlines the many options for starting Outlook beyond the obvious icons on your desktop.

Outlook's installation routine automatically creates two program shortcuts: one on the Desktop, and one in the Quick Launch bar. Selecting either one will start Outlook and display a folder view based on how the program was installed.

- A new IMO installation opens Outlook in the Outlook Today view (see the section "Outlook Today" in Chapter 3).

- A new CW installation prompts you for a profile to open Outlook with. Once a profile is provided, the program opens in the Inbox folder.

- An upgraded Outlook installation (IMO or CW) starts in the same view the previous version was configured to start in.

The following sections explain how to change these default startup options globally or as a separate program instance.

Changing Your Startup Folder

Outlook can be configured to open in one of seven predefined folders: Outlook Today, Inbox, Calendar, Contacts, Tasks, Journal, or Notes. To change your startup folder, go to Tools → Options → Other and click on the "Advanced Options" button. Under the General Settings section, select a folder from the drop-down list provided (see Figure 2-22).

To start Outlook in a folder view not displayed on this list, create a custom shortcut as described in the section later in this chapter, "Starting Outlook from a Custom Shortcut."

Starting Outlook Automatically

Many people find it convenient to have Outlook start automatically every time they turn on their computer. To do this, add a program shortcut to your Windows Startup folder as follows:

- From the Windows Start menu select Settings → Taskbar and Start Menu (or right-click the taskbar itself and select Properties). On the Advanced tab (in Windows 2000 Professional; in NT4/Win9x the tab is called Start Menu Programs) click on the Add button. Browse to the folder containing Outlook (typically *Program Files\Microsoft Office\Office*) and select the *outlook.exe* program file. Windows 2000 requires you to manually complete the full path to Outlook as shown in Figure 2-23 (left).

- Finally, from the Select Program Folder dialog (Figure 2-23, right), select Startup as the folder to contain your new shortcut.

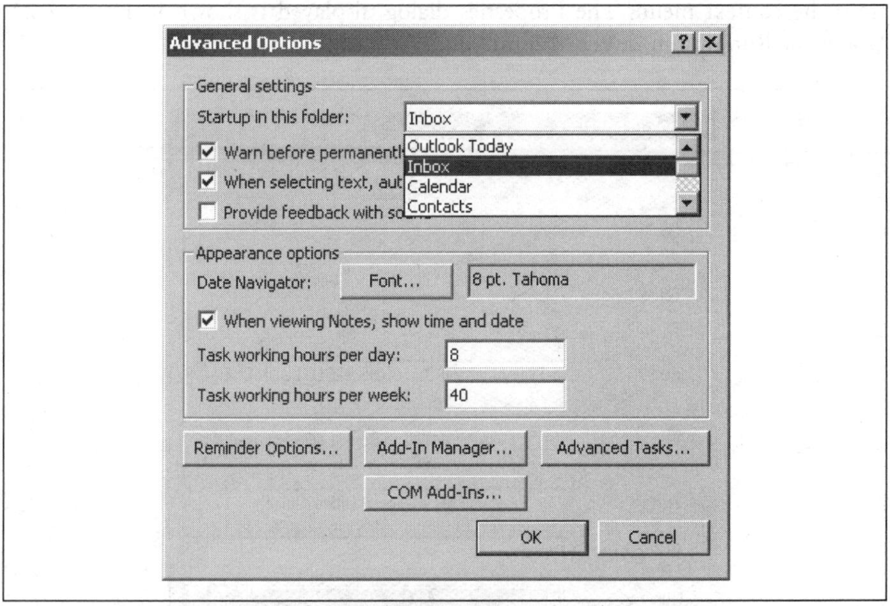

Figure 2-22: Choosing a startup folder from the Advanced Option dialog

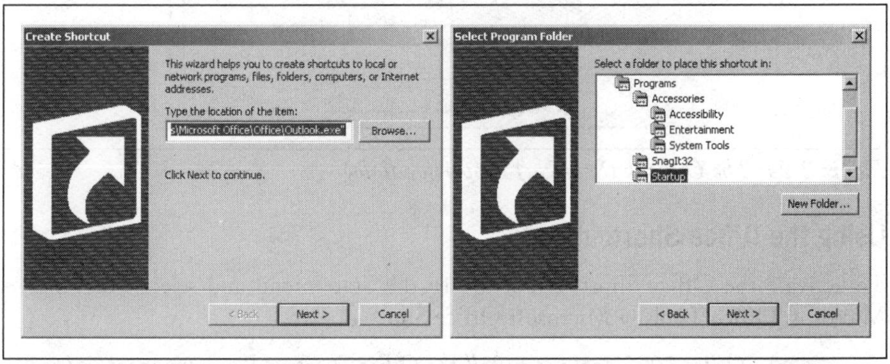

Figure 2-23: Configuring a shortcut to start Outlook automatically: the Create Shortcut dialog (left) and the Startup folder location (right)

- An alternative way is to open the "Explore Start menu" from the Advanced button in Taskbar Properties and browse the Programs → Office section of the Start Menu shortcuts. Copy the Outlook shortcut to the Startup folder.

If you want Outlook to automatically start minimized to the Taskbar, one more step is necessary. Go back to the Taskbar and Start Menu Properties dialog and on the Advanced tab click on the Advanced button. This will open an Explorer window with your Start Menu displayed in the right pane. Select the subfolder named *Startup*, right-click the Outlook shortcut in the right pane, and choose Properties from the context menu. The Properties dialog displayed is shown in Figure 2-24. Under the Run option, select Minimized.

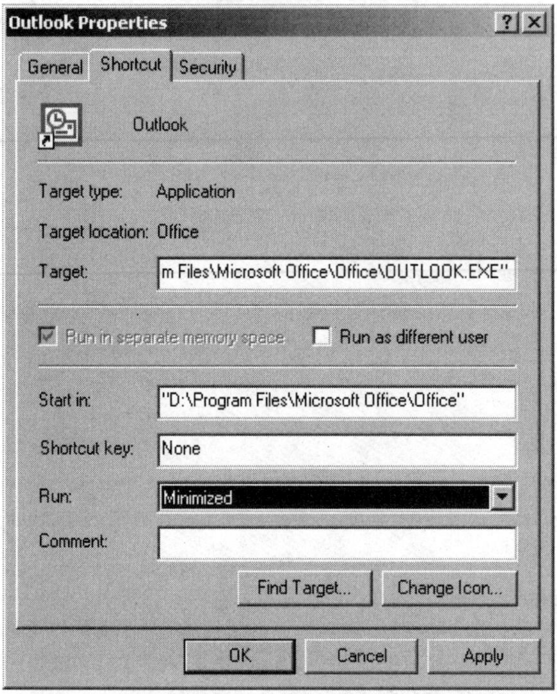

Figure 2-24: The Outlook (Shortcut) Properties dialog

Using the Office Shortcut Bar

To activate the Office Shortcut Bar, go to the Start menu and select Programs → Microsoft Office Tools → Microsoft Office Shortcut Bar.

> **NOTE** *Office 2000 does not install the Office Shortcut Bar component unless you specifically select it. The default setting for this feature, however, is "Run on First Use" so the first time you will be prompted for your Office CD. To install the Office Shortcut Bar manually, see the sidebar earlier in this chapter, "Adding or Removing Outlook Components."*

The Office Shortcut Bar (shown in Figure 2-25) provides you with the means to create a new Message, Appointment, Task, Contact, or Note without directly starting Outlook. Using the Shortcut Bar goes a long way to saving you precious system resources if you already have several programs running, as it only runs enough of Outlook's code to start the component you select. It also eliminates the three-step process of opening Outlook, switching to a component view, and creating a new item.

Figure 2-25: The Office Shortcut Bar

To customize the Office Shortcut Bar, select the Office logo in the upper-left corner or right-click the context menu and choose Customize. Keep in mind as you read the next section on command-line options, that these same tricks can be applied to the icons on the Office Shortcut Bar as well.

Starting Outlook from a Custom Shortcut

The icon Outlook's installation program placed on your desktop is not a true shortcut—it is a direct representation of Outlook itself. (Notice there is no overlaid arrow on it.) To see the difference between a shortcut and the quasi-shortcut this icon represents, right-click on Outlook and select Properties from the context menu. You should see something similar to Figure 2-26 (left). Now do the same with the Outlook icon in the Quick Launch region of the Taskbar.

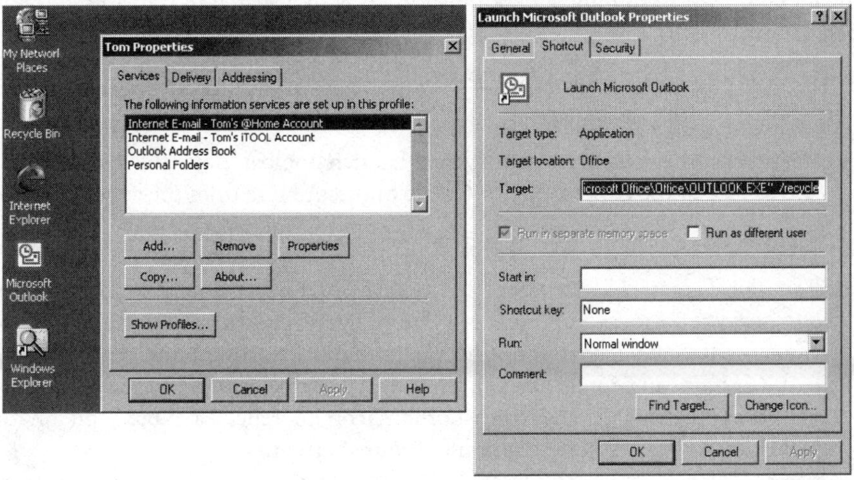

Figure 2-26: The Properties dialog from Outlook's Desktop icon (left) and Properties dialog from Outlook's Quick Launch icon (right)

The properties dialog shown in Figure 2-26 (right) represents a program *shortcut*.

Why might you want to modify a shortcut? Because a plain-Jane shortcut will always give you the same behavior when it is activated—it will open Outlook according to the options you set in the section on "Changing Your Startup Folder." However, *command-line switches* exist that open up a whole new world of program startup options and configurations. These switches are the focus of this section.

TIP # 12

Command-Line Switches

A full list of the command-line switches supported by Outlook can be found in Appendix C.

Let's say, for example, there are times you would like to open Outlook without displaying the Outlook Bar. Go to the Start menu → Run command and type the following:

```
outlook.exe /folder
```

Or perhaps you normally run CW with one profile, but occasionally need to start it with an alternate one. Again, go to the Run command and type:

```
outlook.exe /Profile "profilename"
```

Of course, all this is well and good for infrequent administrative chores, but if you find yourself using a switch to start Outlook on a routine basis, why not create a shortcut on your Desktop to save yourself some typing? The following is a functional example of combining a desktop shortcut with a switch to start Outlook in a specific way.

We are going to create a Desktop shortcut that starts Outlook and displays a new Note form. Here are the details:

1. Right-drag the icon from the Quick Launch toolbar onto the Desktop and release it. Choose either Copy or Create Shortcut Here from the context menu.

2. Right-click your new shortcut and choose Properties from the context menu.

3. Edit the Target field to read: `"C:\Program Files\Microsoft Office\Office\ OUTLOOK.EXE" /c ipm.stickynote`. (The program path may vary depending on your installation.) Pay attention to the quotation marks around the executable path (since it can contain spaces); there are no quotes around the switch. While you're configuring, change the shortcut icon to reflect a Note, and on the General tab type a new description for your shortcut.

The finished product is shown in Figure 2-27. Now that you've managed to get Outlook installed and running, and you've learned all the tricks of the trade to manipulate the program through the command line, we're going to look at one last detail: how to fix things when they break.

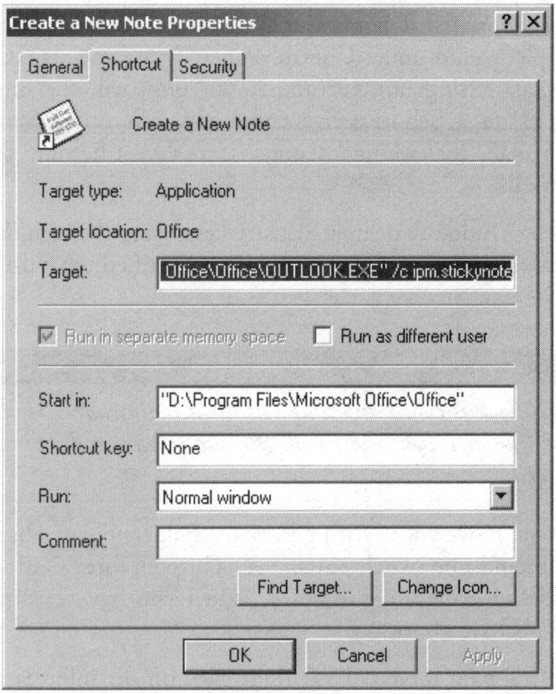

Figure 2-27: Custom Note shortcut using the ipm.stickynote switch

When Things Go Bump in the Night

If you use Outlook long enough and hard enough, eventually you are going to end up breaking something vital, and either the program will not run at all, or it will start to act like it is possessed. This behavior can result from a long list of possibilities, including: damaged or corrupted configuration files, damaged or corrupted information stores (PSTs or OSTs), a damaged DLL, or an overwritten Registry key. The list is long, but the point here is that the problem could be in any number of places, perhaps even more than one.

Given the complexities of today's software, it is often not practical—from a time perspective—to look too deeply for the problem. Sometimes it is quicker to just reinstall from your original CD. You could easily spend an hour scouring through Registry keys and configuration files and come up empty-handed; on the other hand, a reinstallation typically takes less than 20 minutes.

Here are the steps to follow if you are asked to do an exorcism on Outlook:

1. Reboot your system. You'd be amazed at how many gremlins you can chase away by simply rebooting a system and clearing the cobwebs from memory.

2. Locate and run `scanpst.exe` (typically located in *\Program Files\Common Files\System\MAPI\1033\NT*), to scan the PST or OST file for errors.

3. Make sure all your configuration information is copied down, and then delete all your mail accounts. Reboot your system, and re-enter this information via the Mail applet found under Control Panel (*before* you start Outlook). When Outlook's mail settings are corrupted, not only will the program hang (or possibly lock) on a Send/Receive command, but other components totally unrelated to mail (for example, Contacts or Notes) become sluggish or unresponsive as well.

4. Try rebuilding Outlook's default Registry keys using the command [`full path`] `Outlook.exe /Cleanprofile`. For a complete list of command-line switches, see Appendix C.

WARNING

Make sure Outlook is closed any time you use a maintenance/repair command line switch or the scanpst Inbox repair tool. We also recommend that all other programs be closed as well.

---

5. Close Outlook, move your existing Personal Folders file to a backup folder, and run the command-line switch `/cleanpst`. This will force Outlook to generate a new PST file and open in this store. When you have a corrupted PST file, Outlook will behave erratically.

   To find the full path to your PST, right-click on the information store mail is delivered to (typically, the folder displaying the Outlook Today icon), and from the context menu choose Properties. On the General Tab, click on the Advanced button. The Path field will give you the information you need.

6. All of these steps should take you no more than 10–15 minutes. If you have not solved the problem, drag out your original CD, insert it in your drive, open My Computer, and from your CD-ROM's context menu choose Install or Configure. The Office installer will run. From the first dialog displayed, choose Repair Office. The Reinstall/Repair Office dialog is shown in Figure 2-28.

   The "Reinstall Office" option will do precisely as it says—it will reinstall Office with the options and settings used the last time an installation was run. The "Repair errors..." option scours your installation and checks all program files, DLLs, and other associated program components for the correct time/date-stamp/filesize according to information contained on the installation CD-ROM. If the repair process finds a file that is out of sync with the CD's setup information, it is replaced. Both options take about the same amount of time to run, so you're probably better off with the Reinstall option.

7. Finally, when all else fails, uninstall Office completely (Control Panel → Add/Remove Programs), run Microsoft's Office Registry cleaner program (see Tip # 13), and reinstall. While this may sound a little dramatic to the uninitiated, trust us, it is not the huge undertaking it appears to be at first glance.

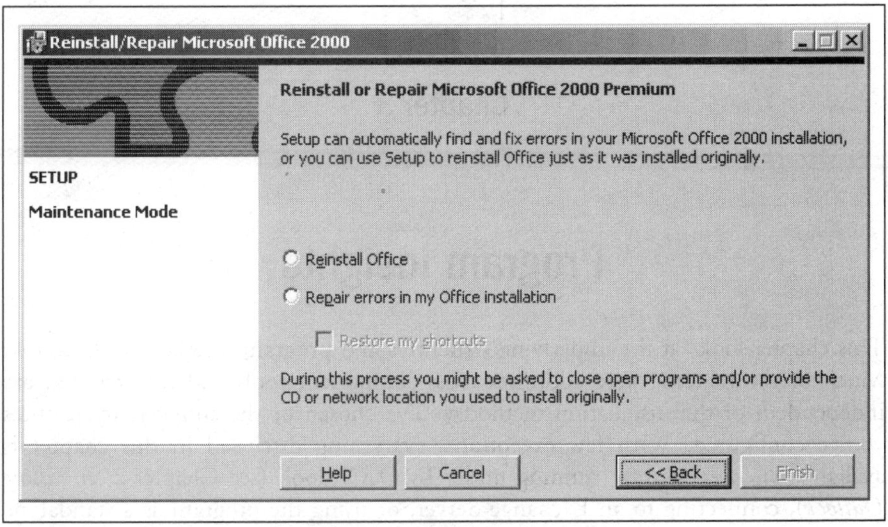

Figure 2-28: The Office Reinstall/Repair dialog

Uninstalling Office does *not* remove any of your data or configuration files, so the whole process (uninstall, run the Registry cleaner, reboot, and reinstall) typically takes less than 20 minutes. Considering, as noted previously, that it is easy to spend half an hour poking around the Registry and still not find any tangible solutions to the problem, this is an efficient—and usually effective—way to exorcise software demons. This, however, should be the last step taken. If your troubles reside in a corrupted PST file, the uninstall/reinstall process will do nothing to resolve your problem.

TIP # 13
Cleaning Up After Office

Microsoft has acknowledged that when uninstalling Office, certain keys are not properly removed from the system Registry. They have provided a small program to address this issue, and it can be found by searching the Microsoft Knowledge Base (http://search.support.microsoft.com/kb/c.asp) for article Q239938: "OFF2000 Utility to Completely Remove Remaining Office Files and Registry Entries" (the current filename is eraser2k.exe).

Chapter 3

Program Insights

This chapter looks at the underlying structures and program interfaces of Outlook. Much of the material here addresses cross-component tools and features that are independent of the installation method you've chosen or the connectivity features you've configured. With few exceptions, everything discussed in this chapter is available whether you are running under IMO Outlook (see Chapter 2, *Installing Outlook*), connecting to an Exchange Server, or using the program as a standalone Personal Information Manager.

In the pages to follow, you are going to read about *Information Stores*, *Address Books*, *items*, *folders*, and *properties*. These are the fundamental building blocks of Outlook. In order to understand the program and use it effectively, it is very important to grasp how these terms relate to the data you create and the tools Outlook provides to manipulate and view that data.

There is also considerable material in this chapter on *views* and *forms*. Views are the mechanism used to display the items contained in a folder. Outlook installs with a preconfigured set of views, and as you will soon discover, these default views are customizable in a dizzying number of ways. Forms are the structural containers used to input and display individual data records. When you open a Note or Calendar entry, it opens in a form; when you create a contact record, you enter the details in a form.

All in all, there is a lot of very densely packed material in this chapter. It is a functional necessity, however, to understand how to nail two pieces of wood together before you can build a house. And before you can build a house, you need a foundation to attach everything to. So first up is a discussion of Outlook's very foundation: Information Stores.

Outlook Information Stores

Outlook saves records in a flat-file (nonrelational) database called an *Information Store*. Every installation has one or more information stores, and, depending on how Outlook is installed and what features are configured, these stores can be one of several "flavors."

Personal Folder Files (PST, or Personal Store)

PSTs are the default information stores used by IMO Outlook and, optionally, by CW. PSTs are created with a predefined set of system folders (see Chapter 2) when configured as the delivery location for email messages. Outlook supports one, and only one, delivery location. You can, however, use multiple PSTs to organize and store your Outlook items. Creating and using multiple PSTs is discussed in Chapter 13, *File Management*.

Exchange Mailboxes

If you use Outlook as an Exchange client, information stores can also be located on the server in the form of a user mailbox. Exchange mailboxes are structurally similar to PSTs and can contain all the same folders a PST does (Inbox, Outbox, Sent Items, Contacts, etc.).

Offline Folder Files (OST, or Offline Store)

Offline Folders are only available under CW Outlook and are local replicas of a user's Exchange mailbox. Offline folders are used when you do not have a persistent connection to Exchange: for example, when your working system is a notebook. You can have only one OST file on your system, and this OST is always defined as the default delivery location for messages. (See Chapter 17, *Outlook and Exchange*, for details on using Offline Folders.)

 An OST file and a PST file can coexist on a system should you find it necessary to keep an archive of records apart from your "working" information store.

Public Folders

Public Folders are another form of information store that reside on an Exchange Server. Public folders are shared databases, accessible by anyone with the appropriate permissions, that can contain any of Outlook's item types (discussed in the following section). In addition, public folders can also store documents, threaded discussions, newsgroup feeds, and scheduling information. Public folders are the backbone of many of Exchange's collaboration features. Details on creating and using public folders can be found in Chapter 17.

Inside Information Stores

An information store contains two additional object types:

Folders

Folders are the organizational structure for Outlook's individual records. They are type specific (Mail, Calendar, Contact, Task, Note, or Journal) and are arranged in a hierarchical tree-like format just like the filesystem on your hard drive, with the "root" represented by the information store itself. The default information store contains several "system" folders that are required, and cannot be renamed, moved, or deleted. They are: Inbox, Outbox, Sent Items, Deleted Items, Drafts, Calendar, Contacts, Tasks, Notes, and Journal.

Outlook's Achilles Heel

Outlook's use of a flat-file database for storing information is a fundamental weakness in program design. While reasonably robust, a nonrelational database does not lend itself well to extensibility or associations.

Contact data in particular is by its very nature dynamic and relational. A contact works for a company, has a wife and two children, is related to another contact, etc. Outlook handles these relationships, but only in a superficial way, and with kludges—not truly extensible associations.

For example, entering a date into a contact's birthday field creates an automatic link to that date in Outlook's Calendar. But what if you want to add a spouse's birthday? That's a manual entry. And what if a contact has more than four phone numbers or three email addresses? Yes, you can create a user-defined field to handle this information, but the linkages and functionality of Outlook's default phone fields are lost by this approach.

Until Outlook graduates to a fully relational database structure, the program's potential will continue to be limited by design.

Items

> Items are the individual records you create. Items are type specific as well, and could be a new contact record, an email message stored in your Inbox, or a doctor's appointment. Items are comprised of fields that store the details of an entry—for example, the subject of a message, or the duration of a meeting.

In addition to folders and items, information stores also contain important details about their own properties: which messages have been downloaded from your mail server, table size, passwords, etc. Some of these properties can be modified by the store's properties dialog (see the section on "Information Store (PST) Properties" later in this chapter), while others are controlled by Outlook and not configurable by the user.

Figure 3-1 shows an overview of how Outlook's various structures and components fit together.

 Outlook scatters program settings and configuration options all over your hard disk (see Chapter 13 for a comprehensive list). Technically, views do not exist within an information store—folder settings are stored there, but you can also find view information in the Registry and user folders. The intent of Figure 3-1 is to provide the reader with an overview of the relationship between Outlook structures.

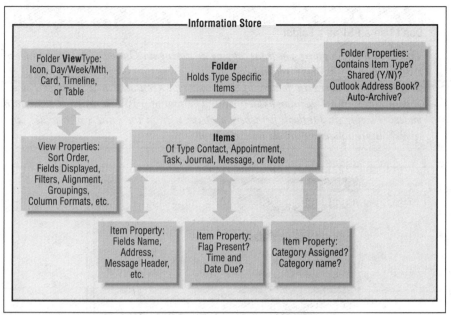

Figure 3-1: Outlook's Information Store and its internal structures

PST, Folder, and Item Properties

Outlook's design and functionality revolve around the concept of properties. Everything in Outlook has a property. A view has a type property (Day/Week/Month, Timeline, Table), and the type property has subproperties (sort order, filters applied, columns displayed, etc.). Outlook items have properties: unread, flagged, format, ad infinitum. For the most part, the concept of properties is hidden from view by the use of names or labels, except when you're working with Outlook's structural elements: information stores, folders, or items. All these elements have dialogs that allow you to view and change selected properties associated with these objects.

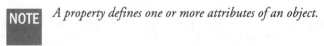 *A property defines one or more attributes of an object.*

Information Store (PST) properties

The default information store created by Outlook is named Personal Folders, and is represented by an icon displaying a house on both the Outlook Bar and the Folder List. To see the properties for an information store, right-click either of these, and select Properties from the context menu. The dialog displayed is shown in Figure 3-2.

TIP # 14

Don't Use a PST as a Folder

There's nothing stopping you from copying or storing an Outlook item in the root of a PST, but we strongly recommend against doing so. Why? Outlook items are designed to be stored in folders of the same type (contacts in a Contact Folder, appointments in a Calendar Folder, etc.). The root of a PST is designed to contain folders. Placing an Outlook item here orphans it from the context of a folder, and severely limits what you can do with the item.

Figure 3-2: The Personal Folders Properties dialog

The name of the information store is displayed at the top of the dialog. Although it looks like you can change this name from here, you can't—you need to do so from the Advanced button.

Description

Provides a text field to note any comments about the PST.

When posting to this folder

Sets the default form used for new items posted to this folder (but not for importing items, nor does it change the form used by existing items in the folder).

Automatically generate Microsoft Exchange views

Generates views that are compatible with Microsoft Exchange. If you share a folder (see Chapter 14, *Collaborating with Outlook*) with people who use Exchange, make sure this option is enabled.

Deliver POP mail to this personal folders file (IMO only)

This determines the location that Outlook delivers email to. Enabling this option generates a set of default system folders used by Outlook for managing email (Inbox, Outbox, Sent Items), plus a system folder for each unique item type (Calendar, Contacts, Tasks, Notes, Journal).

TIP # 15

Changing Your Default POP Location

IMO Outlook only supports one POP delivery location and, as you will note in Figure 3-2, this option is unavailable once set. So the question is, how do you change the location where Outlook delivers messages? The answer is easy, but far from intuitive. First create a new PST (see Chapter 13 for details). Open the properties dialog of this new PST, and select the "Deliver POP mail to..." option. Outlook warns you this change will not take place until you exit and restart Outlook. When you do, a new set of system folders is created and the delivery location is changed.

The folder size button opens the dialog shown in Figure 3-3 (left). This shows the subfolders contained within the PST, plus each subfolder's size. Don't trust these numbers. They indicate size according to items contained within the folder, but do not take into account folder overhead—the forms used by a folder, the view used and its state, and links to other folders.

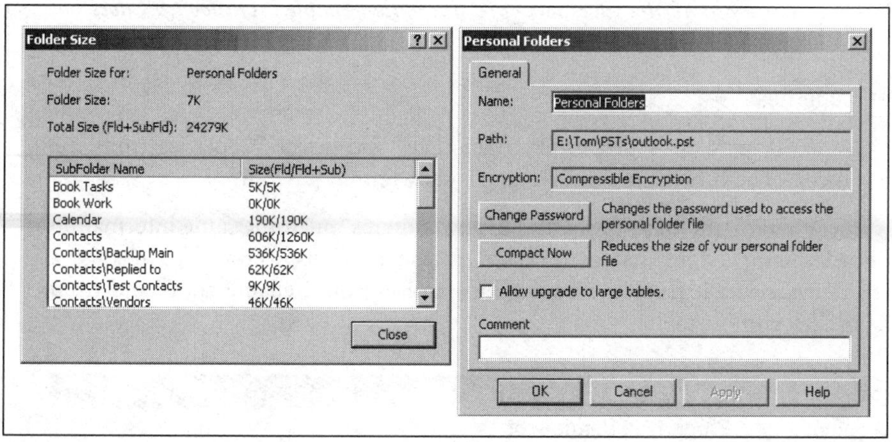

Figure 3-3: The PST Folders size dialog (left) and the Advanced properties dialog (right)

The Advanced properties dialog (named simply Personal Folders) shown in Figure 3-3 (right) contains the following options:

Name
> *This* is where you can change the name of a PST.

Path
> Displays the fully qualified path to the PST. This field is not editable. You might want to write this information down somewhere safe for reference.

Encryption
> Displays the compression and encryption properties of a folder. These properties can only be set when a store is first created. Creating new PSTs is detailed in Chapter 13.

Change Password
> Changes or assigns a password to a PST.

Compact Now
> Recovers the space previously occupied by deleted items. PST and folder maintenance are also topics of Chapter 13.

Allow upgrade to large tables
> Increases the storage capacity of a PST. Unchecked, an information store is limited to approximately 16,000 folders and 16,000 items per folder. With this checkbox selected, this capacity is increased to approximately 64,000 folders and 64,000 items per folder.

> **NOTE** *Selecting "Allow upgrade to large tables" changes the format in which Outlook saves items. Once this format is changed, items created under the large table format cannot be exported and imported in an Outlook information store that does not have this option enabled. Outlook 97 does not support large tables.*

Folder properties

To view/change a folder's properties, right-click, and select Properties from the context menu. The Inbox Properties dialog is shown in Figure 3-4.

The General tab of a folder's properties dialog contains much the same information as the information store dialog discussed in the previous section. To change a folder's name, select it from the Folder List, and use the Rename command from the right-click context menu.

TIP # 16

A Folder's Type Property Is Permanent

You can't change the item type of an existing folder; if you make a folder of the wrong type, you must delete it and recreate it again.

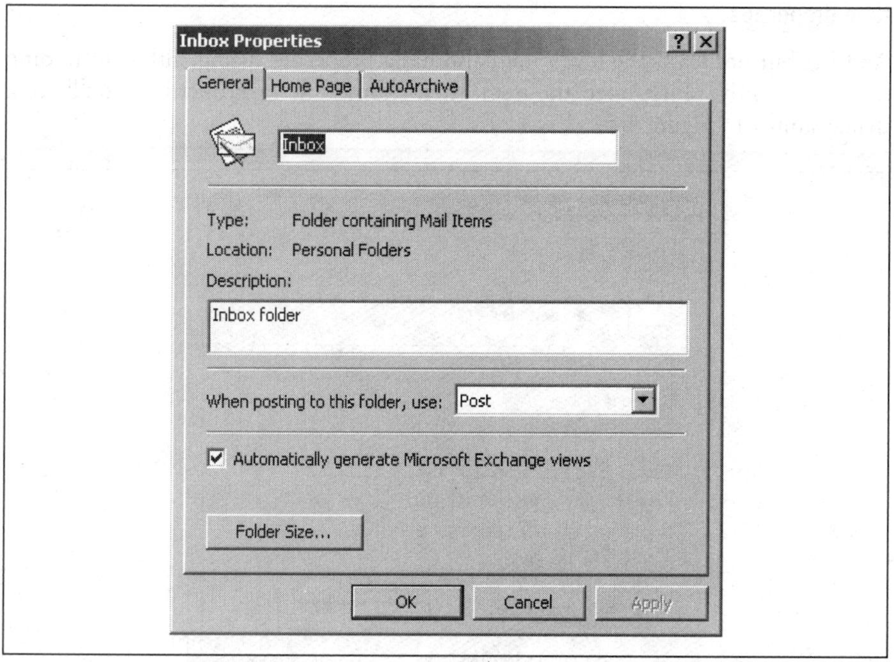

Figure 3-4: The Inbox Properties dialog

Depending on folder type, the Properties dialog also displays several additional tabs:

Home Page (not available for Contact folders)
Associates an HTML page with a folder. Configuring a Home Page is covered later in this chapter under the section "Outlook's Two Special Views."

AutoArchive (not available for Contact folders)
Determines which items from a folder are archived, when, and if items are deleted after they are archived. AutoArchive is discussed in Chapter 13.

Sharing
Displayed when a folder is shared using Outlook's Net Folders feature. Configuring and using Net Folders is detailed in Chapter 14.

Outlook Address Book (Contact folders only)
Lets you define a Contacts folder as an Outlook Address Book. On Contact folders other than the system default, there is also a field on this tab to rename the folder.

Activities (Contact folders only)
Defines the activities Outlook associates with contacts.

Item properties

And last but not least, the lowly item also has a properties dialog, although finding it is not intuitive. First open the item, then choose File → Properties. You'll see a dialog similar to Figure 3-5.

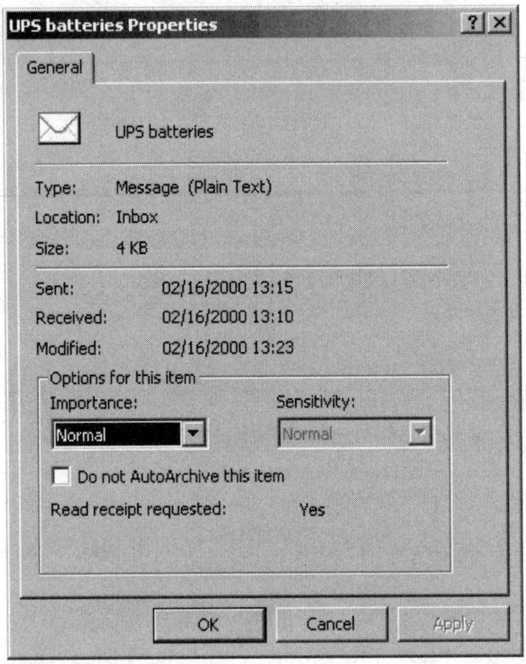

Figure 3-5: The Item Properties dialog

The dialog displays several informational fields (type, format, location, size, date stamps, etc.). You can also set the item's Importance field (Normal, Low, and High), view (but not set) Sensitivity, and mark the item for exclusion from Outlook's AutoArchive feature.

Address Books

In simple terms, an address book is where Outlook stores contact information. Address Books are a messy topic because:

- There can potentially be more than one, confusing users no end. Quickly now, what's the difference between the Outlook Address Book, a Personal Address Book, the Global Address Book, and the Windows Address Book?

- The name suggests a separate, discrete entity. And in some situations, this is indeed the case (the Personal Address Book, for example). In other situations, the term address book refers to an *interface* that collects and synchronizes contact information.

- Address Book dialogs are both visually and organizationally different than the form displayed when a contact record is opened from the Outlook Contacts folder. Because of this, the relationship between the Address Book and the Outlook Contacts folder is not readily apparent.

Let's try to clear this topic up as clearly and as concisely as possible. Depending on your Outlook installation, you can have one or more of the following Address Books on your system:

Outlook Address Book (OAB)—IMO

OK, this is the toughest nut to crack, so we might as well do it first—everything else is relatively easy after this. IMO Outlook saves contact information to the *Outlook Address Book*. The Outlook Address Book is a *property* assigned to a source of contact information. This source can be the Outlook Contacts folder or the data store used by Outlook Express.

The data store used by Outlook is automatically selected as an OAB: you cannot configure this. The default information store used by Outlook must contain a folder called Contacts. This folder is also automatically given the property of OAB. You have no say in this either. You can, however, create additional contacts folders within this (or another) information store and optionally assign one or more of them the property of Outlook Address Book.

The *Address Book* is the *interface* (see WAB, next), represented by a dialog, used to view or create entries in the Outlook Address Book.

Putting all this information together, under IMO Outlook you have at least two sources of contact information, and adding or updating a record in one synchronizes that record in the other. For example, if you add a new entry for Joe Snipps from Outlook Express, this entry is also added to the Contacts folder of Outlook. The inverse is true as well. Note, however, that an email message received by Joe in Outlook Express has no linkage or association to Outlook whatsoever. We're talking address books here, not information stores.

 Any data stores assigned the property of Outlook Address Book are automatically synchronized.

Windows Address Book (WAB)

Go to the Windows Start Menu, select Run, and type in WAB. You have just started the *Windows Address Book* (WAB). The WAB is a collection of *DLLs* and an executable file installed as part of Outlook Express (OE), which is now typically installed as part of the Windows operating system (or when you install/upgrade IE). In addition, some of Outlook 2000's functionality relies on installing Outlook Express, so whether you like it or not you're probably going to have the WAB program files on your system. The WAB program files are responsible for the Address Book dialog discussed previously.

TIP # 17

Quick Contact Updates

You can run the Windows Address Book using the Windows Run command (Start → Run, enter WAB*) and create or modify contact records, even if both Outlook and Outlook Express are closed. Entries made via the WAB automatically update contact information contained in both OE and Outlook.*

In addition to providing synchronization between OE and Outlook, the WAB also contains the hooks for the Start Menu command Search → For People. The Find People dialog, which is a subroutine of the WAB, is displayed. You can reach this same dialog by opening the WAB (or Address Book from either Outlook or Outlook Express) and clicking the Find People toolbar icon. From the Find People dialog you can search any address book shown in the "Look in" drop-down list. The entries displayed here include any Outlook Contact folders designated as an Outlook Address Book or any directory service configured in either Outlook or Outlook Express.

Global Address List (GAL)— Exchange-based
The *Global Address List* contains a list of all the recipients in an Exchange organization. The GAL is more than just people though. The GAL is a list of any object that can receive messages, which can be a mailbox, a Distribution List, a Custom Recipient (email addresses for contacts outside the company), or a Public Folder. The Exchange administrator assigns user permissions to entries in the GAL.

Offline Address Book (OAB)—CW only
A subset of the GAL, stored in a local file, the *Offline Address Book* can be used when a LAN or Internet connect to Exchange in not available. The OAB can contain all or part of the GAL, depending on permissions assigned.

 Outlook must be configured to use Offline folders before an Offline Address Book can be created.

Personal Address Book (PAB)—CW only
Before the arrival of Outlook 2000, the only way a user could create a distribution list was via the *Personal Address Book*. Outlook 2000 now supports distribution lists natively, so for most users the need for a PAB has gone away. If you're using CW Outlook to access one or more mail servers, and your contact information is stored on the server, PAB still retains value. The PAB allows you to copy contact information from diverse sources to one file (for example, multiple mail servers), and then add personal contacts if so desired.

The Address Book is accessed from Outlook by clicking the standard toolbar icon or via the Tools → Address Book command (Ctrl+Shift+B). This opens a dialog similar to that shown in Figure 3-6 (top).

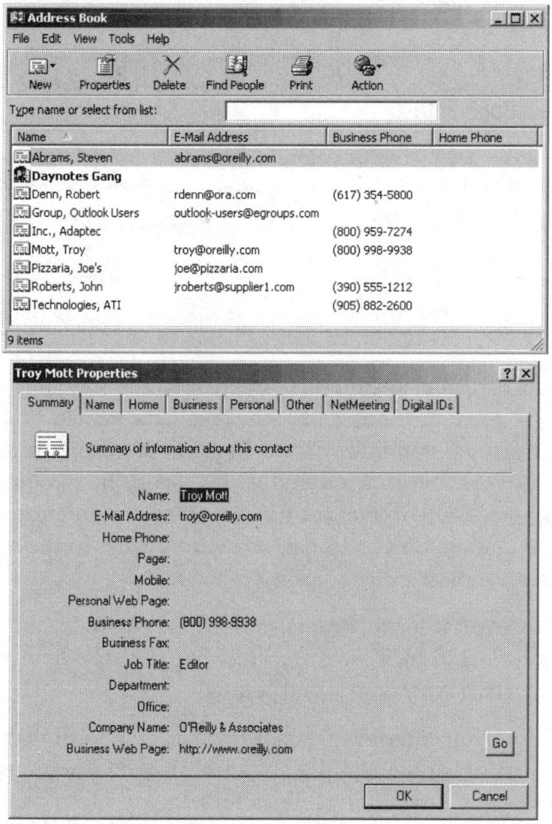

Figure 3-6: Outlook's Address Book dialog (top) and Contact Properties dialog (bottom)

NOTE *Clicking the "To" button on a new message form opens the Select Contacts dialog. This dialog is just a modification on the Address Book dialog allowing you to quickly select recipients from your Outlook Address Book.*

As noted previously, modifying, adding, or deleting an entry from the Address Book dialog is functionally equivalent to working directly in Outlook's Contacts folder. Clicking on the New toolbar icon of the Address Book allows you to add a new Contact or Group to your Contacts folder, using the Address Book dialog. (Group in this context is equivalent to a Distribution List—see Chapter 6, *Mail*, for details on creating and using Distribution Lists.)

Double-click an existing record from the Address Book dialog (or select a record and chose Properties from the toolbar) to open the Properties dialog shown in

Figure 3-6 (bottom). Tabs across the top of the Properties dialog take you to subsets of information pertaining to the open record. Again, note that while the information is arranged and grouped differently here, updating a field on any of the tabs displayed on the Address Book Properties dialog updates the equivalent field found in Outlook's Contacts folder.

TIP # 18

Magic Address Book Entries

If you find entries appearing in your Address Book (and Contacts) folder that you did not make, based only on an email address, you have the option set to automatically add "Replied to" addresses to the Contacts folder (Tools → Options → E-mail Options).

Forms

Information stores provide a structure and container for your data; forms are predefined "boxes" used to input and view that data. When you open a record, Outlook retrieves the required information from the store and displays it in a form. Forms are also customizable in a variety of ways, and, in combination with VBA and VBS (see Chapter 18, *Working with VBA*), allow you to create custom applications that leverage Outlook's existing data structures. Later in the section we'll show you how to build a template using a form.

Figure 3-7 shows a typical form. Recognize it? That's correct, the default Outlook email editor is actually a form. Forms are also what you see when you open a record in Calendar, Contacts, Tasks, Notes, and Journal.

In addition to letting you enter/view data, the fields on a form may contain formatting rules. The name, address, and phone fields on the General page of a Contact form, for example, have parsing capabilities to help you fill in names and addresses correctly. These capabilities are built in to the Outlook executable, so you won't see the rules in the control's properties sheet. When you save an entry, the form simply hands off all its fields to Outlook, which then stores this data dutifully away—in the format provided—in your database.

Much of Outlook's functionality for collaboration centers on exchanging data as email or attachments to email. When Outlook exchanges a message with another email client, that data is bundled in a combination of text and a proprietary binary attachment (typically, *winmail.dat*); inside this binary attachment are the specifications for the form Outlook wants to use to display the data. The email client on the receiving end opens the message, reads the text, and tries to decipher the form Outlook wants the data displayed in.

This explains why some messages are not always translated as intended. When another email client (sometimes another Outlook email client using a different message format) receives a message and it does not understand the attached

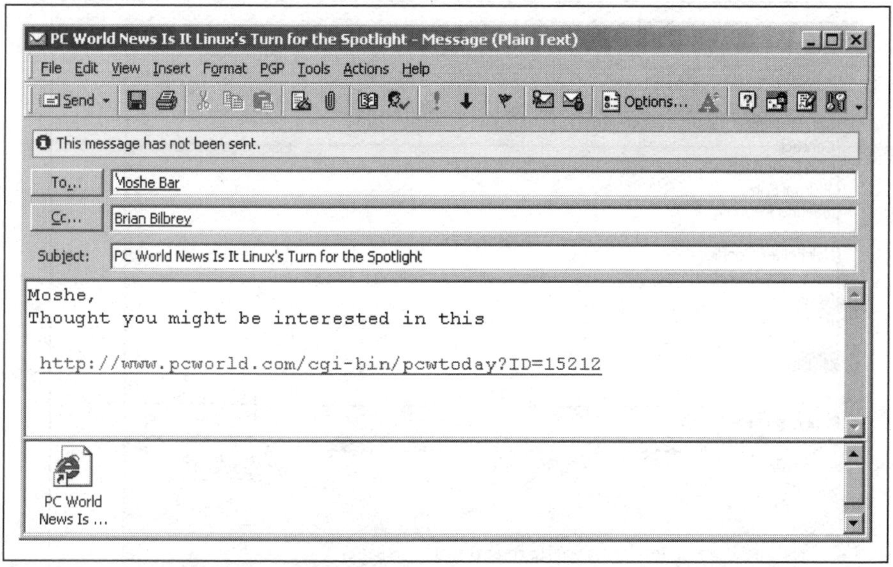

Figure 3-7: A typical Outlook form

winmail.dat file, it resolves this by displaying the text part of the message and either discarding or attaching the binary information. Such scenarios are notoriously common when you try to exchange Task or Meeting requests with other users (see Chapter 9, *Tasks*, and Chapter 7, *Calendar*).

Default Forms

The default forms used by Outlook are found in the Standard Forms Library. The Tools → Forms → Choose Form command displays the Choose Form dialog shown in Figure 3-8. The Details button toggles a section with additional information about the selected item.

The Standard Forms Library (available from the Look In drop-down list) contains Outlook's main component forms. Open a form, fill it in, and click Save or Save and Close. You've created a new Outlook item just as you would by invoking the New command in the form's associated component.

The Look In list, shown in Figure 3-9, specifies storage locations for forms. The Library entries are fixed locations; other entries enable the Browse button, letting you select an Outlook folder or filesystem location. The "User Templates in File System" option references the folder you've selected to store Office templates, usually Templates\Outlook (you can see the path to the Templates folder from Word, for example, in Tools → Options → File Locations). An Outlook template (file extension *.oft*) is simply a form saved to an external file location.

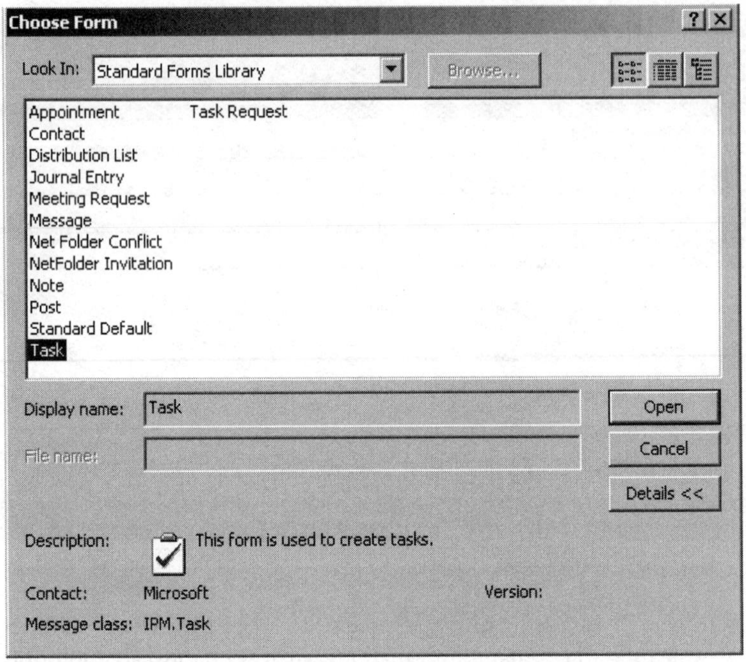

Figure 3-8: The Choose Form dialog

Figure 3-9: Choosing forms from other places

TIP # 19

Form or Template?

Outlook makes a distinction between a form and a template. Forms can be of two varieties: Standard (supplied by the program) and Personal (created by you). Templates, on the other hand, are existing forms, saved with a specific layout and/or text, which can be used as a basis for new entries. Note the difference—forms are created; templates are saved copies of an existing form.

Designing a Custom Form

The first thing to understand about creating a custom form in Outlook is that *it must be based on an existing Outlook form.* This is why the Tools → Forms → Design a Form command only allows you to select from existing forms, not to specify a new name. This means you can only create a customized form based on an existing form from one of the locations found on the Look In list of the Design Form dialog.

 NOTE *Customized forms may be used to standardize information distribution or collection, or to personalize postings with, for example, a company logo. However, they can go far beyond this. An entire application can be based on custom forms, which have little or no resemblance to any of the standard Outlook forms.*

Figure 3-10 shows a new custom form in progress; the new form is based on a Message form selected from the Standard library.

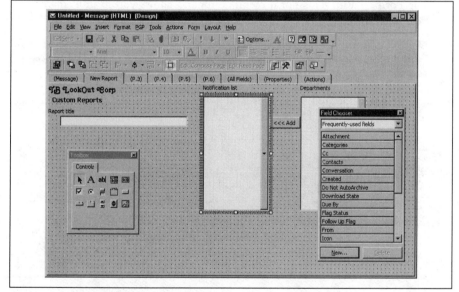

Figure 3-10: Designing a new report form based on a Message form

Layout and design is accomplished with the *Controls Toolbox* and *Field Chooser* tools; the placement commands are found on the Layout menu.

Keep the following points in mind when designing custom forms:

- All Outlook forms (except the Note form) are multi-tabbed forms, with a fixed set of pages. One or more pages are displayed, and the others (P.2 to P.6) can be made visible and used for your purposes. However, you can't create new pages on a form. So if you need more than six pages, you are out of luck. In addition to the pages with controls, there are also pages that display form properties, fields, and actions.

- It is important to start with an existing form that contains the fields required by your custom form. Layout can be changed, but available fields can't. The original form defines which main toolbars and menus are shown and enabled.

- Invisible pages are indicated by tab names in parentheses. At least one page must be visible, and if only one page is visible, you won't see any tabs. Visibility is set for a selected tab with the Form → Display This Page toggle. While the total number of tabs varies depending on the type of form chosen, you can design five custom pages using the extra pages originally labeled P.2 to P.6.

- The All Fields tab provides direct access to most database fields associated with the form. Here you can inspect field properties and customize additional data fields as required.

- The Form → Run This Form menu command allows you to immediately use (test) your form.

 Deleting a user-defined field from the database does not remove it from any items where the field has been used. The field is only removed from the list of available fields for future selection.

Each form has associated properties and actions, defined by the last two tabs. Figure 3-11 shows a typical Form Actions list.

| (Message) | New Report | (P.3) | (P.4) | (P.5) | (P.6) | (All Fields) | (Properties) | (Actions) |

Enabled	Action name	Creates form of type	Address form like	When responding	Prefix
Yes	Reply	Message	Reply	Respect user's default	RE
Yes	Reply to All	Message			
Yes	Forward	Message			
Yes	Reply to Folder	Post			
Yes	Reply with Appointment	Appointment			

Form Action Properties

Action name: `Reply with Appointment` ☑ Enabled

This action creates a form of the following type:

Form name: `Appointment` Check

Message class: `IPM.Appointment`

Characteristics of the new form

When responding: `Attach original message`

Address form like a: `Response`

☑ Show action on
  ● Menu and Toolbar
  ○ Menu only

This action will
  ○ Open the form
  ○ Send the form immediately
  ● Prompt the user to open or send

Subject prefix: `AREQ`

[OK] [Cancel]

[New...] [Properties] [Delete]

Figure 3-11: Defining a new Appointment action

To illustrate the associated Actions subdialog, a new action to send an Appointment form was created for this screenshot. The Form Action Properties dialog specifies the form type created by the action, response type, and any prompts. One option here is to make the response completely automatic, but in most scenarios you want the form to open for the user to fill in and send a response. The custom subject prefix for the response action is added to the generated response in the same way that "RE" and "FW" are added for replies and forwarded messages, respectively. Adding a subject prefix to a message is useful when responses are filtered and managed by mail rules, since a unique prefix makes rules-based message identification very easy.

These defined actions are reflected in the menu and toolbar options presented with the form when it is used. In the dialog, there is the option to restrict this addition to the menu only.

Figure 3-12 shows the Properties tab for a form under design. This provides several fields for form management information, password protection, linking to a particular contact, and room for describing what the form is for. Note the "Use form only for responses" checkbox, which makes the form available only in contexts where replying to a received item is possible.

| (Message) | New Report | (P.3) | (P.4) | (P.5) | (P.6) | (All Fields) | (Properties) | (Actions) |

Category: _____ Version: _____
Sub-Category: _____ Form Number: _____

☐ Always use Microsoft Word as the e-mail editor
Template... _____ [Change Large Icon...]

Contact... _____ [Change Small Icon...]

Description: _____ ☐ Protect form design:
[Set Password...]

☐ Send form definition with item
☐ Use form only for responses

Figure 3-12: Properties for the form

Publishing a Form

After the design is complete, you are ready to publish the form. The Tools → Forms → Publish command opens the Publish Form As dialog shown in Figure 3-13.

The Look In field determines where the form is saved. Forms saved in the Personal Forms Library are accessible from any Outlook component or folder; saving a form to a specific folder makes it available only from that folder.

 NOTE *You cannot save a custom form to the Standard Forms Library. This library is owned and operated by Outlook, and off-limits.*

Although you can also save a form with File → Save As in a variety of formats to specific filesystem locations, this does not make it easily usable from within Outlook. You should publish the form to a folder or library frequently, and also

---

Deleting Custom Forms

There is a way to delete custom forms, but only from CW Outlook (apparently, Microsoft decided that IMO users do not need to delete old forms). Here is one method:

1. Go to Tools → Options → Other.

2. Click the Advanced Options button.

3. On the Advanced Options dialog, click the Custom Forms button.

4. On the Custom Forms dialog, click the Manage Forms button.

5. On the Forms Manager dialog, you can delete forms or copy them to other locations, using the two panes provided.

You can also get to the Forms Manager from a folder's properties sheet (again, only under CW Outlook).

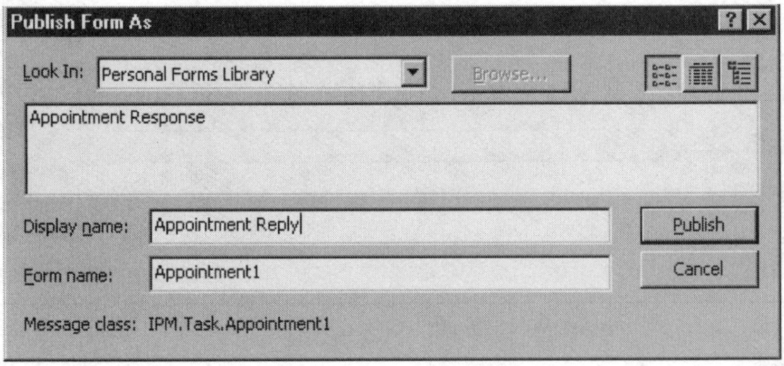

Figure 3-13: Publishing a form in the Personal Forms Library

save it (Save As, *.oft* file, not just Save) to a template file, as a backup. Just saving simply saves the form as an Outlook item.

Sending and Receiving Forms

Forms can be sent and received as email attachments as a means of exchange. To send a form to another user:

1. Go to the library containing the form and open it (Tools → Choose Form).

2. Save the form as an Outlook Template (File → Save As, Type: Outlook Template).

3. Open a new message, address it, and attach the form (now template) you saved in the previous step. (It might be a good idea to add the following instructions so the recipient will know what to do with the attachment when it arrives). Send the message.

When you're on the receiving end of a form attachment, do the following to add it to your library:

1. Open the message, and double-click the attachment. This opens the form.

2. Now publish the form (Tools → Forms → Publish Form) to your Personal Forms Library or to a shared forms library, as appropriate.

Forms as Templates

Do you routinely send messages, structured in a specific way, to the same people? For example, every Friday you send a status report to your editor. It details the progress made (or lack thereof) for each chapter you're working on, projected completion dates, plus comments and questions. Instead of repeatedly entering the same information every week, create a message containing the details that remain fixed and save this message as a form.

 NOTE *We use an email message in this example, but the same principle works for any Outlook item you enter or send on a routine basis.*

Here are the steps:

1. Create a new email message. Add the recipients, subject, and details that remain constant; exclude information that varies. Open the message's Options dialog (View → Options) and enter a Contact link, a category, and any special delivery options applicable. An example is shown in Figure 3-14.

2. Go to Tools → Forms → Publish Form As.

3. The Personal Forms Library is selected as the default location. Save the form here if it is for your own personal use. Publicly available forms are typically saved to an Organizational Forms Library on a shared network drive.

4. In the Display name field, name the form. This is the name that appears in the Look In drop-down list. In the Form name field, type a name for the form if you want it to be different from the displayed name.

5. Select Publish. Unless the form you used already has the "Save Form Definition with Item" option selected, the dialog shown in Figure 3-15 is displayed. It's important to answer Yes if your form contains any custom menus or fields.

When you want to send a message based on this form, go to File → New → Choose Form. Select the location and template, add any additional information, and click Send. Outlook does not add any of this additional information to the template unless you republish the form.

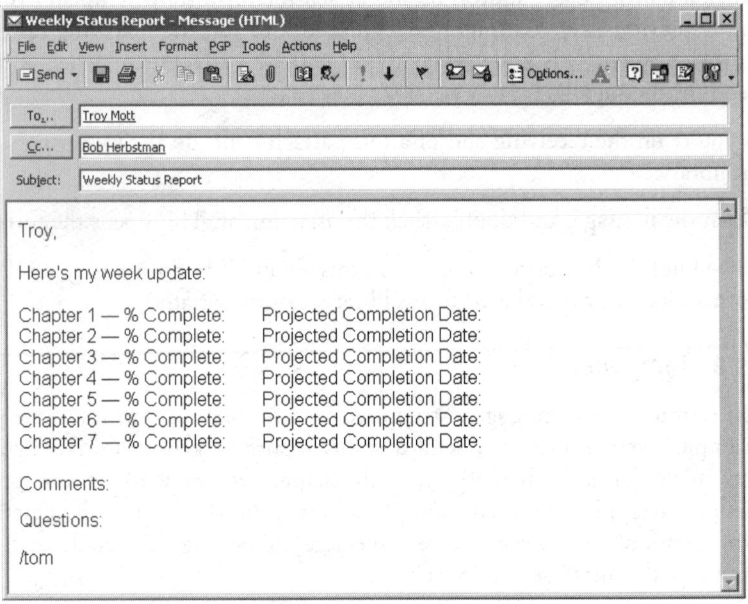

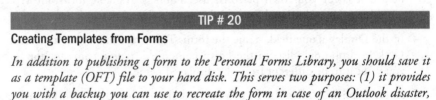

Figure 3-14: Using a form as a template

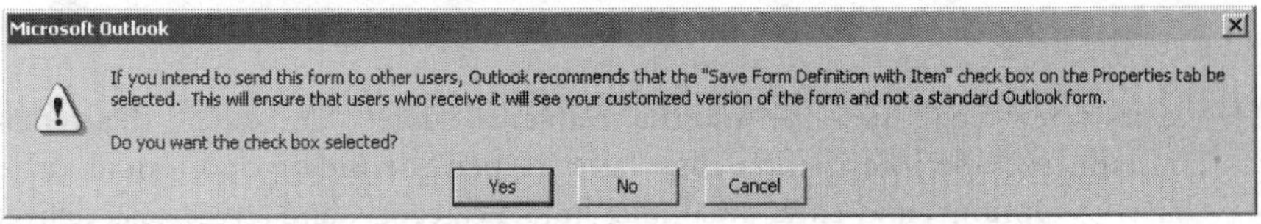

Figure 3-15: The "Save Form Definition…" warning dialog

To add fields to your New Message form, you need to customize the form in the Outlook Forms Designer as detailed earlier in this section.

TIP # 20

Creating Templates from Forms

In addition to publishing a form to the Personal Forms Library, you should save it as a template (OFT) file to your hard disk. This serves two purposes: (1) it provides you with a backup you can use to recreate the form in case of an Outlook disaster, and (2) template format is necessary for some Outlook features. For example, if you're designing an automatic reply to use in conjunction with a Mail rule (see Chapter 6), you must use the OFT file type.

A Primer on Views and Print Styles

Views are one of the key program elements of Outlook. Views display the contents of a folder in a defined way. There are five basic view styles; some are graphical layouts (for example, Calendar's Day/Week/Month views); others are structured as tables in the traditional row and column format. Print Styles are a close cousin to views, and define how an individual item, or the contents of a folder, is printed.

Understanding views is important. Using the right view for a given data set allows you to focus on the records you need to see, in an order that brings important details to the surface, in a format or layout that's conducive to what you're trying to accomplish. And when you can't find an appropriate view for the task at hand, understanding the options available for a view allows you to create a new, customized view that displays the information you need to see, how you need to see it.

Table 3-1 lists Outlook's default views, the folder type they are associated with, and the print styles that can be used from a given view. These are Outlook's out-of-box defaults. Within certain limitations, all views and print styles can be customized.

 NOTE *We use the terms "default" and "preconfigured" synonymously when referring to views. When Outlook is first installed, a default or preconfigured set of views is created for each item type. These default views can then be customized to suit user preferences and work style. A customized default view can be reset to its original state; a view created from scratch (that is, not modified from an existing view), cannot, as there is no default state.*

Table 3-1: Outlook's Default Views and Print Styles

Outlook Folder Type	Default Views	Print Styles
Mail	Messages	Table, Memo
	Messages with Auto-Preview	Table, Memo
	By Follow Up Flag	Table, Memo
	Last Seven Days	Table, Memo
	Flagged for Next Seven Days	Table, Memo
	By Conversation Topic	Table, Memo
	By Sender	Table, Memo
	Unread Messages	Table, Memo
	Sent To	Table, Memo
	Message Timeline	See Tip # 21
Calendar	Day/Week/Month	Daily, Weekly, Monthly, Tri-fold, Calendar Details, Memo
	Day/Week/Month with AutoPreview	Daily, Weekly, Monthly, Tri-fold, Calendar Details, Memo

Table 3-1: *Outlook's Default Views and Print Styles (continued)*

Outlook Folder Type	Default Views	Print Styles
	Active Appointments	Table, Memo
	Events	Table, Memo
	Annual Events	Table, Memo
	Recurring Appointments	Table, Memo
	By Category	Table, Memo
Contacts	Address Cards	Card, Small Booklet, Medium Booklet, Memo, Phone Directory
	Detailed Address Cards	Card, Small Booklet, Medium Booklet, Memo, Phone Directory
	Phone List	Table, Memo
	By Category	Table, Memo
	By Company	Table, Memo
	By Location	Table, Memo
	By Follow Up Flag	Table, Memo
Tasks	Simple List	Table, Memo
	Detailed List	Table, Memo
	Active Tasks	Table, Memo
	Next Seven Days	Table, Memo
	Overdue Tasks	Table, Memo
	By Category	Table, Memo
	Assignment	Table, Memo
	By Person Responsible	Table, Memo
	Completed Tasks	Table, Memo
	Task Timeline	See Tip # 21
Notes	Icons	N/A
	Notes List	Table, Memo
	Last Seven Days	Table, Memo
	By Category	Table, Memo
	By Color	Table, Memo
Journal	By Type	See Tip # 21
	By Contact	See Tip # 21
	By Category	See Tip # 21
	Entry List	Table, Memo
	Last Seven Days	Table, Memo
	Phone Calls	Table, Memo

TIP # 21

Printing a Timeline View

You cannot print a Timeline view. You can, however, select an individual entry (or entries) within a Timeline view and print your selection in Memo style.

Default Views

Outlook supports five basic view styles:

Table view

> Displays Outlook items in a table format with individual records shown as rows, and fields within that record as columns.

Card view

> Represents a folder's contents in a style similar to index cards. A title is shown on the top line of the card, with selected fields in rows below this. The title is typically the field the folder is sorted or indexed on, but it can be any other field of your choosing.

Day/Week/Month view

> Displays your records in a familiar calendar style format, showing the contents of a folder by date and displayed in either a day, week, or month format.

Timeline view

> Displays items chronologically as an icon on a horizontal bar. Timeline views are typically *grouped* (more on this term in a moment) according to a property, with records depicted by icons and spaced on the timeline according to date received or created.

Icon view

> Displays individual records as icons representing the item type, and a caption or title below the icon.

Note that while each of the default views is often thought of in a component-specific context (for example, Card view for Contacts and Day/Week/Month for Calendar), you can create customized views that display the contents of any folder in any view style. There is nothing stopping you from creating a Card view to display your Notes. As a matter of fact, there will be individuals who much prefer the layout and capabilities of such a view to the icon default. Such is the power of views—ultimate user customization.

We'll get to the details of customizing a view shortly, but first some background is in order. Before you start hacking the defaults, it is important to understand what exactly it is you're configuring and the tools at your disposal for doing so.

Understanding Views

By now you should be familiar with the concept of properties, as it's been a central thread throughout this chapter. Everything you've learned applies to views as well. Views are a program element, either associated with a specific folder or shared among similar item-type folders; as objects, views have one or more properties. The following is a list of just a few of the properties a view can have:

> View type (Table, Card, Icon, etc.)
> Shared or folder constrained
> AutoPreview and/or Preview Pane
> Fields displayed
> Grouping
> Sort order
> Filters
> Font (typeface, size, color)—automatic or manual
> Gridlines

To see the properties assigned to a given view, go to View → Current View → Customize Current View. This opens the View Summary dialog shown in Figure 3-16.

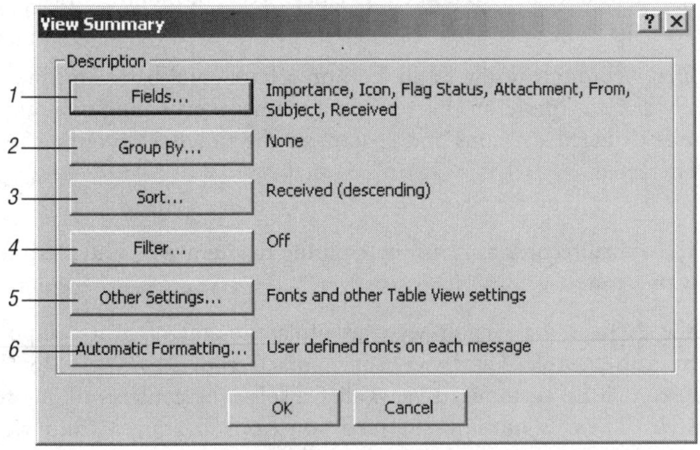

Figure 3-16: The View Summary dialog shown for a table view (Inbox)

The View Summary dialog is the place to head when you're modifying, customizing, or just curious about the settings used by a view. Each button on the left of the dialog opens a subdialog containing the options available for the current view:

1. Fields opens a two-paned dialog that enables you to add, remove, sort, and maintain the fields displayed by a view. The Fields option is not available in Note and Timeline views.

2. Group By allows you to group a view on one or more fields. Grouped views apply to timeline and table views. For this reason, Note, Day/Week/Month, and Card views do not support grouping.

3. Sort determines the order in which items are listed in a view. Timeline and Day/Week/Month views do not support sorting.

4. Filter lets you configure under what conditions an item is displayed. All views support filters.

5. Other Settings contains font, gridline, in-cell editing, Preview Pane, Auto-Preview, and column sizing options. The options contained on the Other Setting dialog vary according to the type of view being modified. For example, for a Card view table gridlines and column fonts have no meaning; these are replaced by Card heading font, body font, Card dimensions, and an option to suppress empty fields from the view.

6. Automatic Formatting lets you set the format (font face and color) of an item within a view according to user-configured rules.

 Certain Outlook views do not support the full range of properties shown in the View Summary dialog. For example, you cannot add fields to or group an Icon view.

Modifying Views

The following section looks at the various properties of a view that can be modified, where it's done, and what's involved. As a side benefit, each individual topic provides you with insights on the building blocks that comprise a view, so when the time arrives for you to create a custom view, you will know exactly what to add and why.

Modifying column widths

By default, Outlook displays all the fields assigned to a table view within the view pane. If you have more columns than space to display them, they are compressed and the information contained within is truncated. This is not an issue for views that contain two or three columns like the default Messages view used by the Inbox, but when you get into a view like the Contacts Phone List, important columns are often unreadable.

Assuming you want to keep all the columns displayed (the easiest solution, of course, is to just remove a field you do not use or need—we'll get to that shortly), there are several possible solutions to this problem:

- Resize the column you need to see. Place your mouse cursor on the line separating any two column titles, and drag left or right. With "Automatic column sizing" enabled (View → Current View → Customize Current View → Other

Settings) this compresses columns in the direction you are resizing, but keeps all fields displayed within the view pane.

- Turn off Automatic column sizing. Now when you resize a column, all other columns retain their width but are pushed out of the view pane. Use the scroll bar to move to a column not visible.

- Use the context menu shown in Figure 3-17 (right-click anywhere on the column title bar). Select Best Fit. This sizes all columns in the view just wide enough to show their contents. This is not a persistent setting. If you manually resize a column, the Best Fit setting is discarded.

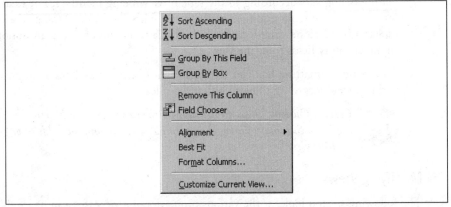

Figure 3-17: The view configuration context menu

TIP # 22

Learn a View's Context Menus

Outlook's context menus are a fast and efficient way to accomplish common tasks. This is especially true when working with views. Make it a habit to explore a view's contexts menus and learn the commands they contain.

Modifying sort order

Sort order determines the order in which items are displayed within a view. For example, the default sort order for the Contacts folder is File As, for Inbox is Received (descending), and for Tasks (Simple List view) has no defined order.

 Views that do not have a sort order explicitly set display items in the order in which they were created or received.

There are a number of ways to modify a view's sort order:

- Table views indicate which columns the view is sorted on with a gray triangle next to the column's title. When the triangle points up, the sort order is ascending; when the triangle points down, the sort order is descending. To change the sort order, click the column title. If the view is already sorted on this field, this action reverses the sort order from ascending to descending, or vice-versa. Clicking on a column with no triangle changes the existing sort order to this field.

- Right-click the column title bar of a table view and choose Sort Ascending or Sort Descending from the context menu.

- For views that support sorting (some do not; for example, Calendar's Day/ Week/Month views and Tasks Timeline view), open the View Summary dialog (View → Current View → Customize Current View) and click on the Sort button. This opens the Sort subdialog shown in Figure 3-18.

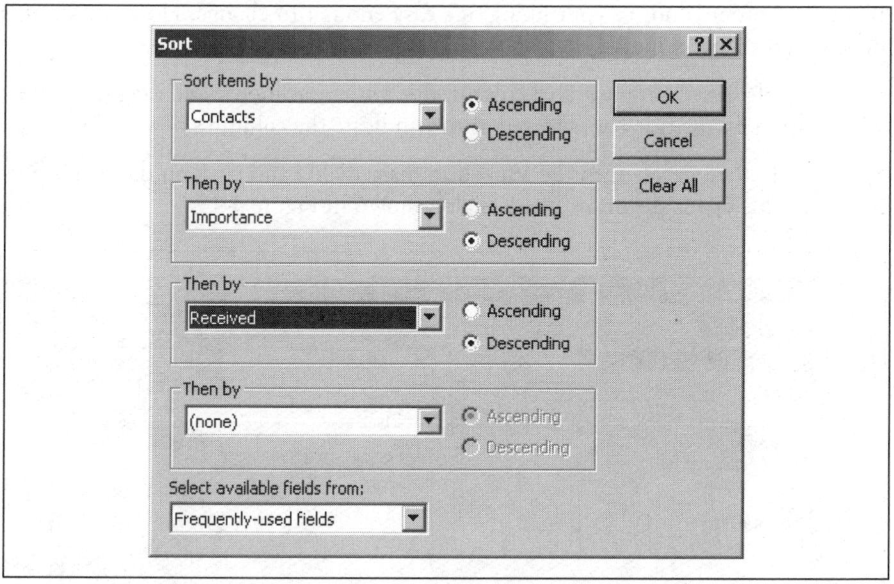

Figure 3-18: The Sort subdialog

TIP # 23

Sorting on Multiple Fields in a Table View

To sort a table view on more than one field, hold down the Shift key while clicking on column titles. Continue to hold the Shift key and click a second time to reverse Ascending/Descending. The "Sort by, Then by, Then by..." order is determined by selection sequence.

Outlook supports sorting up to four levels deep; choosing a field enables the drop-down list for the next level down. If the field you want to sort on is not on the drop-down lists, go to "Select available fields from" and try another group of fields.

To remove all sort order from a view, go to Customize Current View →
Sort, and click on the Clear All button.

Modifying field order

Sort order determines how *items* are ordered within a view. Field order, on the
other hand, determines the order in which the *fields* are displayed within a view.
For example, the default view for the Inbox folder is a table displaying the following
fields from left to right: Importance, Icon, Flag Status, Attachment, From, Subject,
Received. To see the field order of a view, open the View Summary dialog (View →
Current View → Customize Current View); the list of fields displayed and their
order is shown next to the Fields button.

If the field order is not to your liking, it's easy enough to change. How you do this
depends on the view in use:

- For table views, simply grab a column title with your mouse and drag it to a new
  position on the title bar. The red arrows indicate the column's new position.

- For all other views, open the View Summary dialog and click on the Fields button. This opens the Show Fields dialog shown in Figure 3-19.

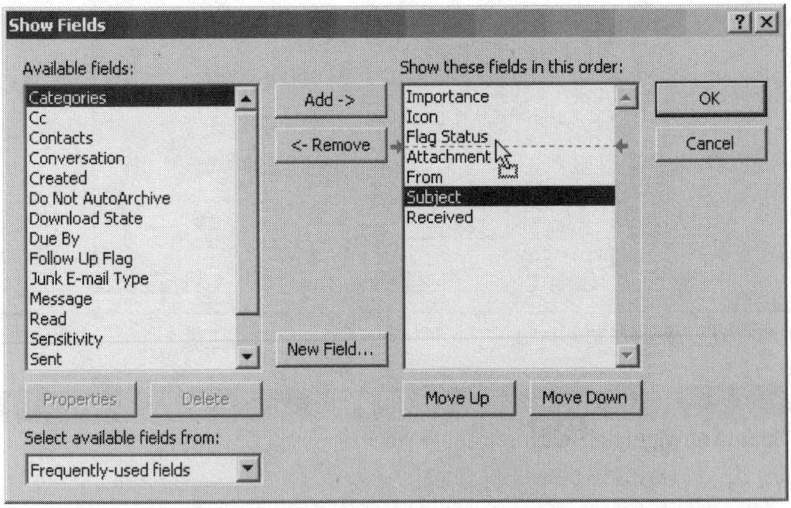

*Figure 3-19: The Show Fields dialog—reorder fields by dragging them while holding
down the right mouse button*

To change a field's display order, select it and drag it to a new location (illustrated by the dashed line in Figure 3-19), or use the Move Up/Down buttons.

Modifying fields displayed

Any given view in Outlook typically displays only a subset of the actual fields available. This is done for two reasons:

- The sheer volume of information hidden behind the façade of a view would overwhelm most users.

- When not entering or modifying data, you do not typically need access to all the fields associated with a given item type.

Everyone is unique, however, so the fields that are pertinent to you may not be pertinent to the next person. To add and remove fields from a view, open the View Summary dialog (View → Current View → Customize Current View), and select the Fields button. The "Show Fields" dialog opens (see Figure 3-19). The right pane shows the fields currently displayed in the view and their order. The left pane shows available fields as defined by the "Select available fields from" drop-down list. To remove a field, drag it from the "Show…" pane to the "Available…" pane; to add a field, reverse the process.

To remove a field from a table view (only), select a column title and drag it off the column title bar or right-click the column title and select "Remove this Column" from the context menu. Sorry—there are no fancy shortcuts to get your fields back again. You'll have to go back to the Show Fields dialog, or reset the view (View → Current View → Define Views, select the view, and choose Reset). Be careful, though, as this will undo all your customizations for the view you are resetting.

An alternate method for adding fields to a table view is to activate the Field Chooser by right-clicking anywhere on the column title bar, and selecting this command from the context menu (see Figure 3-17).

With the Field Chooser dialog displayed, simply locate the field you want to add to your view from the list provided and drag it to the column title bar. The example shown in Figure 3-20 demonstrates this process. Note the two arrows to the left of the Received column. These arrows denote where—in relation to the existing table layout—the dropped field will be positioned.

Creating new fields

You are not limited to the fields Outlook provides in its default views. To create a new field:

1. Go to the View Summary dialog (View → Current View → Customize Current View) and click on the Fields button. From the Show Fields dialog, select New Field (see Figure 3-21).

2. Type a name for the field you wish to add, select a Type from the drop-down list, and then a format for your new field.

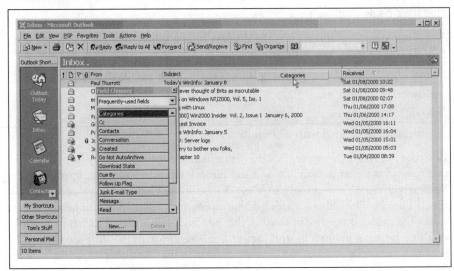

Figure 3-20: The Field Chooser dialog in action

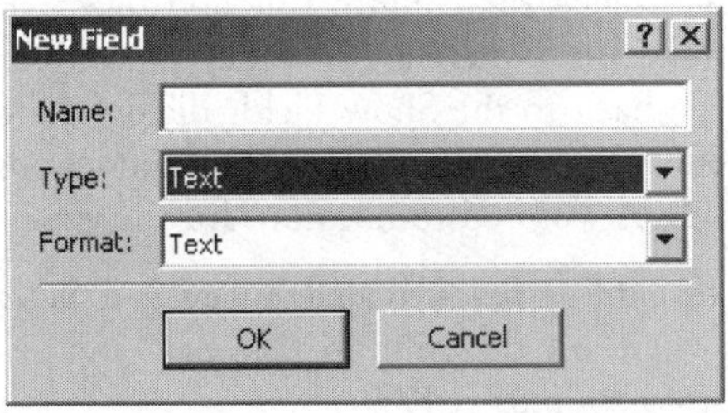

Figure 3-21: The New Field dialog

Before you create a custom field, consider the following:

- If at all possible, use one of Outlook's built-in fields. Using a built-in field enables you to export the data it contains using the Import and Export commands on the File menu. It is also easier to reference a built-in field if you need to write a custom piece of code using VBA or VBS (see Chapter 18).

- Not all of Outlook's preconfigured fields are shown on the program's default forms. To see a list of the fields available for an item type, switch to a view of that type (for example, Contacts or Notes) and open the Field Chooser dialog shown in Figure 3-20. From the drop-down list at the top of the dialog, select All item-type fields.

- If you do create a new field, carefully consider the name you give it. Make sure the name is not already in use, and avoid punctuation marks, property, method, or keyword names.

Filtering items

A filtered view displays only items that meet specified criteria. A good example of a filtered view is the Last Seven Days option available for Mail folders. Any messages older than seven days are not displayed.

TIP # 24

Now Where Did That Record Go?

Filtered views display the text Filter Applied in the upper-right corner of the view pane. Make it a habit to consciously look for this reminder. More than one Outlook user has "lost" a record that was not really lost at all—just hiding behind a filter.

To modify a filtered view, select the Filter button from the View Summary dialog or (when available) choose the Filter command from the right-click context menu within a view. The Filter dialog is shown in Figure 3-22.

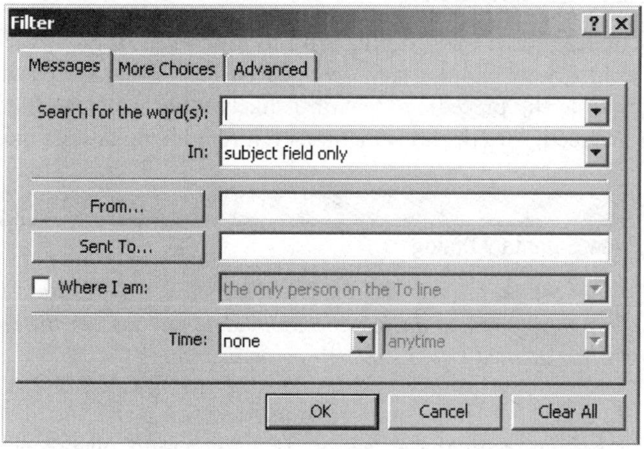

Figure 3-22: The Filter option dialog

Does the dialog look familiar? You've probably seen it before—it's a variant of the Advanced Search dialog discussed later in this chapter. The major difference is that in this case it's being used to hide information, not find it. The Filter dialog contains the following tabs:

`[Item-type specific]`

The first tab is context specific and is labeled according to the view you're filtering. In the example shown in Figure 3-22, the filter command was invoked from a message view. The tab's content varies according to item-type. In case of messages, you can define a word in a specific field, the sender/recipient, your relationship to the messages, and the time frame they were received/sent in.

More Choices

Filters on category assigned, read status, importance, whether the item has attachments, and the size of those attachments.

Advanced

Lets you create advanced filters based on criteria you define. These rules are based on a field, a condition, and a value. For example, the City field "is empty," or the Street Address field contains the value "123."

Grouping items

All of Outlook's Table views can be *grouped* on one or more fields. The concept of groups is simple enough: items within a folder are arranged according to the value of a specific field. For example, a table grouped on Flag status has two groups: one when the value of Flag status is Normal (no flag), and another when the Flag status is Flagged. Items are listed under the appropriate group according the properties of the Flag status. When you start using views with multiple groupings, however, things can get complex in a hurry.

Just like sort order, Table views can have up to four levels of groups. Not too difficult, you say? OK, how about a view grouped on four levels, sorted on four levels, *and* filtered? While the preceding scenario is likely a bit far fetched, grouped views are typically grouped, sorted, and sometime even filtered, on at least one level.

TIP # 25

Use the View Summary Dialog

A good rule of thumb for working with complex views is to use the View Summary dialog as an entry point to all modifications. This lets you see the various groups, sorts, and filters applied before and after customization.

The Group By dialog is identical in form and function to the Sort dialog discussed earlier in this section, with the exception of an Expand/Collapse default list (see Figure 3-23).

Set up the groups using the drop-down lists provided; remember, if you cannot find the field you desire on a list, use the "Select available fields from" drop-down list to broaden the range of fields shown.

 NOTE *To clear all groupings from a view, select the Clear All button on the Group By dialog.*

There is an alternative to using the View Summary dialog—you can arrange a view's groupings visually using the Group By box. This opens a pane above the displayed view, allowing you to simply drag column titles into this area and arrange groupings according to the relative position of where the field box is dropped. Figure 3-24 illustrates the Inbox with the Group By box open.

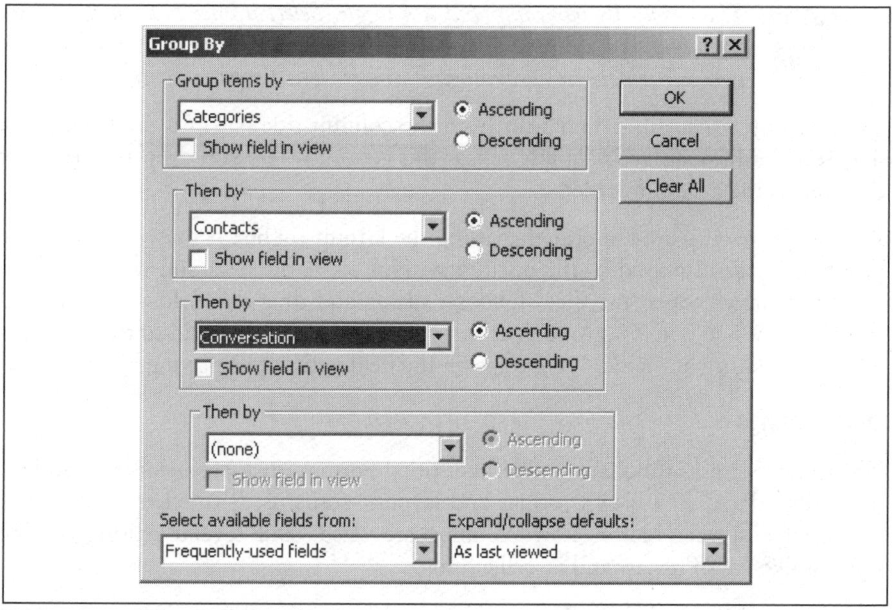

Figure 3-23: The Group By dialog

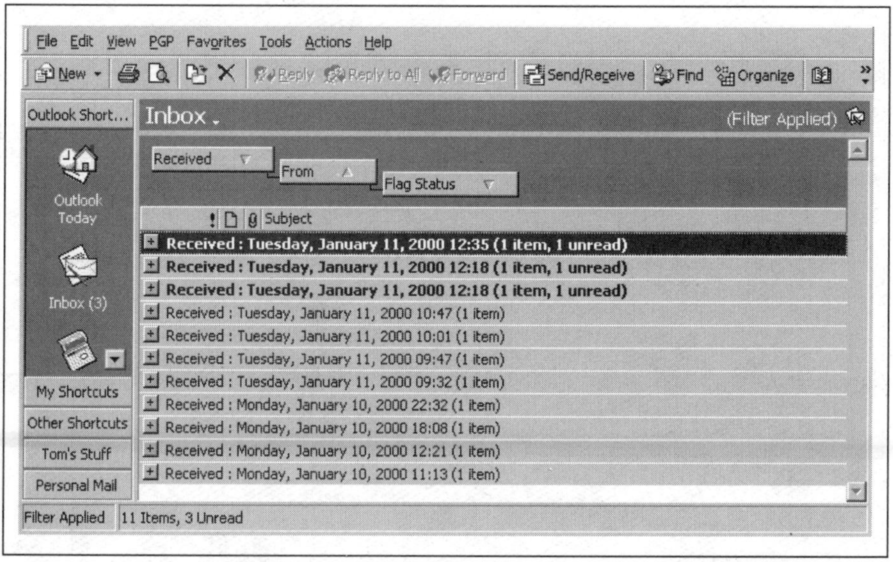

Figure 3-24: The Group By box shown open, grouped on Received, From, and Flag Status

To open the Group By box, right-click the column title bar and choose this command from the context menu.

The Group By box command is a toggle. Select it once to open the Group By pane, and a second time to close it again. Closing the Group By box does not remove any groupings; it simply closes the pane.

To group by a field, drag that field from the column title bar into the open pane. To create additional levels, simply repeat this action; where you drop the field box determines the grouping order.

At first glance, it would appear that using the Group By box is only functional for grouping fields displayed in the open view. Not so. If the field you want to group on is not shown, open the Field Chooser dialog and drag any fields not displayed from here. When you do, Outlook asks if you want to add this field to the view: Yes adds the field to your table, No groups on the field without displaying it.

Other settings

The Other Settings subdialog (sometimes titled Format *view-type*) contains options primarily related to a view's format and layout—fonts used, whether gridlines are displayed and their color, how columns are sized, and several editing/viewing options like AutoPreview and in-cell editing.

The Other Settings dialog (View → Current View → Customize Current View → Other Settings button) for a table view is shown in Figure 3-25.

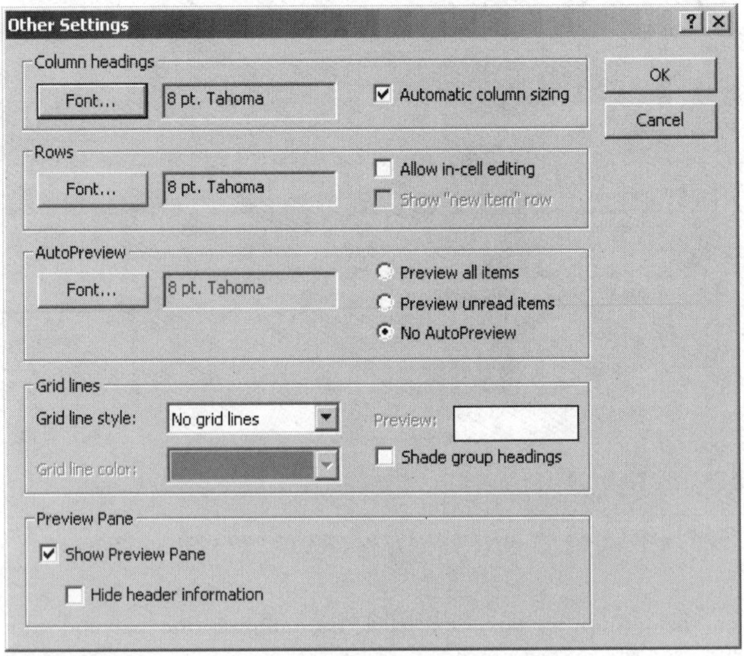

![Other Settings dialog box. Column headings: Font... 8 pt. Tahoma, checkbox checked Automatic column sizing. Rows: Font... 8 pt. Tahoma, Allow in-cell editing unchecked, Show "new item" row unchecked. AutoPreview: Font... 8 pt. Tahoma, Preview all items, Preview unread items, No AutoPreview selected. Grid lines: Grid line style: No grid lines, Grid line color, Preview, Shade group headings unchecked. Preview Pane: Show Preview Pane checked, Hide header information unchecked. OK and Cancel buttons.]

Figure 3-25: A Table view—Other Settings dialog

Column headings

Contains options for setting the font (typeface and color) used in column titles, and enabling "Automatic column sizing." See the topic "Modifying Column Widths" earlier in this section for an explanation of the functionality of this option.

Rows

Contains options for setting the font used for the rows of a table. Enabling the "Allow in-cell editing" option lets you edit the contents of a record directly in the table itself without opening the item in its Add/Edit form (not available in Note table views). Enabling in-cell editing allows you to further choose the "Show 'new item'" row option, which places a separate entry row at the top of the table view. This lets you add new records directly from the table view without a trip to the menu or toolbar to select New *item*.

AutoPreview

To enable AutoPreview for a table, select "Preview all items" or "Preview unread items" from the radio button group. The Font button lets you set the font face and color used by AutoPreview.

Grid lines

To display grid lines in a table, choose a style from the drop-down list provided. Selecting a style shows a preview to the right of the style list. Enabling a Grid line style enables the "Grid line color" list. Enabling the Shade group headings option (unrelated to Grid lines) grays the title of Group By views, distinguishing the group heading from its contents.

Preview Pane

Finally, the Preview Pane section provides options to enable the Preview Pane, and a checkbox to Hide header information. The header information display varies by item type. For example, an email message header displays the contents of the From, Subject, To, and Cc fields; a Task header displays Subject, Status, Due Date, and Owner.

The options in the Other Settings dialog are dependent on the view it is invoked from. For example, Calendar's Day/Week/Month views (see Figure 3-26, left) have properties for time scale and displaying time as a graphical clock (as opposed to text). Format options for a Timeline view (see Figure 3-26, right), focus on fonts, week numbering, and label width.

Resetting a view to its original state

If you've changed the properties of any of Outlook's preconfigured views, you can return them to their original state. Open the Define Views dialog (View → Current View → Define Views) and select the view you want to restore. The Reset button remains grayed if the chosen view has not been modified from its original settings.

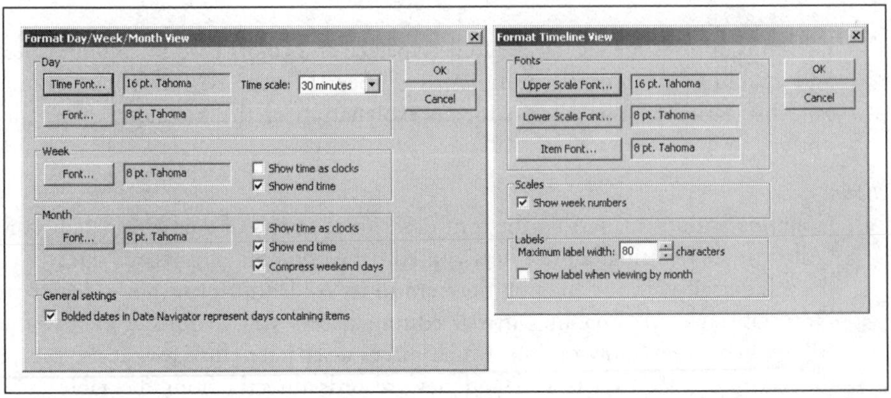

Figure 3-26: Variations on the Other Settings dialog—a Day/Week/Month view (left) and a Timeline view (right)

TIP # 26

You Can't Reset a Custom View

Custom views cannot be reset, because Outlook has no baseline to restore them to. Before you modify a custom view, make a copy of it, so you have a backup should things go awry. Go to View → Current View → Define Views, select your custom view, and click Copy.

Creating Custom Views

When creating custom views, it is important to remember that views are item specific. For example, if you create a custom view for your Inbox folder, that view can only be used for Mail items. This means that you could use this custom view for your Outbox and Sent Items folders, but not for your Contacts or Notes folders. If you want similar views for different types of Outlook items, you need to create a custom view for each different Outlook type.

Custom views can be created from an existing view, configured, and saved as a new view, or you can create a custom view from scratch. We'll tackle the easy one first—creating a view by copying the properties of an existing view.

Creating a custom view based on an existing view

The recommended way to create a new custom view is to begin with a copy of an existing view and modify it to suit your preferences. To do this:

1. Open a view in the Outlook item type you want to use the new view for (for example, Contacts). Then select View → Current View → Define Views.

2. Choose an existing view to base your new view on. Try to pick a view that is close in properties to the custom view you want to create.

3. Choose Copy from the Define Views dialog. The Copy View dialog shown in Figure 3-27 is displayed.

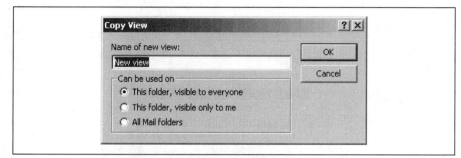

Figure 3-27: The Define Views → Copy View dialog

4. Name the new view, and select one of the three options listed to determine who has access to the view and where the view can be used:

   – "This folder, visible to everyone" makes the view available only from the folder in which it was created. Anyone with permission to access this folder also has access to the view.

   – "This folder, visible only to me" makes the view available only from the folder in which it was created, and only the person who created the view can use it.

   – "All *item-type* folders" makes the view visible from any folder containing the same item type the view was created under.

Now customize this copy using the option and techniques outlined earlier in this chapter under "Modifying Views."

Creating a custom view from scratch

There are times when none of Outlook's predefined views offer a good starting point for creating a custom view to suit your needs. In this case, you'll have to create a new view from scratch. This is not a huge undertaking. Basically, you are taking a blank view, and assigning all display properties to it. To create a new custom view from scratch:

1. Open a view containing the Outlook item type you want your new view to be based on. Again, remember that views are type specific. You cannot create a view for a Contacts folder and use it to display the contents of a Notes folder.

2. Choose View → Current View → Define Views, and click the New button. The Create a New View dialog, shown in Figure 3-28, is similar to the Copy View dialog discussed in the preceding section; but for this operation you need to specify both a name for the view and the type of view to base this new view on.

Your view type choices are: Icon, Day/Week/Month, Card, Timeline, and Table.

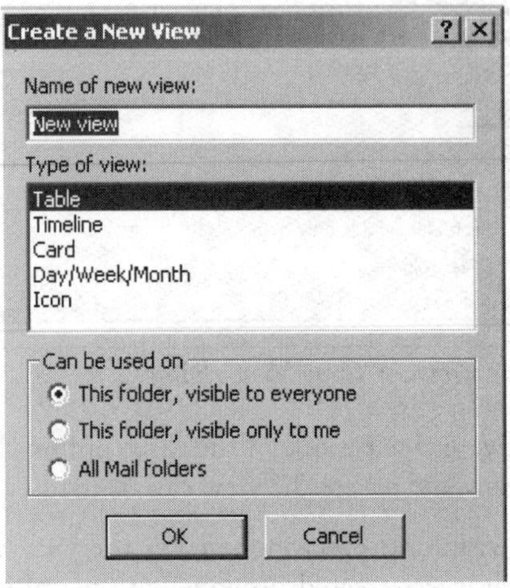

Figure 3-28: The Define Views → Create a New View dialog

The view type determines the view's base layout (for a description of these view types, see "Default Views" earlier in this chapter) and cannot be altered after the view is created. In short, choose wisely.

Deleting a view

The rules for deleting views are very simple:

- You can delete any of the views *you* create.

- You cannot delete any of the views *Outlook* creates.

The latter includes a default view that you have customized—it still belongs to Outlook, despite your hard efforts.

To delete a view:

1. Make sure you have the item type selected for the view you want to delete. If you made the view available under only one specific folder, you must have that folder selected.

2. Go to View → Current View → Define Views. Select the view you want to delete from the list displayed. You'll know immediately if it is a default view or not—if it is, the Delete button is not visible.

3. Choose Delete. Outlook asks you to confirm your action.

Print Styles

The ideal of the paperless office is lofty, but we're not there yet. At some point in time, you're probably going to want to print out something from Outlook. And when you do, it will be based on a print style. Print styles are a combination of format and page layout options.

Like views, Outlook serves up several predefined print styles. The rules for views also apply to print styles: you cannot delete the defaults, you can create custom print styles, and you can't reset a custom print style—only delete it. Are you seeing the pattern here?

On the other hand, print styles are not tied to a specific folder or item type like a view. Print styles are based on a view, but the styles available for a given view are more generic. For example, once a custom print style for a table view is defined, it can be used in any Outlook component using a table view. We refer the reader back to Table 3-1 at the beginning of this chapter for a list of the print styles available for each Outlook view and item type.

Clicking the Print button on Outlook's standard toolbar (or File → Print, or Ctrl+P) opens the Print dialog shown in Figure 3-29, allowing you to select a printer, print options, and choose from an available print style.

WARNING

Mail views immediately spool the selected item to the printer when you click the Print icon on the toolbar. If you have a specific option you want to set before printing a mail item (page range, number of copies, etc.) use the File → Print command or the keyboard shortcut Ctrl+P.

The options found on the Print dialog are:

Printer
Choose a printer from the drop-down list; the Properties button opens a document properties dialog (paper source and layouts) specific to the selected printer. The information fields under Printer show you the current printer's status.

Print Style
Select an available (defined) print style for the item type. The Page Setup and Define Styles buttons open their respective dialogs, each discussed in sections to follow.

 Several options on the Print dialog are not available for the Memo print style under Mail views—you cannot alter page setup properties or redefine the style. It also always prints one record per page.

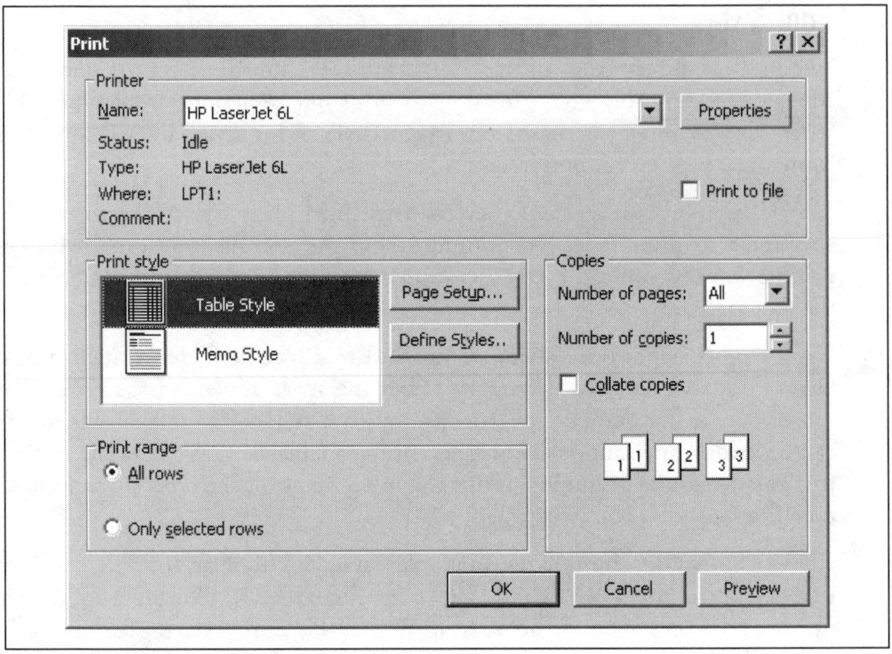

Print [?][X]

Printer
Name: HP LaserJet 6L ▼ [Properties]
Status: Idle
Type: HP LaserJet 6L
Where: LPT1:
Comment: ☐ Print to file

Print style
| Table Style   [Page Setup...]
| Memo Style   [Define Styles..]

Copies
Number of pages: All ▼
Number of copies: 1 ▲▼
☐ Collate copies

Print range
◉ All rows
○ Only selected rows

[OK] [Cancel] [Preview]

Figure 3-29: The Print dialog—Contacts view

Print Range

The options listed here vary according to the print style. For example, Table Style lets you choose between printing all rows, or only selected rows; Memo Style lets you choose select options to start each item on a new page and print attachments.

Copies

Lets you select the number of pages to print, the number of copies, and—if supported by your printer—a collate option.

Page Setup options

Each of Outlook's predefined print styles has a range of page layout options available. These options are organized under three tabs: Format, Paper, and Header/Footer. Figure 3-30 shows the Page Setup dialog for a Contacts view, Medium Booklet Style. The Format tab is on the top, the Paper tab is on the bottom.

 NOTE *Outlook's print formatting capabilities are miserably limited. All you can change are some default selections for the header and footer, margins, and fonts. You can't change the layout or selection of fields on the report page. This makes Outlook virtually useless for any but the simplest report printing.*

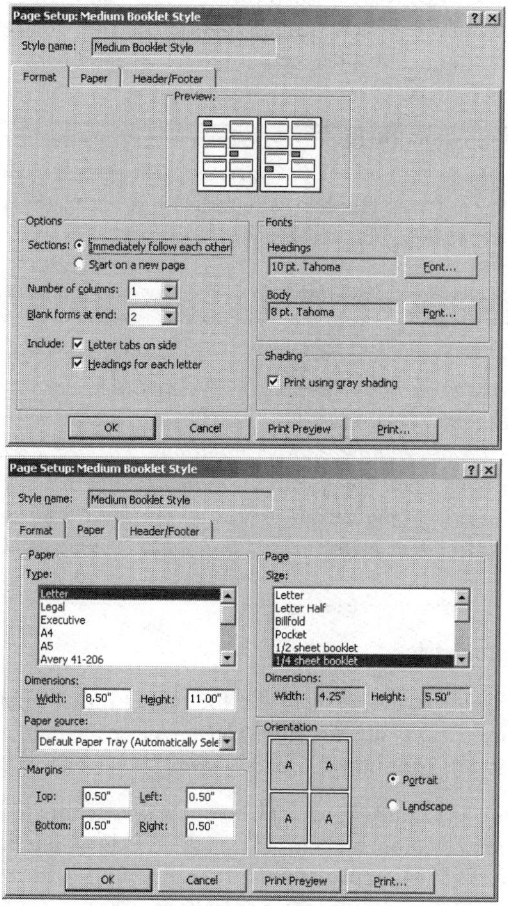

Figure 3-30: The Page Setup dialog for Contacts: the Format tab (top), and the Paper tab (bottom)

From the Format tab (Figure 3-30, top) you can select options to:

- Have each alphabetical section follow the next or start on a new page

- Set the number of columns each page contains

- Print blank pages at the end of the print request (to add contacts or notes pertaining to contact records)

- Include letter tabs at the side of each page

- Print headings for each alphabetical section

In addition, you can set the font used to print headings (the contact's name) and the body text (the contact's address, phone number, etc.). The Shading option determines whether headings are printed on a gray background.

The Paper tab, shown in Figure 3-30 (bottom), lets you define the paper type, set custom dimensions, select a paper source, define the print margins, choose a page size, and set orientation. The Header/Footer tab (not shown) contains fields for custom headers and footers.

It is beyond the scope of this book to describe every option for every page layout available. All options contained on the various print option dialogs are straightforward and relatively intuitive. The best way to learn about page layouts and format is to experiment—after reading Tip # 27.

TIP # 27

Use Print Preview

Print styles are based on the view you choose—and there are 11 of these. Page layout options are based on a combination of print style, the printer you use, and the paper you use—which leaves hundreds of permutations. The best advice we can offer is to use Print Preview before you print anything. It only takes a moment, and this allows you to touch up any details before committing the document to the printer. You'll soon learn what prints how, and what styles and layouts need special attention.

Memo and table print styles

Memo and Table print styles are available for most Outlook item types (again, see Table 3-1). The exceptions are timeline views (select an item within the view to print it in memo style), and some Contact views.

Memo style prints one item per page, with your name as the title, and the details of the record under this. Memo is a simple, quick and dirty, one item at a time print style. The only configurations available are the title and field fonts, paper options, and the contents and fonts used by the header/footer.

The Table print style is available under any Table view, and prints that view just as you see it in Outlook: with each item on a separate row, and the fields displayed as columns. Like memo, Table print styles have limited configuration options.

Calendar print styles

With a Calendar view displayed, you have the choice of six print styles:

Daily and Weekly
> Prints your calendar just as the associated views display it. Page layout options include printing one or two days per page, the inclusion of TaskPad, whether a Notes section is printed (lined or unlined), and the range of hours to include.

Monthly
> Monthly style prints one month of your calendar. Options exist (Print → Page Setup) to print a single month over two pages, include a TaskPad region

(containing a list of current Tasks), include a Notes region (lined or unlined), and exclude weekends. New to Outlook 2000 is the option to print exactly one month per page. When enabled, this forces the Monthly style to print starting the first day of the month through to the last; when disabled, if you have a partial month displayed in the view Outlook prints it exactly as shown (for example, beginning on the fifteenth of the month).

Tri-fold

Prints your calendar in three sections (left, middle, and right); you can select which style to include in which section. Options include: daily, weekly, or monthly calendar, TaskPad, and a Notes section (lined or unlined).

Calendar Details

Prints a detailed view of the activities for the selected day, including any text contained in the Notes field.

 Calendar printing under Outlook 2000 is vastly improved over previous releases. For example, previous versions truncated text that wouldn't fit in the space provided by the page layout; Outlook 2000 automatically wraps text.

Contact print styles

There are five print styles available for Contact items:

Card

Prints your contacts just as you see them in Card view. Options include the number of columns per page, whether to start a new alphabetical section on a new page, and how many blank forms to print at the end of the request (useful for adding new contacts).

Small and Medium Booklet

Booklet style prints your contacts in sections—from one to eight—with or without an alphabetical banner down the right margin of the page. Pages can then be folded into small booklets and carried in a pocket or a flap of your briefcase.

Memo

Prints each contact on a separate page. Details include Full Name, First and Last Name, Business Address, Business Phone and Fax, E-mail, any categories assigned to the contact, and any notes you've added to the Notes field.

Phone Directory

Prints name and phone numbers, separated by a line of running ellipses. The number of columns per page is adjustable (two works well).

TIP # 28

Print Options Are Persistent

After using a specific print style, always ensure you check all options before printing again in another style. Options like page orientation, columns to use, and header/ footer details are persistent. If, for example, you print your contact list in portrait Small Booklet, and then print this same list again using Phone Directory, your page orientation remains that used by the previous style.

Print Preview options

To open the Print Preview window:

- Go to File → Print Preview.

- Go to File → Print, and click the Preview button.

- Select the Print Preview button on the Advanced toolbar.

- From any of Outlook's Page Setup dialogs (File → Page Setup) click the Print Preview button.

One example of the Print Preview window is shown in Figure 3-31.

The toolbar at the top of the screen contains the following commands:

1. Page up/Page down—if there are multiple pages in the print request, this displays the previous/next pages respectively.

2. Actual Size—displays the first page of a print request, actual size. Use the Page Up/Down buttons to move through the range of pages.

3. One Page—displays the first page of a print request, with the full page visible in the Print Preview window.

4. Multiple Pages—displays multiple pages of a print request; click an individual page to open it in a One Page view. This is a quick, useful way to locate and view a single page in a multi-page print job.

5. Page Setup—opens the Page Setup dialog (for example, Figure 3-30).

6. Print—sends the current selection to the selected printer.

7. Close—closes the Preview Pane and returns you to the view it was invoked from.

At the bottom of the Print Preview window is a status bar. In multiple page layouts, this shows you the page number in view, and the number of pages in total.

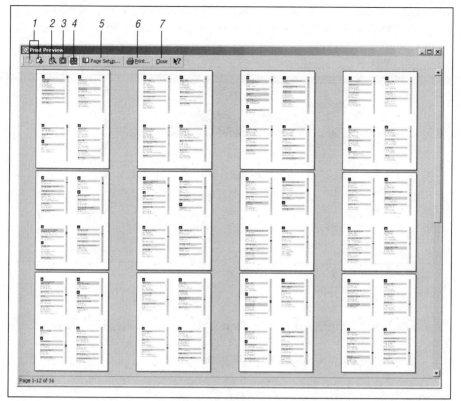

Figure 3-31: The Print Preview Window, shown under Contacts with Medium Booklet Style selected

Custom print styles

If you find yourself adjusting certain print options on a routine basis, we suggest you do not edit one of Outlook's default print styles, but instead create a custom print style. Why?

- If you modify one of Outlook's default print styles, you no longer have a base template to create new print styles from. You can return the modified view to default by resetting it, but you'll lose your customizations.

- If you modify a default print style, and that print style becomes corrupted for whatever reason, you lose both your custom print style and the default print style.

- As a matter of principle, we do not recommend modifying any of Outlook's default program elements without first creating a copy.

To define a custom print style, simply take all the information you've gathered in the preceding sections, select the item type you want to create the style for, and go to File → Page Setup → Define Print Styles. Make sure you select a view that has a print style you want to base your custom style on; you cannot simply create a new print style from scratch. Figure 3-32 shows the Define Print Styles dialog invoked from a Contacts Card view.

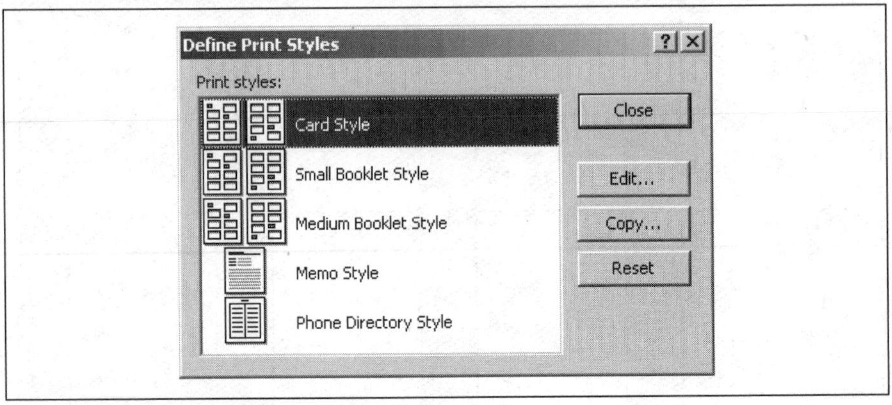

Figure 3-32: The Define Print Styles dialog

Resetting and deleting print styles

Like views, Outlook's default print styles can be reset and custom print styles can be deleted. And just like views, you can't really go wrong here—the Delete button is not available for any of Outlook's default print styles.

To delete a print style, go to File → Page Setup → Define Print Styles. Select the style you want to delete, and press the Delete button.

Outlook's Two Special Views

Outlook has two special views: Home Page (which is technically a folder property) and Outlook Today. While neither view has the same form or inherent customizability of the other Outlook views we've discussed so far in this chapter, they are—nonetheless—ways to organize and select data from within Outlook. The format of the data that feeds both these views is identical: HTML.

Home Page views

Home Page views are new to Outlook 2000. This feature allows you to associate an HTML page with a folder. This HTML page can exist locally on your system, on a LAN, or on the Internet. If you can view a page in your browser, you can associate it with a folder. To see an application of this feature, right-click Outlook Today from either the Outlook Bar, or from the Folder List. Select properties, and click on the Home Page tab. You should see something similar to the dialog in Figure 3-33.

Selecting "Show home page by default..." displays the page listed in the Address field any time the folder is accessed. The Address field accepts any HTML source file, local- or network-based. In the case of Outlook Today, this file is *outlwvw.dll/ outlook.htm*. Yes, that's right. Outlook Today is simply a page coded in HTML,

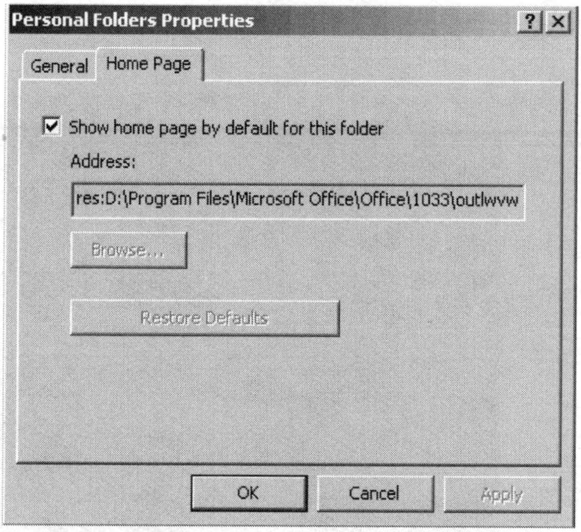

Figure 3-33: The Personal Folders Properties dialog with the Home Page tab selected

displayed by Outlook (via the *outlwvw.dll*) using the Home Page properties of a folder. We'll come back to Outlook Today in the next section.

All well and good, you say, but what can this do for me? Actually, quite a bit, especially if you have a full-time Internet connection. For example:

• You have a folder specifically for activities, contacts, and email related to a company you do business with on a routine basis. If the company has a web page, you can associate that page with a folder. Or you can create a new folder, and use this folder as a web shortcut. Click on the folder, and the page appears in Outlook's view pane.

• Your company stores a series of HTML-based help files on a local server. Create an Outlook folder (for example, HELP!), and associate the main index page with this folder. Click the folder to get help, right from Outlook, without activating an external browser.

• You browse the same Internet sites every day. Create a folder (Daily Surfing, for instance), and create subfolders for each site you visit. Click a folder to visit a site. Presto-pocus. An example of this is shown in Figure 3-34. A new Personal Folder was created called Daynotes. Under this folder are subfolders named Bob, Brian, Jerry, and Matt. The top-level folder opens the *Daynotes.com* site; the subfolders link directly to the sites of Bob, Brian, Jerry, and Matt.

To associate an HTML page with a folder:

1. Right-click the folder, go to the Home Page tab.

2. Enter the URL of the page you want to display.

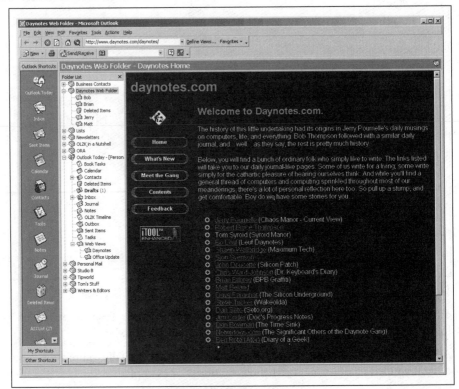

Figure 3-34: Outlook's Home Page folder property in action

3. Select the "Show home page by default for this folder" if you want the page displayed whenever the folder is accessed. If you disable the default display of this page, you can still view it by selecting the folder and, from the View menu, choosing Show Folder Home Page (see Figure 3-35).

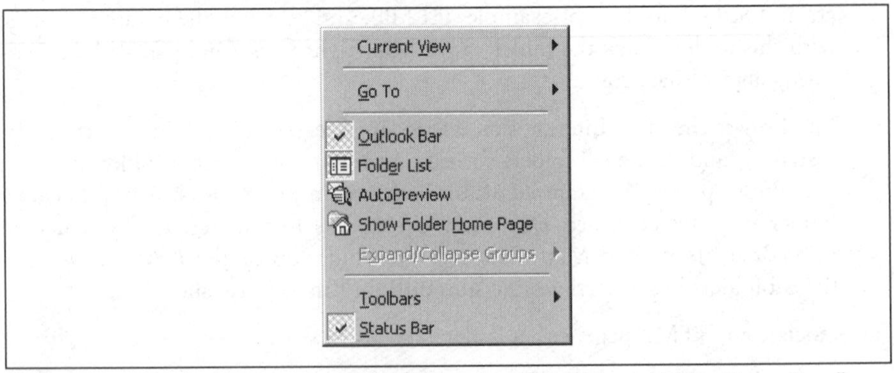

Figure 3-35: Outlook's View menu displaying the "Show Home Folder Home Page" command

---

TIP # 29

Show a Folder's Home Page

Whenever a folder has a Home Page associated with it, the View Menu gains a new command: Show Folder Home Page. Use this command to display a folder's Home Page when it is not configured to display by default.

Outlook Today

Outlook Today is a customizable "Day-at-a-Glance" view of select message folders, Calendar activities, and Tasks as shown in Figure 3-36.

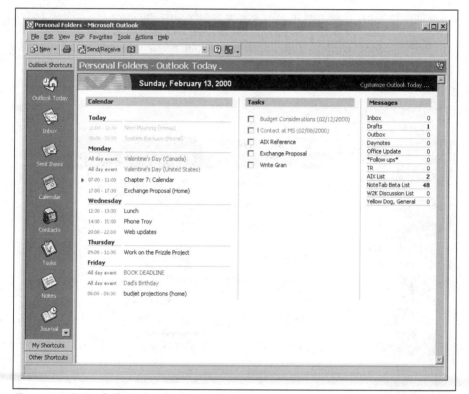

Figure 3-36: Outlook Today displays Calendar activities, Mail folders, and a Task List

Here's how to read and use Outlook Today:

Calendar

Appointments occurring earlier than your current system time are shown in light gray; Holidays are shown in green. The appointment or meeting closest to the current time has a red arrow pointing at it.

Tasks

Overdue tasks are shown in red; tasks flagged as important show in red and are preceded with an exclamation mark. To mark a task complete, click in the checkbox.

Messages

Mail folders containing unread messages show in bold; the number of unread messages displays in the column to the right of the folder.

To customize the contents and format of Outlook Today, click the "Customize…" text in the upper-right corner of the view (or lower-right corner depending on the style applied). Figure 3-37 shows Outlook Today in customization mode.

 There is no way to select a view for the tasks displayed in Outlook Today, without getting very deep into HTML and custom ActiveX controls. This limits Outlook Today's functionally for people who rely heavily on their task list.

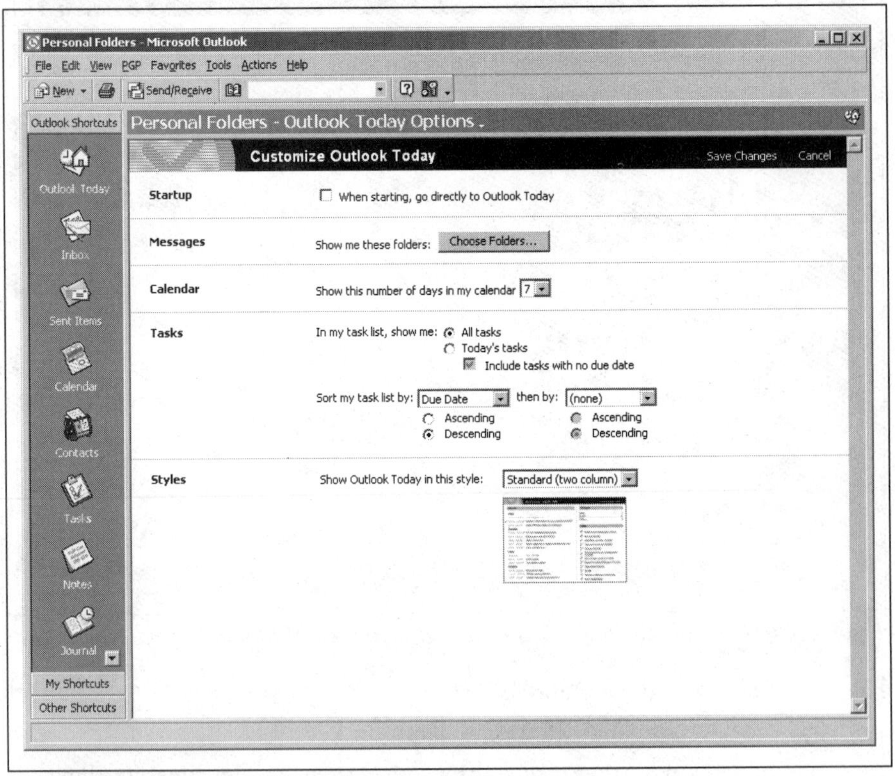

Figure 3-37: Customizing Outlook Today

Startup
> Select this option to display the Outlook Today view when Outlook starts. This option can also be set from Tools → Options → Other → Advanced Options dialog under Startup in the Folder.

Messages
> Opens a folder tree dialog, where you can select which folders are listed in the view. Outlook Today does not show the contents of these folders—it shows the presence of any unread messages (the folder name turns bold) and how many.

 Top-level folders of a PST do not show unread messages; you must choose a folder that actually contains messages.

Calendar
> Select the number of days (one to seven) of your Calendar displayed.

Tasks
> Configure which tasks are shown (all tasks, today's tasks only), whether tasks with no due dates are displayed, and the sort order (up to two levels).

Styles
> Change the color/layout of Outlook Today. Options are Standard, Standard (two columns) (shown in Figure 3-37), Standard (one column), Summer, and Winter. A small preview pane shows the format of each selection.

When you're done, click Save Changes.

We noted earlier in this section that the Outlook Today view is actually just an HTML page on your system. To view (and optionally configure) this page, go to your browser and enter:

```
res://<drive>:\Program Files\Microsoft Office\Office\1033\outlwvw.dll/
outlook.htm
```

The page appears, without links or data. Choose (on your browser menu) View → Source to display the HTML code in Notepad, as shown in Figure 3-38.

You can now print the code, or edit it at your own peril. We suggest that if you're going to experiment, make a backup copy first (File → Save As in Notepad).

The Power of Categories

A category is a keyword or phrase you associate with an Outlook item. You can then use this category as a way to sort, group, or filter a view, to find a lost item, or to organize a group of records, related by topic, but scattered across a diversity of item types. Outlook's categories are unique in today's world of software features—they're simple, powerful, and flexible.

```
🗐 outlook[1] - Notepad                                                      _□x
File  Edit  Format  Help
<!DOCTYPE HTML PUBLIC "-//IETF//DTD HTML//EN">

<html>
<head>
        <!-- OLKBASEHREF -->

<style>
a                           {color:windowtext;}

body                    {margin-top:0px;margin-right:0px;margin-left:0px;}

.CalendarSubjectLocation                  {}

.CalendarStartEnd            {}

.InboxCount                     {font-weight:bold;}

.InboxCountZero                      {font-weight:normal;}
.options
{color:white;font-family:Tahoma;font-size:8pt;text-decoration:none;}
.date                       {margin-bottom:4px;color:white;font-family:Arial;
                                 font-size:11pt;font-weight:bold;  }
.itemNormal             {font-size:8pt; font-family:Tahoma;
text-decoration:none;color:windowtext;  }
.times                  {font-size:7pt; line-height:11pt; font-family:Tahoma;
text-decoration:none; cursor:hand; color:buttonshadow;}

.PastTimes                      {color:buttonface; line-height:11pt; font-size:7pt;
                                    text-decoration:none; cursor:hand; }
.SplitDayTimes                  {color:teal; font-size:7pt; line-height:11pt;
                                    text-decoration:none; cursor:hand; }
.allDayEventTimes               {color:teal; line-height:11pt; font-size:7pt;
                                    text-decoration:none; cursor:hand; }
.TskDone                    {font-size:8pt;color:gray; text-decoration:line-through; }

.itemImportant   {color:red}

.dayHeaders             {font-family:Tahoma;font-size:8pt;font-weight:bold;
                            width:100%;  height:100%;
                         border-color:#CCCCCC;
                            border-width:.1em;
                         border-bottom-style:solid;
                         border-top-style:none;
                         border-right-style:none;
                         border-left-style:none;
                         color:windowtext;
                         cursor:default;
```

Figure 3-38: Outlook Today's source code displayed in Notepad

NOTE *There is one key to categories—you have to use them.*

Using Categories is much like investing in a compound interest savings account. At first, the money you put there doesn't seem significant or even all that useful. But as time goes on, and your investment grows, the day arrives when your discipline and efforts are rewarded many times over. Think of your data as an investment and categories as the tool that leverages its growth. The analogy here is to start small and simple—categorize all the records you create that have long-term potential. As your investment in categories grows, you'll soon be using them to manipulate data in ways you never expected. For example:

• Categories allow you to sort and view related items stored in the same folder. You can track business and personal tasks in the same folder and use the Business and

Personal categories to sort, group, or filter your view. Every Outlook component has a View → By Category command specifically for this purpose.

- When you start a new project, create a category for it. Assign this category the people, meetings, appointments, notes, tasks, and journal entries you make as your work progresses. At any point in time, you can gather together, in one screen (hint: Advanced Find), all entries related to your project.

- Items can be assigned to more than one category. This has particular relevance when working with contacts that do not fit neatly into one clearly defined group. This allows you to assign an important customer to three distinct categories: Key Customer, Business, and Christmas Card List.

TIP # 30

Which Items to Categorize?

The short answer is everything. A more realistic answer is: any Outlook item you plan to keep on your system for more than few days. The time it takes to assign a category pales in contrast to the value of your data over time.

It takes more to organize your data than just randomly assigning categories, though; your categories need to be meaningful, and you need a way to assign them that is repeatable and structured. That's where the *Master Category List* comes in.

The Master Category List

During installation, Outlook creates a base set of 20 categories called the Master Category List. This list provides a quick way to assign a defined category to an item.

So what's the difference between a *defined* category and an *undefined* category? Ah, good question. There are two ways you can assign a category to an Outlook item: use the Master Category List just described, or simply type a word or phrase in the item's category field. The first is a defined category; the second is an undefined category. It is extremely important to understand the difference between the two if you are going to use categories effectively.

The Categories dialog is shown in Figure 3-39. The items shown under "Available categories" are all defined in the Master Category List, *except* the Errata entry. Note that this item shows "not in Master Category List" in parentheses. This is indeed a valid category assigned to the item in question, however this category *cannot be assigned to another Outlook item using the Master Category List*.

The point of categories is to assign them consistently. If you rely solely on memory and your keyboard skills, you could end up with the following three categories assigned to a "Business" contact:

business
Business
busines

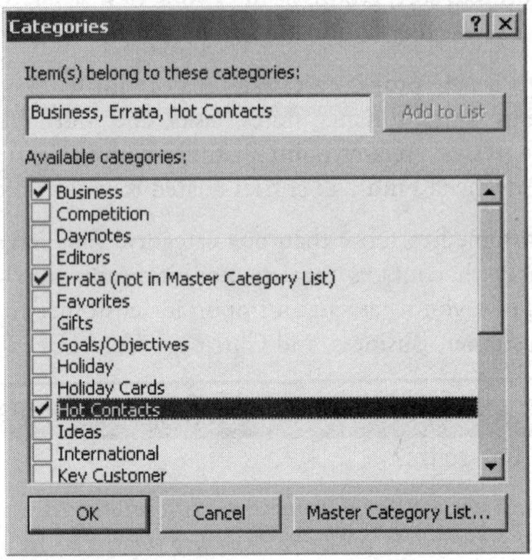

Figure 3-39: Outlook's Categories dialog

Each of these three entries is considered by Outlook to be a distinct category. The consequence of this is when you filter your calendar to show only those appointments related to "Business," you're only going to see one entry.

> **NOTE** *Make it a rule to always select from the Categories list. If you need a new category, add it to the Master list first.*

There are two ways to add an entry to the Master Category List:

- From the Categories dialog (see Figure 3-39) type the category you want to add in the text field at the topic of the dialog. To add more than one category, separate the entries with commas. Click Add to List.

- Click the Master Category List button on the Categories dialog. This opens the Master Category List dialog, shown in Figure 3-40. Type your entry in the New category field, and click Add.

   From this same dialog, you can also delete existing entries, and Reset the user's Master Category List. See the sidebar "The Master Category List Revealed," later in this chapter, for details on what the Reset button does.

> **NOTE** *Deleting a category from the Master Category List does not remove that category from any items it has been assigned to.*

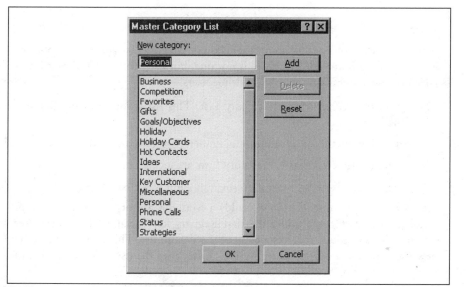

Figure 3-40: The Master Category List dialog

Exporting Your Master Category List

So you've diligently saved and categorized all your Outlook items, but your boss just showed up with a new computer for you or perhaps you just want to share those categories with a colleague. Where, you ask, is my Master Category List stored? Why, in the Registry, of course. Here's how to export and save your Master Category List:

WARNING

Always back up the Registry before doing any modifications there. And know how to restore it. Mistakes in editing the Registry may render your system unusable.

1. From the Run command on the Start Menu, type `regedit`.

2. Locate the Registry key `MyComputer\HKEY_CURRENT_USER\Software\Microsoft\Office\9.0\Outlook\Categories` in the hierarchy displayed. This exports the user's Master Category List, not Outlook's default Master Category List (see the sidebar "The Master Category List Revealed"). The default Master Category List is located under `\HKEY_LOCAL_MACHINE\Software\Microsoft\Office\9.0\Outlook\Categories`.

3. With the `Categories` key highlighted choose File → Export and type in a file name of *eight characters or less*. This is important—the exported name should be in DOS 8.3 format and cannot contain spaces.

4. Choose a location and save the file. Regedit automatically adds the extension *.reg* to the file.

The Master Category List Revealed

Now that we've told you all about the Master Category List and how important it is, we should point out that there is not one, but *three* (or more) Master Category Lists on systems that support multiple users.

The first is the *default* Master Category List. This list is found in the Registry under the key:

```
\HKEY_LOCAL_MACHINE\Software\Microsoft\Office\9.0\Outlook\Categories
```

The second (third, etc.) Master Category Lists are located under the *user's* key:

```
\HKEY_CURRENT_USER\Software\Microsoft\Office\9.0\Outlook\Categories
```

Here's how it all works. Outlook builds a Master Category list at the time of installation and stores it under the first Registry key (default). Each new user recognized by Outlook receives a copy of the default list. This then becomes the new user's personal Master Category List. Categories the user adds are added to this personal list only.

This is the reason for the button labeled "Reset" on the Master Category List dialog. Clicking it replaces the user's personal list with the original default (after a warning, of course).

The moral of this story is that in order to fully back up a multiuser system, you need to either back up the Registry or back up both the default Master Category List plus the Categories key from all the system's users. Short story: back up the Registry on a routine basis.

Now you can attach the file to an email, store it on floppy disk, or post it to a shared folder on your LAN for others to access.

To add the exported list to another user's system, double-click the file. When prompted to Save or Open, choose Open. Your Master Category List is imported to the new user's Registry.

WARNING

Importing a Master Category List to another user's system replaces the existing list with the imported one.

We also advise you to use this procedure to keep a current backup of your own Master Category List somewhere safe, just in case.

Assigning Categories

All Outlook items support the assignment of categories. There are numerous ways to access the Categories dialog:

- All Outlook items have a Categories command on their respective context menus (right-click on the item) that opens the Categories dialog shown in Figure 3-39. This command also supports multiple selections allowing you to assign one or more categories to a group of items in one pass.

- Most Outlook items have a Categories button on their respective forms that displays the Categories dialog. One exception is the Notes form. To assign a category from a Notes form, click the small note icon (upper-left corner), and choose Categories from the menu.

- Mail is the other exception. You can assign a category to a received message by selecting it and using the context menu command, but there is no button or field for this purpose on the default email editor form. You have two options: use the Edit → Categories command, or open the View → Options dialog and enter a Category in the field provided.

TIP # 31

Use Templates with a Predefined Category

If you routinely send email to a specific individual or individuals, and those messages are categorized the same, create a message template (see "Forms as Templates" earlier in this chapter).

Finding Your Stuff

Some days, it seems like "stuff" was designed to be lost. So it goes with Outlook items as well. Even if you systematically sort and file your records in a well-designed folder structure, there are still days when you simply cannot see the forest for trees. Enter Outlook's Find commands.

Simple Find

There are two implementations of the Find command in Outlook. The first, a simple search, is accessed either from the standard toolbar, or from the Tools → Find command. A Find pane opens above the current view, using a predefined set of search parameters. Type a search phrase in the "Look for" field, and click the Find Now button. Figure 3-41 shows a search on the "Yellow Dog, General" folder; the search phrase is `cable modem`. The results replace the contents of the current view.

Note the following regarding the Find command:

- You must have at least a general idea where to begin your search. The basic Find command operates on the folder selected and *only* searches that folder.

- The search parameters are predefined depending on the folder type. The folder searched in Figure 3-41 contains message items, and for this folder type the basic Find command searches the fields From and Subject only. You also have

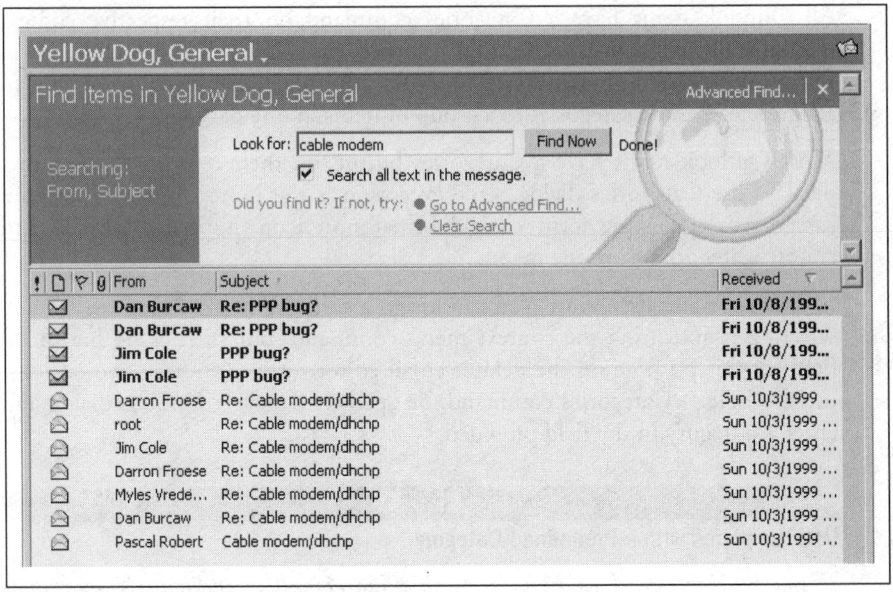

Figure 3-41: Simple Find command, showing open Find pane

the option (which is enabled by default) of searching all text in the message as well. Table 3-2 shows the search criteria used for a simple search based on folder type. Searching all message text can take a long time if some or all of the following are true: your computer is slow; the folder you are searching contains many messages; the messages are large; or the search string is long.

• The search results are displayed using the folder's current view. Changing this view after a completed search discards the search results. Hint: pick the view your want your results displayed under (for example, Messages, By Conversation Topic, Sent to, etc.) before beginning a search.

TIP # 32

Filters and Find

Using a filtered view excludes all filtered records from the search. Keep this in mind when you're using views and Find (both simple and Advanced).

• When the search is complete, two options appear under the "Look for" field: Advanced Search, and Clear Search. Advanced Search (which is discussed in the next section) keeps the search results and presents the Advanced Find dialog allowing you to narrow or refine the search criteria; Clear Search clears the "Look for" field and restores the view's original contents. To close Find, click the close icon in the upper-right corner of the pane (x) or reselect the Actions → Find command.

Table 3-2: Search Parameters Based on Folder Type

Folder Type	Search Parameters
Message	From, Subject
Calendar	Subject, Location, Attendees
Contact	Name, Company, Addresses, Category
Task	Subject, Company, People Involved, Category
Journal	Subject, Body, Entry Type, Contact, Company
Note	Subject

Advanced Find

The Find command is good for quick and simple searches if you know where to begin and the item you're looking for can be defined by one of the preset fields offered. But when you need to search more than the basic fields, search on criteria such as times and dates, or search access multiple folders, use Advanced Find.

Advanced Find has one serious flaw: searches are restricted to a single information store. If you use multiple PSTs (see Chapter 13 for details), this may mean searching more than one location for records.

There are three ways to open the Advanced Find dialog shown in Figure 3-42:

- Open a basic Find search and click on the Advanced Find button in the upper-right corner of the pane.

- Select Tools → Advance Find (or Ctrl+Shift+F).

- From the Outlook Bar or Folder List, right-click the folder you want to search, and from the context menu choose Advanced Find.

The Advanced Find dialog opens configured to search for an item type based on the folder the command was invoked from. In Figure 3-42, for example, Advanced Find was invoked from a message folder, so it is preset to search for Messages. Clicking the down arrow on the "Look for" list, however, presents the additional choices shown in Figure 3-43 (top).

The Advanced Search dialog contains fields and options based on the item type selected; some fields are not displayed for specific item types. Keep this in mind as you read the following descriptions.

The Browse button opens the Select Folders dialog (see Figure 3-43, bottom). Select the folders to search (again, noting that you can only select folders from one information store). Below the folders pane is an option to search subfolders and an area showing your current folder selections.

The Advanced Find dialog is grouped on three tabs. The first changes to reflect the item type. For Messages, the fields are:

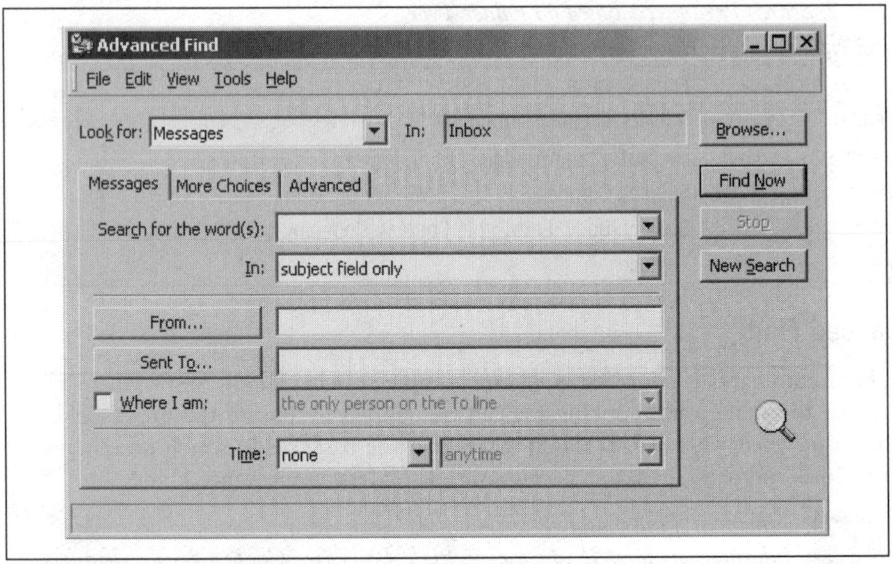

Figure 3-42: The Advanced Find dialog in a Messages context

Search for the word(s)

Enter the word or phrase to search on. A "most recently used" list is displayed when you click the down-arrow button.

In

Select the fields to search. The choices are: subject field only, subject field and message body, and frequently used text fields. Text fields searched vary according to the item type.

From

Searches the From field for the word or name you enter (pertinent, of course, to message items only). Click the From button to open the Select Names dialog, where you can pick from entries contained in your Contacts folder. For a generic search, enter a name (or names, separated by semicolons or commas). For example: matt, bob, don finds all messages from any of these individuals and includes messages from both Don Smith and Don Johnson.

Sent to

Searches the To field of messages. Otherwise, the "Sent to" option functions just like the From option.

Where I am

Selecting this option enables the drop-down list, and allows you to select your relationship to the message. Options are: "only person on the To line," "on the To line with other people," and "on the CC line with other people."

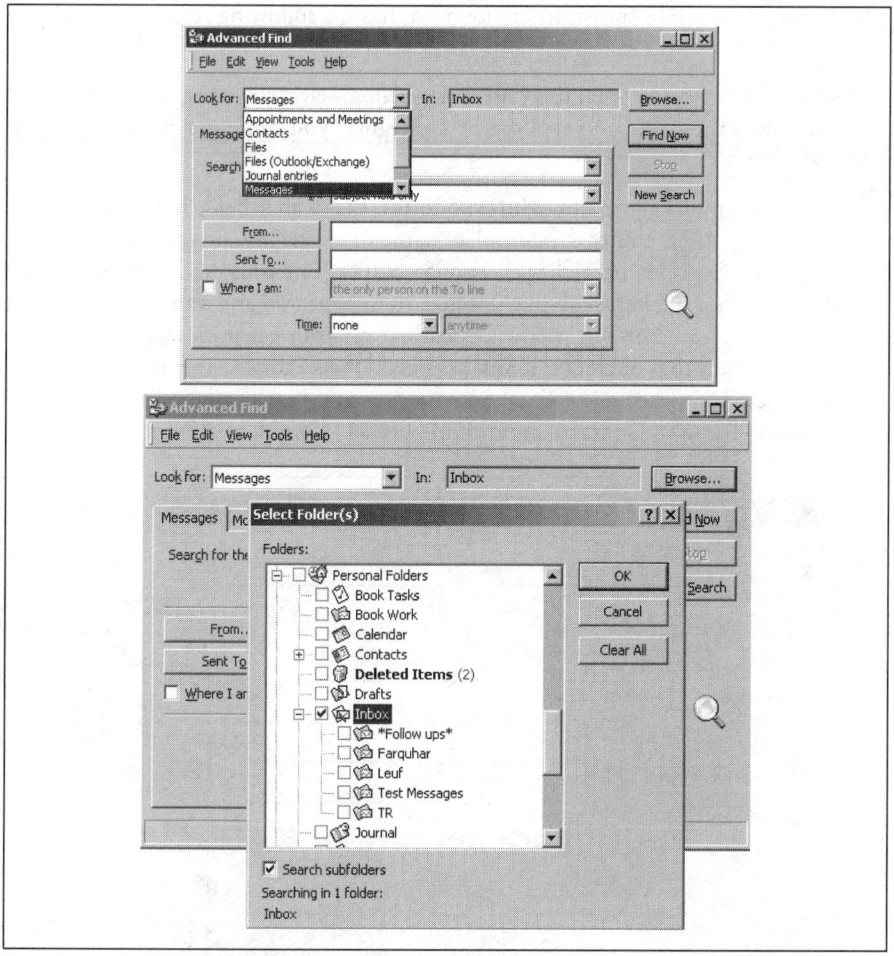

Figure 3-43: The Advanced Find dialog showing the Look for list (top), and Select Folders subdialog accessible from the Browse button (bottom)

Time

Searches message time/date fields for the specified criteria. Selecting any field other than "none" (received, sent, due, expires, created, modified) from the first list enables the date range list next to it. Predefined options are: anytime, yesterday, today, in the last 7 days, last week, this week, last month, this month.

TIP # 33

Search for Specific Dates or Times

Other than "Search for the words," all the drop-down lists on the Advanced Find dialog are predefined—you can't enter your own text. If you want to define specific dates or date ranges, go to the Advanced tab and create custom search criteria.

The More Choices tab, shown in Figure 3-44, has the following search options:

Categories
> Click the button to open the Categories dialog; select the categories to search. If you know the name and spelling of a category, you can enter it directly in the text field.

> There is a much more powerful way to use this search field, however. Say you either do not remember the complete name of a category, or you want to search multiple categories named with similar letters. Entering day, con in the text field searches all items of the selected item type for any categories with the letters "day" or "con" in them. Depending on your categories, this produces a search result that includes items assigned, for example, the categories Day, Daynote, Day Event, Daytime Activity *plus* any items assigned the categories Contact, Business Contact, Important Contact, Confidential Notes, etc.

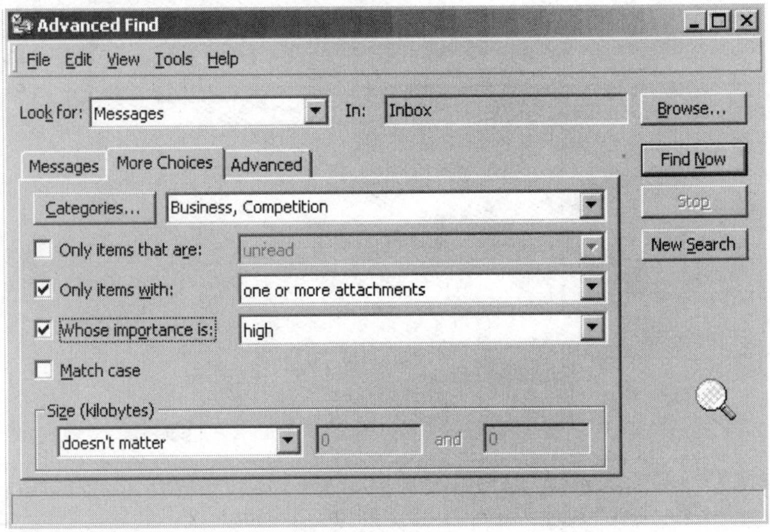

Figure 3-44: The Advanced Find More Choices tab for a Message type

Only items that are
> Options include Read or Unread. Note that any Outlook item can be marked with this status, although the property is typically associated only with email.

Only items with
> Search for items containing "one or more attachments" or "no attachments."

Whose importance is
> Normal, high, or low.

Match case

Selecting this checkbox forces the search to match the case used in your entry on the *first* tab under "Search for the word(s)."

Size

This search criterion relates to item size, not attachment size. Most users have no idea how big individual Outlook items are, so the usefulness of this setting is limited. You might find it useful to search for an abnormally large item, but again, you'd have to have some idea of what "abnormally large" was in relation to "normal."

The Advanced tab, shown in Figure 3-45, lets you create your own custom search criteria. Fields can be chosen from *any* Outlook item type, although pertinence to the folders and items you're searching for impacts on the search results.

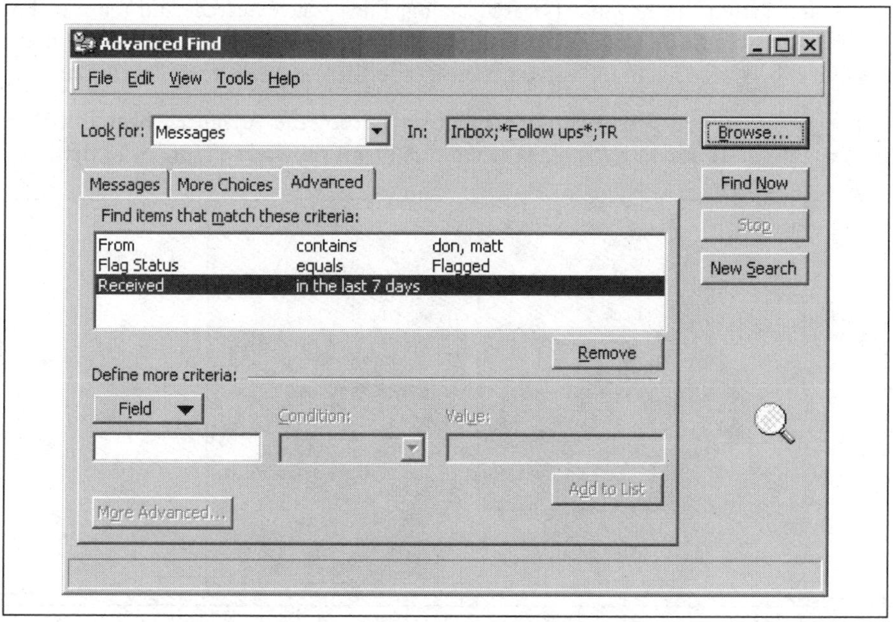

Figure 3-45: The Advanced Find dialog with the Advanced tab selected

To define custom search criteria, select a field from the drop-down list, a condition, and depending on the condition, a value. Select the "Add to list" button. Continue until your search is fully defined.

NOTE *The search criteria defined on the Advanced tab are processed in the order shown, and new entries are added to the bottom of the list. Unfortunately, there is no option to reorder the list. If you get the order wrong, your only option is to delete entries and recreate the list again.*

Once you have your search criteria fully defined, click the Find Now button. Stop pauses the search, and New Search clears all fields.

Advanced Search: Tips and Techniques

The Advanced Search dialog is an "option-rich" feature, and we could easily fill a whole chapter on describing fields, drop-down lists, and ways to create custom criteria. Due to the diversity of the selections here, inevitably we'd miss the one combination you were looking for. Instead, we'll leave you with a few tips and techniques and a suggestion: explore the Advanced Search dialog and learn how to leverage the options here to create searches specific to your data. The time you spend will be wisely invested.

 Outlook lacks any provision for "Find and Replace." There are ways around this, however, one of which is detailed in Chapter 12.

- If you routinely search for the same items, using similar criteria, save your search (from the Advanced Search dialog, File → Save Search) and reuse it. For searches requiring minor changes, make adjustments as appropriate—just don't save the search again unless you want to add these changes to your template.

- Search results can be manipulated directly from the Advanced Search dialog. Right-click an item to display the context menu shown in Figure 3-46 (left).

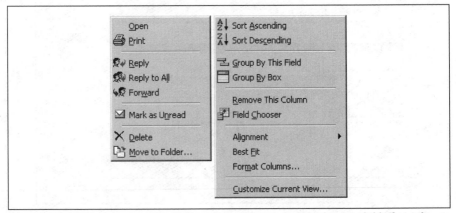

Figure 3-46: The Actions menu (left) and the Views menu (right) available from the Search Results pane

- The format and layout of the search results pane is fully customizable—it's a view! Right-click on any column title to display the context menu shown in Figure 3-46 (right).

- Remember, a search is based on all criteria defined across all tabs. It's easy to forget this if you get involved in creating a complex search. If your results are not what you anticipated—and you're sure the items exist somewhere in the folders selected—review all search options.

- Punctuation is important when entering text in a search field. Enter two (or more) words delimited by commas or semicolons, and Outlook interprets this as a Boolean OR search (match if *either* word is present). Two words with no punctuation constitute a Boolean AND search (match only if both words are present). If you want to search for a phrase containing punctuation (for example: socks, shoes, and shirt), you must enclose the phrase in double quotation marks ("socks, shoes, and shirt").

- Outlook's search engine assumes you want to also find plurals. Entering dog also locates items containing dogs. Unfortunately, Outlook is not smart enough to find both goose and geese.

- As many as ten words and phrases previously used in the Search for the Word(s) field are saved in the MRU drop-down list for reuse.

- Outlook saves phone numbers in a format applicable to regional conventions. If you're searching for a phone number or area code, type it exactly according to the format displayed under the phone fields shown in Contacts (for example, (803) 555-1212).

- "Look for: Files" searches your filesystem. "Look for: File (Outlook/Exchange)" searches Outlook and Exchange items for attachments.

Organize

Outlook's Organize feature (Actions → Organize) is similar to Find. It opens a pane above the current view, and acts on the contents of the folder displayed. Instead of finding items, it allows you to organize them in preconfigured ways, using a combination of drop-down lists and text fields. Figure 3-47 shows the Organize pane open for the Inbox.

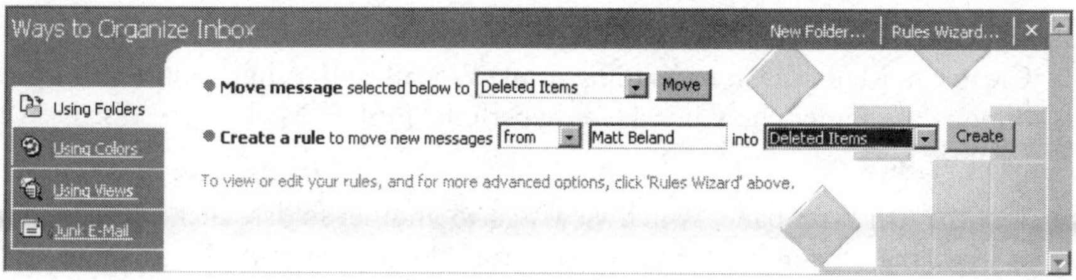

Figure 3-47: Outlook's Organize feature, invoked from the Inbox

Depending on the Outlook folder type displayed, two or more option groups are listed at the left of the Organize pane (Using Folders, Using Categories, Using Colors, Using Views, and Junk E-Mail):

Move message
Moves the selected item (or items) to the folder selected in the drop-down list. This is the same MRU (Most Recently Used) list displayed by the Move to

Folder command found on the standard toolbar. The New Folder button at the top-right of the pane allows you to create a folder.

Create a rule

The predefined rule created is to move new messages from [the item selected] into [folder list]. The Rules Wizard button opens the Rules Wizard dialog. See Chapter 6 for details on creating and managing Mail rules.

Add [item type]

Assigns the category selected from the drop-down list to the items selected in the view. The list displayed is the user's Master Category List.

Create a new category

Adds the category entered in the text field to the user's Master Category List.

Using Views

Displays a list of the views available for the selected folder. Selecting an entry changes the view. The Customize Current View link in the upper-right corner of the pane opens the View Summary dialog.

Using Colors

Message items (only) can be set to display in a color based on formatting rules. For example, messages from Joe Snipps are dark blue in your Inbox. On the top line you can choose what messages to color according to the details of the selected item. Change the name if you wish and the color, then choose Apply Color. All messages that match these settings change color immediately. Click on the Automatic Formatting for more detail. This opens a dialog showing all formatting rules in effect.

 Color options only apply to a single item. If you select multiple items, the rule is applied to the first item in the list.

Junk E-Mail

Creates a Mail rule for handling Junk E-Mail and Adult Content. Further options are under the Click Here hyperlink. Junk E-Mail is also discussed in Chapter 6.

To close the Organize pane, switch views, go to another folder, click the close icon (x), or select the Organize command again from the toolbar or Actions menu.

Table 3-3 summarizes the options available for a given folder type.

Table 3-3: Ways to Organize Options Based on Folder Type

Folder Type	Using Categories	Using Views	Using Folders	Using Colors	Junk E-Mail
Mail		Yes	Yes	Yes	Yes
Contacts	Yes	Yes	Yes		
Calendar	Yes	Yes			

Table 3-3: Ways to Organize Options Based on Folder Type (continued)

Folder Type	Using Categories	Using Views	Using Folders	Using Colors	Junk E-Mail
Journal	Yes	Yes			
Notes	Yes	Yes			
Notes	Yes	Yes			

Getting Help

Even advanced users need help with Outlook at times. The program is just too complex for anyone to fully grasp. Luckily, Outlook has been around long enough and enough people use it that if you have a question there is probably an answer. Like all things computerish, you just have to know where to look. In order of usefulness, here is a list of resources to turn to when Outlook leaves you stumped:

- A colleague who has experience with Outlook

- Internet web sites and Newsgroups (see the Preface for a list of useful web resources)

- Other publications like this one

- Outlook's online helpless system

Unfortunately, Outlook's online help is generally clueless. It (sometimes) gives cursory answers to basic queries and tells you how to modify program options, but is silent about *why* you might want to use a given feature or the consequences of changing setting A to B. It is usually unable to provide any information about common "How do I..." questions, and often returns answers that are entirely unrelated to the question.

 It doesn't hurt to ask "Clippit" or "The Dot" a question when you're stuck—you never can tell what these annoying little creatures might come up with. And while the answers they provide may not go anywhere toward solving your problem, Microsoft's Office Assistants are nonetheless entertaining.

The Office Assistant

The Office Assistant (OA) is actually the interface to Outlook's online help system. Pressing F1 or selecting Help from the menu no longer opens a Help window; it opens a balloon above the animation where you can choose from list of topics, or type a phrase to search the help index on. This balloon dialog is shown in Figure 3-48.

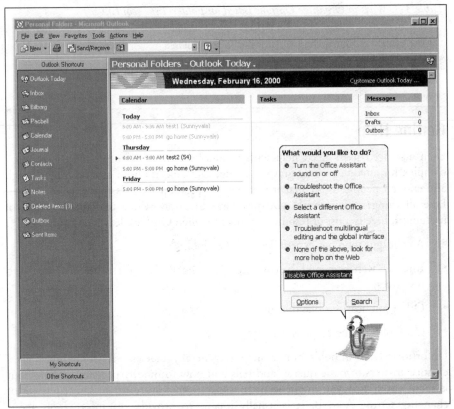

Figure 3-48: The Office Assistant Search dialog

TIP # 34

Killing Clippit

To turn off the Office Assistant, choose Options from the Help search dialog and clear the "Use the Office Assistant" checkbox. This does not disable Outlook's online help, just the animated figure on your Desktop.

The OA animations are also purported to be "intelligent," in that they monitor user actions within an open program (if so configured; see the topic on setting OA options later in this chapter). The OA offers tips as you work at a particular task, and reacts to perceived confusions by offering suggestions. There is also some linkage present between the OA and error messages. For example, if the OA is enabled and you try to permanently delete a message, the normal confirmation dialog is replaced by a balloon caption above the animation.

Choose Options from the assistant balloon to customize how the OA responds to your inputs, and the answers/tips it provides. Outlook displays the dialog shown in Figure 3-49.

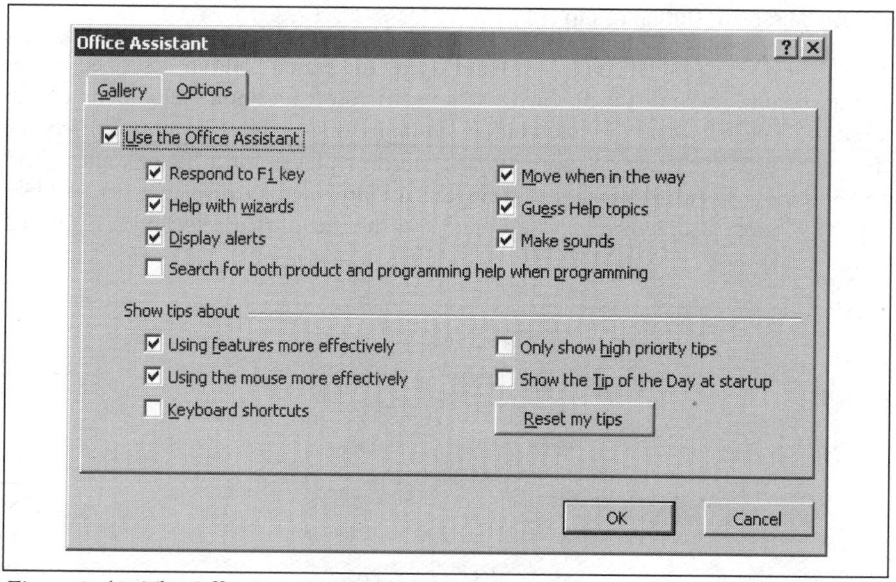

Figure 3-49: The Office Assistant Options dialog

> **NOTE** *Any options you select in the Outlook Office Assistant dialog affect the Assistant in all Office programs.*

Right-click on the Office Assistant, and a context menu displays containing the following items:

Hide

Temporarily hides the Office Assistant; the next time you select Help → Microsoft Outlook Help (or press F1), the Assistant reappears along with the Help search balloon.

Options

Opens the Office Assistant options dialog shown in Figure 3-49.

Choose Assistant

Displays the Office Assistant dialog shown in Figure 3-49 with the Gallery tab selected. If you're bored with Clippit, you can choose a different assistant to annoy you.

Animate

Causes the Office Assistant to perform animated tricks for you. Select this option if you do not have anything constructive to do at your computer.

The Outlook Help Menu

The following commands are available from the Outlook Help menu in Figure 3-50.

Help → Microsoft Outlook Help (F1)

When the OA is enabled, this command opens the search balloon described earlier in this section. If the OA is disabled, Help → Microsoft Outlook Help opens a Help window. The left pane of this window contains three tabs: Contents (a tree-like display of topics), Answer Wizard (type a word or phrase for a list of topics), and Index (type a keyword or choose from the list provided to display a list of Help topics). Choose a topic from the left pane and the text of that selection is displayed in the right.

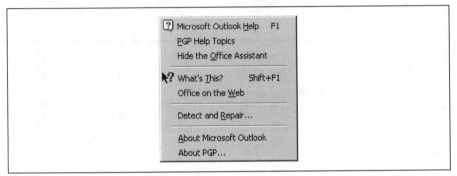

Figure 3-50: The Outlook Help menu

Help → Hide the Office Assistant

This command is the functional equivalent to the right-click Office Assistant command discussed in the previous section—it hides the animated help figure temporarily. Once hidden, the menu description changes to Show the Office Assistant. If you disable Office Assistant by deselecting the Use the Office Assistant option shown in Figure 3-50, you can enable him (or her? or it?) again with this command.

Help → What's This? (Shift+F1)

Adds a question mark to your mouse cursor. With this option enabled, point to a menu command, screen region, or entry field and a text pop-up appears with a description of the item under your cursor.

Help → Office on the Web

Selecting Office on the Web opens Internet Explorer and takes you to the Microsoft Office Update site (at the time of this writing, *http://officeupdate.microsoft.com/welcome/outlook.asp*). Here you can obtain program updates, download add-ons, read tips and tricks, and get the latest information on the complete Office product line. This is an excellent resource for Outlook-specific files and HOWTOs. The site is updated regularly, so make it a habit to check here on a routine basis.

Help → Detect and Repair

Detect and Repair activates a utility that scans the time/date/version stamps for all files Outlook needs to function. If the program finds anything amiss, you are prompted to insert the Office CD, and the correct files are restored. Note that if you have installed patches or updates (for example, 128-bit encryption for Outlook), these have to be reinstalled after the utility has run.

Help → About Microsoft Outlook

Selecting About Microsoft Outlook opens the dialog shown in Figure 3-51.

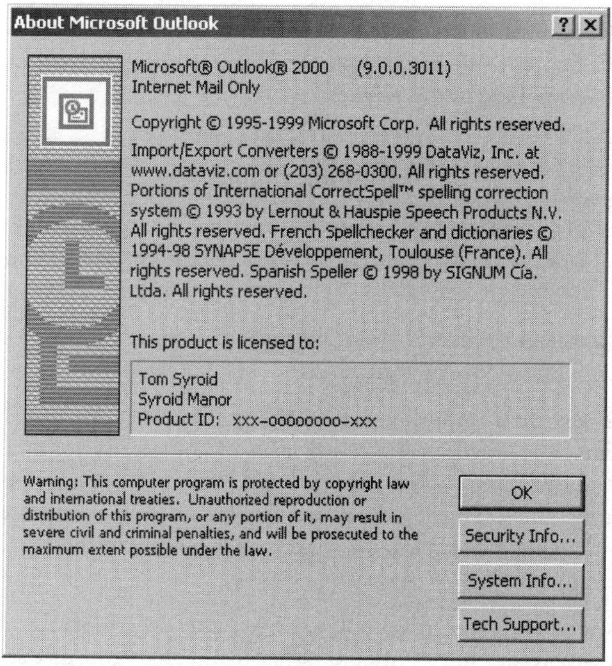

Figure 3-51: The About Microsoft Outlook dialog

The top line of this dialog shows the version of Outlook installed (2000), and the build number (9.0.0.3011). You may be asked for this information if you phone Microsoft Technical Support with a problem relating to Outlook.

On the second line is the Service Option the program is running under (No E-mail, Internet Mail Only, or CWCW).

The About Microsoft Outlook dialog contains four buttons:

OK
> Cancels and closes the dialog.

Security Info

Displays information about the cipher strength supported by Outlook. Due to export restrictions, the default is 40-bit. There are patches available from Microsoft's Office Update site (*http://officeupdate.microsoft.com*) to increase Outlook's internal encryption to 128-bit. Security and encryption are the topic of Chapter 15, *Security and Encryption*.

System Info

Opens the Windows System Information program. From here you can look up details on hardware installed, hardware resources (IRQs, I/O address ranges, DMA channels in use, etc.), and software configurations.

Tech Support

Opens a Help window with a hyperlinked list of resources for contacting Microsoft Support or finding answers to technical issues through one of Microsoft's web-based support sites.

Outlook Online

You may have noticed that this book is somewhat shy on Outlook 2000's new "online" features (integrated web browser, et al.). There are several reasons for this:

- Something had to give. We simply could not cram 1500 pages of material into 600 without leaving features out.

- We are less than impressed with Microsoft's "Web Browser Everywhere" campaign. It's added an unneeded layer of complexity to an already complex product, along with a slew of bugs that can no longer be traced to a single program. Connectivity-related problems now point vaguely to the OS and to the tangle of DLLs and services that no one in their right mind can sort out any more.

- At least one author of this book has been after Microsoft for years to integrate a newsreader into Outlook, rather than hanging it off a separate product (Outlook Express). The integration of IE—in his humble opinion—is a huge waste of time and resources that could have been funneled in other directions. If a newsreader was not a priority, how about fixing some bugs that have been around since Outlook 97?

Chapter 4

Outlook's Navigation Tools

Once upon a time, menus were simple devices. They provided the user with an easy way to display a list of program commands. Then along came toolbars that contained a fixed selection of button-images to quickly access frequently used commands. These days, the situation is very different. In Outlook 2000 we now have menus that are customizable and adaptive; toolbars that are customizable, selectable, and adaptive; and a dizzying array of context menus. Some of these features are fully automatic, while others display a complex mix of automatic and manually configured behavior. This chapter attempts to bring some order to using and customizing Outlook's navigational tools.

Normally, menus and toolbars don't get a lot of attention—that is, until you either cannot find a command, the command you eventually find is not where you expected it, or something does not work as advertised. For these frustrating scenarios, help is at hand. By the time you've finished with this chapter, you should be able to find those missing or vanishing commands, build custom menus and toolbars, or simply rearrange an existing menu or toolbar to better suit your work habits.

In addition to menus and toolbars, Outlook also provides two tools that can be utilized as navigational aids, but also function as indispensable file management tools: the *Outlook Bar* and the *Folder List*. Both of these tools are discussed later in this chapter.

We begin this chapter with a look at the concept of adaptive menus and toolbars. As you read the following section, keep in mind the difference between the terms *adaptive* and *context*. Adaptive refers to the ability of a menu or toolbar to learn and remember the commands you use most often; this is a feature in Outlook that can be turned on or off. Context defines what commands are available when working in a given component or in a specific region (pane) of a component. For example, the commands displayed on a menu or toolbar under Outlook's Journal component will be different than the commands available when viewing a Note.

 Adaptive menus and Personalized menus are one and the same. We have chosen to use the term Adaptive for consistency throughout this chapter.

129

Adaptive Menus and Toolbars

All Office 2000 programs default to what Microsoft has termed "adaptive" menus and toolbars. When you first begin using Outlook, each of these navigational aids display only a subset of their items. The thinking behind this "feature" is to narrow the array of commands displayed to the basics to prevent confusion and make finding the commands you need easier. As you work with the program, it learns the commands you use most often and those that you do not use. The program will then display the most frequently used commands and toolbar buttons at first glance, and hide the less frequently applied tools. As your usage habits change over time, your menus will follow suit. A menu or button command that gets promoted can disappear if it is not used for a specified period.

 Outlook uses a complex formula for determining what commands are shown on adaptive menus and toolbars. The computation involves the number of times the application is launched and for how many successive launches a given feature goes unused. As you use commands, the ones you use more frequently appear on the menu, and the ones you don't are suppressed.

While this feature is built on good intentions, three immediate problems arise with adaptive menus and toolbars (the latter, perhaps, to a lesser extent):

- What is a basic command for one user may not be a basic command for another. For example, a developer would consider Publish As, Run Form, and Script Debugger commands as basic; someone using Outlook to simply send and receive mail would not.

- Some users rely entirely on quickly scanning through all the menus when uncertain about which command to use—with adaptive menus active they will see only a (small) subset of what is available.

- It can be enormously confusing, even for a moderately advanced user, to reach for a command that was on menu or toolbar "A" yesterday, but is gone today. (Now where did that command go... I was sure it was right here somewhere.)

To access the hidden commands, Microsoft added a small double-caret (>>) graphic in both toolbars and menus indicating the presence of hidden commands. Clicking this graphic expands a menu to show all the items it contains. Alternatively, if you activate a menu and wait about five seconds before selecting a command, Outlook will assume you have not found what you are looking for and will fully expand the menu selections.

Adaptive menus are guaranteed to provoke love or hate, but never indifference. Thankfully, this controversial feature can be turned off from the menu and toolbar Customize dialog, which we cover in the next section.

The Customize Dialog

The Customize Dialog (Figure 4-1) centralizes all the menu and toolbar configuration options. This dialog is accessed by right-clicking on the menu bar or any toolbar and selecting the Customize command, or by selecting Tools → Customize. Note that this is a common dialog used by all Office 2000 applications. Some options selected here affect all Office programs; others—such as toolbar and menu customizations—remain local to the program.

Invoking this dialog signals the Office application where it is opened that you are in "customization" mode. As long as the Customize dialog is open, the program interprets any actions involving menus or toolbars as modifications, not commands.

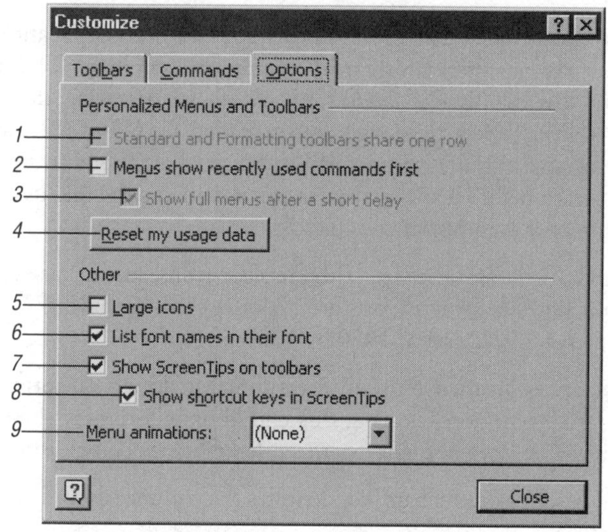

Figure 4-1: The Customize dialog Options tab, with adaptive menus turned off

The Options tab, shown in Figure 4-1, contains options relating to the various display features and arrangements of menus and toolbars. Most of the choices listed on this tab apply globally to all Office applications; there are two exceptions, and they are noted in the descriptions that follow.

1. "Standard and Formatting toolbars share one row" is selectable in contexts where both a standard and a formatting toolbar are displayed (for example, the Outlook mail editor). Where this context is not applicable, the option will be grayed, as shown in Figure 4-1. This is one of two options on this tab that when activated only apply to the program from which they are toggled. While putting two toolbars on the same row increases the editing space available, you also decrease the number of visible buttons. This is partly remedied through the use of adaptive

commands discussed in the previous section. Over time, infrequently used commands will be dropped and frequently used commands will take their place.

2. "Menus show recently used commands first" toggles the adaptive feature on or off for both menus and toolbars. Deselecting this option displays all menu items for a given context, and will resolve your vanishing command problem.

3. "Show full menus after a short delay" is used in conjunction with adaptive menus. If you hold your mouse cursor on an open menu without making a selection, after a short pause all menu commands available will be shown. Infrequently used commands are shown as grayed and recessed. If you elect to enable adaptive menus and toolbars in Office, make sure this option is selected. If it is not, the only way to access hidden commands is by clicking on the double-caret symbol.

4. "Reset my usage data" deletes the history stored for an application and restores the default set of commands for all menus and toolbars. This is the second option on this tab that is *application specific*, so resetting the usage data in Outlook will *not* affect the usage data recorded for Word. Be aware that after resetting an application's command history, it takes about an hour of working in the program before it learns your tastes and adapts the menus and toolbars to show a subset of their actual commands.

5. "Large icons" increases the size of the toolbar icons, just in case you need to see them from ten feet away or you are lucky enough to have a 21-inch monitor with the screen display set at 1920 by 1200 pixels.

6. "List font names in their font" displays font lists found on formatting toolbars in their actual typeface. Clearing this checkbox will display these lists quicker, as the font name does not have to be rendered before being displayed.

7. "Show ScreenTips on toolbars" to identifies the commands for icon-only buttons.

8. "Show shortcut keys in ScreenTips" will show you many of the more obscure keyboard commands when turned on.

9. "Menu animations" controls how the system displays menus. The options are None, Unfold, Slide, and Random. Unfold displays menus from the top edge out and down; Slide displays the menu from the top-left corner out and down; and Random is a mix of the previous two animations.

TIP # 35

Disabling Adaptive Menus

Adaptive menus are a useful feature if you use the same basic commands every day. For new users, however, we recommend disabling this feature at least until you become familiar with Outlook's menu structure and what commands are found where. (Tools → Customize → Options → uncheck "Menus show recently used command first" box).

The Customize dialog has two additional tabs: Toolbars and Commands. Both of these relate specifically to menu and toolbar customizations and are covered in their respective contexts in the sections that follow.

Customizing Menus

Outlook's Menus are fully customizable—you can add and remove commands, rearrange the order they are listed in, change the text that describes a menu item, and even alter the keyboard shortcuts used to activate them.

 Any customizations you apply to toolbars and menus are program specific. For example, customizing the Tools menu in Outlook has no consequence to the Tools menu in any other Office application.

The first step in customizing any of Outlook's menus is to open the Customization dialog shown in Figure 4-1. Activating this dialog is the toggle that alerts all Office products to the fact that you want to modify a menu rather than use it.

With the Customize dialog open, clicking on a menu will highlight the menu title with a bold black rectangle, as shown in Figure 4-2 (left).

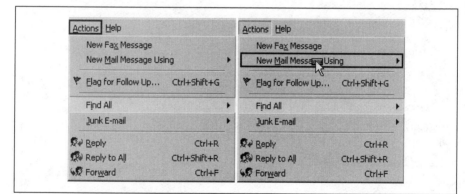

Figure 4-2: Customizing menus—the Actions menu selected (left); a command selected for modification (right)

Selecting a menu command produces a rectangle around that item and a "handle" under the cursor (Figure 4-2, right). There are many different ways to customize menus:

- To move a selected command to another location, hold down the mouse button and drag. When you've settled on a new home, release the mouse button in the desired location and the command will "anchor" itself there. Note that you can move a command to another position on the currently open menu, to a submenu of that menu, or to an entirely different menu.

- To move a complete existing menu structure to another location on the menu bar, select the menu title (e.g., View) and drag it to the desired position. Suppose you prefer your Favorites menu to the right of Help instead of to the left of Tools—just drag it there.

- To remove a selected command from a menu, simply drag it off the menu pad. The same action will remove a complete menu by dragging the menu title off the menu bar.

- To add a new command to a menu, select the Commands tab on the Customize dialog. Choose an entry from the Categories list box. Selecting a category displays the commands available for that group in the right list box. Choose a command and drag it from the Customize dialog to a menu (see Figure 4-3). Take some time to acquaint yourself with both the categories and related commands found on these two lists. Many of them are either not found on Outlook's default menus at all, or are buried deep in sub-submenus. By bringing your most frequently used commands to the surface—either by moving them to a higher menu level or by creating a custom toolbar (see "Customizing Toolbars" later in this chapter)—you will save yourself a great deal of time and effort rifling through menus.

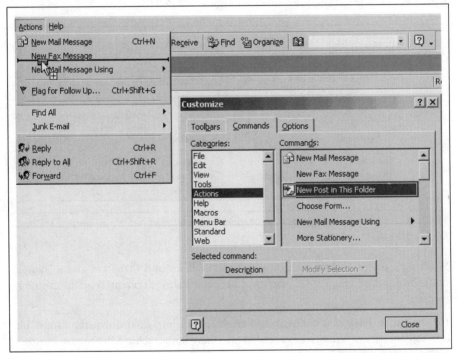

Figure 4-3: Adding a command to a menu—New Post in This Folder is added to the Actions menu under New Fax Message

- To create a new menu, select the New Menu category and the New Menu command in the right list box. Drag this item to the desired location. Note that this location can be anywhere—on the existing menu bar, on an existing menu (which, in effect, creates a submenu), or on an existing toolbar. With this new menu anchored, repeat the steps previously listed to create the items for the new menu.

TIP # 36

Gotcha—Modifying Outlook's Favorites Menu

The contents of the Favorites menu cannot be modified from within Outlook. You can move the location of the menu on the menu bar itself, and modify the menu's properties, but not the URLs it contains. This "Gotcha" is a result of the way Microsoft chose to implement the integration of Internet Explorer and Outlook. The contents of the Favorites menu displayed in Outlook must be modified from IE5 or Windows Explorer.

Before we move on to more advanced modifications, let's pause for a moment and look at a few common challenges you might encounter and how to correct them.

Note that there is no Cancel button on the Customization dialog. This means there is no way to back out of a menu customization if you find your efforts are not producing the intended results. Never fear, though, there are ways to restore your menus to their original pristine state. For example:

- You decide you don't need Help with Outlook and drag this menu off the menu pad into never-never land. A week later, you change your mind and want it back because the program is not as simple as you first assumed. Open the menu Customize dialog, select Menu Bar from the Categories list, Help from the Commands list, and drag it back to the menu pad.

- You make extensive modifications to the Tools menu, add commands, and shuffle menu items to other locations. After using your modified menu for a day, you decide you want the defaults back. Open the menu Customize dialog, and right-click the Tools menu. Select Reset from the context menu shown. Your Tools menu is restored to original the program defaults.

- Your menu customizations are extensive, stretch over several menu groups, and you have lost track of what exactly was altered where. It is possible to restore all your menus to their original defaults (that is, in the form they were when Outlook was first installed). Open the Customize dialogs referenced in Figure 4-1, and go to the Toolbars tab. Select Menu Bar from the list shown, and then use the Reset button. Note that using this option removes all customizations from all menus.

Now that we know how to restore menus to their defaults, we can take the modification process to the next level.

Open the menu Customize dialog. As previously noted, if you right-click a menu, a context menu will appear that allows an even deeper modification of either an existing or custom menu. To customize the properties of a menu item (as shown in Figure 4-4), click the menu title, then right-click the menu item you wish to modify.

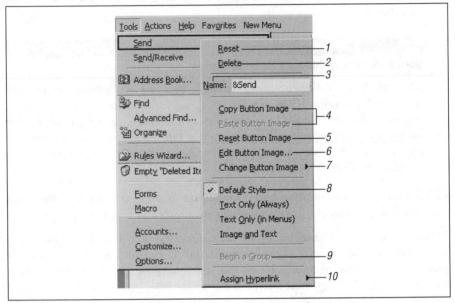

Figure 4-4: Customizing the properties for the Tools → Send menu

1. Reset restores the selected menu to its default as discussed previously.

2. Delete removes the selected menu or menu item. This is identical to dragging a menu item off the menu pad.

3. Name sets the title of the menu or menu item. If you prefer your Help menu title to read "911," enter this here. This field is important when you create a custom menu. The default title of a new menu is—you guessed it—New Menu, which does not do much to explain its purpose. The ampersand (&) sets the keyboard shortcut for the menu. For example, on a top-level menu like Tools, placing the ampersand before the T in the Name field allows this menu to be opened with the keyboard shortcut Alt+T. On a second level menu, the ampersand will denote what further key must be pressed to select this menu item. So the full keyboard shortcut to access the Send menu item shown in Figure 4-4 would be: Alt+T-S. The ampersand also places an underscore under the letter to visually denote it as a shortcut.

4. Copy/Paste Button Image can be thought of as mini-clipboards for transferring button images. If a menu item does not have an image associated with it, or the image it uses is not to your liking, select a command with the image you want and copy/paste that image to your customized entry. Keep in mind that this handy little tool is not restricted to button images found in Outlook; it can be utilized in any Office application. If there is a menu icon you fancy in Word,

for example, use the menu customizing tools there to copy the button image and paste it to a menu in Outlook. The copy/paste functions also tie in nicely with the Edit Button Image tool discussed later in this list.

5. Reset Button Image resets the button image to its original default state. Any button customized by you for the command is removed and any default button associated with it is restored. If you crafted your own button with the Button Editor, it will be forever lost unless you cut and paste the image elsewhere before resetting the button.

6. Edit Button Image allows you to make your own button image. Select the menu command you want to customize a button for, right-click, and select Edit Button Image from the context menu. The Button Editor, a component shared across all Office applications, is displayed (Figure 4-5).

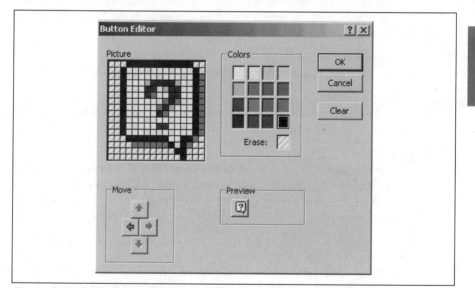

Figure 4-5: The built-in Office Button Editor

If the command you select has no button image associated with it, you will get a blank palette to create from. When you find an image that is close to your needs, use the copy/paste commands to add it to your menu item first, and then edit the button to your preferences by replacing pixels with different colors or by moving them around.

7. Change Button Image allows you to add a button image to a command that lacks one, or change the default image associated with a command. The selection available is rather limited, but some choice is better than none. The palette displayed from this command is shown in Figure 4-6.

8. Default Style defines the way a command displays on the menu or toolbar. Default Style refers to how the command normally displays—some commands

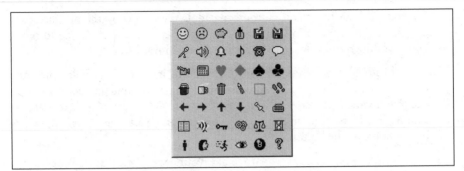

Figure 4-6: The Change Button palette

display only an icon (such as the Print icon on the standard toolbar), some commands show both icon and text, while other commands have no icon associated with them (such as Send). Experimentation with the following options will allow you to pick a display style that suits your needs:

Text Only (Always)
> Display the command as text, *always*, in both menus and toolbars.

Text Only (In Menus)
> Display the command as text only, in menus. Any default style icon associated with the command is still shown when the command is on a toolbar.

Image and Text
> Forces any associated icon to be displayed to the left of the command text. This applies only to the menu item being added, not to the same command that may already exist on another menu, or to a toolbar version of the command.

9. Begin a Group is a toggle, which when activated inserts a divider above the selected item. This, in effect, creates a visual "group" of menu commands. When toggled again, the option is turned off. Top-level menu titles can be grouped in the same way—the divider is then inserted to the left of the selected item. When you move an existing menu or toolbar into another, this also creates a group around the moved item.

10. Assign Hyperlink (displayed in Figure 4-7) is common to all Microsoft Office applications, and allows you to assign a hyperlink to a menu, toolbar, or document.

Toggling any of the four choices shown on the "Link to" icon bar on the left lets you select the type of hyperlink to insert or assign, and shifts the context and choices available in the central part of the dialog.

Existing File or Web Page
> This presents you with a field in which to type the name of a file (already existing on your system) or enter an Internet address in the form of a URL.

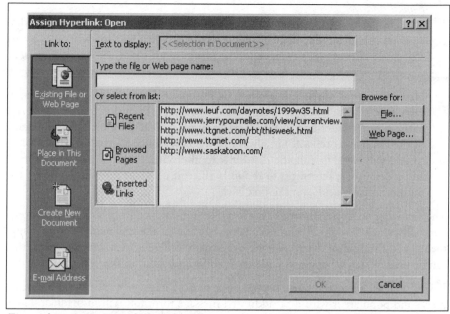

Figure 4-7: Assign Hyperlink dialog

You can also select from one of the lists displayed: Recent Files, a list of recently accessed files stored by the operating system; Browsed Pages, a list of recently accessed pages stored by Internet Explorer; or Inserted Links, a list of recent links you have cut/pasted or otherwise inserted into documents recently.

If you still haven't found exactly what you are looking for, the "Browse for" buttons on the right edge of the dialog opens a common Windows Browse dialog (File), Internet Explorer (Web Page), or opens a dialog allowing you to locate a bookmarked section of your document (Bookmark). The latter is not functional within Outlook unless you are using Word as your mail editor.

Place in This Document

Like the Bookmark button just discussed, this option applies to Office documents supporting bookmarks; unless you are working in such a context from within Outlook, you will see an "unsupported" message when you choose this option.

Create New Document

This provides you with the means to create a new document, specify the path where it will be stored, and choose whether you want to edit the document now or later. Notice that by choosing the "later" option, you would place a hyperlink to a new uncreated document on a menu or toolbar, and create that document by accessing this command.

E-mail Address

This has particular relevance to Outlook users. With this hyperlink option you can create a toolbar or menu item that when selected will open a new email message with the address filled in as specified, and—if you so desire—a subject line as well.

Note that for all these link options, as you enter the type of link in the applicable field (E-mail address, New Document, etc.) the name you provide for this entry in also transcribed to the "Text to display" field. In most cases, the name of the link you enter will not always be the best choice for the displayed name, so you will want to edit the display field afterward. There is also provision to add a descriptive screen tip to the link, the text of which will display when the mouse cursor is held over the link itself.

The following example illustrates both creating a new menu, and using the previously discussed Assign Hyperlink dialog. Although the following example uses menus and the *mailto:* hyperlink, there are many different hyperlink protocols that can be used, which we cover in Chapter 5, *Mail Editors*.

If you send email to the same people on a routine basis, why not build a custom menu and populate it with a preaddressed message form for each individual? Then, instead of opening a new message form and manually locating the recipient's address, all you have to do is select a menu item and Outlook will do all the work for you. Here is the drill:

1. Right-click anywhere on Outlook's menu, choose Customize, and go to the Commands tab. From the Categories list select New Menu; from the Commands list select the New Menu item. Drag it to the desired location on your menu.

2. Right-click the title (which, by default, will be named "New Menu"), and go to the Name field on the context menu displayed (see Figure 4-8). Rename your new menu something appropriate—in the example shown, we've chosen "Email Contacts." If you want to associate a hot-key with this menu, use an ampersand before the desired letter.

3. Click on your new menu (that's left-click, not right-click) to display an empty menu pad. Go back to the Customize dialog, and choose a command to add. At this point in time, your only consideration should be whether you want an icon displayed with the entry. If you do, choose a command with the icon you desire. Any command will work, as we will be adapting its behavior in a moment. While creating a menu item, you are restricted to choosing an icon from the palette shown earlier in this section (see Figure 4-6). If you want to use an icon associated with an existing Outlook command, you have two choices. You may either copy the whole command (including icon), then edit the associated command behavior, or you can create a new menu item, then use the icon copy/ paste feature to modify the icon afterwards. For this example, we'll use the "Mail

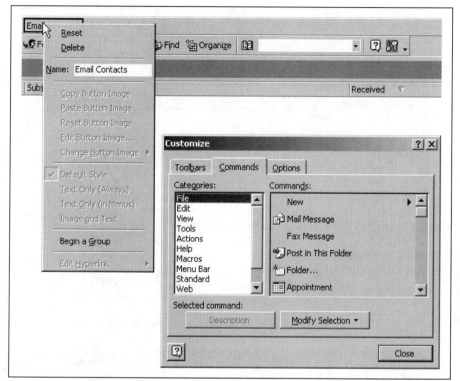

Figure 4-8: Creating a new menu for email contacts

Message" command so we pick up the associated mail envelope icon. Drag whatever command you've chosen and place it on your new menu.

4. Now right-click this new menu item. From the context menu displayed, type a name in the text box provided. Again, if you want to hot-key to this contact, use an ampersand before the letter. Now from this same context menu, choose Edit Hyperlink → Open. From the Edit Hyperlink dialog select "E-mail Address" from the "Link to" icon bar.

5. Type an email address in the field provided as shown in Figure 4-9. Outlook automatically inserts *mailto:* in front of your entry. Note that you have no provision to call up an address list from this dialog. This means you will have to either know the address you want to enter, or have copied it to the clipboard from another source beforehand. The Subject field is optional. If you do elect to use it, what you type here will appear as the initial text in the Subject line of every message you send via this menu item.

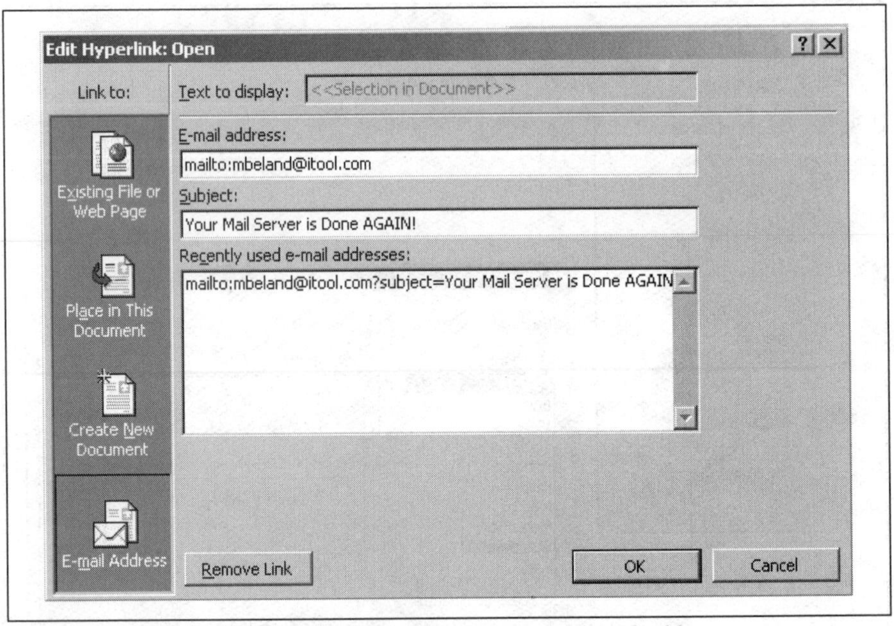

Figure 4-9: Using the Edit Hyperlink dialog to assign an email address to a menu item

---

TIP # 37

Displaying ScreenTips on Custom Buttons

Once you've created a custom toolbar with "mailto:" hyperlinks, how do you remember which button sends mail to whom? Hold your cursor over an icon and it displays the recipient's email address plus the subject, if you used one. Providing, of course, you have the "Show ScreenTips" option enabled (Tools → Customize → Options → "Show ScreenTips on toolbars").

Context Menus

Context menus appear when you right-click specific screen regions in an active window. The menu displayed contains a subset of commands appropriate to the Outlook component in use at the time. Three key factors determine the contents of a context menu: component, screen region, and view:

- *Component* reflects the Outlook component you are working in. Obviously you will be trying to accomplish different things working in Journal than you would in Calendar; the context menus displayed in each component reflect what you can do there.

- *Screen region* is a function of the program layout. Item views occupy the central area of the active window; the Outlook Bar and Folder List are anchored to the left edge of the active window; and the preview pane is displayed below the item view. Each of these regions has a different function and the context menus displayed change to reflect this.

- *View* reflects the way in which Outlook items are filtered, sorted, and displayed. For example, when a contact list is displayed in any of Outlook's table views, a context menu is provided when you right-click the table's header row. This menu provides commands for sorting, filtering, and grouping the view; these options are not applicable when a contact list is displayed as Address Cards.

Menu variations can be produced by subtle context changes, such as selecting more than one item at a time, or the properties of a particular view.

Right-clicking on dialog field descriptors or program options will often produce a text pop-up with information about the field or option's function. For example, right-clicking on the "Web page address" field descriptor in a Contact Add/Edit dialog will display the pop-up information shown in Figure 4-10.

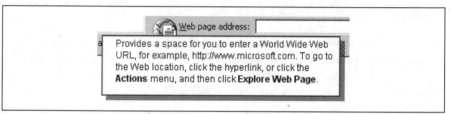

Figure 4-10: Pop-up context descriptor for Contact field

Get in the habit of frequently checking for the presence of context menus. These menus provide a quick overview of common actions appropriate to a given task or view. The commands often take you directly to a dialog that would otherwise require a long, convoluted sequence of menu selections.

Figure 4-11 shows a good example of a highly useful and frequently used context displayed when an Inbox message is right-clicked. Note that the item selected has a file attachment, so the "View Attachments" command is accessible. If the item had no attachments, this command would not be shown. Similarly, if the item had a completed flag associated with it, the "Flag for Follow-up" entry would change to Flag Complete.

Unfortunately, context menus can only be customized using an add-in with VBA, which is beyond the scope of this book. For a general overview of using VBA in Outlook, see Chapter 18, *Working with VBA*.

Toolbars

Outlook installs with several preconfigured toolbars that give one-click access to common commands. Like menus, toolbars are context sensitive (for example, a

Figure 4-11: Inbox item context menu

Message view displays different buttons than a Contacts view) and adaptive (buttons no longer display on a formatting toolbar if you fail to use a particular command for a given length of time). The default toolbars available in Outlook depend on the installation mode chosen (see Chapter 2, *Installing Outlook*).

An Internet Mail Only (IMO) installation preconfigures three toolbars: Standard, Advanced, and Web. The context menu shown in Figure 4-12 is used to display and customize these toolbars and can be accessed via the View → Toolbars command or by right-clicking anywhere on a toolbar or empty toolbar area.

Figure 4-12: The Toolbar submenu—IMO installation

When Outlook is installed in Corporate Workgroup (CW) mode a fourth preconfigured toolbar is added: Remote. The commands on this toolbar relate specifically to reading, marking, and retrieving message headers off a mail server that supports this function.

Toolbars are normally "docked" or "anchored" to the top edge of Outlook's interface. They can, however, be "undocked" and float anywhere on your screen, anchored to any side of Outlook's interface window, or resized to show more or less of the command buttons displayed.

- To resize a floating toolbar, move your cursor over any edge until it turns into a double-headed arrow, and then drag that edge of the toolbar in the desired direction.

- To resize a docked toolbar that shares a row with another toolbar, position your cursor over the "move handle" (the vertical raised bar on the left edge of the toolbar) until it turns to a four-headed arrow and drag *horizontally* in the desired direction (see Figure 4-13).

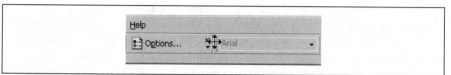

Figure 4-13: Four-headed arrow displayed when resizing a vertical toolbar

- To undock a toolbar, place your cursor over the move handle and when the four-headed arrow appears, drag *vertically* (generally out of a toolbar area).

- To dock a floating toolbar, position your cursor over the title bar and drag it to one of the four sides of the program's interface.

Toolbars remember both their location and state. If, for example, you float a toolbar on your screen and minimize or close Outlook, it will return to the same location and state when you maximize or restart Outlook.

When a toolbar is docked and hiding command buttons, a double-caret symbol (>>) appears on the right edge of the toolbar. Selecting this symbol displays any buttons or drop-down lists not currently in view as well as an "Add or Remove Buttons" pad. Holding your cursor on this pad opens a context menu similar to that shown in Figure 4-14.

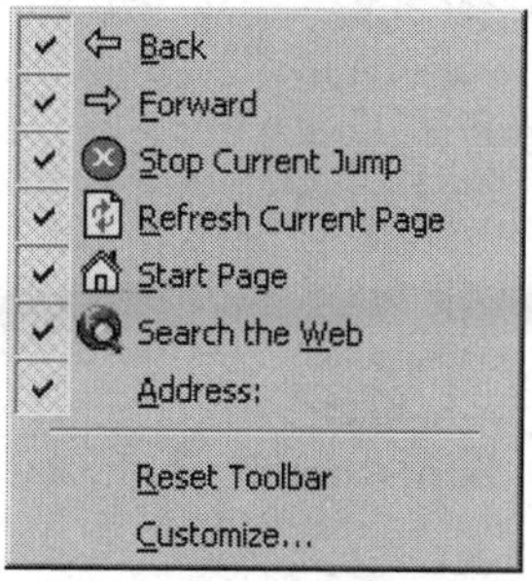

Figure 4-14: Toolbar Context menu—the Web Toolbar

This is a very fast and handy way to customize a toolbar. Deselecting a command causes it to be hidden. Toggling the same command item again (restoring the checkmark) redisplays it on the toolbar. The Reset Toolbar toggle returns the toolbar to its original state before any customizations, while the Customize toggle opens the customization dialog discussed later in this chapter in the "Customizing Toolbars" section.

On floating toolbars there is a down-arrow in the top-left corner of the title bar. This arrow calls up the context menu shown in Figure 4-14.

Although most toolbar buttons simply echo commands that are found on the normal menus and submenus, the Standard and Advanced toolbars also act like context menus by adapting the function of some of the buttons displayed to the current component in use. For example, the Find button sets up a context-specific search scope, and the Organize button opens a "Ways to Organize" pane with preselected options specific to the Outlook component you are working in.

In the next sections we explore in detail the Standard, Advanced, and Web toolbars.

Standard Toolbar

The minimum Standard toolbar in Figure 4-15 mirrors the essential File and Tool commands. In this example, the encryption application *PGP* is installed (see Chapter 15, *Security and Encryption*), which adds the red key-icon to the far right.

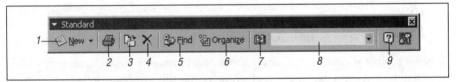

Figure 4-15: The Standard toolbar, PGP component icon at far right

The icons on the standard toolbar are:

1. New (with context-dependent icon, plus list down-arrow) indicates the current default "New" (Ctrl+N) command, which will vary depending on which component view you are working in. The down-arrow button accesses the same submenu entries given by File → New in the current context.

2. Print sends the item(s) currently selected in the view to the default printer for immediate printing—there is no confirmation dialog displayed and no opportunity to change printing options. Use File → Print Preview (or the Advanced toolbar button with the same name) to see what your document will look like. By contrast, the File → Print command (Ctrl+P) calls up the print settings dialog first.

3. Move to Folder, again acting on the currently selected item(s), first shows a submenu with your most recently accessed Outlook folders as selectable destinations. Once the list reaches ten folders, your most recently accessed folder is added to the top and the bottom entry is dropped. At the bottom of the list is

the general Move to Folder command, which opens a dialog to choose from all folder destinations.

4. Delete moves the selected item(s) to Outlook's Deleted Items folder. Holding down the Shift key and clicking this icon deletes an item permanently.

5. Find opens a context-sensitive Find pane above the current view. If you are working in a Contacts view, for example, the Name, Company, Addresses, and Category fields are searched for the text string entered here. (See Chapter 3, *Program Insights*, for a detailed discussion on using Find.)

6. Organize is similar to the Find icon, but opens a context-sensitive Organize pane above the current view. From this pane you can move or copy the selected items, create a mail rule based on the current item's message header, or mark a selected message for inclusion on the Junk Mail list. Organizing your data across all Outlook components is also covered in Chapter 3.

7. Address Book opens the Windows Address Book (WAB), which is actually an alternate interface for viewing the records contained in your Contacts folder. See Chapter 3 for a full explanation of the ins and outs of Outlook's Address Book.

8. Find a Contact (entry field and drop-down list) searches the Contacts folder for matches to the text string provided. A successful result is displayed in an opened Contact details form. If there are multiple matches to the entered name, a Choose Contact dialog allows you to select from those entries found. The drop-down list associated with the entry field lists previous successful matches for quick reference.

9. Help opens Outlook's Help/Search dialog shown in Figure 4-16. Enter a word or phrase and select Search. To open the Office Assistant dialog (Help options), select Options.

TIP # 38

Search with Find a Contact

The Find a Contact search field is a powerful and handy tool, once you gain a sense for what to enter as a search phrase. Names, partial names (for example, "to"), URLs, and email addresses all produce results—usually even with only a few key letters. Other fields that might be obvious candidates for a search result return a blank or confusing response. Examples of nonsearchable fields are: any part of an address (city, street name, or state), phone numbers, and company name. For industrial-strength contact searches, see the section on "Advanced Find" in Chapter 3.

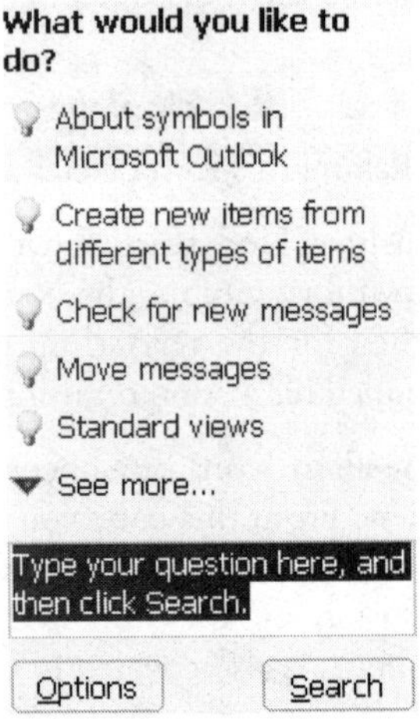

Figure 4-16: The Outlook Help dialog

Advanced Toolbar

The Advanced toolbar is shown in Figure 4-17 and mirrors the Outlook folder navigation and view commands. The first group complements the menu command View → Go to → Folder.

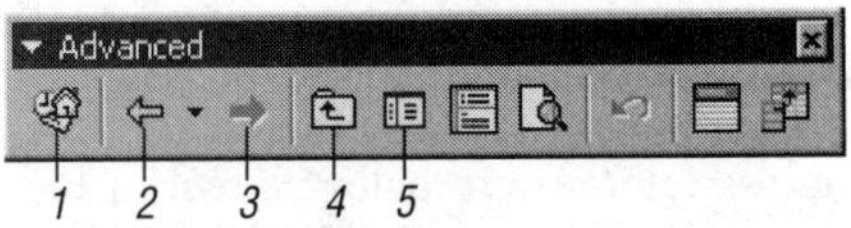

Figure 4-17: The minimum Advanced toolbar

The special toolbar actions here are:

1. Outlook Today is a one-click shortcut to the summary view Outlook Today, discussed in Chapter 3.

2. Previous Folder (and History down-arrow) takes you back to the previous folder view when several folders have been selected in the current session. Otherwise it is grayed out. The visited-folder history is shown in a submenu list when the down-arrow is selected, from which any previous folder can be selected.

3. Next Folder advances to the next folder in the history list. If there is nothing in History to advance to, the button is disabled.

4. Up One Level (parent folder) moves the view up a level in the folder tree, i.e., to the one where the current folder is shown as a child.

5. Folder List toggles the left view pane that shows the folder tree, like View → Folder, on and off.

When browsing web folders, the Previous and Next history echoes the corresponding Web toolbar history, which can be useful if the latter is hidden or disabled.

Web Toolbar

Figure 4-18 shows the Web toolbar, which contains the Outlook Web navigation commands. These are relevant when Outlook is used as a web browser. This toolbar does not change context like the others. All the buttons on this toolbar function the same as they would in Internet Explorer—which makes sense, since Outlook uses Internet Explorer 5 Dynamic Link Libraries (DLLs) for the code to produce its internal browsing features.

Figure 4-18: The Web toolbar

The icons on the Web toolbar are:

1. Page Back returns to the previously visited page

2. Page Forward (shown as unavailable in this screenshot) allows you to move forward through pages already browsed.

3. Stop stops the current request for a page.

4. Refresh "refreshes" the page displayed, requesting a fresh (updated) copy from the server it is resident on. In the case of a local file folder, it will refresh the contents of that folder to reflect any changes made since it was last displayed.

5. Start Page opens your default Home page as configured in Internet Explorer under the Tools menu, Internet Options → General tab.

6. Search the Web starts Internet Explorer and takes you to the Microsoft search site (see Figure 4-19). Note that this site may differ depending on the version of Windows installed on your system.

7. Address provides a text box to enter a URL address. The most common use of this is, of course, an Internet address in the form of *www.somewhere.com* (Internet Explorer will, by default, provide the prefix *http://*). Do not forget that if Outlook's File Management features are installed (see Chapter 2), you can also use this entry box to type a local filesystem path (of the form `c:\My Documents`) or a network file path (of the form `\\server\share`). Using the

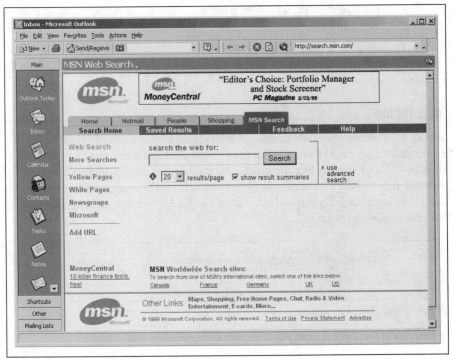

Figure 4-19: Search the Web from within Outlook

latter will bring up a file manager-like window with that folder displayed in the Outlook window.

The visited-page history is shown in a drop-down list using the down-arrow button. Selecting an item from this list allows you to quickly redisplay any recently visited sites or files without concern for the order of visit.

Customizing Toolbars

Like menus, Outlook toolbars are fully customizable with regard to both the command buttons shown, and the location of those buttons on the toolbar. Much of the technique involved in modifying Outlook's toolbars is functionally identical to customizing a menu, so only details unique to toolbars are discussed here.

To customize a toolbar, right-click on any displayed toolbar or the menu bar and select Customize from the context menu (or from the View menu, Toolbars → Customize).

The Toolbars tab in Figure 4-20 displays a list of Outlook's default toolbars, plus any custom toolbars created. Toolbars can be turned on or off from this dialog by selecting an entry and using the checkbox provided. Despite its presence on this list with a checkbox, you cannot turn the Menu Bar off.

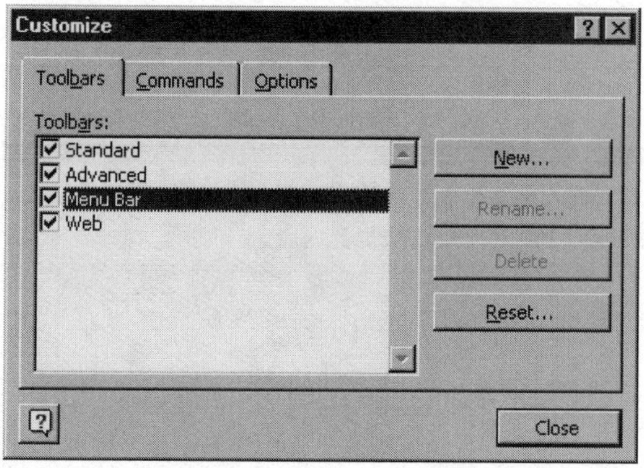

Figure 4-20: The Customize dialog Toolbars tab

The Reset button will return the selected entry to the original commands and placements used when Outlook was first installed. Any customizations you have added to the toolbar are lost. Note that the Reset command works for the Menu Bar entry as well—as a matter of fact, this is the only way—as noted earlier in the menu section—to reset *all* Outlook's menus to their default state in one fell swoop.

> **NOTE** *The Rename and Delete commands on the Customize Toolbars tab are only available for custom toolbars; not Outlook's default toolbars, and not a customized default toolbar.*

The basic procedure for customizing an existing toolbar is the same one used for menus: go to the Commands tab on the Customize dialog, choose a command category from the list on the left, and drag a command from the right pane onto the toolbar you wish to modify.

Figure 4-21 illustrates this procedure. As you drag a command the cursor will provide a visual reference to where you can drop the command (x for not allowed, + for allowed), and when in a permissible location an I-beam will indicate where on the toolbar the command will be added. Release the mouse button to drop the command button in the desired location.

Keep in mind that you are not restricted to using the lists displayed in the Customize dialog as your only source for commands. If the Standard toolbar is displayed and there is a command on it you want to copy to the Advanced toolbar, for example, hold down the Ctrl key and drag the command from one toolbar to another.

Figure 4-21: Drag a command from the Customize dialog to an existing toolbar

TIP # 39

How to Copy When Dragging

The default behavior when dragging commands between two toolbars (or menus) is to move the command; to copy it, hold down the Ctrl key while dragging. And don't restrict yourself to thinking about toolbars and menus as discrete objects—they are all fair game when the Customize dialog is open. See a command on a menu that would look nice on your custom toolbar? Go get it!

With the Customize dialog open you can also rearrange the order of a toolbar by selecting a button and dragging it to a new location. To remove a command, select it and drag it off the toolbar pad.

Removing a button from any of Outlook's default toolbars does not actually delete them; it simply stops them from being displayed. You can reset the display of any of these commands through the Add or Remove Buttons submenu accessible from the small down-arrow displayed next to the toolbar title (this same arrow can be found on the far-right edge of a docked toolbar). In Figure 4-22, the Start Page icon has been removed from the toolbar. To restore it, open the submenu and select the appropriate entry from the list displayed.

Be aware that this technique only works for Outlook's default toolbars. If you remove a command from a custom toolbar, the only way to restore it is to add it back using the Reset Toolbar command.

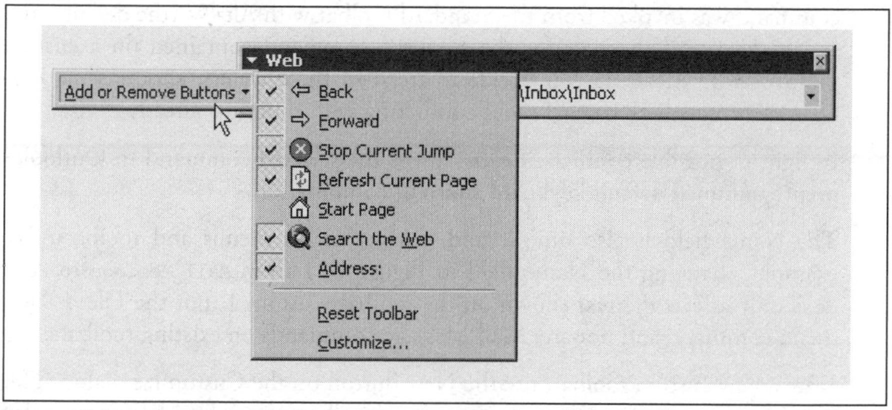

Figure 4-22: Restoring or hiding toolbar buttons; the Add or Remove Buttons submenu is accessed via the small arrow shown to the left of the toolbar title—in the example pictured, "Web"

Like menus, toolbar images and the text displayed can be modified. Again, the Customize dialog must be open to gain access to the context menu displayed in Figure 4-23.

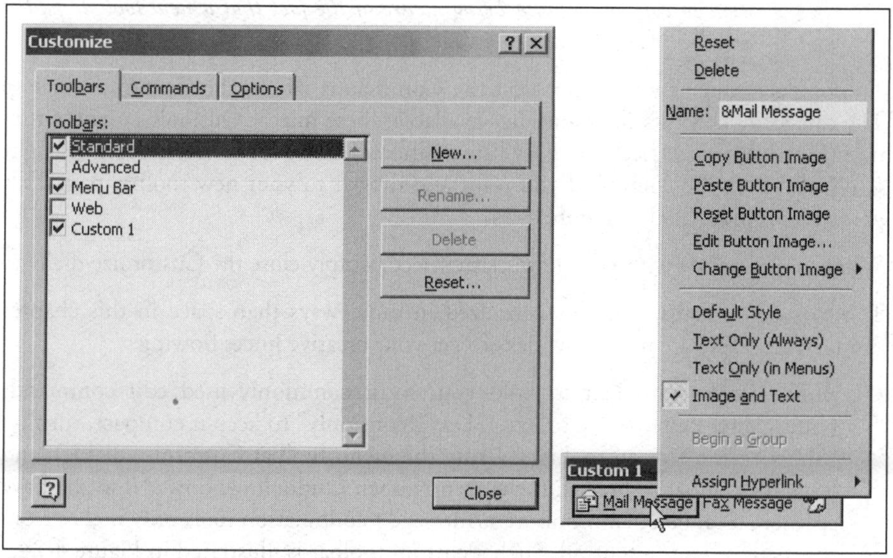

Figure 4-23: Customizing a toolbar button image or name

When using this menu in the context of toolbars, be aware of the following:

• The & in the Name field works the same for toolbars as it does for menus—the character following it will become the keyboard shortcut (Alt+key). You can, however, use a different keyboard shortcut for separate instances of the same command. For example, you could customize Outlook such that the Forward command was invoked from the Standard toolbar with Alt+W (the default) and set the keyboard shortcut for the Forward command contained on a custom toolbar to be Alt+F. If you decide to tread in these waters, choose your keyboard shortcuts with care to avoid conflicting with shortcuts already in use.

- In light of possible conflicts, Reset returns the selected command to Outlook's preprogrammed default keyboard shortcut combination.

- The Name field is also unique and distinct across menus and toolbars. For example, changing the Name field in Figure 4-21 from Mail Message to Mail Mess only affects the text shown on the toolbar Custom 1, not the File → New menu command and not any Mail Message commands on existing toolbars.

To create a new custom toolbar, use the New button on the Customize dialog. This command invokes a dialog prompting you for a toolbar name. The default provided is Custom 1, which can be accepted if a creative name escapes you at the time; don't forget, a custom toolbar can be renamed by using the Rename button on the Toolbars tab.

 The toolbar "pad" created with the new command is only large enough to hold one icon, which makes it hard to find if it ends up laying on top of the Preview Pane divider—which is often the case. There is no direct solution to this, other than being aware of the fact that a new toolbar pad is small and can be easily overlooked.

To populate your new toolbar, select the Commands tab on the Customize dialog. The categories box lists the groupings available; these mirror Outlook's menu structure (File, Edit, etc.). Each category lists a different subset of commands in the right scroll box. Pick the command you want and drag it to your new toolbar pad. This procedure is illustrated in Figure 4-24.

When you're happy with your new masterpiece, simply close the Customize dialog.

Toolbars, like menus, can be customized in more ways than space in this chapter can provide. Here are just a few ideas to get your creative juices flowing:

- Build a custom toolbar to hold your most commonly used edit commands (Cut, Copy, Paste, Move to, etc.). Use "Icons only" to keep it compact, turn on "Show ScreenTips on toolbars" (from the menu-toolbar Customize dialog), and leave the toolbar to float in the currently open Outlook window. Now you have access to a range of common item/message manipulation tools only inches from the focus of your attention. Such a custom toolbar is illustrated in Figure 4-24.

- Create a toolbar for quick access to your favorite web sites. Drag a command from the Customize dialog to a new or existing toolbar.

 Some commands from the Customize dialog cannot be reconfigured to activate a hyperlink (For example, Category → File/Command → New).

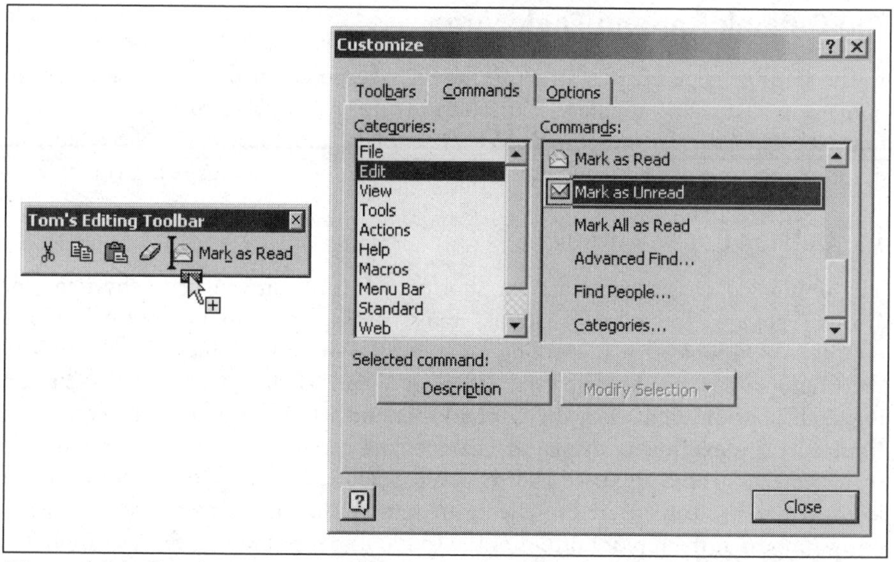

Figure 4-24: Creating a custom toolbar

Right-click the command, select Assign Hyperlink from the context menu, and click Open. This will display the dialog shown in Figure 4-9. Choose a link to assign from one of the options available. Right-click the button again and change the displayed Name.

- Any custom toolbar you create should have commands for Categories and Flag for Follow-up on them. These are two of the most potentially useful organizational tools in Outlook and we recommend you use them frequently.

- If you find yourself switching views on a routine basis, add the Current View command to your all-purpose editing toolbar discussed earlier. This will give you a drop-down list of view choices that switch with context.

- If you close either the Outlook Bar (discussed in the next section of this chapter) or the Preview Pane, you have to make a trip to the menus to turn them back on again; put them on a toolbar for quick access.

- The Address text box (from the Web toolbar) is a good candidate for inclusion on a custom toolbar. With it you can not only quickly go to an Internet URL, but also open a local filesystem folder.

- In general, consider any command you have to dig for on a sub-submenu a worthy candidate for a custom toolbar. A good example of this is the New Mail Message Using → Plain Text menu option. My default email format is HTML, but I have several people I correspond with on a daily basis who prefer Plain Text format. Rather than digging through two menu levels, this command is on a custom toolbar.

The Outlook Bar and Folder Tree

In the spirit of good chapter structure, we've saved the best for last. In addition to numerous menus and toolbars, Outlook provides two further methods of navigation: the *Outlook Bar* and the *Folder Tree*. These graphical folder views are the quintessential means of quickly moving around Outlook and organizing your files.

The Outlook Bar

The Outlook Bar is a container for shortcuts. On it you can place shortcuts for Outlook folders, individual Outlook items, or shortcuts to programs and files external to Outlook (that is, residing on your local or network filesystem). Icons on the Outlook Bar can be displayed Large or Small as shown in Figure 4-25. To toggle this option, right-click the Outlook Bar and select the appropriate command from the context menu displayed. Large icons present a better target for file management, a topic discussed shortly, while small icons allow you to display more icons in a group. If there are more icons in a group than the pane can display, scroll arrows appear at the top or bottom of the Outlook Bar to indicate this fact (note the left Outlook bar shown in Figure 4-25).

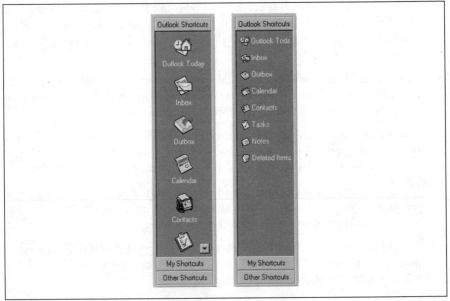

Figure 4-25: The Outlook Bar shown with Large and Small icons respectively

The Outlook Bar can be hidden from view with the context menu command Hide Outlook Bar. Once hidden, you need to use the View → Outlook Bar menu command to restore it.

NOTE	*For details on taking advantage of file management with the Outlook Bar, the Folder List and the Web Toolbar (to access system files within Outlook itself) see Chapter 13, File Management.*

In its default configuration, the Outlook Bar is divided into three Groups: Outlook Shortcuts, My Shortcuts, and Other Shortcuts. To move to a different group, simply click the title. You can add groups to this configuration, rename an existing group with a more meaningful title, or remove a group you no longer use.

- To add a new group, right-click anywhere on the Outlook Bar and choose the Add New Group command from the context menu (Figure 4-26). New groups are always added at the bottom of the Outlook Bar. Type a name for the group in the highlighted space, followed by Enter. To change the display order of the groups on the Outlook Bar, see the "Reordering the Outlook Bar" sidebar later in this chapter.

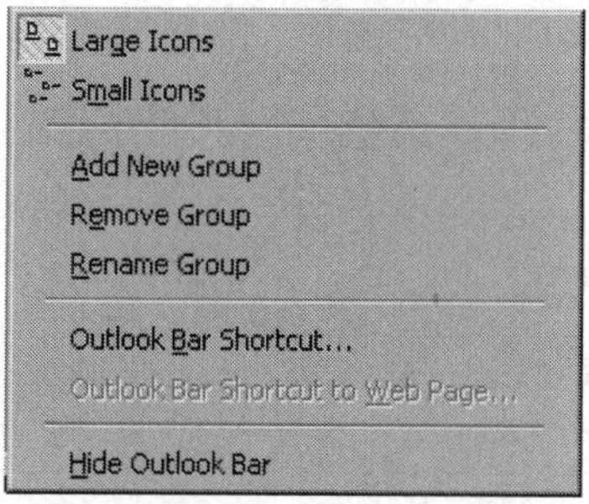

Figure 4-26: The Outlook Bar context menu

TIP # 40

Outlook Bar Limits

The maximum number of groups you can have on the Outlook Bar is 12. Counting the three preconfigured groups Outlook creates, this means that you can add an additional nine groups before you run up against this program limitation. To add more than 12 groups, you have to delete an existing group. Once you reach this limit, the Add New Group command is no longer available.

- To delete an existing group, right-click on the group title button or ensure the group you want to remove is displayed and right-click anywhere within the group. *This is important.* If you inadvertently delete the wrong group, there is no way to undo this action. Select Remove Group from the context menu. A dialog will appear to confirm this action. Note that this dialog does not display the title of the group you are deleting.

- To rename an existing group, right-click on the group title and select Rename from the context menu. Type a new name in the highlighted space provided.

Right-clicking any item (shortcut) on the Outlook Bar invokes the context menu shown in Figure 4-27.

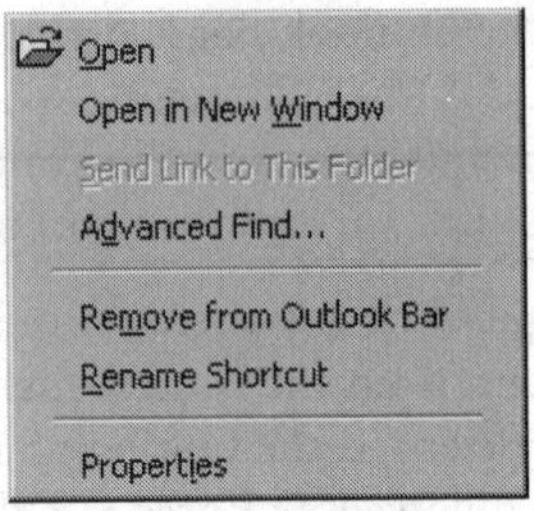

Figure 4-27: The Outlook Bar item context menu

TIP # 41

You Can't Replicate the Outlook Bar

The Outlook Bar is located in the user's Windows folder in a FAV file. Each user's FAV file is unique to that user's mail configuration, so this file will not work if copied from one system to another. The Outlook Bar shortcuts look for a specific signature when attempting to connect to Inbox or Sent Items. Because each Personal folder file (PST), server Mailbox, or other item folder has a unique signature, using the same Outlook Bar shortcut file will not work on a second user's computer. This feature allows Outlook to maintain the integrity of the shortcut destinations.

Open
　　Is essentially a useless command for this context menu. It is no different than clicking on the Outlook Bar icon to navigate to that folder or shortcut.

Open in New Window
　　Opens the shortcut selected in a new window, without the Outlook Bar or Folder Tree displayed. It is often useful to have more than one Outlook window open while you work. For example, you could have your Inbox running in one window with the Outlook Bar and/or Folder List displayed for fast file management chores, and in a separate window (typically minimized) your Calendar displayed in the view of your choice, devoid of any navigation tools. An example of this functionality is shown in Figure 4-28.

Advanced Find
　　Opens an Advanced Find dialog preconfigured to search the selected folder. This is a particularly useful shortcut to remember, especially if you use multiple Personal Folders (see Chapter 13, *File Management*, for a discussion of the merits of multiple PSTs and Chapter 3 for details on the Find/Advanced Find command).

Remove from Outlook Bar and Rename Shortcut
　　Removes or renames the selected shortcut.

Reordering the Outlook Bar

To change the order in which the default groups (Outlook Shortcuts, My Shortcuts, Other Shortcuts) are displayed on the Outlook Bar, follow these steps:

1. Close Outlook. If you are running Outlook in CW mode, make sure you select Exit And Log Off from the File menu.

2. Go to the Windows Start Menu, select Find → Files Or Folders.

3. In the Named box, type `*.fav` and click Find Now. You are looking for the file *Outlook.fav* (or `Profile Name.fav` in the case of a CW installation), which is usually found in the folder: [`path varies`]/*Application Data/Microsoft/Outlook*.

4. Right-click this file, and select Rename. Give it a new name (for example, `Outlook.bak`).

5. In the Search Named box, type `Outlbar.inf` and click Find Now. Right-click the file, and then click Edit to open it.

6. Look for the following section, about one-quarter of the way down in the file:

   ```
   [DefaultOutlookBar]
   AddGroup=OutlookGroup,MailGroup,OtherGroup
   ```

7. Here's the translation on these entries listed by their default titles:

   ```
   OutlookGroup = "Outlook Shortcuts"
   MailGroup = "My Shortcuts"
   OtherGroup = "Other Shortcuts"
   ```

8. Change the AddGroup entry order to the order you want. For instance, if you want the MailGroup (My Shortcuts) to be on top, edit the entry as follows:

   ```
   AddGroup=MailGroup,OutlookGroup,OtherGroup
   ```

9. Save the file and close the editor.

10. Restart Outlook. Outlook will look at the *.inf* file to build the *.fav* file and rearrange the order of the groups on the Outlook Bar. You will see a message asking you to wait while Outlook rebuilds the Outlook bar.

You can only change the order of the three default groups Outlook provides, not of additional groups you have added.

Properties

Opens the properties dialog for the shortcut selected. The properties dialog gives you access to details such as folder size, archive settings, and in the case of a top-level folder, the Advanced → Compress Folder command. Outlook folder

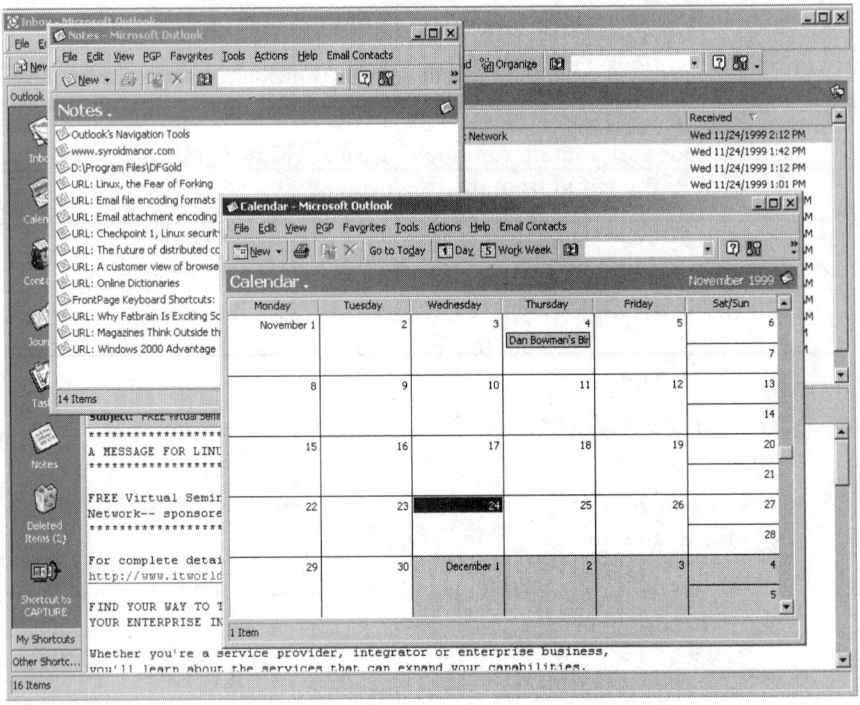

Figure 4-28: Opening multiple Outlook windows using the "Open in New Window" command

properties are discussed fully in the "Data Structures" section in Chapter 3. If the shortcut points to a filesystem folder or program (for example, Favorites, My Computer, or a shortcut to a program), the properties dialog shown will be the same as the one available from Windows Explorer.

Adding shortcuts to the Outlook Bar

Any time you create a new folder in Outlook the program offers to place a shortcut to that new folder on the Outlook Bar (providing you have not turned this feature off). The dialog displayed is shown in Figure 4-29.

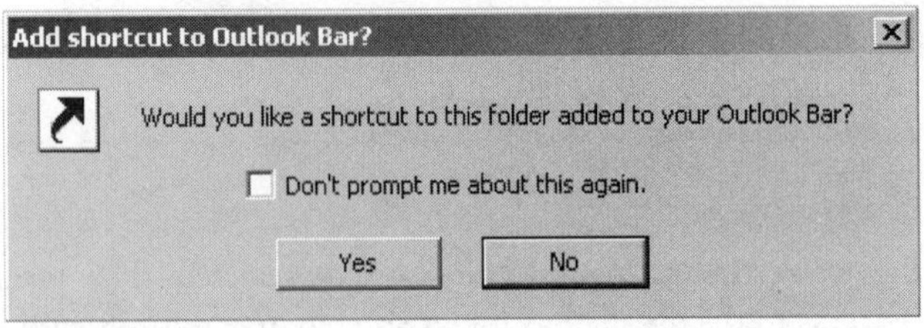

Figure 4-29: Add shortcut to Outlook Bar dialog

Selecting Yes places a shortcut to this newly created folder in the group My Short-cuts. Selecting "Don't prompt me about this again" turns off both the prompt and the automatic placement of shortcuts on the Outlook Bar.

Automation aside, you can add four different types to the Outlook Bar: Outlook Folders, Outlook items, Desktop or program shortcuts, and web pages. Like every-thing else in Outlook, there are a variety of ways to do this depending on the shortcut type, and your mood of the moment:

To add an Outlook Folder using the Folder List (View → Folder List)
Select the folder you want to add and drag it to a group on the Outlook Bar. A line indicates where the folder will be placed. To add the folder to a different group than the one currently open, hold your cursor (with the mouse button still depressed) over the title of an alternative group and it will open. Alter-nately, select a folder from the Folder List pane, and choose "Add to Outlook Bar" from the context menu. This method skips all dialogs and simply adds the selected folder to the *open* Outlook Bar group.

To add an Outlook Folder from the Outlook Bar itself
Right-click in a group and choose "Outlook Bar Shortcut" from the context menu displayed (or from the File menu, New → Outlook Bar Shortcut). This will open the dialog shown in Figure 4-30 (left).

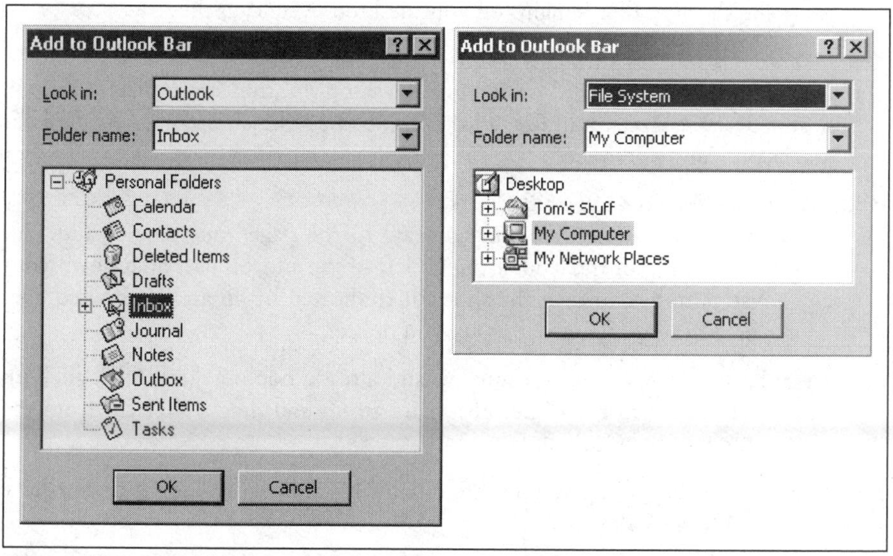

Figure 4-30: The Add to Outlook Bar dialog—Outlook Folder view on the left, filesystem view on the right

From the tree shown, select a folder. It will be placed in the group that is currently open. If the shortcut added ends up in a different group than you intended, simply drag the new shortcut to another group.

To add a program or file from the Outlook Bar

Go to the Add to Outlook Bar dialog as described previously. Under the "Look in" option, choose Look in File System. The dialog now displays the contents of your filesystem as shown in Figure 4-30 (right). Expand the list to display the desired file or folder and select OK.

It is also possible to add system files or folders to the Outlook Bar using Windows Explorer. The easiest way to do this—considering you will likely have multiple windows open, perhaps covering each other—is to begin by minimizing Outlook to the Task Bar. Open Windows Explorer, locate the file you want to add as a shortcut, and drag it to the minimized Outlook icon. Outlook will open after a short pause. Continue holding down the mouse button and drag the shortcut to the Outlook Bar. If the group you want to add the shortcut to is not currently open, hold your mouse cursor over the group title and that group will open.

To add an individual Outlook item to the Outlook Bar

Outlook does not support adding an item of its own kind (for example, a mail message or contact record) to the Outlook Bar directly. There is a way around this, however. Open the folder containing the item you want to add to the Outlook Bar. Drag that item to your desktop and drop it there. Next, drag the item shortcut created on the desktop onto the Outlook Bar. Now go back and delete the shortcut that remains on your desktop. Magic, as they say.

To add a Desktop shortcut to the Outlook Bar

Simply drag the shortcut from your Desktop to the appropriate Outlook Group. If necessary, minimize Outlook and drag the shortcut to its Taskbar icon as previously described.

To add a web page to the Outlook Bar

Open Internet Explorer (IE) and navigate to the page you want to add. Put your cursor on top of the icon at the far left of the address bar, hold down your left mouse button, and drag the shortcut (indicated by an arrow imposed over the cursor) to the Outlook Bar group you desire.

If you have the web page you want to add already bookmarked in IE, click on the Favorites icon in the Other Shortcuts group and drag a shortcut from the view window to the Outlook Bar.

Here are a few creative suggestions for organizing and using shortcuts you have added to your Outlook Bar:

- Create a group for your favorite sites. Ensure you read the section in Chapter 3 first so you fully understand how Internet Explorer integrates with Outlook. Internet Explorer does lose some functionality when launched from within Outlook.

- Keep your most frequently accessed shortcuts near the top of the Outlook Bar. That way, if you have more icons in a group than can be displayed at one time, you won't have to continually scroll through the group to find the icon you want.

- If you find yourself accessing a Control Panel applet frequently (for example, Internet Options), add it as a shortcut to your Outlook Bar. In order to do this, you will have to follow the procedure outlined previously for adding an individual Outlook item—that is, drag the Control Panel applet to your desktop first, then drag it to the Outlook Bar.

- If you find yourself accessing the same document day in and day out (like a book chapter, for example), create an icon for it on your Outlook Bar.

TIP # 42

How to Rebuild a Corrupted Outlook Bar

If you corrupt your Outlook Bar, here is how to restore it: close Outlook. Go to Start on the Windows taskbar. Select Run and in the Open box type: Outlook.exe/ ResetOutlookBar. Entering this will start Outlook and rebuild the Outlook Bar to its default configuration and layout.

While the Outlook Bar is a good container to organize frequently accessed files, folders, and web sites, it is more much more than a shortcut bar; it is your gateway to "drag and drop" between Outlook's various components. For example, you receive email from your associate Joe Snipps asking you to attend a meeting next Tuesday and you want to add it to your calendar. Go to your Inbox (or wherever the message is located), select it, and drop it on the Calendar icon. This action will create a new calendar entry, with the Subject field prefilled and the body of the email entered into the free-form notes field. Fill in the start time and date, add a note or two, link the contact field of the calendar entry to the person sending the email, and you're done.

To sum up the preceding example:

- Dragging an email message to any of Outlook's other components (Calendar, Contacts, Tasks, Notes, and Journal) creates a new record with the message details transposed to the new item entry.

- Dragging a Calendar entry to the Inbox icon creates a new message with the appointment subject as the subject of the message, and the appointment details transferred to the Notes field.

- Dragging a Calendar entry to the Contacts icon creates a new entry there based on the owner (creator) of the appointment item.

- Dragging a Calendar entry to Tasks, Notes, or Journal creates a new record according to the component it is dropped on.

Dragging a Task, Note, or Journal entry to another component works in a similar manner. The point here is that you can save yourself a tremendous amount of time and keyboard entry by dragging and dropping Outlook items onto Outlook Bar icons.

The Folder List

The Folder List displays your Outlook folders in a familiar tree structure, and is arguably one of the most useful combination navigation and file management tools available in Outlook. The fastest way to access the Folder List is to click the folder title displayed in the upper-left of your active window, as shown in Figure 4-31.

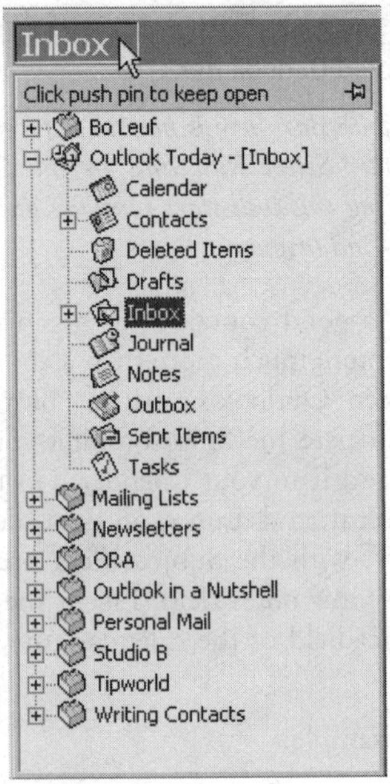

Figure 4-31: The Folder List pane

Note the small pushpin icon in the upper-right corner of the Folder List pane. Much of the functionality of the Folder List is dependent on whether this pushpin is "inactive" (as shown in Figure 4-31), or "activated" (as shown in Figure 4-32).

Figure 4-32: Folder List, with pushpin activated, or "locked"

If you open the Folder List by simply clicking on the title and you do not press the pushpin, this open pane becomes a quick navigational tool. Clicking any displayed folder displays it as the active view, and the Folder List conveniently closes again.

You can navigate to subfolders in the same manner by first clicking the tree expansion square (+) and, after the tree expands, selecting a folder to display. Outlook will obediently wait for you to select a folder before making it active and closing the Folder List pane.

TIP # 43

Folder List Magic

To quickly move one file, you do not need to "lock" the Folder List open. Select the item to move (or copy), hold down the left mouse button, and drag it to the Folder List title. Continue to hold down the left mouse button, and after a pause the Folder List will open. Release the item on the folder of your choice. To copy an item, hold down the Ctrl key as you drag.

On the other hand, if you need to do extensive file management chores, or you simply prefer to use the Folder List as your primary navigational tool rather than the Outlook Bar, "lock" it open. This can be accomplished in one of two ways:

1. By opening the Folder List with the View → Folder List command

2. By opening the Folder List using the "title shortcut" (demonstrated in Figure 4-31), and then pressing the pushpin

Here are some examples of file management shortcuts that can be used with the Folder List open:

- To move an Outlook item from one folder to another, select it and drag it to the destination folder displayed in the open Folder List. To copy a file from one folder to another, hold down the Ctrl key during your drag and drop action. See Figure 4-33.

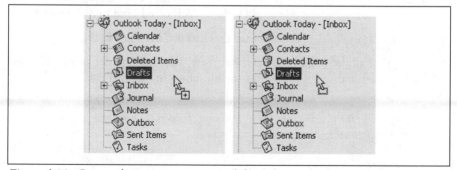

Figure 4-33: Cursors during copy operation (left) and move operation (right)

- To move a folder from one location to another, select the folder and drag it to a new a position; to copy it, use the Ctrl key as described in the previous paragraph.

TIP # 44

Copy Versus Move

A quick way to tell whether you are moving or copying an item is to watch the mouse cursor. During the move operation, the cursor displays a small blank rectangle under the mouse pointer as shown in Figure 4-33 (right); during a copy operation, the cursor displays a + in addition to the rectangle as shown in Figure 4-33 (left).

- To rename a folder, click once, pause, and click a second time. Type the new name in place of the old.

- To delete a folder, select it and press the Delete key.

 Outlook has several key folders inherent to its operation, called System Folders (see Chapter 3). You cannot delete, move, or rename a System Folder (e.g., the Inbox or Contacts folders).

To navigate around the Folder List using the keyboard:

- Use the Home/End keys to position your selection at the top or bottom of the displayed tree. The up and down arrow keys navigate up and down the tree. To expand a branch, position your selection on the folder containing subfolders and press the right arrow key; the left arrow key collapses the branch again.

- To quickly move to a specific folder name, use your keyboard's letter keys. For example, to move to the first folder beginning with the letter "T", press the T key; if you have more than one folder that begins with this letter, Outlook will walk down through the Folder List and when it reaches the bottom (or top) of the tree, reverse direction.

- Select a folder and press F3 to open the Advanced Find dialog. For tips and tricks on harnessing the power of Outlook's Advanced Find, see Chapter 3.

- To create a new folder, the keyboard shortcut is Ctrl+Shift+E.

And finally, for all you "Mouseketeers" out there, selecting a folder and clicking the right mouse button displays the context menu shown in Figure 4-34.

 The Folder list truly comes into its own as a file management tool when you start using multiple Personal Folders. This topic is addressed in Chapter 13.

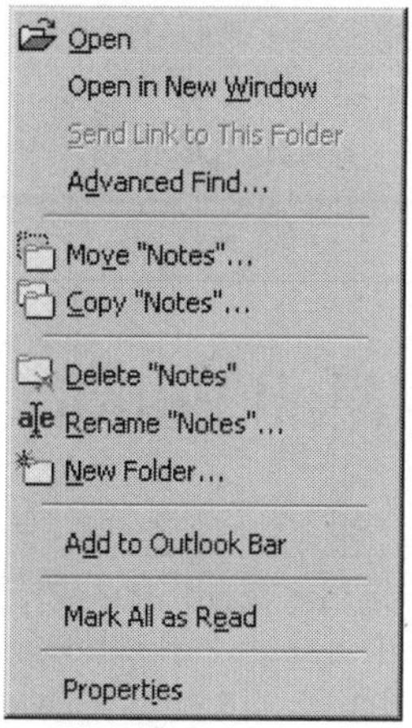

Figure 4-34: Folder List context menu

Navigation
Tools

Folder Navigation Without a Mouse

Many of Outlook's navigation tools are designed to be used with some form of pointing device. For example, the Outlook Bar has no keyboard shortcuts associated with it. You can, however, navigate around your folder structure quite nicely without a mouse if you know the shortcut keys.

1. Press Ctrl+Y to open the Go To Folder dialog.

2. Press the Tab key to access the Folder Name list, which includes all folders on the Outlook Bar. The Folder Name list includes all folders on the Outlook Bar. If you press the Tab key a second time, you can select from a hierarchical list that includes all available folders.

3. Press Up Arrow or Down Arrow to select the folder that you want.

4. Press Enter to open the folder.

5. A comprehensive list of keyboard shortcuts can be found in Outlook's online help system. Press F1 (or Help → Microsoft Outlook Help) and type keyboard or keyboard shortcuts in the search dialog.

Chapter 5

Mail Editors

Every time you create, respond to, or forward a message you interface with a mail editor. At first glance, the editor may seem straightforward. From the perspective of the interface itself, this is true (finding commands aside). But behind the scenes of the editor are myriad options that dictate how a message is formatted, where replies are saved, whether a read or delivery receipt is automatically requested, whether a signature is attached, and how a message is encoded. All of these options, and more, are available as global settings, providing you know where to look.

Many of Outlook's messaging options are not something you need every day. Read receipts are a great way to confirm an important message was received and (perhaps) read by someone, but hanging a read receipt on every message you send is a waste of good Internet bandwidth and unnecessary for most everyday communications. A similar situation exists for message formats. Plain Text is good enough for the majority of everyday correspondence, but situations do arise when placing a picture or graphic in a message helps to convey an important point that words alone cannot.

For this reason, we've structured this chapter in two distinct parts. The first sections explain Outlook's editor choices, message formats supported, the multitude of default options available, and how each one impacts the messages you send. Starting with the section "Using Outlook's Editors" we show you how to override these default setting on a per-message basis.

If you can't find a topic in this chapter, try Chapter 6, *Mail*. Here you'll find a reference to the menu commands specific to Outlook's Mail component. We've tried to keep redundancy to a minimum, and this involved making some choices about where to put certain topics. Generally speaking, menu commands are found in Chapter 6; broader subjects (message formats, stationery, signatures, encoding, etc.) are found here.

Mail Editor Choices

Outlook's default mail editor, shown in Figure 5-1, is actually based on one of Outlook's internal forms discussed in Chapter 3, *Program Insights*. It is full-featured and works capably with all of today's current message formats.

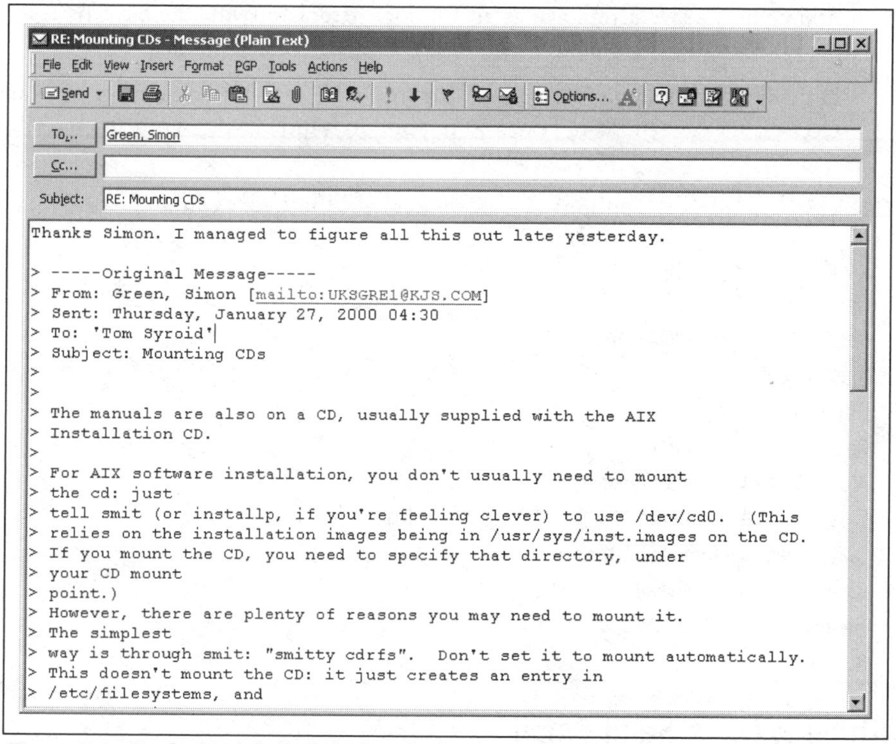

Figure 5-1: Outlook's default form-based editor

Depending on the message format, you can set fonts (family, weight, and style), specify paragraph styles and alignment, and even add bulleted or numbered lists. It has options to view message headers, send Bcc's (blind carbon copies), specify the mail server through which a message is sent, set a message's importance and sensitivity, link contacts and categories to a message, and set an expiration date. Configuring and using these features are the topics of this chapter.

If you install Outlook as part of Microsoft Office, you can instead use Word as your mail editor, using a special Word template called *email.dot*. Word is a powerful, full-featured word processor that supports all the previously listed formatting features, plus several productivity enhancements not available in Outlook's editor, for example, AutoCorrect, a thesaurus, and spellchecking as you type.

On the downside, Word is a *big* program and overkill for sending a simple message. Running Word with Outlook can tax system resources, turning the simple task of replying to a message into an exercise in patience.

In addition, Word does not support several options available under the Outlook editor. In particular, Word does not:

- Support attaching Outlook items to a message (see the section "Attachments" later in this chapter).

- Allow you to save a message as an Outlook template (with the Save As command). Creating a template based on a message is detailed in Chapter 3.

- Let you switch message formats on-the-fly. With the Outlook editor, you can receive a message in Plain Text, and respond to it in HTML. Word supports no such tricks.

Table 5-1 compares the options available for each of Outlook's editor choices.

Table 5-1: Comparing Outlook's Editors

Option	Word Editor	Outlook Editor
Batch/on-the-fly spellchecking	Yes/Yes	Yes/No
Auto-correct	Yes	No
Grammar checking	Yes	No
Context menu thesaurus	Yes	No
Attach Outlook items to a message	No	Yes
Create Outlook templates	No	Yes
Switch message formats on-the-fly	No	Yes
Create tables in a message	Yes	No
Themes	Yes	No
Stationery	No	Yes

Three Ways to Send Email

Outlook supports three message formats for sending email: HTML, Microsoft Outlook Rich Text Format (MS-RTF), and Plain Text. The global configuration for this setting is located under Tools → Options → Mail Format. This selection determines the *default* format used (regardless of editor choice) when a *new* message is created. Replies or forwards are sent in the same format in which the message was received.

 For an explanation of how to change the format used when replying or forwarding a message, see the topic "Changing a Message Format" under the section "Using Outlook's Editors" later in this chapter.

Generally speaking:

- HTML is the *lingua franca* of Internet communications. It offers limited control of message format (font, color, style, etc.) and is supported by most mainstream email clients, which means that compatibility is no longer a major issue. But depending on your needs, this may not be the most efficient and productive format to use. Said another way, it's easy to get caught up in messing with fonts, colors, and "pretty" backgrounds when the task at hand is to get the message out the door and get back to work. If you are truly *using* the capabilities of HTML to enhance communications, this is a good choice. In addition, some of

Whither the Resources?

In case you were wondering why your system becomes sluggish when using Outlook with Word as a mail editor, consider the following information gleaned from the Task Manager Processes tab (available only on Windows NT installations) with both these programs running:

```
WORD.EXE        21,080K
OUTLOOK.EXE     12,876K
```

A quick bit of math reveals these two programs alone use over 32 MB of available memory. "Ah," you say, "but that's with both Outlook and Word running, and closing Word drops these requirements down to 13 MB." Like everything about Outlook, the response to this is, "No, not exactly."

When you use Word as your messaging editor, as long as Outlook is open, a stub of Word is open too. Just to demonstrate, we closed all open programs, rebooted, and started just Outlook. The particulars are as follows:

```
OUTLOOK.EXE     10,012K
WORD.EXE        10,200K
```

So even with just Outlook open, and no message editor formally invoked, memory requirements for the above system are over 20 MB. And let's not forget, that does not include any other system processes or programs. Even with 64 MB of system memory, it does not take long to tax this resource. As soon as all available RAM is exhausted, the system begins to page and/or swap to and from the disk. Depending on your system's configuration and the paging activity, this might slow down your computer considerably. So before you choose Word as your mail editor, consider both your system's ability to handle the load and your true needs.

Outlook's collaboration features (for example, Task requests and Meeting requests) require HTML or MS-RTF to work properly.

- Microsoft introduced MS-RTF in the latter part of the 1980s as an interchange format between operating systems and platforms (including the Mac), primarily as a format for word processing documents. MS-RTF is a viable alternative to HTML, and offers many of the same formatting options regarding fonts and page layout. MS-RTF, however, is a proprietary format and will leave your messages unreadable by some email clients. For example, Outlook Express does not support messages received in MS-RTF. If you are going to use MS-RTF, make sure you're only communicating with other Outlook users or an Exchange Server.

- Plain Text does not support text formatting, paragraph styles, or embedded graphics (although they can be included as attachments). It is this spartan quality that keeps this message format a popular choice for email correspondence.

Plain Text can be thought of as the lowest common denominator of email. A Plain Text message is readable by every mail client on the planet. Plain Text is a good choice if most messages you send do not require a specific font or layout, or if you're unsure of the capabilities of the recipient's mail client. Plain Text also creates the smallest message size of the three formats offered.

TIP # 45

Message Formats and Message Size

Few people realize that message format has a tremendous effect on message size. Plain Text messages are much smaller than messages created in RTF or HTML. For example, one 50-line message in Plain Text format (no attachments) occupies 1 KB of hard disk space. The same message in HTML occupies 8 KB. So the size of Plain Text messages alone is good reason for using this message format unless you really need the capabilities of HTML or MS-RTF.

Unsolicited Advice

So which editor should you use? And which message format? We'll offer our recommendation, developed from many years of email correspondence and far too many hours wrestling with the inner workings of Outlook.

We suggest using Outlook as your default editor, and Plain Text as your default message format. In our opinion, this serves as the best daily working combination, while still leaving numerous options open for those situations that demand the formatting options found in HTML. We do not recommend the use of MS-RTF in anything but a closed Exchange Server environment—it is quirky and has unexpected consequences when used in conjunction with non-Microsoft email programs.

There are several obvious (and a few not quite so obvious) benefits that result from the Outlook editor/Plain Text combination. They are:

- The Outlook editor is more than good enough for everyday correspondence. It demands fewer resources than Word, and is a capable editor.

- Plain Text delivers a smaller message footprint than HTML or MS-RTF, and by using it for daily correspondence alleviates the "Can they read this?" question. When you think about it, very few messages really demand the formatting characteristics of HTML. As an added bonus, most email power-users appreciate the use of Plain Text.

- When circumstances dictate, Outlook's actions menu allows you to easily compose a message in HTML or MS-RTF (see Figure 5-2). This same menu also allows you to use the Word editor on a per-message basis (New Mail Message Using → Microsoft Word). The only drawback here is that if you're using Plain Text, and want to create a message in HTML with Word, you'll have to switch your default format first—which is really a small price to pay for the flexibility you'll gain.

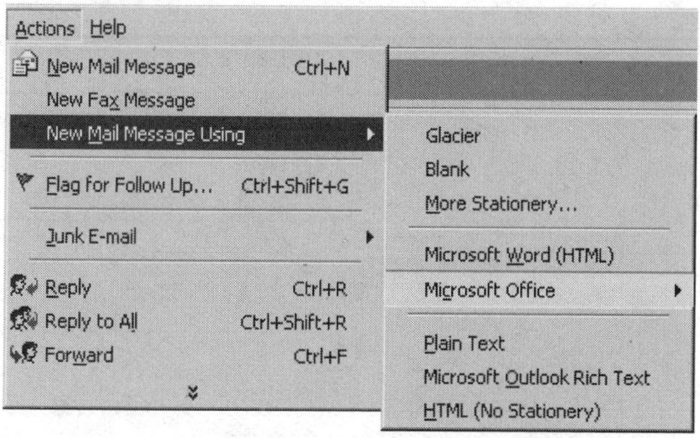

Figure 5-2: Mail editor options available under the Actions → New Mail Message Using submenu

So there you have it. You know the options available for editors, and you have the knowledge needed to make an educated choice about which message format to use. It's now time to do some dialog mining to find out where to locate all these settings.

Default Message Options

One of the biggest challenges in Outlook is to find the right dialog for the option you want to configure. Microsoft engineers seem to have taken perverse delight in scattering configuration settings in some of the most illogical places (un)imaginable. Default message format settings are on one dialog; reply and forward format settings are on another—buried beneath a button simply labeled E-mail Options. While we can't explain this madness, we can guide you through this maze of dialogs, and in the process explain which option does what, where, and why.

This section details default options that, once changed, apply to all subsequent messages, unless overridden for a particular message. Most of these settings apply to both mail editors; exceptions are noted where applicable. To change a configured option for a single instance of a message, see "Using Outlook's Editors" later in this chapter.

Mail Format Options

The Mail Format tab (Tools → Options) is shown in Figure 5-3.

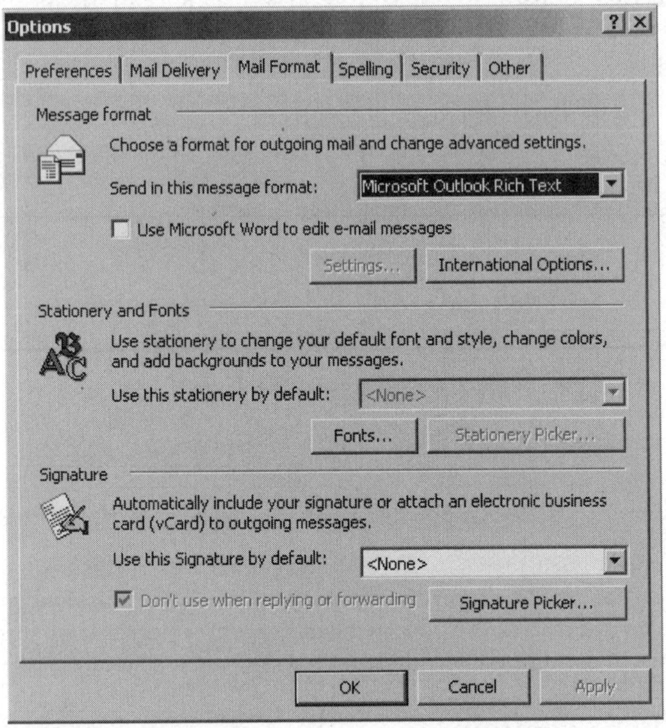

Figure 5-3: The Mail Format tab from the Tools → Options dialog

The key settings to note are under the Message Format heading:

Send in this message format

> The drop-down list provides three options: HTML, Microsoft Outlook Rich Text, and Plain Text. Your choice here determines the default font Outlook uses for *new* messages.

Use Microsoft Word

> Select this to use Word as your default mail editor; deselect it to use the Outlook editor.

> *Choosing a default editor addresses the question of which program starts when you create, reply to, or forward a message. Opening a message from any Outlook Mail folder opens that message in an Outlook form (which is the basis of the Outlook editor), even if you are using Word as your mail editor.*

Options for stationery and signatures are covered later in this chapter.

Font options

To set the font used by your default message format, select the Fonts button on the Mail Format tab (Figure 5-3). This opens the Fonts dialog shown in Figure 5-4.

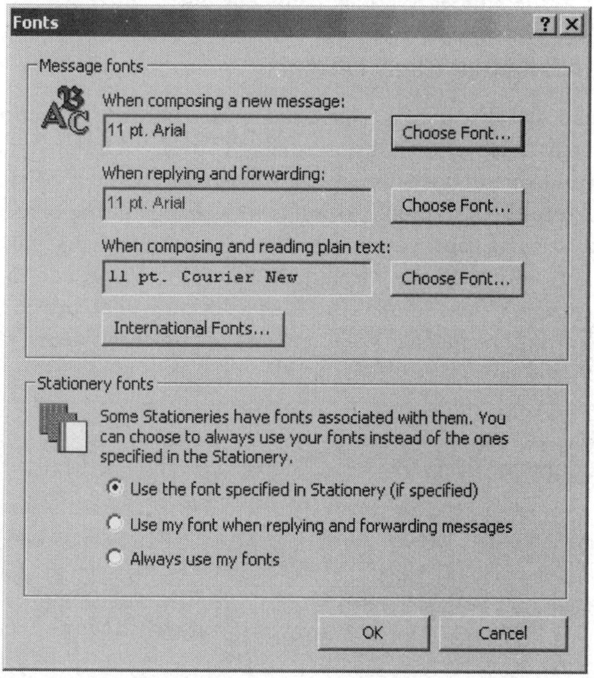

Figure 5-4: The Fonts option dialog

You can specify separate fonts for new messages, replies, forwards, and for composing and reading Plain Text messages. A different color is often used for replies and forwards to make them stand out from the original message. Note that colors are only available when using HTML or MS-RTF as a message format.

The International Fonts button opens the Fonts subdialog that specifies the display font used for messages that use an international character set. Drop-down lists let you select a proportional and fixed-width font, font size (smallest to largest), and a default *encoding* to use. International options are discussed later in this chapter.

The Stationery fonts option provides you with a mechanism to chose which font wins out when a conflict arises between the format used in a stationery template, and the settings used for default message fonts (new message and reply/forward; Plain Text is never an issue because it is not an option applicable to stationery).

- "Use the font specified in Stationery" does just what it says—no matter what your default message font is set to, when stationery is used, the font specified in the stationery is used.

- "Use my font when replying and forwarding messages" is Outlook's idea of a truce. The stationery wins for new messages; your font preference wins when you reply to or forward a message.

- "Always use my fonts" is your refusal to give up any ground—stationery or not, the fonts specified under "Message fonts" are always used.

Message Handling and Reply Formats

The dialog that contains message handling and reply format options is accessed from the Preferences tab of the Options dialog (Tools → Options). Click on the E-mail Options button to open the dialog shown in Figure 5-5. Here you'll find settings that control how Outlook responds to a change in the contents of an open message window, what happens to original messages when you reply to them, and how replies and forwards are formatted. There are also two buttons labeled "Advanced E-mail Options" and "Tracking Options" that provide access to yet another level of option dialogs. We'll get to the Advanced and Tracking settings momentarily.

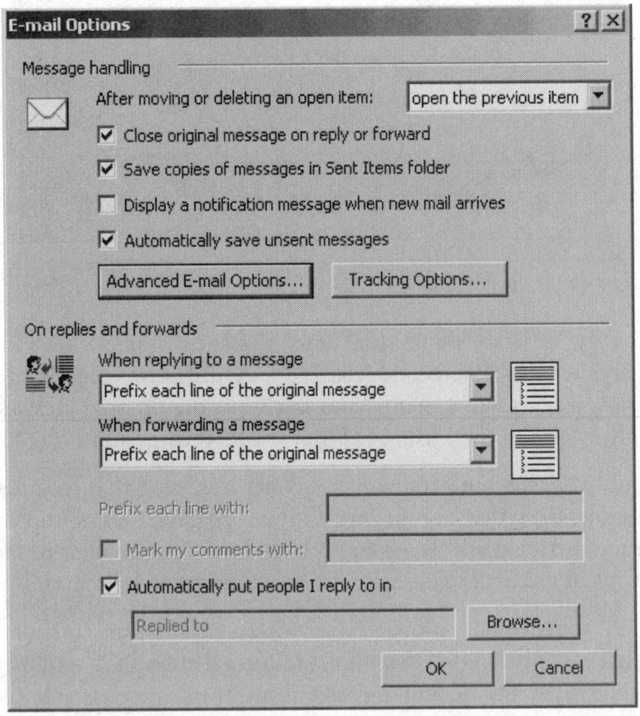

Figure 5-5: The E-mail Options dialog contains settings for message handling and reply/forward formatting

After moving or deleting an open item
> Determines what happens after you move or delete an open message. Your options are: open the previous item, open the next item, and return to the inbox (close the open form).

Close original message on reply or forward
> With this option deselected, clicking on reply or forward from an open message will leave you with two open windows—one containing the original message, and one containing the reply or forward.

Save copies of messages in Sent Items folder
> When selected (default), Outlook saves a copy of all sent messages in the Sent Items folder. If you need an audit trail of what messages you have sent and to whom, leave this option selected.

Display a notification message
> Displays a dialog when new messages arrive. Selecting Yes from this dialog opens the message; No closes the dialog. This is a useful option for users who typically work with multiple windows open and want immediate notification of new mail. If you receive large volumes of mail, however, these dialogs get old fast.

 If you have mail rules enabled (see Chapter 6) you might open a notification only to receive a message that the item has been moved or deleted.

Automatically save unsent messages
> This is the on/off switch for Outlook's AutoSave feature detailed under the "Save and Send Options" section later in this chapter. We recommend you leave this option on unless you have a good reason for disabling it. No, we don't know why the on/off toggle is on one page and the configuration settings for AutoSave are on another.

When replying to a message
> A drop-down list (see Figure 5-6) provides five options for how a reply is formatted: Do not include original message, Attach original message, Include original message text, Include and indent original message text, and Prefix each line of the original message. The icon to the right of the list shows a graphic representation of your selection. "Prefix each line..." is not available when using Word as your mail editor.

When forwarding a message
> The same option list described for reply formats is also available for forwards. The Word editor does not support this feature.

Prefix each line with
> This option is enabled only if you choose the "Prefix each line..." format for either replies or forwards. The character specified is used to prefix the original text of a reply or forward, distinguishing it from your message.

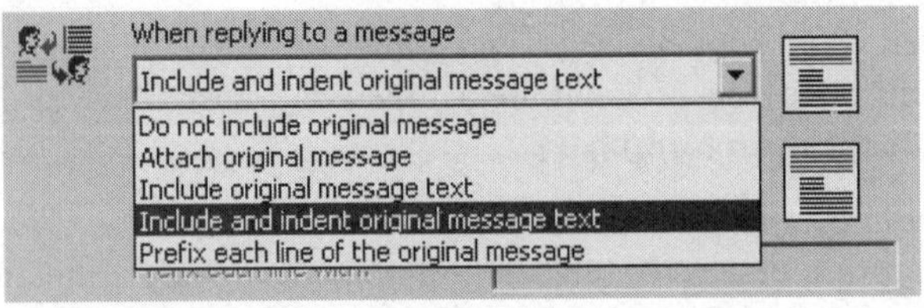

Figure 5-6: Reply and forward format options

Mark my comments with

Automatically enters the text you specify in square brackets (for example, [tms] or [Tom replies]) preceding any text you enter within the body of a received message. Three "ifs" are tied to this option:

— You must be replying to a message *within* the body of the original text before this feature works.

— The *original* message to which you're replying must have been sent in HTML or MS-RTF. This feature does not work if you convert a Plain Text message to a different format.

— You cannot use Word as your editor. Word uses revision marking as an annotation tool.

Automatically put people I reply to in

Enabling this option automatically creates an entry in the specified folder for anyone you reply to who does not already have a matching record there. If you use this option, we strongly advise against using the default folder Outlook suggests (Contacts). When Outlook creates these automatic entries, while it supplies a name when available, it bases record uniqueness on email address. This inevitably results in multiple entries for the same contact for messages sent from different email addresses. In our opinion, *nothing* should *ever* be automatically entered in your Contacts folder that you do not verify first. A better solution to updating your contact records from received messages is described in Tip # 46.

TIP # 46

Adding Contacts from a Received Message

To add a contact to your address book (a.k.a. your Contacts folder) from a received message, open the message and right-click the address displayed on the From line. From the context menu, choose Add to Contacts. This creates a new contact item, and opens a form for you to confirm and edit the details of the entry.

Save and Send Options

The Advanced E-mail Options dialog shown in Figure 5-7 (Tools → E-mail Options → Advanced E-mail Options) contains program defaults for where Outlook saves unsent messages, where replies are saved, new mail notification settings, and several options for configuring how a message is sent.

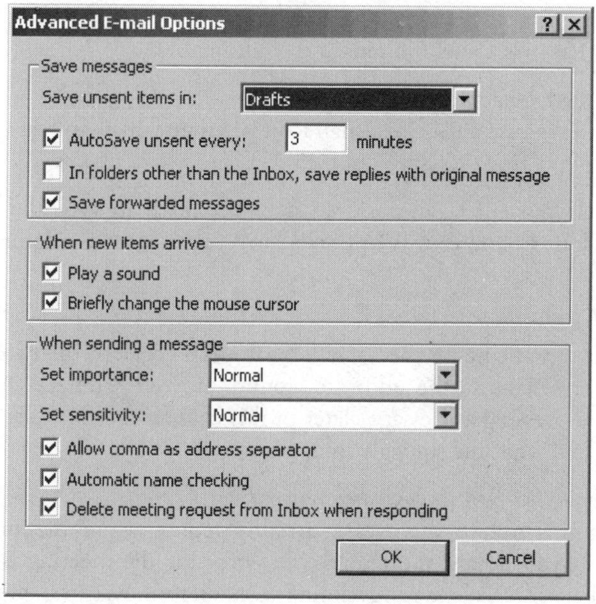

Figure 5-7: Outlook's Advanced E-mail Options dialog

Save unsent items in

Rather than send a new message immediately, you can save it as a draft and review or complete it later. This option specifies where unsent messages are saved. The folder choices are: Drafts, Inbox, Sent Mail, or Outbox. The default setting is the Drafts folder. Unless you have a good reason for doing so, this setting should be left as is.

AutoSave unsent every

The checkbox turns AutoSave on; the minutes field determines the AutoSave frequency.

 NOTE *To manually save an unsent message, use the Save button on the message form's toolbar, or choose File → Save.*

In folders other than the Inbox

Outlook saves a copy of all messages sent from the Inbox in the Sent Items folder. When this option is selected, a copy of your reply is saved in the folder from which it is sent. This is a useful option if you prefer to have all related correspondence in one location (i.e., the original message and your reply).

Save forwarded messages
By default, forwarded messages are saved in the Sent Items folder. Uncheck this option if you do not want to keep a copy of forwarded messages.

Play a sound
Announces new mail with a sound. The wave file played is set from the Windows Control Panel (Sounds and Multimedia).

Briefly change the mouse cursor
Changes the mouse cursor to a mail icon when new mail arrives

Allow comma as address separator
Multiple address entries in the To, Cc, or Bcc fields are typically separated with a semi-colon. Enabling this option allows you to use a comma for the same purpose.

Automatic name checking
Enables automatic name checking. This forces a check of the name entered in a new message against the addresses found in your Contacts folder. See the section "Addressing a Message" later in this chapter for an explanation of name checking and what the squiggly line means.

Delete meeting request from Inbox when responding
Checking this option removes a meeting request from the Inbox after you respond. If you accept the request, an entry for the meeting is automatically entered in your Calendar; declining a request moves the message to your Deleted Items folder (see Chapter 7, *Calendar*, for details on meeting requests).

Read Receipts

The configuration settings covered in this section apply globally to all read receipts Outlook processes. For an explanation of how to assign a single-instance read receipt to a message, see "The Message Options Dialog" section later in this chapter.

Read receipts are the electronic equivalent of a double registered letter: you attach a receipt request to an outgoing message, and when the recipient opens your message a reply is generated and returned to you. The reply shows up back in your Inbox bearing a special icon denoting it as a read receipt (Figure 5-8), with the subject line Read: the subject of your original message.

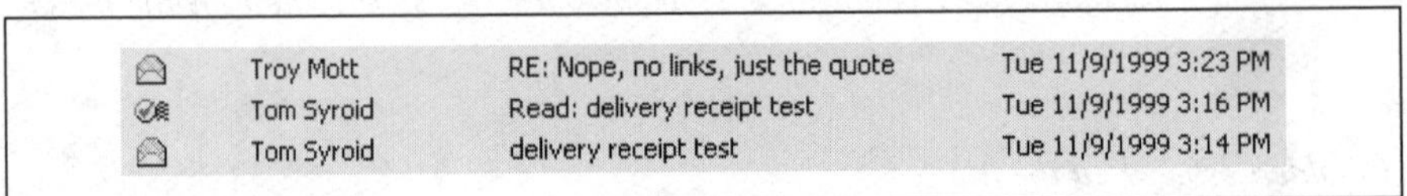

	Troy Mott	RE: Nope, no links, just the quote	Tue 11/9/1999 3:23 PM
	Tom Syroid	Read: delivery receipt test	Tue 11/9/1999 3:16 PM
	Tom Syroid	delivery receipt test	Tue 11/9/1999 3:14 PM

Figure 5-8: A Returned read receipt (the second item)

Read Receipts Versus Delivery Receipts

A *read* receipt is a different animal than a *delivery* receipt. The difference lies in where the receipt is processed. Read receipts are a client-side process; delivery receipts are a server-side process.

When you send a message requesting either form of receipt, it is written into the header of the message before it is sent. When the message arrives at your mail server, the header is examined and if a delivery receipt is requested, the *mail server* responds (if this feature is supported) by sending a message back to the sender. This message simply confirms that the message was received by the server and transferred to the recipient's mailbox.

A read receipt is a *client-side* process. Servers ignore any reference to a read receipt and simply pass the message to the client when requested. The client reads the header, and if a read receipt has been requested, generates the response.

A short message is attached to the returned receipt indicating the date and time the email was read:

```
Your message

    To:  Tom Syroid
    Subject:  delivery receipt test
    Sent:  11/9/1999 3:13 PM

was read on 11/9/1999 3:15 PM.
```

Read receipts are useful for occasions when it is important to know a message was received and read, but only if the recipient of your request wants to play the same game as you. Consider the following:

- A returned read receipt tells you the message to which it was attached reached its destination and was opened, but *not necessarily read*. In the context of Outlook, simply previewing a message marks it as read (if this configuration option is set).

- In the spirit of personal privacy, most (Outlook 97 is an exception) email programs that support read receipts, also give the user the option of turning the feature off completely, or denying them on a per-message basis.

Outlook's Tracking Options configuration dialog is shown in Figure 5-9 (Tools → Options → E-mail Options → Tracking Options).

The upper half of this dialog contains options for how and when read receipts, and voting/meeting requests, are processed:

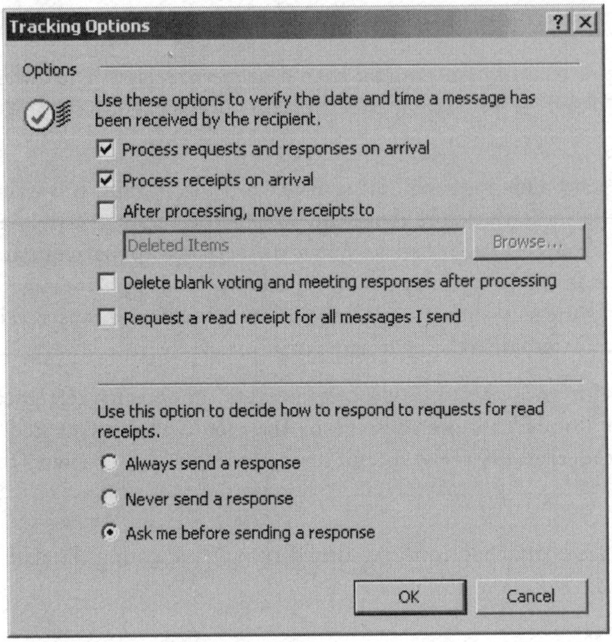

Figure 5-9: Read receipt configuration dialog

Process requests and responses on arrival

    When this is selected, Outlook performs the processing options selected in Resource Scheduling options under Calendar (Tools → Options → Calendar Options → Resource Scheduling). Unless the resource scheduling options are specified in this location, this radio button is meaningless. See Chapter 7 for a full explanation of Meeting and Task Requests.

Process receipts on arrival

    Select this option to have Outlook process *scheduling* receipts on arrival. For example, if a Task request is declined, the matching record in your Tasks folder will be immediately updated with this information on its arrival.

After processing, move receipts to

    If you prefer to keep a record of the receipts you receive, select this option and specify a folder.

Delete blank voting and meeting responses after processing

    If you receive a meeting request or voting form that is blank (i.e., it contains no comments, updates, or notifications), the request is automatically moved to the Deleted Items folder.

Request a read receipt for all messages I send

    Selecting this option generates a read receipt request for every message you send.

Request a delivery receipt for all messages I send (CW only)
> This option is similar to the previous option, but requests a delivery receipt. See the sidebar "Read Receipts Versus Delivery Receipts" for an explanation of the differences between these two options.

The settings found on the lower half of the dialog determine how Outlook responds to a request for a read receipt:

Always send a response
> When a read receipt is requested, one is generated and sent automatically.

Never send a response
> All requests for read receipts are denied automatically.

Ask me before sending a response (IMO only)
> Any time someone requests a read receipt the dialog shown in Figure 5-10 appears. Yes sends a receipt; No denies the request. Selecting the "Don't ask me ..." checkbox and selecting Yes sends a receipt and resets Outlook's global read receipt option to "Always send a response." Selecting this checkbox and choosing No refuses the request and resets the global read receipt option to "Never send a response."

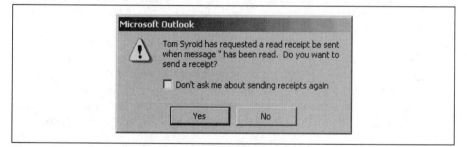

Figure 5-10: The read receipt request confirmation dialog

 To send a one-time read receipt, use the Message Options dialog discussed later in this chapter under "Using Outlook's Editors."

Stationery (Outlook Editor)

Outlook gives you the option of sending mail based on special templates called Stationery, but only for messages based on HTML.

Stationery templates are similar to word-processing templates: they set the background color, font, page layout, and embedded images. Stationery templates are HTML documents, so tuck this in the back of your mind as you read through the following material; it will come in handy later if you create a template of your own.

To access the stationery settings, go to the Tools → Options → Mail Format dialog shown in Figure 5-11 (left). You'll find a pick-list next to the "Use this stationery by default" option.

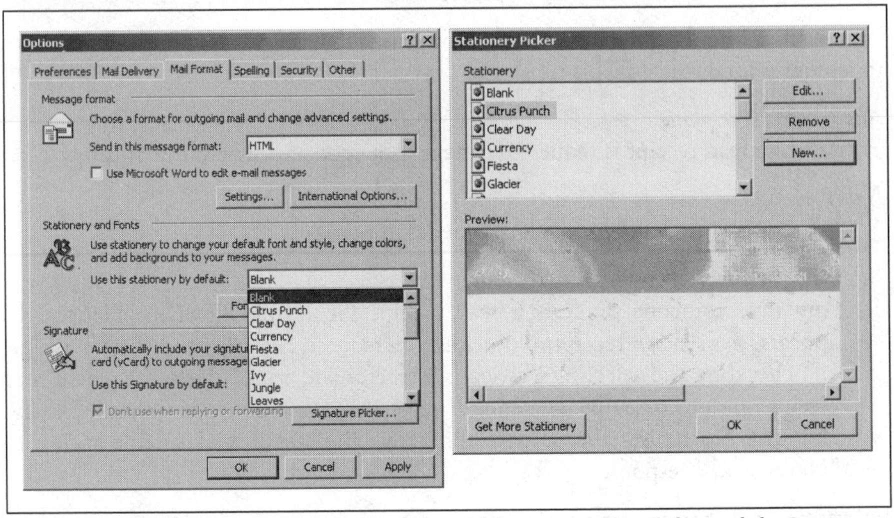

Figure 5-11: Stationery drop-down list from the Options dialog (left), and the Stationery Picker dialog (right)

Outlook ships with 24 predefined stationery templates; how many are actually installed on your system depends on the setup options chosen at the time of installation. To view a stationery template, select the "Stationery Picker" button (hidden under the drop-down list displayed in Figure 5-11, left). The Stationery Picker dialog, shown in Figure 5-11 (right), allows you to view, edit, delete, and create stationery.

To a preview a template, select it from the Stationery list. If the selected stationery is installed, a preview is displayed in the lower pane of the dialog; if it is not installed, a text message is shown informing you that the selected template will be installed the next time you compose mail. This is not terribly handy, as it implies that you need to install a stationery template by name alone—there is no provision available to view the template until such time as it is installed on your system. On the other hand, there are dozens of sites on the Internet that provide free downloadable Outlook stationery, and most provide at least a screenshot of what the template looks like.

> **NOTE** *The view pane on the Stationery Picker dialog only displays the background for the named template; it does not show you the fonts used in the template or if there are any other embedded images associated with the design.*

Selecting the "Get More Stationery" button in the lower left of this dialog launches your browser to *http://officeupdate.microsoft.com/downloadcatalog/dldo2kstationery.htm*, where you can find additional Microsoft stationery templates for your collection.

A Word of Caution About Stationery

Using stationery quickly swells the size of an email message. If you use stationery, try to keep the background simple and superficial distractions (animated GIF images come immediately to mind) to a minimum—both for file size and readability. Also think about the contrast between text color and background. Blue text on a purple background is not very readable.

Remember that the purpose of a message is to communicate. Formatting that does not enhance your message, hobbles it instead. Also, be considerate of people with slow dial-up connections. Waiting twenty minutes to download a 10 MB email message that plays background music and says only "What are you up to these days?" is a good way to annoy people.

Stationery management

Between the Stationery Picker dialog and the Actions → Message Using commands, Outlook stationery can be managed in a fairly simple manner. Here are a few suggestions for managing stationery and stationery templates:

- To send a one-time email based on a stationery template without configuring Outlook to use stationery on a default basis, use the Actions → New Mail Message Using → More Stationery command. This opens the Select Stationery dialog, similar to the Stationery Picker, without any editing commands. Selecting a name from the list provided displays that design in the view pane provided. If the chosen stationery is not installed, the dialog pictured in Figure 5-12 is shown.

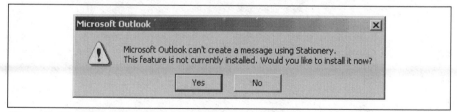

Figure 5-12: The Stationery not installed warning dialog

Selecting Yes loads the stationery requested from your installation CD; No cancels the process and opens a blank HTML message form.

- To use a stationery template for all outgoing messages, go to the Tools → Options → Mail Format tab. From the "Use this stationery by default" list,

Mail Editors

select a template. To reverse this process and return to an HTML message format without stationery, select <none>.

- To delete a stationery template from your system, go to the Tools → Options → Mail Format tab. Open the Stationery Picker, select a template, and click the Remove button.

- To edit an existing stationery design, go to the Tools → Options → Mail Format tab. Open the Stationery Picker dialog, and select Edit. This opens the Edit Stationery [*name*] dialog shown in Figure 5-13. The options in this dialog are:

1. Change font changes the default font used by the stationery.

2. Picture chooses a different background image either from the list provided or from a location on your filesystem.

3. Color sets the background to a solid color (which displaces the Picture option).

4. "Do not include…" removes all background images—both Picture and Color—from the template.

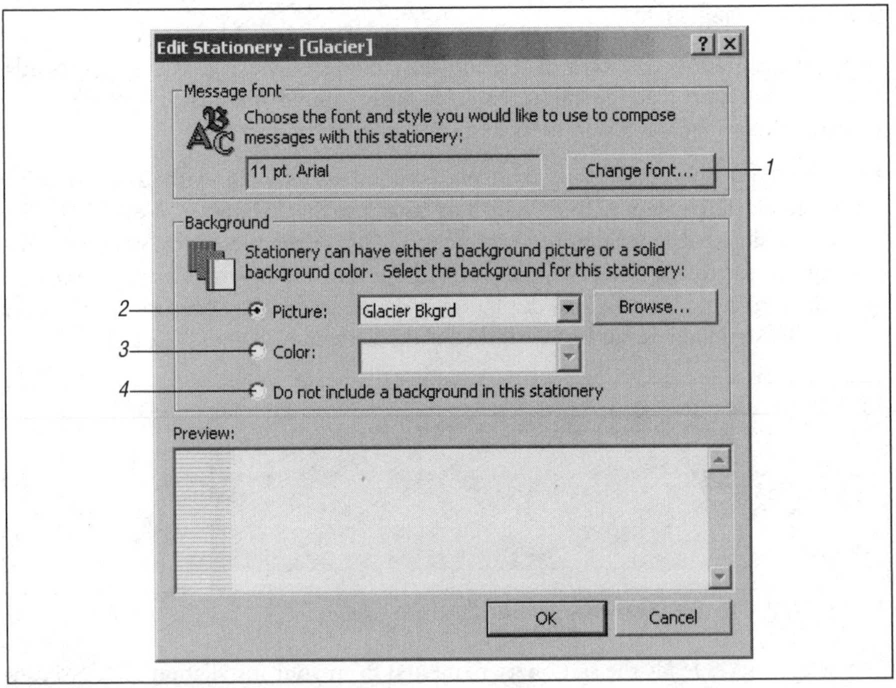

Figure 5-13: The Edit Stationery dialog

If you elect to alter an existing template, we suggest that you either write down the settings before you change them, or back up the Stationery folder before you begin—changes made from this Edit dialog cannot be saved to a different filename.

NOTE *Outlook's stationery files (both HTML and GIF images) are stored in: <drive>:\Program Files\Microsoft Shared\Stationery.*

- To design a new stationery template, go to the Tools → Options → Mail Format tab, and from the Stationery Picker dialog (see Figure 5-11, right) select New.

Enter a name in the Create New Stationery dialog (Figure 5-14). From here you have three options as to how you want to create your stationery: start from scratch, start with an existing stationery template, or use an existing file as a basis for the template. Your selection opens in the Edit Stationery dialog shown in Figure 5-11, which is not terribly handy considering the size of the viewing pane available.

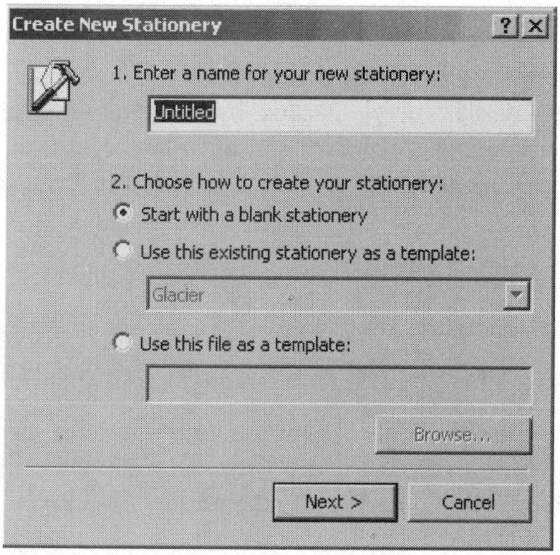

Figure 5-14: Create New Stationery dialog

Our advice is that if you want to create a stationery template, do so in a full screen HTML editor (for example, FrontPage) where you can see just what it is you are creating. Once you're happy with a design, either save it directly to the Stationery folder (at which time it displays on the Stationery Picker list on the Options dialog), or save it in a folder of your choice and use the Create New Stationery dialog's "Use this file as a template" option to add your design to Outlook's menus and drop-down lists.

TIP # 47

Remember, Stationery Is Just HTML

Outlook does a good job of sheltering the user from this fact, but remember that stationery is just a page of HTML. This means you can view and modify stationery in any HTML editor. This also explains why stationery can only be used when your message format is set to HTML.

Themes (Word Editor)

Themes are Word's rendition of Outlook's stationery option. The program includes a multitude of named themes, shared across supported Office components, which you can use when Word is your Outlook mail editor.

Themes, a.k.a. Stationery

You will note in the Word Theme dialog that there are several duplicates listed. This is because any stationery installed by Outlook is seen as a theme by supported Office products. If you create or download a custom stationery design for Outlook, and store it in the correct folder, it can be used by any Office product that supports Themes.

Follow these steps to configure Word to use a Theme for new messages:

1. In Outlook, start a new message using Word as your email editor.

2. Go to the Word menu Tools → Options, and select the General tab. Click on the E-mail Options button; on the Personal Stationery tab, click the button labeled Theme. This opens the Theme or Stationery dialog shown in Figure 5-15.

3. Under Choose a Theme, click the name of a Theme. If the Theme is not installed, you are asked to insert your Office CD.

4. After you have made your selections, click OK to exit all dialog boxes. You will not see your changes in the current untitled message. Close your untitled message without saving and create a new message to see your changes.

TIP # 48

Use Themes Sparingly

Themes are like Outlook stationery—they swell the size of your messages tremendously, so use them sparingly. Also note that messages sent using a Word Theme are proprietary HTML, so unless your recipient has Office installed on his system, chances are he is not going to see your message as you do.

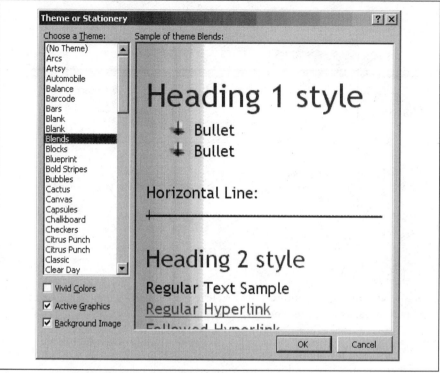

Figure 5-15: Word's Theme or Stationery selection dialog

We leave this topic with a caution about using Themes in Word 2000. This is one of the few features in Word 2000 that does not translate to Word 97 format, so if you switch documents between Word versions, don't use Themes.

Signatures

Signatures are boilerplate text appended to a message. Typically, this text contains your name, job title, phone number, email address, and, optionally, a web page URL. Outlook can append a signature to every new message, or append a signature only to messages you designate. The dialogs and method for creating signatures differ significantly enough between Outlook's two editor options to warrant separating the details that follow.

Creating a signature: the Outlook editor

To create a signature for use with the Outlook editor, start by going to the Tools → Options → Mail Format tab. The Signature Picker button opens the dialog pictured in Figure 5-16.

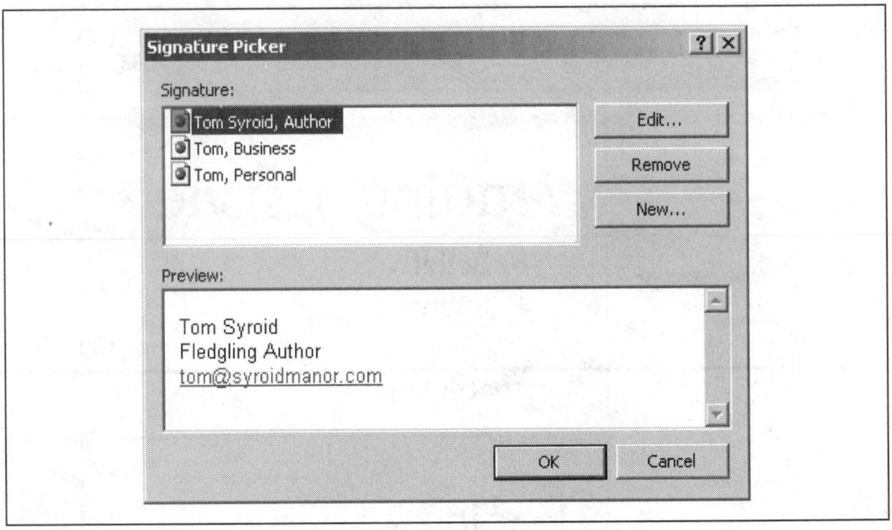

![The Signature Picker dialog]

Figure 5-16: The Signature Picker dialog

If you have existing signatures, they are listed in the top pane; select an entry to display it in the lower pane. You have three options:

Edit

Opens the Edit Signature dialog shown in Figure 5-17 (left). The upper pane functions just like a mini-editor with similar rules and conventions. The four buttons below this pane let you change the font used, paragraph alignment (left, center, right, and bullet), clear (delete) the displayed signature, and open your signature in an advanced editor (which is whatever program is associated with the file extension (*.htm* or *.html*).

Below the editing buttons is a pick list and creation option for attaching a vCard to your signature in addition to the text.

> *For details on attaching a one-time signature to a message, see the topic "Attaching a Signature" later in this chapter.*

Remove

Deletes a selected signature from your hard drive.

New

Opens the Create New Signature dialog shown in Figure 5-17 (right). Here you name your signature, and then select a creation option. You choices are: start from scratch, use an existing template and edit it, or use an existing HTML file as a template, and again modify it to suit your needs.

With your signature complete, go back to the Tools → Options → Mail Format and check the configuration listed under the "Use this Signature by default" option.

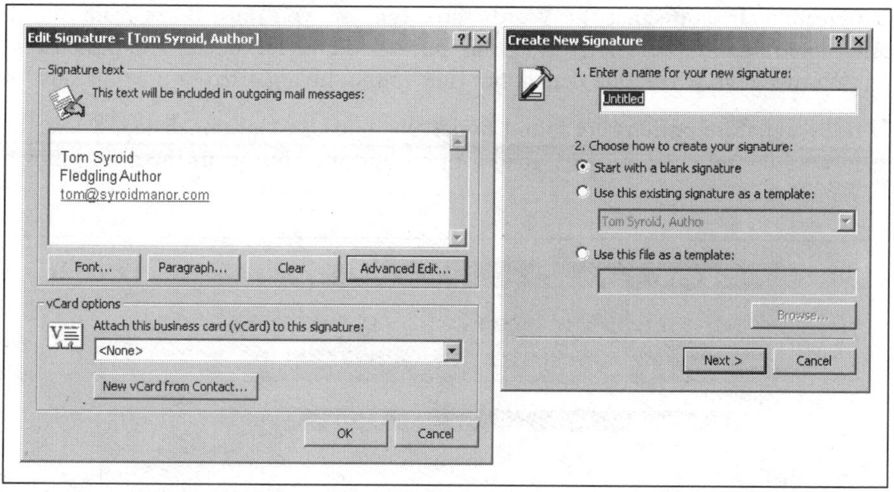

Figure 5-17: The Edit Signature dialog (left) and the Create New Signature dialog (right)

Many people like to use signatures occasionally, but do not want a signature attached to every message. Any time you create or edit a signature, this signature is set as a default attachment to all messages.

We leave you with the following tips and caveats regarding signatures under the Outlook editor:

- Changing message formats (for example, from HTML to MS-RTF) leaves the text of a signature in place, but layout information is usually lost. This is due to how, in the example given, MS-RTF interprets and renders HTML.

- Signatures are stored in the folder *<drive and document path>\username\ Applications Data\Microsoft\Signatures*. You might want to remember this for several reasons:

  - If you've painstakingly created one or more favorite signatures, you'll probably want to make sure you back them up for safekeeping.

  - There's nothing stopping you from directly editing a signature file with another HTML (or text) editor.

  - The Signature Picker dialog (Figure 5-16) has no provision for renaming signatures once they are created—to rename a signature, you'll have to go to the above folder and do so manually.

Creating a signature: the Word editor

Word handles signatures differently than the Outlook editor does. Rather than storing them as separate HTML files, the Word editor stores signatures as Auto-Text entries in the *normal.dot* template file.

Mail Editors

To create a signature that the Word editor can use, you must do so from Word. Any signatures you've created using the Outlook editor can be cut and pasted into the Word signature creation dialog, but they cannot be imported or used directly.

Word's signature options are found under the Tools → Options dialog. Select the General tab, and click on the E-mail Option button. This opens the dialog shown in Figure 5-18.

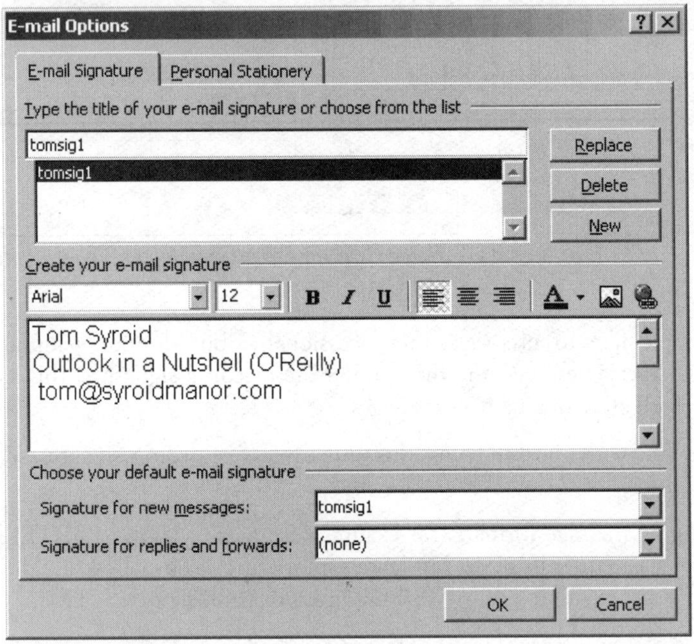

Figure 5-18: The Word E-mail options dialog with the E-mail signature tab selected

The process of creating a signature here is similar to the steps outlined for the Outlook editor. The exceptions are: a Replace button instead of an Edit button, formatting commands are readily available on the toolbar above the editing pane, and you can configure the signature used for new messages, replies, and forwards, directly from this dialog.

TIP # 49

Multiple Signature Sets

If you use more than one message format on a routine basis, you may need to create several signature sets (one for each format). MS-RTF or HTML formatting within a signature block does not always transpose correctly from one format to another.

Spellchecking

Both of Outlook's mail editors feature capable spellcheckers, so whichever editor you choose, you no longer have an excuse for incorrect spelling in your email messages. The methods and dialogs used by each editor differ enough that, again, it's simpler to cover each section separately.

Spellcheck: the Outlook editor

The Outlook editor's spellchecker does not have all the bells and whistles found in Word's (sorry, no grammar checking or as-you-type spellchecking), but for everyday tasks it is more than good enough. Automatic spellchecking is not enabled by default, however, so if you want this option turned on the first order of business is to find the switch. Go to the Tools menu and select Options → Spelling. The Spelling options tab is shown in Figure 5-19.

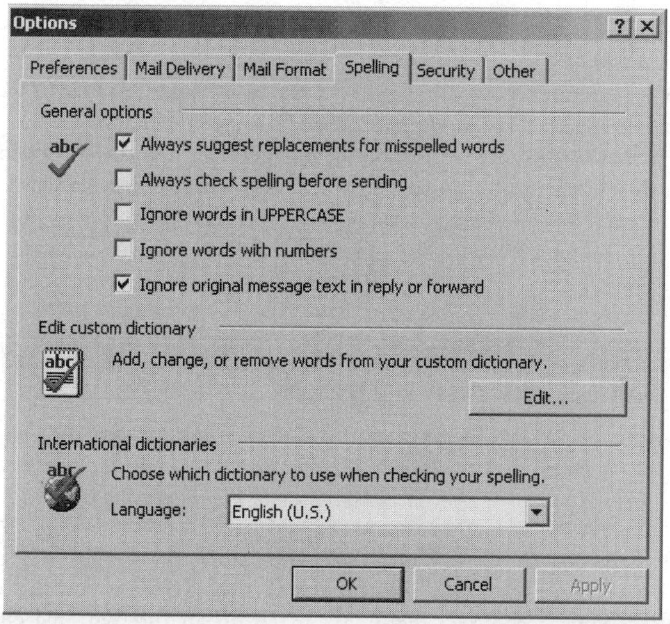

Figure 5-19: Outlook's spelling options tab

The important options to be aware of on this dialog are:

Always suggest replacements for misspelled words
> With this option enabled, when Outlook finds a word in a message that is not in its standard dictionary or the user's custom dictionary, it suggests a replacement; if this option is disabled, misspelled words are highlighted but no suggested replacements are provided.

Always check spelling before sending

This is the off/on toggle for automatic spellchecking. When enabled, Outlook invokes its spellchecker before sending a message. Note that this option forces a manual check-before-send whether you're using Outlook's built-in editor or Word.

Ignore original message text in reply or forward

If the message you're creating is a reply or forward, and you have selected the option to include the original message text in your response (see the section "Message Handling Options" earlier in this chapter), then Outlook spellchecks only text added to the original message.

There is a caveat to this option: if you opt to include original text with replies and forwards and select the option to prefix each line of this original text with a character (typically a >), then Outlook insists on checking the whole document even with the "Ignore original message..." option enabled.

Edit custom dictionary

Outlook maintains a custom dictionary for each user, *CUSTOM.DIC*, stored in the folder *<path>\Username\Application Data\Microsoft\Proof.* This is a simple text file that lists all the words you have added through the spellchecker dialog. If you mistakenly add a misspelled word, or wish to remove a word, this is the place to go. Click the button, and your custom dictionary opens in your default text editor—which will be Notepad, unless you've changed your file associations.

TIP # 50

Merge Spelling Dictionaries from Other Apps

If you have another application with a spellchecker and the data file that application uses is also a Plain Text file (which is often the case), merge the two files. This saves you the tedious process of rebuilding your custom dictionary one word at a time.

International dictionaries

If you have more than one language installed on your system, this drop-down list allows you to choose a dictionary based on an International character set; the default is English (U.S.).

Spellcheck: the Word editor

One of the draws of using Word as your mail editor is that both spelling and grammar can be optionally checked as you type (from Word's Tools menu, Options → Spelling and Grammar); words not found in Word's dictionaries are underlined with a red wavy line, and questionable grammar is underlined in green. To see suggested corrections, simply right-click the underlined word or phrase and a context menu is displayed (see Figure 5-20).

Figure 5-20: Word's spelling context menu

At the top of this menu is a list of suggested corrections; select a word from the list and it's inserted in place of the underlined one in your message. Below the list are these options:

Ignore All

Leaves all instances of the underlined word (or phrase) unchanged for the duration of the current editing session.

Add

If you're confident you're right and Word is wrong, you can add the word to a custom dictionary for future reference. Once a word is added to the custom dictionary, Word no longer highlights it for correction.

AutoCorrect

Adds the spelling error and the correction you choose to Word's AutoCorrect list. The next time Word encounters the same misspelling, it automatically substitutes the error with the correction. If the word substitution you are looking for is not shown, go to Tools → AutoCorrect and enter it manually in the list provided. A scan of this list provides many good examples of how Auto-Correct can be used for more than just spelling corrections.

Language

Gives you the option to change Word's default language dictionary on-the-fly for either the individual word in question or as a default.

Mail Editors

TIP # 51

Exclude Words from the Spellchecker

To exclude a specific word or phrase when Word spellchecks a document, select the text, and from the context menu go to Language → Set Language. Check the option "Do not check spelling and grammar." Word's spelling and grammar checker skips whatever you selected, for just the open document.

Spelling

Invokes Word's full spellchecking dialog (which adds only a button to go to Word's spelling option dialog and the option to ignore one instance of a word).

By default, automatic spelling and grammar checking are enabled in Word. To disable this automation, open Word's Spelling and Grammar dialog (Tools → Spelling and Grammar → Options), and deselect the option "Check spelling as you type."

Manual spellchecking

If you prefer to check spelling manually, simply press F7 (in either editor). In manual mode, you can:

- Spellcheck an individual word by highlighting it (double-click the word), and pressing F7. If the word is spelled correctly, Outlook offers to check the rest of the "selection," meaning the rest of the document. Click OK to continue, or Cancel to quit. If the word is spelled incorrectly, Outlook displays the spelling dialog (see Figure 5-21) and offers a suggestion—if this option is enabled on the spelling options tab described previously. You then, once again, have the option of quitting or continuing the spellcheck process.

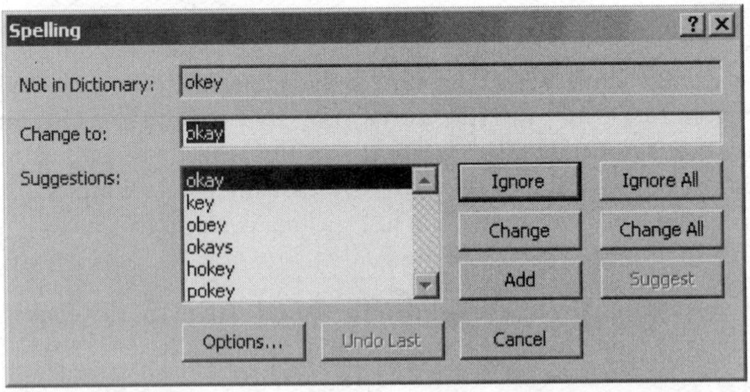

Figure 5-21: Manual spellcheck dialog for Outlook's built-in mail editor

- Spellcheck only a section of the document, by highlighting that section and pressing F7. When the check is complete for that section, the spellchecker offers to continue checking the rest of the document.

- Spellcheck from a specific point forward by placing your cursor at a starting point and pressing F7. The spellchecker walks through the message, stopping at any words not found in its dictionaries. When the spellchecker reaches the end of the document, it automatically moves to the beginning and proceeds back to the point where you began. You can cancel the process at any time.

Figure 5-21 shows the spellcheck dialog displayed when the Outlook editor finds a word not in its dictionary. The word being questioned is shown in the "Not in Dictionary" field at the top of the dialog. Suggestions are displayed in the lower pane; selecting an entry here moves it into the "Change to" field. The buttons on the right side of the dialog determine what actions are taken.

You can also force a manual spellcheck in Word using F7. While functionally similar to the Outlook spellcheck dialog, Word's spellcheck dialog (see Figure 5-22) has two notable exceptions:

- The "Not in the Dictionary" field used by Outlook's editor is locked; you manually modify a word's spelling in the "Change to" text box. Word merges these two dialogs into one; you both view and modify a word's spelling from the "Not in Dictionary" text box.

- Word adds an AutoCorrect button to its dialog. This adds the word highlighted as incorrectly spelled to its AutoCorrect list, pairing it with the suggested correction. In the example shown in Figure 5-22, clicking the AutoCorrect button would add "Ahhh" to the AutoCorrect list, and set up a rule to substitute all further occurrences of this word with (in this example) "Ash." Give some thought to the words you add to AutoCorrect.

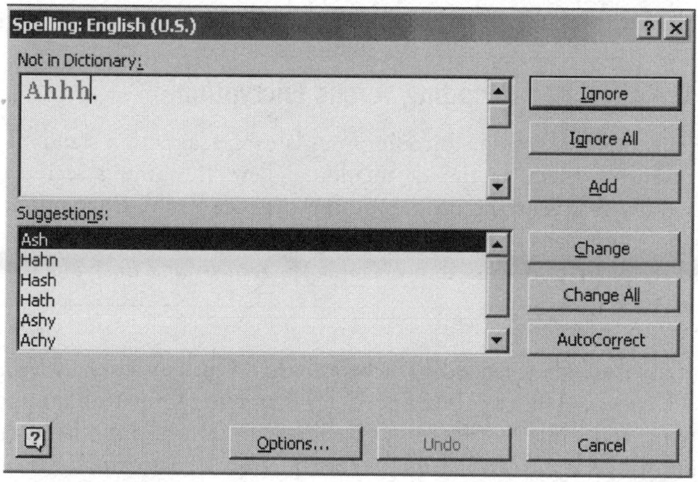

Figure 5-22: Word's manual spellcheck dialog

Encoding Options

Encoding is the process of translating a message into another format for transmission. This is done to make the transmission faster, easier, or better. You could consider a letter to be a form of encoding; you are creating a message and encoding it in another form for transmission to the recipient. You might do this because you can't speak to the recipient directly, because a written message can be delayed, or to create a record of the conversation.

For our purposes, encoding is a means of translating your message in Outlook as it appears on your screen to a format that can be sent over the Internet to another user. If the message is encoded correctly, the recipient will be able to view the message as intended, regardless of the client used to view it.

Why bother? Well, if all email were in the form of Plain Text English, there wouldn't be much need for encoding. When you include stationery, embedded images, and binary attachments, the situation gets more complicated. Add in the myriad possible operating systems and email clients your recipients may be using, and it gets even more complicated. Enter encoding.

For example, many older mail systems were designed to transfer only ASCII (7 bits/byte) data. Because they strip off the eighth bit, such mail systems cannot transfer binary data, such as images or program files, which require 8 bits/byte. Unless, that is, the 8-bit data is first encoded as 7-bit data. Such encoding expands the data, because it must add additional bytes to flag those bytes in the original data that includes a significant eighth bit. The encoded data is larger than the original data, but contains only 7-bit characters, which the mail system can transfer properly. The recipient's mail client (assuming it understands the encoding method used) can then decode that encoded data back to its original 8-bit form.

Encoding Versus Encryption

Encoding is not encryption. Encoding translates messages to a standard format, and reassembles them at the destination. There is nothing secretive about encoding; any recipient should decode the message easily. Encryption, on the other hand, is a means of keeping a message undecipherable to everyone but the intended recipient, as discussed in Chapter 15, *Security and Encryption*.

There are two standard encoding schemes that Outlook uses: *UUencode*, and *BinHex*. UUencode (Unix to Unix Encoding) is an older format still in use on many Unix systems, and some PC systems as well, and BinHex is essentially restricted to the Macintosh world. *MIME* (*Multipurpose Internet Mail Extension*) is not technically an encoding method. It is a standard way to organize the contents of a message. A MIME message can contain a variety of data types, including text or binary data that has been encoded in various ways, such as Quoted Printable or

Base64. Outlook primarily uses MIME, but includes the capability to encode and decode UUencode and BinHex.

The Settings button beneath the messaging editor option opens the configuration dialog shown below. Note that this option is only available when the messaging format is set to HTML (Figure 5-23, left) or Plain Text (Figure 5-23, right); MS-RTF does not support encoding. For this reason, MS-RTF should only be used for communicating with other Outlook users.

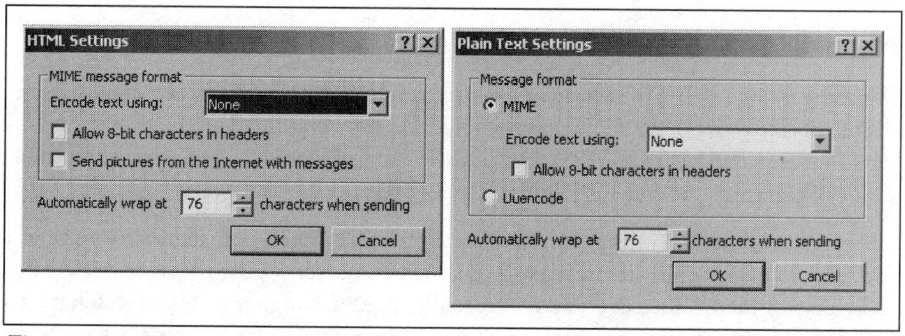

Figure 5-23: Message Format option dialogs—HTML Settings (left) and Plain Text Settings (right)

Both settings dialogs contain a drop-down list that allows you to select the bit and binary formats for encoding a message. The options are: None, Quoted Printable, and Base 64. Under most circumstances, there should be no need to edit these options. By default, Outlook uses the simplest form of MIME encoding to divide the message into text and binary components. Aside from very rare occasions, these options do not require user intervention.

There are also options to "Allow 8-bit characters in headers" and "Send pictures from the Internet with messages." The 8-bit character option specifies that foreign character sets, high ASCII, and double-byte character sets (DBCS—for example, Unicode) are allowed in a message header. Turn on this option only when absolutely required and then only on a per-message basis. Many mail servers still expect 7-bit data in headers, and reject messages they encounter with 8-bit data in them.

The "Send pictures" option specifies that messages should include any embedded graphics instead of simply including a URL or file pointer. This option is useful if you know the recipient does not have access to the graphic; for example, if a graphic embedded in your message is located on your local computer. Use this option when needed, but due to the potential of dramatically increased message sizes we suggest you do not use it as a default.

Finally, both HTML and Plain Text dialogs provide a field to specify line length in characters. When you create a message using either of Outlook's mail editors, the text automatically wraps to the window width as you enter it. When the message is sent, however, the text is wrapped to the value (30 to 132 characters) entered here.

This value should not be set higher than 76; some mail clients, particularly Plain Text clients, cannot accept longer line lengths. When the option to attach or enclose original message text in a forwarded or reply email is set, line lengths can exceed the value set, in which case extra line breaks are inserted. None of the message text is lost, but it does make it hard to read. If your correspondence typically falls into a long series of replies and counter-replies, you might want to set this number to 70 or even 65, or consider manually deleting older portions of the discussion.

International Options

We now know that all messages sent or received by Outlook are encoded and decoded. But where do language options fit into all this? Language options are based on installed character sets, and the selection of languages available are a direct result of the character sets installed on your system.

Character sets and encoding are not directly related. When you send a message in a foreign language, information regarding which character set the message was created in is placed in the message header—usually (see "Changing a Message Character Set" later in this chapter for dealing with messages that lack this information). The message itself is then encoded no differently than it would be if it contained a file attachment or embedded graphic. When the recipient receives the message, it is decoded and Outlook reads the header to determine what character set to use for display and reply. The character set used to send the message is not encoded into the message—it must be installed on the recipient's system.

 The reason for this clarification is that Outlook labels many of the International options (dialogs and menus) using the term "encoding." This is not technically accurate. Anything to do with language options should read "character sets," not encoding.

Figure 5-24 shows the International Options dialog. The options available here are relatively straightforward, and apply specifically to users who are either corresponding in a different language or have a non-English version of Outlook installed and want to reveal some (or all) of a message header in English. The options are as follows:

Use English for message flags
This option sets message flags such as High Importance or Flag for Follow-up to English; the balance of the message's header information, as well as the message text itself, uses the language set for outgoing messages.

Use English for message headers on replies or forwards
This option translates the message header fields in a reply or forward to English; the message body displays in the language set for outgoing messages.

Figure 5-24: Message Format—International Options settings

Use this encoding for outgoing messages
> This option sets the default language used for new messages. Note the list displayed depends on the languages installed at the operating system level.

Use this encoding for unmarked received messages
> This option sets the default language in which an incoming message is displayed, providing the sender did not specify a language for the message when it was sent. Again, the language options available here reflect only those already installed on your system.

Using Outlook's Editors

Until now, we've been dealing with Outlook's global/default editor settings. In the following section we are going to show you some tips and tricks related to using Outlook's editors, as well as describe how to stray from the default settings you've so carefully tweaked without delving back into option dialogs.

Addressing a Message

Addressing a message in Outlook is a reasonably straightforward process, right? Well, yes and no. It is if you only have two or three contacts you communicate with regularly, or if you have a good memory for names and their spelling. But as your contacts file grows, so do the number of Johns and Bills and Marys. And then there's your friend Dan who has three email addresses: one for business, one for home, and one he keeps for a spare when the other two aren't working.

Like everything else in Outlook, you can use two approaches to getting the address you want entered in a new message: brute force, and cunning. We'll show you the brute force approach for completeness, but this section focuses on the cunning— quick shortcuts that save time, effort, and keystrokes.

Brute force first. When you can't remember any part of Whatshisname's name, maybe looking at a list will help jog your memory. On the new message form, click the To button next to the address field. This opens the Select Names dialog shown in Figure 5-25.

 NOTE *The Select Names dialog displays the contents of your Contacts folder and contains the same dataset used by the Windows Address Book (and the Outlook Address Book). Outlook's implementation of Address Books is "addressed" (pardon the pun) in Chapter 3.*

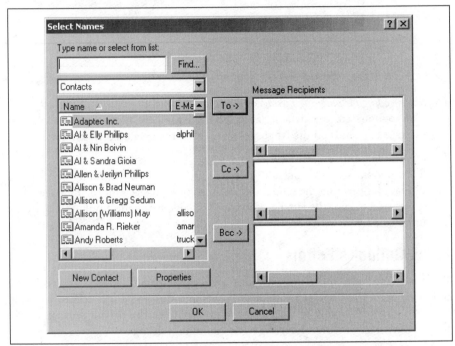

Figure 5-25: Using the Outlook Address Book to address a message

Typing a letter, or series of letters, in the "Type name..." field takes you to the first occurrence of that letter. When you've found who you're looking for, select the name (or names) and click the To, Cc, or Bcc buttons as appropriate. You can also examine the details of a contact record using the Properties button, or create a new record with the New Contact button.

If you happen to know who you're looking for, however, and you have a passion for efficiency, there are better ways to go about this.

You want to send a message to Dave. You don't how to spell his last name, and you haven't a clue as to his email address. You do have one bit of useful information, however: his first name. For Outlook, this is enough. Begin by simply typing Dave in the "To" field. As soon as you tab out of this field, Outlook responds in one of four ways:

- It does nothing, which means it did not find a match anywhere in your contact records for what you entered; the name you entered remains just as you typed it (which is seldom the case if you have any number of contacts entered in your address book).

- It underlines what you entered with a wavy *red* line; this tells you it's on to something but needs some help to narrow the choices.

- It underlines what you entered with a wavy *green* line, and fills the balance of the name in for you.

- It finds a unique name match and underlines it in black.

The first option is pretty simple; you need to give Outlook more information or try another name. What is the difference between the second and third scenarios? Quite a bit, actually...

In scenario two, illustrated in Figure 5-26 (left), the red line is telling you that Outlook needs help in deciding who this message is for. If you ignore the red line, finish the message, and try to send it, Outlook presents you with the Check Names dialog shown in Figure 5-27. In other words, you need to make a decision or this message is not going anywhere.

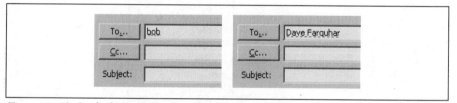

Figure 5-26: Outlook's name lookup feature showing a partial name match (left) and a historical name match (right)

As you can see, Outlook has narrowed the choices for you, but does not know *which* Bob is the intended recipient.

The green wavy line, shown in Figure 5-26 (right), is another matter altogether. Outlook has already taken Dave and filled it out to Dave Farquhar. You can fill in the message body (or mess Dave up by not putting anything in the body), press the Send button, and the message is dispatched without protest. In this case (green line), Outlook makes a guess based on a historical match—in other words, you've addressed a message to Dave Farquhar recently.

Now let's try another scenario: I want the message to go to Dave, but Dave has more than one email address. The entry listed under the first email field of a contact's record is always the default used, but in this case you want the message to

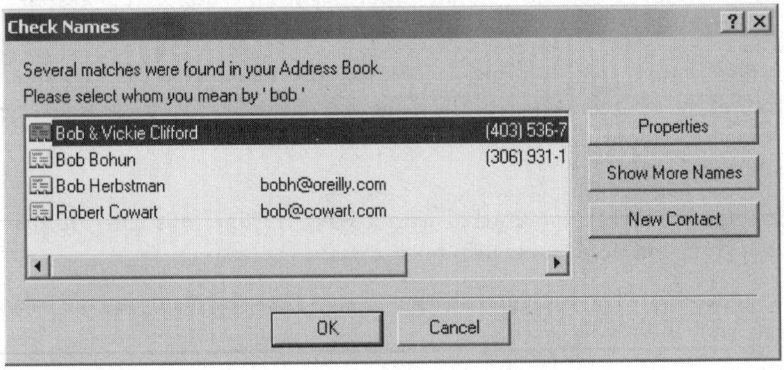

Figure 5-27: Check Names dialog

go to another address. Simple, really—right-click on Dave, and up pops a context menu with all his addresses listed—and more (see Figure 5-28).

Figure 5-28: Check Names context menu (green wavy line)

From this menu I can choose from one of three addresses, choose a different contact altogether, look up Dave's "Properties" (the name, address, and phone details of his contact record), create a new address for dave (note that this is derived from my original entry of dave, the assumption here being that Outlook did not correctly match my search criteria), or open the Address Book for more scouring.

The same context menu trick works for our Bob example, only this time we are asked to narrow our choice before we can access any email addresses (see Figure 5-29).

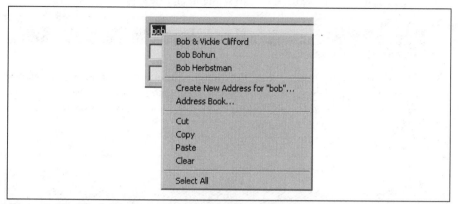

Figure 5-29: Check Names context menu (red wavy line)

Here are some more name-search tips (and gotchas) for filling in an address field:

- If you do not remember the person's name, but you do remember all or part of his domain, enter that. For example, if you have several contacts with email addresses hosted by @Home, typing home in the address field of a new message will provide you with a context menu of everyone with an email address containing @Home in it.

- Any number of letters of a name invokes a search. For example, simply typing the letter a gets you a context menu of all the names in your address book beginning with "A" *plus* any contact with an "a" in their name. While this is not terribly practical for common letters, if your contact has a last name beginning with "Z," typing just this letter alone will net you surprisingly good results.

- The entry does not have to begin with what you enter for a search parameter. For example, entering USA results in a list of all your contacts that have USA anywhere in their name (or probably more accurately, their company name).

The Message Options Dialog

An overlooked and underused feature of Outlook's mail editors is the Message Options dialog shown in Figure 5-30. Using this option dialog, you can override many of Outlook's default message delivery options, hold a message in your Outbox until a specified date and time, choose a different account through which the message is sent, and assign Contact/Category links to a message. One of the biggest draws of this option dialog is that you can set a multitude of flags and message parameters from a single location. This is one dialog Outlook's engineers got right.

The Message Options dialog is accessed via the View → Options command on the Outlook editor menu (*not* Outlook's menu); there is also an Options button on both the Word and Outlook editor's toolbar. As an alternative, select a message from any mail folder, and from the context menu choose Options.

TIP # 52

Reconfigure Sent Messages

Many of the options contained on the Message Options dialog must be set before a message is sent (for example, Security and Delivery options). On the other hand, certain options—notably the Contacts and Categories links—can be entered for a message that has already been sent.

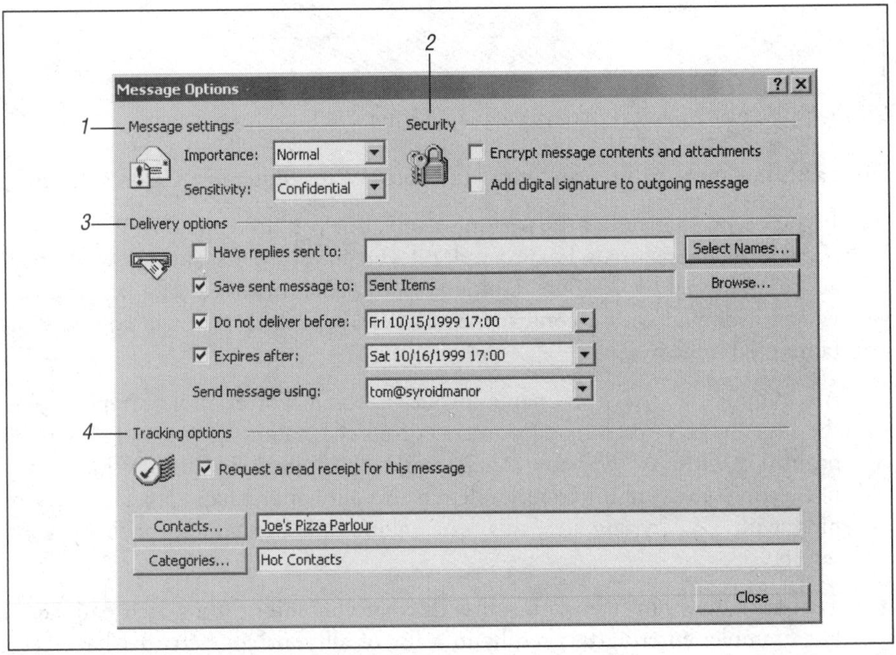

Figure 5-30: The Message Options dialog

The Message Options dialog gives you access to many of the key fields of a message, and allows you to change these options on a per-message basis. Any changes reflected here apply only to the selected message. This is also the only place you find the option to set delivery and expiration dates.

1. Message Settings lets you assign both an Importance and Sensitivity to a message. Messages arriving in a recipient's Inbox with an Importance flag attached display both an icon next to the Subject Line (for Low [↓] and High Importance [!], see Figure 5-31), as well as a notification above the message header when it is opened.

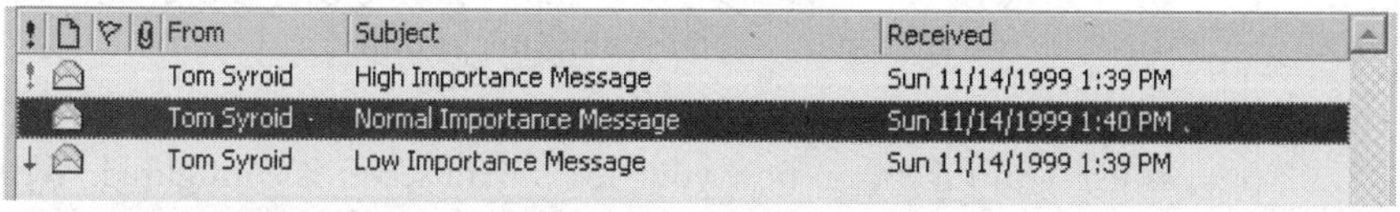

!	□	▽	⌀	From	Subject	Received	
!	✉			Tom Syroid	High Importance Message	Sun 11/14/1999 1:39 PM	
	✉			Tom Syroid	Normal Importance Message	Sun 11/14/1999 1:40 PM	
↓	✉			Tom Syroid	Low Importance Message	Sun 11/14/1999 1:39 PM	

Figure 5-31: Three examples of message importance flags

Sensitivity flags do not have attached icons, but they add a notification in the header of the message when it is opened, as shown in Figure 5-32. Sensitivity flag options include Normal (default), Personal, Private, and Confidential.

> **NOTE** *Sensitivity flags are really meaningless. Setting a sensitivity flag simply informs the recipient that you consider the message to be of whatever sensitivity you specified. These flags would be more meaningful if, for example, setting "Confidential" prevented Outlook from forwarding the message to a third party.*

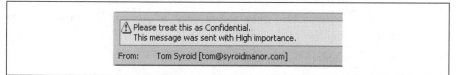

Please treat this as Confidential.
This message was sent with High importance.

From: Tom Syroid [tom@syroidmanor.com]

Figure 5-32: A Mail message sent flagged as Important and with a sensitivity set to Confidential

2. The Security section provides checkboxes for encrypting a message and/or attaching a digital signature to it. Encryption and digital signatures are the topic of Chapter 15. This section is only available when you have a digital certificate installed.

3. Under Delivery Options you can:

   – Send replies to the message to someone other than yourself, a handy feature if you're going on vacation, making an inquiry on behalf of another individual, or you want your assistant to handle follow-ups.

   – Set the folder where the message is saved. The default location for saving message replies is the "Sent Items" folder. While it's possible to configure Outlook to save replies with the original message (Tools → Options → E-mail Options → Advanced E-mail Options), this only works when you reply to a message located somewhere other than the Inbox. This option allows you to reply to a message from the Inbox and save a copy of your reply in a folder of your choosing.

   – Mark the message with a "Do not deliver before" date. Enabling this option keeps the message in your Outbox until the date and time you specify. Sneaking out of town for the weekend? Set up a series of emails to send your boss so he or she thinks you're at home poring over the Tibbles contract. Just don't forget to leave your computer running.

— Set an expiration date for a message. Your mileage is going to vary with this one, as it is contingent on how your ISP's mail server is configured. When functional, you can set a date for a message to expire; if this date passes, and the recipient has not yet picked it up, then it is deleted by the server. This is a useful option if you send a message that is time limited, but again note that it is not well supported.

— Specify which account to send the message from. If you have more than one mail account, you can use this option to select the account to which the message is sent. A word of caution: some ISPs do not allow messages originating from an address not recognized as belonging to a subscriber to be sent through their mail server. They do this to prevent bulk mailers from bouncing messages through their system.

4. Under Tracking Options (IMO only) you can:

— Request a read receipt when the message is opened. Use this option to request a one-time read receipt.

— Link a contact to the message.

— Associate a category with the message.

TIP # 53

One-Time Read Receipts

If you're looking for a place to send a one-time read receipt, the Message Options dialog is the only place in Outlook where you will find such a provision.

The Message Options dialog is a powerful center for configuring messages for circumstances that fall outside the parameter of your default settings, without digging through three or four layers of option dialogs.

Changing a Message Format

For most correspondence, Plain Text is appropriate. It produces compact messages, and, despite the proliferation of HTML, Plain Text remains the universal standard for electronic messaging. No matter which email client your recipient uses, it can read a Plain Text message.

Sometimes, however, using HTML or MS-RTF is necessary or desirable. For example:

• If you're sending a Task request or Meeting request, you and the recipient must *both* use HTML. MS-RTF sometimes works, but is unreliable.

- If you're sending a message to a recipient on a corporate mail system that is Exchange-based, use MS-RTF. While Exchange can handle both Plain Text and HTML, some of its collaboration features are designed around MS-RTF (pre-Exchange 2000).

- If you want to dress a message up with embedded pictures or horizontal lines, HTML is the only format that supports these features.

 The following instructions apply only when you are using the Outlook editor. There is no easy way to change the format of an existing message when your default mail editor is Word, although there is a kludgy workaround that we'll get to in a moment.

To send a new message in a format different from your default setting, open a new message form and select the Format menu. If you do not see all the format options shown in Figure 5-33, read on.

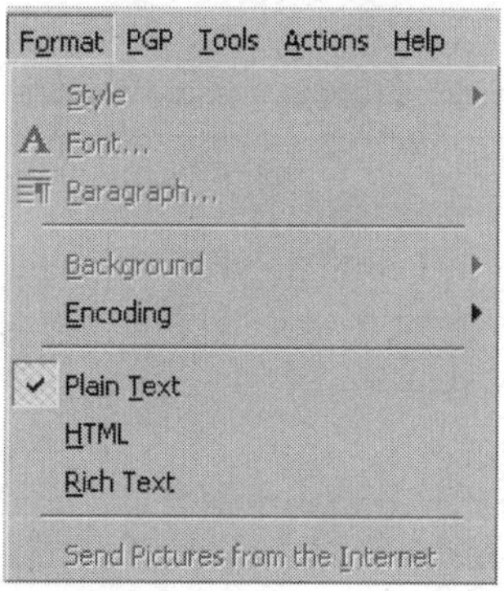

Figure 5-33: Format menu (Outlook's built-in editor)

Selecting an alternative message format can be tricky, depending on the format you are starting from and which format you want to switch to. Here are the steps:

- If your default font is Plain Text, you can go directly to either HTML or MS-RTF.

- If your default font is Rich Text or HTML, you can go directly to Plain Text. When you switch from Rich Text or HTML to Plain Text, you risk losing some of the formatting contained in the message and Outlook warns you of this fact.

- If you want to switch from MS-RTF to HTML (or visa versa), you have to switch to Plain Text first. For example: your default message format is HTML and you need to send an email in MS-RTF. Here is the sequence you'll need to follow: HTML → Plain Text → MS-RTF.

When you reply to or forward a message, Outlook does so using the format in which the message was received. If you want to change the format of your response, the previous steps apply, but you *must* click on the Reply or Forward button first—you cannot change the format of a message that is simply open for viewing. You need to kick Outlook into edit mode first.

We noted earlier that this material applies only to the Outlook editor. If you are using Word as your mail editor, changing from your default format for a *new* message is a snap. Go to the Actions menu and select one of the options found under the New Mail Message Using command as shown in Figure 5-34.

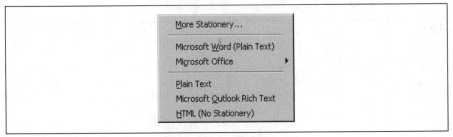

Figure 5-34: The New Mail Message Using submenu

In the example shown, Word is configured as the mail editor and Plain Text is the default message format. To send a new HTML message, choose the HTML (No Stationery) option; to send a new message using MS-RTF choose the Microsoft Outlook Rich Text option.

Now here's the kludge we referred to earlier: if you use Word as a mail editor, there are no menu commands available to change the format of an *existing* message. If you must reply to or forward a message in a format other than the one in which you received it, there are two ways to do this:

1. Switch back to Outlook's built-in editor (Tools → Options → Mail Format tab).

2. Select the text of the original message (Ctrl+A) and copy it to the clipboard. Open a new message with the New Mail Message Using command discussed earlier, and paste the original text into this new message. Describing this takes longer than doing it.

This cut-and-paste method does not transfer address information; you'll have to readdress the new message as a separate step.

Changing a Message Background

This option is only available when your message format is HTML. If you're using the Outlook editor, the command is Format → Background. The Color option produces a pick menu (see Figure 5-35). The Picture option opens a dialog allowing you to browse for a file.

Figure 5-35: The Background → Color submenu showing the fly-out color picker (HTML only)

The Word editor command is the same (Format → Background), however, the color picker is the first option presented off the Background selection. To insert a picture, choose Fill Effects and select the Picture tab.

Changing a Message Character Set

When you receive a message in a different language, the message must contain information about the character set (alphabet) that was used to create it before Outlook can display the message correctly. When you forward or reply to the message, Outlook maintains the character set of the original message and bases your reply on this information.

When you receive a message that contains no character set information, Outlook uses the default language setting specified for your system (Control Panel → Regional Settings). This default setting also appears in the International Options dialog box (Tools → Options → Mail Format tab → International Options).

This default setting might not work for some of the international messages that you receive. For example, if your default is Western European and you receive an unmarked message (that is, a message lacking information about the character set in the header) that uses a Greek character set, the message might display boxes or question marks instead of readable text. To fix this problem, you need to change the character set used to display that specific message.

To change the character set of a received message:

1. Open the message.

2. Select View → Encoding, and choose the character set you want to use.

When you send a message, Outlook automatically uses the default character set specified by your Regional setting. You can, however, apply character sets on a per-message basis.

To change the character set of a message you are sending (new, reply to, or forward):

1. Create or open the message.

2. Select Format → Encoding. The first submenu displays a list of recently accessed encoding selections; the encoding option currently in use has a checkmark in

front of it. Choosing the More option displays a complete list of all the languages installed on your system. A fully expanded view of this menu and its resultant submenus is shown in Figure 5-36.

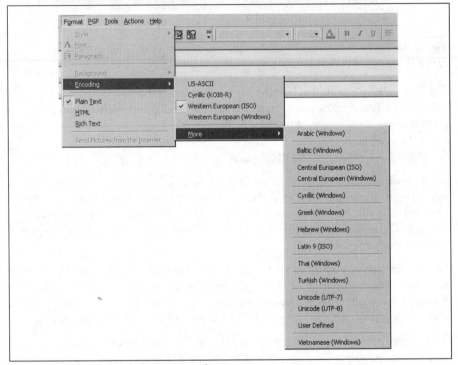

Figure 5-36: Outlook's language Encoding menu

If Word is your default mail editor, go to Tools → Language → Set Language, and from the Language list displayed choose an alternate. Note that in Word this changes the language used for all messages and documents based on the *normal.dot* template. Our suggestion is that if you work with multiple character sets on a routine basis, use the Outlook editor.

Hyperlinks

Outlook supports no less than 12 different hyperlink protocols that can be entered in a message to create active links to files, servers, web pages, or even local Outlook records. As you scan through the following list, note that some protocols require a double slash to be fully qualified (*http://*) and others do not (*mailto:*).

TIP # 54

Qualified Hyperlinks

The difference between a fully qualified hyperlink and text that Outlook may (or, as you're about to find, may not) see as a valid hyperlink is as follows: http://www. somewhere.com is a fully qualified link; www.somewhere.com is not. Note that a fully qualified link begins with the name of the protocol used, e.g., http:// or mailto:.

Here, then, are hyperlink protocols supported:

file://
> A protocol used to access a file on an intranet or local filesystem.

ftp://
> File Transfer Protocol (FTP), the most common method used to transfer files over the Internet.

gopher://
> A protocol used to make menus of material available over the Internet. Gopher was the predecessor to HTTP and has been largely supplanted by it.

http://
> Hypertext Transfer Protocol (HTTP) is the protocol synonymous with the transport of web pages on the Internet.

https://
> Hypertext Transfer Protocol (Secure) is a protocol designed to provide secure communication of web pages.

mailto:
> A protocol used to send a message to an email address. When the recipient of a message clicks a *mailto:* hyperlink, a new message is created in their default mail client with the email address supplied entered in the "To:" address field.

news:
> A protocol used to send a message to a member of a newsgroup. This is similar to the *mailto:* protocol, but the message is sent to a NNTP server rather than a mail server.

nntp://
> Network News Transfer Protocol is a protocol used to distribute, inquire, retrieve, and post Usenet news articles over the Internet.

Outlook: or Outlook://
> A protocol used to access an Outlook record or folder. This protocol is only supported between Outlook clients (see Table 5-2).

Mail Editors

prospero://

> A distributed filesystem protocol used to collect documents from multiple sites using one address along with specific search parameters. Prospero is also used for communication between clients and servers in the Archie system.

telnet://

> Telnet is a widely used protocol for logging onto a system from a remote location.

wais://

> Wide Area Information Servers (WAIS) is a protocol used to retrieve documents from a remote location based on keywords you supply.

Table 5-2: Outlook's Internal Hyperlinks

To Link to This Item or Folder	Type This
Inbox	Outlook: Inbox
Contacts	Outlook: Contacts
An Outlook folder	Outlook: *foldername\subfolder*
Calendar	Outlook: Calendar
A specific message in your Inbox	<Outlook: *Inbox/~Subject of message*>
A specific contact in your Contacts Folder	<Outlook: *Contacts/~Name of Contact*>

To insert a hyperlink into a message:

- Using the Outlook editor and a message format of Plain Text or Outlook Rich Text:

    - Any text entered that begins with www.*anything* is recognized as a hyperlink. It is converted after the first period is typed.

    - An email address entered in the form of *joesnipps@somwhere.com* is *not* converted to a hyperlink; it must be fully qualified (proceeded by mailto:).

- Using the Outlook editor and HTML:

    Both URLs and email addresses can be unqualified (not prefaced with either mailto: or http://).

- Using the Word editor and any message format (HTML, Plain Text, or MS-RTF). Both URLs and email addresses work as they do with the Outlook editor—links do not need to be qualified and are converted to hyperlink format when a space is encountered. *Providing*, that is, you have AutoCorrect set to transpose "Internet Links and Network Paths" to hyperlinks (in Word, Tools → AutoCorrect → "AutoFormat as you Type" tab).

In addition to keeping your editor and message formats straight, keep the following in mind when you enter hyperlinks into messages:

- If the hyperlink contains spaces, the entire address must be enclosed in angle brackets (< >). For example, `<file://C:\My Documents\My File.doc>`.

- The address following the protocol prefix must be valid. While this may sound like a no-brainer, you would be surprised how many addresses we receive in a week that do not work because they are spelled wrong.

- The recipient's system must support the same protocols as the sender's. Not all email clients support the range of protocols Outlook does, nor do all email clients implement protocols in an identical fashion.

 To be safe, any time you are in doubt about either the behavior of the editor you are using or the capabilities of your recipient's email client, enter a hyperlink fully qualified.

Attachments

The following sections detail attachments to a message. Most people think of attachments strictly in terms of files. As you are about to find out, Outlook is capable of much more.

File attachments

For once, we do not have a slew of "if-and-or" qualifiers regarding file attachments—both editors support them, and the mechanism is the same for both.

The source file (or files) can be located on your local hard drive, on a removable drive (for example, a Zip or Jaz drive), on a floppy, or, if you have the appropriate access, on a drive available on your network. If you can access a file with Windows Explorer, you can attach it to a message. Just because you can attach a file, however, does not mean the recipient of your message will be able to view it. Executables and zip files are relatively safe bets. However, if you're sending someone an AutoCad document, make sure they have the means to open and read the file when it arrives.

TIP # 55

Send from Explorer Is Always Plain Text

When using the Send To → Mail Recipient selection from the right-click context menu of a file in Windows Explorer, Plain Text is always used for the new message, even if it is not your default message format. This is good information to tuck away, especially for HTML users; Plain Text seems to have fewer problems handling attachments.

To attach a file to a message:

1. From your mail editor's menu bar, choose Insert → File. This opens the Insert File dialog shown in Figure 5-37.

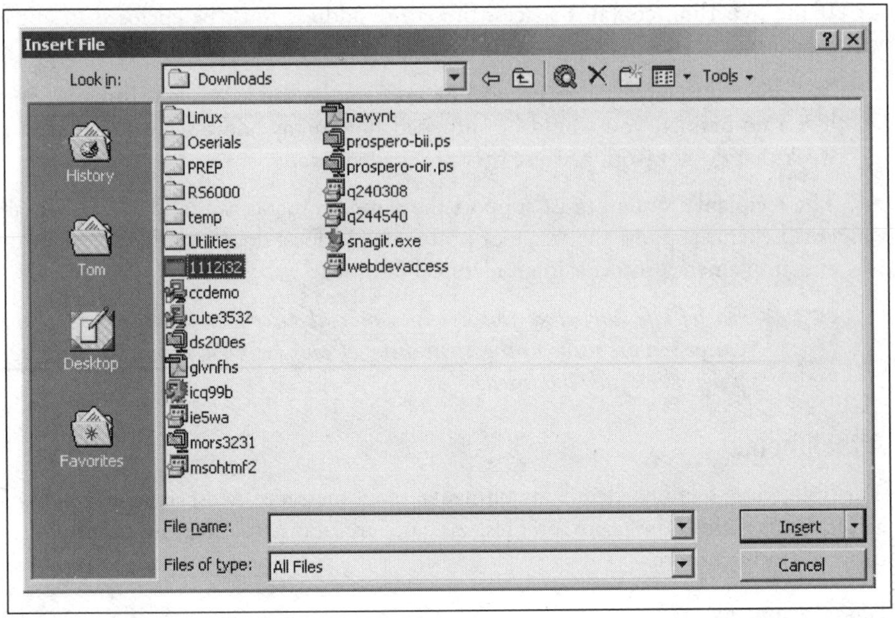

Figure 5-37: Insert File dialog

2. Navigate to the folder containing the file you want to attach, then select the file.

3. Choose insert. A pane at the bottom of the mail editor window displays the attached files (see Figure 5-38).

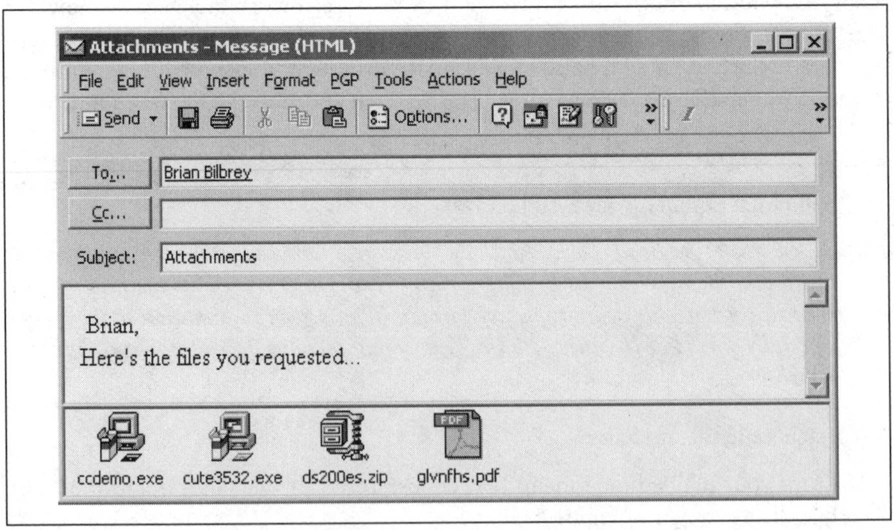

Figure 5-38: Email message showing attachments in lower pane

TIP # 56
Quickly Add Attachments to a Message

Once a message contains at least one attachment, there's a faster way to add files than going all the way to the menu bar. Right-click anywhere in the attachment pane, and choose Add from the context menu. Another easy way to attach files is to drag them from a folder or Explorer window and drop them anywhere in the message pane.

A word of caution regarding sending file attachments to someone: the proliferation of computer viruses transmitted by file attachments means many people refuse to open email attachments. You can take several steps to show that you are doing everything possible from your end to prevent the spread of viruses:

- Get a digital signature (see Chapter 15) and make it a point to sign messages containing file attachments. Deliberately-sent attachments that are signed provide some level of comfort for the recipient.

- Tell the recipient that you're sending a file attachment before you send it. Send an email explaining that you're sending an attachment, and specify the file name you will use. Use a name that helps identify the file as being from you. Do not, whatever you do, send a Word document to someone named text.doc and expect him to open it.

- Do your part to ensure your system is clean. Install a good anti-virus program and scan files before you attach them to a message. Practice safe computing.

Attaching Outlook items (Outlook editor only)

If you correspond routinely with other Outlook users, it's easy to share Outlook items by attaching them to a message. This command is only available from the Outlook editor, and only works between Outlook clients. Outlook items are a proprietary format, and not readable by other email programs.

To send an Outlook item to someone, from an open message form select Insert → Item. This opens the dialog shown in Figure 5-39 (top).

Choose the folder containing the item or items you want to attach from the upper pane, and the item itself from the lower. The "Insert as" and "Attachment" radio buttons let you choose between inserting the item as text in the body of the message or as a separate attachment. Note that you can mix and match these two options in the same message (see Figure 5-39, bottom).

The advantage of inserting an item as an attachment (versus text) is the ease with which your recipient can add that item to his or her own records. It's simply a matter of opening the message, dragging the attached item to the Outlook bar, and dropping it on a folder icon. As an alternative, right-click the attachment and choose Save As from the context menu displayed.

Mail Editors

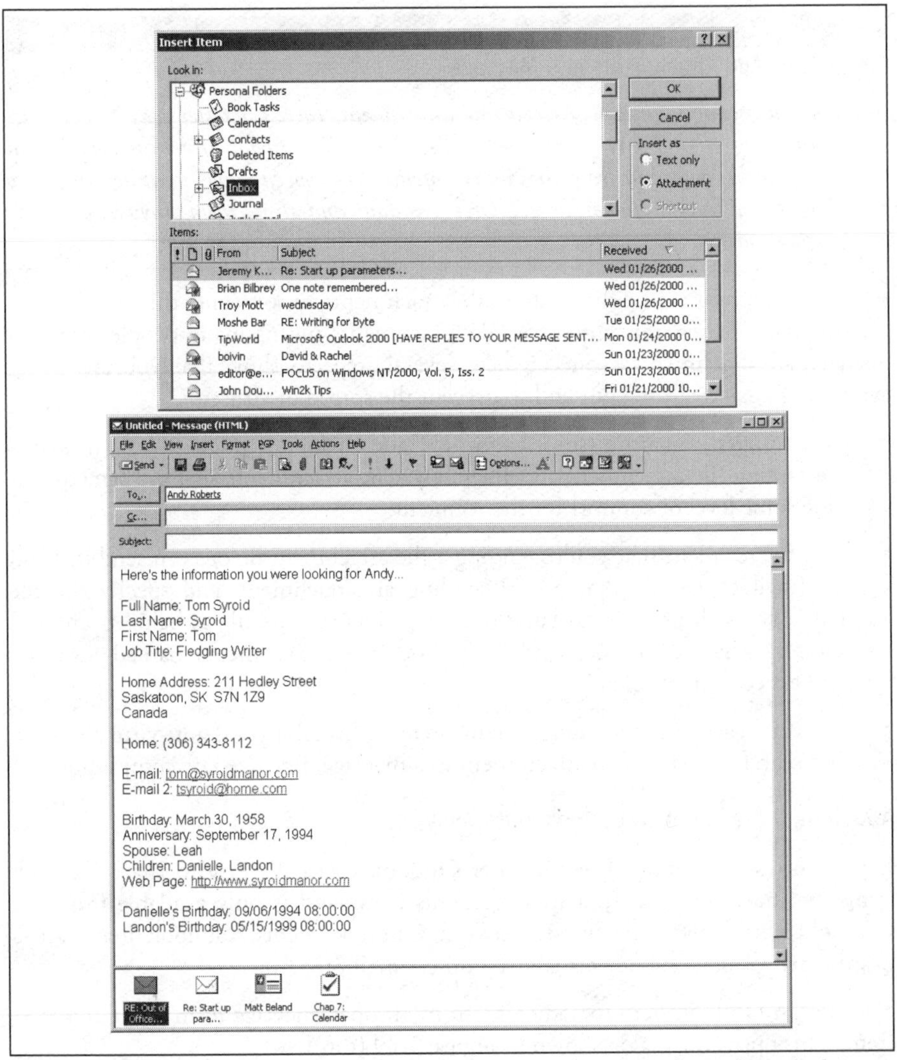

Figure 5-39: Outlook's Insert Item dialog (top), and an example of mixed Outlook items inserted or attached to a message (bottom)

Attaching a vCard to a message

Outlook supports the *vCard* standard, which is a means of exchanging contact information between supported email clients. When you receive a vCard as a message attachment, simply drag-and-drop it on your Contacts folder and a new item is created (see Chapter 8, *Contacts*, for more details on creating and using vCards).

This is all well and good, but how do you attach a vCard to a message? There are actually three approaches: from your Contacts folder, as an external file attachment, and automatically as a signature:

1. To attach a vCard to a message from your contacts folder, select the contact you want to send, and from the Actions menu choose Forward as vCard. Address the message and send it. To send more than one vCard in the same message, hold down the Ctrl key while you select contacts.

2. The first solution is a one-shot deal—every time you want to send a vCard, you have to repeat these same steps. If you send the same vCards on a repeated basis, or you want more flexibility in the attachment method (for example, you want to add a vCard to a message you've already started composing), export the vCard to a convenient location on your hard disk.

   Go to your Contacts folder, open a record (sorry, this only works with one record at a time), and select File → Export to vCard file. This saves the record as an external Outlook item (in the *.vcf* format), which you can attach to a message at any time using the Insert → File command. There's one caveat to this approach: if you update or modify an exported contact, don't forget to refresh the external file.

3. If you'd prefer to attach your vCard to a signature file, either open an existing signature or create a new (perhaps blank) file using the directions given in the "Signatures" section earlier in this chapter. At the bottom of the Edit Signatures dialog, you'll find a provision for attaching a vCard; the procedure is self-explanatory.

TIP # 57
Multiple vCards

Attaching your own vCard to a signature file is a popular way to share your contact information with others. But there may be some details you don't want to distribute to just anyone. The solution is simple. Create two contact entries for yourself: one with personal information, and another with business-only details. Give this second record a unique name (for example, Tom Syroid, Business vCard) and attach this one to your signature file.

Inserting pictures

Outlook's HTML message format supports the insertion of pictures in the body of a message.

TIP # 58
Size Your Picture Before Inserting

Pictures inserted in a message display the same size as the original file does in the graphics program that created it. To keep large images presentable, create a reduced-size version of the picture before inserting it. The free program IrfanView is a good way to do this (http://stud1.tuwien.ac.at/~e9227474/).

To insert a picture in a message:

1. Position your cursor where you want the picture to appear.

2. From the editor menu, choose Insert → Picture. The dialog shown in Figure 5-40 is displayed. If the Picture command is not available, either your message format is not set for HTML or your cursor is not in the message body.

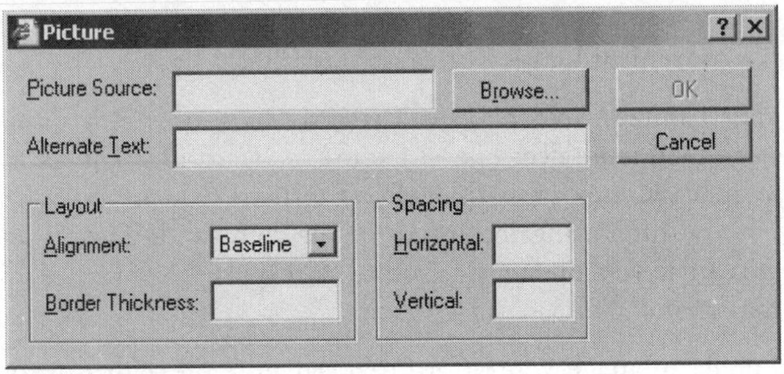

Figure 5-40: Insert Picture dialog

3. Use the Browse button to locate the picture source file. The Browse-for-file dialog supports the following picture file formats: *.art, .bmp, .gif, .jpg, .wmf,* and *.xbf.* You can also use the *.* option to locate another format not listed (for example, *.png*). When sending pictures over the Internet, try to stick to common picture formats, especially if you do not know which email client your recipient uses.

4. Use the Alternate Text field to enter a description of the picture being sent. The text you enter here is shown in place of the picture if your recipient's mail client cannot display the format sent.

5. The Alignment drop-down list sets the picture's alignment within the message. Options include: Not Set, Left, Right, Texttop, Absmiddle, Baseline, Absbottom, Bottom, Middle, and Top. If you want to have existing text wrap around the picture, experiment with a combination of alignment settings and spacing (discussed in Step 7).

6. Entering a number in the Border Thickness field places a border around the picture; this number reflects the border size in pixels. To remove a border, clear the field or enter 0.

7. The Spacing fields determine how much distance is maintained between the picture and other elements in the message (for example, text).

Inserting or Changing a Signature

As noted earlier in this chapter, you can configure Outlook to automatically append a signature file to all outgoing messages. If you prefer not to add a signature to every message you send, you can instead insert a signature on a per-message basis. The same principle holds if you have more than one signature and you want to change it for a select message. The method used to insert or change a signature varies according to your mail editor.

 The process of inserting or changing a signature assumes you have already created a signature file (and in the case of changing, that you have more than one). For instructions on creating a signature file, see the section "Signatures" earlier in this chapter.

To add a signature to a message using the Outlook editor, go to Insert → Signature and chose an entry from the list displayed. Insert → Signature → Other opens a dialog so you can view a signature before inserting it. Alternatively (Outlook editor only), you can use the Signature button on the toolbar of an open message form—it's the writing hand with the paper behind it.

To change an existing signature, you must delete the original and insert an alternate using the menu command. Word stores signature files as *AutoText* entries. To insert a signature, position your cursor where you want it to go and simply start typing the name of you gave your signature. In the example shown in Figure 5-41 (left), the signature file is named Word Signature.

The popup displayed lists the first two lines of the signature file itself. To insert this signature, press enter when the pop up is displayed; if this is not your intent, simply keep typing and the pop up disappears.

Mail Editors

As noted earlier in this chapter, you c use more than one signature, you can sv

In the Outlook editor, go to the Tool

When using Word

Business
Personal
Word Signature
E-mail Signature...

Tom Syroid
This is Series...
mailto:tom

Tom Syroid
This is Serious Folks

Figure 5-41: Changing a signature with the context menu (left) and entering a signature with AutoText (right)

If you already have a signature inserted in your messages, you can change it by right-clicking on the signature text. Figure 5-41 (right) shows an example of the context menu displayed when you do. Use this tip to your advantage by giving each signature file you create in Word a unique, easy to remember name, such as "work" and "home," or something similar.

Part 2

Menu Reference

Chapter 6

Mail

The following menu reference chapters describe the menu commands for Outlook's six program components: Mail, Calendar, Contacts, Tasks, Notes, and Journal. Commands shared by more than one component (for example, Organize and Find) are detailed where applicable, and covered from a cross-component perspective in Chapter 3, *Program Insights*.

The topic order of these chapters reverses Outlook's left-to-right menu presentation on the assumption that the most commonly referenced commands will be actions on an item. Hence all chapters in Part 2 begin with the Actions menu; the remaining menus are discussed in an order that flows naturally with the content.

Outlook was designed primarily as an email client. The growing importance of email means you're likely to spend a lot of time working in Mail. In Chapter 5, *Mail Editors*, we covered aspects of Mail specific to editors: choosing and configuring an editor, message format options, tricks for addressing a message, stationery, etc. In this chapter we focus on the following menu commands that are Mail-specific and weren't covered in Chapter 5:

- *Actions* details mail management—creating and replying to messages, flagging messages for further action, finding messages with specific criteria, and marking junk messages.

- *Tools* focuses on the mail-specific entries found on Outlook's Tools menu, e.g., sending and receiving messages and creating mail rules to automatically manage your Inbox.

- *Edit* covers the commands for marking email messages as Read and Unread.

- *View* describes the preconfigured views Outlook provides for Mail folders, and how to use them to sort, filter, and group the data they contain.

Information about configuring mail accounts can be found in Chapter 2, *Installing Outlook*, along with technical details on mail protocols and message headers.

Mail

Mail → Actions Menu

The Actions menu, shown in Figure 6-1, contains commands for creating and responding to mail.

New Mail Message	Ctrl+N	
New Fax Message		
New Mail Message Using	▶	
Flag for Follow Up...	Ctrl+Shift+G	
Find All	▶	
Junk E-mail	▶	
Reply	Ctrl+R	
Reply to All	Ctrl+Shift+R	
Forward	Ctrl+F	

Figure 6-1: The Mail Actions menu

TIP # 59

Learn Mail's Shortcut Keys

It's worth the effort to learn Mail's principal keyboard shortcuts: New, Reply, Reply to All, and Forward. Creating and replying to email is primarily a keyboard task. Keeping your hands—and mind—focused here increases productivity dramatically. See Appendix A, Keyboard Shortcuts, for a list of Outlook's keyboard shortcuts.

Actions → New Mail Message

The New Mail Message command is one of the most commonly used commands in Outlook. For this reason, it can be invoked in one of several ways:

- From any Outlook component using the File → New → Mail Message command or the global keyboard shortcut Ctrl+Shift+M.

- With any mail folder selected (Inbox, Outbox, Sent Items, etc.) using the menu command Actions → New Mail Message, the keyboard shortcut Ctrl+N, or the New toolbar button.

- Double left-click in the empty space below the messages in any mail folder.

Depending on your choice of mail editor (Tools → Options → Mail Format), this command opens either a new message form (Figure 6-2, left) or Word's *mail.dot* template (Figure 6-2, right). See Chapter 5 for information on choosing and configuring a mail editor.

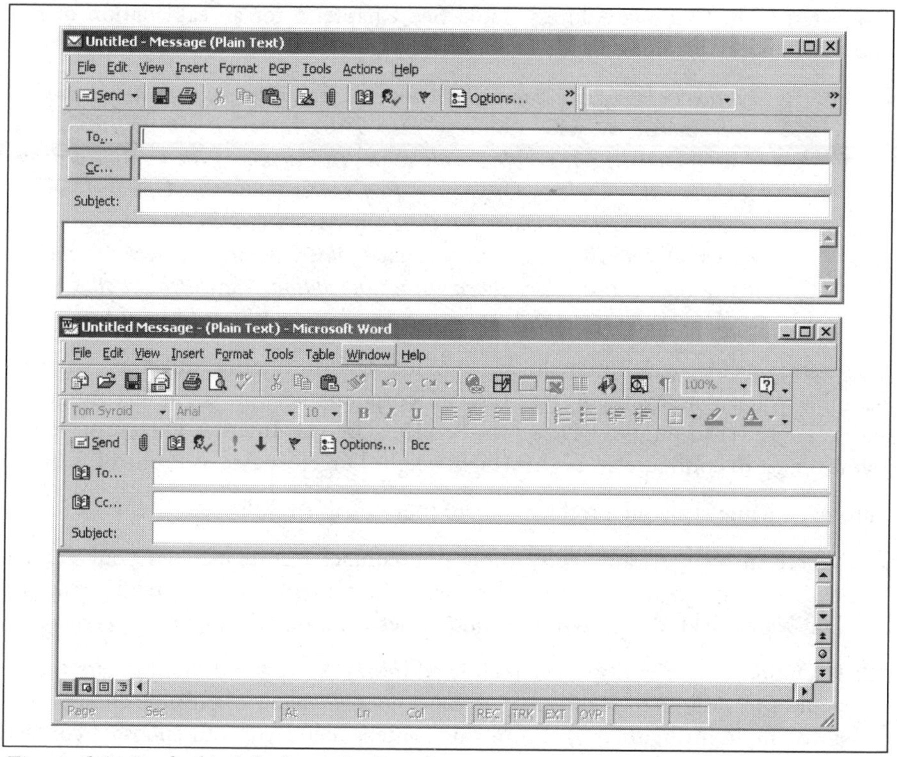

Figure 6-2: Outlook's default mail editor forms

All entry fields are initially blank (unlike when you Reply to a message) and include three header items plus the actual mail body:

> To: (recipient of the message)
> Cc: (carbon-copy recipients)
> Subject: (the subject of the message)
> Text: (the message body)

TIP # 60

Displaying the Bcc Field

Use the Bcc (Blind Carbon Copy) field to send a copy of a message to a recipient without allowing other recipients to see that the Bcc has received a copy. To display the Bcc field, use the View → Bcc Field command available from an open message form.

The Tab key moves forward one field; Shift+Tab moves back one field.

If Outlook is configured for "Automatic Name Checking" (Tools → Options → Preferences → E-mail Options → Advanced E-mail Options), addresses entered in the To, Cc, and Bcc fields are checked against the E-mail field of any Contact folder designated as an Outlook Address Book. See Chapter 3 for an explanation of the inner workings of Outlook's address books.

> **NOTE** *Outlook offers an option to have anyone you reply to via email automatically added to your Contacts file. This feature is controlled by the "Automatically put people I reply to in" checkbox and the associated droplist selection (Tools → Options → Preferences → E-mail Options). When enabled, the default folder for these entries is Contacts, but you have the option of specifying any existing contact folder. We strongly recommend not using the default folder when using this option—no entries should go in your Contacts folder that are not screened and confirmed by you first.*

These entry fields may optionally be checked against external directory services, assuming you can access them (e.g., on your corporate network). This is configured under Tools → Accounts → Directory Service. Use the Internet Directory Server Name dialog to configure an LDAP (Lightweight Directory Access Protocol) server.

Automatic name checking produces one of four possible results:

1. Where there is no ambiguity (only one contact record matches your entry), Outlook replaces the entered address with the contents of the matching record's Full Name field, designated by a solid underline under the name.

2. If Outlook finds multiple or unclear addresses, a wavy red line appears under your entry. Right-click the entry to see a context menu of possible choices (see an example in Figure 6-3). From this context menu you can choose a contact from the list displayed, create a new address for your entry, or open Outlook's Address Book.

3. If there are multiple addresses found for that contact, a green dashed line appears under your entry; the one shown was selected in a previous match. Select an alternative by right-clicking on the entry, as above.

4. If the email address you gave was not found but is in the correct URL format *name@domain.com*, Outlook assumes you entered a valid address.

Here are some practical examples to clarify your entry options:

- Typing one or two letters in an address field typically generates a large number of potential matches (indicated by a wavy red or green dashed line under your entry), but only when you tab out of the field. Right-clicking this entry opens a context menu similar to the one shown in Figure 6-3.

  Note that the entries displayed on this menu include names with the letters you've supplied (in this example, mi) anywhere in the name or email address. In addition, be aware that while this list includes company names, it is *not* generated by a search of the Full Name and Company fields—the list is generated by searching the File As field. This is another good reason to choose your Contact's Save As field wisely.

TIP # 61

Forced Lookup with Ctrl+K

Tabbing out of the To field and then reaching for your mouse to open a context menu is inefficient. As an alternative, type two or three letters in the address field, then select Ctrl+K. This opens a Check Names dialog with the same potential match list provided on the recipient context menu.

Aylmer Schmid
Bruce Kumitch
Fred & Betty Smith
Gordon Fleming
Hayes Microcomputer Products
Joe Smit
Juliana Aldous
MacMillian Publishing Canada
Midwest Detroit Diesel
Mike & Krys Van Arem
More...

Create New Address for "mi"...
Address Book...

Cut
Copy
Paste
Clear

Select All

Figure 6-3: The context menu displayed by right-clicking a name from an entered address, in this case, "mi"

- You correspond with Joe Smit several times a week, and Outlook remembers this fact. Typing Joe in an address field results in Outlook checking for the last "Joe" you sent a message to, filling in the field with this contact's full name, and underlining the entry in dashed green. To choose another Joe, right-click the name. If the name supplied is the correct one, simply send the message.

- Entering a full email address, tsyroid@home.com, forces Outlook to check your Address Book(s) for an exact match. If it finds one, this entry is replaced with the contact's full name, formatted with a solid underline (Tom Syroid). If no match is found, Outlook assumes that the address provided is correct and valid, and underlines it.

For more on address entry tricks, see the section "Addressing a Message" in Chapter 5.

TIP # 62

Enter New Addresses with Care

Any time you enter a new email address from a message field (To, Cc, or Bcc), be absolutely sure you have the correct spelling. This is especially important if you have Outlook set to automatically add new addresses to your contact file. A lack of attention to detail here may result not only in an undeliverable message, but perhaps also inaccurate records being added to your database.

Actions → New Fax Message

This command, which appears only if a Fax component is installed, is functionally equivalent to creating a mail message, but this command alerts Outlook to create it for the fax component and then dispatch it through your defined fax account (via fax modem) rather than SMTP. The "fax account" is a fictional mail account for the fax component similar to the ordinary fax driver routine that appears as an installed printer driver to other applications.

The fax component bundled with Outlook is currently Symantec Fax Starter Edition, and is only available under an IMO installation. It is possible to use the older Microsoft Fax component, by installing it as a service when running in Corporate Workgroup mode. In Windows 98, you can install the fax server (*awsnto32.exe*) from the following CD location: \tools\oldwin95\message\us.

Actions → New Mail Message Using

The New Mail Message Using submenu contains commands that give you complete control over the format and mail editor that Outlook uses for a new message.

In Chapter 5 we recommended that you use Outlook's default form-based editor and Plain Text for your everyday messaging needs. This combination gives you a capable editor that demands half the resources of Word, and sends your messages in a format readable by any email client. But using Word has advantages. It supports table creation, AutoCorrect, and automatic as-you-type spellchecking. For those messages that demand industrial strength editing, the Actions → New Mail Message Using menu is the place to be.

This submenu is shown in Figure 6-4. The contents of this menu are determined by your default message format (Tools → Options → Mail Format) and whether you installed Outlook as a standalone program or as part of the Office 2000 package.

Why is this menu so powerful? As an example, assume you have Outlook configured to use the default (forms-based) email editor set to HTML format. This avoids the high overhead of loading Word as your editor for routine correspondence, and allows you to create messages quickly and easily in a rich text format, usable by most

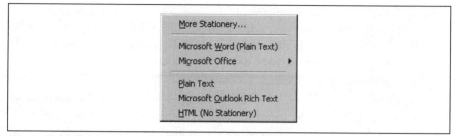

Figure 6-4: The Actions → New Mail Message Using submenu

of the people you correspond with. With the New Mail Message Using menu, you still have the option to:

- Create a quick email in Plain Text when the message has no need for HTML formatting (New Mail Message Using → Plain Text).

- Send a message to someone who prefers Rich Text format (New Mail Message Using → Microsoft Outlook Rich Text).

- Create a monthly budget projection using Excel, and if your company is standardized on the Office platform for all internal correspondence, send this to your boss in native format (New Mail Message Using → Microsoft Office → Microsoft Excel Worksheet).

And all without having to reconfigure your default mail editor.

The following is a list of the full range of menu options available for New Mail Message Using:

(Most recently used stationery template)
This is a context-dependent entry, which only appears when a stationery template has been selected previously; see next item.

More Stationery
Opens the Select a Stationery dialog, with a list of installed stationery (themes with background image and preselected fonts) and a preview pane for the currently selected list item.

> **NOTE** *See Chapter 5 for information on using, creating, and managing stationery.*

Note the button Get More Stationery. You might reasonably expect this to access further stationery files on the installation CD or from some other disk media, but this actually forces a connection (automatic dial-up if necessary) through your default browser to a Microsoft web site where you can download additional stationery files to your computer. Once this download is complete, those templates are registered on your system and available for selection from this dialog. Stationery templates can be useful for the odd special occasion email, but be warned that they quickly inflate the size of your messages. Also be aware: an email that uses stationery is an HTML document, and some people have mail clients that can't read a message in this format.

Microsoft Word (Default Message Format)

This command overrides your default editor settings, and opens a new message window using Word. The parentheses show the message format Word will use, which is determined by settings chosen under Tools → Options → Mail Format. For example, if your default message format is Plain Text, selecting this command opens a new message in Word using Plain Text. Unlike Outlook's default editor, there is no obvious way to change a message's format from Word. There is a baroque way, however. If, for example, your default message format is Plain Text, and you want to create a new HTML message using Word, take the following steps:

—   Use the Microsoft Office → Microsoft Word command discussed later in this list.

—   Enter a recipient and subject, and type your message in the body of the document.

—   Choose File → Save As, name your document, and select a file format from the "Save as type" drop-down list. Use the option Web Page for HTML.

—   Go to File → Send To and choose Mail Recipient or Mail Recipient (As Attachment). Click the Send a Copy command from the displayed toolbar.

Microsoft Office

This command presents a submenu list dependent on installed Office components. Figure 6-5 shows an example. Typical choices are Word (document), Excel (worksheet), PowerPoint (presentation), or Access (data page). Selecting any item on the list opens a new document window using the chosen application, with a mail header form displayed above the editing window.

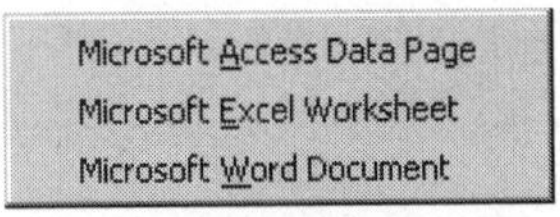

Microsoft Access Data Page
Microsoft Excel Worksheet
Microsoft Word Document

Figure 6-5: One example of the selections available from the Microsoft Office submenu

Plain Text

This opens a new message in the default mail editor (Word or Outlook), using Plain Text mode. Use this format if you are at all uncertain about what mail program recipients use, or what mail formats their program can handle. Plain Text is also the Outlook editor's default mail format.

Microsoft Outlook Rich Text
> This opens a new message window (Word or Outlook) in MS Rich Text mode. The Rich Text format is not as widely readable as Plain Text, but is readable by a wider range of older mail programs than HTML. Outlook Rich Text is the preferred format for sending messages to a recipient on an Exchange Server.

HTML (No Stationery)
> This starts your default mail editor in standard HTML mode, without stationery.

Actions → Flag for Follow Up

Setting a flag on a message item marks it for further action or follow-up. You can only flag one message at a time—the menu choice is unavailable if more than one item is selected. The menu entry is duplicated on the context menu for a single selected item. You may also use Ctrl+Shift+G.

The Flag for Follow Up command opens the dialog box shown in Figure 6-6.

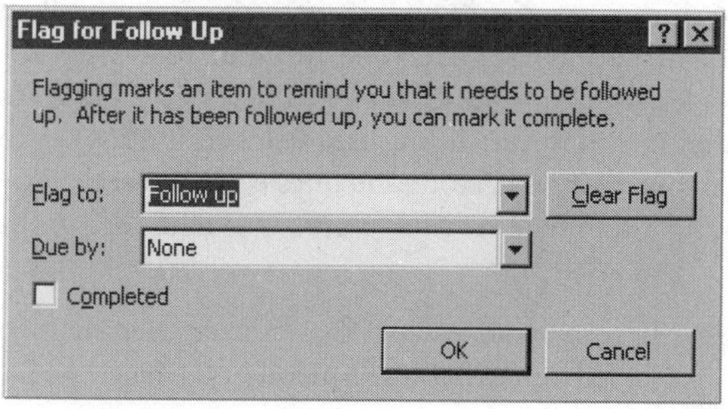

Figure 6-6: The Flag for Follow Up dialog

Here are some of the fine points of flagging a message:

- Pressing Enter or selecting the OK button in the dialog flags a message with the default values shown. The message is marked for "Follow up" and the due date set to "None."

- Selecting the drop-down list "Flag to" offers further choices for the flag type description. These are component-dependent, and for Mail include:

  Call
  Do not Forward
  Follow up (default selection)
  For your Information
  Forward
  No Response Necessary
  Read

Reply
Reply to All
Review

TIP # 63

Enter Your Own Flag Description

You are not restricted to the descriptions shown on the "Flag to" drop-down list. Simply type a description of your own choosing in the field, and it is assigned to the flag. We recommend entering meaningful descriptions whenever you flag a message. Remember, flags are meant as reminders, so the more detail you assign them at the time of creation, the easier it is to remember the reason for the flag later.

- The default selection "Follow up" suffices as a simple follow-up flag. However, being more specific in your initial selection provides you with a valuable resource if you later want to find, organize, or manipulate your messages based on the "Flag to" field.

- Selecting the drop-down list "Due by" presents a graphical calendar enabling you to choose a specific date and time for your follow-up. Clicking on a day inserts that date (and a default time of 17:00 hrs or 5 p.m.) into the "Due by" field. Note that like most intelligent date fields in Outlook, you can enter plain language date shortcuts here, along the lines of "next week" or "next Friday at 2 p.m." Assigning a due date to a flag pops up a reminder on the date and time entered.

- The Clear Flag button removes any flag from a selected message. This command is also available from the context menu of a flagged item.

- Setting the Completed check box retains the flag attached to the message, but changes the color of the flag icon beside the message from red to transparent, to indicate that it has been addressed. This command is also available from the context menu of a flagged item.

Taking the time to flag items pays off later. It transforms a simple list of messages into a powerful task-organization tool. In particular, it allows you to sort flagged items into numerous useful grouped and filtered views, far beyond what the simple visual cue of a red flag in the message might suggest. See the topics relating to flag views in the section "Mail → View Menu" later in this chapter.

Actions → Create Rule (Message Form Menu Only)

Outlook is hardcoded to place all incoming mail in your Inbox. If you receive 10 or 15 messages a day, this is not a problem. But if your Inbox fills faster than you can empty it, mail rules can help you manage the flow.

A mail *rule* checks messages as they arrive. Creating a rule defines what to do with the message based on conditions, actions, and exceptions. The Rules Wizard guides the mechanics of this configuration process. Manually configuring a rule is the topic of the "Tools → Rules Wizard" section later in this chapter.

Unfortunately, manually configuring a rule can not only be a complex process, but it's a hit and miss venture at times. You need to carefully select appropriate conditions and actions, as well as think through possible exceptions you want to account for. Thankfully, a little-known hidden command can help you create mail rules.

The Create Rule command is only found on the Actions menu of an open message form (and not on any of Word's menus when you use this program as your mail editor). When you invoke Create Rule, Outlook looks at the header and body of the message, and sets up a series of preconfigured conditions, actions, and exceptions based on the information it finds.

Figure 6-7 illustrates the conditions the Rules Wizard has automatically generated for an open message. From this introductory dialog, you can further define a rule as outlined in the "Tools → Rules Wizard" section later in this chapter.

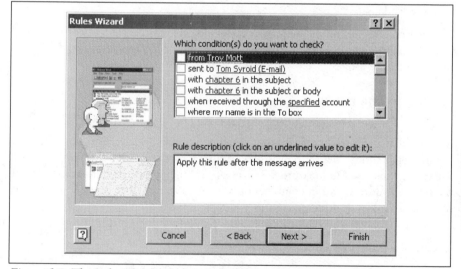

Figure 6-7: The Rules Wizard dialog invoked from an open message form

The key point to note with the Actions → Create Rule command is that it predefines the basics of a mail rule for you. In most cases, it provides you with the basis for a functioning rule that you can then tweak to precision.

Actions → Find All

Find All opens a submenu containing two options: Related Messages and Messages from Sender. Both commands open Outlook's Advanced Search form, the difference being in the preset search criteria each Command uses. While this search form is preconfigured with specific values, there's nothing crippled about the form—you are free to reset any field shown and to search for an item unrelated to the defaults.

 The Actions → Find All commands are preset to search specific folders for a preconfigured string of text. Using Advanced Find as a general search tool is detailed in Chapter 3.

Actions → Find All → Related Messages

The Related Messages command opens an Advanced Search form preconfigured to search the "subject field only" of all messages located in the Inbox, Drafts, or Sent Items folders, and find any messages that match the criteria of "Conversation is (exactly) subject."

Actions → Find All → Messages from Sender

Find All → Messages from Sender opens an Advanced Search form using preset options similar to Related Messages, but the criteria for this command is "From is (exactly) sender."

This option searches for all messages that exactly match the contents of the From field defined by the selected message's header. The Messages from Sender tab is shown in Figure 6-8.

Actions → Junk E-mail

Junk mail or *spam* is on the rise. Loosely defined, junk mail is any unsolicited message that arrives in your Inbox. Whether innocuous advertising or offensive "adult" solicitations, the fact remains you didn't ask for it and it's cluttering up your Inbox. Fortunately, Outlook provides a means to highlight such messages, based on the sender's address, and in combination with mail rules, either delete it directly or move it to a folder.

The Junk email options are activated from the Organize pane (Tools → Organize). The Junk E-mail tab is shown in Figure 6-9.

To configure Outlook to recognize an email as junk, begin by turning on the Junk and/or Adult Content rules with the buttons provided. Then select a message you consider to be typical of a junk message and apply the appropriate rules using the drop-down lists provided.

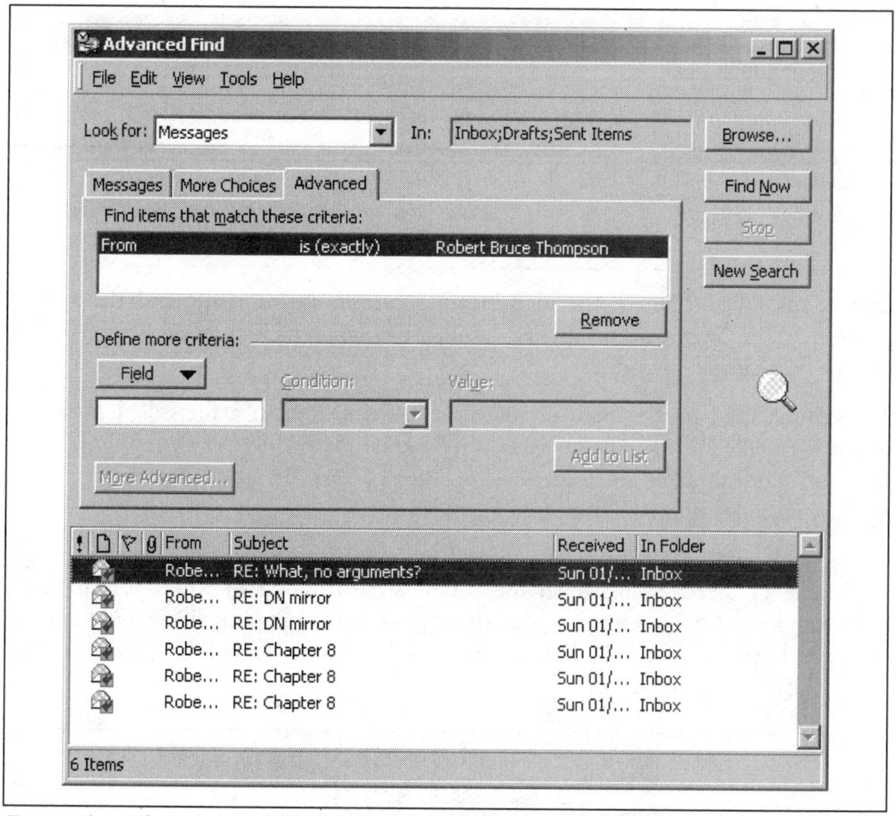

Figure 6-8: The Advanced Find form preconfigured to find all messages from a selected sender

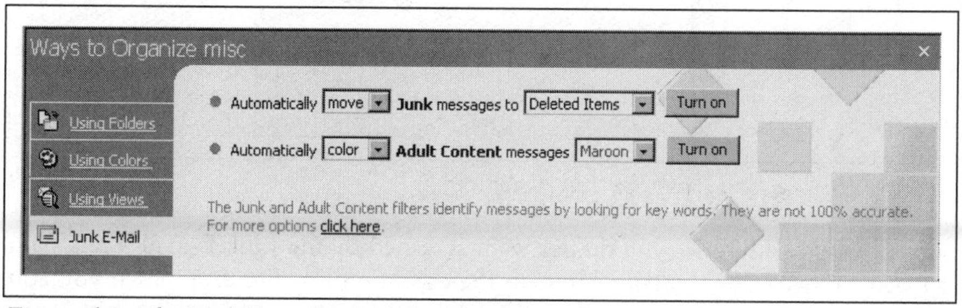

Figure 6-9: The Junk E-mail tab of the Organize tool

Coloring Junk Mail

Setting your junk email color to gray makes questionable messages appear faded but still visible enough to read, ensuring that important mail is not accidentally over-looked. The point of visually color-coding the junk items—rather than simply deleting them out of hand—is to allow you to skip, verify identification, or just delete a message, without having to read the mail's content.

After a rule is configured, the identification process is automatic and the appropriate marking or moving is applied to all subsequent mails received whose sender matches the sample provided.

The criteria used by the built-in filters are documented in a file called *filters.txt*, which is installed by default in *<drive>:\Program Files\Microsoft Office\Office*. You can also find updated information on these filters on the Web from *http://officeupdate.microsoft.com/Articles/newfilters.htm*.

Outlook also provides the means to add exceptions to your junk mail rules. To view, add, or delete items, open the Rules Wizard (Tools → Rules Wizard) and locate the Exception List entry in the upper pane of the opening dialog. Clicking on the underlined exception list link in the lower pane opens the Edit Exception List dialog shown in Figure 6-10.

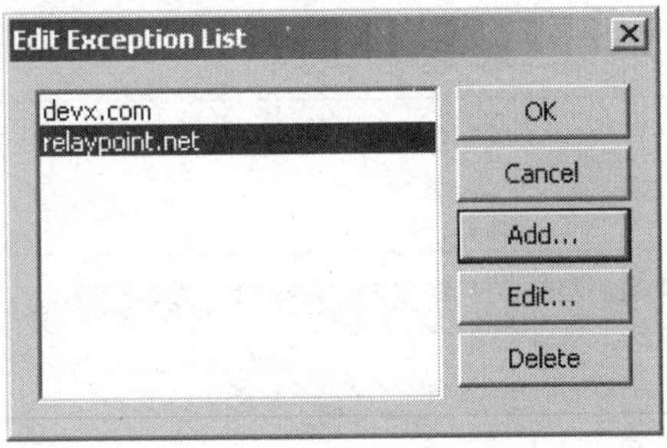

Figure 6-10: The Edit Exception List dialog

Enter the email addresses you do not want screened by the Junk E-mail filters. You can also add part of an email address to the exception list. For example, if you add the phrase host.domain.com, no email address containing *host.domain.com* will be filtered out. Thus, any email sent to you by user@host.domain.com, regardless of its subject, would not be flagged as junk email.

Actions → Junk E-mail → Add to Junk Senders List

This adds the selected email address to the junk list. Any subsequent messages arriving in your Inbox that match a sender added to this list are colored according to the options set in the Organize dialog.

Actions → Junk E-mail → Add to Adult Content Senders List

This adds an email sender's address to the Adult Contents list. Behavior here is identical to the Junk Senders List described previously, with the only exception being the color options set for Adult Content via the Organize pane.

To edit the contents of either your Junk or your Adult Content Senders List, open the Organize pane, click on Options, and from the new pane displayed select the Edit Junk/Adult Content Senders link. This opens a list-edit dialog as shown in Figure 6-11. From this dialog you can Add, Edit, or Delete list items.

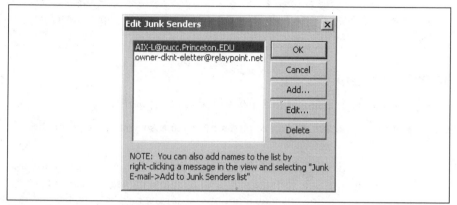

Figure 6-11: The Edit Junk Senders dialog

 There is an update link on the Junk mail filters Organize pane that claims to update your mail filters. In fact, all this link does is take you to a page on Microsoft's web site that explains the filters.txt file described at the start of this section.

Actions → Reply

This command is used to reply to a received message. When replying, a new mail window opens with the email address of the sender (using the Reply to header information, if present, and otherwise the From header) already in the To field. The subject of the message being replied to is included on the Subject line, prefaced by "RE:" (regarding, or in reference to).

Depending on your mail option settings (Tools → Options → E-mail Option, under the section "On replies and forwards"), the body of the message reply is either blank, or contains the text of the original message. When the original message text is included, the option settings determine if the original text is attached, included, included and indented, and any prefix (for example, ">") added to the beginning of each line. See Chapter 5 for details on setting message options.

Actions → Reply to All

The Reply to All command sends a response to everyone a message was addressed to, including recipients specified in the Cc field. Beyond this, Reply to All functions exactly like a reply.

TIP # 65

Check Your Message Header Before Replying

Before you select Reply or Reply to All, take a minute to check the message header. What you are replying to could be a Cc, a Bcc, or a forward. The original recipient of the message may have a bearing on the tone and style of reply you send, or if a reply is even necessary.

Actions → Forward

Forwarding a message is similar to Reply, with these exceptions:

- Forward does not fill in any recipients by default, so you must fill in the To, Cc, and Bcc fields yourself.

- You can forward multiple messages; neither the Reply nor Reply to All commands support multiple message selection. Multiple messages are forwarded as attachments, overriding any global options set for the format of replies and forwards.

- When a message is forwarded, attachments contained in the original are sent with the message. Attachments are not sent with a Reply. This last point is important: if you receive a document attached to an email that you want to send to someone, Forward is the only type of reply command that will do this.

 When multiple messages are selected for forwarding, they are sent as attachments to the new message. Some mail clients and mail account providers (notably AOL) do not handle multiple attachments properly.

Actions → Resend This Message (Message Form Menu Only)

Like the Create Rule command discussed earlier in this section, Resend This Message is only found on an open message form's Action menu—not Outlook's main Action menu (and not on any of Word's menus when you use this program as your mail editor).

There are numerous reasons that a sent message might be returned "Undeliverable":

- The recipient's email address could be wrong.

- There is a failure on the MT (message transfer) route. This could be a result of a mail server being down, a DNS server not responding, or a firewall failure.

• The recipient may have switched service providers, and therefore has a new email address.

First and foremost, examine the notification of delivery failure message, which often describes the problem specifically, for example:

```
550 <username@domain> … user unknown
```

which indicates that the recipient you entered does not exist, or:

```
Transient delivery failure…
Warning: message still undelivered after 4 hours
Will keep trying until message is 5 days old
```

which indicates a temporary problem in connectivity between your SMTP server and the recipient's SMTP server.

Often, the subject line of the delivery failure notification message provides enough information to deduce the cause of the failure, e.g., "Warning: could not send message for past 4 hours" or "Returned mail: User unknown." If the message indicates a problem with the address, double-check the recipient's address. Once you're sure the address is correct, open the message and use the Resend This Message command. If your message is returned a second time, you might want to wait before sending it again (see the second point in the preceding bulleted list) or make a phone call to ensure the address you are using is correct.

TIP # 66

Finding the Cause of "Undeliverable"

When you receive an undeliverable message, it is prefaced with a paragraph explaining the (possible) cause of the failure. Read this information carefully. If you see the text "mailserver.com not found," this tells you the recipient's mail server is not accessible—but not why.

Mail → Tools Menu

The Tools menu, shown in Figure 6-12, contains several cross-component commands discussed at length in other chapters.

Detailed discussions of Address Books, Find, Advanced Find, Organize, and Forms can be found in Chapter 3. Macros are discussed in Chapter 18, *Working with VBA*, and creating and modifying Accounts is detailed in Chapter 2. Program options are examined throughout the book where appropriate.

If Outlook is installed as a Corporate/Workgroup client (CW), your Tools menu will contain additional commands specific to installed connectivity options. The Synchronize, Remote Mail, and Out of Office Assistant commands configure their respective options or features for an Exchange Server account.

```
                    Send
                    Send/Receive                    ▶

            📖 Address Book...        Ctrl+Shift+B

            📑 Find
                    Advanced Find...      Ctrl+Shift+F
            🔍 Organize

            📩 Rules Wizard...
            📁 Empty "Deleted Items" Folder

                    Forms                            ▶
                    Macro                            ▶

                    Accounts...
                    Customize...
                    Options...
```

Figure 6-12: The Tools menu (IMO installation with a direct Internet connect)

 NOTE *The topic of Outlook as a client for Exchange could easily fill a book in itself. We touch on several important troubleshooting and configuration issues in Chapter 17, Outlook and Exchange, so we refer you there for further insights.*

The first topics of the "Mail → Tools Menu" section cover the Send and Send/Receive commands. These are followed by a detailed explanation of creating and modifying mail rules.

Tools → Send

Choosing Tools → Send causes Outlook to check the Outbox for any pending messages and sends them to the appropriate account.

If you have multiple accounts configured, selecting Send, Send/Receive → All Accounts or Send/Receive → *account* causes Outlook to automatically switch your connection as required. In these situations, you *should* see the warning dialog shown in Figure 6-13. If you don't, you can re-enable this warning by going to the Dial-up Options tab (Tools → Options → Mail Delivery) and selecting the "Warn before switching dial-up connection" checkbox.

This dialog displays your current active connection and presents you with two choices plus a disable warning checkbox:

Hang up and dial account
> Disconnects from the current account and attempts to establish a new connection as defined in the specified account's dial-up properties (Tools → Accounts → *account* → Properties → Connection).

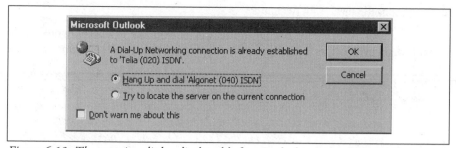

Figure 6-13: The warning dialog displayed before Outlook switches from one active connection to another

Try to locate the server on the current connection
> Keeps the current connection active and tries to authenticate you with another server. This will not always prove successful—see the sidebar "'Deny Relay' Explained" for the reasons why.

Don't warn me about this
> Use with care. Whatever behavior you select now becomes the automatic response in future situations of this kind.

If you want to send only those messages meant for a particular mail server (thus potentially preserving an active connection), use Send/Receive and select the appropriate account from the submenu.

TIP # 67
Why Send Only?

Use the Send command in situations when you either need to send a message quickly to free a phone line, or when you know you have mail with attachments waiting but the quality of connection speed would make the download a painful process.

Tools → Send/Receive

Outlook doesn't have a "Receive Only" command, just the combined Send/Receive command. To manually check your accounts for new mail, you have three choices:

- The menu command Send/Receive → All Accounts.

- The keyboard shortcut F5 or the toolbar button Send/Receive; both options are functionally equivalent to the "All Accounts" menu command.

- The menu command Send/Receive → *Account*, which allows you to select an individual account.

The following sections describe these Send/Receive commands and how they differ.

Tools → Send/Receive → All Accounts

Tools → Send/Receive → All Accounts attempts to connect to all configured mail accounts that have the "Include this account in Send and Receive All" setting selected.

 To edit the "Include this account in Send and Receive All" property of an account under IMO Outlook, go to Tools → Accounts, and select the account. Click Properties, select the General tab from the resultant dialog, and select or deselect the checkbox as required. In a CW configuration, the correct dialog is accessed via the Tools → Options → Internet E-Mail tab.

With each successful account connection, Outbox messages for that account are sent, and messages are retrieved and placed in your Inbox. With the Tools → Send command, active connections may be terminated, possibly without warning, in order to establish new connections to check your other accounts.

Tools → Send/Receive → Account List (user specific)

Under the Send/Receive command is a list of all defined mail accounts. Selecting one initiates a connection to that service, followed by a Send/Receive session for that account.

Selecting Send/Receive for an individual account is useful when you have several mail accounts that you don't check every day. For such accounts, de-select the "Include this account in Send and Receive All" and check them manually using the Send/Receive → Account command.

> **WARNING**
>
> *Closing Outlook in the middle of a mail check could hang the program. Always ensure Outlook is finished sending and receiving mail before exiting the program.*

Tools → Send/Receive → Free/Busy Information (context specific)

Tools → Send/Receive → Free/Busy Information forces an update of your Free/Busy data. Setting up, configuring, and using Outlook's Free/Busy feature is discussed in Chapter 14, *Collaborating with Outlook*.

Tools → Rules Wizard

Rule-based sorting is an important feature in any mail client. It allows you to automatically sort and manage large volumes of mail by applying conditional rules to incoming messages. These rules can be simple ("Move all mail arriving from Joe Smith to my Followup folder") or complex ("Move all mail arriving from Joe Smith to my Followup folder if X is in the subject line and it is not CCed to Mary Smith"). The simplest and most effective way to construct a mail rule is to think about what you want to manipulate and how, then write it down. If you can put a rule into words and the appropriate destination folders, conditions, and actions exist in Outlook, then you can create that rule.

"Deny Relay" Explained

In response to a flood of junk email, ISPs are configuring their mail servers to deny *email relaying*. This term is a misnomer, and originates from the old days when messages were relayed from one server to the next until they reached their destination. Today, most messages are sent directly from the source server to the destination server.

In simple terms, *deny relay* means you can't send mail to an SMTP server without first being authenticated. This authentication may be enforced in several ways:

- Addresses (or domains) of known mass mailers are blocked at the mail server.

- A server can be configured to deny access to any address except the one associated with the user's account.

- The SMTP server can be configured to validate the "From" address of a sent message against a POP server.

- The SMTP server can be configured to refuse access to any user not connected to the local network of which the server is a member. That is, you may be able to use your ISP's SMTP server only if you are dialed in to the ISP directly rather than accessing the server across the Internet.

- The SMTP server can be configured to use "SMTP-after-POP" authentication, which allows a user, once authenticated via POP, to send messages via the SMTP server for some limited time.

What does all this mean? If you have more than one email account, you might have to disconnect from one before you can send or receive mail from the other.

TIP # 68

For Novice Rule Makers

If you are new at creating mail rules, the wealth of options provided by the Rules Wizard can be overwhelming. For this reason, we suggest you get a feel for the process by using the option discussed earlier in this chapter under the topic Actions → Create Rule. This command automates much of the creation process for you, based on an open message. Once a rule is created, you can tweak it using the many conditions, actions, and exceptions available from the Rules Wizard proper.

Rules impose only minor performance penalties in mail processing in return for automated message handling, so use them when appropriate. Experiment with care though, as a permanently deleted message is gone forever. One way around this is to create a "holding" folder for messages you want to delete with a rule. Your rule can send messages to this folder, where you preview them prior to deletion. If the behavior of the rule over time is as expected, then you can modify the rule to delete messages instead of moving them.

The Tools → Rules Wizard command opens the dialog shown in Figure 6-14. Defined rules are displayed in the upper pane. Rules that are active are checked. Selecting a rule displays its description in the lower pane. The description provides details on what the rule does, and the conditions that trigger it. Clicking on an underlined value allows you to edit it via the same dialogs used to define the value originally.

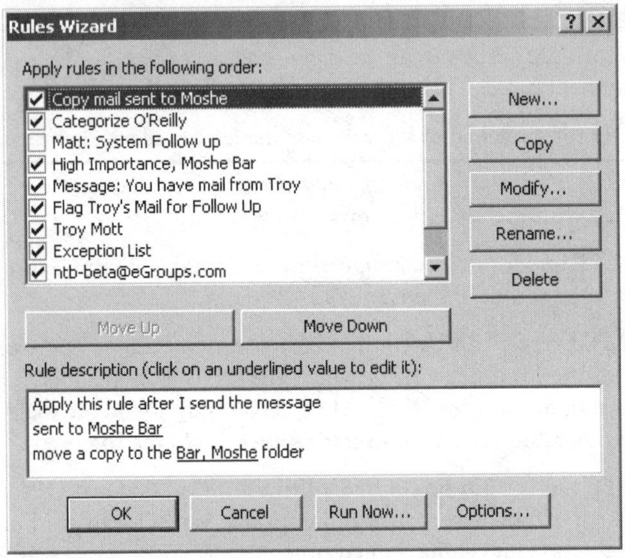

![Rules Wizard dialog]

Figure 6-14: The Rules Wizard dialog

NOTE *Using the upper right X (Close) button is equivalent to canceling a rule creation or edit, and discards all changes. A newly created rule is only saved when you exit the Rules Wizard using the OK button.*

Rules can be applied to incoming messages, outgoing messages, and existing messages stored in any Mail folder. While most rules are applied automatically, it is also possible to manually apply a rule. Some practical rule examples appear at the end of this section.

The buttons on the right edge of the Rules Wizard dialog invoke the following functions:

New
Starts the Rules Wizard and the process of creating a new rule.

Copy
Creates a copy of an existing rule, which you can modify for a different purpose. This is a very important command, and serves two purposes: (1) it allows you to use an existing, proven rule as the basis for a new rule, and (2) it allows you to make a backup copy of an existing rule before you modify it.

Modify
> Starts the Rules Wizard, allowing you to edit a selected rule.

Rename
> Renames an existing rule.

Delete
> Deletes an existing rule.

Move Up and Move Down
> Changes the processing order of defined rules. This order can be critical, because rules are applied in the order in which they appear. It also allows you to intentionally disable a sequence of rules by placing the "Stop processing all the following rules" rule ahead of them.

TIP # 69

Back Up your Rules

Always make a backup copy of a rule before you modify it. Stuff happens, and it's easy to revert back to a saved copy if things go awry. It is also a good idea to ensure you have a backup copy of your entire current rule set tucked away on floppy somewhere safe (Rules Wizard → Options → Export). It can take months of trial and error to build a good set of mail rules—protect your investment.

At the bottom of the Rules Wizard dialog are the Run Now and Options buttons:

Run Now
> Calls up the "Run Rules Now" subdialog, allowing you to select one or more rules for execution. This dialog contains options to specify which folder and which messages to apply the rule(s) on (All Messages, Read Messages, or Unread Messages). This process may be repeated as many times as necessary before closing the dialog.

Options
> Opens a subdialog allowing you to export rules to files or import rules to append to the existing list. This allows you to create named rule sets and backup files (*.rwz*).

To begin creating a new rule, click on the New button and the wizard guides you through the necessary steps. The following sections detail each of the dialogs involved in building a rule: Selecting the rule Type, applying Conditions, defining Actions, specifying Exceptions, and naming/testing. You may move freely between the dialogs with the Next and Back buttons, refining and modifying details until you are satisfied.

Underlined words in the Rule description pane are variables that link to subdialogs where you can set or edit the specific values used by a rule. Undefined, these words are simply descriptive placeholders (underlined blue); otherwise they show the current values (underlined black) that the rule uses.

Mail

The variables that define a rule can take on one or more of the following values:

Names

A name (an email address or distribution list) selected from the Rule Address subdialog, which gives a list of names based on contacts files, and a simple find function. You may add any number of names to the list (right-click on a selection to remove a name from the rule). To specify a name not in your contacts list, you must create a new contact entry, which you can do from this subdialog.

Folders

A single destination or source folder is selected from a subdialog that shows the Outlook folder tree. If the folder does not exist, create it from this subdialog.

Fields

A predefined field value is assigned to a triggered action. Depending on the rule type/action/condition used, these actions can include: a Flag assignment, category assignment, notification messages, importance or sensitivity flags, a response by form or template, or the execution of a program.

Words

A word or phrase list. Conditions are often based on a search for words or phrases in a specified field or in the body of a message. These comparisons are performed as a simple logical "and" of the list provided, in no particular order.

All values must contain valid entries before a rule is considered complete; only then can it be saved to your list. A new rule is not saved until the Rules Wizard is exited using the OK button.

Tools → Rules Wizard (Type)

The first step in creating a rule is to choose a rule type. Figure 6-15 shows the first of four dialogs displayed by the Rules Wizard. Selecting a rule type from the list provided copies its description to the lower pane. Some of the rule types offered are simple checks ("Check messages when they arrive"); others are a predefined set of checks, conditions, and actions ("Apply this rule after . . . from . . . move it to . . .").

TIP # 70

Quick Rule-Making

Several of Outlook's simpler rule types can be defined directly from the first dialog of the Rules Wizard. One example is the "Move new messages from someone" rule. Select it, then choose a sender and a folder to move the message to. "Finish" automatically assigns your rule a name based on the sender, and even turns it on for you.

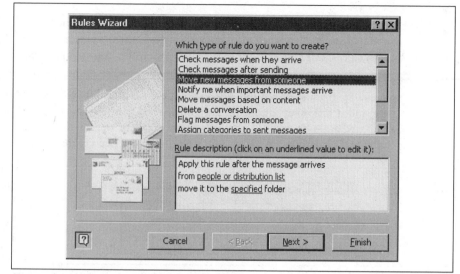

Figure 6-15: The Rules Wizard rule type dialog

The following is a list of the rule types available:

Check messages when they arrive or after sending

Outlook applies mail rules from two starting points: items received and items sent. The former is the starting point for most of the rules to follow, but you can also apply a rule to outgoing messages.

Move new messages from someone

This rule checks the mail header of arriving messages and moves messages from a specified sender to a specified folder.

Notify me when important messages arrive

The first trigger for this rule is if the To field of an arriving message contains the same name used by the E-mail Address field for Outlook's default mail account (Options → Tools → Accounts). If it does, and the importance of the message matches the value used to define the rule, a user-specified notification message is displayed.

Move messages based on content

Checks the subject and body of arriving messages for specific words or phrases. A match triggers a move based on this content. Unless you can provide some very specific phrases, the effectiveness of such a rule varies. Consider using a rule with a narrower search focus.

 If you receive a lot of large messages, rules that check for content can dramatically slow Outlook's processing of incoming mail.

Delete a conversation

> This is similar to a *spam* filter (see "Actions → Junk E-mail"). If specified words occur in the subject field, the message is moved to the Deleted Items folder. Use this rule with care, specifying a unique subject line pattern for known junk email.

Flag messages from someone

> Arriving messages from specified individuals (or a distribution list) are assigned a Flag type and a follow-up due date. Assigning a value of "0" days opens a reminder immediately on arrival. This rule is an excellent option for priority messages that can be defined by simply knowing the sender (see Figure 6-16).

Figure 6-16: The rule-based Flag Message dialog

Assign categories to sent messages

> Here's another powerhouse rule. Users always complain that they don't have time to categorize messages—so have Outlook do it for you! With this rule you automatically assign a category to any messages sent to a specified contact.

> *Be careful assigning categories with rules. There is no pick-list or access to the Master Category List from the dialog used to assign a category to a rule. This implies that you will need to know the exact spelling of the category you enter here, or risk not having it available to other Outlook components. For an explanation of the implications here, see the "The Power of Categories" in Chapter 3.*

Assign categories based on content

> This rule works on received items. You define one or more categories to assign to a message based on specific words found in the subject or body text fields.

Move messages I send to someone

> This rule acts on messages sent to a defined recipient and moves a *copy* of your reply to a specified folder; the original goes to the Outbox. By default, Outlook places a copy of all sent messages in the Sent Items folder. Using separate folders to archive messages received from people you routinely correspond with is a good organization strategy (see Chapter 13, *File Management*). Using this rule, you can automatically copy your message replies to these same folders as well.

Stop processing all the following rules

> This terminates further rules processing in the list. Rules are disabled by moving them below the "stop processing" rule, and reactivated by moving them

up into the active section of the list. You can manually run disabled rules at any time from the opening dialog of the Rules Wizard (select and Run Now).

Tools → Rules Wizard (Conditions)

The Conditions dialog of the Rules Wizard is shown in Figure 6-17. From this dialog you define further conditions to the actions discussed in previous sections. Depending on the rule type you chose at the beginning of the creation process, you may already have a fully defined rule in place. If so, click Next or Finish.

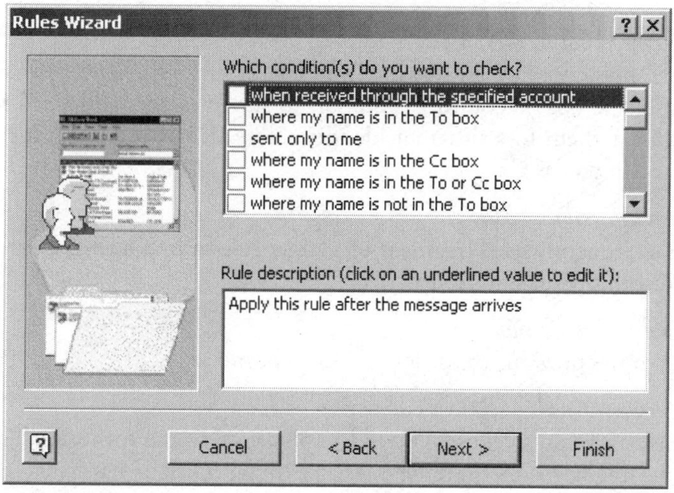

Figure 6-17: The Rules Wizard conditions dialog

> **NOTE** *Finish names the rule for you, based on values specified, and automatically turns it on. We do not recommend this approach. Use Next to advance to the final dialog, and name the rule manually with a name that is meaningful to you, not Outlook. Then, if possible, test the rule.*

The exact order of conditions shown is context-dependent on the chosen rule. In addition, a particular rule may already have selected and specified some conditions. The full list is:

When received through the specified account
This condition acts on a message received through a specified mail account. You might, for example, want to sort all messages received from your corporate account in different ways than those received via your private home account.

Where my name is in the To box
Actions depend on your name being found in the To field. This does not necessarily mean you are the only addressee, since there may be more than one recipient specified.

Sent only to me
> Addressed to you, with no Cc specified or any other names in the To field. This narrows the previous condition to you, and you only.

Where my name is in the Cc box
> The message is addressed as a copy to you; someone else is the main recipient. This condition is a way to filter or collect some kinds of broadcast or list mail.

Where my name is in the To or Cc box
> Apply the current rule to any message that is addressed to you, directly or indirectly.

Where my name is not in the To box
> Traps all messages not addressed to you (the inverse of "Where my name is in the To or Cc box"). Use this condition to sort messages addressed to an alias and redirect them to a different identity. Note that it implicitly includes mail addressed to you as Cc.

From people or distribution list
> This is a frequently used fragment of a larger rule to trap messages arriving from a specified individual or group.

Sent to people or distribution list
> Similar to the previous condition; it tests sent messages.

With specific words in the recipient's address
> Use this condition to specify a word or phrase to search for in the To field. An example might be to examine messages directed to a particular domain or subdomain, no matter who is listed as the recipient.

With specific words in the sender's address
> Similar to the previous condition; it searches the sender's address field for a specified word or phrase with `specific words` in the subject. Specify which words to search for in the Subject field. Trigger words are often used in subject lines to encourage placing a message in a particular category, defined by the recipient. "Urgent" is a trivial example. "Secret XYZ list" is a less obvious one.

With specific words in the body
> You may specify which words to search for in the message text.

With specific words in the subject or body
> This is a combined form of the two preceding conditions. Again, we remind you that invoking searches of a message body can dramatically slow the receipt of incoming mail.

With specific words in the message header
> This search includes all the fields in the header, even those not mentioned elsewhere, e.g., Reply-to, or X-mailer (sending client identification). Use this condition when your filtering is contingent on a word or phrase hidden in the message header.

Flagged for action

This applies to any Flag for Follow Up setting in the message. The default test is for "any" flag, but the subdialog allows you to select a specific flag type. This condition depends on previously assigning suitable flag types.

Marked as importance

This checks for the priority setting in the message, i.e., Low, Normal, or High importance. The main problem here is that you are dependent on the sender's sense of appropriate importance.

Marked as sensitivity

This checks for the sensitivity setting in the message, i.e., Normal, Personal, Private, or Confidential. See caveat noted for the previous condition.

Assigned to category

This finds messages assigned to the specified category or categories. This condition is typically used in rules created to act on messages already received and assigned a category.

Which is an Out of Office message

Incoming messages are checked for this status, and typically moved to another folder or deleted. Out of Office messages are a specific kind of auto response generated by Exchange Server. See Chapter 17.

Which has an attachment

Any messages with one or more attachments satisfy this condition. You may want to consider creating a rule that moves all messages containing attachments to a separate information store (PST). This store could then be scanned with an anti-virus program before any of the attachments were opened.

With selected properties of documents or forms

This condition allows you to match field contents specific to Word documents or HTML forms. The initial subdialog (see Figure 6-18) applies to Word documents, and lets you select named Word document fields to test (from a convoluted button and submenu construction: Field → Document fields → selection). The test conditions are formulated as field + condition + value, each defined in its own entry field, and then added to the list "Match these criteria" to specify the complete test to apply. Examples might be "Keyword contains proposal" or "Creation Time after 2/8/2000." The alternate selection path from the button Field leads to another subdialog (Field → Forms → Select Forms), which is described later in the corresponding specific condition "Uses the form name form."

With a size in the specified range

Clicking on the range link calls up a subdialog allowing you to specify the size range in kilobytes that satisfies this condition, from "at least" to "at most." If the latter remains at zero, the range is assumed open-ended from "at least." This

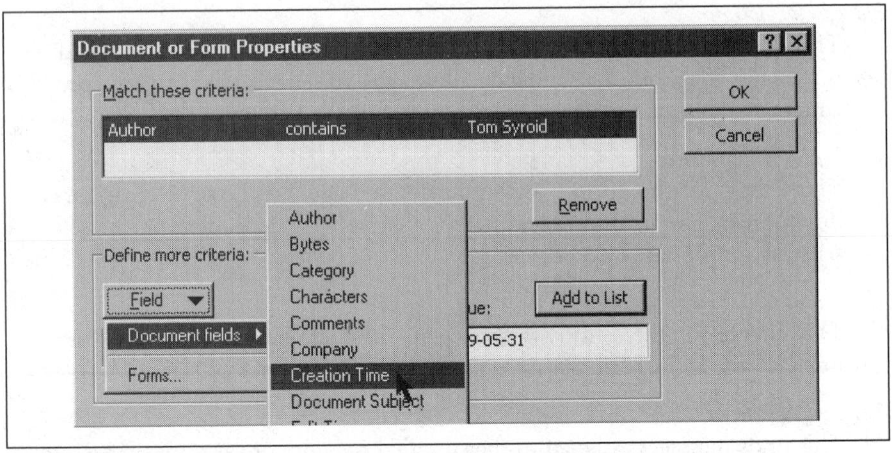

Figure 6-18: The rule conditions dialog for document properties

later condition applies to messages containing large attachments you want handled in a specific way, e.g., stored on an external drive or network file server.

Received in a specified date span

Clicking on the range link calls up a subdialog allowing you to specify the date range that satisfies this condition, based on "after" or "before." The range can be an open-ended or a fully-bounded interval, depending on the fields activated by the corresponding checkbox. The default date shown is the current system date (i.e., "today"). The date fields here are at least partly intelligent in that they accept date entry as well as some intuitive Plain Text input variants of the type "yesterday," "Tuesday last week," and so on.

Uses the form name form

This is a direct selection that corresponds to the Forms subdialog found under the condition "With selected properties of documents or forms," described earlier. The "Uses the *form name* form" condition specifies forms that can be selected from the source lists Inbox, Personal Forms, or Application Forms. Creating, modifying, and managing forms is detailed in Chapter 3.

Suspected to be junk email or from Junk Senders

This condition traps messages that either come from senders on the Junk E-mail list (see the description of this in the "Mail → Actions Menu" section), or have text content that matches messages previously selected as representative of some form of junk email.

Containing adult content or from Adult Content Senders

This condition is similar to the Junk Senders condition, except the Adult Content list is used.

Tools → Rules Wizard (Actions)

When you are done with Conditions, it is time to move on to desired Actions, some of which may already be defined and configured in the previous step. The possible Actions to apply to a message are:

Move it to the specified folder
You specify the destination folder.

Move a copy to the specified folder
Sorry—we didn't write the conditions, Microsoft did. To interpret: *moving a copy* means the original message remains where it is, and a copy is created and moved to the specified folder.

Delete it
Moves a message to the Deleted Items folder. The settings for this folder (Tools → Options → Other tab → "Empty the Deleted Items folder upon exiting") determine when deleted messages are permanently removed from Outlook's information store.

Permanently delete it
The message is erased, not moved to the Deleted Items folder. Use if you are sure that this rule selects messages you *never* want to see, because they will be really and truly, irrevocably gone. Instantly. Use this action with extreme caution.

Forward it to people or distribution list
This rule automates the forwarding of a message to another recipient or Distribution List. When triggered, a Forward form opens allowing you to edit the original message before it is sent.

 Be very careful not to create a mail loop, for instance, by creating a rule that forwards all mail from list@provider.com to list@provider.com.

Forward it to people or distribution list as an attachment
This is similar to the previous rule, except the message is forwarded as an attachment rather than text inserted in the new message body.

Print it
Messages that satisfy the conditions attached are sent to the printer.

Reply using a specific template
This is an important rule, because it allows you to generate automatic replies to specific messages (creating message templates is discussed in Chapter 3). Such automated replies can vary, from just a courteous "message received and I will respond ASAP" to "I am exploring Aztec pyramids and won't be back in the office until November 3."

Notify me using a specific message

This rule generates a pop-up notification containing user-specified text displayed in the top pane of the dialog, and a reference to the message below this (see Figure 6-19).

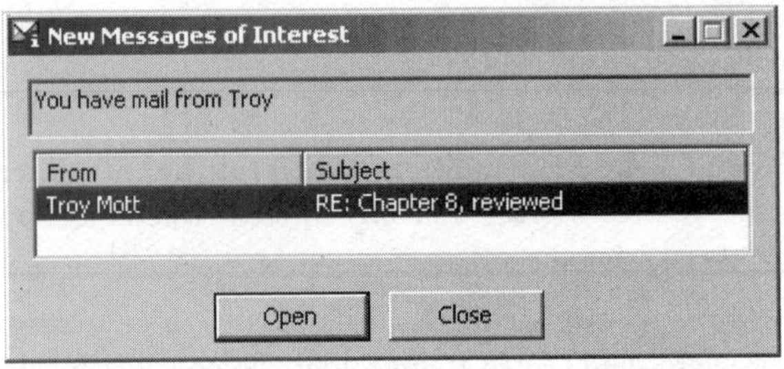

Figure 6-19: Rules generated New Message of Interest

Any of the conditions of this section can be used to trigger this notification (for example: from *person*, with High importance, containing *text* in the subject line). This is a useful rule for trapping and alerting you to the arrival of messages that require immediate attention.

Flag message for action in a number of days

This sets a Follow Up Flag on a triggered message. A flag type should be specified, along with a specific due date. See the section "Actions → Flag for Follow Up" earlier in this chapter for details on flagging messages.

Clear the Message Flag

This clears the Follow Up flag for any messages that satisfy the conditions applied. Flags can normally only be modified or cleared on an item-by-item basis, so this rule provides the user with the means to "batch-process" a group of flagged messages. Note, however, that clearing a Follow Up flag destroys any indication that the flag was ever set or why. Changing flag status to "done" is usually better than automated clearing.

Assign it to the category

Messages that satisfy the conditions are assigned the specified categories. This is a powerful way to automate category assignment, plus manage mail flow— assign category z to messages from Troy with a subject line containing OL2K and then move them to this folder.

See the note earlier in this section regarding working with rules and categories.

Play a sound

This allows you to assign a sound to a message meeting certain criteria. For example, you could select a "you have mail" sound file to play whenever a message is received addressed directly to you. Any available .*wav* format file can be selected using the standard file selector. (There is no "preview" function

here, so you may want to locate available files for suitability using the Control
Panel applet Sounds first.)

Working Together on Successful Mail Flow

*The key to successful mail management is communicating your needs to those people
with whom you routinely correspond. The simple agreed-upon convention of prefacing topic specific messages (for example, prefaced with an all-caps word) simplifies
rule creation, and allows you to better manage priorities.*

Start application

Specify any executable file (*.com, .bat, .exe*) or file associated with any application, to start the application on receipt of specifically addressed or formatted
messages. *Use this action with care!* Allowing a remote message to automatically
start an application on your system opens you to a host of unsafe possibilities.

Mark it as importance

Messages are assigned the specified importance level when previous conditions
are met. A simple example is to force Low importance to messages received
from your boss, and High to messages from his secretary, if that's the way it
plays at your place of business. Another example could be to raise the importance of messages from a client or coworker during a critical time in a project.

Perform a custom action

Custom actions are additional features provided by third-party programs that
can hook into Outlook functionality. These are selected from a subdialog list.
Outlook does not itself include any custom actions so the list is initially empty.

Stop processing more rules

This is a conditional version of the rule by the same name. When the conditions specified are satisfied by a message, this terminates further rules processing
on that message. This is useful in more complex rule structures, such as
defining special exceptions.

Tools → Rules Wizard (Exceptions)

After Actions, the normal order of specifying rules in the wizard is to define any
exceptions to the rule produced so far. If no exceptions are needed, then the rule is
complete and you can skip to the next section. The Exceptions listed are the logical
negatives of the Conditions, specifying when *not* to apply the current rule:

Except if sent directly to me

Do not apply the rule to messages sent with your email address in the To field.

Except if sent only to me

Do not apply the rule if you are the only recipient of a message. In the previous
exception, there may be other recipients specified.

Except where my name is in the Cc box
> Exclude any message sent to you as a copy. This exception is true even if you are specified in both the To and Cc box.

Except where my name is in the To or Cc box
> This excludes any message directed to you—directly in the To field or indirectly as a copy.

Except where my name is not in the To box
> Exclude any message not sent directly to you.

Except if from people or distribution list
> You specify which senders or distribution lists cause the rule not to be applied.

Except if sent to people or distribution list
> You specify the recipient identities or distribution lists that keep the rule from being applied.

Except when received through the specified account
> The rule is not applied to mail received through the specified account.

Except with specific words in the recipient's address
> Exclude messages when the specified words match anything in the recipient's address field, for example, messages addressed to you using a particular email identity or address.

Except with specific words in the sender's address
> When you wish to exclude messages based on some part of the sender's address, such as all messages from a particular origin domain, specify it here.

Except if the subject contains specific words
> Exclude messages based on a match with specified words in the subject field, which is normally a test for a topic or special "attention words," possibly messages directed to lists or automated message functionality.

Except if the body contains specific words
> This tests for any match of the words provided in the message body, which would be a very loose way to exclude a message.

Except if the subject or body contains specific words
> This exception combines the two previous tests in one, and is consequently even broader in scope, but useful when trigger words can be expected in either the subject or the body.

Except if the message header contains specific words
> Word matching is here applied to any one of the message's header fields, even those not normally visible. Compare with the corresponding Condition.

Except if it is flagged for action
> Again, this is the opposite of the corresponding Condition, applicable when you wish to exclude a message from this rule with a specific type of flag.

Except if it is marked as importance
Messages with the specified importance level are not affected by the current rule. The level may be set by the sender, or by you after receiving the message.

Except if it is marked as sensitivity
Messages with the specified sensitivity level are not included in the selection for this rule.

Except if it is assigned to category
Messages assigned to the specified category or categories are excluded.

Except if it is an Out of Office message
Do not apply rule to messages that are Out of Office messages. See the condition of the same name for more details.

Except if it has an attachment
Do not apply rule to messages that have attachments.

Except with selected properties of documents or forms
A message is not processed by the rule when it is a document or form containing the field contents or based on the named form specified in the respective match criteria.

Except with a size in a specific range
Exclude a message from this rule if it is larger or smaller than the size limits specified. The range may be open-ended or bounded.

Except if received in a specific date span
Exclude message if it is received after or before the specified dates. The date range may be open-ended or bounded on both ends.

Except if it uses the form name
This is a special case of the more general document properties condition, where messages based on the form name provided are excluded.

Tools → Rules Wizard (Name)

Now your rule is defined. The final Rules Wizard dialog, shown in Figure 6-20, lets you specify a name for the rule, select an immediate run of the rule on Inbox messages, enable (or disable) the rule, and complete a final review of the rule description.

The Finish button creates the rule, adds it to the bottom of the current rules list, and closes the dialog. Use the Back button to return to various points in the rule creation process to make additions or modifications.

The following two practical examples summarize this lengthy rule creation section.

The first example assumes that you have two email accounts, one through your place of business and one for personal correspondence. Email received via the former almost always has to do with business matters, and the home account always

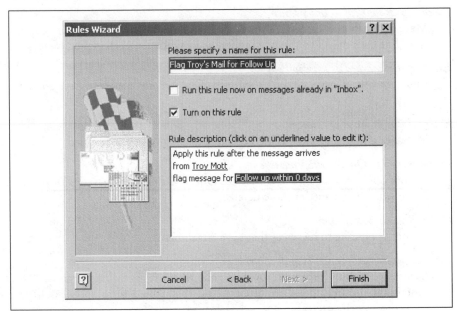

Figure 6-20: The final Rules Wizard dialog to name and apply the rule

has private mail. Both accounts are checked regularly, so a rule to separate the different mail flows automatically is practical.

A simple "business mail" rule can be created by first selecting the "Check messages when they arrive" rule and applying the "when received through the specified account" condition. The variable is replaced with the business mail account selected from the subdialog showing all defined accounts. The action applicable here is "move it to the specified folder," and the variable set to a folder called "business." The rule is complete, so you can skip ahead to the final dialog to name the rule, set it active and finish. Whenever possible, make it a habit to test new rules on mail already in your Inbox. To create the "personal mail" twin to this first rule, create a subfolder under Inbox named "personal," and make a copy of your completed business mail rule. Now modify this second rule by renaming it, and changing the required values to make it a personal mail rule.

An alternative to this procedure is to use the "assign category" action for at least two defined categories: "business" and "private," rather than blindly moving mail. This would keep all unread mail in your Inbox, and allow you to use the By Category view to quickly filter for either business or personal messages.

The second example is a practical solution for someone who subscribes to an Internet mailing list. The list generates 20 to 40 messages a day and you do not want these messages cluttering your Inbox and distracting you from the other messages you need to attend to. In addition, you do not read the messages from this list every day, but prefer to go through them on a weekly basis in a quiet moment.

Start by creating a new contact record with a name appropriate to the mailing list, and add the email address for the list to the record. Next, create a new mail folder to store these messages. Now create a new rule, apply the rule "after the message arrives" under the condition it was "sent to the email address" you just created, then add an action to "move these messages to the specified folder" you created for this purpose. Finally, test your rule on a representative collection of messages in your Inbox to ensure it actually moves the messages you want to the folder you specified.

TIP # 72

Use the Message Header to Tweak Rules

You may find you have to tweak the "sent to" condition by using the "specific words in the message header" option in order for the rule to recognize and act on some message headers. Some mailing lists are notorious for using "To" fields that are inconsistent, making it difficult to adapt basic rules to them.

As you can see from the extensive lists described in this section, rules are a powerful tool for managing mail flow. Expect to spend some time tweaking and refining your rules, however. This is not a reflection of any fault on Outlook's part, but due to the wide range of topics, structures, and conventions of email messages. Most common mail rules are triggered when Outlook scans a message header, and these can be varied and complex.

Last but not least, once you have a working rule collection honed and polished, *don't forget to back it up.*

Mail → Edit Menu

Among the shared items under the Edit menu title, three commands are specific to working with messages: Mark as Read, Mark as Unread, and Mark All as Read (see Figure 6-21). Each provides the user with a way to override the normal automatic changes to the read status of email items. By using a filter or sort on a mail view, you can collect and display messages according to the current status of this flag. See the "Mail → View Menu" section later in this chapter for a description of the distinction between normal and filtered views.

When a message is opened or viewed, Outlook sets the message status to Read, and the header line font changes from bold to normal. There may be times, however, when you want to manually adjust the status of a message or a group of messages. For example, you might open a new message and quickly realize you don't have time to deal with it. In this case, you close it and mark it an unread so it stands out as such in your Inbox.

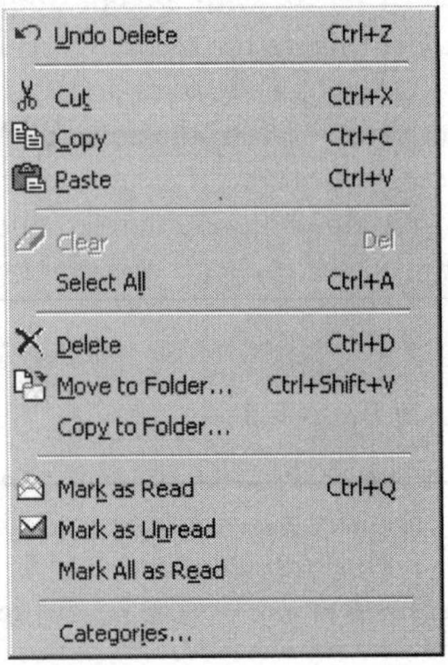

Figure 6-21: The Mail Edit menu

Edit → Mark as Read

Use Edit → Mark as Read, in any view, to change the status of one or more selected messages from Unread to Read. The command is also available on the right-click context menu for one or more selected messages, *provided* at least one of those messages has an Unread status. There is also a keyboard shortcut: Ctrl+Q.

Edit → Mark as Unread

As expected, Edit → Mark as Unread resets the status of the selected messages from Read to Unread. This menu entry is also available on the right-click context menu after selecting one or more message entries, where at least one has the status Read. There is no associated keyboard shortcut for this command.

Edit → Mark All as Read

Selecting Edit → Mark All as Read sets the status of all messages in the current view to Read. This affects only those messages displayed according to the current view and filter selections.

While the command itself is accessible only from the main menu, the same result can be achieved by selecting all (visible) messages in the current view, and then using the command Mark as Read (main menu or context), or as a keyboard sequence Ctrl+A followed by Ctrl+Q.

Mail → View Menu

The View menu contains commands for changing how mail folder content is displayed. Figure 6-22 shows Mail's View menu.

Figure 6-22: The Mail View menu

Message views display items differently according to read, reply, and forward status. New (unread) messages are formatted bold on their description line and the item icon shows a sealed envelope. In addition, the folder they are contained in also displays bold in the Folder List pane, along with a count of how many unread items there are. Read items are depicted by an opened envelope regardless of their reply/forward status.

Some of the views described in this section are sorted, others are filtered, and some are a combination of the two. The distinction is that sorted views show all the items in a given folder ordered in selectable ways, while filtered views show only a predefined subset of those items. It is possible to have a view sorted only, filtered only, or both filtered and sorted.

You may at some point suddenly panic because you are unable to find an item that simply must be in the folder you are viewing. It is possible you are viewing the folder through a filter that is excluding the missing item. Before you go off in a frantic search for your "lost" data, select View → Current View → Messages. This is the default setting, and in effect clears all filters and returns the view to the default sort order.

TIP # 73
Look for the "Filtered" Indicator

Whenever a view is filtered Outlook displays the message "(filter applied)" in the upper-right corner of that view's window. Get in the habit of looking for this indicator before you go searching for lost messages.

For a general discussion of views, filters, sort options, and view customization, see the section "The Power of Categories" in Chapter 3.

View → Current View

The menu options available in the Current View submenu (see Figure 6-23) display your mail folders with various preconfigured sort and filter settings already applied. The preset selections are duplicated in the drop-down list on the optional Advanced Mail toolbar.

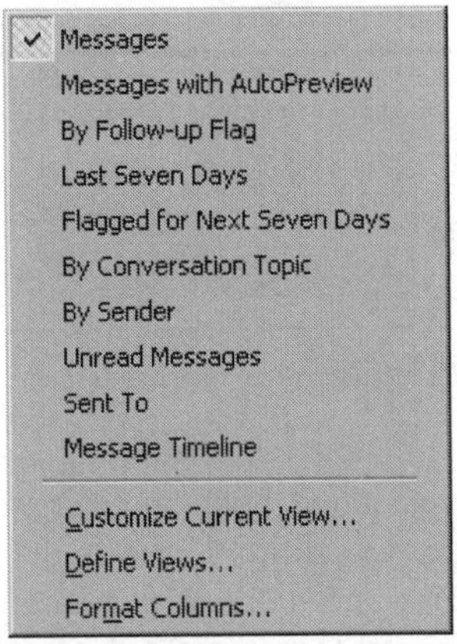

Figure 6-23: The View submenu Current View

Each of these default views can be customized beyond their initial starting point, possibly leading to views totally unrelated to the menu's descriptive label.

TIP # 74

Customize with Care

Changes made to the settings of a default view permanently change how this view is displayed, even after restarting Outlook. To return a default view to factory fresh settings, open the Define Views dialog (View → Current View → Define Views), select the view from the list displayed, and click the Reset button. Only preconfigured views can be reset; custom views have no defined baseline to return to.

View → Current View → Messages

This is the default view for mail messages, and selecting it clears all filter and sort settings. The View → Current View → Messages command shows all items in a selected mail folder, in a table view, sorted on the Received field (descending, i.e., recently received items first).

This view is a good starting point for most users. It displays enough information to allow you to quickly assess the messages contained in a folder, according to sender, subject, attachments (if any), status flags, and the date received.

The first four headings are displayed with flag/status icons in their respective columns: Importance, Message Status (Read, Unread, Replied to, or Forwarded), Flags, and Attachments. This is followed by the headings From, Subject, and Received. As explained in Customizing Views, this order is fully configurable, and easily reordered for the visible fields by simply dragging headings left or right.

Repeatedly clicking any column title toggles between ascending and descending sort orders for that field. Right-click on the column title bar to open a context menu with these same sort commands and choices for further customization options. Remember, any sort-order and customization changes made for this view remain in effect unless you change them back.

View → Current View → Messages with AutoPreview

Messages with AutoPreview display the contents of a folder (see Figure 6-24) with a header row and the first three lines of a message under each item header, but only for those messages with status Unread. For items marked Read, only the message header is displayed. Compare this with the View → AutoPreview command, described in detail later, which ignores read status.

Moving your selection from one message to the next in this view marks a message as Read (depending on your setting under Preview Pane Options) and cancels the display of the AutoPreview lines.

View → Current View → By Follow Up Flag

By Follow Up Flag displays messages in a table view, with a descriptive column for the flag type, and a column noting any due date associated with the flag (this entry is None if no date is set). The view's default sort order is on the Due By (Descending) and Received (Descending) field. It is not filtered; all items—flagged and unflagged—are visible.

Of course, Flag views are not terribly useful without flagged items, so we remind you to take the time to use this powerful tool often and liberally.

As functional as this view is, adding two minor customizations dramatically increases your productivity while managing flags. First, activate in-cell editing as outlined in Tip #75. Second, customize the field layout by adding a Flag Status icon next to the Follow Up Flag column as shown in Figure 6-25. Now you can quickly edit flag descriptions, add reminders to your flags, and toggle an item as Flagged, Completed, or Normal (no flag) by simply clicking on the column and selecting a status from the drop-down list displayed.

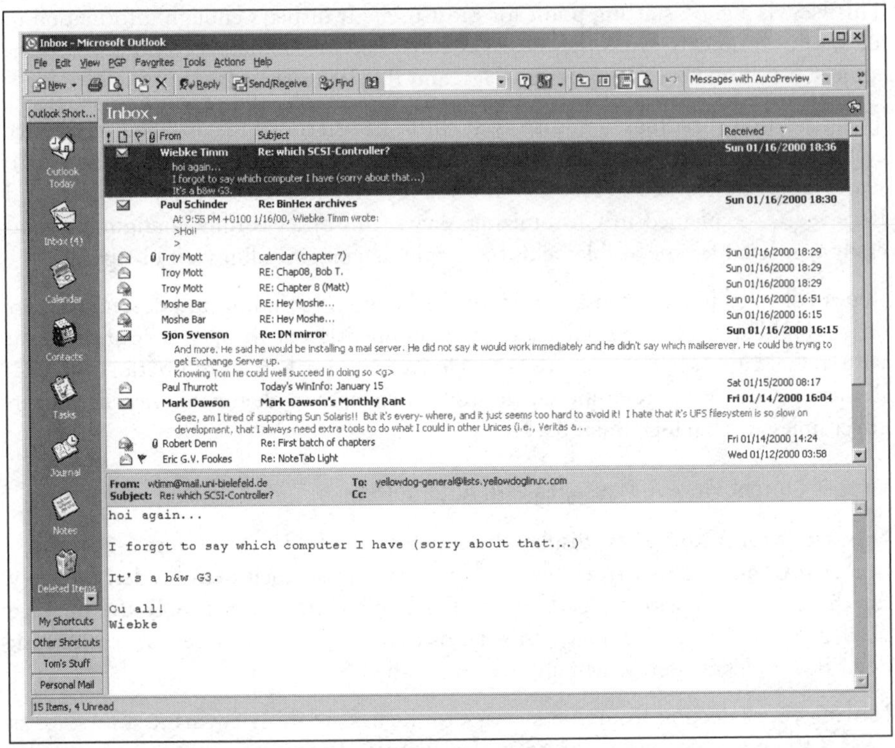

Figure 6-24: Messages with AutoPreview

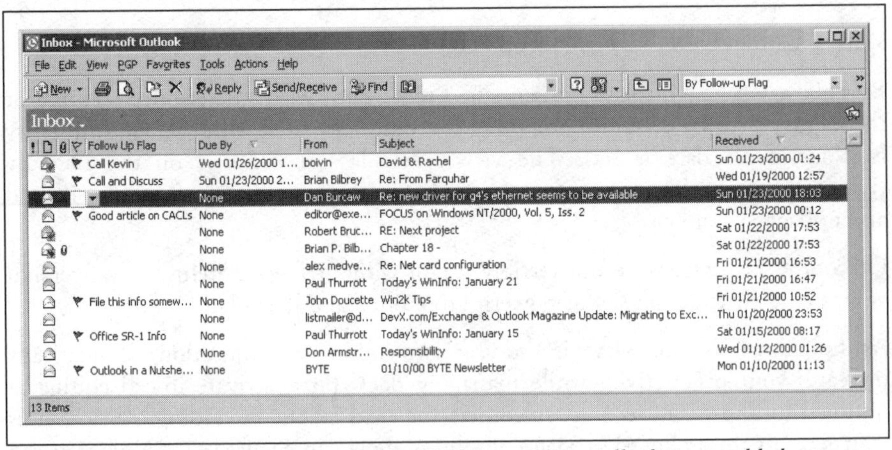

Figure 6-25: Current View → By Follow Up Flag with in-cell editing enabled

Enable In-Cell Editing to Quickly Set Flags

This is an excellent view in which to enable in-cell editing. (Right-click a column title and choose Customize Current View → Other Settings.) Doing so allows you to quickly edit or assign flag descriptions, or add date and time reminders.

View → Current View → Last Seven Days

This view displays messages filtered to show only those items received in the last seven days, determined from the current system time and the received date of message header.

View → Current View → Flagged for Next Seven Days

Displays messages filtered to show only items with a flag set *and* a due date that fall within the next seven days, determined from the current system time. Messages are displayed grouped by flag descriptions and ordered with closest (usually highest priority) due dates first. This view illustrates the functionality of using both descriptive flags and assigned due dates.

View → Current View → By Conversation Topic

This view displays messages sorted by Conversation Topic (which is another way of saying the contents of the Subject line), with an expandable, collapsible tree structure based on this topic list. Messages belonging to a common topic are then listed under one branch, and sorted or filtered according to other settings. The topic line specifies how many items belong to the group, and the heading list is initially presented as collapsed. Figure 6-26 illustrates the view By Conversation Topic.

Clicking on the + or - box in the respective topic header line expands or collapses the list as desired. Selecting a topic (use the up- and down-arrow keys) and pressing Enter also works to expand or collapse a group.

For those who file topical correspondence in unique folders, or archive messages from regular correspondents, this can be an extremely functional view when searching for a particular topic or subject buried deep in old email.

Open All Items in a Group

Right-click a group topic header, and the first item on the context menu displayed is Open All Items. It opens all items contained within that group, each in an individual window. Thankfully, Outlook is considerate enough to warn you if the number of items is "large." If you are dealing with a mailing list, a group could potentially contain hundreds of items. And opening 100 message windows is going to take some time.

Mail

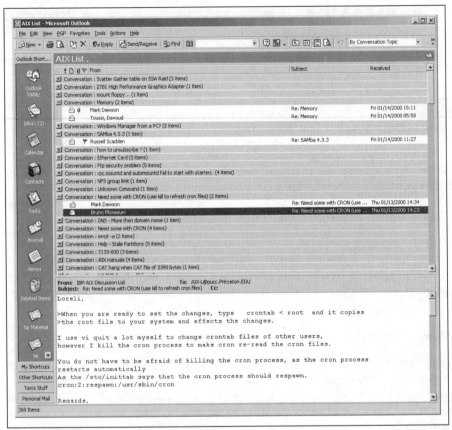

Figure 6-26: The View By Conversation topic

Messages retrieved off an *Exchange Server* or from a newsgroup are listed by their true conversation topic (reply thread) as set by the moderator of the forum or folder, or by the message's author. Again, in such circumstances this view becomes a useful tool to mine through hundreds of messages for a particular topic or thread that interests you.

This view does not mark a message as read when the selection changes. To do this you need to actually open the message, or manually mark the selected message with status Read.

View → Current View → By Sender

This selection groups messages by sender (name or email address), and presents them in an expandable tree-style listing, initially collapsed to a list of sender headings. Clicking on the + sign beside a given header then expands the underlying list to show all individual messages grouped under that sender.

This view is particularly useful when your current folder contains a large number of messages and you are looking for one sent by a certain individual. You may enter the first letter of the name you are searching for to drill down to the start of the list of messages received by that person.

View → Current View → Unread Messages

This filter displays only unread messages, excluding those marked with status Read. Actions that mark a message status read are determined by settings for the Preview Pane. This read status can be modified using the Edit → Mark As... commands discussed earlier in this chapter.

The Unread Messages view is useful for scouring through Mail folders containing a large number of items, and excluding any items you've already read or opened. An example would be a mailing-list folder that you move or copy items to (perhaps using a rule) for perusal at a convenient time. Using the Unread Messages view displays only unread items; after a message is read it disappears from view (*not* from the folder).

View → Current View → Sent To

This is similar to the By Sender view, except that it sorts messages according to the recipient (name or email address) specified in the To field.

View → Current View → Message Timeline

The Message Timeline view is effectively a "sort by date" option, except messages are presented horizontally on a scrollable timeline, like in the Journal view. This gives a graphic dimension to how messages have been received over time, as shown in Figure 6-27. Messages are identified by icon, and if there is room, by subject field.

The top (date) bar's context menu (Figure 6-28, left) provides a number of relevant settings in terms of scaling and grouping, along with date navigational commands. Select the Day command to see a timeline of your messages as they were received throughout the course of a given day, or select the Week command to provide a view as in Figure 6-27. Note that in the Day view the timeline scale is in an hourly format, while Week or Month views change this scale to a weekday/date format and adjust the range shown accordingly.

Outlook's View menu itself also adapts to reflect selections relevant to this view by adding the commands "Day, Week, Month" when a Timeline is displayed (see Figure 6-28, right).

The following tips are applicable when working in a timeline view:

- Any timeline view that has many messages condensed into a short period of time simply shows those messages as envelope icons ("open" for read; "closed" for unread). Holding your mouse pointer over a specific icon will display the

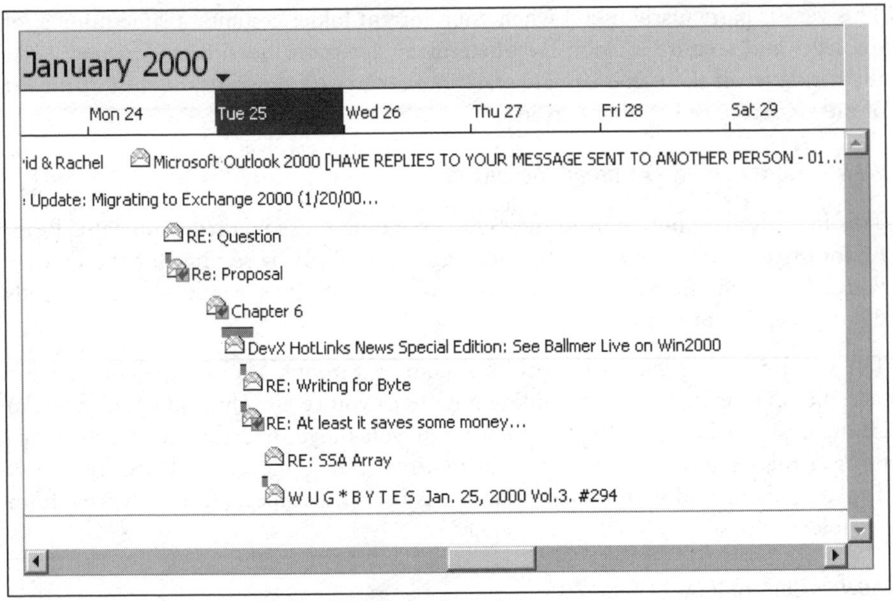

Figure 6-27: A section of a timeline view of messages

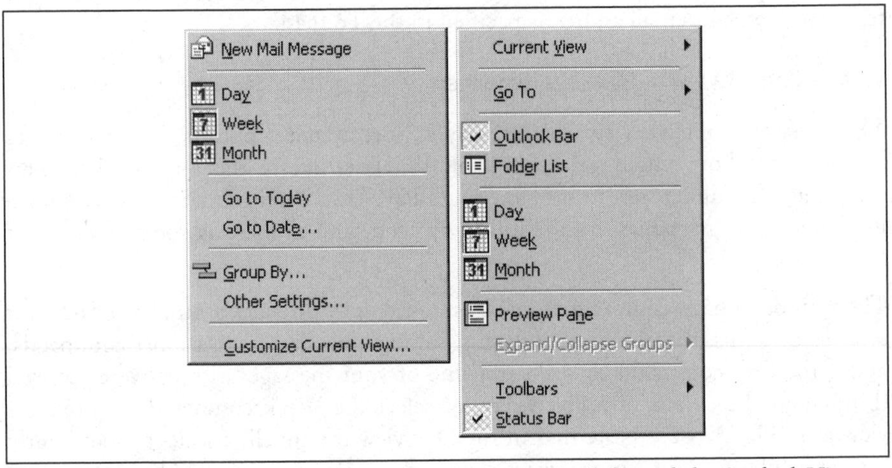

Figure 6-28: The context menu for timeline view settings (left) and the Outlook View menu in for a timeline view (right)

subject of that message. Right-clicking a specific icon produces the same context menu available in most message views. Double-clicking an icon opens the message for viewing.

- To navigate to another date, click on the date bar to produce a pop-up calendar, allowing you to scroll and select any date, or return to Today. This is the same calendar dialog accessed by the down-arrow in the dialog reached from

View → Go To → Go to Date, or via the context menu. The keyboard shortcut for this pop-up calendar is Ctrl+G.

- The date field in the dialog Go to Date does not accept a more detailed specification by hour, only by date, so in a Day scale you must scroll horizontally to the appropriate time.

View → Preview Pane (On/Off Toggle)

This option is an on/off toggle. To activate the feature, select View → Preview Pane once; to turn the option off, select again. When activated, a pane appears in the lower half of your view, showing the contents of any currently selected item. (Compare this with the AutoPreview function, described next.) It's a good idea to activate this in conjunction with the "Single key reading using spacebar" option discussed in the next section to scan through long lists of new mail and quickly find those that need immediate attention, perhaps assigning flags as you go.

The preview pane can be resized by grabbing its upper border (your mouse cursor changes from the default pointer to two horizontal lines when in the correct position), holding down the left mouse button, and dragging this border up or down to a different positional preference.

Options also exist to modify several aspects of what the preview pane displays, how it displays, and when. Right-clicking between the two lines that separate the (table) view pane from the preview pane produces the context menu shown in Figure 6-29.

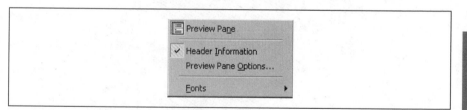

Figure 6-29: The context menu for Preview settings

Preview Pane
    Selecting this turns off the preview pane. (To turn it on again, go to the main View menu or Toolbar button.)

Header Information
    This toggle selection controls the display of basic header information from the selected message (From, To, Subject, and Cc).

Preview Pane Options
    This leads to a second-level dialog (Figure 6-30) with the following selections that control Preview behavior.

Mark message as read in preview window

When selected, the previewed message is marked with a Read status when it has been in the preview pane for the time specified in the associated field: "Wait (x) seconds before marking item as read." This is useful for keeping the unread status on messages you are just skimming through (you should also *deselect* the "Mark item as read when selection changes" option).

Mark item as read when selection changes

When selected, the message previewed is marked with status Read when you move from one message to the next.

Single key reading using spacebar

This option allows you to step through the display shown in the Preview Pane using the spacebar. Once the end of the message is reached, the next item listed in the upper message window is automatically loaded and the step-preview continues. In this way you can just keep reading through an entire list of messages, sequentially, with a single key.

Preview header, Font

This lets you specify the typeface, style, and size used to display the optional header information, as enabled in the context menu item Header Information. The currently selected font is given in the box. The button calls up a subdialog to specify a new font.

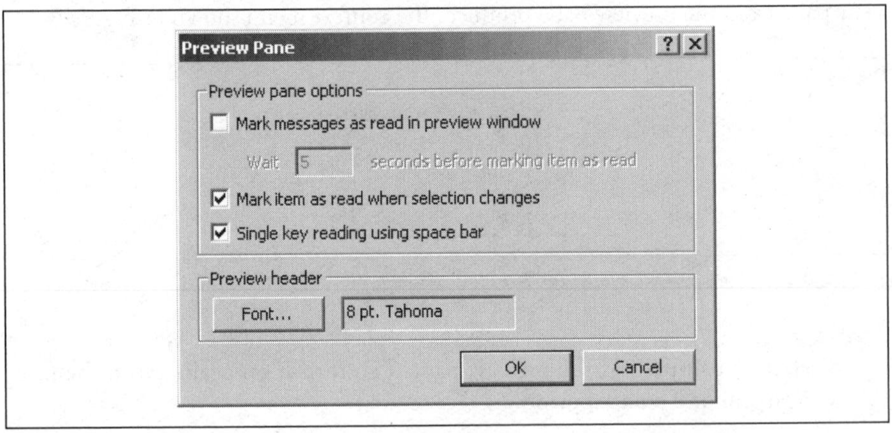

Figure 6-30: The Preview Pane options dialog

Fonts

Sets the font size used in the preview pane. Five choices are available: Largest, Large, Medium, Smaller, and Smallest. Note that this setting is only applied to HTML-formatted messages (font size steps relative to the default size), not Word-doc style (themed) mail, which tends to have internally specified fixed font sizes, nor Plain Text messages, in which case the menu selection is grayed out.

View → AutoPreview

The View → AutoPreview command toggles the AutoPreview function on or off, but unlike the View → Current View → Messages with AutoPreview menu command discussed earlier, the function here applies to all messages in the view, irrespective of their read status. You may additionally have the Preview Pane option active at the same time, which can affect the read status of selected messages if previewing is configured to mark messages as Read (see Preview Options earlier in this section).

When AutoPreview is active, the first three lines of each message are displayed underneath the respective message header. AutoPreview is useful for quickly scanning a list of newly received messages for relevance and attention priority without having to open them individually. It can also help you quickly search for a specific message in an older or archived message folder.

Be aware that the format of the message determines whether the three preview lines under the header are meaningful or not. While all Plain Text messages as a rule display a useful preview, HTML material may not. HTML messages are sometimes structured with formatting information at the head of the document.

Note the difference between the functionality of AutoPreview and Preview Pane: AutoPreview lists the first three lines of a message under the header information, while Preview Pane shows the full text of a message in a separate, scrollable window below the table view of message items.

Some users may prefer the more detailed AutoPreview display with the initial contents of several messages visible, to the split display with headers in one pane and a separate single preview in another. Others may find this too cluttered—YMMV (Your Mileage May Vary).

Chapter 7

Calendar

Calendar is a time-management tool that provides an electronic means to track and manage appointments, multiday events, birthdays, anniversaries, meetings, and anything else you don't want to forget. Each of these activities can be one-time or recurring (daily, weekly, monthly, or yearly), and reminders configured as needed. Like Outlook's other components, Calendar provides a selection of preconfigured views for arranging and sorting your schedule on a range of time-scales, or narrowing the items displayed to a specific type of activity—for example, active appointments or annual events.

There is a great deal of functional overlap between Tasks (see Chapter 9, *Tasks*) and Calendar items. Outlook treats each item as a distinct type because tasks (optionally) have a start and/or end date, but have no provision for a time property.

Outlook recognizes three unique types of Calendar activities:

- *Appointments* are activities that occur at specific times on specific days.

- *Meetings* are also date- and time-specific, but include other people and sometimes resources (like a conference room or an overhead projector).

- *Events* are special occasions, such as birthdays, anniversaries, or holidays that occur on a recurring basis. Events can also be one-time activities, such as a project or a multiday trade show. Events differ from appointments and meetings in that they do not occur at specific times.

Items created as one type can be easily changed to another. For example, if an appointment you've created as a personal reminder turns into a meeting, simply open the item, click the Invite Attendee button on the form's toolbar, and enter a list of people you want to invite.

And herein lies the real power of Calendar—its integration with Outlook's other components. Meetings can be planned by first consulting the recipients' Free/Busy times, and booking a conference room. Invited members can then be sent meeting requests via email, allowing the recipient to reply by accepting, declining, or marking their response as tentative. If a meeting is rescheduled, all attendees are automatically informed when a change is made.

Figure 7-1 shows a Day view of Calendar with these options and features displayed:

1. *The time bar.* The left edge of Day and Week views displays a time bar that divides a day into intervals. Right-click on the time bar to select a different increment. You can configure and display a second time zone and quickly switch between the two using the Change Time Zone command from the time bar's context menu.

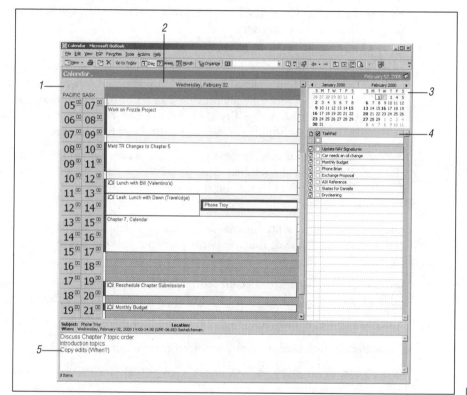

Figure 7-1: Outlook's Calendar component

2. *The Calendar view pane.* The center pane of a Calendar view displays appointments, meetings, and events. According to the view selected (View → Current View), entries are shown in either a graphical layout (Day/Week/Month), or in a table layout with preconfigured groups and/or filters applied. Like all Outlook components, these views can be customized beyond the defaults provided (see Chapter 3, *Program Insights*). The current view can serve as simply a display of Calendar items (double-click an entry to open it), or as directly editable records. Position your cursor on a time slot and start typing to create a new entry; select an existing entry and click once with your mouse to edit the record. Day/Work Week/Week views support rescheduling of entries via drag and drop. You can also change duration by dragging an entry's upper or lower border.

3. *The Date Navigator.* In the upper-right corner of a Day/Week view window is the Date Navigator. This graphical calendar allows you to quickly navigate to a specific day, week, or month. It can also be used to change your current view. Select one day to open a Day view; hold your cursor to the left of a week to open a 7-day Week view; drag your cursor across any group of less than seven days and a Work Week view is displayed; click anywhere in the day-of-the-week header to get a Month view. You can even select noncontiguous days. You'll find more details on the Date Navigator in the section "Calendar's Date Navigator" later in this chapter.

4. *The TaskPad.* Below Date Navigator is the TaskPad. This is not a distinct component of Calendar per se, but a window on your Tasks List available from specific Day/Week/Month views. Entries and updates made here are saved to your Tasks folder. Context menus provide a range of preconfigured views for the TaskPad (All Tasks, Active Tasks, Overdue Tasks, etc.). The view used by the TaskPad is distinct from the view used by the Tasks folder proper.

5. *The Preview pane.* All Calendar views (graphical or table) can optionally display a Preview Pane under the selected view. The Preview Pane shows the contents of the free-form text field located on the item's entry/edit form. Text displayed here cannot be edited, only viewed.

This chapter details the menu commands central to Calendar and is arranged to help you gain familiarity with this component without missing any vital, need-to-know details:

- *Calendar Options* details the default settings for Calendar and how your choices influence the creation and management of appointments, meeting, and events.

- *Date Navigator* shows you how to quickly move between Calendar entries.

- *Actions* details commands to create appointments, meetings, and events.

- *View Options* details the View → Current View → Customize Current View and Define Views commands.

- *View* covers Calendar's preconfigured views, their displays, and how to use them.

How you configure Calendar's options has a big impact on the default behaviors of many aspects of creating and working with activities. For this reason, we begin this chapter with a look at Calendar's various options, and how to change the defaults to suit your work style.

Calendar's Option Settings

Calendar's option settings begin on the Tools → Options → Preferences tab shown in Figure 7-2.

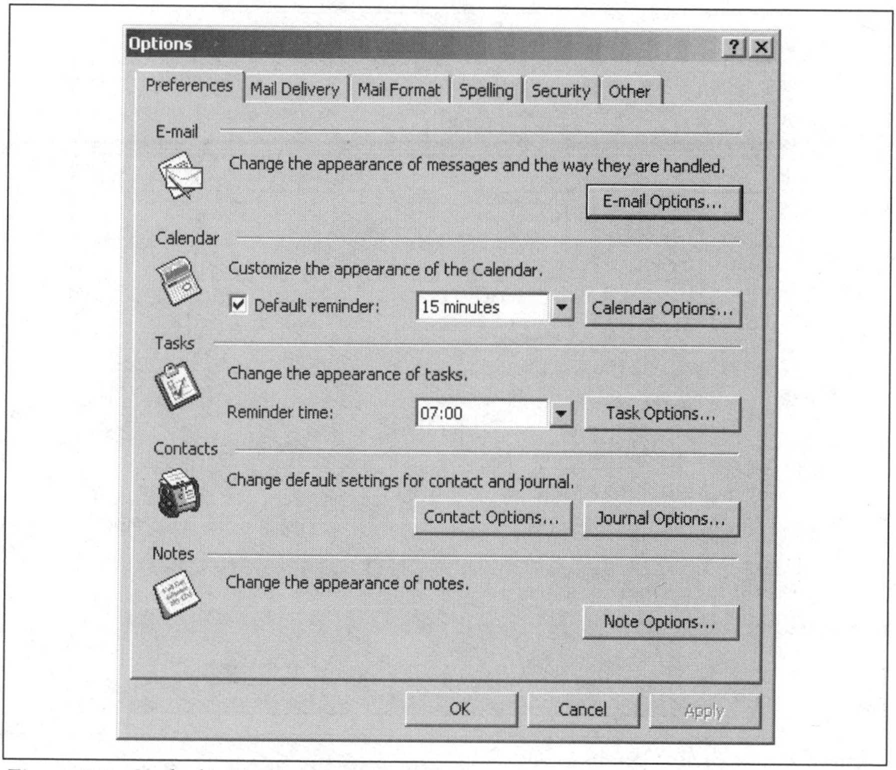

Figure 7-2: Outlook's Tools → Options dialog

Under "Customize the appearance of the Calendar" you'll find the setting for reminders. Selecting this option adds a default reminder to all new Calendar items. Next to this is a drop-down list for selecting the time in advance of the activity a reminder displays. You can choose from this list, or type a time of your choosing. See the Sidebar "More Date (and Time) Entry Shortcuts" later in this chapter for tips on shortcut time field entries.

Clicking Calendar Options opens the dialog shown in Figure 7-3, where you find most Calendar configuration options; each option is described in the sections that follow.

Calendar Work Week

At the top of the Calendar Options dialog is a section to configure your "Calendar work week." Selections here have a large impact on how many of Calendar's views are laid out, and how several important drag-and-drop features function, so consider your options carefully:

Work week
> Specifies which days of the week are considered working days. Your selection determines the days displayed under Work Week view (this can be changed by

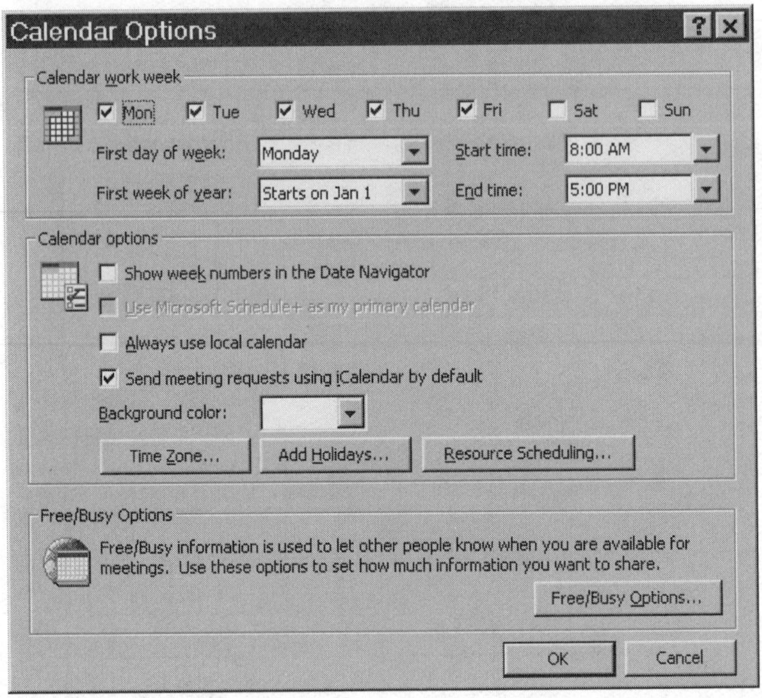

Figure 7-3: Calendar Options dialog

selecting dates from the Date Navigator). The default is Monday through Friday.

First day of the week

Defines any weekday as the first day of the week. It also shifts the dialog display accordingly as shown in Figure 7-4. The left column of Calendar's Week and Month views start with the chosen weekday.

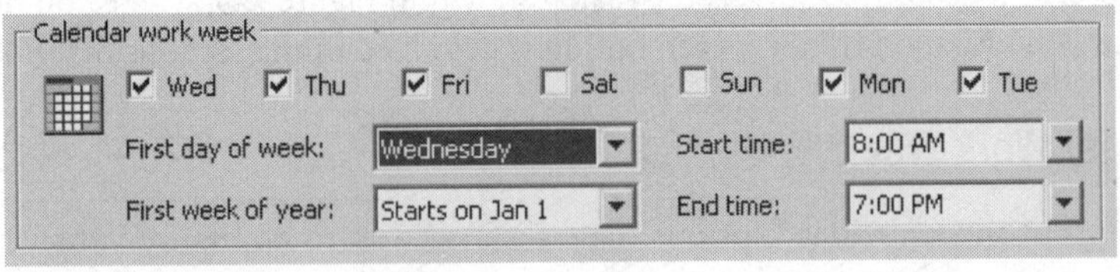

Figure 7-4: Wednesday was made "First day of the week"

First week of year

Companies in many countries use numbered weeks in corporate planning, but different national (and corporate) calendars can have different rules for what constitutes "week 1" in any given year. You can choose from Starts on Jan 1, First 4 day week, and First full week. Set this option to match your local rules or customs.

Start time and End time

These two selections define the standard hours for a workday. Hours between Start and End time display in the background color chosen further down the Calendar Options dialog, while hours outside of this range display in a grayed shade of this same color (this setting applies to Day and Work Week views only). This allows you to quickly visualize your working day and any appointments and meetings that may need rescheduling. Pay attention to the Start time setting: there are numerous shortcuts to creating a new appointment or meeting in this chapter, and many of them base the default Start time of the new entry on the setting of the Start time field on this dialog. Pick a time that best reflects when the majority of your activities begin, even if this is not the true start of your workday.

Calendar Options

The Calendar Options section groups a general assortment of settings:

Show week numbers in the Date Navigator

This numbers (1–53) the weeks of the year at the left edge of the Date Navigator. The Date Navigator is displayed in many of Calendar's drop-down date lists, so if you use week numbering in your scheduling, this is a good option to select.

Use Microsoft Schedule+ as my primary calendar

Some organizations have not migrated to Office 97/2000 and still use Schedule+ as a basis for their scheduling needs. Selecting this option replaces Outlook's Calendar with Schedule+, allowing you to share your calendar with Office 95 users.

Always use local calendar

Applicable only when Outlook is installed in Corporate Workgroup (CW) mode (see Chapter 2, *Installing Outlook*). Enabling the local option in CW mode limits referencing to your own Calendar folder when resolving meeting requests or scheduling conflicts. Deselected, Outlook is allowed to look externally for any relevant Free/Busy information (for example on an Exchange Server).

Send meeting requests using iCalendar by default

Outlook can send meeting requests in either native or iCalendar format. See the section later in this chapter, "Actions → New Meeting Request" for the pros and cons of this option.

Background color

Select the background color for Day and Work Week views from the drop-down list. The selections are unfortunately limited to a fixed range of solid and dithered colors. We recommend one of the three solid colors (white, yellow, or light blue), as the dithered colors make text hard to read.

Time Zone

Calendar's Time Zone dialog (see Figure 7-5) allows you to assign a label to your current time zone, and optionally add a second time zone to the time bar shown under Day and Work Week views. This is useful when you travel between two different time zones and prefer to work in and view your calendar under local time.

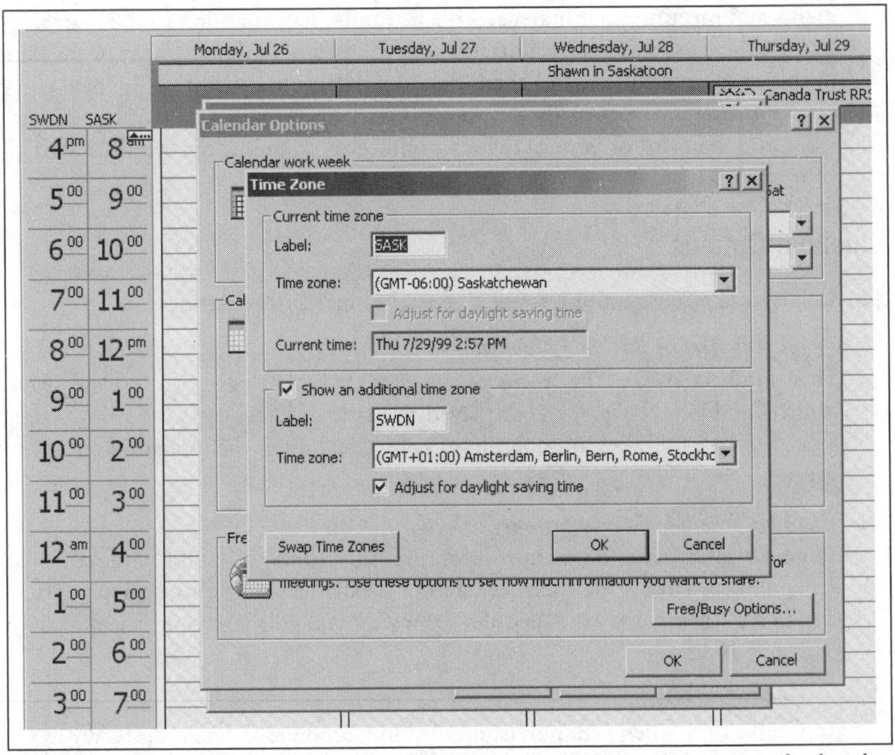

Figure 7-5: Time Zone configuration dialog—note the additional time zone displayed

The Label field accepts any string of text; try to keep your entry here as concise as possible. Depending on the font size chosen for the time bar, anything more than approximately eight or nine characters is truncated.

The Time Zone field is selectable via the drop-down list provided. Set your current time zone for your home location, and leave it. If you're going to adjust time zones for travel, use the additional time zone. The additional time zone translates dates and times according to the primary time zone, but any entries made while the additional time zone is displayed are recorded in your database according to the setting of the current time zone.

The Time Zone display only applies to views with specified hour slots—Day and Work Week views. The Swap Time Zones button swaps the additional time zone with the current one, affecting which zone is displayed, and also the time your activities show under.

TIP # 77

Quick Swap Time Zones

To quickly change your time zone, right-click the time bar and select Change Time Zone from the context menu. This opens the Time Zone dialog. Click Swap Time Zones, and OK. Changing Outlook's current time zone changes the time zone used by Windows.

Add Holidays

Add Holidays opens the dialog shown in Figure 7-6, allowing you to add location-specific holidays to your Calendar.

Figure 7-6: The Add Holidays to Calendar subdialog

While at first glance this may seen like one of those "Good Things To Do," we caution against using this automated approach to adding holidays to your calendar. Here's why:

- Outlook reads selected locations from a text file (*outlook.txt*) and copies them to your Calendar folder as events, not recurring or annual entries. In addition, the dates added only span the years 1998 to 2002.

- If you add more than one locale, you often end up with duplicate entries. For example, adding holidays for United States and Canada adds two entries for Valentine's Day, Easter, Christmas Day, etc.

- This text file is not always accurate, nor does it adequately specify days when businesses or shops are closed. For example, despite having the error pointed out repeatedly, Microsoft still inexplicably believes that Thanksgiving Day in the U.S. falls on Wednesday rather than Thursday.

- What Microsoft defines as a holiday, and what you define as a holiday, may be two different things. (Groundhog Day: a holiday?)

WARNING

Although a warning dialog appears if you try to add holidays from a country list already installed in your calendar, ignoring this warning results in duplicate entries.

Our advice is to add those holidays important to you, properly (as annual recurring events), once, and be done with it. Automation is nice, but this is definitely a case of automation doing more harm than good.

Resource Scheduling

The Resource Scheduling button opens the subdialog shown in Figure 7-7.

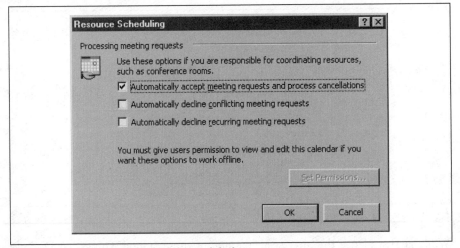

Figure 7-7: The Resource Scheduling subdialog

This dialog relates directly to public meeting resources (conference rooms, audio-visual equipment, etc.) and the people responsible for administering these resources.

The "Automatically decline conflicting meeting requests" and "Automatically decline recurring meeting requests" checkboxes are unavailable unless the "Automatically accept meeting requests and process cancellations" checkbox is marked. The term "meeting" is used in all the following options, but in the context of a resource, this implies someone trying to schedule, for example, a conference room. We'll use this example in the following list to clarify the terms used for each option:

Automatically accept meeting requests and process cancellations
If someone sends a request for the conference room and it is free, give them the room and show it as "booked;" if someone cancels the conference room, accept the notification and show the room as "free" to the next person asking.

Automatically decline conflicting meeting requests
If the conference room is booked, and someone requests it, decline the request.

Automatically decline recurring meeting requests.
If someone tries to book the conference room for every Friday for the next two years, decline the request.

The Set Permissions button is used to administer the resource, for example, to assign another member of the workgroup administrative rights.

Free/Busy Options

Outlook's Free/Busy feature allows you to share your scheduling information via special *.vcb* files accessible on a corporate LAN or Internet server, or from a corporate mail server. Other Outlook users can then access this information for group scheduling purposes. Schedules are displayed as time blocks that show Free (no appointments scheduled) or Busy (appointment scheduled), with the further options of Tentative and Out of Office. See the "Actions → Plan a Meeting" section later in this chapter for more on how this is used.

You access the configuration settings for publishing Free/Busy information with the Free/Busy Options button on the Calendar Options dialog. Entries dictate how much and how often this information is published, as well as the URL where Outlook stores and searches these files (see Figure 7-8).

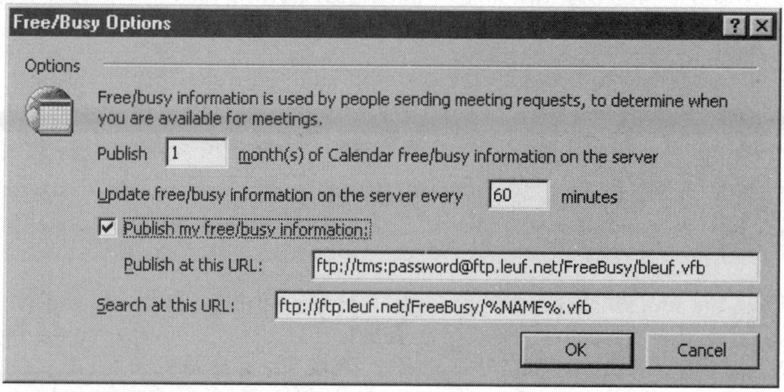

Figure 7-8: Setting Free/Busy publishing options

NOTE *The actual appointment details of any Busy times published in this way are not public, only the labeled time blocks.*

Setting up and publishing Free/Busy information is an involved process, covered fully in Chapter 14, *Collaborating with Outlook*.

Calendar's Date Navigator

Unlike Outlook's other components, working in Calendar often means moving from one record to another in a nonlinear manner. The Date Navigator, shown in Figure 7-9, helps you move quickly to a different day or month with a single mouse click.

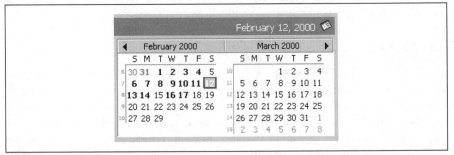

Figure 7-9: Calendar's Date Navigator

The Date Navigator is only available under Calendar's graphical Day/Month/Week views, and, by default, shows a two-month time window.

Here are some tips and tricks for reading and using the Date Navigator:

- The current day—determined by your system's internal clock—is indicated by a red square; the day, or range of days, displayed by the current view is shown in gray. Days for which appointments have been entered are displayed in bold.

- Click on a date to bring up the corresponding Day view in the calendar pane. Click to the left of a week row (on a week number if this is displayed), and that week is highlighted and appears in a Week (7-day) view.

 NOTE *If your view is Work Week, clicking a date in the Date Navigator shifts your calendar to the Work Week view containing that day.*

- Drag the mouse cursor over a range of days, and those dates are displayed in a suitable calendar view. The display rule is that a selection of seven days gives a Week view, while less than this gives a Work Week style view (multiple days in hour column format). More than seven days is adjusted to even weeks and displayed in a Month-like format.

- To move between contiguous months, use the arrows to the right or left of the Navigator's title bar. To quickly move to a noncontiguous month, click and hold on the month's title to display the selection pop-up seen in Figure 7-10. The list of months scrolls if you hold the cursor down above or below the box.

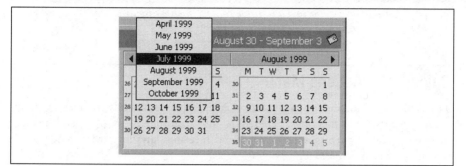

Figure 7-10: The Date Navigator with the pop-up month list

- Clicking on the weekday region just below the month bar selects the entire calendar month and displays it in a Month view.

- By default, the Date Navigator displays two months at a time. Dragging the left or lower boundary of the Navigator pane increases the display at the expense of the Calendar and TaskPad panes respectively. In Figure 7-11, the Navigator pane has been expanded downward to fit four months—note the resize cursor with up/down arrows.

Figure 7-11: Expanding the Date Navigator view by dragging the lower separator bar

TIP # 78

See into the Future

Outlook provides a second way to jump to a specific date: the Go To Date command. Right-click an open area on your Calendar (or use the Keyboard Shortcut Ctrl+G) and select Go to Date from context menu displayed. See View → Go to Date later in this chapter for details.

Calendar → Actions Menu

The Actions menu, shown in Figure 7-12, contains commands to create appointments, events, and meetings. There are also commands to plan and manage meetings, create recurring appointments and meetings, and forward Calendar items to contacts as email messages.

Figure 7-12: Calendar's Actions menu

Appointments are activities that occur on a specific day (or days), at a specific time, and have a specific duration. Meetings are also date- and time-specific, but involve other people; events are activities that occur on a specific day without reference to a specific time. We begin this section with the basics: creating appointments.

Actions → New Appointment

Appointments are the fundamental building blocks of Calendar. We make this distinction because meetings and events are really just appointments with specific properties applied. Meetings are appointments with one or more attendees. Events are appointments with the "All Day Event" option toggled, which, in effect, simply removes the time property fields from the record.

Changing a Calendar Item Type

The relationship of Appointments to Meetings and Events is an important one. You can create a Calendar item of any type and change it to another type by simply adding or removing certain properties. For example, to create a meeting from an appointment, simply click the Invite Attendees button on the open form and fill in a list of contacts to invite. To switch an All Day Event to an appointment, deselect "All Day Event" on the open item's form.

To create an appointment:

- From the Actions menu, select New Appointment.

- Use the global keyboard shortcut Ctrl+Shift+A from anywhere in Outlook; use Ctrl+N from within Calendar.

- Double-click in an open region of a Calendar view. Under Day or Work Week view, the time slot you click on becomes the appointment Start time. Under Week or Month view, double-clicking on a day creates a new All Day Event. In a table view, this creates an appointment for the current system date, with the start and end times set around the current time of day.

- Select a date and time slot from Day or Work Week view, right-click, and from the context menu choose New Appointment. This creates a new appointment according to the parameters chosen. In Week or Month view, this creates a new appointment for the day selected, with the time set for the first working time slot of the day as defined by your settings under Work Week (Tools → Options → Calendar Options).

- Drag your cursor over a series of time slots in a Day or Work Week view, and select New Appointment from the context menu. This creates an appointment with Start and End times matching the times spanned.

- Drag a task entry from TaskPad (only available from Day/Week/Month views) and drop it on a date. A new appointment is created for that date, the Start time is set to the first time slot defined by your Work Week, and the appointment duration defaults to the interval used by Day and Work Week's time bar.

- From any Outlook folder (Inbox, Tasks, Notes, etc.), select and drag an item and drop it on the Calendar icon on the Outlook Bar. This creates an appointment, date, and time set to your system, the item's subject copied to the appointment subject line, and the details of the dragged item entered in the notes field.

Any of these actions opens a new appointment form, similar to that shown in Figure 7-13. Other than the date/time preselection tricks noted, the form is blank.

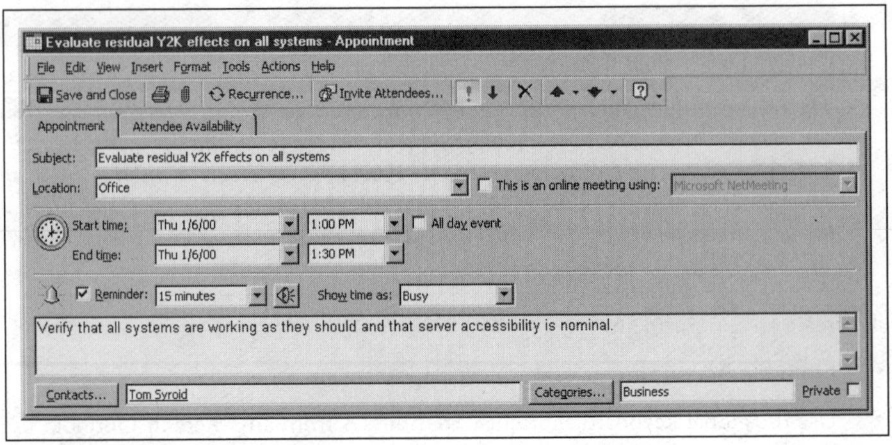

Figure 7-13: Calendar's New Appointment form

Defining an Appointment

An Appointment form contains the following fields:

Subject

Describes the purpose of the appointment or meeting. Put key words at the beginning of the description so they are visible under views with narrow columns (for example, Month view). Subjects need not be unique—it takes both subject and date/time to define an appointment—but for the sake of clarity it is better if they are.

Location

Defines the appointment or meeting location. Click the drop-down arrow to the right of the field for a list of your ten most recent entries.

Start time

This is the date and time your appointment begins. See the entry tricks at the beginning of this section for details on timesaving methods for preconfiguring this field and the next.

Times can be changed using the drop-down list or by entering a date and time directly in the appropriate field. See the sidebar "More Date (and Time) Entry Shortcuts" for some examples.

TIP # 80

Default Appointment Durations

The default interval used for an appointment is a function of the scale selected for the time bar displayed to the left of Day and Work Week views (right-click the bar to see your options). If your time scale is set to 30 minutes, a new appointment that starts at 7 a.m. defaults to 7:30 a.m. as an end time. Similarly, setting your start time to 7:10 a.m. automatically shifts the end time to 7:40 a.m. The default duration is set from the Customize View dialog (View → Current View → Customize Current View → Other Settings).

End time

The time interval between start time and end time defines the duration of the appointment. When you specify a start time, Outlook automatically changes the end time so that the duration of an appointment remains unchanged. You can change the end time, however, without affecting the start time.

In Day and Work Week views, appointment duration is indicated by a white block spanning the appropriate time slots; Week and Month views indicate appointment duration by times (or optionally clocks) to the left of the entry.

All Day Event

Selecting the All Day Event turns an appointment into an event. See Actions → New All Day Event later in this chapter for more details.

Reminder

If the checkbox is selected, a reminder dialog pops up on your screen at a specified time before an appointment. You can set a time not shown on the drop-down list by entering it directly in the field. Fractional times are rounded (8.5 minutes is converted to 8 minutes). Click the speaker icon to open the Reminder Sound dialog (see Figure 7-14).

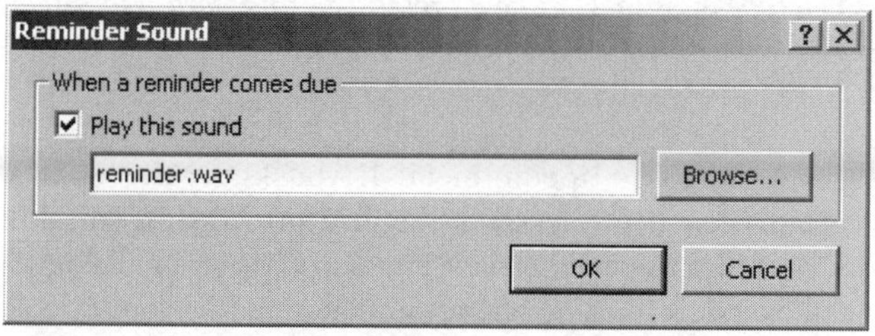

Figure 7-14: The Reminder Sound dialog

Deselect the "Play this sound" option to display a dialog only; the Browse button lets you assign a sound file of your choice to the reminder. See the section on "Reminders" later in the chapter for details on reconfiguring default reminder settings.

Show time as

By default, Outlook classifies all appointment times as Busy. From the "Show time as" drop-down list you can reclassify an activity one of four ways: Busy (shown as a blue border in Day and Work Week views), Free (white), Out of Office (purple), and Tentative (light blue).

Classifying an activity gives you a quick visual guide to your commitments. It also provides useful information for others when you share your calendar information either directly (for example, in an Public Folder on an Exchange Server) or by posting your Free/Busy times to a server. Configuring and using the Free/Busy property is a topic of Chapter 14.

Notes (not labeled)

The Notes field occupies most of the lower half of the Appointment/Meeting form. It's often useful to jot notes in here at the time an appointment or meeting is created, adding details not accommodated by the form fields, or listing topics that need to be covered in a meeting. This is also where attached documents or files are displayed.

Contacts

Clicking the Contacts button opens the Select Contacts dialog, allowing you to select a contact to associate with the appointment. An entry in this field creates a two-way link between the activity and the contact record it is linked to. Any activities linked in this way are also displayed under the contact's record (Activity tab → Show → Upcoming Tasks/Appointments).

TIP # 81

Leverage the Power of Outlook

Outlook is a tremendously powerful program, but it needs your help to leverage the linkages between components. Whenever possible, you should be associating contacts and categories with your activities—even activities that do not seem significant at the time. You'll be astonished at how easy it is to find, sort, and display the relationships between two or more items long after they were created.

Categories

Assigns a category to an appointment. If you know the exact spelling of an existing category, enter it directly in the field provided; if you do not, click the Categories button to open the now familiar Categories dialog. See Chapter 3 for a general overview of using and assigning categories to Outlook items.

Private

Place a checkmark here to hide the appointment from anyone you share the Calendar folder with. See Chapter 14 for information on sharing Outlook folders.

In addition to the basic fields outlined here, there are several important features for Calendar items located on the open item's form, toolbar, or Actions menu. These

More Date (and Time) Entry Shortcuts

Outlook has intelligent date fields. They accept entries in the form of next thursday, two weeks ago, three months from now, 8 days from yesterday, second day of next week, etc. We've detailed many of these shortcuts in other chapters (see *Chapter 6, Mail* and *Chapter 9, Tasks*, for example), so we won't repeat the basics here. But we've been holding back a few tricks for this chapter:

- In addition to describing your date in words, you can also use abbreviations. For example, 15m means 15 minutes from now, 3w means three weeks from now, 2mo means two months from now, and 5y means five years from now. In each case, "now" is from the time shown in the Start Time field.

- If your appointment spans more than one day, you can enter decimal numbers. For example, 1.5d or 2.75w.

- You can also combine these abbreviations: 1mo 4d translates into "one month and four days" from now.

- In the time fields, Outlook interprets your entry based on the current time. So entering 4 after 12 noon converts to 4:00 p.m. If it's 4:00 a.m. you're after, enter 4a.

- You can increment a time field containing a "whole hour" entry to a "past the hour" entry by typing xm, where x is minutes. So typing 10m in a time field containing 7:00 would increment it to 7:10; entering 40m increments the field to 7:40.

include a status or information bar, a command to set recurring activities, and options to set reminders.

Appointment status

A status bar is displayed on the item's form. This gives you important feedback on conflicts, when an appointment or meeting is due, whether invitations have been sent, how many attendees responded, and a bevy of other valuable details. Figure 7-15 shows the status bar of an open item that conflicts with the scheduling of another calendar entry.

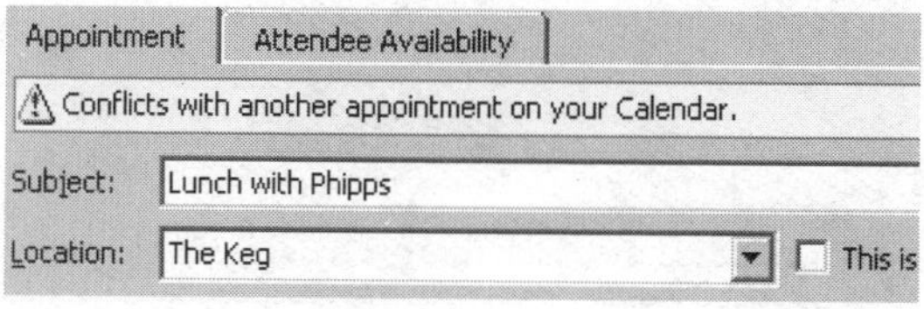

Figure 7-15: A warning message displayed in the status bar of an appointment

Recurring activities

Any Calendar item that repeats at a defined interval can be set up as a recurring activity. Once configured, Outlook generates a series of entries for that item according to the settings provided in the Appointment Recurrence dialog. Good candidates for recurrence are birthdays, weekly sales meetings, or weekly system backups.

Recurrences are set up two ways:

- Open an existing activity and choose Actions → Recurrence, or click the Recurrence button on the form's toolbar.

- Select a date from any Calendar view and choosing "New Recurring *activity*" from the context menu.

Either approach opens the Appointment Recurrence dialog shown in Figure 7-16.

TIP # 82

Activity Recurrence the Easy Way

The fastest, most efficient way to create a new recurring activity is as follows: go to Work Week view, and select the day you want your recurrence to begin. Highlight the time slots to define the time you want to use (if any), right-click, and choose New Recurring type_of_activity. This opens a new Appointment form behind the Appointment Recurrence dialog. The values you chose in the previous steps are already filled in the appropriate fields. Tweak, and click OK.

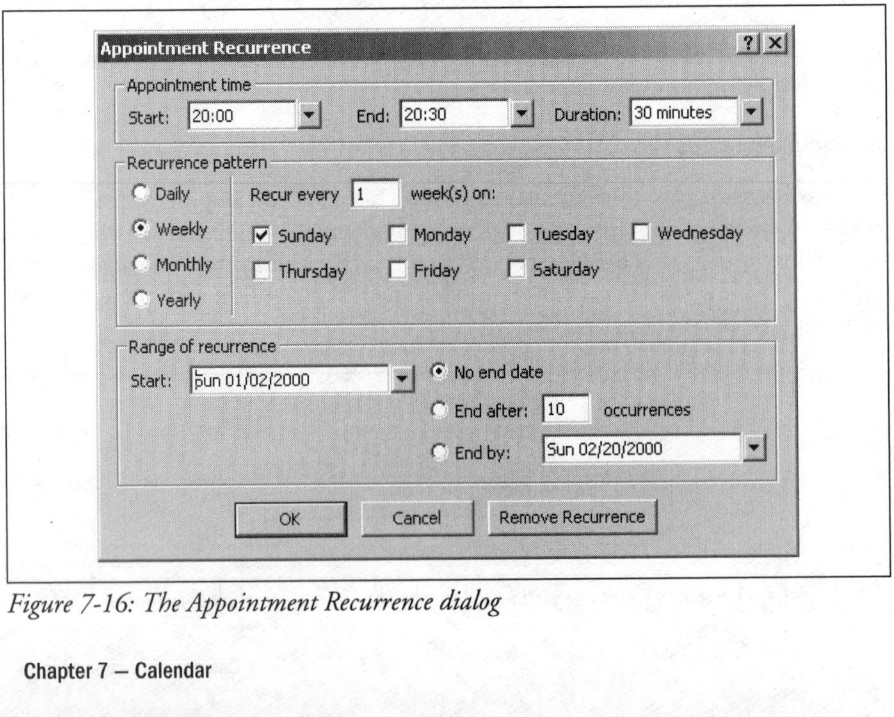

Figure 7-16: The Appointment Recurrence dialog

Setting a recurrence is a matter of configuring *when, how often,* and *for how long.*

The top row of the Appointment Recurrence dialog sets the *when*: Start time, End time, and Duration. Drop-down lists provide common entries for each field. If you don't find the time or scale you're looking for, enter it manually. Note the following:

- Change the Start time, and the end time changes to reflect the duration set.

- Change the End time, and the Duration adjusts accordingly.

- Change the Duration, and the End time changes to reflect the correct time between Start and End.

 To create a recurring All Day Event, set the Start and End times to "00:00" and the Duration to "1 Day."

The Recurrence pattern section defines *how often* the activity occurs. There are four patterns: Daily, Weekly, Monthly, and Yearly. Each choice produces a different set of configuration options, as shown in Figure 7-17.

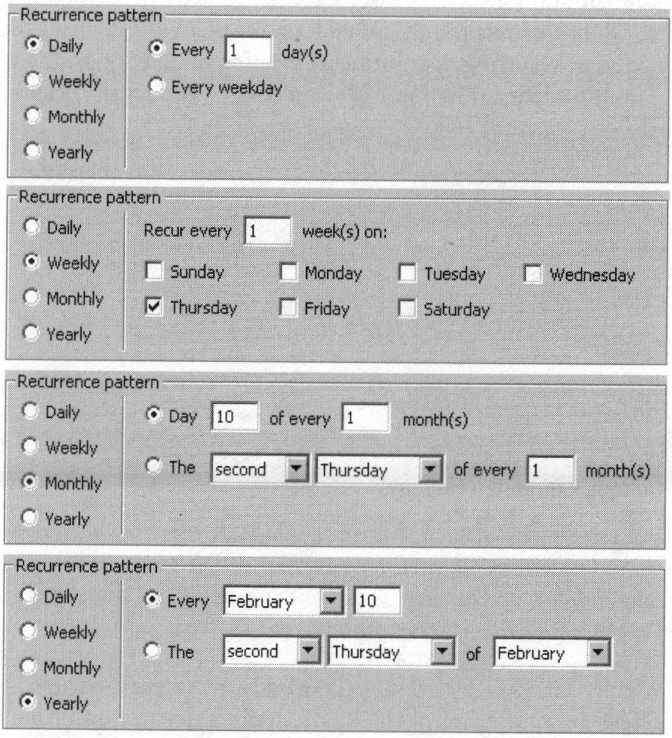

Figure 7-17: The four possible Recurrence patterns: Daily, Weekly, Monthly, and Yearly

Daily

Options include "Every *x* day(s)" for activities that repeat, for example, every second or third day, and "Every weekday" for activities that occur on every day in the work week (excepting Saturday and Sunday, given the default work week). The start date in this case is the next valid time on a working day.

Weekly

Options include the number of weeks between recurrence, and the day of the week the activity falls on. Here's where you'd set up a sales meeting that occurs every second Friday.

Monthly

Options include either a specific date every *x* months, or a specific day of the week every *x* months. Use this pattern to set up a recurrence for a users group meeting that takes place on the third Tuesday of every month.

Yearly

Options include a specific date every year (a birthday or anniversary), or a specific day of the month every year (commonly used for holidays; for example, Mother's Day—the second Sunday in May).

The final configuration necessary for a recurring activity is: *for how long* (see Figure 7-18). "Range of recurrence" provides a drop-down list to set the start date (if you created your recurring appointment, meeting or activity on the wrong day), and three options to define duration: "No end date," "End after *x* occurrences," and "End by *date*."

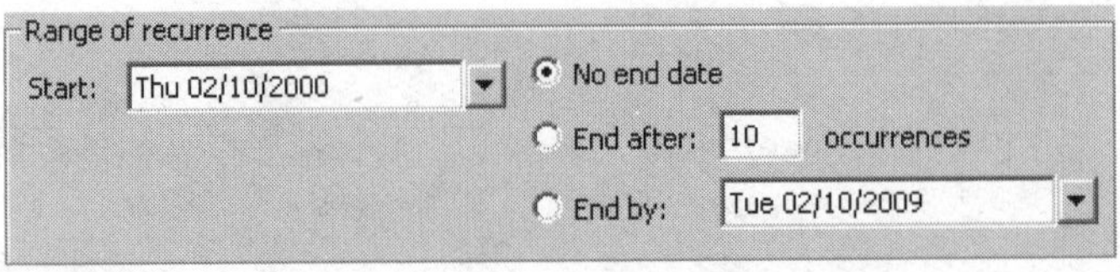

Figure 7-18: The Range of recurrence section of the Appointment Recurrence dialog

TIP # 83

Fixing Outlook's Imported Holidays

When you import predefined holidays into Outlook, they are added to your calendar as individual all-day events and not recurring activities (see the sidebar "Pitfalls of Importing Holidays"). One way to fix this is to delete all but one occurrence of a holiday and redefine it as a recurring activity.

Figure 7-19 gives an example of how a weekly recurrence pattern looks when configured. The top screenshot of the figure shows a description of the recurrence, which replaces the Start/End time fields in the activity's form. The lower part of

Figure 7-19 show a recurring series of appointments in a Work Week view. The two semi-circular arrows denote the activity as recurring.

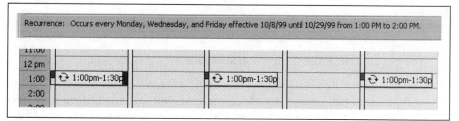

Figure 7-19: The information field found on a recurring activity form (top), and a recurring activity shown in a Week View (bottom)

Any time you open a recurring activity, you'll see the dialog shown in Figure 7-20.

Figure 7-20: The Open Recurring Item dialog

Your options in this dialog are:

Open this occurrence
> Opens a *single instance* of the item. You can tell you are working with a single instance of the recurrence because date and time fields are displayed. Any changes made to the open item apply to the open item only. For example, you created a series of recurring appointments as a reminder to do weekly backups every Friday at 8:00 p.m. This Friday, however, you're going to be out of town. To reschedule your reminder, open a single occurrence of the series, and change the date. This modification does not affect the original occurrence series: you are still reminded the following Friday to do your backups.

Open the series
> Opens the recurrence *series* for modification. In this case, the open form displays the information text shown in Figure 7-19 (top). Changes made on this form affect every event in the series *ahead* of the date opened. Continuing the example used in the previous item, Fridays are not a good day and you want to change your scheduled backups to Sunday. Open the series and click the

Calendar

Recurrence icon on the toolbar, and modify the Appointment Recurrence dialog to reflect the desired changes.

Reminders

Here is a brief summary of using reminders:

- You can set a reminder for any Calendar item.

- The default setting for Calendar's reminders is located on the Tools → Options → Preferences tab, under the Calendar section. Selecting the Default Reminder checkbox sets reminders for all new Calendar activities. The default lead-time for reminders is set via the drop-down list. If you don't like any of the interval options provided, enter your own.

- You can override these default settings on an item-by-item basis from the record's Appointment form using the Reminder options.

- When a reminder is displayed (see Figure 7-21), you have several options:

Dismiss
Close the dialog and cancel the reminder.

Snooze
Close the Reminder dialog and be reminded again after the time period shown in the drop-down list. The contents of this drop-down list are fixed—you cannot add your own custom snooze times. If you Snooze an item, when the item pops up again after the selected Snooze time, the default Snooze time remains as you set it for one more occurrence. If you Snooze it again, the next time it pops up, the default Snooze time is reset to five minutes.

Open Item
Open the activity attached to the reminder. The reminder remains active until you select Snooze or Dismiss.

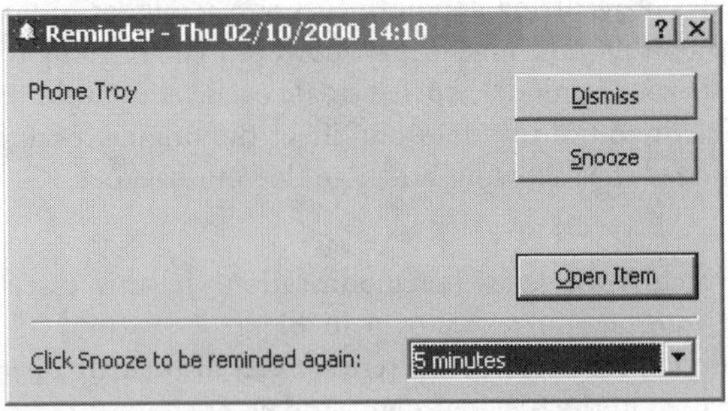

Figure 7-21: Outlook's Reminder dialog

- There is a further reminder option dialog located deep in the bowels of Outlook's options dialogs under Tools → Options → Other → Advanced Options → Reminder Options. This dialog determines whether a reminder is displayed, a sound is played, neither, or both. You can also select the default sound associated with a reminder using the Browse button.

Load-Balancing Your Calendar

Rescheduling activities is a fact of life. When you find your calendar getting out of sorts, shuffle your activities the easy way—with drag and drop. Open one of Calendar's graphical views (Day, Work Week, Week, or Month), select an activity, and drag it to a new date.

Under Day or Work Week, you can also adjust appointment durations by simply dragging the upper or lower edge of an entry's border.

Actions → New All Day Event

An all-day event is an activity that occurs on a specific day (or days). Events differ from appointments and meetings in that they have no times attached. Candidates for Events include deadlines, birthdays, anniversaries, holidays (please see the sidebar "Are Holidays Annual Events?" later in this chapter), or trade shows.

As noted in our discussion of appointments earlier in this chapter, Calendar items can easily be changed from one type to another (see Tip # 79). This results in three ways to create an All Day Event:

- Open an existing appointment or meeting and select the All Day Event option.

- Create a new All Day Event using a menu command.

- Double-click a date in Week or Month view.

TIP # 84

Fast Path to a New Recurring Event

The Actions menu doesn't have a New Recurring Event command, but Calendar's context menus do. Right-click any open area of a Calendar view and you'll find the command listed.

The Actions → New All Day Event command simplifies the two-step process of first creating an appointment and then designating it as an event, and instead creates an appointment with the All Day Event option preselected, as shown in Figure 7-22.

All Day Events are defined with a Start time of "00:00" and an End time of "00:00," spanning one or more days, and displayed as a banner under the day heading of Calendar's graphical views (Day/Week/Month).

Calendar

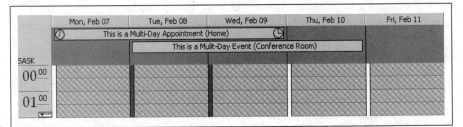

Figure 7-22: The All Day Event option—when selected, it hides the time fields

Note the distinction between a multiday event and a multiday Appointment, illustrated in Figure 7-23. A multiday event is based on a 24-hour duration, and as such, spans whole days only. A multiday appointment can span part-days (for example, starting at 7:00 a.m. on Monday Feb 07 and extending to 3:00 p.m. on Wednesday Feb 09), although the banner shows it as blocked for the whole width of the day's column. The easiest way to tell the difference between the two is the presence of a small clock on either end of a multiday appointment.

Figure 7-23: A Work Week view showing a multiday Appointment at the top, and a multiday Event below

All Day Events can be set for reminders and recurrences, and forwarded to others (via the iCalendar format or regular email). You can edit the subject of an event directly in the banner, or open it in an appointment form by double-clicking. You can also adjust the dates of an event from a Day or Work Week view by dragging the left or right edge to increase or decrease the duration as desired.

Actions → New Meeting Request

New Meeting Request is Outlook parlance for creating a meeting. Creating a meeting implies scheduling and inviting attendees, choosing a location, and booking resources.

> **NOTE** *Meeting Requests and Task Requests (see Chapter 9) are functionally similar; they get other people involved in your commitments by leveraging Outlook Mail.*

Planning and creating a meeting with Outlook is straightforward. As we pointed out in the "Actions → New Appointment" section, a meeting is just an appointment with the addition of several properties added to accommodate the collaborative elements of any group gathering:

- You need to invite and inform people of the meeting.
- You need to know who can attend.

- You need to schedule any resources required.

- Optionally, you need a way to determine a time slot that fits with the other attendees' (and resources') existing commitments.

This is all accomplished through the Appointments form, modified to accept and manage these new elements. This New Meeting Request form can be invoked in the following ways:

- From the Actions menu, select New Meeting Request, or from any Outlook component use the keyboard shortcut Ctrl+Shift+Q.

- Select a date and time slot from Day or Work Week view, right-click, and from the context menu choose New Meeting Request. Like New Appointment, this creates a new meeting for the day selected, with the time set for the first working time slot of the day as defined by your settings under Work Week (Tools → Options → Calendar Options).

- Drag your cursor over a series of time slots in a Day or Work Week view, and select New Meeting Request from the context menu. This creates a meeting with Start and End times matching the time slots selected.

- Open your Contacts folder, select one or more contacts, and drop them on the Calendar icon on the Outlook Bar. This creates a new meeting request pre-addressed to the contacts selected.

Calendar's Meeting entry/edit form is shown in Figure 7-24 (bottom).

In contrast to the Appointment form shown in Figure 7-24 (top), the Meeting form simply adds a To field above Subject. You can quickly convert an existing appointment to a meeting using the Invite Attendees button.

TIP # 85

Save a Meeting Request for Later

If for some reason you are not ready to send a meeting request, you can use the Cancel Invitation command and save the item as an appointment instead. Outlook hides the attendee information you've entered, but it reappears if you later open the appointment and click Invite Attendees.

The To field specifies the email addresses of everyone invited to the meeting. Entries are resolved against any defined Outlook Address Books (see Chapter 3) and support all the same features as addressing an email under Outlook. See Chapter 5, *Mail Editors*, for details on the shortcuts available for addressing a message. Clicking the To button opens the Select Attendees and Resources dialog shown in Figure 7-25.

Meeting attendees can be of three types: Required (necessary to the meeting), Optional (guests), and Resources. Double-click an entry to add that contact to the Required list. To add entries to the Optional or Resources list, you must first select

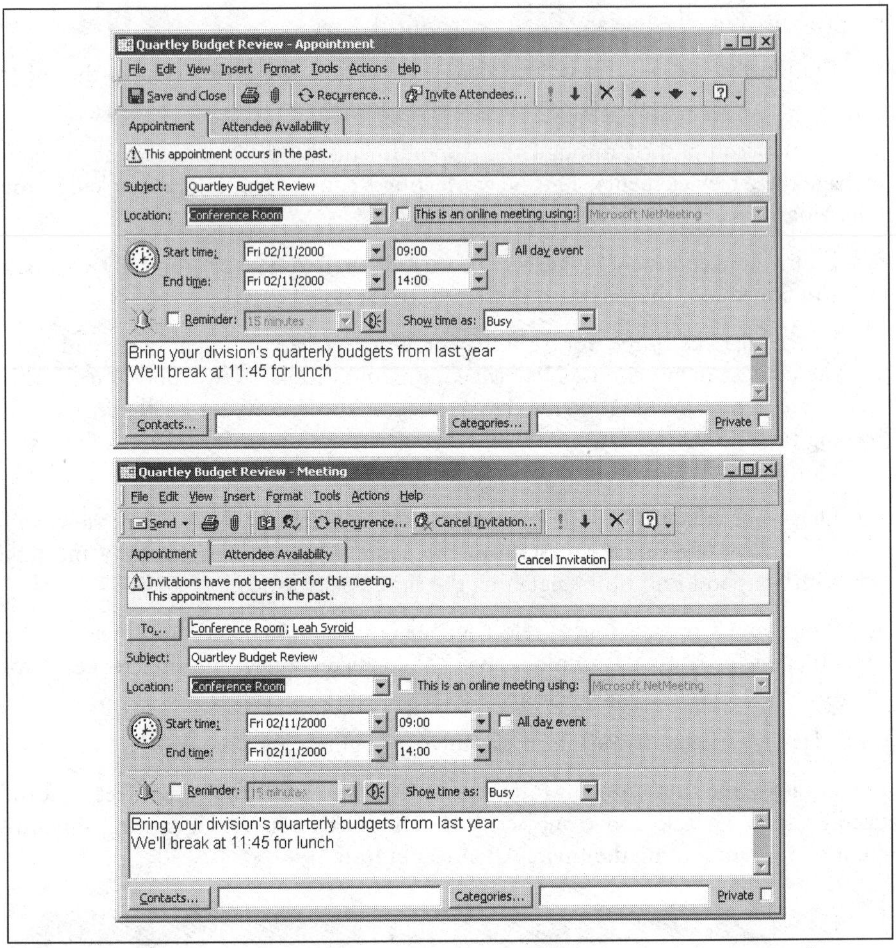

Figure 7-24: Calendar's New Meeting Request form, showing an Appointment form (top) and a Meeting form (bottom)

the person or resource from the left pane, and then use the respective button. When you're done, click OK. This will insert your selections in the To field of the Meeting Request.

TIP # 86

Using Distribution Lists for Meeting Requests

If you routinely send meeting requests to the same group of people, save time typing by creating a Distribution List (DL). This ensures that you don't miss anyone important. Irregular attendees can be added to the address field as required. For details on creating Distribution Lists, see Chapter 8, Contacts.

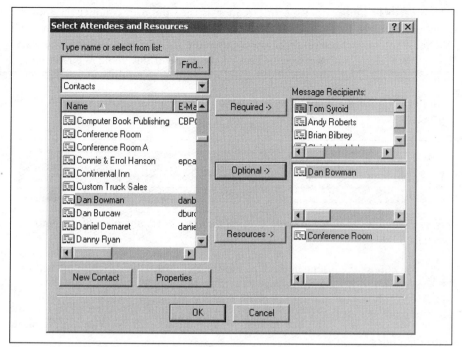

Figure 7-25: The Select Attendees and Resources dialog accessed from the Meeting form To button

Meetings under Outlook always have a Meeting Organizer (just as Task Requests are always owned by one person). That organizer is always displayed under the Required/Message recipient's list (distinguished by a blue index card—all other recipients are shown as a green card), although he or she is not sent an invitation.

Using Resources Under Outlook

Resources are tools or facilities required to conduct a meeting. These might include a conference room, slide projectors, overhead projectors, whiteboards, etc. The notion behind "inviting" a conference room to a meeting is to ensure it is available, and if it is, book it in your name so everyone else in your group or organization knows that it is occupied for the specified period.

The functionality of this feature under Outlook relies on access to some form of shared scheduling system. One example of this is connectivity to an Exchange Server where you can share the contents of your Calendar, and resources have a special mailbox or account specifically set up by the administrator.

Trying to schedule resources without the features of such a messaging system doesn't work. Resources, just like flesh-and-blood meeting participants, need an email address and some kind of mechanism to confirm their availability.

The other field unique to a meeting request is the option to conduct the meeting "Online." Online meetings under Outlook use the features of NetMeeting and NetShow to conduct a virtual conference over the Internet or a local area network. Using NetMeeting and NetShow is beyond the scope of this book. We refer you to *Windows 98 in a Nutshell* (O'Reilly) for more details on using these products.

Selecting "This is an online meeting using" enables and expands a section of the form as shown in Figure 7-26.

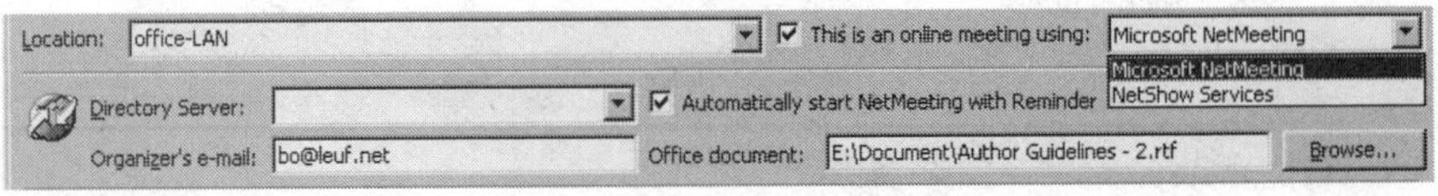

Figure 7-26: The expanded selection showing the protocol options available for online meetings

Once you choose the online option, you must select either NetMeeting or NetShow Services from the drop-down menu.

If you want your PC to automatically establish the online connection when it's time for the meeting, check the box labeled "Automatically start NetMeeting/NetShow with Reminder."

> **NOTE** *The Subject description for the Meeting Request becomes the conference name in a NetMeeting session.*

The NetMeeting-specific fields and options are:

Directory Server
This is required. For NetMeeting, you must specify the connection server's *TCP/IP* address (or URL). Your System Administrator typically provides this address.

Organizer's email
This address defaults to the meeting creator, and is required.

Office document
This is optional. Only a single document is accepted here; browsing or selecting a second document replaces the first. Outlook opens the document in collaboration mode when the meeting starts.

NetShow Services is a way to broadcast streaming content (audio, video, whiteboard, chat) over the Internet, and has only one field:

Event Address
This is the required URL for the NetShow event broadcast site. This is where whiteboard actions are sent for distribution to all attendees. The NetShow tools are used to create the events to be broadcast.

The Appointment form also contains a tab labeled "Attendee Availability" illustrated in Figure 7-27. The functionality and features of this element of the form are detailed in the "Actions → Plan a Meeting" section of this chapter.

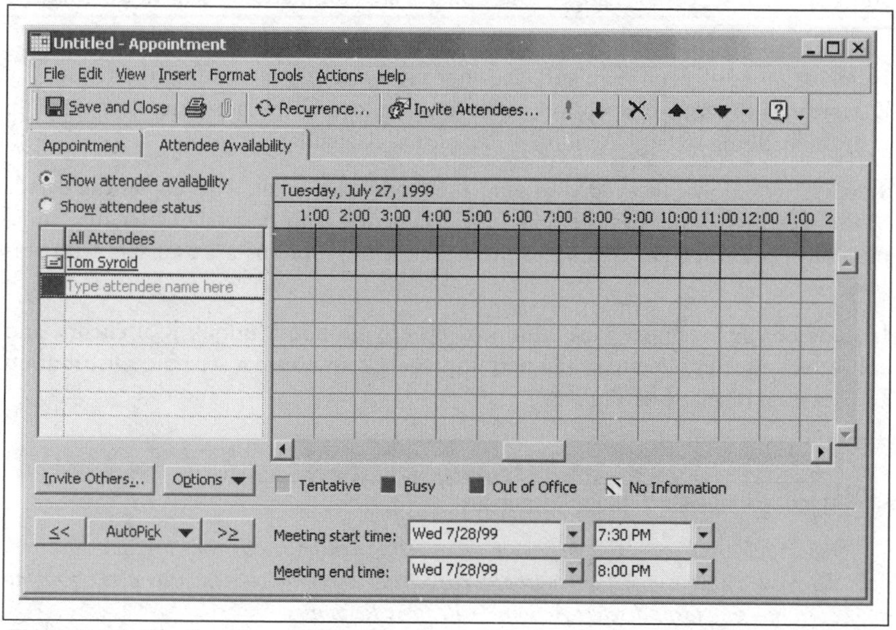

Figure 7-27: The Appointment/Meeting form with the Attendee Availability tab selected

When you're satisfied with the details of the meeting, click Send on the form's toolbar. This saves the item, adds the entry to your calendar, and dispatches the request to all the recipients named.

TIP # 87

Mark a Meeting as Tentative

If the meeting you're scheduling is tentative, mark it as such using the "Show time as" field on the Appointment form. This displays the meeting with a light blue border in both your calendar and the calendar of any recipients of the Meeting Request.

Meeting requests can be sent in one of three formats:

- As an Outlook item—the default.

- In iCalendar format, manually or as a program default configured under Tools → Options → Calendar Options.

- As a regular email, discussed under the "Actions → Forward" command later in this chapter.

The scheduling program used by each individual recipient dictates your choice here. Sending a meeting request as an Outlook item is the best choice, as this method is the most functional. The meeting is automatically added to the recipient's calendar, and responses, schedule changes, and updates are automatically sent to the meeting creator.

If one or more of your recipients does not use Outlook, forwarding the request by iCalendar is the next best option; however, you lose Calendar's automatic tracking features by doing so (see "Actions → Forward as iCalendar").

The least functional method is to send the request by email. This copies the details of the meeting to the message body; the recipient has to manually enter this information in her calendar. Again, no message tracking options are available with this option.

If some of your recipients use Outlook, others use non-Outlook iCal clients, and still others use simple email, the best approach is to create a separate Distribution List for each format (see Tip # 86).

TIP # 88

Meeting Requests Without Responses

Responses are the default behavior for meeting requests, but they are not required. To send a meeting request without requesting a response from attendees, from an open meeting form deselect Actions → Request Responses.

Tracking a meeting request

Once a meeting request is sent, it is what we term "committed." You can still cancel the meeting, but not via the Cancel Invitation button on the toolbar; you must use the meeting form's Action → Cancel Invitation menu command. The toolbar command toggles an entry between an appointment and a meeting, up until the meeting is committed. The menu command *deletes* the meeting entry from your records, after first asking you if you want to send a cancellation notice to all attendees.

If at any time you need to reschedule a committed meeting:

- Open the entry and change the time fields, or

- Drag the entry to a new time in any of the Day/Week/Month views, or to any day in the Date Navigator.

Doing so produces the warning dialog shown in Figure 7-28.

Clicking Yes opens the record so you can add a reason or explanation to the notes field; send the update by clicking Save and Close on the form's toolbar. Selecting No reschedules the meeting in your calendar, but sends no update.

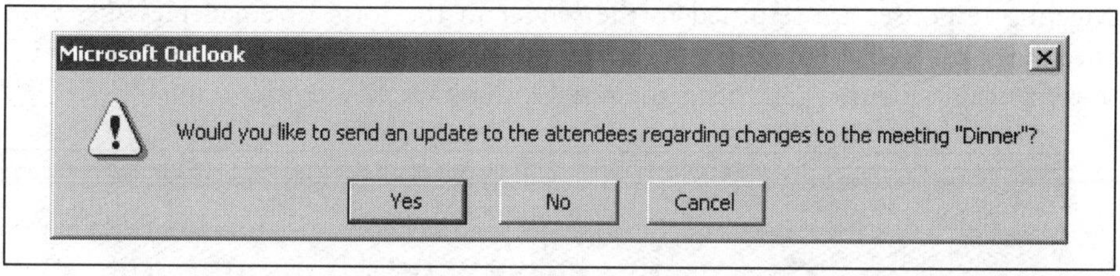

Figure 7-28: The Warning dialog display when a committed meeting is rescheduled

When the recipient receives the meeting request—providing his email client supports the iCalendar standard—he can either Accept the invitation to add it to his calendar, Decline it, or select Tentative. Any of these three responses generates a return message to update the sender's meeting record. If the recipient's email client doesn't support this standard, he must inspect the request visually, interpret the content, and respond manually.

> **NOTE** *The Accept/Decline/Tentative options a recipient receives are not the same as meeting tracking. Tracking refers to updates sent when a meeting item is rescheduled, or the content of any of the fields changed. Both Outlook items and iCalendar format supports responses; Outlook items alone support tracking.*

Before the return message is sent, the dialog shown in Figure 7-29 is displayed. The

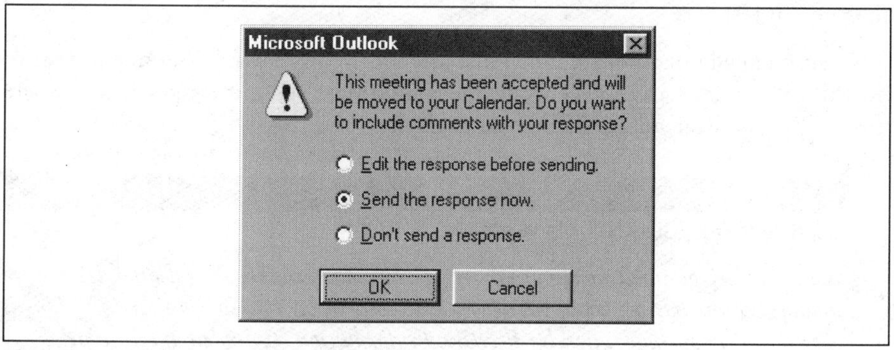

Figure 7-29: The Meeting Accept/Decline dialog

options in this dialog are:

- Edit the response opens the meeting request form for the recipient to add a note or modify any of the item's fields. Click Send when done.

- Send the response now adds the meeting to the recipient's calendar and sends a response.

- Don't send a response adds the meeting to the recipient's calendar and sends no reply.

Meeting responses are returned to the sender in the form of email messages with meeting-specific content. Opening a response updates the sender's meeting entry automatically. Figure 7-30 shows the way Outlook tracks attendee status.

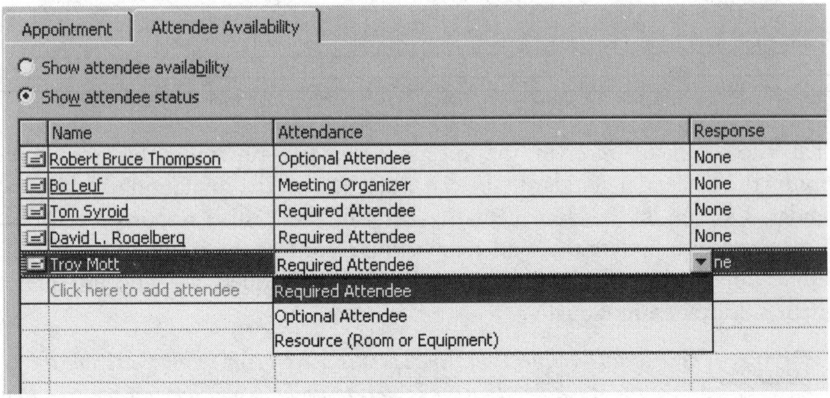

Figure 7-30: The companion Attendee status form, showing the attendance type change for an attendee

The status list (on the Attendee Availability tab of the item's form) provides an overview of which contacts are attendees, what type of attendees they are, and their most recent response.

You can manually manipulate individual attendee status entries. You might wish to do this if a contact cannot generate the appropriate reply messages (perhaps she doesn't have an iCalendar-capable mail client).

TIP # 89

Send Your Free/Busy URL Via vCard

A successfully planned meeting requires a time slot suitable for all attendees. Since available time has a way of changing, you need to be able to monitor this. This is easy to do if you have attendee Free/Busy information. Complete the Internet Free/Busy field on your contact record, and then attach your vCard to messages you send as a Signature. Chapter 5 provides you with the necessary details for doing this.

Actions → Plan a Meeting

When you send a Meeting Request, the subject is defined, the attendees selected, and a time is chosen based on the preferences of the meeting organizer. The request is then dispatched and the attendees, in turn, accept or decline the invitation to attend. It's not too hard to see the inherent problems with this approach. You've got a conference room booked, and ten people invited to an important product review. Unbeknownst to you, three of those people—all key to this meeting—are either tied up with previous commitments or out of town. Wouldn't it be a lot easier if you had some way of knowing, in advance, who was busy when?

Well you do, *providing* the attendees you are planning your meeting around publicly post their schedules somewhere. This "somewhere"—for Outlook—takes one of two forms: a public or corporate server that hosts Free/Busy information, or a mail server (for example, Exchange Server) that lets users post their schedules in public folders.

Calendar's Plan a Meeting command turns the process of arranging a meeting around—first you choose attendees, then you plan the meeting based on an appropriate time slot that fits with the attendee's existing commitments.

 Outlook's Plan a Meeting command relies heavily on access to public schedules. If you do not have access to this information, Plan a Meeting is not going to get you any further than a meeting request—you're still trying to organize an activity in the dark.

Actions → Plan a Meeting opens the dialog shown in Figure 7-31 (if this dialog looks familiar, it should—it's simply the Attendee Availability tab from a Meeting form).

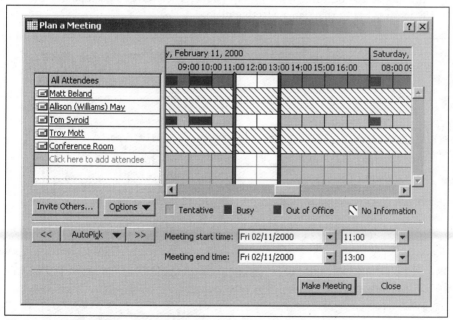

Figure 7-31: The Plan a Meeting dialog

The meeting duration is indicated by the two vertical bars on the timeline graph: green represents the start time, red the end time. Meeting times can be adjusted either with the drop-down lists below the timeline, or directly by dragging a start or end time bar with your mouse.

The creator of the meeting has a special, fixed attendance status as Meeting Organizer. You can remove attendees with the Invite Others button or the context-menu command for the selected attendee. This dialog is explained later in the "Add or Remove Attendees" section. When you save attendee changes to a committed meeting, Outlook then asks whether to send notifications to all attendees, to added or deleted attendees only, or to no one.

 The row to the right of the All Attendees title bar displays the combined schedules for all invited members and resources. This is useful for quickly discerning conflicts.

Options in the Plan a Meeting dialog are as follows:

Invite Others

Opens the Select Attendees and Resources dialog shown in Figure 7-32. Select the meeting attendees from the list on the right. Double-click an entry to add that contact to the Required list. To add entries to the Optional or Resources list, you must first select the person or resource from the left pane, and then use the respective button. When you're done, click OK. This updates the All Attendees list on the Plan a Meeting dialog.

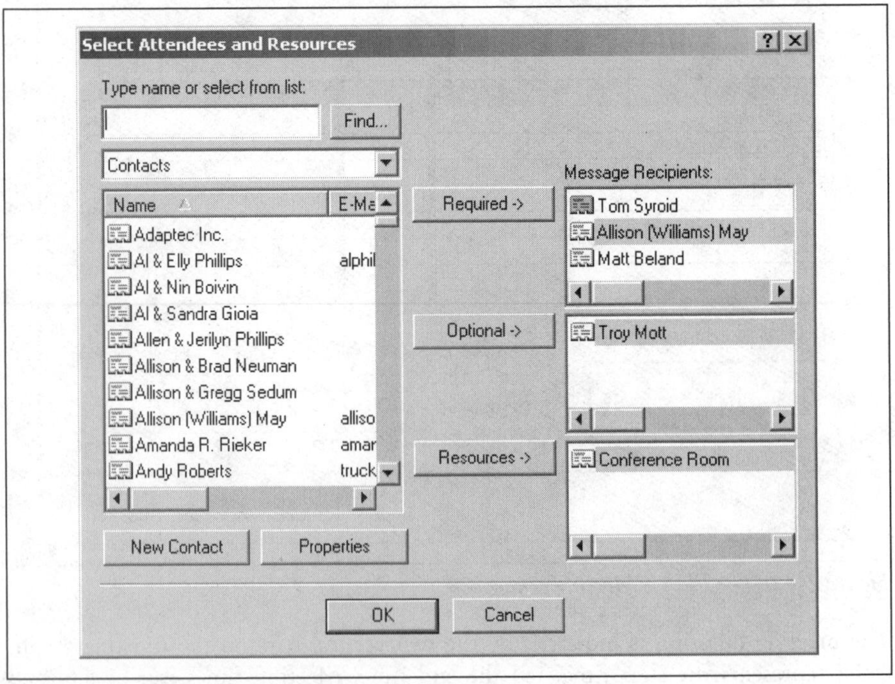

Figure 7-32: The Select Attendees and Resources dialog

Options

Contains three settings: Show Only Working Hours, Show Zoomed Out, and Update Free/Busy (see Figure 7-33, left).

Show Only Working Hours

Limits the timeline scale to the hours you've selected under Calendar Options as representative of your working day.

Show Zoomed Out

Shows a full 24-hour day if the Show Only Working Hours option is selected, and almost three days if it is not.

Update Free/Busy

Forces a refresh of Free/Busy information for all attendees listed. This is a good idea, as most Free/Busy schedules are typically set to refresh only once or twice a day at most, and people's schedules can change quickly. This ensures the scheduling information displayed is current based on the schedules provided.

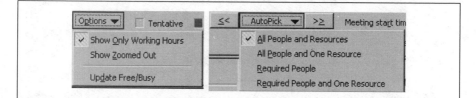

Figure 7-33: The Plan a Meeting Options submenu (left), and the AutoPick submenu (right)

AutoPick

Lets Outlook automatically find the first available time slot. From the drop-down list you can select the range of resources the analysis uses: All People and Resources, All People and One Resource, Required People, and Required People and One Resource, as shown in Figure 7-33, right. Required People uses only those attendees listed under Required on the Select Attendees and Resources dialog; choosing One Resource uses the first resource list on the same dialog.

Clicking the >> or << buttons scans forward or backward in time until it finds the next suitable block of free time available for all of the people and resources involved in the meeting. You cannot scan earlier than the current system time.

When you're done, click Make Meeting. A new Meeting Request form is generated. The attendees from the Plan a Meeting dialog are entered on the To line, any resources identified as rooms are added to the location field, and the time/duration you chose are entered in the Start/End times. Fill in a subject, and click Send.

Actions → New Recurring Appointment/Meeting

We combine these two commands under one heading, as they are functionally identical aside from the fact one creates a new recurring appointment, and the other a recurring meeting.

Earlier in this chapter we discussed the process of taking an existing activity and setting a recurrence pattern for it. Both these "New Recurring..." menu items shortcut this two-step process and create a recurring appointment or meeting directly.

The usual suggestions offered for the creation of other Calendar activities apply here as well: select the date—and optionally a time range—first, then choose the appropriate command from either the Actions menu or the right-click content menu. Whichever approach you pick, a new form opens along with the Appointment Recurrence dialog, as shown in Figure 7-34.

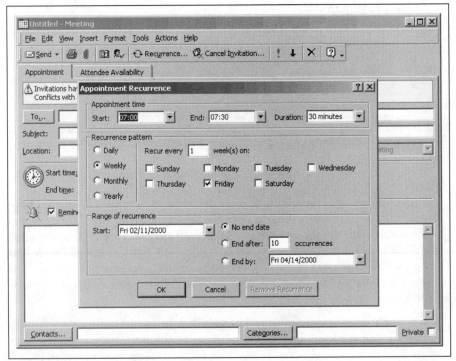

Figure 7-34: Appointment Recurrence dialog for a new Meeting

Step-by-step instructions for configuring a recurring activity are located under the section "Recurring activities" of the "Actions → New Appointment" command.

Actions → Add or Remove Attendees

To enable this command, you must have a meeting selected in your calendar. Right-click and choose Add or Remove Attendees from the context menu (or Actions → Add or Remove Attendees from the menu). This command is simply a shortcut to opening the meeting, selecting the Attendee Availability tab, and clicking the Invite Others button. Using the Add or Remove Attendees dialog is fully described under the "Actions → Plan a Meeting" section earlier in this chapter.

Actions → Forward as iCalendar

iCalendar is an open standard, based on RFC 2445, that enables applications to share calendaring information in a format independent of the program it was created in or the transport used to exchange it. In practice, this means that Calendar items from Outlook forwarded in the iCalendar format should be readable by any other mail client supporting this standard.

Unfortunately, theory and reality are all too often miles apart in the world of computers and computing. iCalendar attachments are not always portable between two mail clients both claiming to support the standard, due to the way each vendor chooses to implement it.

To forward a Calendar item to another person in iCalendar format, select it, and from the Actions menu choose Forward as iCalendar. This opens a new message form in your default mail editor with the record attached. Address the message and send it. Upon arrival, if your recipient uses Outlook, they can simply drag the attachment and drop it on the Outlook Bar Calendar icon to create a new entry. Similar methods for other mail clients vary.

 NOTE   *A meeting sent via iCalendar does not support the automatic tracking of attendees. If the recipient is in fact intended to be an attendee, you need to manually update your attendee list accordingly.*

iCalendar attachments can be saved as separate files (*.ics*). These are Plain Text files that look similar to the text shown in Example 7-1.

Example 7-1: A Typical iCalendar Attachment File

```
BEGIN:VCALENDAR
PRODID:-//Microsoft Corporation//Outlook 9.0 MIMEDIR//EN
VERSION:2.0
METHOD:REQUEST
BEGIN:VEVENT
ATTENDEE;CN="Bo Leuf";ROLE=REQ-PARTICIPANT;RSVP=TRUE:MAILTO:bo@isp.net
ATTENDEE;CN="Tom Syroid";ROLE=REQ-PARTICIPANT;RSVP=TRUE:MAILTO:tom@isp.net
ATTENDEE;CN="Jeffery Thomas";ROLE=OPT-
PARTICIPANT;RSVP=TRUE:MAILTO:jthomas@northern.com
ORGANIZER:MAILTO:bo@isp.net
DTSTART:19990928T070000Z
DTEND:19990928T073000Z
```

Example 7-1: A Typical iCalendar Attachment File (continued)

```
TRANSP:OPAQUE
SEQUENCE:0
UID:040000008200E00074C5B7101A82E00800000000000D0C6211B9706BF010000000000
 000000100000000633BFE1D971D3118848006097F79CFD
DTSTAMP:19990924T121425Z
SUMMARY:milestone evaluation
PRIORITY:5
CLASS:PUBLIC
BEGIN:VALARM
TRIGGER:PT15M
ACTION:DISPLAY
DESCRIPTION:Reminder
END:VALARM
END:VEVENT
END:VCALENDAR
```

If you are unsure about your recipient's mail client capabilities, it is better to simply forward Calendar items as described in the next section.

Actions → Forward

If you need to exchange scheduling information with someone and you're unsure about his or her ability to handle the iCalendar format, use the workhorse of the Internet—simple email. Select a calendar item from any view, and choose Actions → Forward. The default message editor opens with the details of the selected items copied to the notes field of a new message, as shown in Figure 7-35.

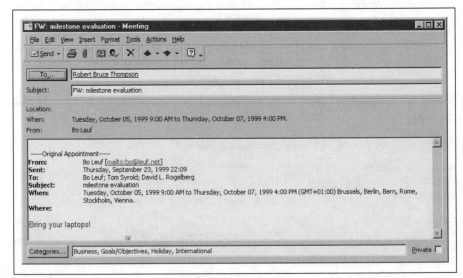

Figure 7-35: Forwarding a meeting request as email

Add any further comments, address the message, and click Send. Note that if the calendar item is a meeting request or update, the recipient of the message is not included in the automatic attendee tracking process.

The Forward command is here primarily to allow users of other email clients to still receive calendaring information—for example, details of an event you have stored in Outlook—electronically. It's not as seamless as sending the information via meeting requests or iCalendar, but it does the job.

Calendar View Options

We're going to break from our discussion of menu commands and look quickly at the configuration options available for Calendar views. These options are found at the bottom of the View → Current View menu (Customize Current View and Define Views), so they logically belong somewhere toward the end of this chapter if we were to follow strict topic-menu order. It's better to be aware of configuration options now, however, before we start discussing Calendar's preconfigured views.

It bears repeating that Calendar supports two types of view: Day/Week/Month and table. This distinction ripples throughout everything to do with views: how they display, the contents of context menus, and the available configuration options.

There's nothing unique about Calendar's Table views; they work the same, act the same, and are configured the same in Calendar as they are in other Outlook components. To open a Table view's options dialog, go to View → Current View → Customize Current View and click on the Other Settings button (see Figure 7-36, left).

TIP # 90

Shortcut to the View Settings Dialog

Accessing a view's settings dialog through Outlook's menus is an exercise in inefficiency. Thankfully, there's a two-click shortcut. Right-click in any open area of a view, and from the context menu choose Other Settings. This trick works for both Calendar and Table views.

The Other Settings dialog, shown in Figure 7-36 (left), contains the options for setting the properties of column headings, rows, AutoPreview, and grid lines for the displayed table. See Chapter 3 for details on customizing table views.

Calendar's Day/Week/Month views, on the other hand, offer several display options not found anywhere else in Outlook. You access the Format Day/Week/Month View dialog shown in Figure 7-36 (right) in one of two ways: from the View menu (View → Current View → Customize Current View, click the Other Settings button), or using the context menu shortcut detailed in Tip # 90.

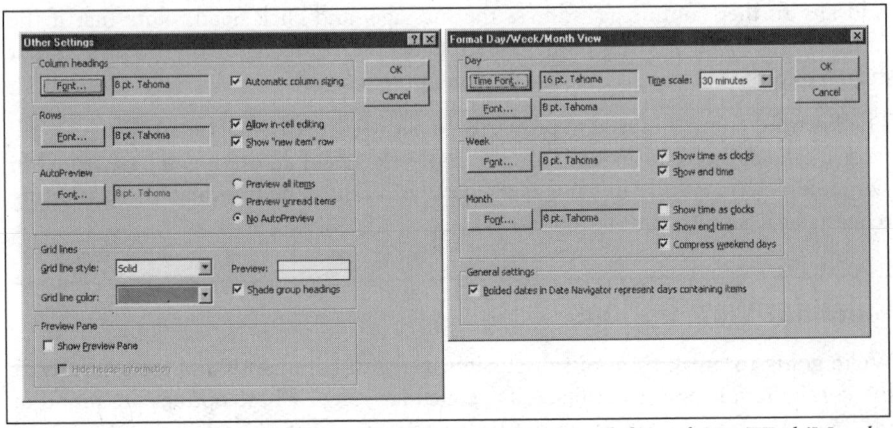

Figure 7-36: Calendar's view options dialogs—Table view (left) and Day/Week/Month view (right)

The Format Day/Week/Month View dialog contains the following options:

Under the Day section

The Time Font button sets the font used by the time bar displayed on the left edge of Calendar's Day and Work Week views. Don't bother trying to set a point size here; it doesn't do anything. The Font button sets the face and point size used to display entries—again, for both Day and Work Week. The point size works for this option.

The Time scale drop-down list sets the time scale for Day and Work Week views. Interval choices are: 5, 6, 10, 15, 30, or 60 minutes. This option also determines the default time interval for a new Calendar item. For example, setting the time scale to "30 minutes" makes the default duration of new appointments or meetings 30 minutes.

Under the Week section

The Font button sets the font (face and point) used by a Week view. "Show time as clocks" uses icons to depict appointment and meeting durations. "Show end time" shows both start and end times; this option works in conjunction with the previous clocks setting.

Under the Month section

You have all the same settings as the Week section, with an added option to "Compress weekend days." This displays Saturday and Sunday together in one cell.

Under General settings

Select the "Bolded dates in Date Navigator..." option to show dates containing any type of Calendar item (appointment, meeting, or event) as bold in the Date Navigator.

Calendar → View Menu

The preceding topics in this chapter have focused on creating appointments, meetings and events. At some point in time, you'll want to display, sort, and analyze all this valuable information. This is the realm of Outlook's View menu.

The view menu contains the Current View and Go To submenus. If the view selected is of the Day/Week/Month format, the menu displays commands for switching the range of days shown (Day, Work Week, Week, or Month) and a submenu for selecting a TaskPad view (see Figure 7-37, left). When a Table view is selected, the Day/Week/Month view and TaskPad commands are replaced with AutoPreview and a submenu for expanding and collapsing groups (see Figure 7-37, right).

 NOTE *The Preview Pane can be enabled for both Day/Week/Month and table views. The Preview Pane displays the contents of an activity's note field. You cannot, however, edit the contents of this field from the Preview Pane.*

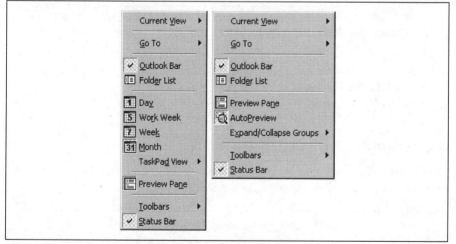

Figure 7-37: Calendar's View Menus—Day/Week/Month (left) and Table view (right)

AutoPreview is a handy—and confusing—feature because of how it is implemented in Calendar's Day/Week/Month views and the design of Outlook's menu structure.

AutoPreview is described by Outlook's Help topic as an option to display "the first three lines of a message" (in the context of an email message). This is not the case. It displays more than three lines, but the rules as to how many and when are not clear. In the context of a Calendar item:

- AutoPreview is available for both Day/Week/Month and table views, even though it is not displayed on the View menu for Day/Week/Month view. To enable AutoPreview under a Day/Week/Month view, select View → Current

View → Day/Week/Month with AutoPreview. To enable AutoPreview for a table view, you must toggle it on or off from the View menu (see Figure 7-37, right).

- Under a Day/Week/Month view, AutoPreview only works for Week (not Work Week) and Month. When enabled, holding your cursor over an appointment or meeting (not an event) displays the contents of the Notes field in a pop-up—all of it, not just the first three lines. Don't confuse this pop-up with the one displayed by default, for all views, that shows the Subject and Location fields if column sizing has cut off part of this information.

- Enabling AutoPreview for a table view displays the contents of the Notes field for *all* items (including events), using the same inconsistent format found in Mail: you see more than three lines, usually, and how much you see varies widely depending on the contents.

If you use AutoPreview, the best advice we can offer is to ensure you put the most important details of a note in the first two or three lines.

TIP # 91

The Current View Menu Remembers State

This is an important tip to use to your advantage: the Current View menu remembers state. This means that if you change your current view (e.g., drag the Due Date field off the title bar) and go to a different view, once you return to the previous view it will be as you left it.

View → Current View

The Current View submenu is shown in Figure 7-38. It contains seven predefined views, plus any customized views you've created.

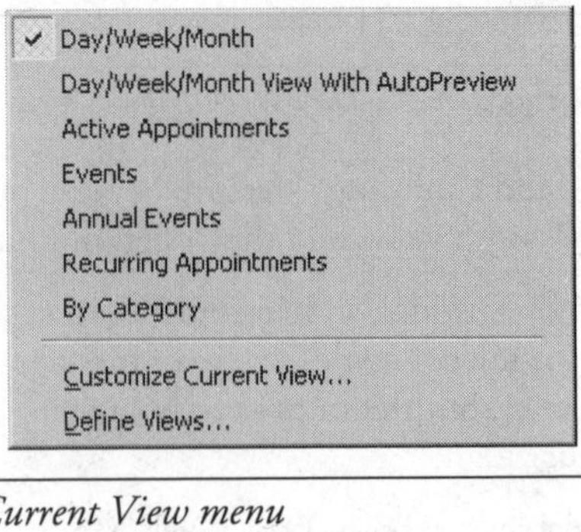

Figure 7-38: Calendar Current View menu

Of the seven listed views, the top two display the content of your Calendar folder in graphical calendar-like views. The remaining views are in table format with records laid out in rows and the fields of that record as columns. You'll find the graphical view more suited to daily scheduling tasks, and table views the choice for sorting, analysis, and followup.

 The format of the displayed date in Calendar is controlled by the date settings found on the Windows Control Panel → Regional Settings dialog.

Views → Current View → Day/Week/Month

Day/Week/Month displays the contents of your Calendar folder in a graphical, calendar-like format. As the name implies, a secondary scale selection found on the toolbar and the view menu (see Figure 7-37, left), determines the range of days shown—Day (1), Work Week (2–14), Week (7), and Month (35).

All Day/Week/Month views share the following characteristics:

- Each Calendar entry shows a description of the activity, based on the Subject and Location fields. If any part of this description has been truncated by column width, holding your cursor over an entry displays the full contents of these fields in a pop-up text box.

- Meetings are differentiated from appointments by a two-headed icon.

- Activity descriptions (Subject and Location) can be edited directly from any view. Simply click the entry, position your cursor, and type.

- Because All Day Events are not time specific, they are shown as a banner at the top of the date(s) on which they occur. All Day Events can be moved and extended by dragging or stretching the banner, respectively.

- Activities can have one of four classifications to further aid you in sorting and prioritizing your schedule: Free, Tentative, Busy, and Out of Office. These classifications are shown as a colored stripe to the left of the activity in Day and Work Week.

- By default, the Date Navigator and TaskPad are displayed in Day, Work Week, and Week views. They are not displayed under Month, but this can be easily remedied (see Tip # 92).

TIP # 92

Changing an Activity's Time or Date

All Calendar's Day/Week/Month views support drag-and-drop for quickly rescheduling an activity's time or date. Select the item, and simply drag it to another time slot. To copy the activity, hold down the Ctrl key while dragging.

The following details the differences between each of the four subviews provided under Day/Week/Month:

Day

Day view (Figure 7-39, top) displays one selected day from your calendar. The current date is shown at the top of the pane, and below this any scheduled Events on this day. On the left edge of the view is a time bar, which shows the time scale used for the view. To change the scale, right-click the time bar. Appointment and meeting durations are depicted by the number of time slots they span. To change the duration of an appointment or meeting, drag the upper or lower edge of the item's box.

Day and Week views show your defined working hours each day as a solid color, and nonworking hours (whatever those are) as grayed. See the section "Calendar's Option Settings" at the beginning of this chapter for details on defining your work week.

Work Week

Displays the range of days selected by the "Calendar work week" checkboxes on the Calendar Options dialog (Tools → Options → Calendar Options); the default configuration is Monday to Friday. Each day is displayed as a separate column with appointments and meetings shown as boxes spanning the appropriate range of time slots (see Figure 7-39, bottom). Events appear under a column's date header; the banner for multiday events spans the days on which they occur.

Due to the column layout used by Work Week, this view tends to get cluttered in short order if you have numerous appointments on one day, but it does support something not found in any other Calendar view—the display of noncontiguous dates. Go to the Date Navigator, hold down the Ctrl key, and select multiple dates in any order. This is very useful for an assortment of dates, weeks or months apart, or copying activities from one noncontiguous day to another. (You can also use this same Ctrl key plus Date Navigator method to add days to the Day view.)

 The maximum number of days a Work Week view can contain is fourteen.

Week

Uses a seven-day week format as shown in Figure 7-40 (top). Days of the week are shown in two columns, Monday through Wednesday as rows in the left column, Thursday through Sunday in the right. Appointments and meetings are listed within these rows, sorted by start time and subject. Events are shown at the top of each day; multiday events do not span days as they do in Work Week and Month. If the number of activities in a day exceeds the dimensions of a day's cell in Week view, a small down-arrow is shown in the lower-right corner. Click it to switch to a Day view of that date. Week view is not as configurable as Outlook's other calendar view. Weekends, for example, are always shown as compressed.

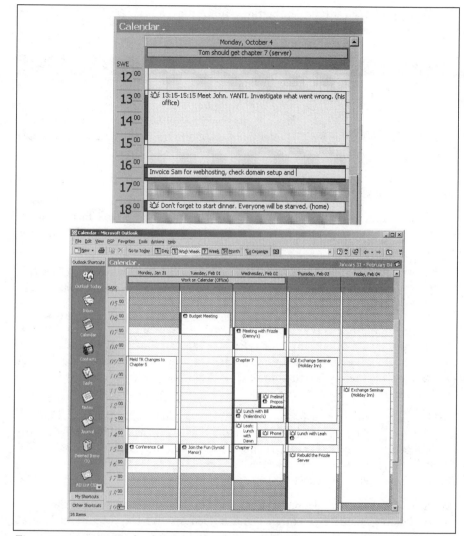

Figure 7-39: An example of a Day view (top), and a Work Week view (bottom)

Configuration limitations aside, for most people Week view is the most functional calendar layout for everyday planning. The subject of most appointments display fully, and the seven-day format gives you enough perspective to plan your week without the distraction of long-term projects.

Month

Uses a traditional western calendar layout, displaying a full month of activities (see Figure 7-40, bottom). Like Week view, activities for a given date are ordered by start time, Events at the top of that date's box. Multiday events are shown as spanning their respective dates. To display Saturday and Sunday as full-size cells, go to Other Settings from the context menu and deselect "Compress weekend days."

TIP # 93

Displaying the TaskPad in a Month View

By default, the TaskPad and Date Navigator are not displayed in a Monthly Calendar view. To display these two components, position your mouse cursor on the right inner border of the Calendar window (where the cursor transforms into two vertical lines) and drag to the left.

Views → Current View → Active Appointments

The balance of the views listed on the Current View menu use a table format. Activities are shown one per row (when no filtering is set); fields are displayed as columns.

Do not be deceived by the use of the word "Appointment" in Calendar's menus and dialogs. In most cases, this term encompasses appointments, meetings, and events.

Active Appointments is a filtered table view summarizing all the appointments, meetings, and events from your calendar that start "on or after Today." The default grouping applied is by recurrence—a group for "(none)," plus groups for each recurrence period found. The default sort within each group is by Recurrence Start Date (ascending).

This is an excellent view for forward planning, providing you have not let Outlook add holidays to your calendar. If you have—as you can see by Figure 7-41—the view loses effectiveness and ends up being cluttered with nonessential items.

Views → Current View → Events

Events are activities that take place on a specific day, but not at a specific time. The Events view is grouped by recurrence and filtered for "All Day Event equals Yes." What this typically leaves you with are appointments explicitly selected as an All Day Event, birthdays and anniversaries (in the grouping Yearly), and holidays automatically generated by Outlook's Add Holiday feature.

Views → Current View → Annual Events

We won't belabor the point any further—holidays are not shown as Annual Events as one might suspect. What this view does give you is a filtered subset of any "All Day Event" activity with a recurrence pattern of yearly, sorted on date (see Figure 7-42).

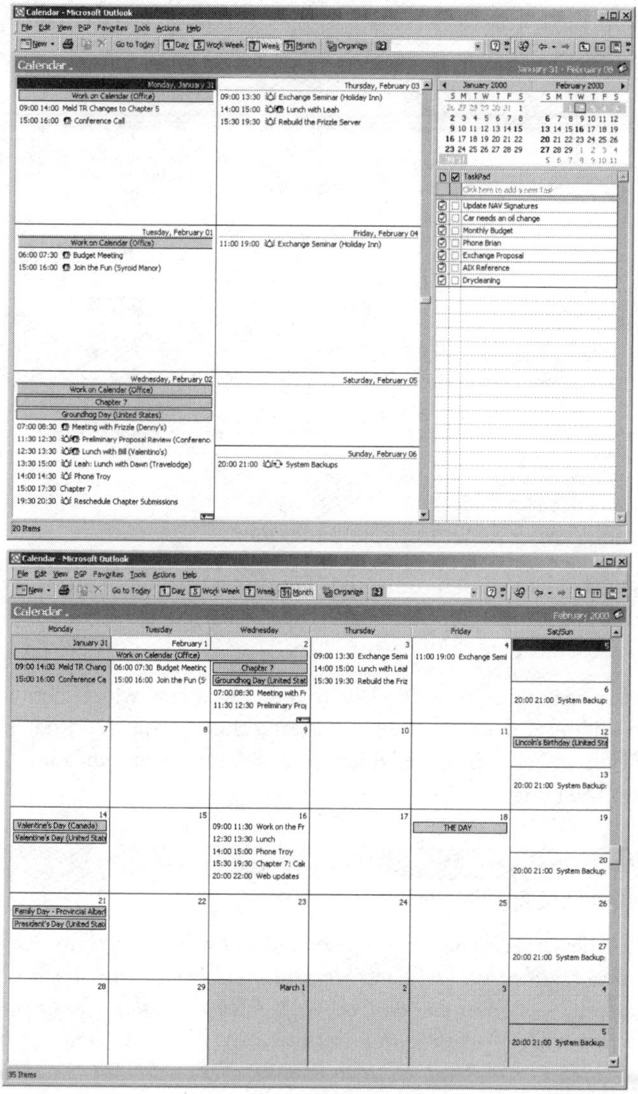

Figure 7-40: Calendar's Week view (top) and Month view (bottom)

NOTE *Birthdays and anniversaries entered from a contact's record (from the Details tab) are automatically added to your Calendar, properly configured as All Day Events, with recurrence pattern set to Yearly.*

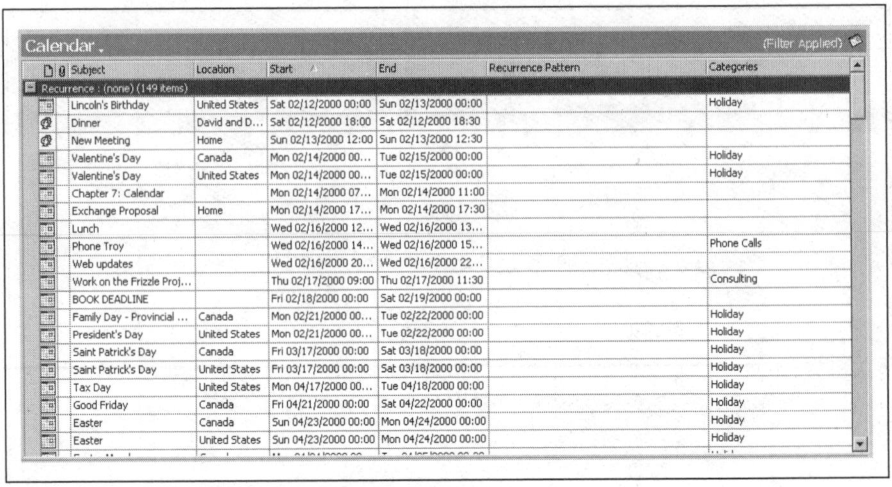

Figure 7-41: The Active Appointments view

Views → Current View → Recurring Appointments

This view is filtered to display only recurring activities (appointments, events, or meetings), grouped by the type of recurrence (daily, weekly, monthly, or yearly), and sorted on the start date of the recurrence.

Use the Recurring Appointments view to quickly assess which activities in your Calendar are ongoing, their recurrence pattern, and the start/end dates assigned to each item. With in-cell editing enabled (the default), you can adjust date ranges directly within the table.

TIP # 94

Delete a Group of Appointments

To delete a group of items in your Outlook calendar, switch to one of Outlook's Table views. Unlike the Day/Week/Month views, Table views support the Select All command (Edit → Select All or Ctrl +A). Choose a table view that groups your Calendar items appropriately (for example, By Category) and apply a filter to display only those records you want to remove. Next, select all the remaining items, and from the context menu choose Delete.

Views → Current View → By Category

Current View → By Category groups your activities by assigned category, sorting items within this grouping first by recurrence (descending) and then by start date (ascending). The By Category view is shown in Figure 7-43.

Categories are an excellent way to organize and group any Outlook item. This is especially true with Calendar entries due to the natural granularity with which they

Are Holidays Annual Events?

You might be asking yourself why Outlook does not list the holidays it automatically adds to your Calendar (see the "Add Holidays" topic under the "Calendar's Option Settings" section earlier in this chapter) as annual events. Good question. The answer lies in the method used to generate holidays.

A list of holidays for a selected location is read from a text file (...\Office\1033\ outlook.txt) and imported into Calendar. This file is comma-delimited, and simply contains a holiday name and five dates beginning in 1998 and ending in 2002. Each date from the text file is added as a separate *appointment*, with the Location field set to the holiday locale, and the All Day Event field is toggled— however, *no recurrence patterns are set.*

Given that both Events and Annual Events use groups and filters based on recurrence, this leaves the holidays Outlooks adds either grouped as "recurrence (none)" in the case of the Events view, or filtered out completely in the case of Annual Events (because this view filters on "Recurrence equals Yearly").

There are three solutions to this poorly implemented method:

- Imported entries are assigned a category of Holiday. Set up a subgrouping for your view based on the category; collapsing or expanding this subgrouping cleans the Events view up substantially.

- Open all your imported holidays and manually change the recurrence type to Yearly. No, you can't use a grouped table view and drag items from a recurrence of "none" to a recurrence of Yearly. Recurrences must be assigned before they can be changed using this method.

- Don't let Outlook import your holidays—enter them manually, correctly, yourself. This is a pain, but when recurrence fields are set properly, a series can be easily edited should the need arise.

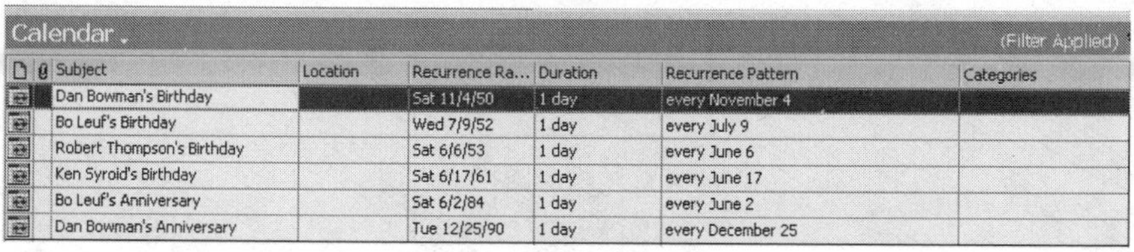

	Subject	Location	Recurrence Ra...	Duration	Recurrence Pattern	Categories
	Dan Bowman's Birthday		Sat 11/4/50	1 day	every November 4	
	Bo Leuf's Birthday		Wed 7/9/52	1 day	every July 9	
	Robert Thompson's Birthday		Sat 6/6/53	1 day	every June 6	
	Ken Syroid's Birthday		Sat 6/17/61	1 day	every June 17	
	Bo Leuf's Anniversary		Sat 6/2/84	1 day	every June 2	
	Dan Bowman's Anniversary		Tue 12/25/90	1 day	every December 25	

Figure 7-42: Calendar's Annual Events view

appear in these views. What, after all, are you going to group an activity on? Subject, location, and times are good sort fields, but do not make good cross-activity groupings. This is where categories come into play. Even assigning a broad

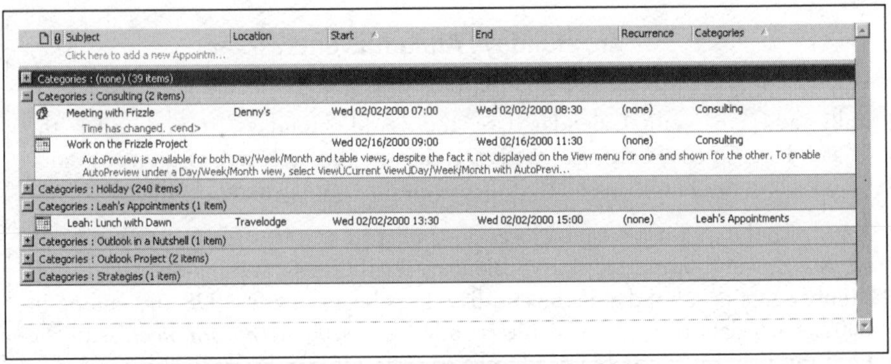

	Subject	Location	Start	End	Recurrence	Categories
	Click here to add a new Appointm…					
Categories : (none) (39 items)						
Categories : Consulting (2 items)						
	Meeting with Frizzle	Denny's	Wed 02/02/2000 07:00	Wed 02/02/2000 08:30	(none)	Consulting
	Time has changed. <end>					
	Work on the Frizzle Project		Wed 02/16/2000 09:00	Wed 02/16/2000 11:30	(none)	Consulting
	AutoPreview is available for both Day/Week/Month and table views, despite the fact it not displayed on the View menu for one and shown for the other. To enable AutoPreview under a Day/Week/Month view, select View\Current View\Day/Week/Month with AutoPrevi…					
Categories : Holiday (240 items)						
Categories : Leah's Appointments (1 item)						
	Leah: Lunch with Dawn	Travelodge	Wed 02/02/2000 13:30	Wed 02/02/2000 15:00	(none)	Leah's Appointments
Categories : Outlook in a Nutshell (1 item)						
Categories : Outlook Project (2 items)						
Categories : Strategies (1 item)						

Figure 7-43: The By Category View with AutoPreview enabled

category such as Business or Personal to your activities allows you to quickly see the natural divisions within your meetings and appointments.

 NOTE *Items assigned more than one category are displayed twice, once in each category grouping.*

Figure 7-43 also illustrates the common drag-and-drop functionality of grouped Table views—you can quickly add more categories to one or more selected items by dragging to the appropriate group. Such an item then appears to be duplicated, because it becomes a member of each Category group it has been assigned to.

View → Go To

The View → Go To submenu, shown in Figure 7-44, contains two Calendar-specific commands: Go To Today and Go to Date.

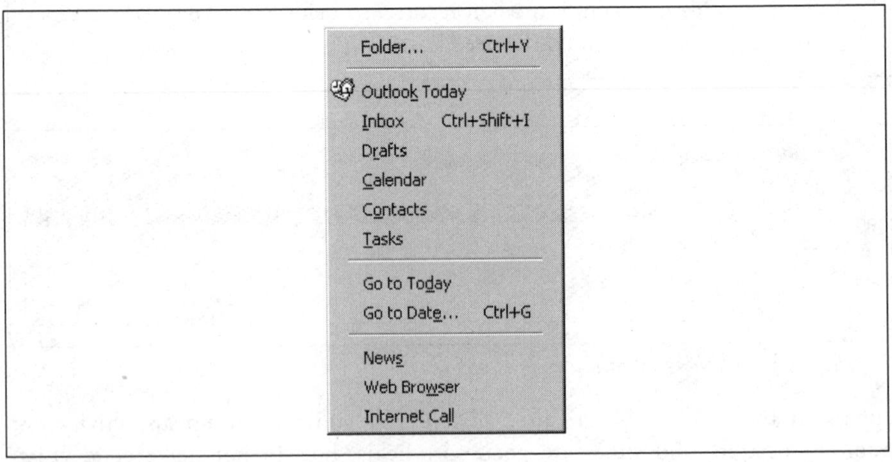

Folder...	Ctrl+Y
Outlook Today	
Inbox	Ctrl+Shift+I
Drafts	
Calendar	
Contacts	
Tasks	
Go to Today	
Go to Date...	Ctrl+G
News	
Web Browser	
Internet Call	

Figure 7-44: The View → Go To submenu

Go to Today

Returns you to the current date from any date or year. This command is only available for calendar views (Day/Work Week/Week/Month). You'll also find the same command on the context menu (right-click on an open area) of all four calendar views, which is a lot faster than using the View menu.

TIP # 95

Go to This Day

There is a little known—but useful—command you should be aware of that is only found on the context menu of the Week (seven-day, not Work Week) and Month views. Position your cursor over a day in either of these two views, right-click, and choose Go to This Day from the context menu. This takes you to the selected date, displayed in a Day view.

Go to Date

Opens the dialog shown in Figure 7-45. As simple as it may seem, this is a powerful tool for quickly moving through your Calendar, as well as switching views. Note that the Date field accepts all the entry shortcuts discussed earlier in this chapter in the sidebar, "More Date (and Time) Entry Shortcuts"

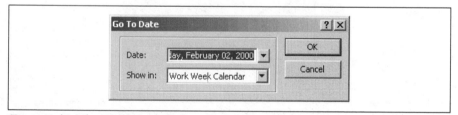

Figure 7-45: The Go To Date dialog

View → Day, Work Week, Week, Month

With one of Outlook's calendar layouts active, the View menu displays four items for switching layouts: Day, Work Week, Week, and Month. There are more efficient ways to switch layouts, however. If your hands are already on the keyboard, use the shortcut keys detailed in Tip # 96; if you're a "mouser," use the respective buttons on the standard toolbar.

Calendar

TIP # 96

Calendar Layout Shortcut Keys

Going to the menu bar every time you want to switch calendar layouts is a pain. Instead, use the keyboard shortcuts associated with these views: Alt+Shift+Y (Day), Alt+Shift+R (Work Week), Alt+Shift+K (Week), and Alt+Shift+M (Month). Round this out with Go to Date (Ctrl+G), and you can view and schedule appointments without your hands ever leaving the keyboard.

View → TaskPad View

The TaskPad (see Figure 7-46) is a miniature view of the contents of your Task folder. The TaskPad is only visible from the Day, Work Week, Week, and Month views.

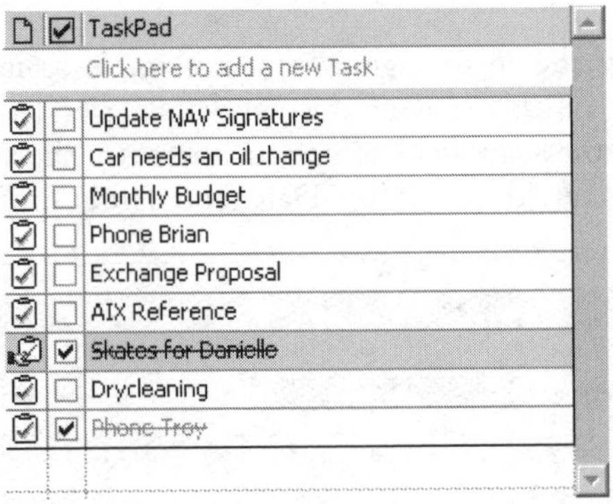

Figure 7-46: Outlook's TaskPad view

The TaskPad shares all the functionality of Outlook's full Task component, so refer to Chapter 9 for full details on the mechanics of creating tasks and task requests.

The TaskPad's default view displays three fields: Icon (a hand under the clipboard depicts an assigned task), Complete, and Subject. This view is no different than any other view in Outlook; you can sort, group, and customize it to your heart's content.

Right-click an open area of the TaskPad (not on a Task item directly) to create a new Task, new Task Request, enable AutoPreview, and to gain access to the TaskPad View/Settings submenus. The New context menu is shown in Figure 7-47 (left); the View and Settings submenus are shown in Figure 7-47 (center) and (right) respectively.

Unless you have a remarkably small task list, filtered views are essential for managing what the TaskPad displays. The View submenu (Figure 7-47) gives you several functional starting points:

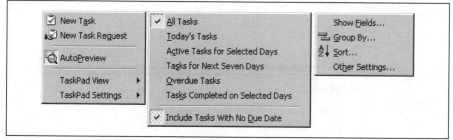

Figure 7-47: TaskPad's context menus—the New Task menu (left), the preconfigured views submenu (center), and the Settings submenu (right)

All Tasks

Shows all tasks, including those marked as complete. If you have a large Task list, this is not the most useful view given the small size of the TaskPad.

Today's Tasks

This is the default TaskPad view and arguably the most useful one. Only tasks not marked as complete are displayed; overdue tasks are shown in red (by default; see the TaskPad Settings → Other Settings command).

Active Tasks for Selected Days

Shows only tasks with due dates that fall within the range defined by the current calendar view. This view-relative filter is handy to focus on tasks that are critical in a given date interval.

Tasks for Next Seven Days

Gives the look-ahead view for planning your week, which includes overdue tasks.

Overdue Tasks

This is the "Round-To-It" view that collects all your overdue task items.

Tasks Completed on Selected Days

Shows a follow-up view, where you can identify which tasks were completed for given date ranges.

Include Tasks with No Due Date

This is a toggle with a self-explanatory function. Timeless tasks may or may not be relevant to your TaskPad view, but using this option you can easily decide whether they should be displayed.

Two additional context menus are available within the TaskPad pane. The first is applicable when working with individual Task items; open it by right-clicking on a TaskPad entry directly (see Figure 7-48, left).

The second (Figure 7-48, right) is an industrial strength view customization menu, and is identical to the context menu you'd find working with a table view directly in the Tasks component. Access this menu by right-clicking on the title bar of the

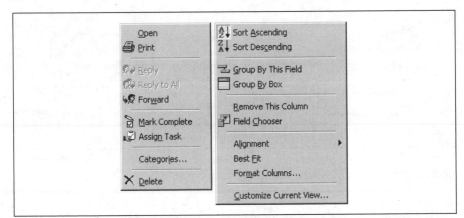

Figure 7-48: TaskPad context menus displayed for working with an item (left), and customizing views (right)

TaskPad. Given the small size of the TaskPad, most of the customization options found on this second settings menu are not very functional to the average user; nonetheless, it is available for complex customizations if you so choose.

Chapter 8

Contacts

While Mail is typically the most widely used component of Outlook, Contacts is the most referenced component. Information, after all, is seldom faceless. Email is sent from someone, to someone; tasks are often shared or collaborated on; meetings are groups of people gathered together to discuss a topic or issue. The rhythm of our daily lives does not occur in a vaccum—it involves people.

Contact records are an extremely important element to Outlook's functionality and its data. They form the basis of many of the program linkages available that allow disparate items to be grouped and referenced across components and data sources.

This chapter references the two menu groups key to working with contact records, Actions and View:

- The *Actions* menu contains the commands for creating new contact records and distribution lists. It also gives you the means to create new Outlook items and associate them directly with an existing contact.

- The *View* menu contains the commands for displaying contact records, plus the commands to modify the preconfigured views provided.

Contacts → Actions Menu

The Actions menu shown in Figure 8-1 contains commands for creating contact records and distribution lists. It also provides commands that transfer information from existing contact records to other Outlook components and external application.

TIP # 97

Outlook's Global Shortcut Keys

Learn the global keyboard shortcut keys shown on Outlook's menus. (For example, Ctrl+Shift+G used by the Flag by Follow Up command.) These are global keyboard shortcuts, functional from any Outlook component. Learning the most common ones saves a lot of mousing around.

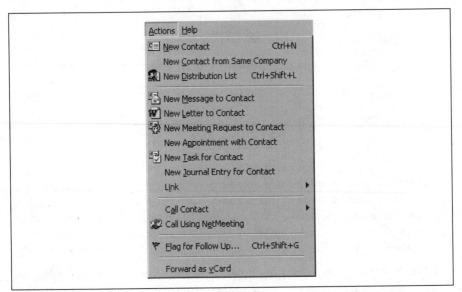

Figure 8-1: The Contacts Actions menu

Actions → New Contact

Actions → New Contact opens a blank new contact form. Because creating contact files is central to the functionality of Mail and other components, the command is always accessible from the File menu (File → New → Contact), and has the global keyboard shortcut Ctrl-Shift+C. In the Contacts component, it is the default New command, used by the keyboard shortcut Ctrl+N and the Standard Toolbar New buttons.

The Contacts form shows five tabbed sections: General, Details, Activities, Certificates, and All Fields. These tabs structure your contact data in manageable and logical chunks of information.

The Actions menu in Figure 8-2 accessed from the Contacts form is subtly different from the one found on Outlook's main menu (Figure 8-1). The Actions menu on the Contacts form includes extra options applicable to an open contact: Display Map of Address and Explore Web Page. These options are enabled if the contact record contains data in the Address and Web Page Address fields, respectively.

TIP # 98

Take the Time to Invest in Your Records

The more information you supply for each contact, the more powerful Outlook becomes down the road when you need to sort, search, or refine your data. It doesn't take long to amass a large contact file. Going back later to add, for example, categories to every entry is time consuming. Always include as much information in a new record as you can when you first create it.

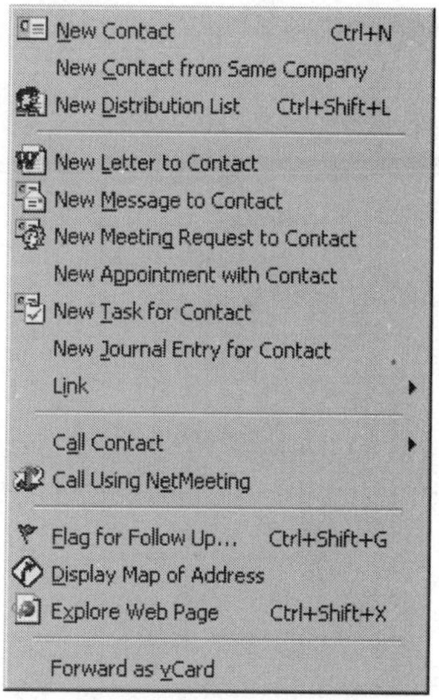

Figure 8-2: The Actions menu in the New Contacts dialog

General tab

The General tab shown in Figure 8-3 displays the key fields of a contact record: name, company, phone, address, email and web links, and a section for free-form notes or attachments. At the bottom of the form is a Contacts button for linking the open record with one or more existing contacts, and a button for assigning a category to the contact. There is also a checkbox for marking the contact Private. All of these features are covered later in this section.

> **NOTE** *If you share a Contacts folder, marking a contact Private means the record is only visible to the person who created it.*

Outlook applies automatic formatting rules to most fields on the Contacts form. For example, entries in the Full Name field are assigned proper capitalization, and an unbroken string of ten digits entered into any one of Outlook's four phone number fields format to (*xxx*) *xxx-xxxx*. Several caveats go along with this "auto-magic" formatting, however, and are discussed where relevant.

Many fields have down-arrow buttons. These allow you to define more than one entry for the field, e.g., alternative mailing or email addresses, and a selection of field descriptors for phone numbers. The Full Name and Address buttons both call up subdialogs that allow more explicitly detailed field entries.

Full Name, Title, Company, File As, and Address fields. The first field on the Contacts form is Full Name. Proper capitalization is not normally required. When you move to another field (Tab for next), your entry is automatically transformed into proper

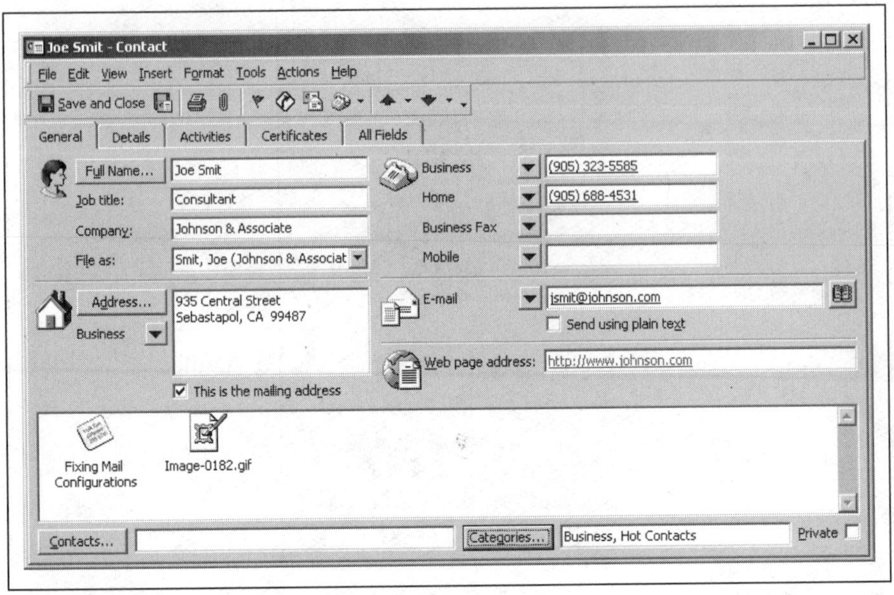

Figure 8-3: The Contacts form General tab

caps. Names can be entered normally (First name/Last name). The field also accepts two paired first names (e.g., a married couple) if the word "and" or the ampersand (&) separates them.

If Outlook can't identify the components of a full name (perhaps you entered only a first or last name), it displays the Check Full Name dialog shown in Figure 8-4.

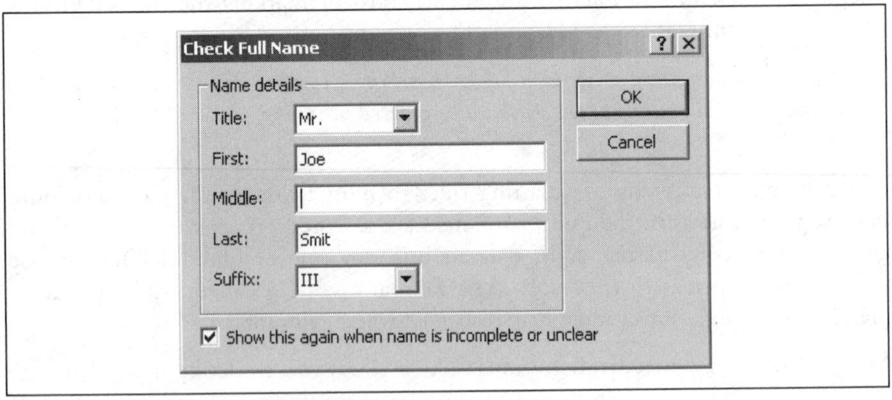

Figure 8-4: The Check Full Name dialog

TIP # 99

Be Careful What You Type

Whatever you enter in the Check Full Name dialog is recorded exactly as you type it. Accuracy is especially important for contact records due to the deep linkages between Contacts and Outlook's other components.

If the contact requires titles (prefix or suffix additions to the name), enter these in the respective fields of the dialog. Common ones can be selected from the associated drop-down lists. Alternately, enter them in the appropriate place before or after the free-form name in the Contacts form (e.g., `Dr. John Smith` or `Bill Smith, PhD`) and see if Outlook can parse the entry properly; it usually will for common titles.

Clearing the "Show this again when name is incomplete or unclear" checkbox disables name checking. If you disable this feature, however, whatever you enter in the Full Name field is recorded exactly as typed.

Outlook's Name-Check Quirks

Outlook's parsing and automatic capitalization of names and titles can be quirky for unusual entries. Mixed case entries (`bill deWinter`) or punctuated titles (`dr. john smith`) leave case unchanged. Hyphenated last names are identified and capitalized properly, unless other factors like mixed case or title suffixes come into play. In short, blindly relying on automatic parsing and case adjustment can be problematic.

We recommend you enter names that require a specific format using the Check Full Name dialog. This is the only way to ensure that the name you enter is displayed as intended.

Like the Full Name field, entries to the Company field are automatically converted to proper-caps. Both the Full Name and Company fields are limited to 256 characters, including spaces.

The personal or company name you enter is automatically entered in the File As field according to the preferences specified in the Tools → Options → Preferences → Contact Options dialog (see Figure 8-5). If you fill in new contact fields in an order different than the normal tab-through sequence (e.g., first Company, then Name), the first filled-in field determines the File As content. The specified filing option is applied when both fields are complete.

The File As field on the Contacts form can be manually configured in five different ways using the drop-down list in the Contact Options dialog. The options are:

> Last, First (default)
> First Last

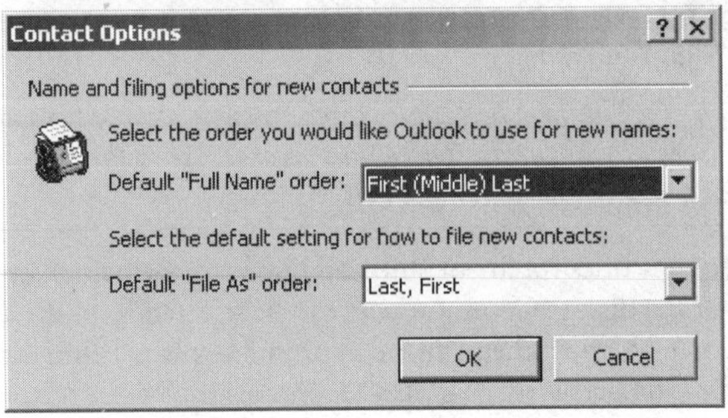

Figure 8-5: The Contact Options dialog

> Company
> Last, First (Company)
> Company (Last, First)

Unknown to many users, the File As field is fully editable. This allows you to reject the automatic content and specify another name variant, a nickname, or any other heading to file the contact under. Remember, this field specifies the *primary index* for your contacts file, which determines how contacts are accessed and the default order in which they are displayed. For this reason the File As name should be easily and uniquely identifiable.

If you have two different contacts with the same name, attempt to distinguish them by adding a middle initial. Avoid duplicate records for the same contact; you should instead be updating or editing the original contact record.

TIP # 100

Organizing Family Member Records

To track activities and birthdays for more than one member of the same family, you can use the Company field for the family name (e.g., "The Smith Family"). Create the first member's record, filling in as many details as possible, and then use the Actions → New Contact from Same Company menu command to add subsequent family members.

Although Outlook accepts duplicate contacts (determined when the field Full Name or E-mail address of an existing record is identical to the new contact being entered) a warning is generated when attempting to save the duplicate as illustrated in Figure 8-6.

The Duplicate Contact Detected dialog gives you the option of adding your entry as a duplicate, or updating the existing record using the details provided. Updating merges the two records, and when there are field conflicts, the newer entry takes precedence. The Open Existing Contact button allows you to view the duplicate record before overwriting it. If you update an existing contact with a duplicate, the

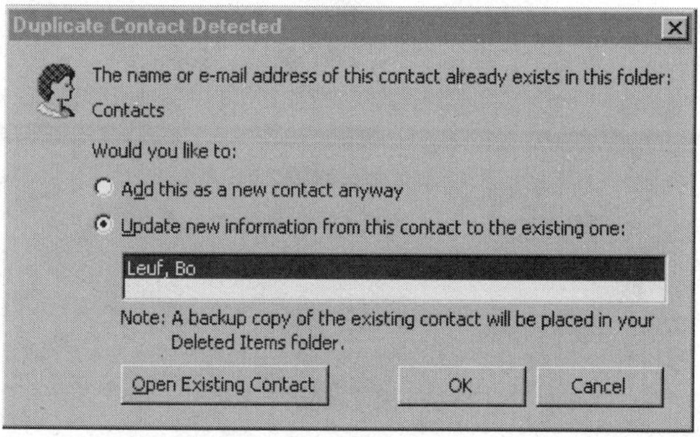

Figure 8-6: The subdialog Duplicate Contact Detected

original record is moved to the Deleted Items folder. This gives you the possibility of recovering it, at least until that folder is cleared.

TIP # 101

Creating Duplicate Contacts Intentionally

It's usually unwise to have duplicate contacts, but there's an exception to every rule. When you send an email to a contact, Outlook defaults to using the first email field of that contact's record. If you have a contact who routinely uses alternating email addresses (perhaps because she has an office email address and a roaming email address), create two contact entries: Contactname, Office and Contactname, Roaming.

The Address box is a free-form entry field. Like the Full Name field (and associated Check Full Name dialog), the Contacts' Address field is modified by "field-checking" rules. An (American style) entry of the following form is correctly interpreted as a valid address:

```
123 Shady Lane Dr. <Enter>
Milltown, CA 91210 <Tab>
```

However, for other formats, or if any part of the entered address is recognized as incomplete or missing (e.g., no Postal Code), Outlook displays the Check Address dialog with the cursor positioned in the field in question. See Figure 8-7, where the Postal Code component was omitted in the original entry.

At the bottom of the Check Address dialog is a checkbox to disable automatic address checking. We recommend leaving address checking enabled to confirm the field placement of free-form entries.

Check Address ? X

Address details

Street: 123 Shady Lane

OK

Cancel

City: Milltown

State/Province: CA

ZIP/Postal code:

Country/Region: United States of America ▼

☑ Show this again when address is incomplete or unclear

Figure 8-7: The Check Address subdialog for specifying address component fields

NOTE *Outlook does not capitalize address fields for you. Type your entries both in the free-form Address field and the Check Address dialog exactly as you want them displayed.*

Outlook's default address type selection is for Business. Use the down-arrow button to the left of the address entry form to select Business, Home, or Other *before* entering address data. Outlook cannot change an entered Business address into a Home address. Although you can cut and paste between fields if you do fill in the wrong selection, this is an awkward and time-consuming fix.

The checkbox labeled "This is the mailing address" makes the displayed address the preferred mailing address, i.e., the address used to create letters or envelopes. This selection applies to only one address (Business, Home, or Other) at a time; clearing the checkbox removes any preference at all. (It may help conceptually to know that the Mailing Address setting is actually a single one-line field shown on the All Fields tab. This field is either empty or contains a copy of the marked address.)

TIP # 102

Choosing a Mailing Address

*The entry chosen as a contact's mailing address is the one used by Outlook to address a letter via Word's New Letter macro. It's also the address displayed in the View →
Address Cards and Detailed Address Cards views.*

Phone numbers. Outlook can store up to 19 phone numbers for each contact. By default, Outlook displays Business, Home, Business Fax, and Mobile, but you can choose any four numbers to display for each record. (See Figure 8-8.) The four fields you choose carry forward to other Outlook menus related to phone functions (for instance, the automatic dialer), so pick those shown for a given contact with some thought.

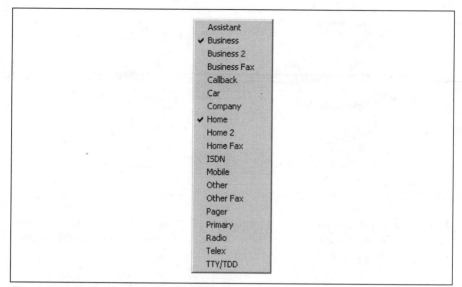

Figure 8-8: Outlook's Phone Field choices

Phone number fields on the Contacts form are largely self-formatting, again with some caveats. The first time a phone entry is made in a new installation, Outlook displays the Dialing Properties dialog. To format entries correctly, Outlook needs to know your area code and dialing preferences. This information is later used by the Windows TAPI (Telephone Application Programming Interface) interface to dial phone numbers directly from Outlook (The New Call command is discussed later in this chapter).

These location properties make several quick entry tricks possible in phone number fields:

- 5551212 formats to (xxx) 555-1212 (where xxx is the regional area code you supplied for your location).

- 3065551212 forces a different area code and formats to (306) 555-1212.

- 13065551212 forces a country code and area code and formats to +1 (306) 555-1212.

 Outlook's automatic phone dialer ignores non-numeric characters. This means, for example, that you can include dialing notes after the phone number ("ext. 1234" or "before 10:00").

If Outlook does not recognize the phone number format, it displays the Check Phone Number dialog shown in Figure 8-9.

This dialog gives you the option to manually resolve the ambiguity or force the entry to be accepted as entered by clicking OK. Like the Name- and Address-check dialogs, clearing the "Show this again..." checkbox disables phone number

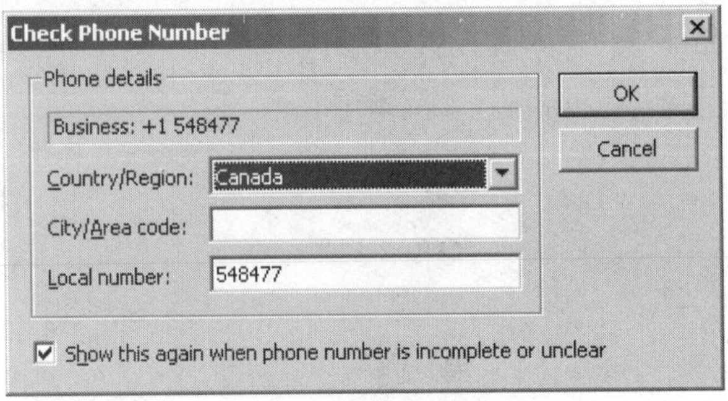

Figure 8-9: The Check Phone Number dialog

checking. To reenable this checking option, double-click on an underlined phone number from any Contacts form. This opens the Check Phone Number dialog, allowing you to mark the "Show this again..." checkbox.

Non-U.S. Phone Numbers

Phone number formatting in other countries may differ significantly from the North American standard AAA-XXX-NNNN, where AAA is area code, XXX is exchange, and NNNN is the number within the exchange. This also means that Outlook may misinterpret non-U.S. local numbers.

If Outlook does not understand the formatting of a phone number, it presents a detailed entry form that prompts the user to specify components exactly. Unfortunately, Outlook often does *not* detect such ambiguities and translates numbers incorrectly without warning.

For example, entering a Swedish phone number as 4655551212 incorrectly formats it as a North American number: (465) 555-1212, even if you prefix it with +. With a Swedish locale setting, this entry also parses incorrectly to +46 55551212 instead of the correct +46 (55) 551212. Include parentheses or spaces around the area code, i.e., 46(55)551212 or 46 55 551212, to force Outlook to format the number properly.

Always verify entry details for phone numbers that do not use the North American standard. Double-clicking the number displays the detailed component dialog for entry or edit.

Email and web page fields.   Outlook allows up to three unique email addresses for each contact, creatively labeled E-mail, E-mail 2, and E-mail 3. The drop-down arrow adjacent to the entry field selects which label is displayed. Always place the preferred email address in the E-mail field, as this is the default used for new messages. Marking the "Send using plain text" checkbox forces Outlook to use Plain Text as the default format for new messages to this contact. You can override this setting from Mail with the menu command Actions → New Mail Message Using.

Outlook displays the contact name in the Mail To: entry field of a new message as an underlined name, e.g., Joe Smith and not joesmith@email.com, making it unclear which email address used when the contact has more than one. Some thought about which email entry should be the default saves confusion later on.

 For tips, tricks, and options related to sending email messages, see the section "Addressing a Message" in Chapter 5, Mail Editors.

The address book button beside the email field opens a Select Contact dialog. Here properties and entry details can be inspected for other contacts in your file. Selecting a contact and accepting with the OK button takes the default email address from this dialog and inserts it in the current contact's email field. This is beneficial in situations that necessitate using the same address for multiple contacts. For example, a company might use *sales@company.com* as the primary email for all members of its sales team.

Below E-mail is the field for recording a web page address associated with this contact or company. Here you would typically enter the main URL for a company's web site, a person's homepage, or whatever other web address seems appropriate. To have more than one such URL listed for a given contact, you need to either put them in the free-form notes section (next topic), or set up a user-defined field for each one.

Free-form notes and attachments. The notes field is the large open area (for some reason unlabeled) in the lower half of the Contacts form. This free-form field can serve several purposes. Use it for notes about your contact. This field can also contain attachments from other Outlook components or shortcuts to files located on your hard drive (local or network).

From the Contacts form (Insert menu command) you can add any of three types of attachments: File, Item, or Object:

File

Inserts data (e.g., images or documents) or executables (programs) found either locally or on a network. The rule is if you can see the file in Windows File Manager, you can also insert it in the Notes field. Once you've chosen a file to insert, you have the following options in the drop-list from the button initially labeled Insert: Insert, Insert as Text, Insert as Attachment, or Insert as Shortcut. A shortcut insertion only works as long as the original file remains available in the location specified.

Item

Inserts one or more Outlook items (mail message, journal entry, contact record, etc.) into the open Contact's text field. Choosing this option opens the dialog shown in Figure 8-10. Outlook's Folder List is displayed in the upper pane, and a list of the selected folder's contents below this. Items can be inserted as Text Only, Attachment, or Shortcut.

Insert Item	? X

Look in:

```
⊟ 🖳 Personal Folders                              ▲    [   OK   ]
     📒 Book Tasks
     📒 Calendar                                        [  Cancel ]
  ⊞ 📒 Contacts                                     ┌─ Insert as ──┐
     📂 Deleted Items (1)                           │  ○ Text only │
     📒 Drafts                                      │  ● Attachment│
  ⊞ 📬 Inbox                                    ▼    │  ○ Shortcut  │
     📒 Journal                                      └──────────────┘
```

Items:

!	🗋	📎	From	Subject	Received ▽
	📄		Lisa Mott	RE: chapters 5 & 6	Wed 01/12/2000 ...
	📄	📎	Swami	Chapter 18	Wed 01/12/2000 ...
	📄		Lisa Mott	FW: chapters 5 & 6	Wed 01/12/2000 ...
	📄		Swami	Da chapter	Wed 01/12/2000 ...
	📄		Troy Mott	RE: Okey. Dokey.	Wed 01/12/2000 ...
	📄		Troy Mott	chapter 3 comments	Wed 01/12/2000 ...
	📄		Troy Mott	RE: Houston...	Wed 01/12/2000 ...
	📄	📎	Troy Mott	RE: heading 8	Wed 01/12/2000 ...

Figure 8-10: Outlook's Insert Item dialog

Object

Inserts anything Windows sees as a registered entity, such as a WordPad document, an HTML file, a media clip, or a wave-sampled sound. From the Insert Object dialog choose Create New or Create from File. The form shown for a new object presents application data types registered with Windows as "object" types. Selecting one lets you create and insert that data type as an embedded (editable) item, optionally just displayed as an icon. To insert an existing file as an object, type in the path or use the Browse button to search the filesystem. In this case, you have the additional option of just inserting a link to the object instead of embedding it.

 NOTE *The Insert → Object command is not enabled unless the cursor's focus is in the free-form text field.*

Any attachments in the notes pane can be viewed by double-clicking on the icon representing the object. This opens the attachment in the corresponding Outlook dialog for the component, or in the application associated with the object type.

Opening a mail attachment from this field invokes a default warning that attachments may contain viruses or scripts that can be harmful. Although you can disable this warning by deselecting the checkbox "Always ask . . ." the dialog does give you the useful immediate reminder and option to save the file to disk instead of simply opening it. This may be preferable to the manual version of the command found in the context-menu for the selected attachment icon. Your own level of paranoia will have to determine whether you want this warning to remain active or not. The global setting that goes with this is found under the Outlook menu Tools → Options → Security → Attachment Security. The choices here are High and None; the latter disables this and most other security warnings.

Contacts. The Contacts button at the bottom left of the General tab opens the Select Contact dialog, allowing you to link related contacts. This linkage can only be made to an existing contact record, as there is no provision to add a contact from this dialog.

Contacts linked via this field appear as underlined names; double-click an entry to open the linked contact's record. This is a two-way link: the current contact becomes a new entry in the corresponding field of the target contact.

Categories. The Categories button at the bottom right of the General tab calls up the dialog shown in Figure 8-11. From this dialog you can classify the type of contact according to a list of existing categories. The Master Category List button leads to a subdialog where further categories can be added, or existing ones removed.

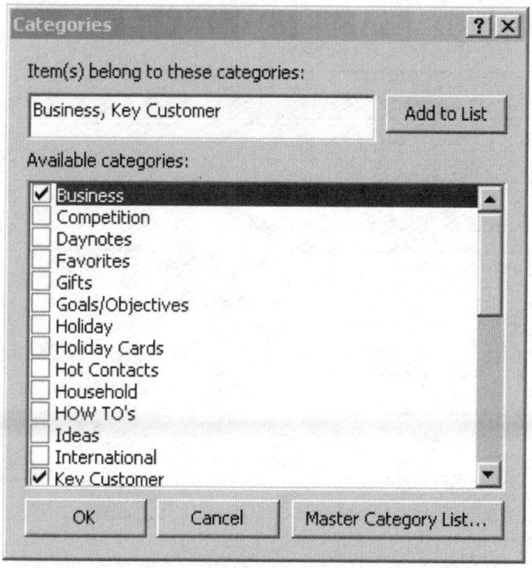

Figure 8-11: The Categories dialog

> **NOTE** *The Category text field at the bottom of the Contacts form accepts whatever you enter there, existing category or not. Only the categories listed on the Master Category List are available to other Outlook components via the Categories dialog. We do not recommend assigning categories to a contact using this field unless you are fully aware of the consequences of a misspelled or inaccurate entry.*

If you want to assign a new category to a contact, first use the Master Category List button and add the category as a new item.

Categories are a powerful organizing tool for managing large contact files. They allow you to select and manipulate groups of dissimilar items that have one or more specified characteristics in common. Take the time to classify each new contact in as detailed a manner as you can. It is hard to know in advance which search or grouping criteria you may want or need to use at a later date. The more information you include here, the greater the possibilities for the future. Remember also to review these assignments from time to time, because things change, jobs change, interests change. See the section "The Power of Categories" in Chapter 3 for a detailed discussion on the role of categories in Outlook.

Details

The Details tab (Figure 8-12) provides a group of predefined fields for recording contact information not necessarily accessed every day, but nonetheless handy to have for some of your contacts.

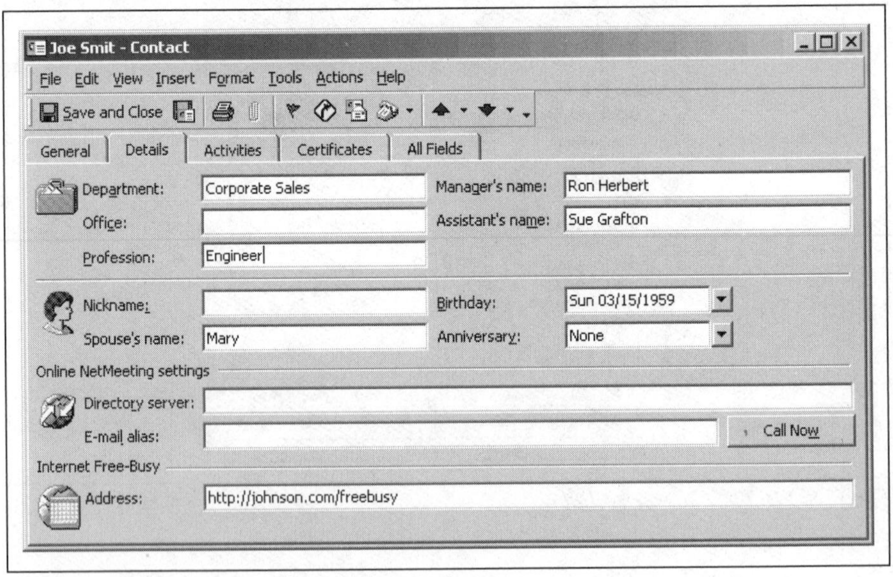

Figure 8-12: The Details tab of a Contacts form

There are five organizational name fields in the upper section: Department, Office, Profession, Manager's name, and Assistant's name. These are all simple text fields with a limit of 256 characters each. You are free to enter whatever strikes your fancy here. Entries made to either name field (Manager or Assistant) are examined by Outlook, and if they resemble a person's name (joe smith, for example), they are parsed and automatically given proper capitalization (Joe Smith). Your mileage with this feature is going to vary, however, and note that it does *not* work quite the same as the corresponding feature for the Full Name field under the General tab.

TIP # 103

Using Outlook's Name Fields

The best advice we can offer when it comes to any text field is to type your entry exactly as you want it displayed. This alleviates the problem of trying to remember what fields have automatic formatting, and what fields support name checking.

Below the divider rule on the Details tab are a number of personal information fields, each with its own formatting characteristics. Nickname and Spouse's name are name fields like those described in the General tab section; anything Outlook recognizes as a name is translated into proper caps.

The Birthday and Anniversary fields are self-explanatory. You can enter dates here several ways:

- Type the date in typical notation (*mm/dd/yy* or *mm/dd/yyyy*); if you enter a date without a year (for example, 12/30), Outlook appends the current year.

- Use the Date Navigator calendar accessible from the down-arrow next to the field.

- Use Outlook's ability to calculate dates for you. If you know a portion of the date (for example, 20 years ago tomorrow), use one of the date shortcut entry tricks described in the sidebar Date Field Shortcuts.

Entering birthdays and anniversaries for your contacts through these fields has a surprise benefit: dates recorded here are automatically transferred to your Outlook calendar and set as recurring events. Depending on your settings in Calendar, these entries can automatically remind you of the event a specified number of days before it arrives. For a full explanation of recurring dates and setting alarms, see Chapter 7, *Calendar*.

Internet collaboration settings. In the bottom section of the Details tab are fields for entering information specific to conferencing with your contact through a NetMeeting Server. The field "Directory server" expects an Internet address of the form `http://netmeeting.server.com`. The prefix `http://` is added automatically if missing. It is also possible to enter an IP number in this field of the form `192.123.200.1`. Again, Outlook adds the `http://` prefix.

Contacts

Date Field Shortcuts

Outlook's date fields support several entry shortcuts that are useful to either speed up or simplify many date entry tasks. Below is a short list of examples to get you started—the syntax is fairly intuitive:

- Typing today fills in the current system date, while tomorrow fills in the following date.

- Typing 1 week from today supplies a calculated date one week from the setting of your computer's clock (the shorter next week accomplishes the same thing).

- Typing 1 year ago (or 365 days ago) supplies a date as requested.

- Typing next thursday calculates and enters the appropriate date from the current "today" date.

- Typing last monday does as expected, working backward from the date of entry.

- Typing 30 years ago will, if the date is 5/8/99 (and the system is using American date format), fill in 5/8/69 for you.

The usefulness of this artificial intelligence feature is quickly apparent with a little experimentation and practice. For example, you may have a friend who is celebrating a thirtieth wedding anniversary on Sunday. Simply type next Sunday 30 years ago in the field Anniversary to enter the correct date.

The associated "E-mail alias" field is usually set to the contact's ordinary email address. This entry is used in conjunction with the Call Now button to establish a NetMeeting link to this contact and start the conference.

Finally, Outlook provides a field for "Internet Free-Busy" information, which gives you connectivity to your contact's shared calendar through an enterprise email product like Exchange Server. In the Address field you specify the URL or server path to your Internet free/busy file. Information on setting up and using Outlook's Free-Busy feature is detailed in Chapter 14, *Collaborating with Outlook*.

Activities

The Activities tab on the Contacts form displays any Outlook items related to a contact. This can take the form of email messages, a Note, a Task, a Journal entry, or another contact linked to the open contact's record. Items displayed on this list must be *explicitly* linked to the contact, except for email items that already carry that linkage implicit in the address fields. For example, a Note associated with a contact shows on that contact's Activities list. (See Chapter 10, *Notes*, for details on how to link a Note to a Contact.) Contact Birthdays and Anniversaries turn up here as well.

Figure 8-13 shows the Contacts Activities tab. The Show drop-down list sets a filter for the items displayed. The options are: All Items, Contacts, E-mail, Journal, Notes, and Upcoming Tasks/Appointments. The view can be sorted by clicking on a column's title (Shift-click for a multilevel sort); right-click for a sorting and grouping context menu. Double-click an item to open it. Right-clicking an individual item opens the same context menu displayed if you performed the same action from a view native to that item type.

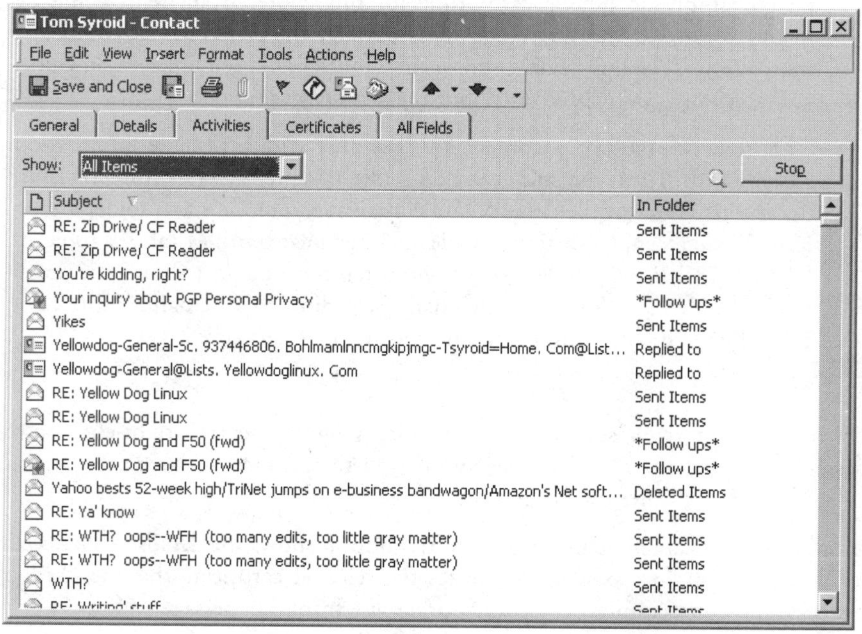

Figure 8-13: The Contacts form, Activities tab

In short, when the Activities tab is filtered to a specific item type, it becomes a view on a view. This makes the Activities tab a very powerful tool for finding and sorting contact related information across Outlook components, providing you create the necessary associations—yet another good reason for taking the time to link and categorize *all* Outlook items, even if at the time of creation some may seem unimportant.

The Activities tab is new to Outlook 2000, and is not without growing pains. See the sidebar "The Activities Tab—Son of Journal" later in this chapter for an explanation of its inherent limitations.

Certificates

The Certificates tab provides a place to store digital signatures you may receive from your contact, either through digitally signed mail, or in a special file (attachment)

The Activities Tab—Son of Journal

The Activities tab is a new feature to Outlook 2000, and appears to be an attempt to overcome the frustrations and complexity users experienced using Outlook's Journal component. It's a worthy first attempt, but has two prominent limitations you should be aware of:

- You still need to explicitly link Outlook items to a contact. However, many people simply do not have the time for this chore. If all items could be seamlessly linked the way email messages are, the Activities tab would be more useful. The downside to this is, like Journal, hidden linkages slow program response, noticeable on all but the fastest systems.

- The Activities tab tracks contact linkages only within a single information store (PST). If you use multiple PST's (see Chapter 13, *File Management*), items moved out of the default PST containing your Contacts folder are no longer listed. This also impacts file maintenance routines (also a topic of Chapter 13). For example, the Activities tab for a contact shows any email replies you've sent to that individual, providing they remain in the Sent Items folder: archive this folder, and they're no longer listed.

that you can import. When you receive a digitally signed message, right-click on the message's From field and select the option Add to Contacts to have the signature added to the Certificates list for that contact.

Selecting a certificate item and the Properties button shows the details of that certificate. The button "Set as Default" makes the selected certificate the one Outlook uses with this contact unless you specify otherwise from the message editor.

For a detailed explanation of encryption and digital signing options available for Outlook, see Chapter 15, *Security and Encryption*.

All Fields

The All Fields tab, shown in Figure 8-14, provides a complete listing of all fields available for data entry under Contacts. These fields are listed alphabetically in the viewing pane under the Name column. Data from these fields is displayed in the right column under the heading of Value. You may freely edit values here, although note that some fields have validation and parsing rules applied—the "intelligent" date fields, for example. Simply click on the relevant field and begin typing to modify the contents of a record. The changed value (if valid for the field data type) is stored as soon as you move out of the field.

To limit the number fields shown, the list is filtered using the drop-down "Select from." This can narrow the range considerably, showing, for example, only Phone

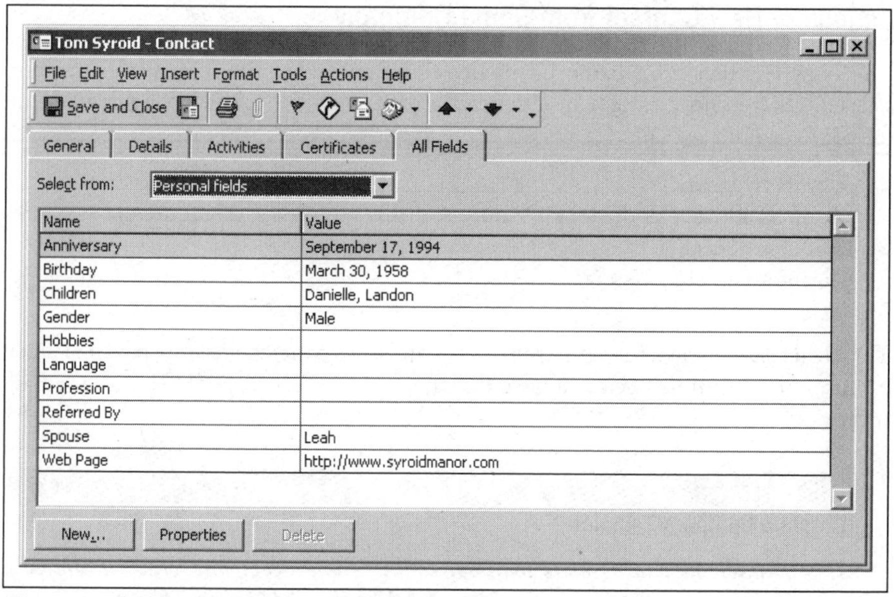

Figure 8-14: The Contacts form, All Fields tab

number, address, or Personal fields. Curiously, the default filter is for user-defined fields, so that the first time you bring up this tab, you usually see no fields at all.

You can inspect the properties (i.e., data type and data format) for any entry shown in the Name column by selecting it and clicking the Properties button at the bottom of the dialog. Properties for the default fields cannot be changed.

The format of a user-defined field can be modified from the item Properties subdialog, but not the field *type*. For example, you could change the display of a customized date field from 05/15/2000 to May 5, 2000. You cannot, however, change a date field to a text field directly, but would have to delete and recreate the item.

To delete a field (again, user-defined only), select it and click the Delete button.

TIP # 104

Exploring Outlook's Fields

The All Fields tab is a good place to spend some time getting a feel for the huge number of fields available in Outlook and the different data types they contain. Did you know that Outlook has preconfigured fields for Government ID, Computer Network Name, and FTP Site?

Actions → New Contact from Same Company

The New Contact from Same Company command takes the information from a selected record and creates a new contact record with the following fields filled in for you:

> Company (name)
> Business address (and Mailing Address, if this was set for this address)
> Business phone(s)
> Business fax
> Telex

The fields *not* carried forward from your previous contact are any personal data (spouse, for example), Contacts and Categories, Web Page URL, and email addresses.

TIP # 105

Create a Company Template

If you anticipate adding more than one contact from a company, create a company template. Open a new contact form and fill in the global fields: Company name, address, phone and fax numbers, etc. Save this record. Now, to add a contact affiliated with this company, use the Actions → New Contact from Same Company command.

Actions → New Distribution List

A Distribution List is a Microsoft term for what other mail programs typically call a Mailing List. If you routinely send mail to a group of contacts, creating a distribution list (DL) lets you address a message to a single recipient instead of having to fill in a lengthy To or CC list of individual recipients.

Figure 8-15 shows a Distribution List form. To create a new Distribution List:

1. From any Contacts folder, select Actions → New Distribution List. The global keyboard shortcut is Ctrl+Shift+L.

2. Give your list a meaningful name (Newsletter Mailing, for example).

3. Use the Select Members button to add members to the list already in your Contacts folder.

4. To add someone to your list that isn't in your Contacts folder, use the Add New button. The "Add to contacts" checkbox at the bottom of the dialog determines whether to add the contact to your records (see Figure 8-16).

The Remove button removes a member from an existing list. The Update Now button refreshes the contents of your list after adding or deleting members. There is

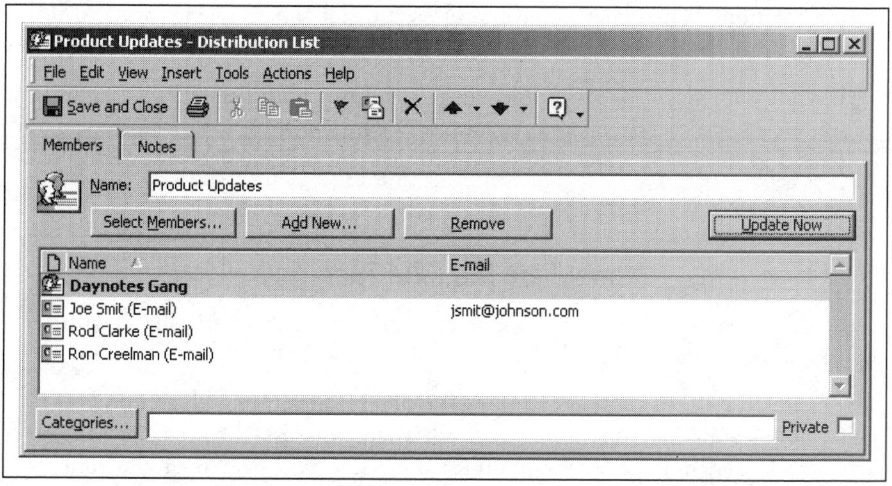

Figure 8-15: Outlook's Distribution List form

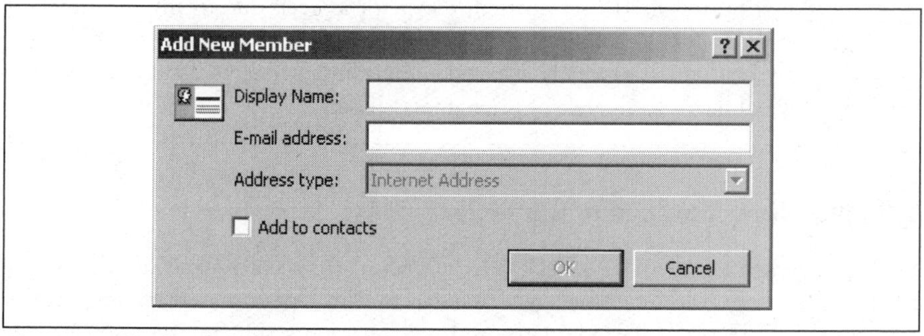

Figure 8-16: The Distribution List Add New Member dialog

also a Notes tab available to record in free form any details or reminders you want to file with the record.

Distribution lists constitute a very powerful tool, and while used predominantly for group email distribution, they are by no means restricted to this task alone. Here are some ways to use a distribution list you might not have considered before:

- Create a distribution list for all those contacts you routinely send Christmas cards to. When the holiday season rolls around, use this list to print out a set of mailing labels for your cards, or merge the contacts on this list with a newsletter created in Word.

- When you switch your Internet provider and get a new email address, change jobs and get a new employer, or move to a new home, create a DL containing a list of people you routinely correspond with. Create a new message, address it to this DL, and attach a vCard to the message containing your new contact

Contacts

information. When they receive your vCard, all the recipients need to do is drag and drop the vCard onto their contacts icon or folder.

- If you maintain a web site and wish to inform your regular readers of any important structural changes to your site, compile a DL of those readers and send a group mailing out before you implement any changes, specifying what they are in advance.

Now Where Did I Put That List?

When you create a Distribution List in Outlook, you are actually creating a special form of contact record.

If you create a DL in another component (Mail for instance) and later find yourself pulling your hair out trying to find where this list is stored, go to your contacts folder and search for it under the name you gave it at the time of creation.

The first distribution list I ever created, I lost for a week due to my misunderstanding of how Outlook stores a DL. Once you know where to look, a Distribution List can be quickly spotted. The contact entry displays an icon showing several heads to the left of the name assigned.

Actions → New Message to Contact

To send a new message to a contact, select a record (or records) and use the menu command Actions → New Message to Contact. This opens a new message form with the To field preaddressed to the selected recipients. Fill in the body of the message form as you would any other email and click Send.

If you select a recipient with more than one email address, the warning dialog shown in Figure 8-17 is displayed. Make sure you remove any addresses not required. If multiple contacts are selected, Outlook uses only one address per recipient: the first email address listed on that individual's contact form.

Figure 8-17: The Warning dialog for an email recipient with more than one address

Actions → New Letter to Contact

To send a letter to a selected contact, go to the Action menu and select New Letter to Contact. This invokes Word and starts the New Letter macro. Contact information is automatically entered into the address fields of the form as shown in Figure 8-18.

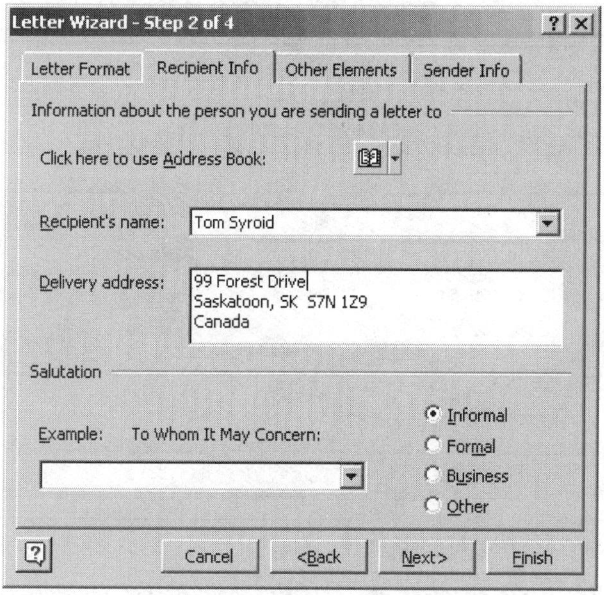

Letter Wizard - Step 2 of 4   [?] [X]

| Letter Format | Recipient Info | Other Elements | Sender Info |

Information about the person you are sending a letter to

Click here to use Address Book: [📖] ▼

Recipient's name: | Tom Syroid | ▼

Delivery address: | 99 Forest Drive|
                       Saskatoon, SK S7N 1Z9
                       Canada

Salutation

Example: To Whom It May Concern: ○ Informal
                                                        ○ Formal
            [   ] ▼   ○ Business
                                                        ○ Other

[?] | Cancel | | <Back | | Next> | | Finish |

Figure 8-18: Word's Letter Wizard invoked from the Actions → New Letter command

 NOTE *Actions → New Letter to Contact is only available when a single contact is selected. Selecting more than one contact disables this command on the menu.*

Fill in the required fields on each of the Letter Wizard's four tabs, and click on Finish.

This command is unavailable if Outlook is installed as a standalone program (as opposed to being installed as part of the Office package).

Actions → New Meeting Request to Contact

Sending a Meeting Request to a contact is remarkably straightforward in comparison to the Appointment and Task topics discussed later. Select a contact (or contacts), and click on the Actions → New Meeting Request to Contact command. A Meeting form opens (see Figure 8-19), with the names of the selected contacts entered in both the Contacts (lower left) and To: fields.

Complete any other required fields on the form (see Chapter 7 for details on sending a Meeting Request), and select the Send button.

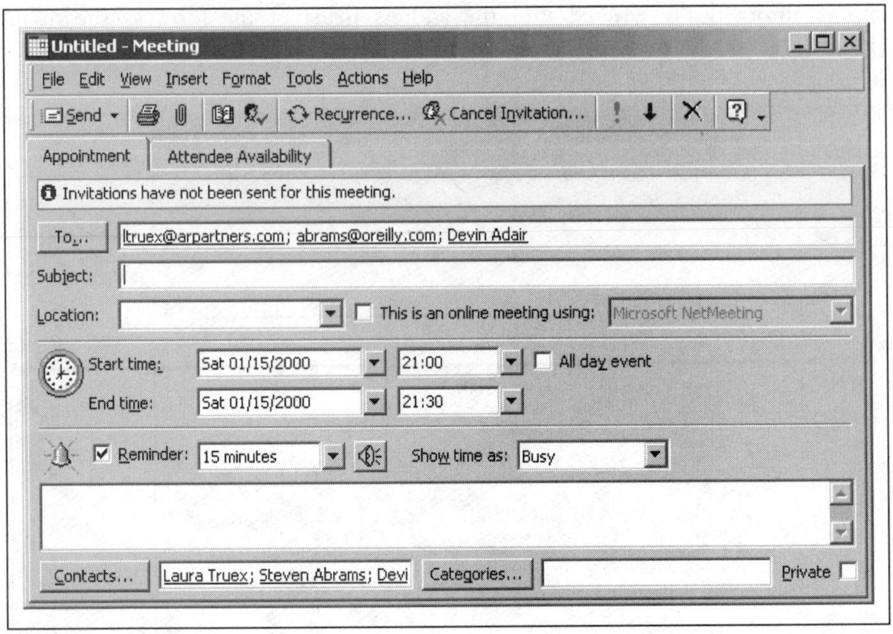

Figure 8-19: New Meeting Request form

> **NOTE** *If a single recipient of a Meeting Request has multiple email addresses defined, all of these are filled in after a warning to remove any you do not wish to use. This does not occur for multiple recipients.*

Actions → New Appointment with Contact

To create a new appointment (Calendar) entry from a selected contact (or contacts), use the menu command Actions → New Appointment with Contact. This opens an Appointment form with the names of the selected contacts entered in the Contacts field (see Figure 8-20).

If you Save and Close the form at this stage, the selected contacts remain as links in the Contacts field. To send an email to these contacts informing them of the pending meeting, you must click the Invite Attendees on the Appointment form's toolbar. Doing so opens a To: field above the Subject line. At this point you must *manually* copy the underlined contact links from the Contacts field to the address field (select the contact, hold down the Ctrl key, select and drag). Now click the Send button (which used to be the Save and Close button) to dispatch your request. Read more about creating appointments in Chapter 7.

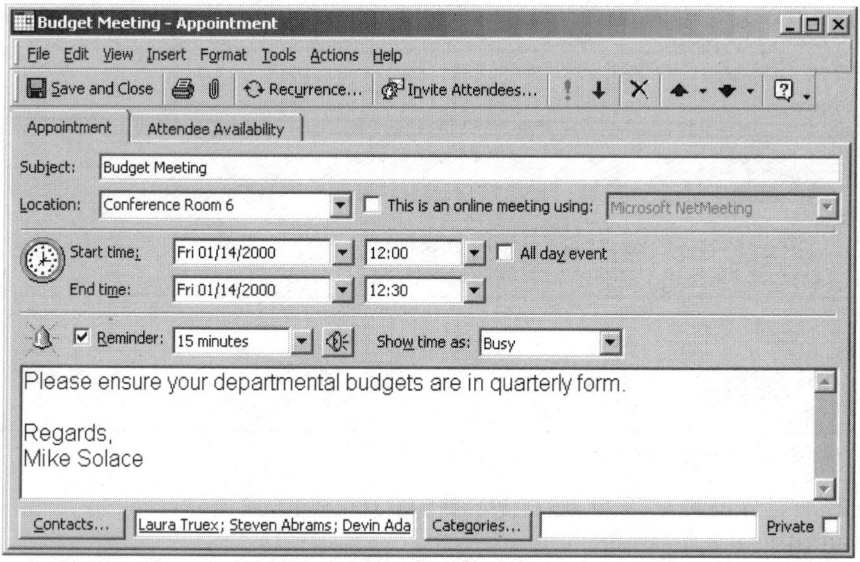

Figure 8-20: The New Appointment form invoked from the Contacts Actions → New Appointment menu command

Actions → New Task for Contact

To assign a Task to a contact, select a record and choose Actions → New Task for Contact. This opens a Task form, shown in Figure 8-21, with the names of the selected recipients preentered in the Contacts field (lower-left of the Tasks form).

From here, you have two options:

- If you want to simply link the selected contacts to the task, fill in a Subject and any other fields desired, then click Save and Close. The record is saved in your Tasks folder and appears on your Task list.

- If you want to email a Task Request to the selected contacts, from the open Task form click on the toolbar button labeled Assign Task. This transfers the contact's email information to the To: line on the Task form and changes the Save and Close toolbar button to Send.

For more details on Outlook's Tasks component, see Chapter 9, *Tasks*.

Actions → New Journal Entry for Contact

To create a new Journal entry from a selected contact, choose New Journal Entry for Contact from the Actions menu. This opens a Journal form with the Subject and Company field filled in, the Contacts field with a link to the contact record,

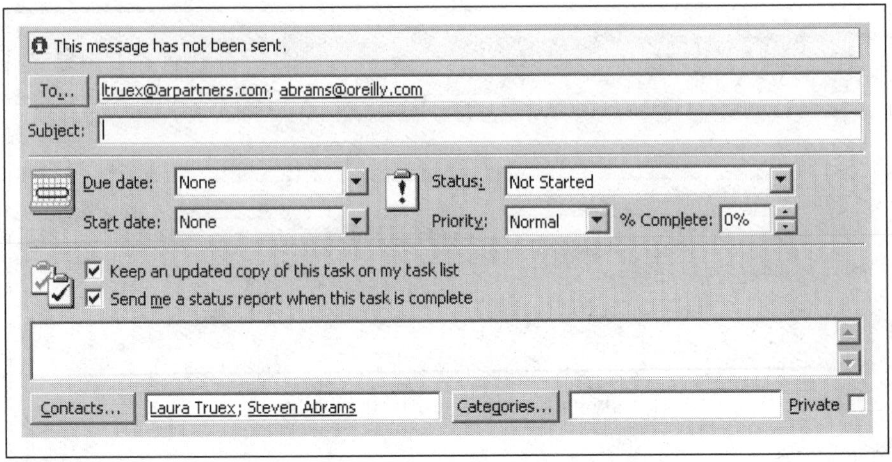


```
❶ This message has not been sent.

To...    ltruex@arpartners.com; abrams@oreilly.com

Subject:  |

  Due date:  None        ▼   ❗  Status:  Not Started                    ▼
  Start date: None       ▼       Priority: Normal ▼  % Complete: 0%  ▲▼

  ☑ Keep an updated copy of this task on my task list
  ☑ Send me a status report when this task is complete


  Contacts...  Laura Truex; Steven Abrams    Categories...  |              Private ☐
```

Figure 8-21: Assigning Contacts to a Task

and the "Entry type" field set to Phone Call (the default). Complete the form as required, and click Save and Close.

There are three gotchas involved with this command:

- Contacts with entries under Company only are not linked; however, the company name is placed in the subject field.

- You can select multiple contacts, but only one is linked to the Journal entry.

- The name placed in the Subject and Contact field of the Journal form is dependent on the order of selection! Selecting Phipps, Joe; Bugworth, Sam; and Slate, Helen; (in this order) creates a Journal entry for Joe Phipps (not Bugworth, as might be expected). In other words, order of selection takes precedence over the alphabetical order of the contacts.

For specifics about using the Journaling features of Outlook, see Chapter 11, *Journal.*

Actions → Link

Links can be established between a contact and an *item* or a *file* (Actions → Link → item or link). Items refer to an existing Outlook record. The following two sections detail the differences between these commands.

> **NOTE** *Outlook's Link commands only operate on one item at a time; selecting more than one item disables the Link menu command.*

Actions → Link → Items

The Actions → Link → Items command opens a dialog (see Figure 8-10 for a screenshot of the Outlook Link Item dialog) allowing you to link a contact with another Outlook item (contact, email, journal entry, etc.) in any open PST file. Once a link is established, it is bidirectional: the referenced Outlook item is listed on the contact's Activity list; a link back to the contact is placed in the target item's Contact field.

Linking Outlook items gives the user a powerful tool for relating topics, ideas, or people in almost unlimited ways.

Actions → Link → File

The Actions → Link → File command establishes a link between an external file (local or network) and the selected contact using Outlook's Journal component. To link a contact to a file:

1. Select a contact. From the Actions menu, choose Link → File.

2. From the Choose a File dialog, locate the file you want to link the contact record to and click on Insert.

3. A Journal form opens with the Subject (the name of the file or document), Company (taken from the contact record), and Entry type filled in. The file you've selected to link the contact to appears as a shortcut in the free-form text field. A link to the contact is placed in the Journal form's Contact field.

4. Once the Journal entry is saved, a link to the entry appears on the Activities tab of the contact record (seen in Figure 8-22).

The linkage established between these two items is two-way. You can open the Journal entry and access the linked file from the free-form text field, and the contact from the Contacts field. To open the Journal entry from the contact's end, go to the Activities tab and double-click the entry there.

Actions → Call Contact

Providing you have a modem connected to your system, Outlook has internal hooks that enable you to dial any of the contact phone numbers listed in your records using the Windows TAPI (*Telephone Application Programming Interface*) system.

Select a contact you want to call and the menu item Actions → Call Contact. A submenu displays containing several choices.

Actions → Call Contact → Selected Contact's Phone Numbers

The first items shown on this submenu are the phone numbers listed under your contact's record, as the example in Figure 8-23 shows. Since Outlook only displays a maximum of four choices in the Contacts form, this is the maximum number that

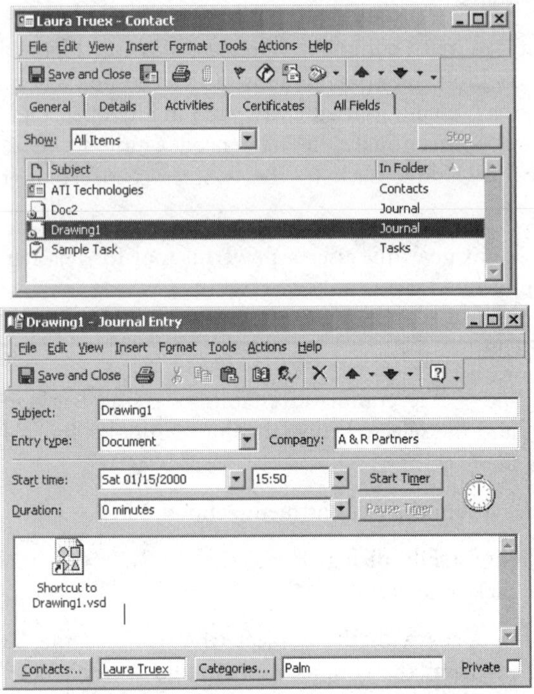

Figure 8-22: The Activities tab of the Contacts' record (top) and the linked Journal entry of the same item (bottom)

can appear on this list. The order the phone numbers are listed in your contact's record determines the display order here. Fax numbers also appear on this list, so select your dialing choice carefully.

Figure 8-23: The Call Contact phone list submenu

Select any of the listed choices and the New Call dialog is invoked (see Figure 8-24). The selected contact's name and calling information are filled in for you. There is a wealth of options available on this dialog. From it you can:

- Type a different name in the Contact field and Outlook will look up and fill in the phone number for this new entry. You must know exactly how this contact is listed in your records, however; there is no search facility for partial names or misspellings.

- Open the contact record for the listed entry with the Open Contact button.

- Choose any of phone number entries for that contact.

- Change the dialing properties used to call the contact—especially useful if you are working from a notebook out of your usual area code.

- Create a Journal entry to log the call being made, including call duration.

- Start the call, which dials the call using your modem, based on the dialing information currently displayed.

- Terminate a call.

- Add this contact and the phone number selected to your Speed Dial list, using the button Dialing Options,

Actions → Call Contact → Redial

The Call Contact → Redial command opens a third-level submenu listing the ten most recent numbers dialed using Outlook. The list shows contact name and the number (in the full record format) and is stored between Outlook sessions. Calls using the fax component are also noted, prefixed "fax:", as are any calls made by manually entering the name and number in the New Call dialog. Select a number from the list to redial it.

Actions → Call Contact → Speed Dial

The submenu selection Speed Dial produces a third-level context menu listing all entries currently saved there, up to a maximum of 20. To add a commonly dialed number to your speed-dial list, first select Actions → Call Contact → New Call as described in the next section, then select the Dialing Options button to open a subdialog for managing the speed dial list. Enter the name the contact is listed under and which number from this record to store in the speed dial. Pressing Tab from the name field automatically fills in the default number from the identified contact's record, but see the following caveat. Both fields are fully editable, and you may use the drop-down list to select an alternate number in case of multiple telephone numbers. The Add button records the new entry. The Delete button removes a selected record from the list.

The Name entry field in this dialog is quasi-intelligent with respect to finding a contact from the name you enter and extracting the correct phone numbers from that contact's record. For example, typing either bo leuf or leuf bo works correctly, assuming the contact exists, and fills in Bo Leuf (properly capitalized), along with the default telephone number. However, typing only tom or syroid goes nowhere in locating the contact and leaves the phone number field blank. The field also remains blank in the case of matching duplicate contacts—not very helpful.

This can work to your advantage, however, if you want an entry stored differently under the speed dial list than it is listed in your contact records. Using the previous example, enter Tom, and manually fill in a phone number to store. The listing on the speed dial menu reflects exactly what you have entered, including contacts and numbers not in your contact records.

Actions → Call Contact → New Call

Selecting the Actions → Call Contact → New Call menu command (Ctrl+Shift+D) invokes the dialog shown in Figure 8-24. The Contact name field is quasi-intelligent in the same way as the Speed Redial command; a correctly identified contact causes the Number field to be filled in automatically.

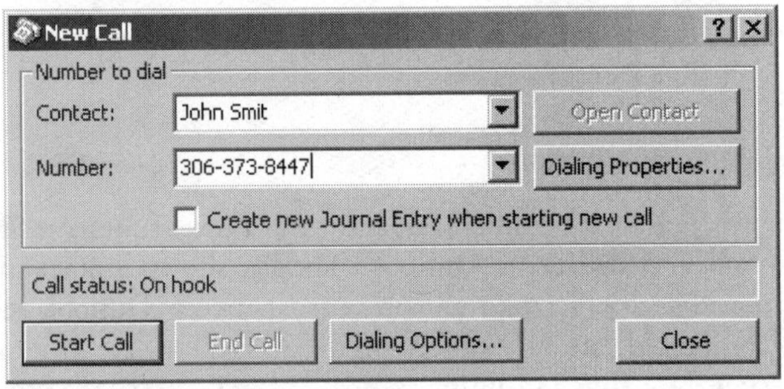

Figure 8-24: The New Call dialog

The Contact field drop-down lists all contacts (successfully) called from this dialog—this is not the same as the Redial listing, and is not stored between sessions. The drop-down list associated with the Number field allows selection of any other phone numbers defined for the current contact.

Actions → Call Using NetMeeting

The Call Using NetMeeting command attempts to connect to the selected contacts according to the defined parameters for NetMeeting in the contact file. This command is functionally identical to the Call Now button on the Contacts form's Details tab. This command requires that the external applications NetMeeting or NetShow are installed and configured.

Actions → Flag for Follow Up

The Actions → Flag for Follow Up command (or Ctrl+Shift+G) allows you to flag one or more selected items using the dialog shown in Figure 8-25. Flagging Outlook items in general is discussed at length in Chapter 3. We also refer you to the section later in this chapter "View → Current View → By Follow-up Flag" for details specific to flagging Contact items.

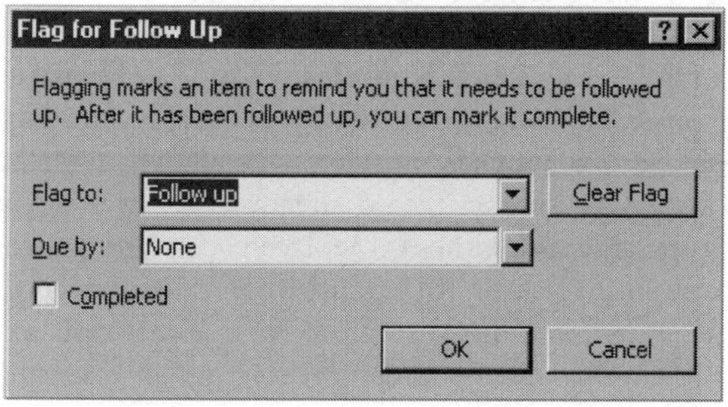

Figure 8-25: The Flag for Follow Up dialog

Actions → Forward as vCard

The vCard concept is an open standard designed to allow users of various brands of contact managers to exchange contact information in a format understood by all programs.

> **NOTE** *For detailed information on the vCard standard, we refer you to the Internet Mail Consortium's web page: www.imc.org/pdi/vcardwhite.html.*

To use this feature, select a contact in any view and choose the command Actions → Forward as vCard. A new message form opens, which you address to the recipient of the vCard. The vCard is appended to the message in the form of an attachment, as shown in Figure 8-26.

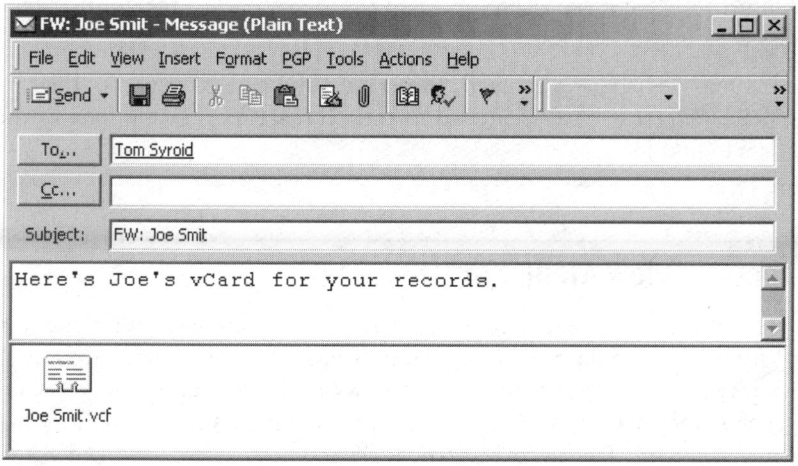

Figure 8-26: New message form with vCard attachment

When you receive a vCard there are two methods of extracting the information contained in it. You can double-click the attachment icon to open it, or drag the icon attachment onto your Contacts icon on the Outlook Shortcut bar and drop it on the Contacts icon. If the contact information is new to your database, an entry is automatically created and a Contacts form opens to allow you to confirm the details of the addition. Should the contact record already exist for this person or business, Outlook gives you the choice to either (a) replace your existing record with the new one (effectively overwriting it), or (b) update your existing record with any fields that are new or different from your current entry. In either case, a copy of the original contact file is left in the Deleted folder, for that just-in-case situation.

vCards are an easy, effective way to keep your friends and associates up to date on any changes to your personal information (like a new email address). They also make for a speedy and efficient way to exchange contact data with fellow business associates.

Finding a Contact

Can't remember Joe Whatshisname's last name? Use Outlook's Find a Contact list on the Standard toolbar (next to the Address Book icon).

Place your cursor in the box and type any part of the name you know (in our example, joe) and Enter. If the information you've provided is sufficient to uniquely identify the person you're looking for, Outlook opens the record in a Contacts form. If two or more contacts match your search criteria, Outlook displays a Choose Contact dialog. Select the entry you want.

Outlook remembers each successful entry found using the Find Contact box. If you forget Joe's last name again (or if you're just lazy), select the down-arrow to display a list of previous searches.

If you cannot remember a contact's name, but you know all or part of their web page URL (and that URL is entered in their contact record), Outlook can use this data to find Joe.

Contacts → View Menu

The View menu (Figure 8-27) contains commands for displaying and altering the many different preconfigured and custom views of your contact records. The following section details the preconfigured views available from the View → Current View menu. Information on the Outlook Bar, Folder List, and Toolbars can be found in Chapter 4, *Outlook's Navigation Tools*. The Preview Pane and AutoPreview commands are discussed in Chapter 6, *Mail*.

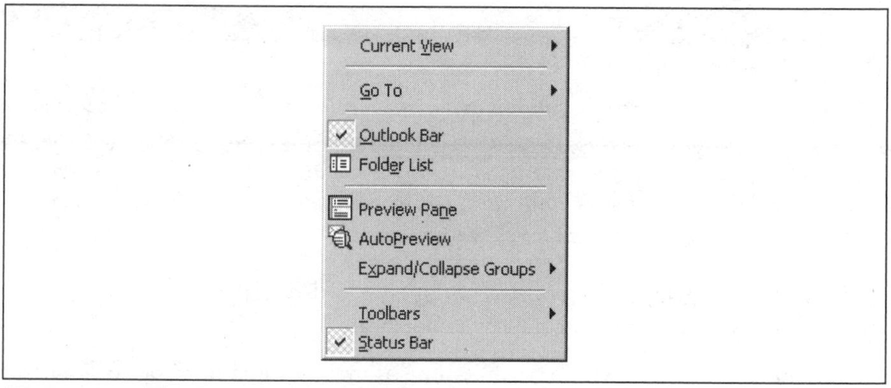

Figure 8-27: The Contacts View menu

For general information about using and customizing views beyond the techniques discussed here, see Chapter 3.

View → Current View

The Current View menu, shown in Figure 8-28, provides you with seven different preconfigured ways to display the information contained in your contact records. Their purpose is to give you a series of useful starting points for displaying your contact records. Each of these views can be further customized to vary both the amount of information presented and the layout it is presented in.

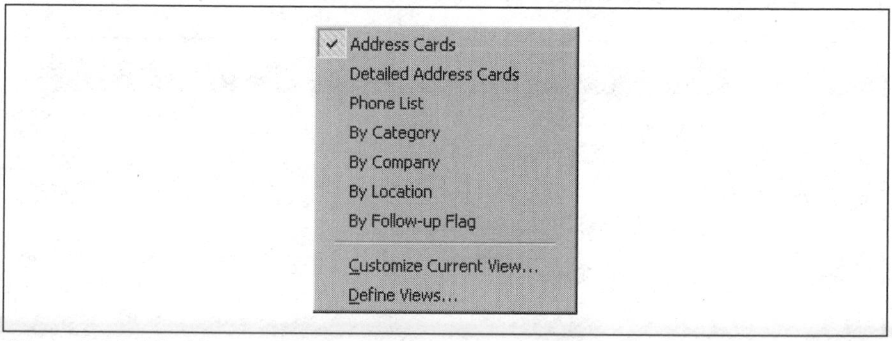

Figure 8-28: The View → Current View menu

Contact views can be classified as either card-based or table-based. Card-based views are visually similar in appearance to Rolodex-style address cards and are useful for quickly looking up frequently used information, like a phone number or address. Table-based views display your contact data in rows and columns with various sort, filter, and grouping options applied.

TIP # 106

Using Context Menus

Right-clicking on a record, column entry, or column header almost always brings up a context menu containing commands that apply to the context you are working in. These context menus not only provide insight about relevant actions you may not have otherwise considered, but also save you frequent trips to the main menu in search of the right command for the task at hand.

Table views optionally allow you to modify a record directly in the table itself or quickly add a new contact from a "new item" located in the first row:

- To modify a record within a table, the "Allow in-cell editing" option must be enabled (View → Current View → Customize Current View → Other Settings). Once it is, click the field you want to modify. When the cursor appears in the table cell, edit the contents as required. Press Enter or select another field to save the record.

- The "new item" row option places a new blank row above the first row of a table (see Figure 8-29). To add a new contact, simply click anywhere in this new row, and begin typing the entry fields according to what column you are in. Use Tab to advance along the columns shown. The record is added when you leave the field row or press Enter. To enable or disable this feature, right-click on the column title row, select Customize This View → Other Settings, and toggle "Show new item row" on or off with the checkbox. "Allow in-cell editing" must also be enabled before the new item row can be selected.

		Full Name	Company	File As		Business Ph...	Business Fax	Home Phone	Mobile Phone	Journal	Categories
		John Smith								■	
		Steven Abrams	O'Reilly and ...	Abrams, Steven						☐	
		Joe Bart	Marketing S...	Bart, Joe, Marketing Strategies		(313) 963-4...				☐	
		Daynotes Gang		Daynotes Gang						☐	
		Daynotes Gang		Daynotes Gang						☐	
		Robert Denn	O'Reilly & A...	Denn, Robert		(617) 354-5...				☑	
		Troy Mott	O'Reilly & A...	Mott, Troy, O'Reilly & Associates		(800) 998-9...				☑	Business, Web Contact
		Outlook Users Group		Outlook Users Group						☐	
		John Roberts	Pizza Dough...	Pizza Dough Supply, Roberts, John		(390) 555-1...				☐	OL2K Test
		Joe's Pizzeria		Pizzeria, Joe's						☐	
		Thumb, Tom		Thumb, Tom						☐	

Figure 8-29: The Contacts Phone List view

Tabled views with groupings also allow drag-and-drop reassignment of field content when you drag items to a different group. A small pop-up box indicates the fields affected when dragging and the new values that will be assigned. Be aware that reassignment is done without confirmation.

View → Current View → Address Cards

This is the default view for Contacts and is displayed in address-card format. As long as it has not been customized from its default settings, this view presents the most important fields from your contact records, as listed in Table 8-1.

Table 8-1: The Default Card View Fields

File As (index field)	Follow-Up Flag	Mailing Address
Business Phone	Company Main Phone	Home Phone
Mobile Phone	Car Phone	Other Phone
Business Fax	Home Fax	E-mail
E-mail 2	E-mail 3	

The default layout used here is a good starting point for most users. It provides quick access to commonly referenced contact information. To edit or add contact information, select an item and double-click or press Enter to access the Add/Edit dialog. If in-cell editing is enabled, records can be modified directly in the Address Cards.

TIP # 107

Showing Empty Fields

Outlook's default behavior in both Address Cards and Detailed Address Cards is to display only fields containing data. To change this option, right-click on the alphabetical index tabs displayed along the right edge of the address card window and toggle the Show Empty Fields option.

You can move through your records in several ways: scroll bar, arrow keys, Tab key, or page up or down keys.

The index tabs along the right window edge bring you to the first matching entry in your records, or the first following entry if the range is empty. To quickly locate a particular record in your contact file, simply start typing the name of the individual or company you want to reference.

 Any significant pause between keystrokes in name entry is interpreted by Outlook as a request to start a new name search.

View → Current View → Detailed Address Cards

This command expands on the simpler Address Cards view by displaying more fields, as listed in Table 8-2.

Table 8-2: Fields Displayed by the Detailed Address Cards View

File As (Main Index)	Follow-Up Flag	Full Name
Job Title	Company	Department
Business Address	Home Address	Other Address

Table 8-2: Fields Displayed by the Detailed Address Cards View (continued)

Business Phone	Business Phone 2	Assistant's Phone
Company Main Phone	Home Phone	Home Phone 2
Mobile Phone	Car Phone	Radio Phone
Pager	Callback	Telex
TTY/TDD Phone	ISDN	Other Phone
Primary Phone	Business Fax	Home Fax
Other Fax	E-mail	E-mail 2
E-mail 3	Web Page	Categories
Notes		

Because of the number of fields displayed, the detailed view is not a common one to use on a daily basis, especially if the majority of these fields contain data. To keep the amount of information you need to scan through in check, use a simpler layout (like Address Cards) to drill down to a specific record, and then select this more detailed view to expand the range of fields shown.

View → Current View → Phone List

Phone List is a Table view, and presents your contact information with the individual records as rows and the fields displayed as columns. The view is initially sorted based on the entry File As. The Phone List view is shown in Figure 8-29.

This is an excellent layout to use when you need to quickly find a specific contact's phone number. Clicking on any of the column headings sorts your data in either ascending or descending order on that field. The exception here is Categories, which cannot be used as a sort order for this view.

It is possible to use the previously described keyboard method (in Card view) to drill down through your contact list and locate a specific entry, but *only* if the feature "Allow in-cell editing" is turned off (Customize Current View → Other Settings). With in-cell editing enabled, typing on the keyboard starts a new record entry if the option "Show new item row" is enabled.

View → Current View → By Category

This is another Table view, and groups your contacts according to the categories assigned to them. Items assigned more than one category are repeated under each category heading. You can assign categories to a contact from this view by right-clicking the selected items and using the Categories context menu command.

Quickly Assign a Category Using Groups

Providing you have a grouping displayed for the category you want to assign to your contact, simply drag the record from the group "(none)" to the group containing the category you want to assign.

If you have categorized your contact records, the Table view By Category is a very powerful and useful tool for working with groups of individuals or companies.

Assume, for example, that you have taken the time to create and assign a category to all the contacts you routinely send Christmas cards to. Selecting the category view would then produce a listing of all the records in your contact file, grouped by their assigned category. You can then open the branch labeled Christmas Cards, select everyone listed there, and choose an action to perform on this group.

How you use and assign categories will reflect how you most often use your contact file. The key here is to *use* them! Categories are a tremendously powerful feature of Outlook and worth the extra effort it takes to assign them. To read more about creating and assigning categories, see Chapter 3.

View → Current View → By Company

This view groups your contacts by their respective company associations. The Company field becomes the first-level grouping, with a second-level grouping on the File As field. You can see the current group hierarchy by right-clicking on the header row and selecting Group By Box from the context menu.

Remember that in all Table views, the groupings described are the installation defaults. If you remove Group By Company, replace it with another field, or add further subgroupings, you have created a new, different view.

If Outlook's default views are customized beyond the default settings, *it is this changed view that is displayed* when you later reselect the same view. To reset this view to its original settings, go to View → Define Views, select By Company and use the Reset button. Be sure to exit with the Apply button if you want the changes to take effect.

View → Current View → By Location

By Location displays a Table view organizing your contact records by the field Region/Country, with a secondary sort order based on File As. This is an appropriate view to use if you are looking for a contact in a particular country or region, or wish to manipulate a group of contacts that share a common location. For example: you're preparing to make a business trip to Toronto and want to call ahead to all your suppliers there to let them know the dates of your visit. Switch to the By Location view, click on the Region column to sort your entries on Canada, then on the State column to invoke a secondary sort. From the resulting table, it is easy to quickly compile a list of the individuals or companies you need to advise of your pending visit. See Figure 8-30 for an example view.

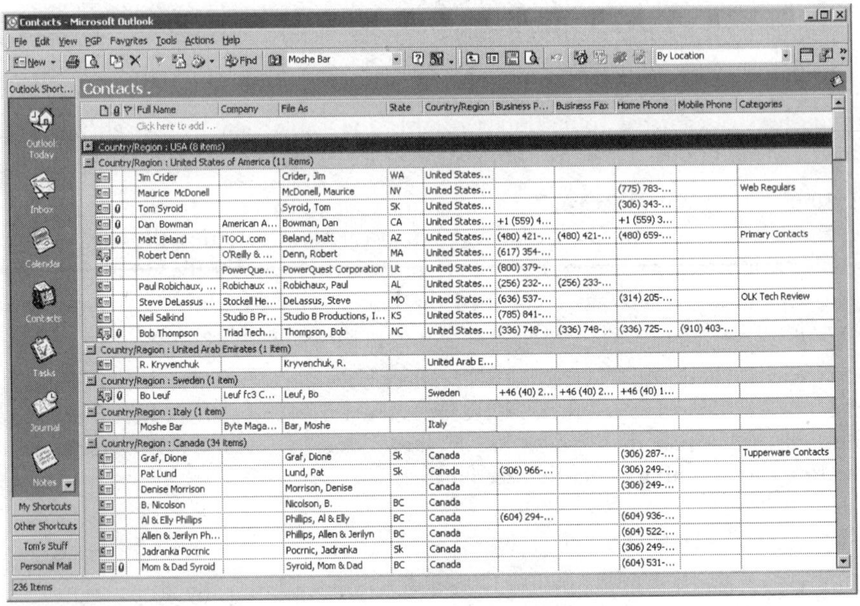

Figure 8-30: The View → Current View → By Location is useful for sorting contacts located in similar regions

Grouping and filtering makes a powerful tool to narrow a large database of contacts down to a select subset for easier viewing or manipulation.

View → Current View → By Follow-up Flag

The By Follow-up Flag view arranges your contacts by the flag *status*, sorted on the field File As. There are three possible status groups:

Flagged
    The item has an active flag attached.

Completed
    The item has a flag attached that has been marked as complete.

None
    The item has no flag attached to it or that flag has been cleared.

Flagged items also support five preconfigured descriptions referenced by the "Flag to" field:

    Follow up
    Call

Arrange Meeting
Send E-mail
Send Letter

The default flag description is simply "Follow up." This is beneficial as a quick reminder, but the reason you flagged an item can be quickly forgotten over time. Flags only become a powerful tool if you take the extra effort to specify the flag type, and where appropriate, a due date for the flag. Doing so provides you with a clear record of why an item was flagged and allows you to sort and manipulate these flags using the power inherent in this view.

TIP # 109

Modifying a Flag Description

Do not be deceived by the list box used for flag description in the Flag for Follow Up dialog. While it appears that this list is a "one-or-the-other" proposition, it is not— you can type any description you want in the "Flag to" field. Use this to your benefit by assigning flag descriptions to an item that make sense to you.

Clicking on the flag icon for a contact item presents a small submenu where you can change the flag status to any of the previously listed values. You can also reassign the flag status for any item by just dragging it into a different group, but be aware that other fields can change as well if other subgroupings are applied to the view. As you drag a record between groups, a small pop-up box shows the affected field and the new value. The Follow Up Flag column shows you the flag type assigned for items that remain active. Double-clicking on an individual item displays that entry's Contacts form.

The following points should be kept in mind when flagging contact items:

- Typing anything into the description field of an unflagged item automatically flags it as active. This is a quick way to assign customized flag types.

- If the flag icon for a contact item is shown, then you can click on it to access a drop-list to change the status.

- To reflag, uncheck the Completed checkbox in the flag dialog, or use the icon method.

- Changing a flag to Completed keeps the flag type (*and* Due By).

- Setting a Due Date on a flag does *not* place a link to that item in your task list or calendar as might be expected.

- Contacts items with attached flags show "Follow Up Flag: `description`" on the first line of a Card view; opening a contact with an attached flag shows the flag description only as an information banner under the form's tabs.

- Right-clicking a selected contact with an active assigned flag allows you to clear the flag or complete the flag via context menu, but *not* assign a date to the flag.

Right-clicking a contact with a flag status of Completed or None, however, produces a context menu with a Flag for Follow Up command on it. Go figure.

It is important to understand the difference between *Clearing* a flag and marking it *Complete*. Clearing a flag removes the flag description, and leaves that item with a flag status of None. Marking a flag Complete, however, only changes the flag status to Complete, keeping the description.

 If keeping a task trail of flagged but addressed items is important to you, mark an item as Complete when it is done, instead of just Clearing the flag. This will help you find an item later on.

View → Current View → Customize Current View

The topic of customizing Outlook's default views is an expansive one, and fully documented under the section "A Primer on Views and Print Styles" in Chapter 3. The following section touches on just a few of the ways a Contacts-specific view can be modified.

The Current View → Customize Current View command opens the View Summary dialog shown in Figure 8-31.

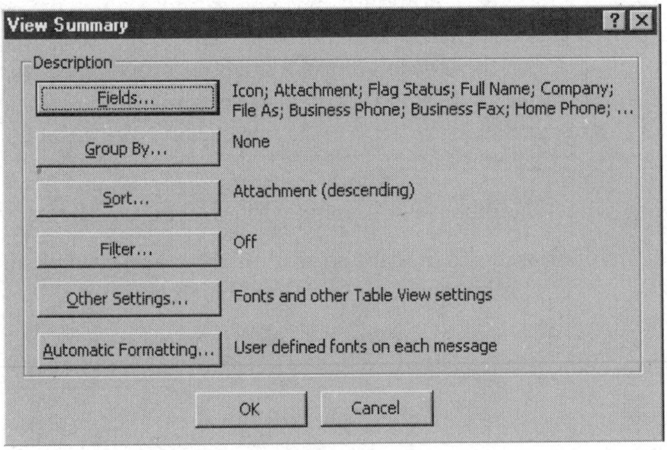

View Summary	? X
Description	
Fields...	Icon; Attachment; Flag Status; Full Name; Company; File As; Business Phone; Business Fax; Home Phone; ...
Group By...	None
Sort...	Attachment (descending)
Filter...	Off
Other Settings...	Fonts and other Table View settings
Automatic Formatting...	User defined fonts on each message
OK	Cancel

Figure 8-31: The View Summary dialog shown in the context of the Phone List view

The view this dialog is invoked from determines the options available. For contact items, the two default choices are Card views and Table views. Card views do not support grouping, so the Group By button is disabled when the View Summary dialog is opened from Address Cards or Detailed Address Cards.

View-at-a-Glance

The View Summary dialog shows you, in one quick glance, which properties are currently assigned to a specific view. By referring to the text descriptions next to each button, you can see what fields the view is configured to display and the order they are displayed in, fields (if any) the view is grouped by, the view's sort field and order, and if any filters are applied.

Outlook also provides access to a number of the customization options contained on the View Summary dialog directly from context menus. Again, these context menus are view specific. The context menu for Card views is shown in Figure 8-32 (left); the context menu for Table views is shown in Figure 8-32 (right). Both menus contain the command Customize Current View, which is a faster route to the View Summary dialog than the using Outlook's regular menus.

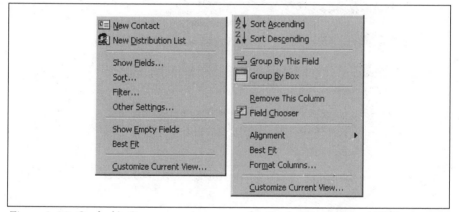

Figure 8-32: Outlook's Contacts context menus for Card views (left) and Table views (right)

In the following two sections, we look at the most commonly used commands for customizing a view in Contacts using the context menus as reference points. We remind the reader that all the commands and options discussed can also be accessed from the View Summary dialog as well.

Customizing Card views. To open the view-specific context menu (Figure 8-32, left) in a Card view, right-click on the alphabetical index bar.

The four commands Show Fields, Sort, Filter, and Other Settings, take you to the same dialogs accessed via buttons on the View Summary dialog. Below them are two toggle commands: Show Empty Fields (self-explanatory), and Best Fit, which automatically sizes your columns to the narrowest possible width without compromising the detail contained in the displayed records.

Show Fields

This command opens a dialog (see Figure 8-33) where you can select which fields are displayed in the current view. You may also move the fields up or down in the list to modify the display order, or define a new user-defined field based on a multitude of types and formats. The standard item mouse selection applies in these lists (click, click and drag, shift-click for block, control-click for disjoint selection, etc.) as do keyboard shortcuts for selection and dialog buttons.

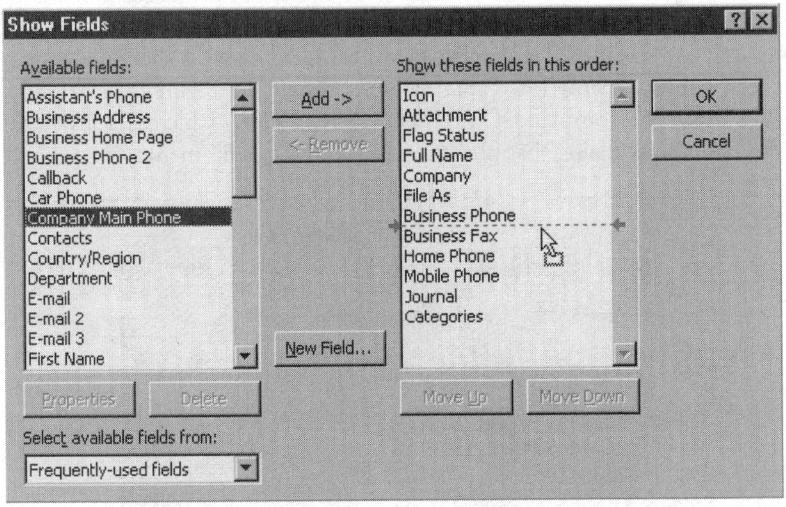

Figure 8-33: The Customize View subdialog Show Fields, showing the Note drag and drop

To add fields to the view, drag entries from the "Available fields" list (left pane) to the "Show these fields in this order" list (right pane). When dragging, the added field is placed in the list position indicated by the red dashed insertion line. Alternatively, you can select the fields and use the Add button, which inserts the selected field *after* the previously selected item in the receiving list.

To remove one or more fields from display, select and drag the other way, from Show to Available, or use the Remove button.

To limit the number of field choices shown in the Available list and see only fields of a particular type, select an appropriate category from the "Select available fields from" drop-down list. Note that user-defined fields belong to their own exclusive category.

To create and add a user-defined field, select the New Field button. In the resulting subdialog, enter a Name for the field you wish to add, and then use the drop-down lists to select appropriate data Type and Format.

To modify or remove an existing user-defined field, select it in "Available fields." This activates the Properties button (to change Format only, as applicable) and Delete button under this list.

 The default contact fields in Outlook are hard-coded and cannot be deleted or have their formats altered. For a full list of the Rules of Engagement regarding default fields and view, see the sidebar later in this chapter titled "Rules for Managing Views and Fields."

Sort

Sort opens a dialog (see Figure 8-34, left) that allows the sort order of the view to be modified. Records can be sorted up to four levels deep, each in ascending or descending order. The list of fields to choose from can be narrowed by selecting a category grouping from the drop-down list at the bottom of the dialog. The Clear All button resets the view to Unsorted.

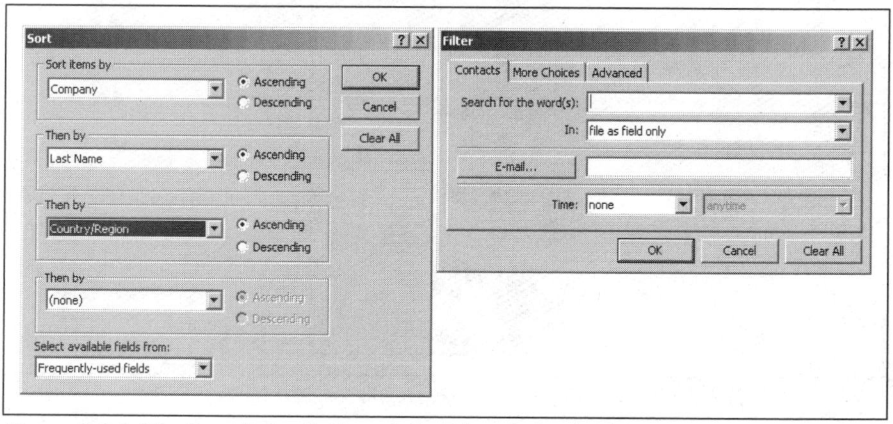

Figure 8-34: The Sort dialog (left) and the Filter dialog (right)

Filter

The Filter command opens the dialog shown in Figure 8-34 (right). This dialog allows you to enter qualifiers that display only a selected subset of data. Once you apply a filter to your contact data, it remains in effect until that filter is cleared. To view all contact entries again, you must select the Clear All button at the bottom of the Filter dialog.

Other Settings

The Other Setting command opens a dialog containing options to format your Card view. Here you set the fonts for card heading and body, toggle in-cell editing, control whether empty fields are visible, and set the displayed card dimensions (width and multiline minimum height).

Customizing table views. Customizing Table views works in principle exactly like Card views; the options are different, however, due to the differences in layouts.

Table views, which include the Phone List and all the "By..." views, can be customized either through the View Summary dialog (View → Current View → Customize Current View) or with the context menu displayed by right-clicking the column title bar. As most commands on the View Summary dialog are also available more directly from the view's customization context menu, we'll focus our efforts here.

The Table view context menu is shown again in Figure 8-35 for reference. The first two options control the order items and are displayed within the current view:

Sort Ascending and Sort Descending
> These two commands duplicate the functionality of clicking on a column header box. The field determining the current sort order is indicated by a shadow-triangle on the header box (sometimes not seen if the column width is too small) indicating which sort direction is in effect at any given time.

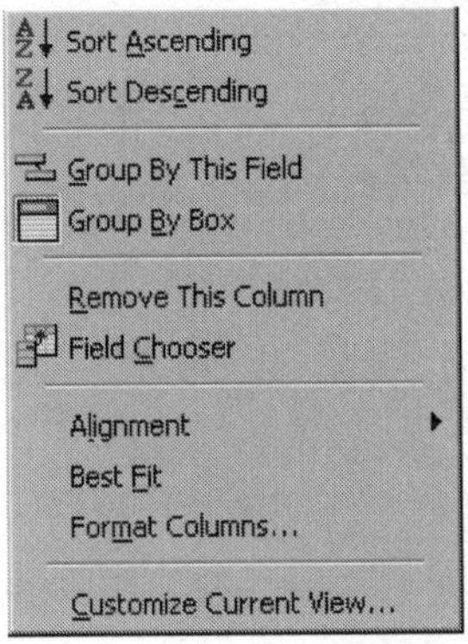

Figure 8-35: The Table customization context menu

Table views can be grouped with the next two commands on the menu: Group By This Field and Group By Box. Grouping a view shows you how many items have the selected field's contents in common. A typical example may be to group contacts by company or location, and these are in fact two of the preset groupings available as Current View submenu selections.

Group By This Field
> This command appends the field for the column you right-clicked to the current grouping structure. If it is the first group, and the group area is not already visible, the table is shifted down and the grouping area shown with the selected field's box in the first position. The table then shows the contacts in groups as determined by the column field selected. Repeat the process with another column header and you produce a further subgrouping within the first groups. The hierarchy is indicated by how the group boxes are linked.

Group By Box

This command simply shifts down the table pane, freeing an area above the table, with one or more title boxes showing the groupings and sort orders currently used. If there is no grouping active, an outlined space labeled "Drag a column header here to group by that column" is shown. Drag and drop any new field title box to a desired position in the grouping area to activate a new (sub) grouping. The arrows in Figure 8-36 indicate the nearest link position when dragging a box inside the grouping area.

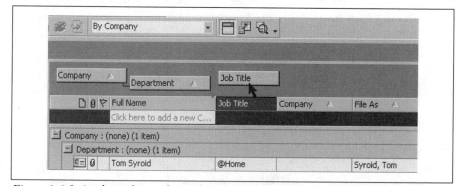

Figure 8-36: A column box is dragged to insert a new subgrouping at the indicated location

---

TIP # 111

Resetting a View

Any modifications made to a default view, such as modified groupings, remain in effect until you change them again. To restore a default view to factory fresh settings, go to the Define Views dialog (View → Current View → Define Views), select the view you want to restore, and click the Reset button.

To turn off grouping by any active field, drag the grouping box out of the delineated area (the dragged box copy is then shown crossed over) and release it. Alternatively, you may right-click any member of an existing grouping and select "Don't Group by this Field" from the context menu. Remaining groupings automatically adjust position. Removing all groupings returns the display to the default order based on the File As field.

A sort affects the order (ascending or descending) of items, either throughout the entire list, or repeatedly on subordinate items nested under a common item. A group, on the other hand, also displays a header for each unique item at a given sort level, and allows you to expand or collapse the list segments under each heading. In addition, groupings can be managed in a more graphic way with the boxes and Group By commands.

Contacts

The next two context menu commands, shown in Figure 8-32, control the column layout of a Contacts table:

Remove this Column

Removes the column under your mouse pointer from the table layout.

Field Chooser

Opens the Field Chooser dialog shown in Figure 8-37. To add a column to a Contact view, select it from the list shown and drag it to the view's column title bar. Two red pointers indicate where, with respect to existing columns, the new field will be positioned relative to existing columns.

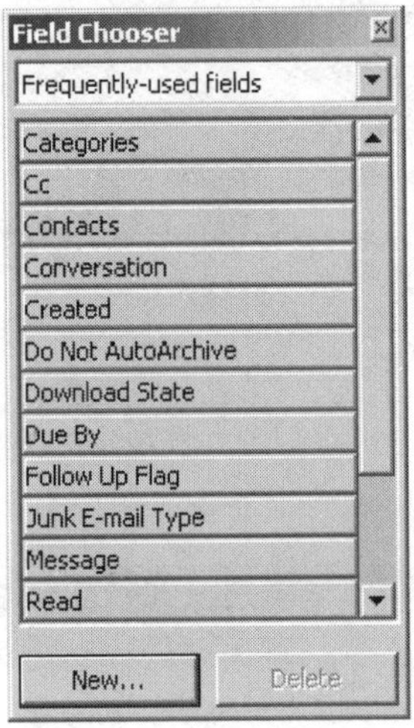

Figure 8-37: The Field Chooser dialog

The remaining three commands on the table view context menu shown in Figure 8-32 relate to column/field format and sizing:

Alignment

Opens a "fly-out" submenu with three justification options for the selected column: Align Left, Align Right, and Center.

Best fit

Best fit sets the column width wide enough to accommodate the longest text entry it contains. (There are some constraints depending on what a column contains and the maximum width set.)

Format Columns

Opens the Format Columns dialog shown in Figure 8-38.

The Available Fields list shows all fields associated with the current view. Selecting an entry from this list displays that field's format properties in the options on the right.

Rules for Managing Views and Fields

The rules for creating, deleting, and modifying views and fields are straightforward and, remarkably enough, consistent across all components of Outlook:

- You can reset a default view, but not delete it.

- You can delete a custom view, but not reset it.

- You can delete a custom field, but you cannot delete any of Outlook's default fields.

- You cannot change a field's type. You can, however, change the display format of a field within the limitations of type. (*Some* user-defined fields are exempt from this rule.)

- Deleting a custom field from the Field Chooser deletes it from the list of available fields but does not remove it from any view in which it is used.

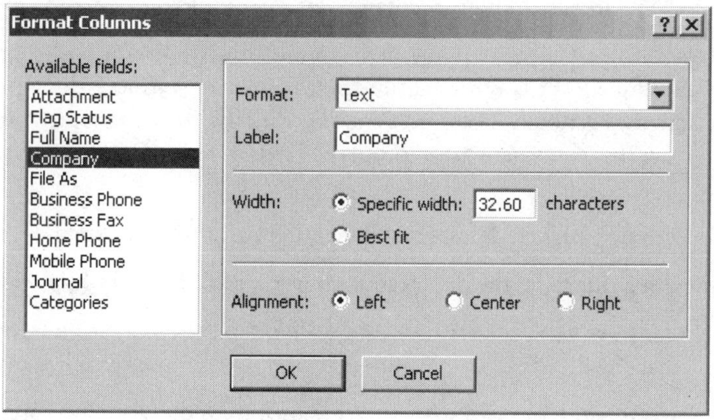

Figure 8-38: The Format Columns dialog

As noted in the "Rules for Managing Views and Fields" sidebar earlier in this section, you cannot change a field's type, but you can change its display format (when a type has more than one format option). The format field on the Format Columns is one place to do this. Selecting Attachment, for example, gives you the option of formatting the column containing this field as Yes/No, On/Off, True/False, and Icon.

The Label option lets you change the column title displayed in the view; this changes the view label only, not the field name itself. The width option lets you specify a column width, or choose "Best fit."

Alignment is a duplication of the content menu command discussed earlier in this section.

Chapter 9

Tasks

Tasks are the electronic equivalent of those to-do notes scattered all over your desk. Tasks are an excellent candidate for electronic organization because, like Outlook's other components, they can be edited, sorted, organized, categorized, and quickly shuffled for priority when all your best laid plans take a turn for the worse.

The real power of Tasks, however, lies in their ability to leverage Outlook's other components to delegate a task to another person. This assignment feature uses email to send a task to someone on your contact list. The task can then be accepted or rejected by the recipient, and on acceptance, automatically tracked until complete.

Tasks are similar to Calendar items in form and function with two subtle twists. Setting a date for a task is optional; under Calendar it is a necessity. In addition, Calendar activities typically occur at a specific time (with the exception of events), but Tasks have no equivalent time property. This gives rise to three distinct task categories:

1. Tasks with no assigned dates: your "when I get around to it" items.

2. Tasks with a due date: the dry cleaning that needs to be picked up on Monday.

3. Tasks that have both a start date and a due date: the manuscript you have to review that's will be ready on Wednesday and needs to be complete by Friday.

Outlook does not support tasks with a start date and no due date; we can only speculate that Microsoft engineers wanted to ensure you finish everything added to your Task list. And while we're talking about quirks, note that a dated Task entry does not show up on your Outlook Calendar as one might expect.

This chapter looks at two menu groups specific to Tasks:

- The *Actions* Menu contains commands to create, delegate, and Forward tasks.

- The *View* Menu contains commands to display tasks in a variety of preconfigured views, each based on a different sort order, filter, or grouping.

Tasks → Actions Menu

The Actions menu for Tasks is shown in Figure 9-1. The following sections describe creating tasks for your own personal use, assigning tasks to other people, setting task orders, and forwarding tasks.

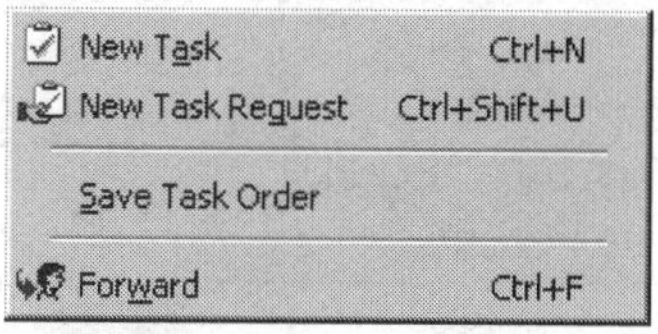

Figure 9-1: The Tasks Actions menu

Actions → New Task

To create a task:

* From the Actions menu, select New Task.

* Use the global keyboard shortcut Ctrl+Shift+K from anywhere in Outlook; use Ctrl+N from within Tasks.

* Double-click in any open region of a Task view.

* Select New Task from one of Tasks' numerous context menus.

* Use the TaskPad (see Chapter 7, *Calendar*).

Any of these actions opens a new Task form (see Figure 9-2). The two tabs below the form's toolbar—Tasks and Details—organize the entry of your task information.

A new task requires, at minimum, a subject. The subject describes the task, and identifies it in all views. We recommend throughout this book that you enter as much information as possible any time you create a new record of any kind. If you're pressed for time, however, make sure you use key words for the subject and that they're detailed enough to remind you why you created the entry in the first place. You'll realize the wisdom of this the first time you find an entry on your task list marked Urgent: Call Supplier and you have no idea when it was created, if there was a due date, or which supplier it was you were supposed to call.

The Task tab

The Task tab contains all the common input fields associated with creating a task:

Subject
> Every new task requires a unique description. The subject line serves as a reference to the task's purpose and distinguishes it from other tasks on your list.

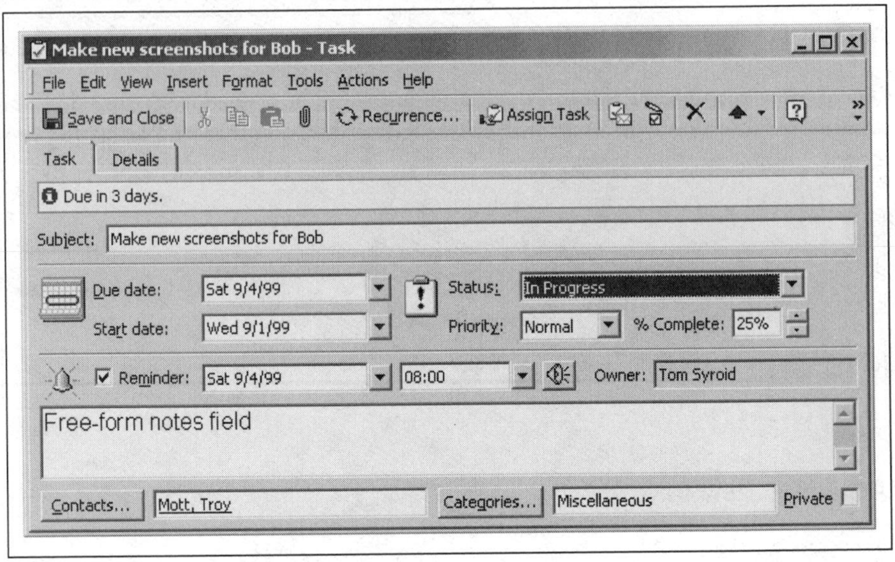

Figure 9-2: The New Task form

From here you may press the Save and Close button on the toolbar. Or you can press the Esc key and Outlook prompts you to either Save or Cancel the record. The Subject field has no formatting tricks attached; what you enter here becomes the task description.

Due date

If you don't use any other field on this dialog, use "Due date." Put an entry here that reflects when you need or anticipate the task to be completed. Overdue tasks are displayed in red (configurable from Tools → Options → Task Options). In addition, setting a due date for a task also works in conjunction with the next field, "Start date."

All the date fields on the Tasks form function in an identical manner. When a new task entry is created, the default date is None. Tabbing into any of these fields allows you to make entries that convert intelligently: Sunday, Next Sunday, 1 week, 2 weeks from next Tuesday, etc. You can also select the arrow button to the right of the field, which calls up the Date Navigator, allowing you to quickly select a date from a graphical calendar.

TIP # 112

Task Due Dates and Start Dates

You can assign a task a due date without assigning a start date. You cannot, however, assign a start date and set the due date to None.

Start date

Setting a start date for a task serves two purposes. It records when you entered the task or scheduled the task to start. Also, used with Due Date and the Task Timeline view, you can view projects in a Gantt-style timeline with start and end dates clearly blocked out. Timeline views are discussed under the "Tasks → View Menu" section of this chapter.

Status

Tracks the progress of tasks. Choices are: Not Started, In Progress, Completed, Waiting on Someone Else, and Deferred. The default entry is Not Started. You need not change this field when entering a new task unless you are creating an entry for a task already started. You typically update this field from one of the task views to keep yourself (or others) up to date on where a given task stands.

Priority

Assigns an importance to the task (Low, Normal, or High).

% Complete

Gives you the option of updating larger projects and monitoring them. Like the status field, this is more likely to be updated after a new task is entered.

Reminder

Lets you select a date, time, and, if you so desire, a sound to play when the task is due. Choosing the Reminder option activates all three associated fields: a trigger date, time, and the sound file to use to announce the reminder.

 The default reminder time for all Outlook items is set from the Preferences tab of the Options dialog (Tools → Options).

Owner

This field labels the Owner or creator of the task and is supplied by Outlook. It is not editable. When you delegate a task to someone, she becomes the owner of the task.

Notes (not labeled)

The Notes field functions the same across all Outlook components. Use it to enter notes about the task that are not accommodated by the form's other fields. This is also where attached documents or files are displayed.

*Contacts**

The Contacts button opens the Select Contacts dialog shown in Figure 9-3. Choose a contact folder from the upper pane, and then select a record from the list provided in the lower pane. A valid contact entry in this field creates a two-

---

* If a contact linked to a task is deleted or archived, the Contacts field on the task still displays a link to the contact. Opening the link, however, presents a warning dialog informing you the contact has been deleted and is no longer a valid Address Book entry. Deleting a task removes it from a contact's Activities tab.

way link between the task and the contact record it is linked to. Any tasks linked in this manner are also displayed under the contacts record (Activity tab → Show → Upcoming Tasks/Appointments). Any changes to the task record from Contacts (including deleting a task) are reflected in all views under Tasks.

TIP # 113

Contact Record First, Link Second

To link a contact not already in your records with a task, you have to create the contact entry before applying the linkage; there is no provision on the Select Contacts dialog for adding a new contact.

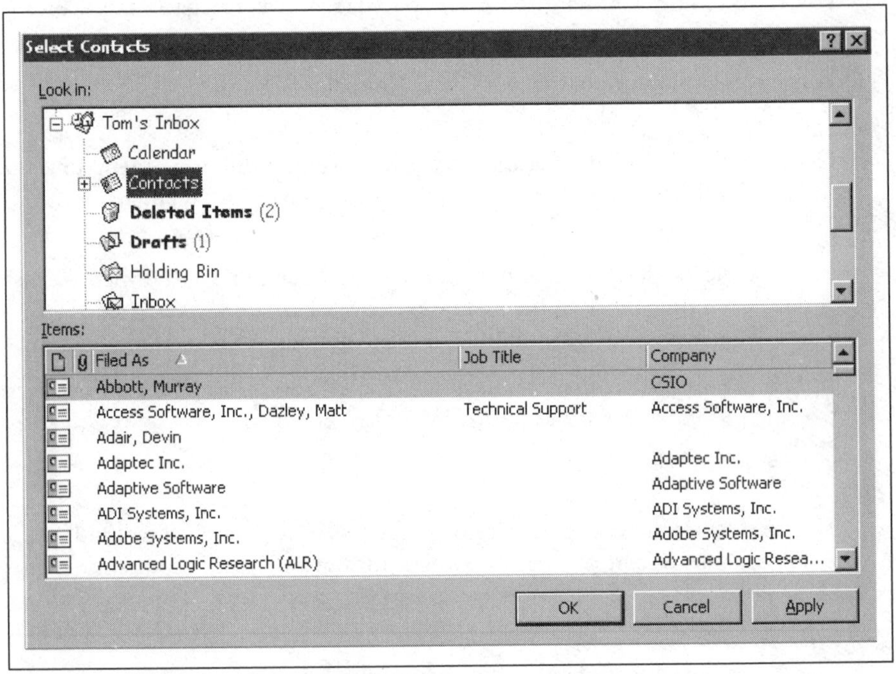

Figure 9-3: The Select Contacts dialog

Categories
Assigns a category to a task. If you know the exact spelling of an existing category, enter it directly in the field provided; if you do not, click the Categories button to open the Categories dialog. At the risk of sounding repetitive, make it a habit to use the Master Category List. See Chapter 3, *Program Insights*, if you do not yet know why.

Private
Place a checkmark in the Private checkbox to hide the task from anyone you share your Tasks folder with.

Link Your Tasks and Contacts

If you want to truly leverage the power of Outlook, take the time to link your tasks with their associated contacts. Doing so provides you with a rich matrix of interrelated items, available from multiple sources.

For example, it's Monday and you need to call Joe Smith about the Pringle account on Tuesday. Create a new task; link both of these contacts to it (Smith and Pringle, Inc.,) using the Contacts field on the task form. On Tuesday morning, before you make your call, open the task and open both links in the Contacts field (double-click). Now you have everything you need in front of you, including a place to make some free-form notes as you talk. When you finish, mark the task as complete to keep existing linkages in place and the task listed in both contact records for reference. If you delete the completed task, both the task and the linkages are lost.

In addition to the fields just described, there are three commands found on an open task form (via the form's toolbar or the Actions menu) you should be aware of:

Recurrence

Recurrence is extremely useful for ongoing items that have a specific pattern: bank loans, weekly meetings, or yearly trade shows. Set up a task once, set the recurrence pattern, and Outlook generates an ongoing to-do list for you.

The upper half of the dialog shown in Figure 9-4 gives a range of settings for a task recurrence pattern. Selecting Daily, Weekly, Monthly, or Yearly in the upper-left panel displays corresponding sets of selections in the upper-right panel. Note the Regenerate new task option, which creates a new task entry at the specified interval after the task is marked complete.

The lower half of the dialog allows you to set the Range of the recurrence. Set a start date, then choose "No end date" for an ongoing task, "End after x occurrences" for a task that you want to occur a specific number of times, or use the "End by" option to stop the recurrence on a specific date.

> **NOTE** *Recurring tasks are added one at a time to your task list. When you mark the current task complete, the next occurrence appears. When the next occurrence appears is a function of the recurrence pattern set for the series.*

Assign Task

Delegates a task to someone. See the "Actions → New Task Request" section later in this chapter for details on how task assignment works. If you assign a task to someone, but change your mind before it is sent, you can use the Cancel Assignment button to restore your entry to an unassigned task format.

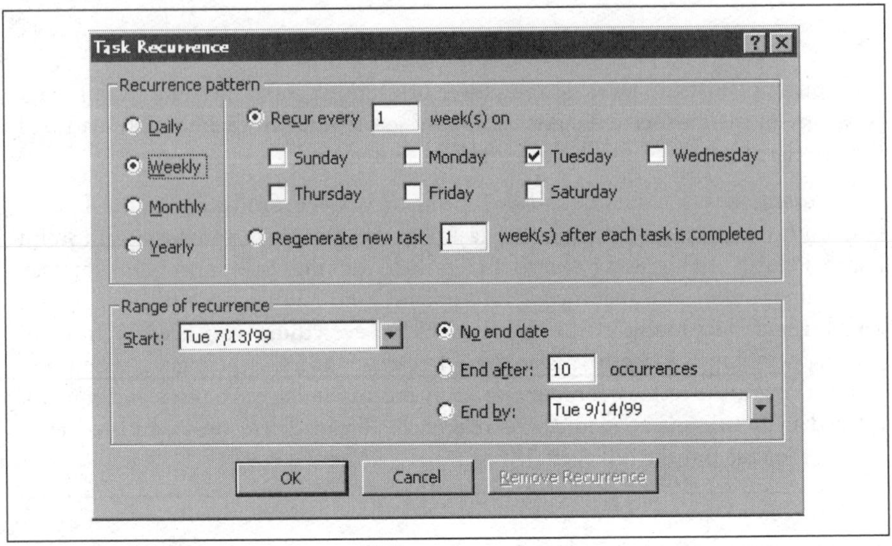

Figure 9-4: The Recurrence option dialog

Send Status Report

Updates the original owner (or owners*) of your progress on a delegated task. Updates for delegated tasks are automatically sent (if requested) when a task is marked complete. For long-term tasks, however, you may elect to send a task update when specific milestones are met—for example, when the task is 50% complete.

TIP # 114

View Specific Date Defaults

Tasks created from a Table view default to "None" in the Start and Due Date fields. New tasks created from a Timeline view, however, set both the Start and Due Date fields to the current date. See the "Tasks → View Menu" section later in this section for details on Task's preconfigured views.

The Details tab

The Details tab of a Task form (Figure 9-5) provides several fields to store additional information about a task.

Date completed

Initially contains the entry None. This field is automatically updated with the current system date when a task is marked complete from any Task view

---

* A task request can only have one owner. In this context, we mean a task that is owned by A, delegated to B, and further delegated to C. Status reports will be sent to everyone in this chain requesting them.

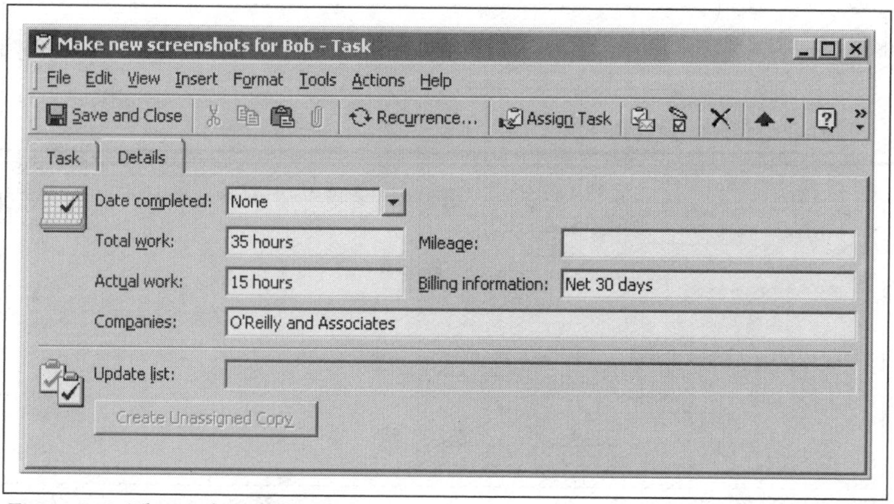

Figure 9-5: The Task Details tab

(including the TaskPad). You can also manually enter a date, or choose from the drop-down calendar displayed when you click the down-arrow button. When a task is marked complete, Outlook automatically sets the Status field (on the Task tab) to Completed and the % Complete field to 100. In similar fashion, if a task is already shown as complete, resetting the Date complete field to None changes Status to Not Started and % Complete to 0.

Total work

Is a measure of time anticipated to complete the task. The typical entry here is in hours, but other units explicitly entered (e.g., 12 days or 2 weeks) are accepted. Large hourly values are automatically converted to days or weeks as appropriate. For example, 100 hours is converted to 2.5 weeks. This conversion is based on the settings found under the Appearance section of the Advanced Options dialog shown in Figure 9-6 (left). (Tools → Options → Other → Advanced Options). The defaults are 8 hours per day, 40 hours per week. Changing these numbers adjusts the conversions made accordingly.

Actual work

Records the actual time expended on a task. The entry rules for this field are identical to Total work.

Mileage, Billing information, and Companies

Whatever you enter here is displayed exactly as you type it. The Companies field does *not* link to your contacts folder, as might be expected.

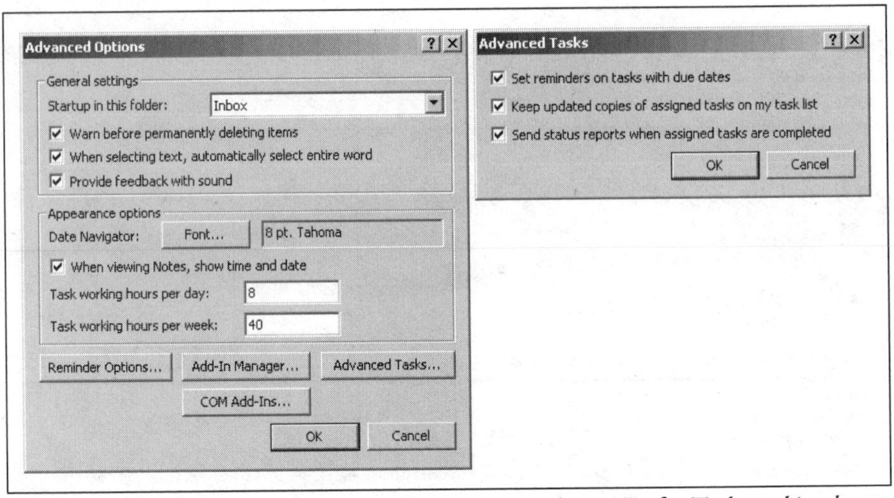

Figure 9-6: The Advanced Options dialog containing the setting for Task working hours per day/week (left) and the Advanced Tasks dialog (right)

TIP # 115

Setting Task Defaults

Default task options are inconveniently hidden in Tools → Options → Other → Advanced Options → Advanced Tasks. The Advanced Tasks dialog (see Figure 9-6, right) sets default behaviors for reminders with due dates, updating status reports for task requests, and whether a status report is sent when an assigned task is completed.

The Task Details tab (Figure 9-5) also contains an Update List field and Create Unassigned Copy button. Both these are relevant to delegated tasks—next on the topic list.

The Update List field becomes functional when a task request is sent to an individual who then chooses to reassign that task to yet another individual. Each person in this chain who chooses to keep an updated copy of the task on his or her task list is displayed here.

For example, Sharon creates a task request and sends it to her colleague Joe. Joe doesn't have time to take on the assignment, so he reassigns the task to his assistant Cindy. If both Sharon and Joe have enabled task tracking, when Cindy receives the request (providing she accepts it) her Update List shows entries for both these individuals. Entries here are displayed in the form:

```
Sharon Smith; Joe Snipps
```

Right-clicking an entry displays the email address task updates are sent to. These addresses are editable, but doing so automatically sends an update to both individuals, informing them the recipient has modified this field.

The Create Unassigned Copy button is only available when an *assigned* task (one you do not own) is open. Use this to break the linkages between the task on your system and the assigned task stored on the recipient's task list.

Accepting OK in the warning dialog shown in Figure 9-7 removes any task assignments from that item and restores ownership to you. If your current tasks view is By Person Responsible (View → Current View → By Person Responsible), the record no longer shows under the group Owner: *previousowner* but instead under Owner: *yourname*. In addition, the subject line now has the word (Copy) appended to it. A notification is automatically sent to the previous owner of the task informing them of your actions.

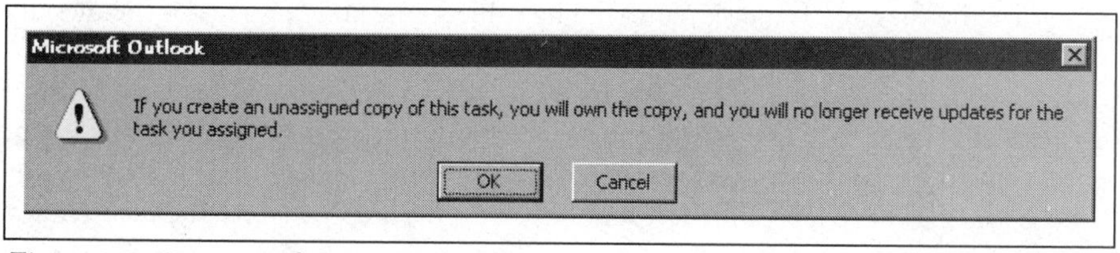

Figure 9-7: Unassigned Copy warning dialog

Actions → New Task Request

Working with Task Requests should be seamless and intuitive. Unfortunately, by making the installation modes for Outlook functionally different in the way they handle and display task messages, Microsoft has made task delegation needlessly complex.

How a task request is received, the format it arrives in, and how it is manipulated all depend on how Outlook is installed on both *your* system and the systems of *any* recipients involved in this collaborative process. The two mail handling options available at installation time are Corporate/Workgroup (CW) or Internet Mail Only (IMO). Details and a comprehensive discussion of setting up Outlook under various mail modes can be found in Chapter 2, *Installing Outlook*.

TIP # 116
Learn to Read Task Icons

The icons displayed by a task (in both your Inbox and Tasks folder) provide a valuable reference to the differences between a task, a task request, an accepted task request, a declined task request, a completed task request, etc. All Tasks' various icons are listed in Table 9-1 at the end of this chapter.

Instead of providing a long, confusing list of "If the sender is using CW/MS-RTS and the recipient is using IMO/HTML, then . . ." we'll be as straightforward as possible:

• Task requests do not work if your message format is Plain Text.

• Both sender and recipient should ideally have Outlook configured as IMO.

Tasks

- Sender and recipient should ideally use HTML as their default message format.

- If you send task requests from a CW installation to another CW installation and both systems have their mail processed by Exchange Server, task requests work as advertised. Your mileage will vary using task delegation in other CW-to-CW installations.

If you choose to depart from this advice, expect complications. For example: if you send a task request from a CW installation to an IMO installation, it will arrive in the recipient's mailbox looking like a normal email message with a paperclip showing an attachment to the message, and the subject line will read Task Request: the name or subject the sender gave the task. First, the recipient will need to recognize the message as a task request. The subject line and contents of the message provide some clues, but they may not be enough for a new user or someone unfamiliar with tasks. Second, the recipient will be faced with the dilemma of what to do with this request. Opening the message simply displays the task details in the notes field. The non-intuitive trick here is to drag the message from the Inbox and drop it on the Task icon on the Outlook bar. This step converts the task request *message* to an actual task.

Having said all this, task requests are an extremely useful and powerful tool for those who need to distribute their workload. If, that is, you can get through all the permutations and "if-then-else" combinations to be wary of, and you know what to do about each scenario and how to adjust to things when they don't work as advertised. And trust us—task requests do not always work as advertised.

There are two ways to create a task request:

- Use the New Task Request command (from the Actions menu or from one of Tasks numerous context menus). This opens a blank Task form.

- Reassign an existing task to someone using the Assign Task button located on an open task's toolbar (or the Actions menu). All information entered in the existing task is retained.

Task requests are deeply tied to the concept of "ownership." According to Outlook's Rules of Conduct, all tasks have one—and only one—owner. If you've created a task for your own personal use, you own that task. When you delegate or assign a task to someone else, you pass ownership of the task to someone else. Keep this firmly in mind as you read through the following material.

TIP # 117

Task Request Limitations

It is possible to send a task request to more than one contact. This, however, breaks the policy of "one-task-one-owner." Task updates do not function under this scenario.

A New Task Request form is shown in Figure 9-8. It is similar to a regular task entry form, with the addition of a To field above the Subject, and checkboxes below the date/status fields that allow the sender of a task to optionally track the recipient's progress as they complete the task.

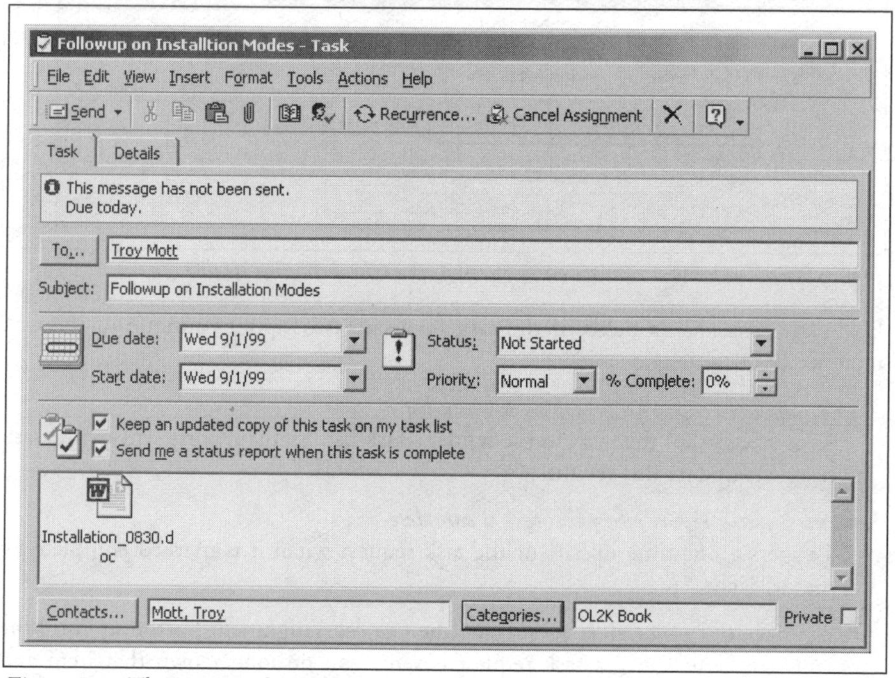

Figure 9-8: The New Task Request dialog

You cannot delegate a task to a contact that does not have a valid email address. Selecting the To button brings up a Select Task Recipient dialog with a list of only the contact records that match this criteria. If you bypass the To button and enter something free-form in this field, Outlook attempts to match this information to a contact record. If it is successful and finds only one record matching your entry, the contact's address is entered in the To field. If more than one record matches your entry, the Check Names dialog is displayed (see Figure 9-9).

From this dialog you can:

• Select one of the matches Outlook found.

• Select one of the matches Outlook found and view that contact's record (Properties button).

• Go back to your address book and choose another entry using the Show More Names button.

• Create a new address for your entry.

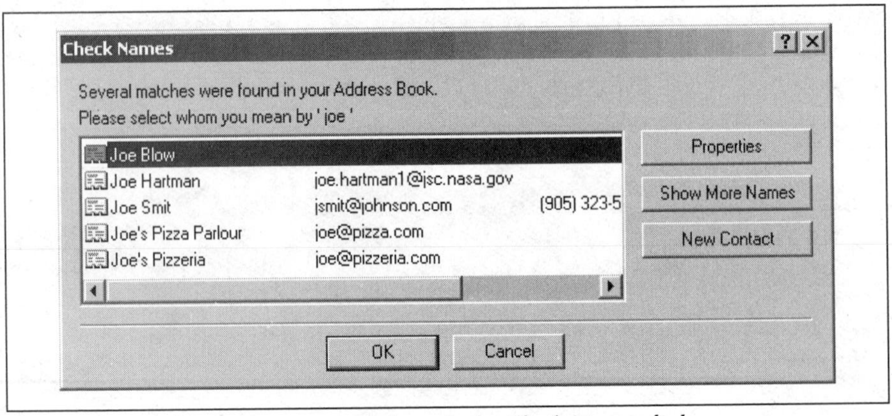

Figure 9-9: Resolving a contact entry through the Check Names dialog

Under the date/status fields of the task form are two options unique to the task requests, both initially enabled:

Keep an updated copy of this task on my task list
> Adds a record of this task to the sender's task list. Status reports sent by the task recipient update this record.

Send me a status report when this task is complete
> Triggers a one-time update of the task request when it is marked complete by the recipient.

You can back out of a task request using the Cancel Assignment button up until the moment it is sent. Once a task request is sent, you no longer own that item and messing with the assignment linkages Outlook embeds can cause havoc for both you and the recipient. If you—the sender—want to cancel a task request, the safest way is to send an email to the delegate asking him to delete the record from his end.

TIP # 118
Use Meaningful Subjects for a Task Request

Using a meaningful description for a task request avoids confusing the recipient. Consider clarifying the scope of the assignment with a few notes in the space provided in the lower half of the dialog. If the task relates to a document, attach it to the task request (from the dialog menu, Insert → File).

Receiving a task request

When you receive a task request from another Outlook user, it arrives in your Inbox, denoted by a special task icon as shown in Figure 9-10.

The sender is shown in the From field, and the subject is prefixed with the words Task Request.

!	D	⊽	0	From	Subject	Received ⊽	
!	📇			**Leah Syroid**	**Task Request: New Task Request**	**Tue 02/08/2000 2...**	
	✉			Paul Thurrott	Today's WinInfo: February 8	Tue 02/08/2000 20:04	
	✉			Ho Park	Fw: HA with SSA RAID5	Tue 02/08/2000 20:03	
	📭			Troy Mott	RE: chap09.r2	Tue 02/08/2000 19:36	
	📭			Troy Mott	RE: chap09.r2	Tue 02/08/2000 19:28	
	✉			J.H. Ricketson	WebWanderings 0200	Tue 02/08/2000 18:18	

Figure 9-10: A Task Request, viewed from the recipient's Inbox

NOTE *More often than not, if the sender and recipient of a task request are using different message formats (one HTML, the other MS-RTF), the new task request form will not display the Accept/Decline buttons. In this case, the recipient has no other option but to enter the task request manually.*

The recipient has a choice: Accept the task, or Decline it (shown in Figure 9-11). Clicking on the Accept button sets into motion several actions:

- The recipient can either "Edit the response before sending" a reply, or simply "Send the response now" from the Accepting Task dialog (Figure 9-12, top).

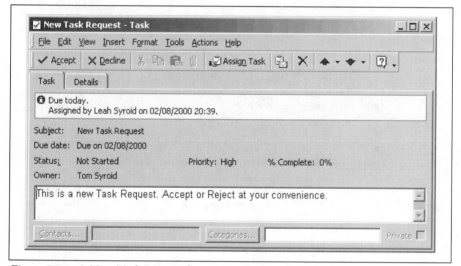

Figure 9-11: A New Task Request form as received by the recipient

- If the recipient chooses to simply send the response without edits, it is sent without further input.

- If the recipient chooses to edit his response, this opens the task request form (see Figure 9-12, bottom) where changes can be made to any of the form's fields (Due date, Start date, etc.). In a typical scenario, if the recipient changed any of the details of the task request he would add a note explaining why, and any other necessary details. Choosing Send returns his response to the sender.

TIP # 119

Add a Contact from a Task Request

The task request form functions just like any other Outlook message form. If you receive a task request from someone not in your contact records, simply right-click the sender's underlined name, and choose Add to Contacts from the context menu.

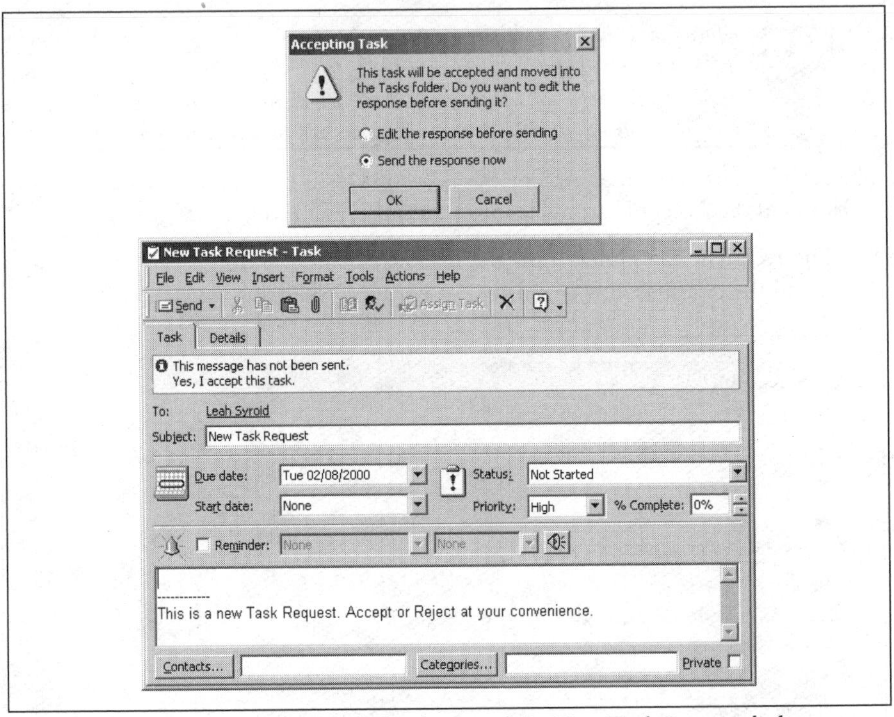

Figure 9-12: The Accepting Task dialog (top) and the New Task Request dialog (bottom)

- In addition to sending a response to the sender, accepting a task request also:
  - Adds the task to the recipient's Task folder
  - Transfers ownership of the task to the recipient
  - Deletes the Task Request message from the recipient's Inbox

The recipient now has full ownership of the task, and as a result, full access to all the information contained on the task's form. He can update the status, priority, or "% Complete" fields at his leisure. The recipient can also, at any time, click the Send Status Report button on the task form. This sends an update to the sender (if he choses the option to "Keep an updated copy . . ."). In addition, the recipient can further assign this task to someone using the "Assign Task" button. In this case, the chain continues—the current owner of the task loses ownership of the task when the next recipient accepts it.

 The key is task ownership. Once a task request is accepted, the recipient owns that task; all the rules and behaviors associated with editing and managing tasks hold true until he further assigns or completes that task.

When the recipient marks the task complete, one of two things happens: if the sender requested a status report on task completion, this is sent; if she did not, the task is no different than a regular task entry—the recipient can delete it or save it for reference.

If a recipient has accepted ownership of a task request and tries to delete it before it is marked complete, the warning dialog shown in Figure 9-13 is displayed.

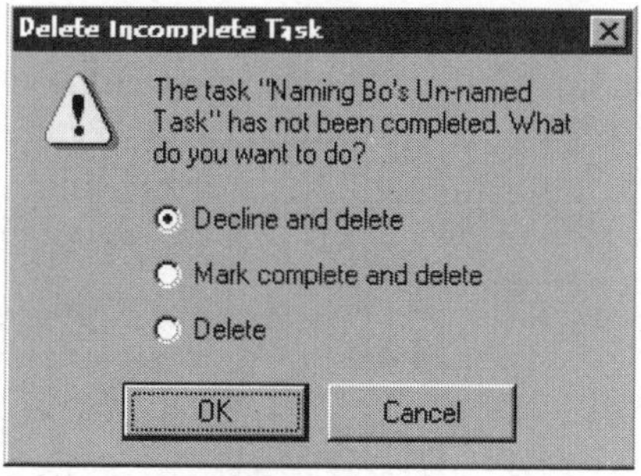

Delete Incomplete Task

The task "Naming Bo's Un-named Task" has not been completed. What do you want to do?

- ⦿ Decline and delete
- ◯ Mark complete and delete
- ◯ Delete

[OK]   [Cancel]

Figure 9-13: The Delete Incomplete Task dialog

Decline and delete
Sends a "task declined" message back to the previous owner of the task and deletes the task from the Tasks folder.

Mark complete and delete
Sends a message back to the previous owner that the task is complete, and marks the task complete.

Delete
Deletes the task request from the current owner's Task folder; no warning of this action is sent to the previous owner of this action.

The warning dialog and subsequent actions occur regardless of the original owner's "update status" settings.

Receiving a response to a task request

Outlook handles the responses received from the recipient of a task request (and there's always at least one response) in various ways:

Tasks

- If the recipient accepts the task, Outlook examines the original request. If "Keep an updated copy..." was selected, Outlook updates the original record to indicate that the request was accepted. If that option was not selected, Outlook deletes the local copy of the task.

- "Impromptu" task updates (sent by the delegate using Send Status Report command) automatically update the owner's task record when the report/message is opened.

- If the recipient declines the task, Outlook returns the task to the sender's Task folder and restores ownership. The owner can then assign the task to someone else, or simply complete it herself.

- If the recipient deletes an incomplete task assignment (as discussed relative to Figure 9-13), the owner receives the task "back" as declined. See the preceding list item.

- When the recipient completes the task request, if the owner requested a "completed" notification, this is automatically generated and sent. Opening this message updates the matching record in the owner's Task folder and marks the task complete. Any previous owners in the chain of delegation also receive the same notification—if they asked for one.

Note the last sentence in the preceding list. Again, we remind you of the ownership principle involved in task requests. If A delegates to B who delegates to C, then C has ownership until the task is complete. If both A and B requested updates and notification on completion, then when C completes the task, both A and B are sent the appropriate updates.

Actions → Save Task Order

In a Table view, tasks can be sorted to any location within the list by dragging them and releasing them as shown in Figure 9-14, *providing* (yes, there's always a catch with fun tricks like this) the view has no sort order, filters, or groupings assigned to it. An example of such a view is Simple List—assuming, of course, you've done nothing to customize it. To quickly see if a view has any of these properties, go to View → Current View → Customize Current View. The descriptions next to the Group By, Sort, and Filter buttons should say None, None, and Off respectively.

TIP # 120

Customizing and Restoring a View

To clear, for example, a defined Group By setting, go to the View Summary dialog. Select the Group By button, and Clear All. To restore one of Outlook's preconfigured views to factory defaults, go to View → Current View → Define Views. Select the view you want to restore, and click Reset. You cannot restore a view that you're created from scratch, simply because Outlook has no baseline to restore it to.

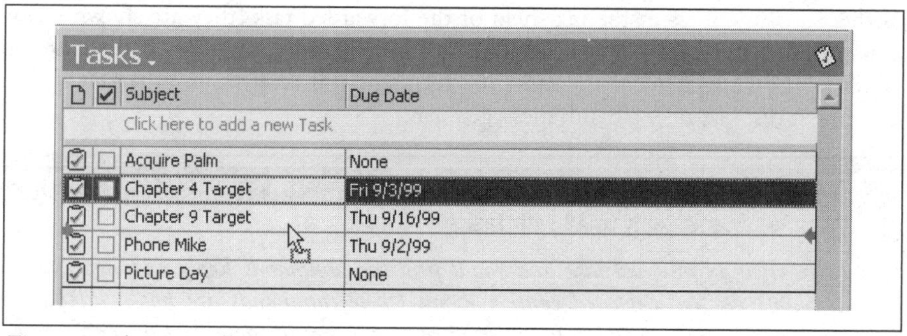

Figure 9-14: Manually sorting your Task List

After you have all your tasks arranged, go to Actions → Save Task Order. This saves the order as the default for any view you switch to that *does not have a preconfigured filter or grouping applied*. For example, if you arrange and save the task order for Simple List and switch to Detailed List, your task order remains in place. Switching to Active Tasks (which is a sorted and filtered view), however, replaces your saved task order with that of the new view. Fear not: your task order is not lost. Switch back to Simple List, and it is restored.

Frankly, we find this "feature" of limited use and wish Outlook's engineers had spent more time putting component option dialogs in logical locations.

Actions → Forward

Sometimes you need to send a task to someone who is either not directly involved in the task, or whose email client is unable to read or process Outlook's task format. If so, use the Actions → Forward command (for task requests you can also use the Reply and Reply to All commands—see Tip # 121).

To forward a task, select an existing entry from any task view, and use the Forward command from Actions or the context menu. This places the item in a new mail message with the name of the task as a subject line. Address the message, optionally add a few sentences to the body of the message explaining the context, then send it as you would any other email. The recipient of your forwarded task receives the information laid out in a format similar to the following example:

```
Subject:      Don't forget to credit Bob Thompson...
Start Date:   Friday, July 09, 1999
Due Date:     Saturday, July 10, 1999
Priority:     High

Status:       Not Started
Percent Complete:  50%

Total Work:       0 hours
Actual Work:      0 hours

Owner:        Tom Syroid (E-mail)
```

If there are any notes in the text field of the forwarded task, they are shown below this text and also enclosed as a separate attachment to the message. If there are no notes in the notes field of the task, the recipient still receives an attachment, but opening it displays only a blank message form.

TIP # 121

Using Reply and Reply to All with Tasks

Right-click an assigned task and you'll find the commands Reply and Reply to All available on the displayed context menu (these commands are not available for unassigned tasks). Replying to an assigned task copies the details of the entry into a new email message (in a form similar to the example shown under Actions → Forward), preaddressed to the owner. Use this approach to query the owner of a task about a detail without formally updating or otherwise modifying the task itself.

Tasks → View Menu

The Tasks → View menu is shown in Figure 9-15 along with the Current View submenu. On the main View menu you'll find the Preview Pane command (selectable for any Task view). This opens a pane in the lower half of the view window that displays the contents of a selected item's note field. AutoPreview—available only for Table views—shows the first several lines of this same note field below the subject of the task. In addition, this menu contains an Expand/Collapse Groups command for views that contain groupings (for example, By Category).

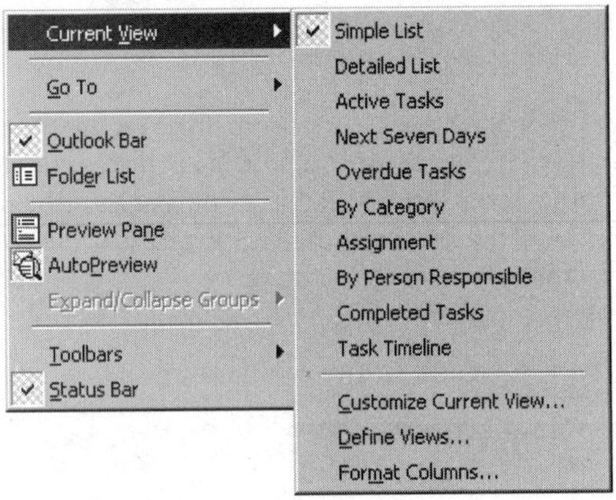

Figure 9-15: The Tasks View menu—the check mark represents the current view

The Current View submenu contains ten preconfigured ways to view tasks. Other than Task Timeline, these are all Table views. Below the menu divider are the three customization commands common to all Outlook views: Customize Current View,

Define Views, and Format Columns. For details on customizing and configuring views beyond what is presented here, see Chapter 3.

View → Simple List

Simple List is the bare bones view of your task list. It is unsorted, unfiltered, and has no groupings applied.

The Simple List view (see Figure 9-16) displays an icon in the left column as a quick reference to what type of task the item is. A personal task is shown as a clipboard with a checkmark on it, a task delegated to you shows a hand under the clipboard, and a task delegated to more than one person shows two hands holding the clipboard. Table 9-1 at the end of this chapter outlines the various Tasks icons and their meanings.

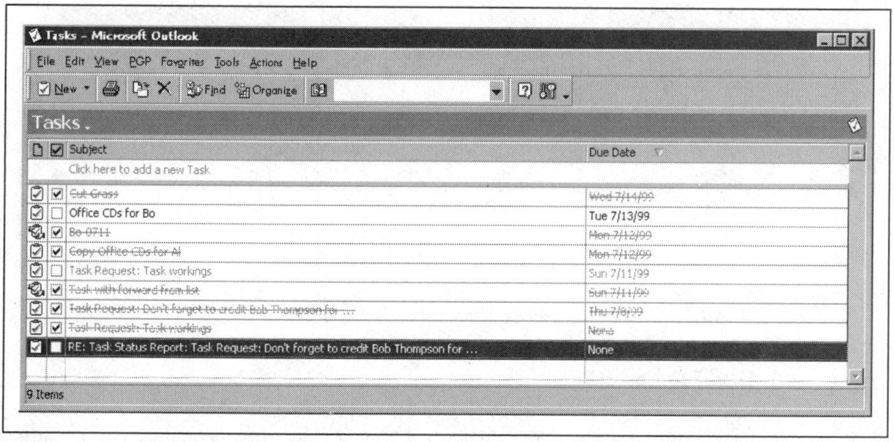

Figure 9-16: The Simple List view—completed items are formatted with a strike-through and grayed, overdue tasks are shown in red and bold

The next field displays a checkmark for completed items, also shown as a strike-through.

> **NOTE** *To configure format options (strike-through, overdue task color, etc.) right-click a blank region of the view, and from the context menu choose Customize Current View → Automatic Formatting.*

The Subject field contains a description of your task, and the Due Date field is self-explanatory.

All Tasks' preconfigured table views have in-cell editing enabled. This means you can edit any displayed field directly in the table (click once on the field you want to edit). Depending on the field type, you can either edit the text or choose from a predefined drop-down list. To save your changes, click a blank region of the view or select another record.

View → Detailed List

Detailed List builds on the Simple List and adds an icon beside the task type to indicate Priority (∅ for low, nothing for Normal, and ! for high) and a column that displays a paperclip if there are any attachments to the task.

Next to the Subject is a field showing the task's Status (see Figure 9-17). The options available are Not Started, In Progress, Completed, Waiting on someone else, or Deferred. To change an item's status, select this field and a list of choices is displayed. Beside the Due Date is the "% Complete" field and to the right of that a column to show any categories assigned to the task.

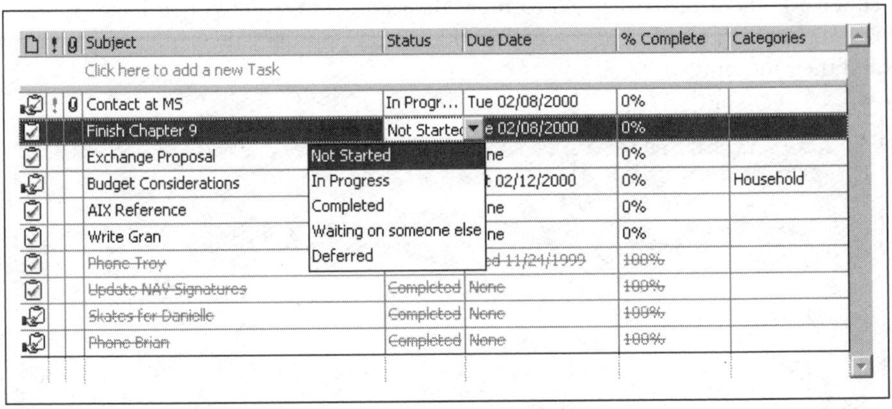

D	!	0	Subject	Status	Due Date	% Complete	Categories
			Click here to add a new Task				
	!	0	Contact at MS	In Progr...	Tue 02/08/2000	0%	
			Finish Chapter 9	Not Started ▾	e 02/08/2000	0%	
			Exchange Proposal	Not Started	ne	0%	
			Budget Considerations	In Progress	t 02/12/2000	0%	Household
			AIX Reference	Completed	ne	0%	
			Write Gran	Waiting on someone else	ne	0%	
			Phone Troy	Deferred	d 11/24/1999	100%	
			Update NAV Signatures	Completed	None	100%	
			Skates for Danielle	Completed	None	100%	
			Phone Brian	Completed	None	100%	

Figure 9-17: Detail List view showing the Status field options

View → Active Tasks

The Active Tasks view displays your tasks in the same column layout as the Detailed List, filtering out any items marked complete. Entries include items that have been delegated or assigned to others. Use this view as a quick check on personal tasks that are in progress or incomplete.

View → Next Seven Days

Next Seven Days is a filtered view and displays only those items with a due date falling within the next seven days, calculated from the current system date. This view hides any items with due dates *outside* this range, and any items marked as complete.

 NOTE   *The Next Seven Days view excludes overdue items!*

By using only this view to plan ahead you are likely to miss allocating the time and resources necessary to address overdue and hidden tasks. Overdue items are addressed separately in the next view.

View → Overdue Tasks

This view displays all tasks that have a Due Date that has passed without being marked Complete. Overdue tasks are displayed in red by default, but this is customizable (Customize Current View → Automatic Formatting). The sort order and layout are identical to the Detailed List view. If you open this view and find it blank, either you're extremely efficient and deserve a pat on the back, or you're not dating task items.

View → By Category

This is one of the most powerful cross-component features of Outlook available (see "Using Categories" in Chapter 3 for details).

The Categories view (Figure 9-18) displays your task list in an expandable and collapsible tree format grouped by category name. If there are any tasks with no assigned category, this forms the first grouping (none), followed by groupings of the tasks that have assigned categories. The default sort order for this top-level category grouping is Ascending, which is a fancy way of saying, "alphabetically from A to Z." To reverse this sort order, open the Group By Box (right-click anywhere on the column title bar) and either left-click the Categories group box displayed there, or right-click this same box and choose Sort Descending.

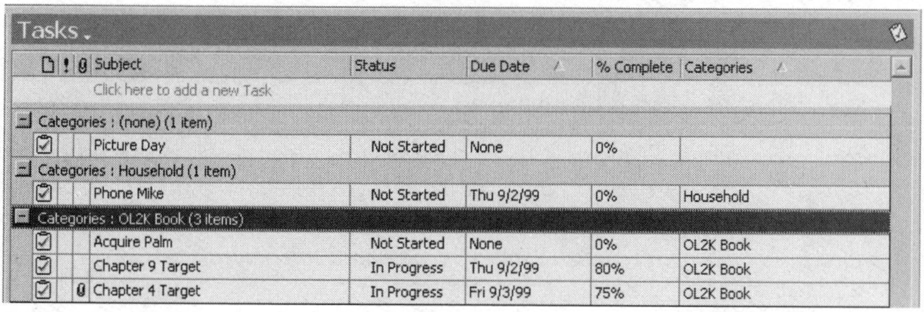

			Subject	Status	Due Date	/	% Complete	Categories	/	
			Click here to add a new Task							
⊟ Categories : (none) (1 item)										
☑			Picture Day	Not Started	None		0%			
⊟ Categories : Household (1 item)										
☑			Phone Mike	Not Started	Thu 9/2/99		0%	Household		
⊟ Categories : OL2K Book (3 items)										
☑			Acquire Palm	Not Started	None		0%	OL2K Book		
☑			Chapter 9 Target	In Progress	Thu 9/2/99		80%	OL2K Book		
☑	0		Chapter 4 Target	In Progress	Fri 9/3/99		75%	OL2K Book		

Figure 9-18: View by Category

Like other Table views, you can edit an item by clicking a field and typing your change or selecting an alternative from the list provided.

We don't recommend adding a category with in-cell editing unless you are confident about both its name and spelling. Instead, double-click the item and use the Category button on the open form. If the category you wish to use is not on the selection list, add it with the Master Category List button.

View → Assignment

When you create a Task Request or assign an existing task to someone, you delegate a task created by you to another individual (see the "Tasks → Actions Menu" section earlier in this chapter). The Assignment view displays any items from your task list that are assigned to someone else. This view is sorted on Owner (ascending) and Due Date (ascending), and filtered by "Assigned equals 'Assigned by Me.'"

Two things regarding task assignment are worth noting here:

- When you *create* a task you automatically become the owner of that task. When you *delegate* a task, you pass ownership of the task to the person or persons it was delegated to.

- This view reflects Assignment according to the Assigned by Me filter. What this implies is that if you have items on your task list that have been delegated or assigned by others *to you*, they do *not* show in this view.

The By Person Responsible view is better to use when dealing with task delegations and assignments.

View → By Person Responsible

This is the big picture of all your tasks whether they are owned by you, delegated by you to others, or delegated by others to you.

TIP # 122

The Premiere View for Task Assignments

View → By Person Responsible is the view to use when you have task assignments (either to others or by others), and you want to see these task groupings in conjunction with your own personal to-do list. It also provides a good overall perspective on which tasks have been completed and which remain unresolved.

By Person Responsible groups your task list by the owner of the task. The "none" group does not exist in this view—in Outlook, all tasks are owned by someone. If you created the task and have not assigned it to anyone else, it is listed under your name. If a task has been delegated to someone else, it is shown under a grouping named for the recipient. Tasks delegated to you by others are shown under the grouping for your name, and the person who delegated the task is displayed in the Requested By column (see Figure 9-19).

The default arrangement for this view is unfiltered, grouped by Owner, and sorted on Due Date (ascending). Completed tasks are displayed with the usual strikethrough. The grouping by owner cannot be modified in this view, as it is intrinsic to the layout. Any of the other fields displayed can be used as a secondary sort.

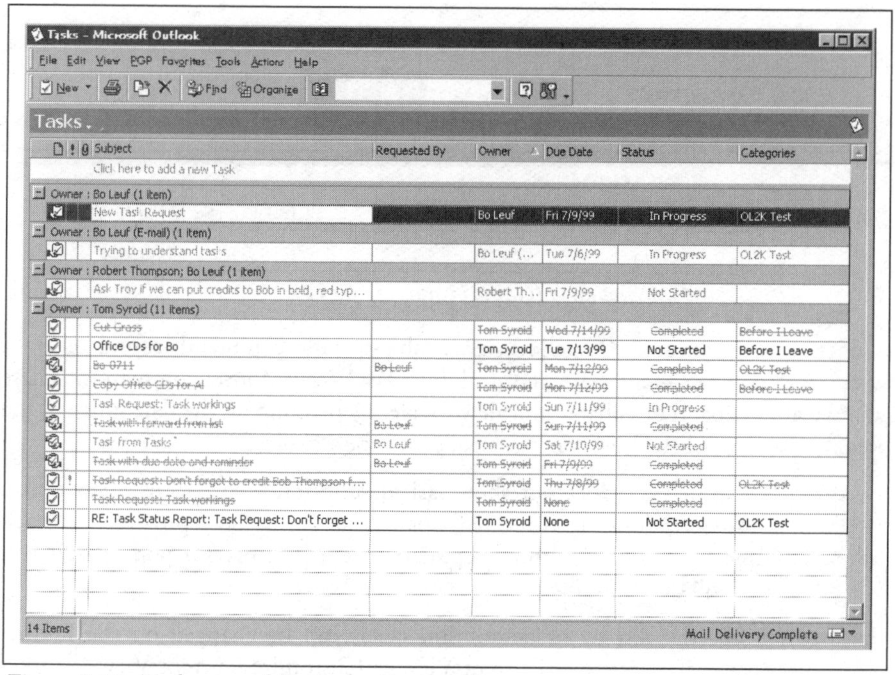

Figure 9-19: Tasks viewed By Person Responsible

View → Completed Tasks

Completed Tasks is the flip side to the Active Tasks view. It filters your task list to display only items marked complete. The columns displayed are Task-Type, Priority, Attachments, Subject, Due Date, Date Completed, and Categories. The default sort order is Due Date (descending). Records in this view are displayed without the text strike-through that is the normal default for completed items.

View → Task Timeline

The Task Timeline displays your tasks in a Gantt-style layout. A Gantt charts graphically depict the time relationships between project tasks using horizontal bars (see Figure 9-20). In the case of the Task Timeline view, horizontal bars show the duration of a task based on the Start Date and Due Date fields.

Tasks with a Due Date assigned, but no Start Date, display as a text/icon entry under that date (for example, Phone Mike in Figure 9-20). Items with both a Start Date and Due Date assigned are shown with a text/icon entry and a bar depicting the task duration. Table 9-1 shows the various Tasks icons and their meanings.

> **NOTE** *Tasks with no dates assigned are not visible under a Task Timeline view.*

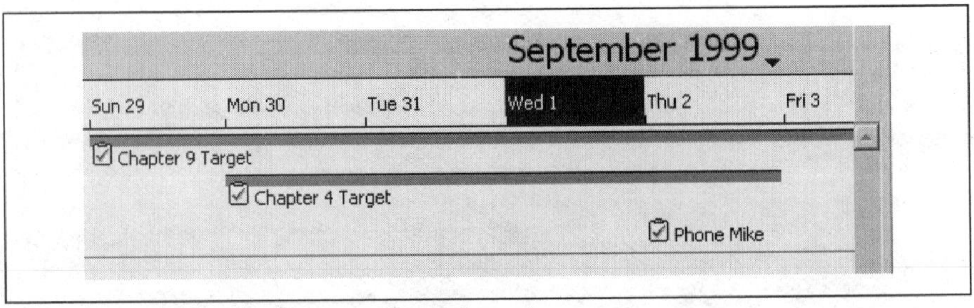

Figure 9-20: Task Timeline view (Gantt layout)

Under any of Outlook's Timeline views, table-specific commands found on both View and context menus are replaced by Day/Week/Month commands. These allow you to expand or collapse the view's scale. Depending on the date range of the item on your task list, Week view is usually your best choice.

By default, Month view does not show task descriptions—just icons. This makes sense, as task descriptions are truncated when tasks fall in close proximity to each other. Holding your mouse cursor over such an entry displays a pop-up text box with the task's full description.

The settings for the display of description labels can be changed on the Format Timeline View dialog (View → Current View → Customize Current View → Other Settings, or choose Other Settings from a timeline's context menu). Under the labels section, select "Show label when viewing by month."

Table 9-1: Task Icon List

Icon Name	Icon Image
Normal (personal) task	
Recurring task	
Delegated task	
Task delegated to more than one person	
New task request	
Task request declined	
Task request accepted	

Chapter 10

Notes

The Notes component of Outlook is a simple but effective tool for organizing all those Post-it notes that adorn your monitor casing. There are several advantages to storing your notes electronically: you can sort and group these notes under individual folders, associate them with a contact, categorize for fast search and retrieval, and edit freely. High-tech functionality aside, probably the best reason for using electronic notes is that they are less likely to fall off your monitor than paper ones.

Like their paper counterpart, the best way to use Outlook Notes is as a place to jot down reminders, ideas, or transitory bits of information. By this we mean lists that will be deleted when complete (daily to-dos or a grocery list), a snippet of information you don't know whether to keep or not (a potentially interesting URL), or the name and phone number of a contact you want to create a permanent record for later.

This chapter describes the two menus used to create and manipulate Notes:

- *Actions* contains the commands to create or forward a note to an email recipient. In addition to Outlook's system menus, the note form itself contains a menu with commands for creating, forwarding, cut and paste operations, saving the text to another format, categorizing, and linking to a contact.

- *View* lets you choose how notes are displayed (in icon or table layouts), as well as the sort order and filters applied to the view selected. Views are also available that group a notes folder according to category or color. Grouped views are fundamental for organizing more than one Outlook item at a time.

At the end of the chapter we show you several ways of moving notes into other documents or permanent Outlook records.

Notes → Actions Menu

In contrast to the same menu in Mail or Contacts, the Notes → Action menu (see Figure 10-1) is sparse. There are only two commands: New Note and Forward. The simplicity of this menu is due to the fact that each note has a command menu, which enables you to assign a contact or category, change the background color, and save in an alternate format.

Figure 10-1: Notes → Action menu

Actions → New Note

There are several ways to create a note in Outlook:

- Select the Notes icon from the Outlook Task Bar, and choose Actions → New Note (Ctrl+N).

- From any Notes view, click the New Note icon on the standard toolbar. Alternatively, right-click an empty area in the Notes view pane and select New Note from the context menu displayed.

- Open an existing note. Select New Note from the form's command menu (see Figure 10-3).

- Double-click anywhere in the open space of the notes view.

- Use the global Outlook keyboard shortcut Ctrl+Shift+N; this shortcut will create a new note from any Outlook component. (This is the equivalent of selecting File → New → Note.)

A new blank note is shown in Figure 10-2. The bottom status bar displays the date and time the note was created or modified.

```
                              7/22/99 2:55 PM
```

Figure 10-2: New Note form

Text entered on the first line of a note doubles as the title. For this reason, keep this line descriptive and as short as possible. Text entered in a note automatically wraps to the width of the form.

There is no Save command for a new or edited note. To save the contents of a note, close the form (using the X on the form's upper-right corner), press the Esc key, or click anywhere outside the note. This nonintuitive save convention introduces the following behaviors when a new note is created:

- If no text has been entered into a new note, pressing Esc or closing the note cancels it.

- As soon as any text has been entered in a new note, pressing Esc or closing the form saves the note to Outlook's database.

In other words, once any information is entered in a note the only way to cancel it is by selecting Delete from the command menu (see Figure 10-3), or by closing the note and deleting it from the view you are working in.

TIP # 123

Looking for the Minimize Command?

Right-click anywhere on the title bar that extends between the note icon on the left and the close icon on the right. The familiar Move, Size, Maximize, and Minimize context menu will be displayed.

To open a note's command menu, click the note icon in the upper-left corner of the note form as shown in Figure 10-3.

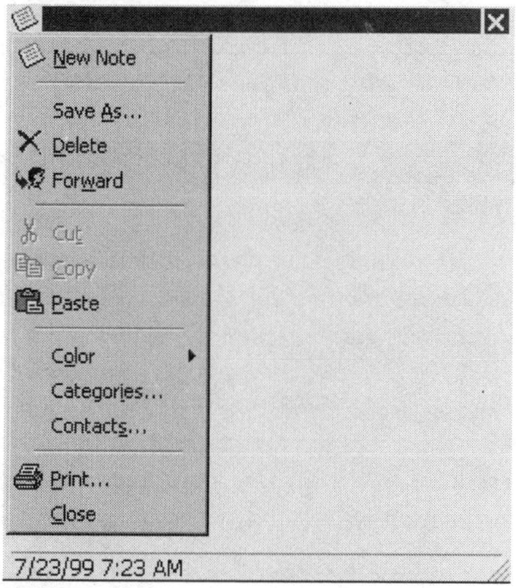

Figure 10-3: Note command menu

In addition to the expected commands to delete, print, copy and paste, or close the note, there are several useful items on this menu.

Save As

The Save As command saves the contents of a note in one of four formats: Text Only, Rich Text Format, Outlook Template, and Message Format. The Text Only and Rich Text Format (RTF) are useful to save information contained in a note for use in another program or document. Both RTF and Plain Text are universal file import/export formats in most current software applications.

Outlook Template format can be used to create a boilerplate note containing information entered on a recurring basis. A simple example might be a note template designed to save key information about downloaded files stored on your computer.

To create such a template, start with a new note and enter the boilerplate text similar to the example text shown in Figure 10-4. Next save the note in Outlook Template format (*OFT*) with a name that clearly indicates the intended function. This template can be stored locally, or on a network server if other users will need access to it.

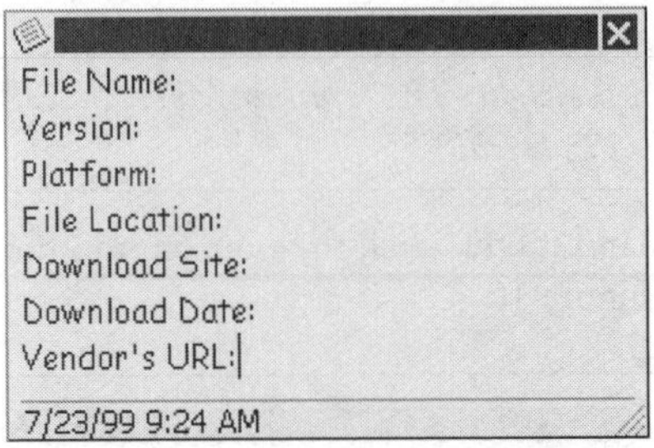

File Name:
Version:
Platform:
File Location:
Download Site:
Download Date:
Vendor's URL:

7/23/99 9:24 AM

Figure 10-4: Note Template showing example boilerplate text

TIP # 124

Templates as Shortcuts

*Tired of digging through four layers of menus and two dialogs to access your Outlook templates? Create a Desktop shortcut for those you access most frequently. Open your template folder in Explorer (to find, use Windows Find and search on *.OFT), right-drag any item to the Desktop, and select Create Shortcut(s) Here. You can also place a template shortcut on the Office Shortcut Bar.*

Finally, to create a new note based on this template, use the menu command File → New → Choose Form, which will display the dialog shown in Figure 10-5.

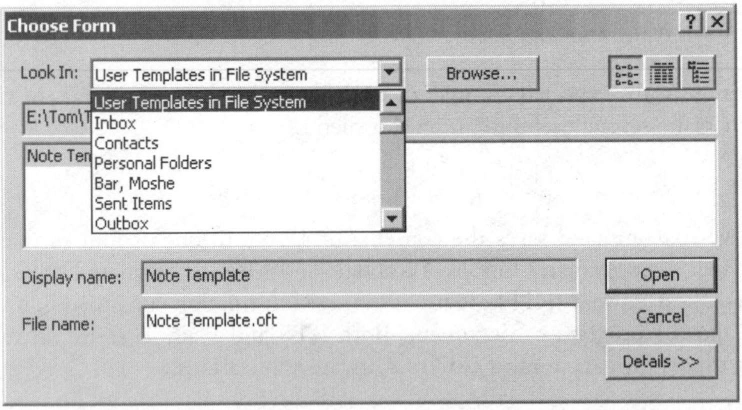

Choose Form

Look In: User Templates in File System

Browse...

User Templates in File System
E:\Tom\T Inbox
Note Te Contacts
Personal Folders
Bar, Moshe
Sent Items
Outbox

Display name: Note Template

File name: Note Template.oft

Open
Cancel
Details >>

Figure 10-5: Outlook Choose Form dialog

Notes

If the template you created was stored locally, select User Templates in File System. Opening the example template will create a new note item complete with the boiler-plate text. From here, simply fill in specifics necessary to finish the entry. A completed note using the example discussed is shown in Figure 10-6.

File Name: 550NT203
Version: 2.03
Platform: NT4
File Location: D:\DRIVERS\DIAMOND
Download Site:
Download Date: 7/3/99
Vendor's URL: www.diamondmm.com

7/23/99 8:59 AM

Figure 10-6: Complete example note using Template Form

TIP # 125

Using Hyperlinks in a Note

URLs embedded in notes are active links; click on the entry and your default browser launches and opens the web page listed. In addition to Internet locations, these links can be email addresses, a Newsgroup server, or a local resource path. See the section "Hyperlinks" in Chapter 5 for a list of supported hyperlink formats.

Saving a note in Message Format creates a copy of that item, external to Outlook's database, in a file location you specify. This file will have an operating system file association of Outlook Item (extension *.msg*). Double-clicking on this file opens it in an Outlook Note form. Outlook does not have to be running to access and view this standalone file.

This same Message Format is used for any data record copied, moved, or saved outside the bounds of Outlook's interface. Common examples of such items are Save As files, message attachments, or a record dragged to the Windows Desktop.

Color, Categories, and Contacts

Referring back to the Note command menu in Figure 10-3, below the Paste command are three menu items useful to organizing notes.

The Color and Category commands work exactly as one would expect: Color changes the open note's background to one of the five available options; Category opens a dialog where you can associate the note with one or more of the descriptions listed. (See Chapter 3, *Program Insights*, for details on working with Categories.) Right-clicking on an existing closed note will also give you access to these commands. So, for example, you can easily change a single note from blue to green. See View → By Color later in this chapter for details on changing the color of multiple notes in a single operation.

The third menu item from this group is Contacts. Figure 10-7 shows the dialog used to assign or modify a contact link to a note.

 The Contacts command for Notes is only found on a note's command menu. Assigning a contact to an existing note is a three-step process: open the note; access the command menu; then select Contacts from this menu.

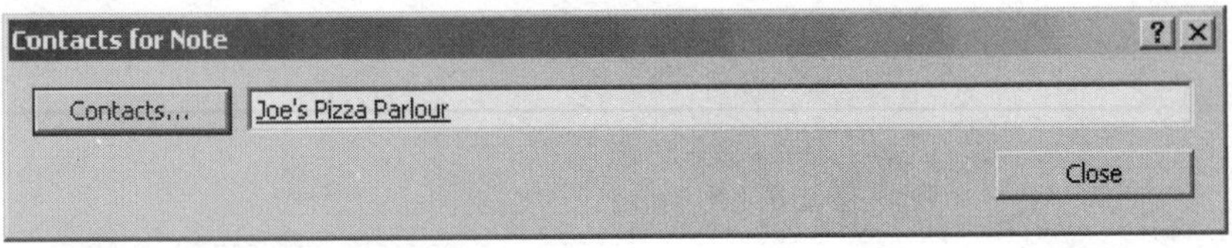

Figure 10-7: Note contact dialog

Select the Contacts button to open the Select Contact dialog. The upper pane of this dialog allows you to choose a contacts folder; the lower pane displays the contents of that folder. Alternatively, you can skip the Contacts button and enter a contact directly in the field provided.

When you enter a contact directly, that entry will not be checked against the records contained in your contacts folder until the note is saved. If the contact does not exist or is misspelled, *Outlook does not warn you*. The note just obediently closes with a nonfunctional link.

TIP # 126

Leveraging Name Resolution

To guard against Outlook's failure to pick up on misspelled or nonexistent contact records, make it a habit to enter a partial name and force the program to provide you with a name-resolution dialog. For example, instead of entering Tom Thumb as a contact, enter just Tom. If there is just one Tom in your address book, then the contact link will automatically resolve itself without further intervention on your part.

Once a link is established between a note and a contact, it is fully bidirectional:

1. Open a linked note and return to the "Contacts for Note" dialog shown in Figure 10-7. Double-click the entry here, and the Contact entry/edit form is displayed.

2. To view any notes linked to a contact, open the form associated with that individual or business, go to the Activities tab, and from the Show drop-down list select Notes.

Actions → Forward

This command attaches a selected note to a new email message. The Subject line will be entered automatically according to the note's title (FW: *Note Title*). If your default mail format is configured for Microsoft Rich Text, the note is inserted into the body of the message as an embedded file. Plain Text or HTML mail formats show the note as an attachment in a pane below the body of the message.

After the message is addressed, send it as you would any other email. If the recipient also uses Outlook, the note attachment will be viewable in Note format. Other email clients display the forwarded note in the message body as either RTF or Plain Text, depending on how the recipient's viewing preferences are configured.

Notes → View Menu

Outlook provides five preconfigured views for displaying notes:

- Icons—displays notes as colored icons, sorted by date created. Icons view contains three subviews:

    - Large Icons shows each note as a large icon, ordered left-to-right, with the first several words of the note title below the icon.

    - Small Icons represents each note as a small icon with the note title to the right of the icon. When the note's title is short, this view orders icons left to right; for longer note titles icons are ordered in rows.

    - List displays your notes as small icons, title to the right of the icon, each note beginning a new row in the view.

- Notes List—Table view with notes sorted by the date/time created or modified.

- Last Seven Days—Table view, filtered to show only those notes created or modified in the last seven days.

- By Category—groups notes in a Table view by category assigned and sorted within each category by date created or modified.

- By Color—groups notes in a Table view by color, and again, sorted within these groups by date.

Select a view using View → Current View, Tools → Organize, or through the Organize button on the toolbar, if available. From the Organize pane, click the Using Views tab, and then choose one of the five options from the list. Changing the view affects not only your view of the notes, but also the options available in the View menu and on the toolbar. The Icon types are only available when the Organize → Icons option is active.

There are distinct advantages to each mode of organization. For example, while the Icon view shows note colors, it provides no way to manipulate or change the color of a group of notes. Switching to View → By Color, however, allows you to drag more than one note from one color grouping to another.

Also remember that the views discussed in the following section are just preconfigured examples. All Outlook views can be extensively customized to accommodate users' preferences and work styles. A comprehensive overview of this topic can be found in Chapter 3.

All Note views can be toggled to display the Preview Pane in the lower half of the current window or to show an AutoPreview of your note's contents. The Preview Pane is a separate window that displays a selected item's contents; AutoPreview is an option available under most Table views that displays the first three lines of a note under a header row.

Configuration options for Notes can be accessed from the Tools → Options tab. The Notes Options button opens the dialog shown in Figure 10-8. The options listed set the default appearance for a new note: background color (Blue, Green, Pink, Yellow, White), size (Small, Medium, or Large), and display font (point size, face, style, and color).

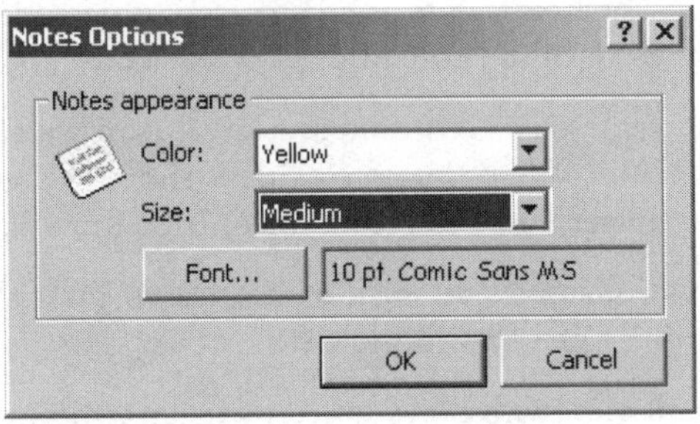

![Notes Options dialog showing Notes appearance group with Color set to Yellow, Size set to Medium, Font button with 10 pt. Comic Sans MS, and OK and Cancel buttons]

Figure 10-8: The Notes Options configuration dialog

 NOTE *While color and size can be modified on a per-note basis, the font settings specified in the Notes Options dialog are global; there is no way to change the font of an individual note.*

View → Current View

The Current View submenu is shown in Figure 10-9. Selecting any of the first five choices from this menu displays the contents of your Notes folder with the preconfigured sort and filter associated with that view. The usual Customize and View commands access dialogs to modify these preset orders. Details on customizing default views can be found in Chapter 3.

Figure 10-9: Notes Current View submenu

View → Current View → Icons

This is the default view for Notes, and displays each folder item as a colored icon with a title. The title is a repeat of the note's first line of text.

Icon view provides three display options: Large Icons, Small Icons, and List. Toggle between these three views using the appropriate button on the Notes toolbar, or by selecting a display option from the right-click context menu.

Large Icons displays a full size icon with the note title below. Small Icons and List both display a small icon with the note title to the right of the icon. Table 10-1 shows the default placement, orientation, and sort order for each of these three views.

Table 10-1: Icon View Placement, Orientation, and Sort Order

Icon View	Icon Size	Orientation	Default Sort Order
Large	Large	Horizontal	Creation Date
Small	Small	Horizontal	Creation Date
List	Small	Vertical	Creation Date

Note that the sort orders referred to in Table 10-1 are defaults. Sort order changes are persistent across all Note views. This means if you re-sort your view in Large Icons to Subject this same sort order will be displayed if you switch to Small Icon view. The exception to this rule is the List view: it is *always* sorted on Date Created.

TIP # 127

Quickly Re-sorting a Notes View

To quickly re-sort an Icon View on creation date, right-click and choose List from the context menu. Right-click again and return to your original view, where your notes will be displayed sorted by Date Created.

The Icon layout has configuration settings not available in other Note views. These settings are accessed from the Customize Current View → Other Settings command, or by opening the context menu of an Icon View and selecting Other Settings. The Format Icon View dialog is shown in Figure 10-10.

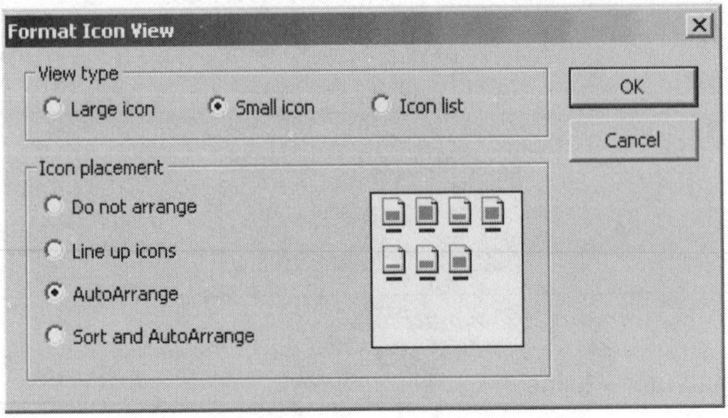

Figure 10-10: Format Icon View customization dialog

Toggling an option button displays the effect of that option in the small virtual desktop to the right of the selections. The gray shaded areas within the icons illustrate sort order. In Figure 10-10 the sort order is None. If you select Sort and AutoArrange, the top-left icon would show the smallest slice of gray progressing to the bottom right icon showing the largest. This depicts an ascending sort order (Figure 10-11).

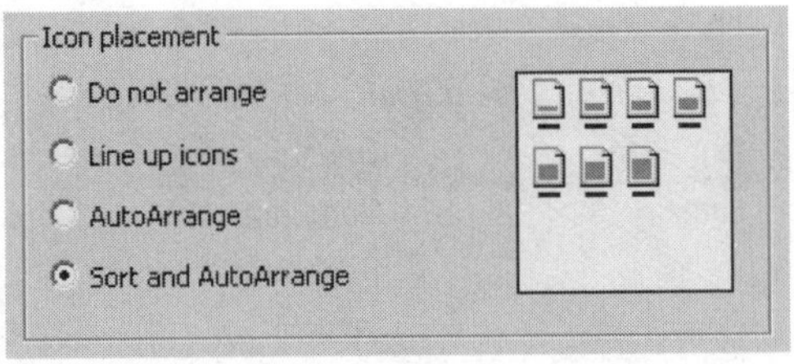

Figure 10-11: Icon Placement with Sort and AutoArrange

"View type" determines the options available for "Icon placement." "Large icon" and "Small icon" can use any of the four placement options. Choosing "Icon list" (shown in the top row of Figure 10-10) grays out these choices and displays all note items sorted alphabetically on Subject (ascending), arranged vertically in the view window.

- "Do not arrange" allows note icons to be placed anywhere in the window. Icons stay where you put them until you move them or choose a different placement.

- "Line up icons" positions your notes on an invisible grid. Moving an icon snaps it to the nearest grid line.

- "AutoArrange" orients the display arrangement horizontally with no sort order. Moving a note within a matrix of other notes makes room for that note in its new position and realigns all notes on invisible grid lines.

- "Sort and AutoArrange" arranges your notes as just described and sorts them on Subject (ascending).

When using icon placements:

- If you select AutoArrange in "Large icon" view and switch to "Small icon" view this setting remains in place. Switch to List view and back to either Large or Small icons and this setting is lost.

- "Line up icons" and "Sort and AutoArrange" are not persistent. That is, they are a quick way to arrange or sort your notes, but moving an icon after applying either command returns placement to "Do not arrange."

View → Current View → Notes List

Notes List is a simple table layout of your Notes folder. Fields displayed are Icon, Subject, Created, and Category. There are no groupings or filters applied. By default, the sort order is descending by note creation date. This view, shown in Figure 10-12, is an excellent working layout for notes as it is uncluttered and functional. All commonly referenced fields are visible, and if the Preview Pane is enabled (View → Preview Pane), items can be quickly scanned for content. Selecting an item and using the right-click context menu allows quick edits of both note color and category. A note can be edited by opening the item, or in the Preview Pane.

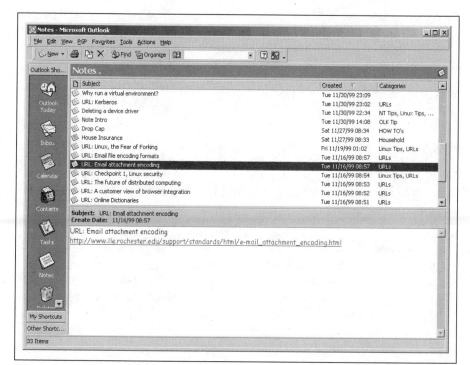

Figure 10-12: View → Current View → Notes List with Preview Pane enabled

Unlike other Outlook tables, Notes does not allow editing directly from the Table view. To modify a note, you must open it.

View → Current View → Last Seven Days

This view displays the contents of a Notes folder in List View, but filters the view to show only notes created or edited within the preceding seven days.

View → Current View → By Category

Like all components in Outlook, you can assign Notes a category to help sort and retrieve them. By Category view displays the fields Icon, Subject, and Created, grouped by header rows on category. Items listed under these groupings are sorted on a note's creation date and time (descending).

TIP # 128

Categorizing Notes

Don't bother assigning categories to temporary notes, but take the time to categorize notes you intend to convert into other Outlook items. Categories you assign to a note transfer to the newly created item.

To assign a category to a note, select it and use the Category context menu command. The Categories list is the same dialog seen across all components of Outlook. Place a checkmark beside the category you wish to associate with the note, or use the Master Category List button to add a new description to the list.

To change a category assignment, invoke the Categories dialog or simply drag the note from its current grouping to a new category grouping. As you drag the item a pop-up displays the new category change.

Dragging a note from (None) to a category grouping assigns that note to the category of the group you drop it on. If a note already has a category assignment, dragging it to another grouping displays a copy of the note under both the original grouping and the new dropped location, and in doing so assigns both categories to the note.

WARNING

Be careful when deleting notes displayed in multiple groupings: deleting an item from one group deletes all instances of that item. For example, if you have a note displayed under both the Home category and the Business category, deleting either entry deletes the note.

View → Current View → By Color

Notes can be created in or changed to one of five preset colors: Blue, Green, Pink, Yellow, or White. The default color used for a new note is set from Tools → Options → Notes Options. The By Color view is grouped on Color, sorted on date last modified, and has no filters applied.

To change a note's color, select it and use the right-click context menu. You can only change color this way for a single note at a time. You can, however, drag several selected notes to another existing color grouping. When you drag selected items to a different grouping, a pop-up displays the new note color. See Figure 10-13.

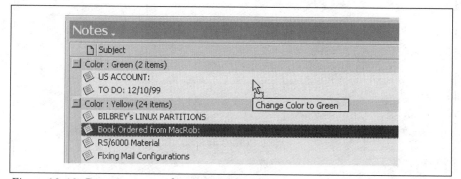

Figure 10-13: Dragging a note from one color grouping to another

Working with Notes

In the beginning of this chapter, we introduced the idea of using notes as a temporary container for ideas or scraps of information. Notes can be deleted when the information is no longer needed. On the other hand, notes gain immense value when you use them to create other Outlook items, or external documents. This section explains how to do that.

 Remember when you exchange data between Outlook items, or with external documents, that data is a copy of the original.

Creating Another Outlook Item from a Note

To create another Outlook item from the contents of a note, drag the note's icon to the Outlook Bar.

• Dropping a note on the Inbox or Outlook Today icon creates an email message containing the date the note was last modified, any categories or contacts assigned to the note, and the text of the note itself (see Figure 10-14, top). The message will be in Rich Text Format; this can be changed using the techniques outlined in Chapter 5, *Mail Editors*.

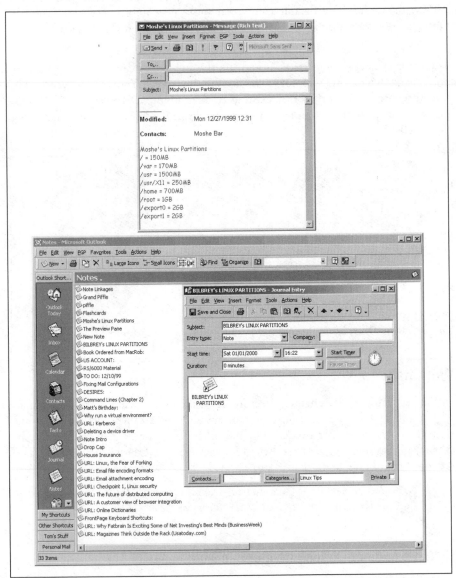

Figure 10-14: A note dropped on the Inbox icon (top); a note dropped on the Journal icon (bottom)

- Dropping a note on the Tasks, Contacts, or Calendar icons creates a new item of the appropriate type. The free-form text field contains the contents of the note, again including any categories or contacts assigned. The first line of the note becomes the subject of the task or appointment.

- Dropping the note on the Journal icon embeds a shortcut of the note in the free-form text field as shown in Figure 10-14 (bottom). The shortcut still points to the correct note, even with modifications, but changes are not reflected in the name of the shortcut. However, deleting the note orphans the shortcut.

In the View → By Category section, we suggested assigning categories to notes that had long-term value. This advice bears fruit here—Outlook always transfers categories assigned an item to new items.

There is another method of creating new Outlook items that gives you more control over how data is copied from the original item. Instead of dragging and dropping the note using the left mouse button, hold down the *right* mouse button. When you release the item, a dialog similar to that shown in Figure 10-15 is displayed. The top option in this dialog reflects the default behavior exhibited by left-click drag-and-drop. Most items are created as "with Text" by default; Journal items are created "with Shortcut" by default. What "Attachment" means depends upon what type of item you create. If you create a message, Attachment is an OLE item. For journal entries, Attachment is a copy, unlinked to the original. Each context is potentially different, due to the different uses of the various Outlook components.

- The first option places the *text* of the note in the new item (substitute Contacts for the Outlook type you're creating). For a new Contact item, this is the drag-and-drop behavior.

- The second option creates a *shortcut* to the note in the new item's text field. This allows you to update the original note from the new item, although changing the note's first line of text will not change the name of the shortcut as it does the name of the note.

- The third option copies the note to the new item, and inserts it as an *attachment* represented by an icon. The note is copied; there is no linkage between the original note and the new item.

- The fourth option *moves* the note from its original folder and inserts it in the new item as an attachment.

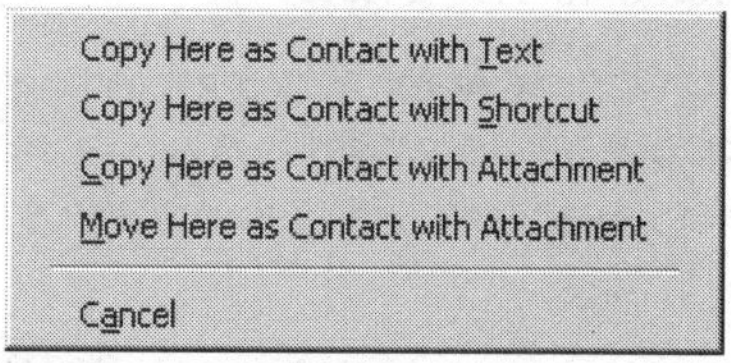

Copy Here as Contact with Text
Copy Here as Contact with Shortcut
Copy Here as Contact with Attachment
Move Here as Contact with Attachment

Cancel

Figure 10-15: Outlook's right-drag context menu

Copying a Note into an Office Document

Outlook notes can also be copied into an Office document (or any other OLE-compliant application, for that matter), where they are inserted as an embedded object.

Office Inconsistencies

Office applications are annoyingly inconsistent when it comes to dragging items between documents. For example, dragging a note from Outlook into Word embeds an OLE object. Drag a note from Outlook into Excel, however, and only the first line of the note's text is copied to the open spreadsheet.

Always experiment before dragging and dropping between Office applications so you know what to expect. Better still, make it a habit to select just the material you want copied, and move it between documents using the Windows Clipboard Cut/Paste commands.

To copy an Outlook note into a Word document:

1. Open Outlook and Word, and position them side-by-side on your Desktop.

2. Select a note from Outlook and drag it to the location in Word where you want it inserted.

To insert the *contents* of a note (versus the note itself), open the note, select the text desired, use the Copy command from the note's command menu, and the Paste command from Word's Edit menu.

Copying a Note to the Windows Desktop

You can also drag a note from Outlook and drop it on the Windows desktop. This is an excellent way to put reminders or a simple scratchpad within easy reach while you work in another application. Remember that Outlook does not have to be running to open and modify a note on the Desktop.

TIP # 129

Use the Right Mouse Button to Drag a Note

If you drag a note from Outlook to the Windows Desktop while holding down the right mouse button, you can choose to copy or move the item from the context menu displayed when you release your mouse button. This tip works for any Outlook item (Note, Contact, etc.).

Once you drag a note onto the Windows Desktop, you can manipulate it just like any other filesystem object. Right-click its icon to display the context menu shown in Figure 10-16.

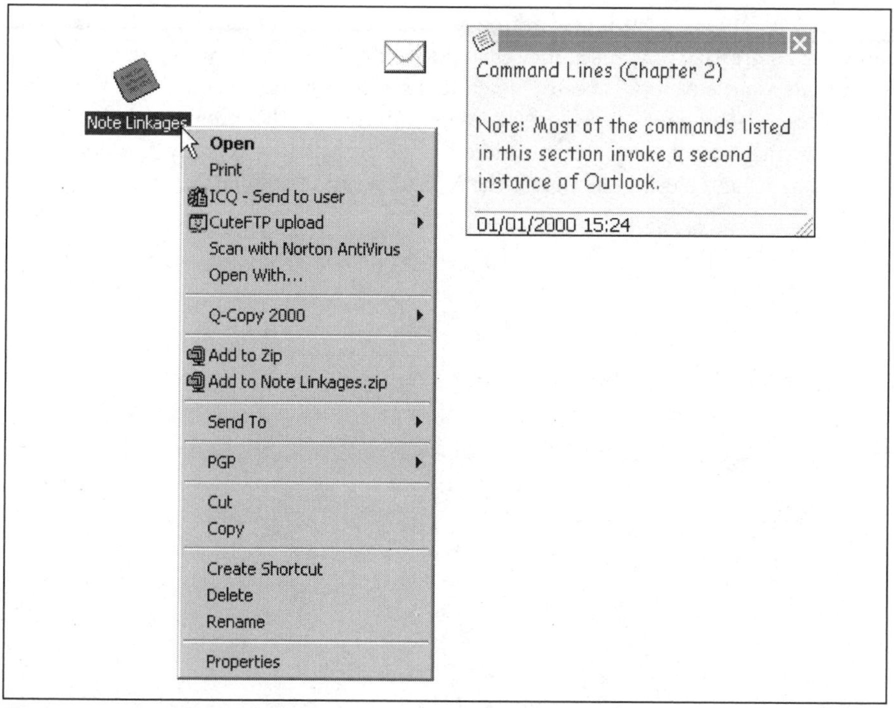

Figure 10-16: The Windows context menu available when an Outlook item is dragged to the Desktop

Working with multiple notes on your desktop is a very powerful way to manipulate discrete chunks of information. Here are just a few tips to consider:

- You can move or copy (the default is move—hold down the Ctrl key to copy) selected sentences or ideas between two notes by simply dragging and dropping.

- You're browsing the Web and find an interesting URL you want to investigate more fully later. Open a new note on your Desktop, and drag the address there. Or perhaps you find a phrase on a web page you want to save; select it, and drag it to an open note.

  NOTE *Instructions for creating a New Note shortcut on your Desktop are in Chapter 2, under the section "Starting Outlook from a Custom Shortcut."*

- You have a note on your Desktop as a reminder to call someone. Instead of opening Outlook to look up the phone number when you make the call, select the record in Contacts, and drop it on the note when you create it. Now you have all the information you need in one place.

• You can drag your Desktop To-Do list to the Recycle Bin icon.

One final comment regarding working with notes on your Desktop. If you look closely at Figure 10-16, you'll notice that the icon for the "Command Lines..." note is depicted as an envelope, because when this screenshot was taken, the note was in the process of being edited. Outlook items external to the program default to a *message* format (.*msg*), and are considered as objects of this type by the operating system. Saving and closing the note returns its icon to the original yellow scratchpad.

Chapter 11

Journal

Journal provides you with tools to track and record daily activities. Journal entries can range in complexity from a manually created record of a phone call to an automatic entry generated every time an email message is sent to a specific contact. In addition to tracking Outlook items and Office documents, Journal also provides the proper context for recording activities not tied directly to your computer, such as a handwritten letter or the receipt of a courier package.

While other components within Outlook provide similar note-keeping abilities, only Journal provides a fast (and optionally automatic) means to date/time stamp an activity, log the entry type (for example, phone call or meeting request), and even track the time spent on an activity for billing purposes.

Journal functions in two distinct modes: *automatic* and *manual*. This chapter begins with a section detailing the preference settings that relate to automatic journal entries. It then covers the *Actions* menu, which provides commands to create and send Journal entries. This is followed by a description of the *View* menu, where the various ways of viewing Journal items are detailed. The chapter ends with a section on the context menus available in Journal.

Journal Options

Journal displays the alert dialog shown in Figure 11-1 the first time you run it. Selecting Yes here activates Journal's *automatic tracking* feature and subsequently leads you to the configuration dialog shown in Figure 11-2.

Selecting No leaves automatic tracking disabled, bypasses the Journal Options dialog, and places you in the default view for Journal (Timeline, By Type). Like many similar dialog boxes, you see this over and over again, until you disable it or select Yes.

To implement Journal's automatic tracking, you must: (a) turn it on, and (b) configure what you want to track. Simply turning automatic tracking on does nothing. You need to tell Outlook what to track and for whom.

If you disable automatic tracking initially, and later want to enable it, choose Tools → Options → Preferences → Journal Options. The configuration dialog displayed is

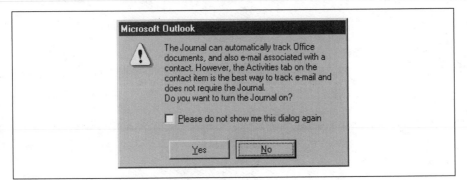

Figure 11-1: Initial alert for tracking option

identical to that shown in Figure 11-2, and all the same "on/off" tracking options (described later in this chapter) apply.

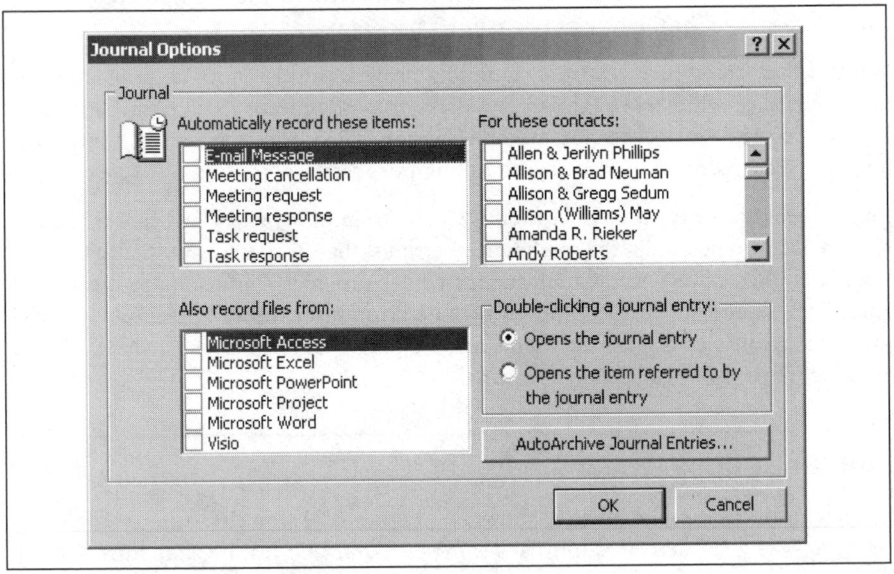

Figure 11-2: The Journal Options dialog

Journal options available to you are:

Automatically record these items

Select from a list of Outlook items to track as Journal entries. All options here revolve around three forms of messaging: regular email, meeting notifications, and task delegation. Item types selected from this list are tracked for the contacts you choose in the next option. Selecting an item to track without choosing a contact for whom to track it does nothing.

TIP # 130

Limitations of Automatic Tracking

Unfortunately, Journal's tracking options are not very flexible. Once you enable E-mail tracking, Outlook tracks every contact checked. You cannot automatically track specific email messages for a contact—it's all or none. You can, however, overcome this limitation by creating manual Journal entries on a per-item basis.

For these contacts

Here you link tracked Outlook items with those contacts for which you want to track them. This automatically creates journal entries for selected contacts. The entry created is identical to that made by dragging an email message to the Journal folder manually.

Only contacts in the top-level Contacts folder can be selected for automatic tracking. You must move (or copy) contacts from subfolders to the main Contacts folder in order to automatically track items for these individuals.

Also record files from

Creates an automatic Journal entry every time an Office application selected from this list creates or accesses a document. The selections available depend on which Microsoft Office applications are installed on your system. In the case of a full Office installation, documents from Access, Excel, PowerPoint, and Word can be tracked.

When automatic tracking is enabled for a particular document type (for example, Word documents), this setting applies to all documents that the application accesses. While this is a useful selection if you only use an application for certain tasks, it may also create many Journal entries filled with information you may not need to preserve. Make this selection with care.

Double-clicking a Journal entry

Double-clicking a Journal entry can open either the entry or the item referred to in the entry. You can override this selection with the context menu while working in the Journal view.

AutoArchive settings

The AutoArchive button is just an oddly placed shortcut to the Journal folder's Properties dialog, tabbed to the archiving settings. See Chapter 13, *File Management*, for details on archiving Outlook's data files.

Deciding whether to create Journal entries automatically, and for which contacts, can be a difficult decision. Poorly implemented, automatic tracking can quickly generate a flood of Journal entries you don't need. Instead, consider what you really need to track automatically. You can always create Journal entries manually, regardless of automatic tracking. This may be a better approach in some situations. Manually creating Journal entries is covered in the "Actions → New Journal Entry" section later in this chapter.

However, there are many situations where selective automatic creation of Journal entries is a powerful tracking tool. Properly configured, Journal entries are created in the background with no further effort on your part.

TIP # 131

Turning Off Automatic Journaling

There is no one-click solution to disabling automatic journaling. To turn this feature off, open the Journal Options dialog (Tools → Options → Journal Options) and clear all the checkboxes from the "record these items" and "record files from" lists. Clearing items selected in the contacts list is not necessary. Remember, automatic journaling consists of tracking items/files for a contact. Breaking the linkage on the "items to track" end is enough.

The following examples offer some insight on how to best leverage this feature:

- You routinely exchange important email with a business associate and you want to track all exchanges for reference. Unless you have a mail rule configured, incoming messages from this associate arrive in your Inbox. You read them, reply to them, and then archive these incoming messages to another folder. But now you have your associate's incoming message in one folder and your reply to him or her in another (by default, Sent Items). Configuring Journal to automatically track all your exchanges places a record of all messages relating to this contact (both received and replied to) in one convenient location. Instead of hunting for your response to a query made two weeks prior, open the Journal entry labeled message subject (Sent) for the date in question, double-click the embedded link, and Outlook takes you to the message containing your response.

  > **NOTE** *If you've set up automatic tracking for a contact that has more than one email address, Journal only tracks messages sent and received using the default address—that is, the entry shown under the E-mail field (not E-mail 2 or E-mail 3).*

- If you make your living writing with Microsoft Word, turning on automatic document tracking for this application provides some very interesting insights into where your days go and what documents you worked in. If you're going to use document tracking in such a scenario, however, be aware of the distinction between how Outlook tracks a document and how Word itself records editing time (via the File → Properties → Statistics tab, under the field editing time).

  Outlook tracks the time a document is *open*; Word tracks the time spent *physically editing* a document (that is, pressing keys). When automatic journaling is enabled under Outlook, as long as a document is open, this time is being recorded, even if you are away from your desk tending to other things. If a record of the actual time spent working on a document is important to you (whether mulling a paragraph, editing, or entering new text), learn to close it when you move on to other things. Using a combination of Word's editing time and Outlook's tracking fields, you can get a realistic picture of how much time you spend doing what.

As demonstrated by the earlier examples, we advise automatic tracking for your critical contacts and for specific applications that benefit from an automatic audit trail. Other items can be placed in the Journal manually as required.

 Once enabled, automatic tracking is always on. A stub of Outlook code runs in the background and monitors the Office applications you've selected to track—even if Outlook is closed.

When using automatic tracking for documents, there is often a significant lag time between when the document is closed and when the entry appears (or is updated) in a Journal view. Also, remember that if the document has been opened previously, the most recent tracking entry does not appear at the top of the list. Journal entries are ordered—by default—according to start date, which in this case would be the *first* time the document was opened or created.

Delays Due to Automatic Journaling

Automatic journaling can cause very long delays during manual or automatic timed saves, as well as when you exit the application. Although it may appear that the application has hung, in fact it is simply saving the journal information. If you experience apparent lock-ups during these procedures, check Outlook to see if automatic journaling is turned on for that application. If so, wait a minute or two to give the application a chance to save your data, and then turn off automatic journaling if it has become too onerous to use.

Journal → Actions Menu

The Actions menu is shown in Figure 11-3. It contains only two commands required to work with Outlook's Journal component: New Journal Entry and Forward. These items are discussed in the following sections.

Figure 11-3: The Journal Actions menu

Actions → New Journal Entry

The Actions → New Journal Entry command opens the Journal Entry dialog, shown in Figure 11-4. The keyboard shortcut for this dialog is Ctrl+N from within the Journal component; Ctrl+Shift+J opens a blank Journal Entry from anywhere within Outlook.

TIP # 132

Two Ways to a New Entry

In all Outlook components, the context menu displayed when you right-click a blank region of a view always lists a New command as the first item. There's a quicker way to open a new entry form, however—simply double-click the same blank region you used to invoke the context menu.

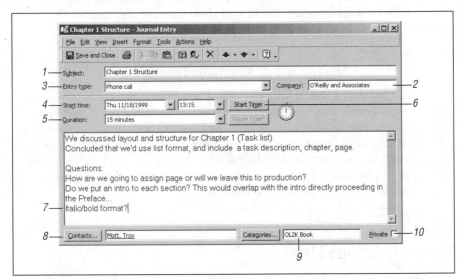

Figure 11-4: The New Journal Entry dialog

As with all other Outlook entry forms, the more information you add when creating a new record, the more leverage you can gain in mining the data later. When creating a new Journal entry, the Subject (see Figure 11-4, Item 1) field is important, as this is the "title" you see in all icon and table views. Name your Journal entries with unique and easily identified subjects.

Outlook automatically generates a name in the Company (2) field when the entry is created through automatic tracking or drag and drop if the company field is defined for that contact. When a manual entry is created, this field is blank. This field is useful when creating groupings or filters in a custom view. Note that this field is not modified when you add contacts manually, as described later in this section.

The Entry Type (3) is one of the key fields for grouping and filtering Journal views, and each type is associated with a unique icon. The drop-list selection for the Entry Type field is shown in Figure 11-5. The selections for external applications shown depend on the Office components installed on your system.

For details on adding entry types to Journal, see the sidebar "Creating New Journal Entry Types" at the end of this chapter.

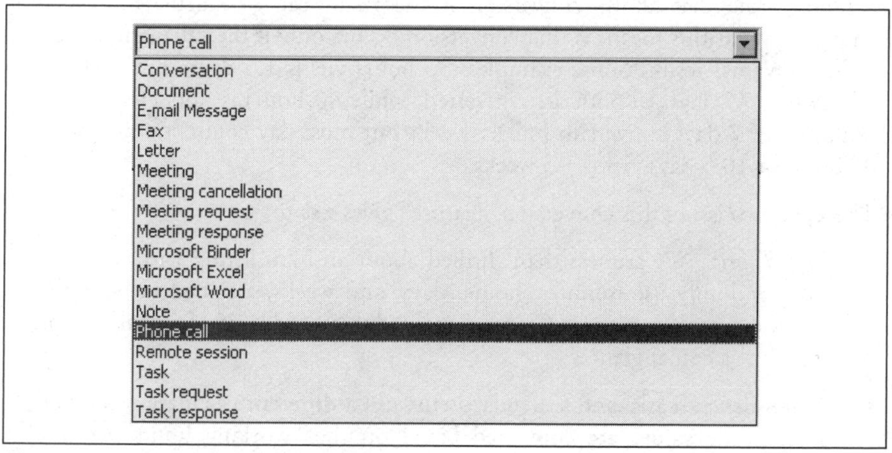

Figure 11-5: Journal's selectable entry types

When automatic tracking is used, Outlook generates Journal entries according to these types. For documents, entry types match the associated application (for example, Word). Manually tracked documents are grouped under "Document."

The "Start time" field (4) records the date and time when a Journal entry begins. For a new entry this field is prefilled with the current system date and time. A different date can be selected using the down arrow, which calls up Outlook's Date Navigator (see Chapter 7, *Calendar*). Outlook translates relative times such as yesterday or last Monday automatically. The time field provides a drop-down list set at 30-minute intervals, but it is also directly editable and accepts entries like 1:15 (a.m.) or 1:15 pm in either 12- or 24-hour format. Outlook converts entries to the format your operating system is configured to display. Changing the date and time of an existing entry does not affect the date stamp of any attachments, nor does it affect the recorded duration of the event in any way.

The Duration field (5) reflects the amount of time a Journal entry spans. A new entry defaults to zero minutes, but this can be modified from either the drop-down list or by typing a number directly in the field. The duration values you enter are interpreted and displayed as minutes unless explicitly followed by some other time unit (hours, days, or weeks). For large values these are converted to display fractional hours, days, or weeks (see the sidebar "Time Conversion Caveats"). When the

Time Conversion Caveats

Conversion in Journal of duration values to days and weeks is mathematically simple (60 minutes, 24 hours, 7 days). Some users may appreciate this.

However, we have found that this automatic conversion should not be relied on to always perform conversions into the next applicable unit. There appears to be a hidden rule that allows conversion if the result can be calculated "evenly enough." What this means is that conversion occurs only if the calculation yields a short decimal result. Some examples: 36 hours yields 1.5 days, and 42 hours results in 1.75 days, so both are converted, while 40 hours is not. Hence, even multiples of 7 days convert to integer weeks but most day counts do not, while 84 hours or 10.5 days yields 1.5 weeks.

There are two issues this conversion "feature" gives rise to:

- *Mixed units.* We are less than thrilled about an item listing with durations that randomly use minutes, hours, days, and weeks, assigned in ways that the user cannot control. Comparing 40 hours and 1.75 days takes more than just a casual glance.

- *Inconsistency.* Tasks and Calendar items use a different calculation method, where time values are converted based on the "working hours per day" (default 8) and "working hours per week" (default 40, implied 5 days) as defined on the Calendar Options dialog. It is far from intuitive that a Journal entry (24-hour days) specifying 3 days and a Task entry (default 8 hour days) also specifying 3 days are in fact very different things.

The conclusion we draw here is that duration logging is a simple feature made unnecessarily complex and confusing by having an automatic conversion feature that is inconsistent and cannot be user-controlled.

timer is used for a Journal entry, the duration recorded is displayed in minutes, however large this count becomes.

Duration can be of critical importance if your business depends upon billable hours and minutes. Judicious use of the timer and duration functions in the Journal component allows more complete project tracking, as well as better information for project planning and justification. Consultants love these capabilities, but for authors under deadline, this is just more sand through the hourglass.

The Timer buttons (6) shown in Figure 11-6 are of special interest for manual Journal entries. Here you can start and pause a timer to interactively record the duration of the activity the Journal entry describes. The Duration field is automatically updated while the timer is running. In addition, you can add time to the Duration field by opening an existing Journal entry and starting the timer. This allows you to accumulate the duration of several phone calls in a single record, for example. The actual times of the separate calls would then have to be manually specified in the notes field, since the "Start time" field only shows when the entry was first created.

Start time:	Thu 99-06-10 ▼	18:00 ▼	Start Timer
Duration:	9 minutes	▼	Pause Timer

Figure 11-6: Dialog detail showing timer running

The Notes field (7) occupies the lower part of the Journal Entry dialog. Here you can enter text or notes to expand on the purpose of the record, cut and paste information found on the Internet relating to a business project, or insert a document. This is also where any attachments are placed as a result of automatic tracking.

 Although any type of information can be placed in the notes field, this data cannot be used to sort or create custom views of Journal. You can search the Notes in the Journal component using the Tools → Advanced Find feature.

The Contacts (8) and Categories (9) fields at the bottom of the Journal entry dialog (Figure 11-7) enable you to classify entries with links to Contacts and Categories. We recommend using these features due to the greater flexibility and power available when organizing and filtering Journal views.

Contacts...		Categories...		Private ☐

Figure 11-7: Contacts, Categories, and Private field from Journal entry form

The Contacts button opens the dialog shown in Figure 11-8. In the upper pane you can select any valid contacts folder from among your Outlook folders. From the bottom pane you choose contacts that you want entered into the contacts field on your Journal entry. Standard shift-click and control-click rules apply for contact selection. Once entered, double-click contacts in the field as a shortcut to open the contact record. Also, contacts are used as a primary sorting field for many Journal views. This is a handy way to locate all of your correspondence and work relating to a specific contact.

The Categories button opens the standard Categories list used by all Outlook components (see Figure 11-9). In the lower pane, you check the categories that are appropriate to the Journal entry. As they are selected, categories are transferred to the upper pane. The Add to List button that adjoins the upper pane allows you to add free-form categories (say, Authors) to the official Categories. Alternatively, you may edit the master category list by selecting the Master Category List button from this dialog.

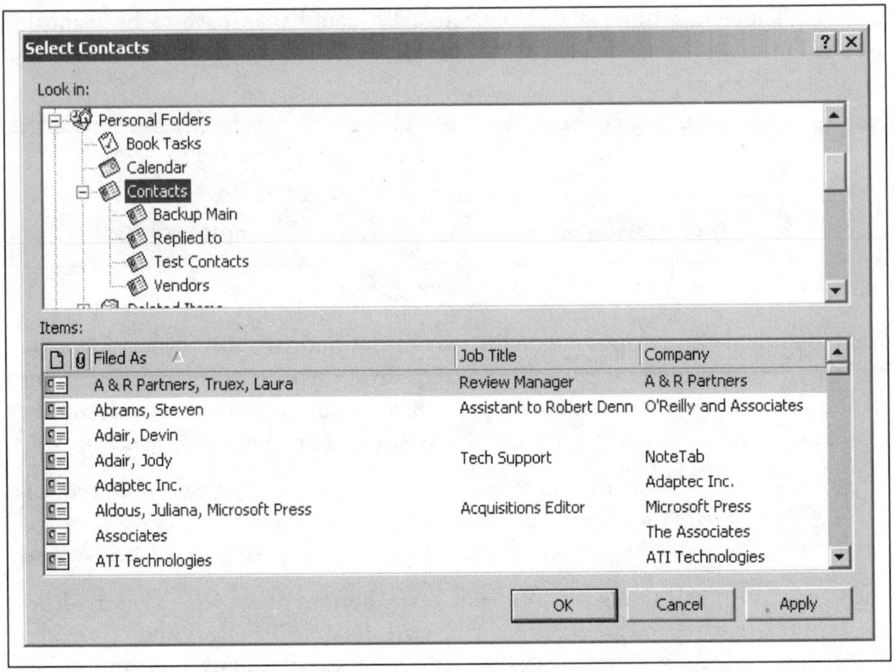

Figure 11-8: The Select Contacts dialog

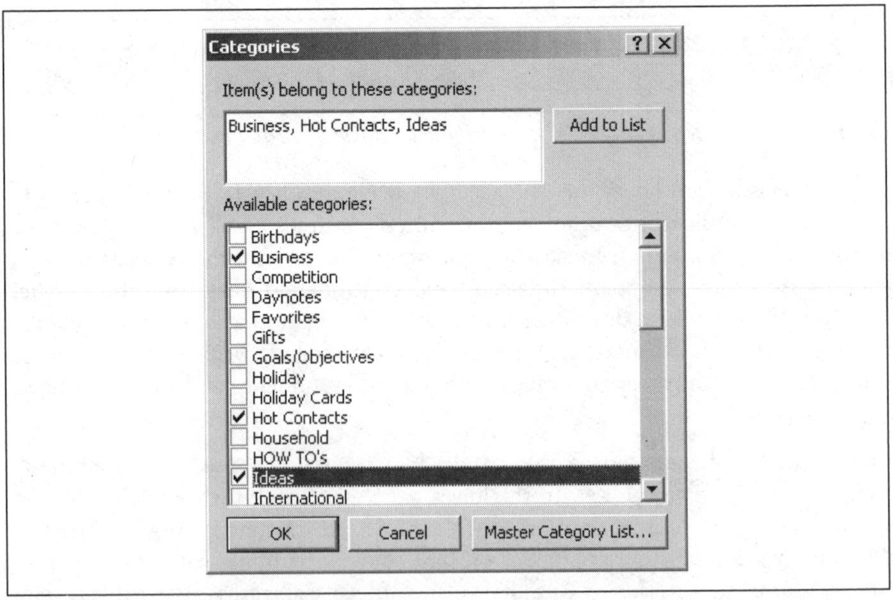

Figure 11-9: Outlook's Categories dialog

Journal

TIP # 133

Assigning Categories from a View

You can also access the Categories dialog from the context menu of a Journal view. Select the entry, right-click, and choose Categories. This is also a powerful way to assign a category to multiple items at once.

If the Private checkbox (10) is selected, the Journal entry is hidden from other users who have shared access to the folder where the item is contained. This option has relevance only if you are using Net Folders (see Chapter 14, *Collaborating with Outlook*) or working from a Public Folder on an Exchange Server.

Linking Documents in Journal

Earlier in this chapter we discussed automatic document tracking. This option links Office documents to Journal entries; a new Journal item is created every time the document type is accessed.

Occasions do arise, however, when you want to link a document to a Journal entry manually. There are several reasons for linking documents manually:

- Only Microsoft Office applications can be selected for automatic tracking. If you use Corel WordPerfect as a word processor and Outlook to manage your contacts, you must track documents manually.

- You could find yourself wanting to add a link to a Journal entry either as a cross-reference or as a shortcut to access the document directly from the Journal entry.

- As noted in our discussion of automatic document tracking, this option is an all or nothing proposition. You may not want to track all your Word documents, but sometimes it is important to track one or two specific documents.

When files are manually inserted into a Journal entry, no automatic time tracking takes place—the document is simply accessible through the Journal entry form (or via a context menu; see the section "Journal's Context Menus" later in this chapter). You can, however, use the Timer function to manually create this field when working on a linked document.

Two methods exist to link a document or file with a Journal entry. While both methods achieve the same result, one is better suited to creating a new Journal entry linked to a document and the other better utilized for linking a document to an existing Journal entry.

To create a new Journal entry linked to a document, select the file from Windows Explorer and drop it on the Outlook Bar's Journal icon or in any open Journal view. A new entry is created with the Subject as the name of the document, and the Entry type is set to Document. A Start time is entered based on the system time and date. This method places a shortcut to the document (or file) in the Notes field. Double-click this shortcut to open the item.

 If you find that the Insert Object command is unavailable, it is probably because your cursor is not positioned in the note field of the form.

The second method involves inserting an *object* into a Journal entry. The Journal entry form provides an Insert menu command that opens the Insert Object dialog shown in Figure 11-10. This dialog has two insertion options (Create New or Create from File) and changes appearance depending on which one is selected.

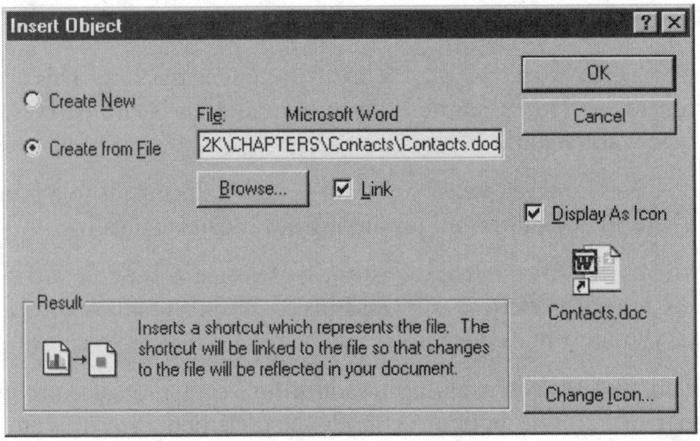

![The Insert Object dialog showing Create from File selected, with File field containing 2K\CHAPTERS\Contacts\Contacts.doc, Browse button, Link and Display As Icon checkboxes checked, OK and Cancel buttons, a Contacts.doc icon, Change Icon button, and a Result description reading "Inserts a shortcut which represents the file. The shortcut will be linked to the file so that changes to the file will be reflected in your document."]

Figure 11-10: The Insert Object dialog (Create from File)

The selections shown in Figure 11-10 insert the document *contacts.doc* as a link to the actual file and display this link as an icon. Clearing the Link checkbox inserts a copy of the file itself as an item. This is significant if you are working in shared folders, where the link may point to a place in your filesystem inaccessible to the other users of the Journal.

Alternatively, you can create a new object, of any registered application type, and insert the object in your journal entry. One use of this feature might be creating a document in some application while on a call.

Some pitfalls arise regarding the Insert Object dialog:

- Check the selections and options before exiting this dialog to ensure you are getting what you want. The default behavior for this dialog is to insert an object as an OLE item (embedded in the notes field), not as a link as most people would expect.

- If you insert a document as an unlinked object, it is inserted as a copy of the document. Changes made to the copy do not update the original. To update the original, open the document from the Journal entry and use the Save As command on the application's File menu to overwrite the original.

- Inserting Office documents with the Display as Icon option unchecked inserts the contents of the document in the free-form text field. If you're concerned about the size of your PST file, avoid this option. Inserting a document from any other application only shows an icon, regardless of the Display as Icon state.

 The duration for a tracked document type is "elapsed time" while the document is open. Contrast this with "total editing time," tracked inside Word documents, based upon keyboard activity. Depending upon the type of work you do, one of these tracking methods should meet your needs.

Actions → Forward

Actions → Forward (Ctrl+F) attaches the selected Journal items to a new email message. The appearance of the forwarded message is dependent on both the default email editor and the message format being used. When the message format is Plain Text or HTML and sent using Outlook's default editor, these attachments are displayed in a separate pane below the message body as shown in Figure 11-11. RTF message attachments, on the other hand, are embedded directly in the message pane itself. When you use Word as the default message editor, attachments are displayed in the "Attach..." field.

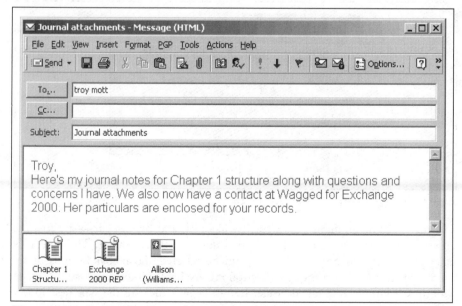

Figure 11-11: Forwarding Journal items to another user

The functionality remains the same, however, across mail editors and message formats. When the forwarded Journal item is received using Outlook it is in the form of an email message with attachments. Opening the attachment displays the entry in a Journal dialog and all fields display the same information for the recipient as they did for the sender. The recipient can drag this attachment to their own Journal icon on the Outlook bar and create an entry there just as they could with one of their own files.

If you create a new (OLE) document in the notes field of a Journal entry (Insert → Object), this document is forwarded with the message and is readable by the recipient (providing they have the means to view or open a document of this type on their system). If the sender creates a link to a document in the Journal entry, this document is only accessible to the recipient if they have access to the filesystem where the original document resides.

For recipients using other email clients, the attachments are received in binary format (named *winmail.dat*) that contains the Outlook-specific formatting and content data. Only the text contained in the free-form notes field is readable.

Journal → View Menu

The Journal → View → Current View submenu (Figure 11-12) contains six preconfigured ways to view Journal entries.

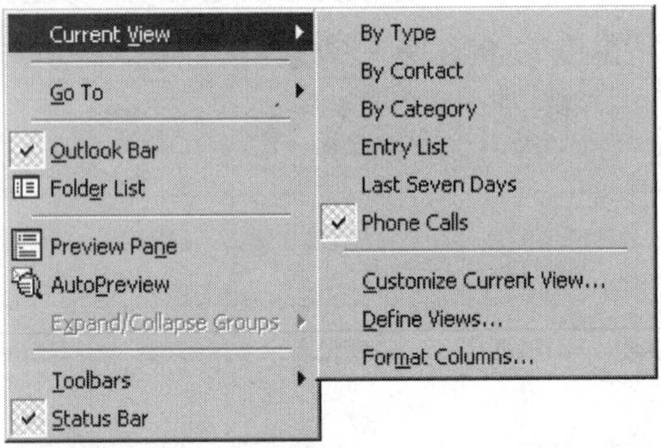

Figure 11-12: Journal's Current View submenu

The first three menu items—By Type, By Contact, and By Category—are *timeline* views, where entries are grouped vertically using the "By..." choice. The timeline's date range is shown horizontally, and can be selected via toolbar buttons or by context menu (right-click the date description). Available options are Day, Week, or Month. Clicking on the raised header button (+ or -) next to the type description expands or collapses the group. Journal entries are represented by icons and are arranged horizontally by date and vertically by time (earlier entries higher on the list). Figure 11-13 shows a timeline view.

TIP # 134

Quickly Expand/Collapse Timeline Groups

When working in a timeline view, Outlook adds an entry, Expand/Collapse Groups, to the View menu. This item mirrors the functionality of the raised header +|- button, but adds the ability to expand or collapse all groups with one command rather than toggling each group separately.

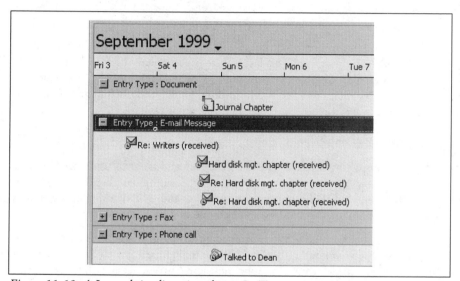

Figure 11-13: A Journal timeline view shown By Type

The next three view selections (Entry List, Last Seven Days, and Phone Calls) display in table format with individual entries as rows and fields as columns. By default, Journal fields cannot be edited in Table views. To edit an entry it must be opened. Alternately, you can enable in-cell editing with View → Current View → Customize Current View → Other Settings, then select "Allow in-cell editing." The disadvantage of in-cell editing is the drop-down lists and dialogs found on an entry's form are not available, but for a quick tweak of an item, in-cell editing works well.

All of the preconfigured views in Journal are customizable in a variety of ways using the three customization commands at the bottom of the submenu. Changes made to these views are persistent, however, so configure with care. If you end up mangling a preconfigured view beyond repair, it can be restored to factory defaults using the Reset button on the Define Views dialog (View → Current View → Define Views). Sorry, no such option exists for custom views. A detailed overview of customizing and configuring views can be found in Chapter 3, *Program Insights*.

A summary of context menus employed throughout the Journal component can be found at the end of this chapter. Note that many of these menus are particularly helpful when sorting or manipulating the views in Journal.

Current View → By Type

Current View → By Type opens a timeline view with Journal items grouped according their entry type (see Figure 11-13) and sorted by date, oldest to the left. The range of the timeline can be expanded and collapsed with the Day/Week/Month buttons on the toolbar displayed for this view.

Double-click an icon to open that item; hold your mouse pointer over an entry to see the text of the Subject line. This last feature is particularly useful when using the Month timeline view, since only icons are shown for each entry. The strength of this view lies in its ability to assist you in finding "that Word document I worked on last Tuesday... What the heck did I call that file, anyway?"

Current View → By Contact

By Contact groups your Journal entries by the contacts assigned using the Contacts field. In this view, an entry appears in as many locations as there are associated contacts. This highlights the power of this view—and that of using the Contacts field consistently. Figure 11-14 shows an example of a By Contact view.

For example, assume that you have automatic journaling enabled for all email sent to, or received by, your contact Bo Leuf. All journal entries created are associated—via the Contacts field—with Bo. One of these entries, "Tasks side-issue" also involves another contact, Dan Bowman. Open the entry and add Dan to the Contacts field. The entry now displays under both Bo and Dan's contact grouping. This not only serves as a visual reminder of who was involved with the item in question, but also leaves you with several options for locating the entry.

Current View → By Category

This view arranges your Journal entries grouped on their assigned categories, and displayed in a timeline format as described at the beginning of this section.

Using categories to organize your work in Outlook is just another example of wise cross-referencing. If you have yet to discover the power of categories for searching and organizing your data, seeing all your Journal entries as a large group of "(none)" is extremely educational. We strongly suggest you read the section on Categories in Chapter 3.

Two examples illustrate the utility of the By Category view:

- Several writers are collaborating on a book project. You can find the messages from any one individual, or on any given topic. But with assigned categories, you can easily group and then locate all of the related correspondence and documents in one view.

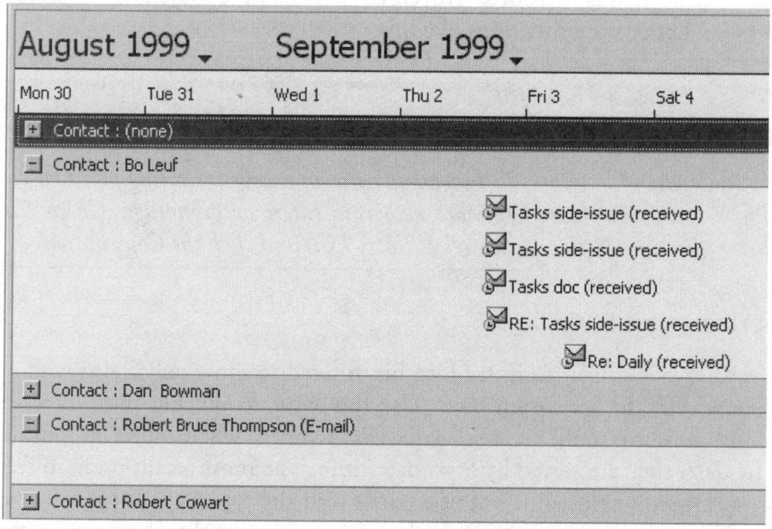

Figure 11-14: The By Contact timeline view showing the details of an expanded group

- If you record phone calls, the By Contact or By Type views quickly become overwhelmingly large. The use of categories as you create these items allows you to organize your data into a more coherent and usable form.

Current View → Entry List

Entry List (see Figure 11-15) is a Table view, unfiltered by default, and sorted with the most recent entry at the top as defined by the start date/time of the item. The columns displayed are Icon, Attachment, Entry Type, Subject, Start, Duration, Contact, and Categories.

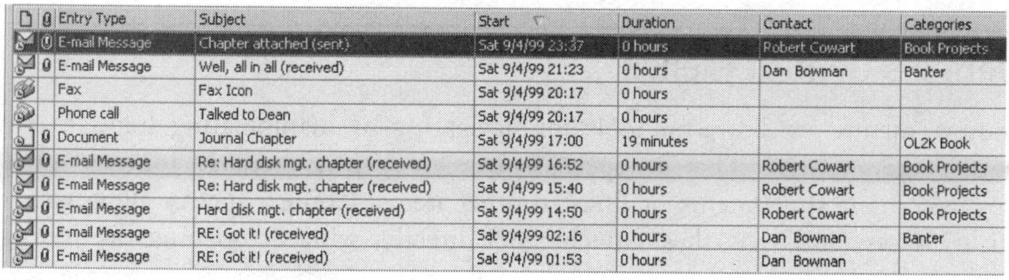

		Entry Type	Subject	Start	Duration	Contact	Categories
		E-mail Message	Chapter attached (sent)	Sat 9/4/99 23:37	0 hours	Robert Cowart	Book Projects
		E-mail Message	Well, all in all (received)	Sat 9/4/99 21:23	0 hours	Dan Bowman	Banter
		Fax	Fax Icon	Sat 9/4/99 20:17	0 hours		
		Phone call	Talked to Dean	Sat 9/4/99 20:17	0 hours		
		Document	Journal Chapter	Sat 9/4/99 17:00	19 minutes		OL2K Book
		E-mail Message	Re: Hard disk mgt. chapter (received)	Sat 9/4/99 16:52	0 hours	Robert Cowart	Book Projects
		E-mail Message	Re: Hard disk mgt. chapter (received)	Sat 9/4/99 15:40	0 hours	Robert Cowart	Book Projects
		E-mail Message	Hard disk mgt. chapter (received)	Sat 9/4/99 14:50	0 hours	Robert Cowart	Book Projects
		E-mail Message	RE: Got it! (received)	Sat 9/4/99 02:16	0 hours	Dan Bowman	Banter
		E-mail Message	RE: Got it! (received)	Sat 9/4/99 01:53	0 hours	Dan Bowman	

Figure 11-15: Journal's Entry List view

This is a good view to use if you are looking for a relatively recent journal entry. Table layouts have a decided advantage over timeline views in that they compress a lot of information into a compact space. But if you use Journal extensively, and the item you are looking for is not a recent entry, this view quickly leads to a lot of scrolling and searching for that proverbial needle in a haystack. A filtered or grouped view better suits situations like this.

TIP # 135

Use Entry List as a Template for New Views

The simplicity of the Entry List view makes it an excellent starting point for customizing a new view based on more elaborate filters or groupings. Go to View → Current View → Define Views, select Entry List, and click the Copy button.

Current View → Last Seven Days

Last Seven Days is similar to Entry List, but filtered to show only items with a Start date/time within the last seven days. Use this view to quickly filter an extensive Journal list to show only recent entries. Remember, when views in Journal are sorted by date, they are sorted by Start date/time. The most recent item, in terms of when it was saved or closed, is not necessarily near the top of the list if it had a long duration. Some events may even be excluded from the list displayed due to the fact that the start date falls outside the filtered range. This caveat also applies to the previous view, and any other date-sorted Journal view.

Current View → Phone Calls

Phone Calls is a preconfigured view filtered to only show items of the type Phone Call. The default columns displayed are Icon, Attachment, Subject, Start, Duration, Contact, and Categories.

This view is useful when you use Outlook's Journal features to track your phone calls. The default Entry Type for a new journal entry is in fact Phone Call. Because a new journal item can be invoked with Ctrl+Shift+J from any Outlook component, logging and timing your phone calls is only a keyboard shortcut away.

Journal's Context Menus

Context menus are powerful tools for navigating or manipulating items in any Outlook component. This is especially true in Journal because Journal entries usually contain attachments or links to other items. Context menus allow you to quickly access and view these attachments directly, without opening the Journal item.

 Some Journal views (particularly Table view with many entries) make it difficult to find the "right" space to click on to open the desired context menu. If this happens to you, scroll to the bottom of the open view and click on the very last row or white space available.

Right-clicking on an empty area of a timeline view brings up the context menu shown in Figure 11-16 (left). The features offered here are selected from the most useful commands from View menu and submenus. Quick and simple view navigation and customization is the order of the day. The context menu shown in Figure 11-16 (right) is displayed when your view is a table format.

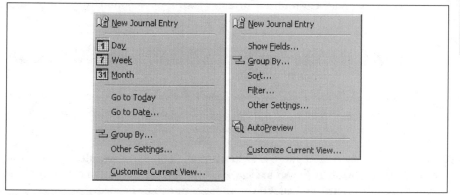

Figure 11-16: The context menu displayed for a timeline view (left) and a Table view (right)

Figure 11-17 (left) shows the context menu displayed when you right-click a *single* item in any Journal view. Open and Open Journal Entry are functionally equivalent. Open Item Referred To opens the journal entry itself (identical, then, to Open and Open Journal Entry) if the item contains no associated external documents (for example, an item containing details of a phone call or meeting). If the entry has an associated document or Outlook item (for example, a Word document or linked email message), this menu command opens the attachment in its native program.

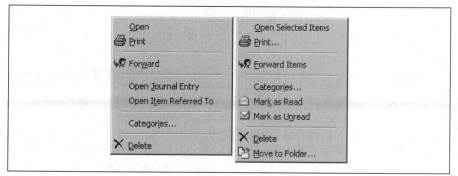

Figure 11-17: Context menu for a single Journal item (left) and for multiple selections (right)

When more than one Journal Entry is selected from a view, the context menu changes to that shown in Figure 11-17 (right). Note the addition of the "Mark as…" commands for Read status (also found on the Edit menu) and the Move to

Folder command. The "Mark as" commands appear for multiples of any Entry Type, even those including no messages.

The Read status can conceivably be used as impromptu importance flags denoting an item that needs further attention or another look. Visually, Unread status renders an entry as bold text in table displays. This can be customized with the format rules for Unread Items under Customize Current View → View Summary → Automatic Formatting → Font.

TIP # 136

Override Your Default "Open" Settings

The Open default behavior (Entry, or item referred to in the Entry) is set in the Tools → Options → Journal Options dialog. The addition of the Open commands to context menus constitutes a handy override to your default settings.

When an entry has one or more attachments, the context menu displays a View Attachments command as shown in Figure 11-18. This opens a submenu listing the attachments for the entry and allows you to select one to be opened.

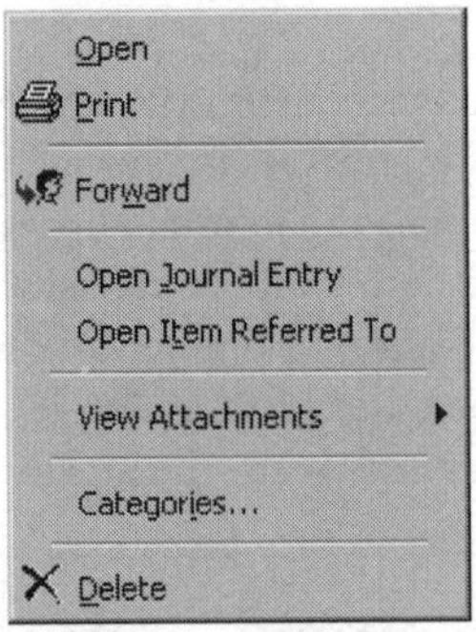

Figure 11-18: Context menu for Journal item with attachment

WARNING

If you've enabled automatic journaling for all entries created by an application (for example, Excel), then every document you create or open generates a Journal entry. If you manually add additional items to the entry, depending on where you place the icon, the Open Item Referred To command may open the manually placed link, even though that item does not show up on the list displayed by View Attachments.

Creating New Journal Entry Types

If you find Journal's default selection of entry types doesn't suit your needs, it is possible to modify this list. The process involves editing the Registry, so before you begin, make *sure* you have a good backup of this critical file. Accidentally changing the wrong key could seriously damage your system.

1. From the Start menu, choose Run. Enter regedit in the Open dialog and navigate to the Registry key My Computer\HKEY_CURRENT_USER\Software\ Microsoft\Shared Tools\Outlook\Journaling.

2. Right-click the Journaling key, select New → Key, and enter a name for the entry type you want to add (for example, Installed Software). Your new key name doesn't have to match the descriptive text that appears in the Entry Type field, but it's easier if it does.

3. Now right-click your new key and choose New → String Value. You need two basic entries, both string values: Description (the text that appears in the Entry Type field) and Large Icon (a number from 1–23 that appears in square brackets, [XX], that determines which icon Outlook displays for this item in a Table view). When you're done, the right Registry pane of your new key should contain a value named Description with a data entry matching your new entry type, and a value named Large Icon with a numeric data entry matching the icon you've chosen. Use Outlook's predefined Journal keys for reference.

That's all you'll need for your new key to work. You can omit the Large Icon value, but then you'll just get a default icon—a blank sheet of paper—for entries of this type. If you omit a Description value, your new entry type won't appear on the Entry Type list when you create a new Journal item.

While you're in the Registry you can also delete any entry types that you don't want, with the exception of the Phone Call entry. Because it's a default entry, Outlook won't allow you to delete it. You can, of course, effectively rename it by simply adding a Description string value with whatever text you like.

These changes only apply to the currently logged-in user, as you may have guessed, because they're under the HKEY_CURRENT_USER class. To share your custom list with others, simply export the \Outlook\Journaling branch of the Registry (either the specific new entry type if there's just one or the entire Journaling key if there are multiple new entry types) to a *.reg* file. This is easily done in the Registry Editor by selecting Registry → Export Registry File.

When your recipient receives the *.reg* file, they can import it in their Registry by double-clicking it. Like magic, it incorporates your new entries seamlessly.

Part 3

Beyond the Basics

Chapter 12

Import and Export

The concept of import/export is simple: avoid unnecessary data entry. If you already have an extensive collection of contacts created in another program, reentering each one in Outlook is a waste of time and energy. And what about all the data you've created with other programs or received from other sources? For organizational purposes, it makes sense to combine all this information in one place, preferably with minimal reentry.

Unfortunately, the simple concepts are often the hardest to apply. Sharing information with others is a way of life, but there is still no widely accepted and implemented universal data format (HTML is close, but not there yet). Software vendors load their products with features, many of which dictate a proprietary data format, making the act of exchanging and combining data sources a frustrating process.

The good news is, Outlook has a decent selection of import and export filters that provide acceptable results with most common data formats. The bad news is no import/export filters are perfect. The more unique the data, the harder it's going to be to get it from one program to another cleanly.

Many people tend to regard import/export as a one shot deal, used to transfer a complete document or dataset between dissimilar programs. Given the diversity of information Outlook is capable of storing, this is limited thinking. You might, for example, use Outlook's import/export tools to:

- Use a filter to export a subset of a single folder (for example, Contacts or Calendar) to share with a business associate. If your associate uses Outlook, this file can be saved to a PST format; if they use ACT!, the file can be saved to dBase format.

- Import the table containing customer names and addresses from a multi-table Access database and merge it with your existing contacts. You can just as easily export contacts out of Outlook into an Access database, then merge the table created into a larger existing customer database.

- Import mail settings from Eudora, Outlook Express, or Netscape Messenger for use in Outlook.

The possibilities are only limited by your needs, your creativity, and a healthy dose of persistence. Before jumping into the details of importing and exporting data with Outlook, it is important to understand the concept and technique of field mapping.

Field Mapping

With the exception of Personal Folder File format, every import/export option in Outlook gives you the opportunity to view and change field mappings. A field map establishes a one-to-one relationship between the contents of a field in the source file, and the field the data is copied to in the destination file.

Field mapping can be used to:

*   Import or export data between dissimilar data structures.

*   View or look inside a data format.

The Map Custom Fields dialog shown in Figure 12-1 is accessible from the Map Fields button located on the last dialog of the Import and Export Wizard.

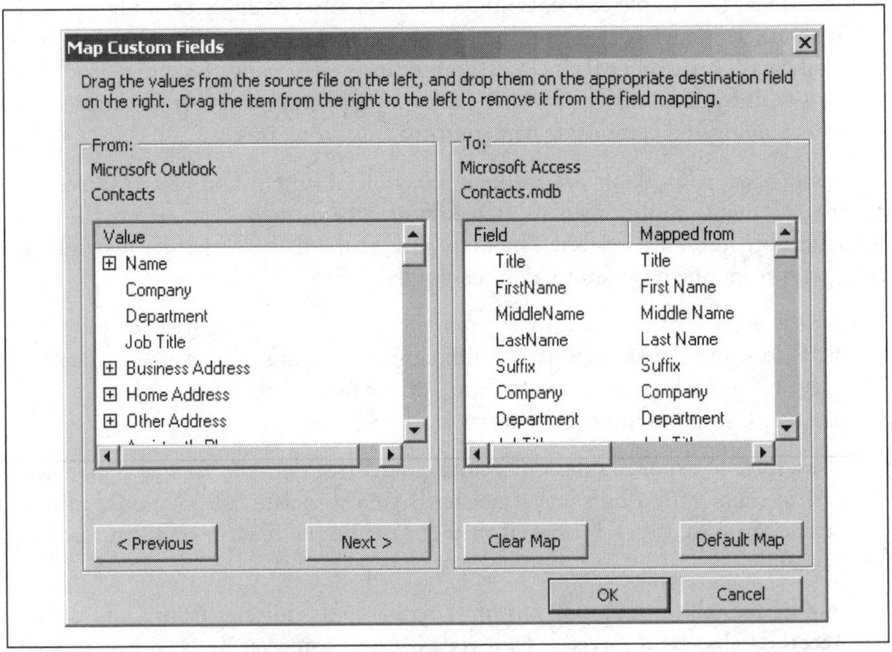

Figure 12-1: Outlook's Map Custom Fields dialog

The left pane shows the values (or fields) from the source file. The Previous and Next buttons shift the contents of the pane from field names to the actual contents. An example is shown in the Figure 12-2, where the view has been advanced to an entry in the Contacts folder.

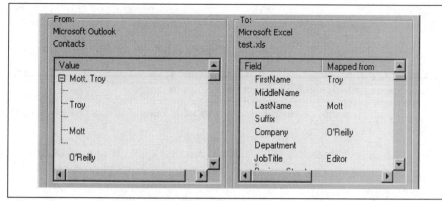

Figure 12-2: Viewing the actual field contents mapped—the Address field is shown expanded

This is a good way to see how a file will import or export before committing to the actual process. It also provides you with the opportunity to see an example of the type of data a field contains if the name used for the value is not intuitive at first glance.

Fields that are expandable into separate components, such as full name or address, are initially shown in the From pane collapsed. Click on the "+" to expand the view and show each component separately.

To use Outlook's field-mapping option:

- Drag a field from the left pane (From) and drop it on an entry under the Field column in the right pane (To). Note there is no requirement to map similarly named fields to each other. There is nothing stopping you from mapping, say, Department in the From pane to Company in the To pane. However, you have to be cautious about field types. Outlook will not stop you from mapping a numeric field to a text-only field, but when the data is actually imported/ exported, the results may not be what you expect. Unfortunately, there is no way to discern a field's properties from the Field Mapping dialog.

- You cannot map a field displayed in the From pane to more than one field in the To pane. For example, if Name is already mapped to FullName, trying to map Name to a second field removes the mapping established to FullName.

- To remove a field from the mapping, drag the field name from the To pane back to the From pane. To remove all mappings and create your own from scratch, click Clear Map. If you get muddled or just want to start over with Outlook's defaults, click Default Map.

- Fields with subcomponents (Name, for example) do not have to be mapped to separate fields in the destination file (the default map). To map a field with subcomponents to a single field, remove the subcomponent fields from the right pane, then drag the collapsed field back to the right pane.

- To reorder fields in the To pane, drag-and-drop them in the list as desired.

- The destination field names are editable—just click on a selected field name and type in your changes. There are two things to consider:

  - Spaces are removed when you confirm with Enter. For example, Job Title becomes JobTitle.

  - New session copies of default names automatically get appended a number. The intent is if you edit a name that already exists, e.g., change "Title" to "Suffix," you instead get "Suffix1," thus ensuring unique field names. Unfortunately, this also means if you remove "Title," change your mind and reinstate it from the left-hand pane, you get "Title1," and you cannot edit this back to just "Title." Repeat the process, and you get "Title2."

  - A further caution: fields are case-sensitive, thus both "Title" and "title" are possible in the same list.

TIP # 137

Outlook's Import/Export Memory

Outlook remembers mapping options based on the source file format and the folder type destination. These definitions are stored in the folder <userdata path>\<username>\Application Data. If you've created complex mappings and want to save them, you might want to add this location to the backup list provided in Chapter 13, File Management.

Importing Data

There are two rules for importing data:

Rule #1: Expect problems.
Rule #2: Plan for problems.

If this sounds a little scary, it should. Data is a precious commodity. Unfortunately, this fact is all too often lost on people until something goes wrong and they are forced to enter 1000 records from scratch. And unless you're dealing with data that was exported from an identical version of the same software you use, importing data can be a hit and miss venture. Fortunately, we have some suggestions that should keep you from getting into serious trouble, and may even make the process reasonably painless:

- Never import data into your working information store. Create a new PST file for the task and use this structure to experiment (see Chapter 13 for details on working with multiple information stores). When you have the data imported in all the proper fields, move (or copy) it from the test PST to your working PST.

This solves two problems. First, if something goes wrong you're not jeopardizing any existing data (or data structures). Second, once you're satisfied you can easily move the data from one PST to another, which is about as safe and seamless as it comes.

- If you're bringing data in from a format foreign to Outlook (which is just about anything other than a PST), take the time to look carefully at the structure of the import file. If it's comma- or tab-delimited, you can view it in Notepad or WordPad. If it's a database file, track down a freeware file viewer on the Internet that's capable of showing you the contents of the file.

  The intent here is to eliminate surprises. Look at the fields, how they are laid out, and most importantly, how they differ from Outlook's. To see the internal structure of an Outlook folder, see the section "Import/Export: Not Just for File Transfer" later in this chapter or use the Map Fields option described earlier in this chapter.

- If you need to map your import file, get out a piece of paper and draw it. The dialogs Outlook uses are not resizable, which means you'll do a lot of scrolling to see fields. It's hard to get a true idea of the big picture in a 4" by 3" square.

  Write out the fields you're importing on one side of the page, and the fields Outlook offers on the other. Think carefully about what to put where. The more you plan, the easier the import.

- Back up your Outlook files *before* you begin—and we mean all of them. See Chapter 13 for the list of files to back up.

 NOTE *To import a Lotus Organizer 2.1 or a NetManage ECCO Pro file, you must have the program that was used to create the file installed on your computer.*

Outlook provides the following import options:

Import a vCard file (*.vcf*)
Import an iCalendar or vCalendar file (*.vcs*)
Import cc:Mail archive
Import from another program or file
Import Internet Mail and Account Settings
Import Internet Mail and Addresses

Under the "Import from another program or file" option, the following program formats can be imported into an Outlook information store:

ACT! Contact manager (2.0, 3.X, and 4.0)
Comma Separated Values (DOS or Windows)
dBase
ECCO (2.0, 3.0, 4.0)

Lotus Organizer (1.0, 1.1, 2.1, and Organizer 97)
Microsoft Access
Microsoft Excel
Microsoft FoxPro
Microsoft Mail
Personal Folder File
Schedule Plus (Interchange, 1.0, 7.0)
Sidekick (1.0, 7.0, and Sidekick 95)
Tab Separated Values (DOS or Windows)

All import/export functions in Outlook are wizard-driven, which—for the most part—guides you through the possible options and routines for a given format.

Importing an Access Database

This section walks you through the import process using an Access database as an example.

1. Begin by creating a new PST for the imported data. As outlined earlier in this chapter, this is a safe way to import any data into Outlook. Next, create one or more folders within this PST to match the data types you are importing.

2. Open the Import and Export Wizard (File → Import and Export), and select "Import from another program or file." Choose Microsoft Access. On the next dialog, locate the source file and determine how you want the records merged. If you're following our advice and using a new, empty PST, your choice here does not matter. When you import to an existing Outlook folder, your best option is to "Allow duplicates."

3. The next dialog, shown in Figure 12-3 (left), displays a list of the tables within the database structures. Selecting a table that does not have fields that match the destination folder automatically invokes the Map Custom Fields dialog.

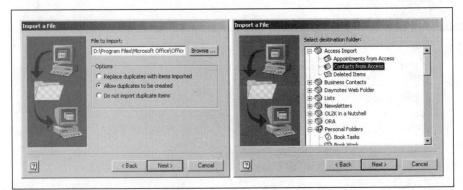

Figure 12-3: The Import Wizard

4. In our example, we have created a new PST called Access Import. This PST contains two folders: *Contacts from Access* and *Appointments from Access* (see Figure 12-3, right). If we select the "Import Customers" option from the list in Figure 12-4 (left), Outlook accepts this action without protest—we have a Contacts folder in the destination file, and Outlook knows how to map the Access table to this folder type. On the other hand, if we select "Import Categories" from the list, the Map Custom Fields dialog opens as shown in Figure 12-4 (right). In this case, despite the fact Outlook knows about categories, it does not recognize the fields (CategoryID, CategoryName, Description) from this table.

TIP # 138

Always Check Field Mappings

Your mileage is going to vary considerably with field mappings, even with a program Outlook knows and recognizes, like Access. Our advice is simple: always double-check mappings, even if the import program appears to know what it's doing with fields.

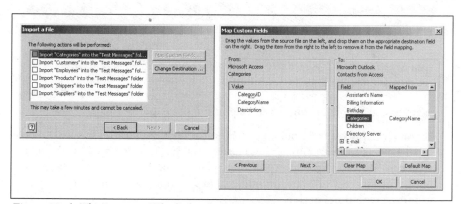

Figure 12-4: The Import a File dialog from the Import and Export Wizard detailing the possible actions to perform on an Access database

5. Once you have selected all the tables to import, doublecheck your settings before clicking the Finish button. Once you commit to the import, you cannot cancel the process; there is no undo option.

Exporting Data

Import and export are really just flip sides of the same coin. When you import, you're trying to save yourself entering data that already exists. When you export, you're trying to save someone else (sometimes you) repetitious data entry.

Anytime you export anything, you should be asking yourself several questions: What is the purpose of the export? Do you need to manipulate the data with another program? Is it for backup purposes? Are you sharing a file or a database with another person? In short, what is it you want to do with the information you export?

Outlook supports the following file export formats:

> Comma Separated Values (*.csv*), DOS and Windows format
> dBase (*.dbf*)
> Microsoft Access (*.mdb*)
> Microsoft Excel (*.xls*)
> Microsoft FoxPro (*.dbf*)
> Personal Folder File (*.pst*)
> Tab Separated Values (*.txt*), DOS and Windows format

Most of the options here are self-explanatory. The Comma and Tab Separated options export only the text and values from a record—all formatting, graphics, and attachments are removed. A Tab Separated format separates each field within a record with a tab. Comma Separated format uses a comma as a field separator; if a field itself contains a comma (for example, Outlook's File As field), the field's contents are enclosed in double quotation marks.

WARNING

When exporting to the Comma Separated Values or Tab Separated Values file format it is best to use the Windows, rather than the DOS, format because the DOS code page doesn't fully support the extended character set. You may lose certain characters unless the Windows format is used.

There are several factors to consider in determining an export format:

- If you are exporting Outlook information for your own use, export to the Personal Folders format. This option creates a subset of data, based on the folder type chosen at the time of export, but preserves both field structure and contents. Your success will vary according to folder contents and format used when exporting with other options.

- If the intent of the export is to share or transfer Outlook data with other people, find out what they have available for programs and use a format that preserves as much data as possible. For example, if your recipients use ACT! as a contact manager, find out if their version supports importing from an Outlook PST. If not, use dBase.

- If you're exporting Outlook information to distribute to a group of people and you don't know who can handle which formats, use the lowest common denominator approach. Export to either a Windows Comma or Tab Separated format.

Exporting to Word, PowerPoint, or Publisher

If you're exporting data for use in Microsoft Word or PowerPoint, select either the Tab Separated Values (Windows) or the Comma Separated Values (Windows) file type. Use the Comma Separated Values (Windows) format for Microsoft Publisher.

The Personal Folders File option exports a folder in the native format used by Outlook's information stores (PST). Note that you cannot export the complete PST—only a folder within the PST. You can, however, export a folder to a PST and then add further folders to this existing export file (see Tip # 140).

Exporting a Personal Folder File (PST)

To demonstrate the export process, we'll use the Personal Folder option. This is one of the safest (least likely to mangle data) choices available; use it whenever you can.

 You cannot export a complete PST using the Personal Folder File option, only folders within a PST. To back up or exchange a complete PST with someone, use one of the options discussed in Chapter 13.

To export a folder in PST format:

1. Go to File → Import and Export. This starts the Import and Export Wizard shown in Figure 12-5.

2. Select "Export to a file" from the "Choose an action to perform" list.

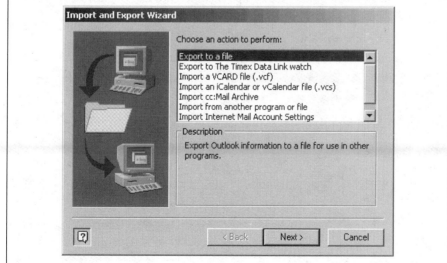

Figure 12-5: The Import and Export Wizard

3. Select a folder to export from the list in the Export Personal Folders dialog pictured in Figure 12-6 (left). To include subfolders, select this option. The Filter button opens the Filter dialog shown in Figure 12-6 (right). This allows you to filter specific items from the export. See Chapter 3, *Program Insights*, for an explanation of the various filter options and what they do.

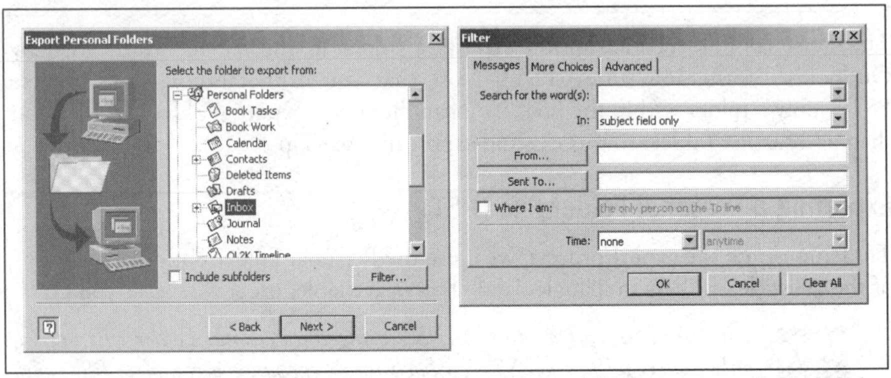

Figure 12-6: The Import and Export Wizard—selecting a folder to export (left) and the Filter dialog accessible from the Filter button (right)

4. In the Export Personal Folders dialog, shown in Figure 12-7 (left), provide a location and name for the exported file. When you select a duplicate option, consider your choice. Outlook doesn't prompt you when overwriting duplicates.

5. If the PST you've chosen for a Save location does not exist, the Create Microsoft Personal Folders dialog opens (see Figure 12-7, right). Fill in a name for the file, and any encryption or password options desired.

6. When you are satisfied with your choices, click Finish.

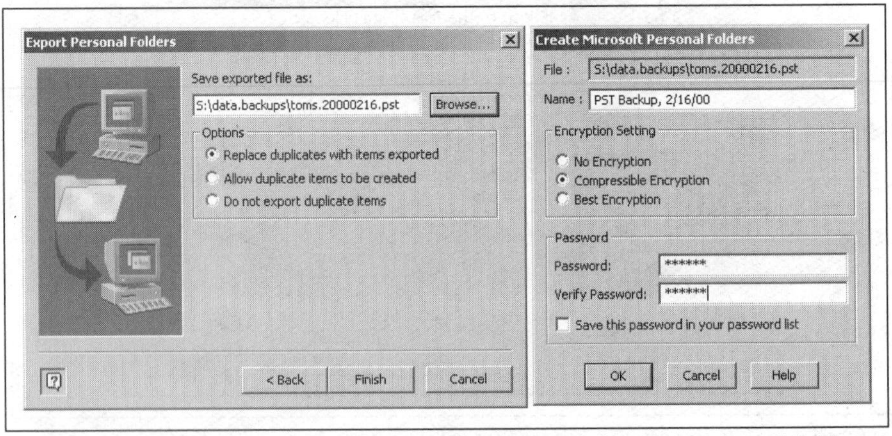

Figure 12-7: The Export Personal Folder dialog (left) and the Create Personal Folders dialog (right)

TIP # 140

Compiling a PST with Export

Generally speaking, we do not advocate importing or exporting to anything but an empty PST. But for every rule, there is an exception. One good use of the Outlook export function is to build up a PST-using data from diverse sources. In this case, you would create a "base" PST, and export files to specific folder types created there. If you use this approach, just make sure you keep your apples and oranges separate— one export to one folder only. You can also combine this technique with the "test information store principle" and build new complex PSTs from a diversity of sources, with little fear of overwriting existing data.

Import/Export: Not Just for File Transfer

Outlook has a glaring omission in its feature list: there is no way to Search and Replace a text string. This presents a vexing problem if you have a field (or fields) that changes for a large group of entries. One of the most common examples is when a new area code is added to a region. You could, of course, filter your contacts to show only those affected and manually edit each record. But there is a better way—export the data you want to change to a program with search-and-replace capabilities, make the required changes, and import the changes back into Outlook.

The following example walks you through this process. We'll use the area code quandary and Access to make the required changes. The following technique can be extrapolated to any Outlook item type and any external program. We chose contacts because they are the most likely candidates for a global change. Our choice of Access reflects the fact that Outlook supports the Access file format (*.mdb*) extremely well, and Access has the Search/Replace capabilities Outlook lacks.

1. Export your Contacts folder to an Access database. Choose File → Import and Export. From the Import and Export Wizard, select "Export to a file," and pick Microsoft Access as the file type. Select the Contacts folder from the selection list shown (see Figure 12-8).

2. Select a location for the exported file.

3. The next dialog lets you verify the folder to export, and via the Map button, view and modify how the fields contained in the folder selected will be mapped to the export file format. If you're using Access, simply let Outlook do its thing and click Finish.

4. Open the exported file in Access and double-click the Table view entry for the file from the Database picker.

5. Select Edit → Replace. The Find and Replace dialog is shown in Figure 12-9.

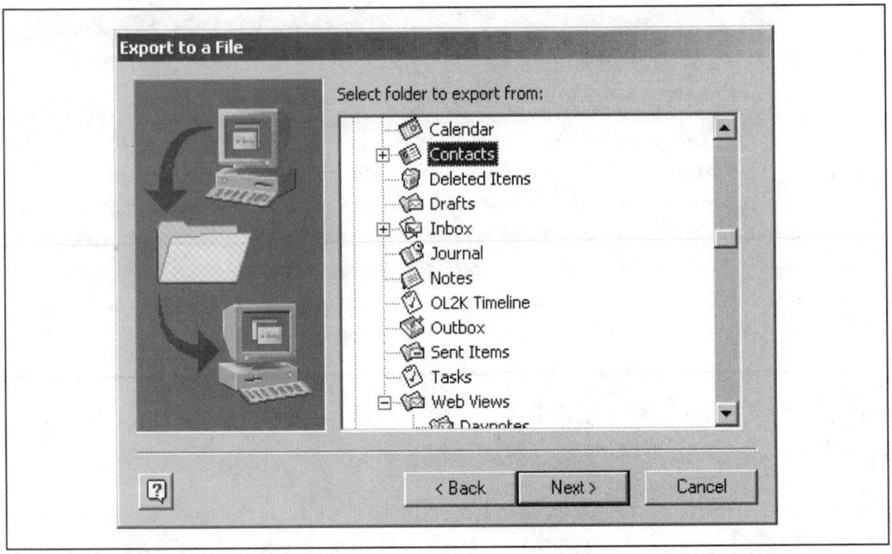

Figure 12-8: The Export to a File wizard showing the folder selection list dialog

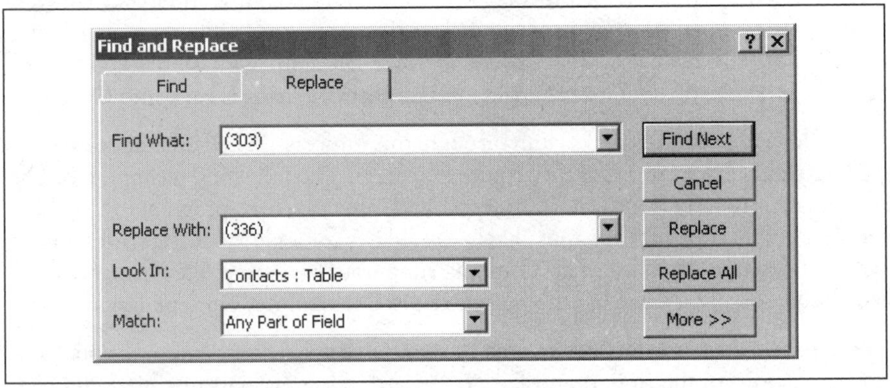

Figure 12-9: The Find and Replace dialog

6. Note the following items specific to the example discussed:

    - Outlook saves phone numbers with parentheses around the area code. To narrow your search/replace operation in Access, add these to both the Find What and Replace With fields. If you don't, Access will find every instance of the digits you provide—including addresses and phone numbers proper.

    - Under Look In, select the whole table (in the example shown, Contacts: Table). The default entry here is the first column of the open table.

    - Change the Match field to Any Part of Field. The default is Whole Field, and the entries in the Find What and Replace With field—providing you're using the method outlined here—will net you no returned matches.

7. Click Find Next to find the first instance of the search string. If this is a valid replacement, click Replace; if not, click Cancel to start over or Find Next to move to the next match. We do *not* recommend the use of the Replace All button unless you are absolutely, positively sure there are no aberrations in your data that might lead to a false match/replace.

8. Access does not have a separate save command. Moving your cursor out of a change field saves that change.

Now import your changes back into Outlook, keeping in mind the rule and tips provided at the beginning of the "Importing Data" section of this chapter. We recommend at the very minimum you do a backup of your PST before importing changes. Importing Access files is generally trouble-free, but it doesn't hurt to use the dummy folder trick just to be sure the changes made are what you want. Again, treat your existing data with the respect it deserves.

9. From Outlook, open the Import and Export Wizard (File → Import and Export).

10. Select "Import from another program or file," and choose Microsoft Access from the list provided. On the file location dialog, shown in Figure 12-10, note the duplication options.

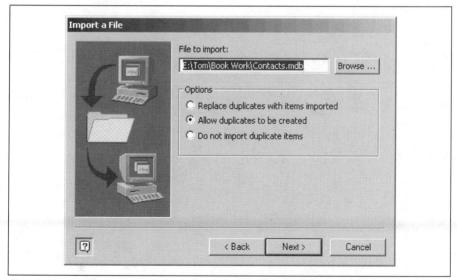

Figure 12-10: The Import a File dialog, which defines the file to import and duplication options

11. If you're importing directly into an existing Contacts folder, choose the "Replace duplicates with items imported" option. Duplicates are defined as two records with the same File As field. Selecting "Allow..." creates two entries for all entries—the record existing in Outlook, and the record being imported

from Access. "Do not import…" would, in this example, import none of the records in the Access table.

12. From the next dialog, pick a destination folder and click Next.

13. The final wizard dialog provides you with once last opportunity to review the import. Take a minute to double-check the details. When you're satisfied, click Finish.

TIP # 141

Outlook and Access—an Excellent Combo

If you are an Outlook power user, you owe it to yourself to get a copy of Access. Outlook supports the Access file format for both import and export, and our experience shows it to work very well. Access has excellent search/replace capabilities, plus a good report generator. In short, Access very nicely complements some of Outlook's shortcomings.

Chapter 13

File Management

File management is the art of keeping your data logically organized and healthy. We say art, because there are hundreds of approaches to managing files. Some work better than others; some people prefer one method to the next. The key is to develop a routine and follow it regularly. If you receive a lot of mail every day, sort and cull it every day, using Mail rules to automate repetitive tasks.

Keeping your data healthy necessitates either deleting or archiving items that are no longer pertinent. It also means making routine backups, complete enough to restore Outlook to a working state, with minimal reconfiguration. This includes not only data, but also key configuration files that are spread throughout your filesystem and Registry. Folders, files, locations, and contents all need to be understood and used properly to maintain Outlook in racing form.

We begin by reintroducing two terms used in numerous places elsewhere in this book. The default information store and the system folders take on another layer of significance, because they define what you can do with certain objects, and why things work as they do:

Default information store
> The location to which Outlook delivers POP mail. It is set from the Properties tab of the information store as explained in Chapter 3, *Program Insights*. Outlook can have only one default information store.

System folders
> When you install Outlook (or when you create a new default store), a set of *system folders* is generated: Calendar, Contacts, Tasks, Notes, Journal, Inbox, Outbox, Sent Items, Deleted Items, and Drafts. These system folders cannot be deleted—even from an information store that is no longer the default.

Archive and Backup

Like most programs, Outlook generates both data and configuration files. Maintaining copies of these files can take one of two forms:

Archiving
> An Outlook feature that copies (and optionally deletes) items older than a specified date to a separate information store. Archiving is typically used to store

records you no longer need to access on a daily basis. It can be invoked manually, or configured to run at specified intervals automatically (AutoArchive). Archiving is done from within Outlook, with the program running. Archiving does not back up the complete information store, nor does it back up any program configuration files. It simply moves items from the default information store to another information store.

Backup

A generic term that typically refers to copying data and configuration files to either an alternate location (for example a network drive) or some form of removable media. In this chapter, we use this term to describe backing up *all* of Outlook's data and configuration files. And as you're about to discover, a comprehensive backup of Outlook is a complex process. In order to back up the default information store, Outlook *must be closed.*

TIP # 142

Outlook Does Not Share Nicely

When Outlook is running, it locks any information stores in use (that is, displayed in the Folder List) for exclusive access. This explains why Outlook must be closed before the default information store can be backed up. It also explains why you cannot simply put a PST on a network drive and share it with others. The first person to open the store locks everyone else out.

Used in combination, these two techniques allow you a great deal of flexibility in keeping your data safe, and your information stores to a manageable size. Different approaches might consist of:

- AutoArchiving system folders that fill quickly, and are not accessed routinely (for example, Deleted Items and Sent Items) every three or four days.

- Manually archiving other folders when the need arises.

- Hourly *xcopy* backups of your primary information store (requires Outlook be shut down using Exit and Logoff in CW and simply Closed in IMO).

- Nightly tape backups of your working information stores.

- A weekly tape backup of all information stores (including archives) and configuration files.

- A biweekly copy of all information stores and configuration files to two CD-Rs—one stored on-site, the other stored off-site.

The approach and combination of tools you use is not as important as ensuring you have good, *restorable* backups of your data and program settings. Backups that are not restorable are worthless.

TIP # 143

Test Your Backups

Make it a habit to test your backups once a month by randomly picking a selection of files and physically restoring them to hard disk.

AutoArchive

AutoArchive is a way to archive items automatically based on their age. If enabled, AutoArchive checks the contents of specified Outlook folders and compares the item dates to the configuration settings for each folder. Items older than a specified number of days, weeks, or months are targeted for archive, and the dialog shown in Figure 13-1 is displayed. Click Yes to archive, and No to cancel the process. Canceling does not turn AutoArchive off; it simply defers it for another *x* days.

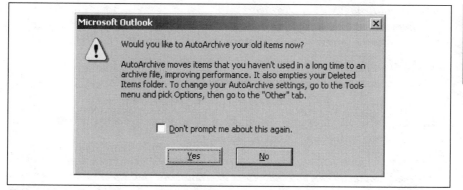

Figure 13-1: Outlook's AutoArchive dialog

Outlook's AutoArchive settings can be configured on two levels: globally (all Outlook folders) and on a per-folder basis. Per-folder settings always override Global settings. Change Global settings using the AutoArchive dialog found under Tools → Options → Other (see Figure 13-2).

AutoArchive every x *days*

Determines how often AutoArchive runs automatically. Each *x* days, AutoArchive automatically checks folders configured to AutoArchive old items. Each folder may have different criteria for "old." Clear this checkbox to disable AutoArchive. With AutoArchive disabled, you can still archive, but you have to initiate the process yourself.

Prompt before AutoArchive

This option, which is enabled by default, prompts you with the dialog shown in Figure 13-1 before the AutoArchive begins.

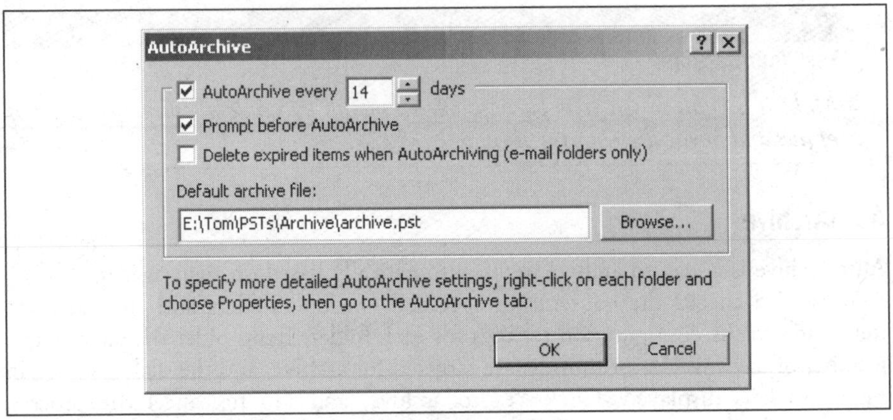

Figure 13-2: Outlook's default AutoArchive setting dialog

Delete expired items when AutoArchiving

Moves any messages that fall within the date criterion for archiving to the Deleted items folder. Note that this option only applies to Mail folders.

Default archive file

Sets the default location where archive files are stored.

These defaults apply to the system folders listed in Table 13-1. Each folder type has a date range that specifies how old an item is before it is archived, based on the criteria shown in the column "Date Range Based On."

> **NOTE** *Contact folders do not support AutoArchive. You can manually archive a contacts folder, but no records are transferred in the process.*

Table 13-1: Outlook's Default AutoArchive Settings for Folder Type

Folder Type	AutoArchive By Default	Archive Items Older Than	Date Range Based On
Calendar	Yes	Six months	Item start date or date of last modification.
Contacts	N/A	N/A	Not archived.
Tasks	Yes	Six months	Completed date or last modified. Uncompleted task are not archived.
Notes	No	Three months	Date created or late modified.
Journal	Yes	Six months	Entry date or last modified.
Inbox	No	Three months	Date received or last modified.
Outbox	No	Three months	Date created or last modified.
Drafts	No	Three months	Date created or late modified.
Sent Items	Yes	Two months	Date sent.
Deleted Items	Yes	Two months	Date moved to folder.

AutoArchive is disabled by default for newly created folders. Archive defaults can be changed on a per-folder basis. To enable or change a folder's AutoArchive settings, select the folder and choose Properties from the context menu. The AutoArchive tab is shown in Figure 13-3.

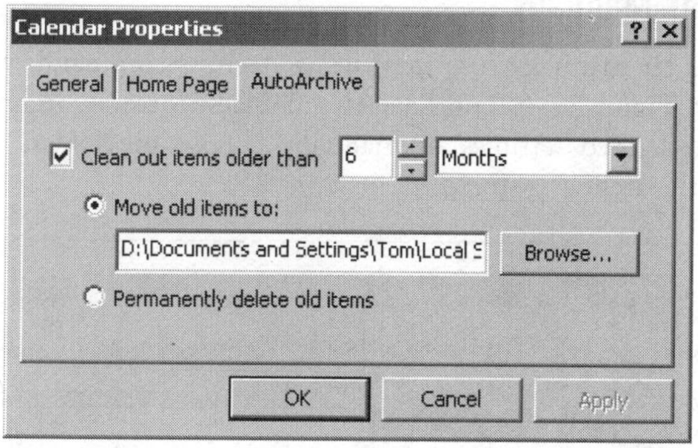

Figure 13-3: The folder Properties AutoArchive tab

Clean out items older than

Specifies the age of the youngest items that will be processed by AutoArchive. With the setting shown, items up to six months old will remain in the main information store, while items six months and a day old or older will be moved or deleted. This is also the on/off switch for AutoArchive. Clear this checkbox to disable AutoArchive for the selected folder.

Move old items to

Specifies the fully qualified filename of the file to which old items will be moved. The default location on a multiuser system is *<user path>\Local Settings\Application Data\Microsoft\Outlook.*

Archives are saved as PST files, with a default filename of *archive.pst*. We highly recommend you name your archive files using some form of date notation (for example, SENTYYYYMMDD–YYYYMMDD would contain archived items from the Sent Items folder from the period YYYYMMDD to YYYYMMDD).

TIP # 144

Create a Separate PST for Your Archives

Consider creating a new PST for your archived files (see the section "Using Multiple PSTs" later in this chapter). Within this PST create subfolders under each item type (Calendar, Notes, Mail).

Permanently delete old items

Selecting this option deletes items older than the period specified. They are not moved to the Deleted Items folder, they are *gone*. This is not a wise option to select except for junk folders, or if you do backups religiously every night.

Archiving Items Manually

To archive a folder manually, use the File → Archive command, which opens the dialog shown in Figure 13-4. You have two choices: force an archive based on the AutoArchive predefined settings, or manually choose the folder, date range, and location where the archive is stored.

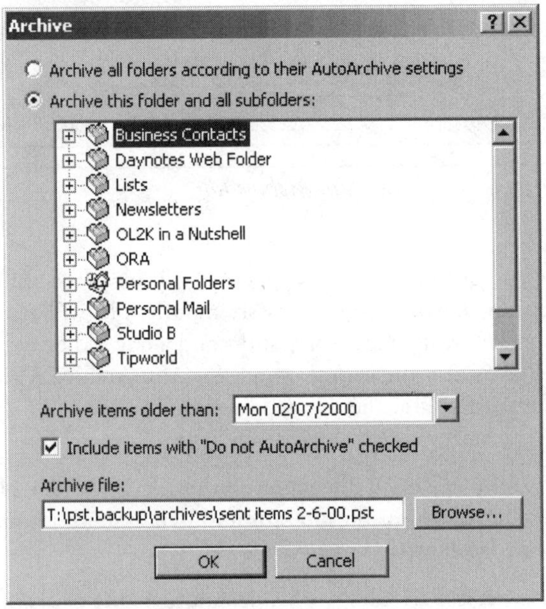

Figure 13-4: Manually archiving an Outlook folder

At the top of the Archive dialog are two radio buttons that determine the type of archive performed. The first is:

Archive all folders

Forces a manual archive, based on the AutoArchive settings for each folder.

TIP # 145

Cancel a Manual (or Automatic) Archive

If you start an archive process then decide you want to cancel it, click the "Archiving . . ." icon displayed in Outlook's status bar (the bar at the very bottom of the active Outlook window), and select Cancel Archiving from the context menu displayed.

Below this is a second option. It allows you to manually archive a selected folder, according to the following parameters:

Archive this folder and all subfolders
> Choose a folder to archive. This can be a PST or a folder within a PST. Outlook archives all items within the selected folder, plus all subfolders.

Archive items older than
> Enter a date. All items before this date are included in the archive process, provided the next option is not selected. Click the down-arrow to display a graphical calendar (the *Date Navigator*, see Chapter 7, *Calendar*) or type a date directly in the field. All Outlook date entry shortcuts (again, see Chapter 7 or Chapter 9, *Tasks*) work here. For example, typing 2mo ago <Tab> converts the current system date displayed to a date two months prior to this.

Include item with "Do not AutoArchive" checked
> Every Outlook item, regardless of type, can be marked for exclusion from all archive activity. To enable this property, open the item and from the Form menu, choose File → Properties. Place a checkmark in the "Do not archive this item" option. Clearing the "Include items with . . ." checkbox causes the archive process to ignore such items. Marking the checkbox causes the archive process to ignore the "Do not archive . . ." flag and process the item according to the date range in effect for the folder that contains it.

Archive file
> Specifies a filename and location.

Backing Up Outlook

Outlook's engineers were certainly consistently inconsistent. Not only are Outlook's option dialogs strewn over a wide range of locations, so are the files that control program settings. This makes doing a complete backup of Outlook ridiculously difficult. The good news is, we've compiled a list that should both help with backups and give you some insights into where to look for a configuration file should the need arise.

TIP # 146

How Often Should You Back Up?

A good rule of thumb is: how much data can you afford to lose if your system went down this instant (and was not fixable)? Your answer to this question determines your backup schedule.

Table 13-2 lists Outlook's information stores and configuration files, their extensions, and common locations. A quick glance at this list should immediately raise warning flags—unless you are doing a complete backup of your hard disk every night, backing up your PST files alone is not enough. To restore Outlook to its currently working state you also need to back up many other key files.

Here is how to read Table 13-2:

File column
> Lists the components that should be included in a full backup.

Extension column
> Is a reference to the extensions associated with the file or files in the first column.

Location column
> Lists common locations where Outlook saves user data and configuration files. These locations vary from system to system due to the way different versions of Windows lay out folder structures. For example, under Windows 98, Outlook saves information stores under *Windows*; NT 4.0 saves stores under *WINNT\ Profiles*\<user>*Application Data\Microsoft\Outlook*; and Windows 2000 saves stores under *Documents and Settings*\<user>\ *Application Data\Microsoft\Outlook*. You can also elect to store your PSTs anywhere your heart desires. This is the reason we provided the Extension column. If you can't locate the files listed using Windows Explorer, use the Windows command Start → Search → "For files or folders" and enter the extension provided.

Table 13-2: Outlook File Locations

File	Extension	Location
Information Stores	.pst	*<user>\Application Data\Microsoft\Outlook*
Offline Stores	.ost	*<user>\Local Settings\Application Data\Microsoft\ Outlook*
Personal Address Book	.pab	*<user>\Local Settings\Application Data\Microsoft\ Outlook*
Windows Address Book	.wab	*<user>\Application Data\Microsoft\Address Book*
Menu and View Settings	.dat	*<user>\Application Data\Microsoft\Outlook*
Outlook Bar Shortcuts	.fav	*<user>\Application Data\Microsoft\Outlook*
Default Program Settings	.inf	*<user>\Application Data\Microsoft\Outlook*
Outlook Nicknames (user mail settings)	.nick	*<user>\Application Data\Microsoft\Outlook*
Rules	.rwz	*<user>\Application Data\Microsoft\Outlook*
Print Styles	None	*<user>\Application Data\Microsoft\Outlook*
User Signatures	.rtf, .txt, .html	*<user>\Application Data\Microsoft\Signatures*
User Stationery	.html	*<user>\Application Data\Microsoft\Stationery*

Table 13-2: Outlook File Locations (continued)

File	Extension	Location
Custom Forms		*<user>*\Local Settings\Application Data\Microsoft\ *FORMS*
Dictionary	.txt	*<user>*\Application Data\Microsoft\Proof
Templates	.oft	*<user>*\Application Data\Microsoft\Templates
Registry Settings	.reg	See Appendix B, in particular, the keys under HKEY_ CURRENT_USER\Software\: Microsoft\Office\9.0\Outlook Microsoft\Office\Outlook Microsoft\WAB Microsoft\Shared Tools\Outlook Microsoft\Exchange \Microsoft\Windows NT\CurrentVersion\Windows Messaging Subsystem\Profiles\Microsoft Outlook Internet Settings

While the list in Table 13-2 is long and obnoxious, there are ways to ease the pain of backing up Outlook. Here is one solution that can serve as a starting point for creating your own tailored solution:

1. Create a folder—preferably on a separate partition—and move all your data files here. Good candidates for subfolders are: PSTs, Templates, Documents, Downloads, and that ever-favorite folder, Stuff. For computers shared by more than one user, the folder structure should be:

   User\<name>\<subfolders>

2. Create four subfolders under the PST location you created in Step 1: *Archives, Registry Backups, Backups,* and *Settings.* You should end up with a folder structure similar to that shown in Figure 13-5.

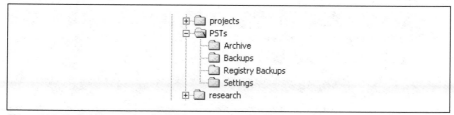

Figure 13-5: One example of a folder structure for PSTs

3. If you installed Outlook as part of Office 2000, go to Word or Excel and set the location for your user templates (Tools → Options → File Locations) to the Template folder created in Step 1.

4. With Outlook closed, move your information stores to the PST folder created in Step 1. When you restart Outlook, it will scratch its head and tell you it can't find the default information store. Point it to the new location using the

dialog displayed. Now you have all Outlook's key *data* files in one place. Unfortunately, there is no easy way to move configuration files to this same location.

5. Download the Personal Folders Backup program outlined in the next section. Configure it to back up your PST files on a suitable schedule (we recommend daily). Point the location of these backups to the *Data\PST\Backups* folder created in Step 2.

6. Once a week schedule 30 minutes to back up Outlook. Complete the following steps:

   - Using regedit, copy the complete HKEY_CURRENT_USER\Software\ Microsoft key to the Registry Backups location under your PST folder.

   - Copy the contents of *\Documents and Settings\<user>\Application Data\ Microsoft\Outlook* (in Windows 2000), or *\WINDOWS\Local Settings\ Application Data\Microsoft\Outlook* (Windows 98) to the Settings subfolder. If you're concerned about losing your Custom Dictionary, Custom Stationery, Signatures, or Custom Forms, copy these files to this same folder using the locations provided in Table 13-2. If you use Outlook as a client to Exchange, copy the contents of the *\Documents and Settings\ <user>\Local Settings\Application Data\Microsoft\Outlook* (Windows 2000) folder to the same location, or create a new folder specific to this data.

   - Now run a removable media backup (tape, CD-R, Zip, etc.) on your Data folder. When it finishes, you will have a complete backup of Outlook in a form that lets you restore anything, from one Registry key to a complete program configuration.

 The paths and structures presented here work for any system configured for multiple users (NT, Windows 2000, or Windows 98).

TIP # 147

Outlook Causes Needless Backups

Each time Outlook opens an information store, it immediately toggles on the Archive bit for that file, even if it has not written to it. That means that any backup method that depends on archive bit status to determine whether a file requires backup will back up any information store that has been opened since the last full backup. So, for example, if you open a 150 MB archive PST file in Outlook to read an old email message, Outlook immediately marks that file as requiring backup, even though its contents have not changed. If you back up to tape, that's no big deal. But if you use xcopy to perform frequent on-the-fly backups, as we do, having large archive files unnecessarily marked for backup is a pain. To fix the problem, display the Properties sheet for the file and clear the Archive check box.

Personal Folders Backup

Until late 1999, Outlook had no internal means to back up information stores. This has been remedied with a program add-on called Personal Folders Backup. At the time of this writing, this file was available from:

http://officeupdate.microsoft.com/2000/downloaddetails/Pfbackup.htm

It's free, the download is small (182 KB), and it provides you with a configurable backup routine directly from within Outlook. Installation instructions are provided on the download page.

 The Personal Folders Backup add-on backs up your PST files only. It does not, however, back up OSTs, your Address Books, or any of the other various Outlook configuration files listed in Table 13-2. In other words, use it for daily backups of PSTs, but make sure you also do routine backups of all your Outlook configuration files.

Once installed, a Backup command is added to Outlook's File menu. Selecting it opens the dialog shown in Figure 13-6.

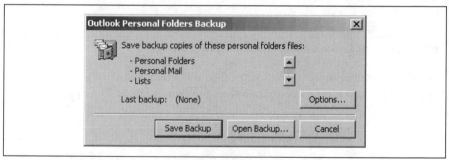

Figure 13-6: The Outlook Personal Folders Backup dialog

This dialog lists the PSTs currently selected for backup, the date the last backup was performed, and buttons to activate the following options:

Save Backup
Starts a backup using the configuration defined on the Backup Options dialog described below.

Open Backup
Selects a backup file to open. Backups are saved as *.pst* files, so you can actually open any PST using this option. Opening a file displays it in the Folder List; view/copy/move items just as you would any other information store.

Options
Opens the Backup Options dialog shown in Figure 13-7. Here you can set a reminder, choose which information stores are included in the backup, and a location and filename for the backup. Each PST listed can be backed up to a

unique location. The default filename is the first word used for the PST description, followed by the word "backup."

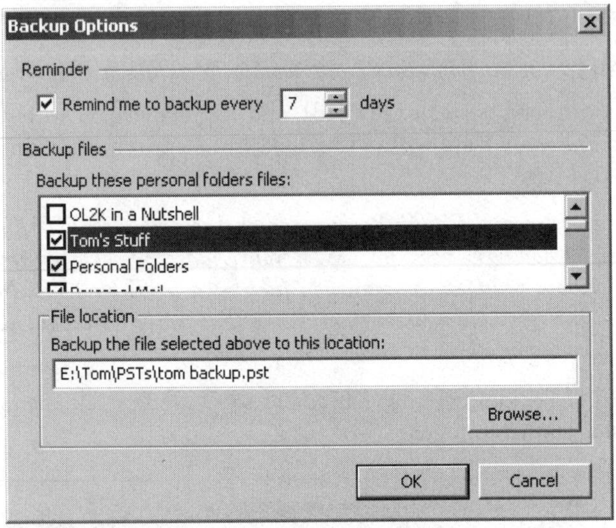

Figure 13-7: The Personal Folders Backup Options dialog

A reminder appears every *x* days identical to the screenshot shown in Figure 13-7. Click Save Backup and an information dialog shown in Figure 13-8 appears.

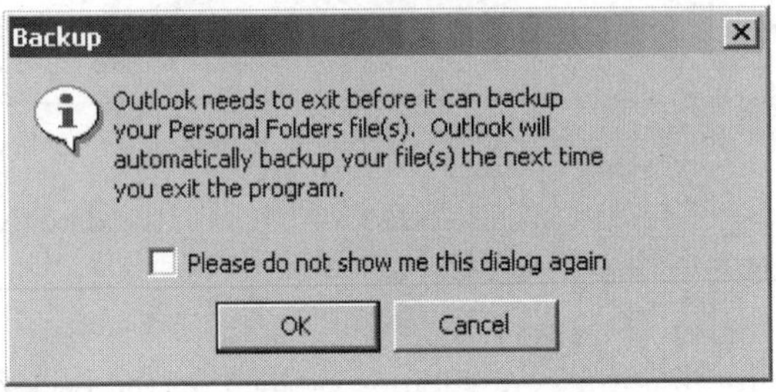

Figure 13-8: The Personal Folder Backup information dialog

To disable Personal Folders Backup, open the Backup Options dialog (see Figure 13-7), and deselect the reminder option and all the information stores listed.

File and Folder Management 101

The following topics are a quick overview of what we consider to be the essential tools for managing Outlook files and folders.

Use the Folder List

The Outlook Bar is a good way to quickly switch folders, and the large icon option provides good targets when you need to create a new item type from an existing record (for example, drop a message on the Calendar icon to create a new appointment). But for serious file and folder management, use a combination of the Folder List and context menus.

TIP # 148

Remember the Pushpin

Whenever you use the Folder List for file management, remember to "lock" the view open using the pushpin icon in the upper-right corner. Context menus are not available until the pushpin is selected.

Using Context Menus

Figure 13-9 shows the context menu displayed when you right-click any information store from either the Outlook Bar (the Outlook Today icon, for example) or the Folder List.

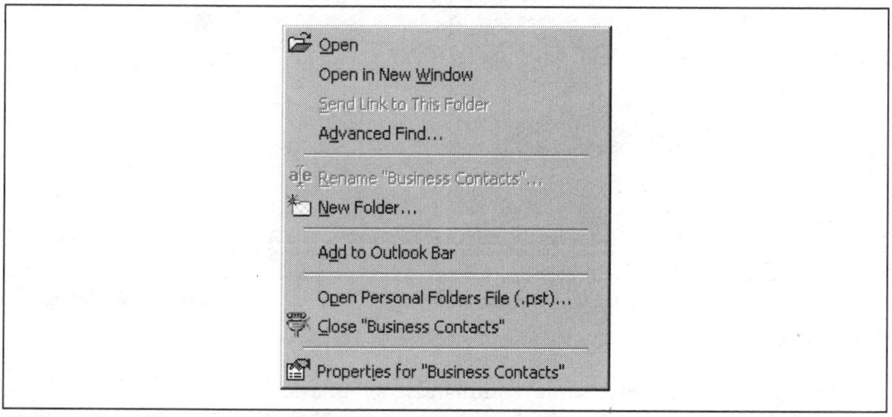

Figure 13-9: The Personal Folders context menu

Open in New Window

Opens the selected store in a new Outlook window, distinct from the existing one. This is useful if you have a need to see the contents of two PSTs simultaneously. For file management chores, working from the Folder List is a better option.

Advanced Find

Opens the Advanced Find dialog, allowing you to search the selected store.

Rename [PST]

This command is always unavailable from the context menu. To rename a PST, select Properties, click the Advanced button, and use the Name field at the top of the Properties dialog.

Add to Outlook Bar

Adds the selected store, as a shortcut, to the Outlook Bar. Adding a *folder* to the Outlook Bar always places it in the My Shortcuts Group. PSTs are added to the *open* group.

Right-click a folder from the Folder List to display the context menus shown in Figure 13-10.

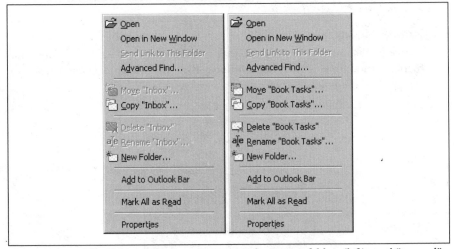

Figure 13-10: The Folder actions context menus for System folders (left), and "normal" folders (right)

In Figure 13-10 (left) some commands are unavailable. This is because the folder selected is a system folder. You cannot move, delete, or rename an Outlook system folder.

TIP # 149

An Optional Source of Context Menus

All the context menus discussed in the preceding section can be activated by right-clicking the title bar above the view; for example, when the Inbox is open, the bar runs between the Inbox label and the small envelope icon.

Multiple Outlooks

The "Open in a New Window" command opens the selected object (right-click either an information store or folder) in a new Outlook window. This is an extremely useful command. For example, you can set the current window to display the Folder List and your Inbox, open a new window containing your Calendar or Task List, and minimize this new window to the Windows Task Bar. You can now refer to your Calendar by simply maximizing it from the Task Bar, rather than switching the current view. View changes made in one window are independent of all other currently open windows. See Figure 13-11 for an example of three Outlook windows open simultaneously.

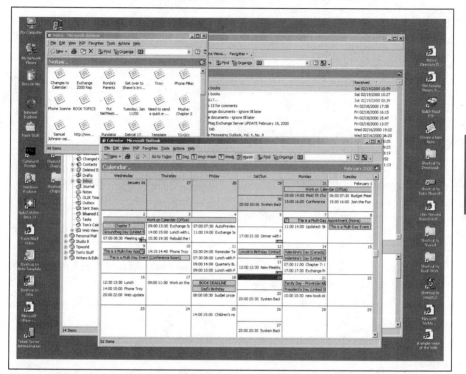

Figure 13-11: Use the Open in a New Window command to display multiple Outlook windows

Managing Deleted Items

Like the Windows Recycle Bin, Outlook does not discard deleted files immediately; they are moved to the Deleted Items folder first. Every information store has its own Deleted Items folder, and it is created automatically when the store is created. You cannot delete this folder; it is a system folder, and as such is owned and protected by Outlook.

There is only one global option affecting the Deleted Items folder, located on the Other tab of the Tools → Options dialog (see Figure 13-12). Selecting this checkbox empties the folder each time you exit Outlook. Note that this empties the Deleted Item folder of the *default information store only*. If you use multiple PSTs, these must be either emptied manually, or set to AutoArchive and "Permanently delete old items."

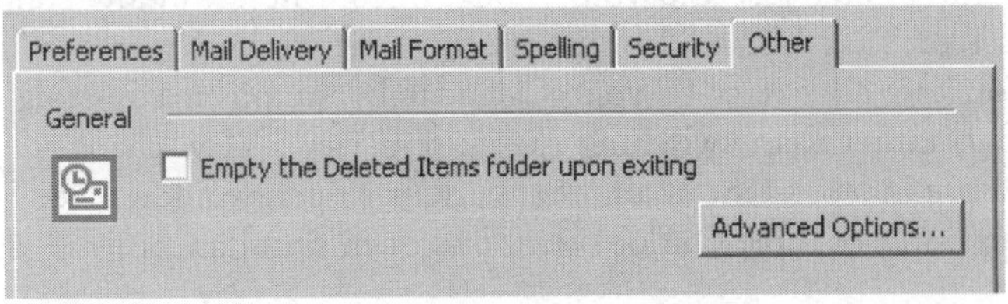

Preferences	Mail Delivery	Mail Format	Spelling	Security	Other

General

☐ Empty the Deleted Items folder upon exiting

[Advanced Options...]

Figure 13-12: The Deleted Items folder option controls whether the folder is emptied when Outlook exits

In addition, to these automatic methods, you can:

- Delete an item and bypass sending it to the Deleted Items folder by holding down the Shift key.

- Empty the Deleted Items folder manually by selecting it and choosing Empty "Deleted Items" Folder from the context menu.

- Empty the Deleted Items folder manually by making it your current view, selecting all items (Ctrl+A), and choosing delete from the toolbar or keyboard.

- Delete individual records from the Deleted Items folder just as you would any other Outlook item.

NOTE *It's not a bad idea to archive the deleted items folder before you manually delete it—just in case.*

Compacting Information Stores

Outlook's information stores are not unlike the filesystem on your hard drive—deleting items leaves holes in the structure that are not immediately reclaimed. This causes the store to increase in size over time, sometimes dramatically.

To reclaim this space, Outlook provides a command to compact your information stores. Right-click a store from either the Outlook Bar or Folder List, and select Properties from the context menu. Choose Advanced and click the Compact Now button.

Using the Inbox Repair Tool

Outlook seldom munges its own information stores. When it does, however, a lot of data hangs in the balance. Fortunately, Microsoft provides the Inbox Repair Tool, which can usually fix damaged *.pst* and *.ost* files successfully. Even files that are so badly corrupted that Outlook refuses to open them can often be fixed. Running the Inbox Repair Tool performs eight checks on the designated information store, and allows you to make a backup of the damaged store before making the repair attempt. Even if the Inbox Repair Tool is unable to fix the damaged file entirely, it at least salvages as much data as possible.

To run the Inbox Repair tool, change to *Program Files\Common Files\System\Mapi\ 1033\NT* and double-click *scanpst.exe* to display the Inbox Repair Tool dialog. Enter the full path and filename of the *.pst* file you want to check, or use Browse to select it. Once you have entered the name of a *.pst* or *.ost* file, the Inbox Repair Tool activates the Start button, as shown in Figure 13-13.

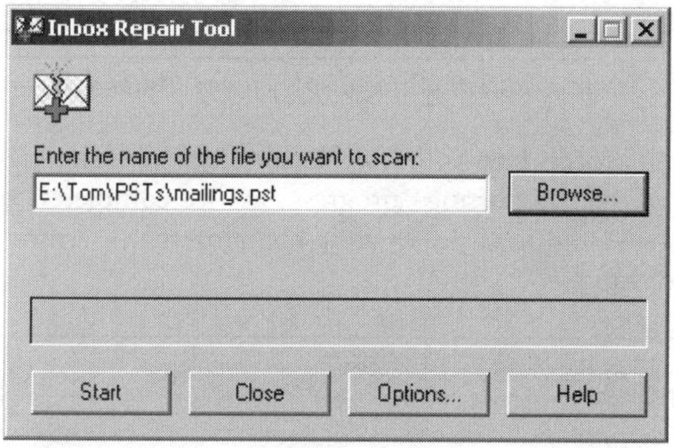

Figure 13-13: Outlook's Inbox Repair Tool dialog

Click Options if you want to set logging options for the repair process. You can elect to disable logging, add to an existing log, or replace the existing log, as shown in Figure 13-14.

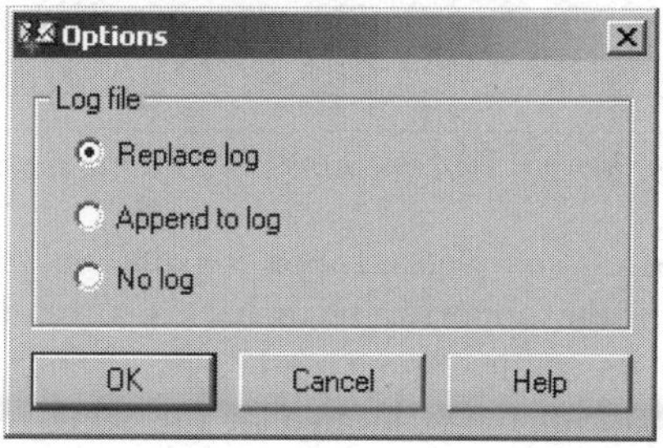

Figure 13-14: Scanpst's log file options

The Inbox Repair Tool requires exclusive access to the *.pst* file it attempts to repair. If you have not closed Outlook, or if for some other reason the Inbox Repair Tool is unable to lock the file for exclusive access, the dialog shown in Figure 13-15 appears. The most likely cause is that you have not closed Outlook, or you have closed it using the Exit command rather than the Exit and Log Off command (in CW mode). To remedy this, open Outlook again, choose File → Exit and Log Off, and then click Start on the Inbox Repair Tool dialog again. If the warning dialog appears again, some other process has the *.pst* file locked. Sometimes shutting down and restarting the computer clears this problem. We have seen one incident, however, where even this did not remedy the situation. In this case, the *.pst* file was corrupted beyond the ability of the Inbox Repair Tool to fix it.

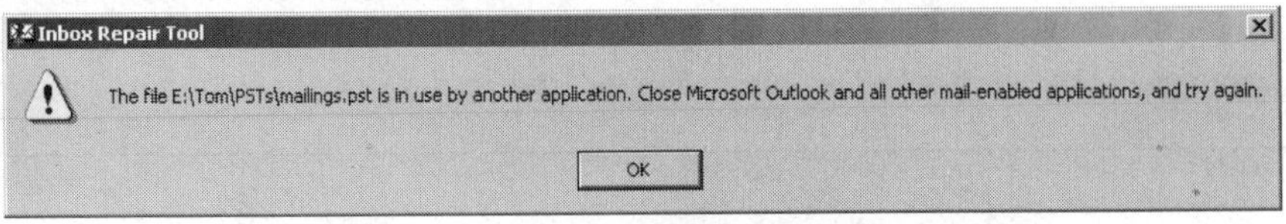

Figure 13-15: The Scanpst caution dialog display when Outlook is running

Once the scanning process begins, Inbox Repair Tool performs eight separate passes through the *.pst* file, reporting progress as it completes each phase (See Figure 13-16). If the file is large, or if it contains many errors, this process can require an hour or more.

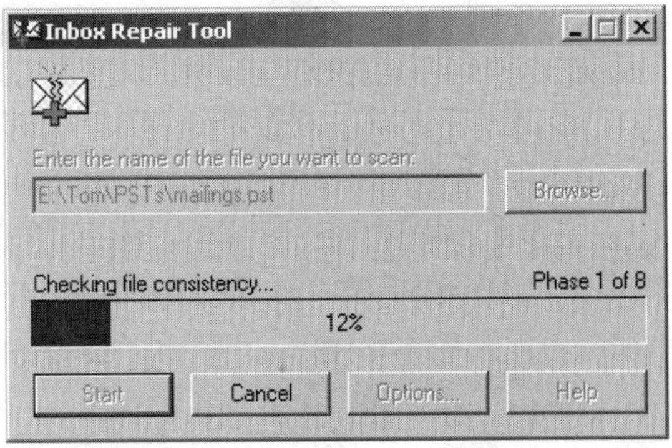

Figure 13-16: The Inbox Repair Tool checking a PST's file consistency

When the scanning process completes, Inbox Repair Tool displays a report of what it found and offers you the opportunity to back up the damaged *.pst* file before attempting repairs, as shown in Figure 13-17. By default, the backup option is enabled. The default backup file is located in the same folder and has the same name as the main *.pst* file, but with a *.bak* extension. To attempt to repair the *.pst* file, click Repair.

When the repair process completes, you're usually greeted with the happy dialog shown in Figure 13-18, which indicates that errors have been repaired and no data was lost. If Inbox Repair Tool finds errors that it cannot fix, it informs you and does its best to save whatever data is salvageable.

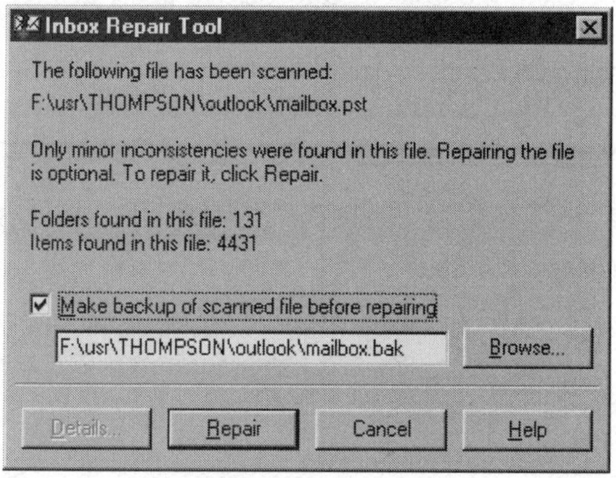

Figure 13-17: The Inbox Repair Tool dialog if a damaged file is detected

Figure 13-18: The Inbox Repair Tool "Repair complete" dialog

Using Multiple PSTs

Typically, people who use Outlook accept the program defaults at installation. Outlook creates one PST for each user, and stores all that user's data here.

Multiple PSTs offer several advantages relative to storing data in one file:

- They offer a logical way of organizing related topics (for some suggestions, see the "File Management Synopsis" section at the end of this chapter).

- If a PST becomes corrupt (it doesn't happen often, but it does happen), you do not lose all your data, just a subset. Given that you're doing routine backups, it's relatively easy to restore a subset of data to a useable working state.

- It keeps the memory demands of your system in check. Most people do not need access to all their data, all the time. Every PST Outlook has open consumes memory resources. Using multiple PSTs means that you can keep information stores not in use closed (for example, a PST of old Calendar items or an Archive of messages).

- PST files are horribly inefficient in the way they store data. Many items within an information store are replicated due to the flat-file structure used. Also,

PSTs do not reclaim the space used by deleted items well (Folder Properties → Advanced → Compact Now). This means that PSTs get *big* in a hurry. It's not uncommon for a PST with several thousand records to be over 200 MB. Splitting your information stores into smaller chunks keeps them manageable, and allows you to keep backup copies on media like Zip disks.

TIP # 150

Outlook Remembers PST State

Outlook remembers which PSTs were last in use when you close the program. If you have store A, B, and C open, and exit Outlook, the next time you start the program it will open stores A, B, and C. So close the stores you are not actively using before exiting Outlook.

There are, of course, some drawbacks to multiple PSTs. When using multiple information stores, keep the following points in mind:

- If you use mail rules (see Chapter 6, *Mail*) for managing your Inbox, and one of those rules copies/moves items to a separate store, that store must be open and accessible when Outlook is running.

- Outlook's Find command does not work across multiple PSTs. You can only search the contents of one store at a time.

- Alarms and reminders only work for items contained in Outlook's default information store

The most important factor in using multiple stores successfully is the forethought you put into the structure and naming conventions you use. Figure 13-19 illustrates one example of using multiple PSTs under Outlook. Like mail rules and categories, the up-front effort is dramatically repaid in usability down the road. Take the time to think about how PST files can best be adopted to your organizational needs. We find it useful to consider them in the same manner as you might approach splitting up your physical files among several filing cabinets. Are these obvious groupings for your files? Do you need access to everything every day? What labels can you put on the drawer fronts that quickly identify the contents?

Here are some suggestions for PST groupings:

Newsletters
Weekly or infrequent subscriptions, with subfolders named for the site or publication.

Lists
Newsgroup subscriptions.

Personal Mail
Friends and family, with subfolders in the form Lastname, firstname.

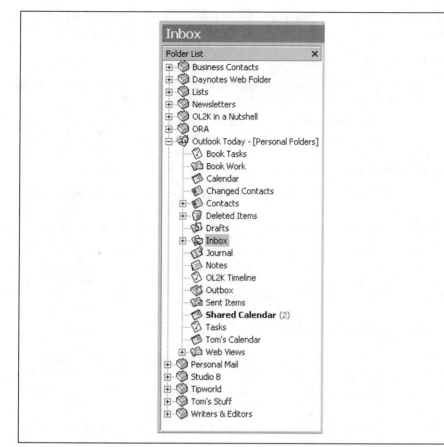

Figure 13-19: Folder List view showing one example of a multiple PST structure

Ideas

Backburner stuff.

Business Contacts

Organized by company.

Archives

Archive records and create a subfolder structure based on item type and date.

Tips

Organized by product. There are hundreds of daily mailings out there with useful tips on just about any software product imaginable. Keep the good ones for future reference.

For example, a PST could be created to organize a project. This PST could contain folders for Notes, Mail, Calendar, and Journal entries. Messages arriving in your Inbox relating to the project can either be copied or moved (the default is move) to the appropriate folder. Dropping an email on the project's Calendar folder will automatically create an appointment, filling in the subject and time, and copies the details of the message header (From, Sent, To, and Subject) to the Notes field.

With all this structural and logistical discussion out of the way, creating multiple PSTs is a relatively easy process:

1. Go to the File menu and select New → Personal Folders File (PST).

2. The usual Office "Create New File" dialog is displayed. Select a folder location and give the PST a name. We recommend storing all your PSTs in one folder for backup and file management simplicity. The name you give the PST here can be different than the name actually displayed in your Folder list.

3. The next dialog lets you name the PST; what you put here will be the name displayed in your folder tree. You can specify encryption and assign a password to the PST. The PST is then created and displayed in your folder tree.

4. From here, drag a subfolder from your main PST to the newly created PST. The default drag and drop action is a move; to copy a folder hold down the Ctrl key as you drag (or right-click on an item and drag it). Note that each individual store has its own Recycle Bin, specific to that PST.

File Management Synopsis

In this chapter we've shown you how to archive and back up data, manage files and folders, and organize PSTs into separate information stores. Now let's tie all this information together, along with the tips and tricks presented in other chapters. Here are some suggestions for managing your Outlook data:

- Use separate information stores to structure and organize your records. While Outlook's Find command does not work across information stores (Arrghh), if you organize your PSTs logically, it should be easy to quickly find the information you need.

- Use Flags. Jot a note or two about why the message is important, then move it out of your Inbox into the appropriate destination. The flag field can hold up to 255 characters, but try to make the note concise and include keywords (for example, "Read this article, Exchange 2000"). If you're looking for a message, search the appropriate store using Find with one of your keywords.

- Use a Note and make a list of the keywords you use most frequently. Refer to this list to jog your memory when a search comes up blank or you don't find what you're looking for.

- Build a Master Category List appropriate to the information you manage every day. Categorize everything that has even a remote chance of being valuable one day. This translates to: categorize every item you do not delete.

TIP # 151

Defrag Your Hard Disk

Disk fragmentation occurs when files grow and are saved back to disk spread across noncontiguous clusters. All files are subject to performance impacts from disk fragmentation, Outlook more so due to the size PSTs frequently grow to. Keeping a 300 MB file in contiguous regions of your hard disk is damn near impossible, especially when that file is in frequent use. Defragmenting your hard disk on a routine basis goes a long way toward keeping Outlook running optimally.

Chapter 14

Collaborating with Outlook

When used as an Exchange Server client, Outlook provides rich server-based collaborative features. Running as a standalone mail client and PIM connected to the Internet or a corporate LAN, Outlook provides more limited collaborative features using peer-to-peer techniques.

This chapter looks at two of these features: Net Folders and Internet Free/Busy. Although these peer-based collaboration methods have the advantage of not requiring a server, people with low tolerance levels should not attempt to use either of these features. When they work, they work well, but getting them to work can be an exercise in frustration. This chapter should alleviate at least a part of this frustration.

Net Folders

Using Net Folders, an Outlook client can create shared folders, which can be accessed by other Outlook clients on the local network or via the Internet. Data in a shared folder can be added, changed, or deleted by any authorized user. Changes are replicated, using standard Internet mail protocols, to all participants. The only prerequisite for using Net Folders is that all members of the sharing group must have an email address. Even non-Outlook clients may participate in some aspects of shared folders, although with reduced functionality.

Some potential uses for Net Folders are:

- Collaborate with co-workers on a project

- Exchange and update appointments and schedules with friends or family

- An alternative to a mailing list or listserver

- Share a common set of business contacts with colleagues

- Share book drafts with a co-author on the other side of the globe

Throughout this chapter the terms *Net Folders* and *Shared Folders* are used interchangeably. Technically, Net Folders is the feature and Shared Folders are the shared folders themselves.

When a Net Folder is activated, a copy of that folder and its original contents are automatically replicated to the default PST (that is, the location email messages are delivered to) of anyone designated as a member of or subscriber to that folder. The creator of the share assigns permissions to each subscriber, which determines the level of access that user has to the shared folder. Permissions range from read-only to full edit-delete. Items changed by subscribers are automatically replicated to everyone on the members list.

A subscriber who does not use Outlook is forwarded copies of the folder contents as email messages. The replicated folders are not created on his system and he does not have direct access to the shared folder's contents.

Calendar or Contact items stored in a shared folder are not readable by other email clients. Any items stored and updated by Net Folders using a message format (posts, messages, notes, or journal entries) are.

Installation

You must install the Net Folders component before you can share an Outlook folder. By default, Net Folders is configured to Install on First Use. The first time you share a folder, Office Setup prompts you for your Office CD and adds the necessary files to activate the feature. If you prefer to install the files manually, go to Control Panel → Add/Remove Programs and choose the Office 2000 entry. Click Change. When the Update Features dialog appears, expand the list under Microsoft Outlook for Windows and set Net Folders to Run from My Computer, as shown in Figure 14-1.

Net Folders: Constraints and Cautions

Before you share a folder, it is important to understand several constraints and cautions regarding their use:

- You cannot share a "root" folder. By root we mean the topmost folder of a PST file (or information store).

  For example, in the folder structure shown in Figure 14-2 you cannot share the default system folder (Outlook Today – [Personal Folders]) or any of the other top-level folders pictured (Personal Mail, Tipworld, Topics du Jour, etc.) each of which corresponds to a separate *.pst* file. You can, however, share subfolders within a PST, with the following exceptions:

  - You cannot share the Inbox folder. Outlook flatly refuses to do this.

  - You cannot share the Outbox folder successfully, although Outlook allows you to define a share for it without warning you that doing so is disastrous. Sharing the Outbox folder causes Outlook to enter an infinite loop, *rendering this folder and its contents useless.* Do not go there unless you have an affinity for rebuilding information stores.

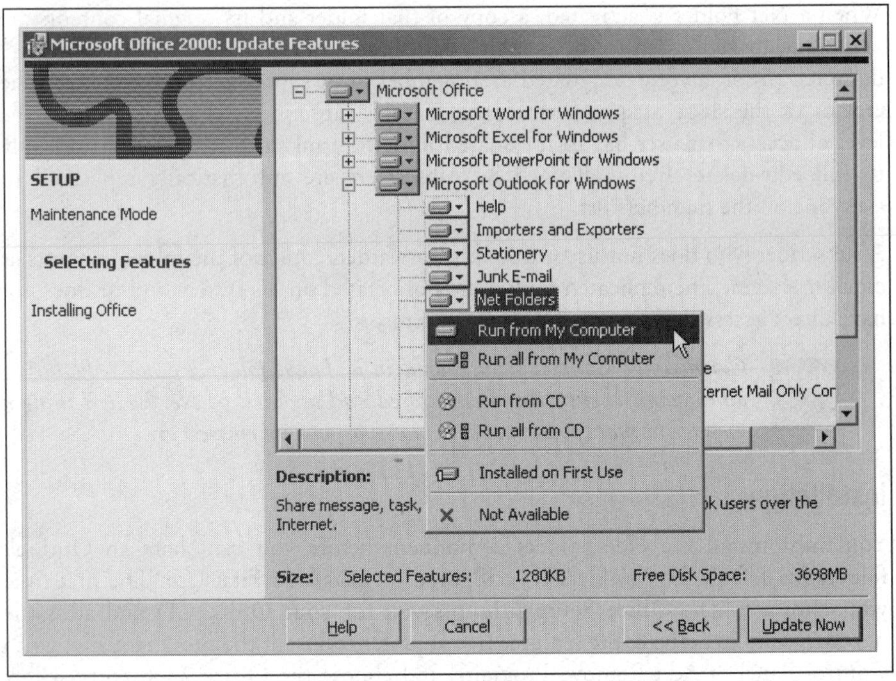

Figure 14-1: Installing Net Folders from the Office 2000 Update Features dialog

- You cannot share Exchange folders or an Offline Folder (*.ost*). If you are using Outlook as a client to Exchange Server, you can only share local Personal folders (*.pst*).

• Sharing a folder containing Mail, Note, or Post items is an all-or-nothing proposition. If you share one of these folders, every item in the folder is visible to every member with access to that folder. Calendar, Contact, Journal, or Task items can be marked "Private" from their respective entry forms. Doing so hides that item from everyone but the entry's creator.

• Shared material is transferred and updated in clear text using the SMTP/POP email transport protocols, and is therefore vulnerable to hacking. Do not risk exposing sensitive or confidential material by placing it in a Net Folder.

• Any time you create a new folder in Outlook, you must define the type of Outlook item that folder contains. The available choices are: Mail items, Appointment items, Contact items, Journal items, Note items, or Task items. Once a folder type is assigned, it cannot be changed, so careful consideration should be given to this choice. Folder type directly affects what can be stored in a shared folder.

- Mail folders are the most flexible. You can post or copy *any file or Outlook item* to a shared folder set up to contain Mail items. This is the preferred option for *ad hoc* discussion and collaboration folders.

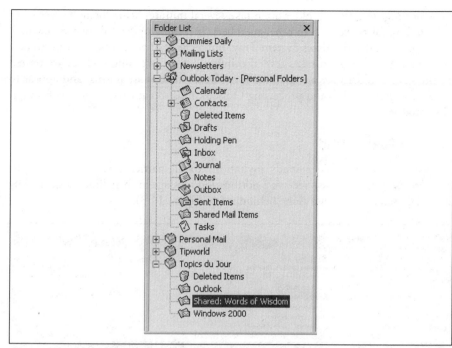

Figure 14-2: A sample PST structure viewed from the Folder List

- Note folders are second in versatility. You can post new Word or Excel documents, Excel charts, or PowerPoint presentations to a shared Notes folder. But you cannot copy existing documents here (as you can with a Mail folder). You can, however, insert an existing document into a posted item within a Notes folder. For details on how to do this, see the section "Adding an existing Office document to a shared mail folder" later in this chapter. A shared Notes folder is a good choice if you want to restrict the type of items a shared folder contains.

- Shared Appointment, Contact, Journal, and Task folders are restricted to containing the corresponding item type or Office documents. Use one of these folder types if you are creating a shared folder to, for example, make your calendar available to a coworker and you want to ensure only appointments are entered. In this scenario you would probably also want to assign restrictive permissions as well—see the "How Net Folders Work" section, later in this chapter.

Finally, be aware that latency issues exist when using Net Folders. All the underlying replication and synchronization of these folders takes place automatically, in the background, and without overt action or notification to the user. And while this behind-the-scenes automation is not a bad thing, it does produce program behaviors that at times seem quirky.

New postings to a shared folder often take several minutes before being processed to the Outbox for replication to other members. Incoming updates display a new mail notification in the Windows System Tray, but a check of your Inbox reveals no new messages. Again, it often takes several minutes before incoming updates are posted to the shared folder they are destined for. These latencies are normal and appear to reflect the extra sorting and processing Outlook must do as part of the synchronization process.

How Net Folders Work

Activating a shared folder sends invitations to all participants specified by the *member list*. Outlook users receive a notification message in their Inbox indicated by a special folder icon with a globe behind it (see Figure 14-3).

!				From	Subject	Received
				Tom Syroid	**New subscription to OL2K Timeline**	**Fri 02/18/2000 20:40**
				Troy Mott	FW: Windows 2000	Fri 02/18/2000 20:34
			0	Troy Mott	RE: Chap 12 for comments	Fri 02/18/2000 17:35
				Matt Beland	RE: Exchange documents - ignore till later	Fri 02/18/2000 16:31
				Matt Beland	RE: Exchange documents - ignore till later	Fri 02/18/2000 16:15
				Paul Thurrott	Today's WinInfo: February 18	Fri 02/18/2000 15:57
				Matt Beland	Exchange documents - ignore till later	Fri 02/18/2000 15:47
				Windows 2000 E...	Win2000Mag Exchange Server UPDATE February 18, 2000	Fri 02/18/2000 13:37
				Moshe Bar	How is everything?	Thu 02/17/2000 12:08
		0		Brian P. Bilbrey	activities tab	Wed 02/16/2000 19:22

Figure 14-3: A Net Folder notification message display in the Inbox

Opening this message displays the Accept/Decline dialog pictured in Figure 14-4.

This message invites the recipient to participate in the share, and in the body explains how to install Net Folders should the Accept/Decline button not show on the form. Below this is a brief description of the folder being shared and any notes from the creator describing the folder's purpose or contents.

TIP # 152
Folder Subscriptions Are Sent in MS-RTF

Folder subscriptions are always sent to members in MS-RTF format. RTF format allows the Accept/Decline buttons to be displayed. In addition, important folder properties (permissions, contents, etc.) are encoded within this message format. Keep in mind that Microsoft's version of RTF may not work with clients such as Eudora. In the world of email clients, the Rich Text message format is not a standard.

The recipient can specify where the replicated folder resides and give it a name. For the reasons described in the Naming Convention sidebar, we recommend that you do not accept the defaults, but instead supply your own folder name and location.

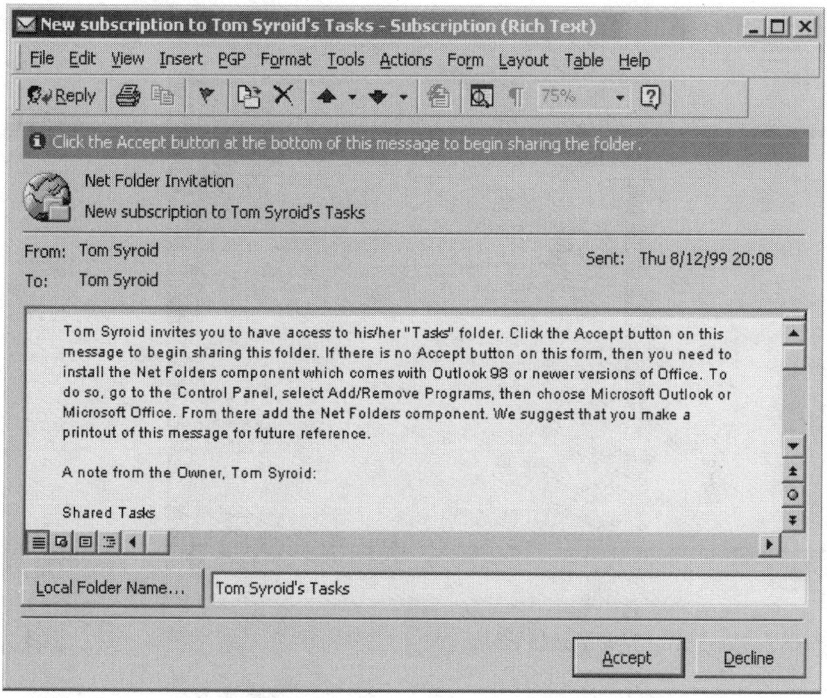

Figure 14-4: Net Folder Invitation message form

Accepting the invitation sends an automatic response to the share creator, clears the "(waiting for response)" notation from that entry on the member list, and initiates the replication process between the two computers.

If an invitation is declined, a Declined notification is sent back to the creator of the shared folder, and the sender's entry in the members list is automatically removed.

Net Folder Setup

Unless you have a specific reason to do otherwise, we recommend creating a new folder, and then sharing it. Doing so allows you to better manage its contents.

To create a shared folder, choose New → Folder from the File menu (or Ctrl+Shift+E from whatever view you happen to be in). The Create New Folder dialog is shown is Figure 14-5.

Enter a name for the new folder (see the sidebar "Folder Naming Conventions"). Select the type of item the folder will contain using the guidelines provided earlier in this chapter. The location of the folder is not critical. A shortcut placed on the Outlook Bar makes the actual location seamless to the user anyway.

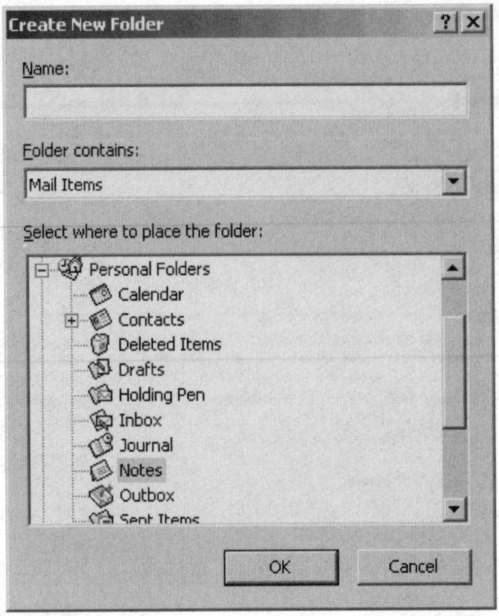

Figure 14-5: Create New Folder dialog

Folder Naming Conventions

Consistent naming conventions are a big part of making your Outlook folder structure intuitive and workable. Give some thought to how you name your folders, especially with regard to their purpose and location in your existing folder structure.

Net folders display no unique icon to indicate their special status. Hence it is in your best interests—for both clarity and future reference—to name shared folders in a way that denotes their purpose.

Referring to the folder tree in Figure 14-2, you can see three subfolders under the "Topics du Jour" PST. Although all three of these folders are shared, the only clue to this fact is the naming convention used for the "Shared: Words of Wisdom" folder. The other two folders have no such visual cue to remind the user that they are shared folders.

As an alternative, you may want to consider creating a new information store specifically for shared folders. The PST could be named something unique like "Net Folders" and the subfolders named to reflect their contents (for example, "Net Contacts" and "Net Company Calendar").

TIP # 153

Shared Folders Must Be Accessible

If a shared folder exists outside your default information store (usually named Personal Folders), it must be kept open so it is accessible to updates.

To share an *existing* folder, first select it from the Folder List, and then choose File → Share. The Share submenu (see Figure 14-6) contains four options.

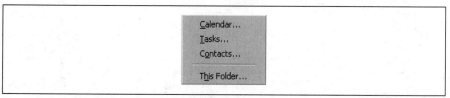

Figure 14-6: The File → Share submenu

The first three selections—Calendar, Tasks, and Contacts—refer to the system folders they are named for and provide a quick way to activate them as Net Folders.

TIP # 154

Do Not Share Your System Folders

We do not recommend sharing any of Outlook's system folders. These folders are critical to the program's operation, and their contents and structure should be guarded religiously. Always create a separate folder for shared items, and then copy an applicable subset of your data there.

The fourth selection, This Folder, shares the current open folder. This is the recommended sharing option, preferable to the previous options that apply to the default Outlook folders. Most users only want to share select information from an existing folder. For example, you have a selection of business contacts that you want to share with several of your colleagues, but these contacts exist in a folder containing personal contacts as well. The solution is to create a shared Business Contacts folder, copy (or move) the relevant contacts to this new location, and share this folder, not your personal Contacts folder.

Selecting any option on the Share submenu starts the Net Folder Wizard. This Wizard guides you through the process of specifying which users can access the folder, and what permission level they have for the items it contains. Figure 14-7 shows the Member List dialog of Net Folder Wizard.

The Add button opens the Select Contacts dialog of the Outlook Address Book (OAB). Contacts are added to the Member List with a default permission of Reviewer. Outlook does not let you add a contact that does not have an email address.

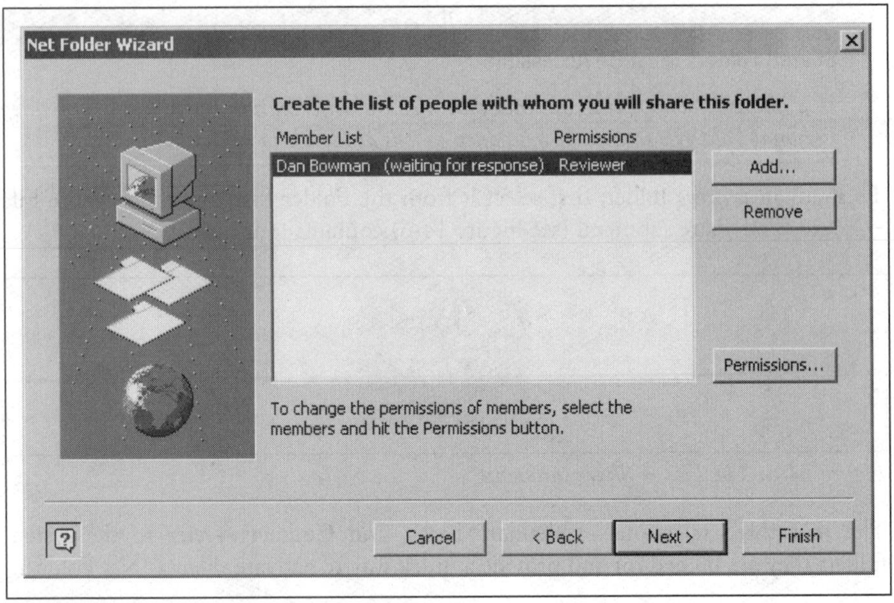

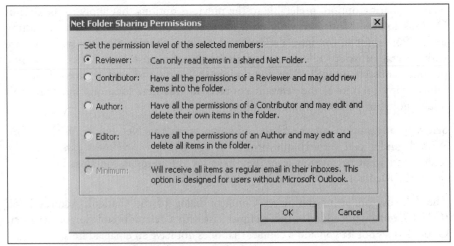

Figure 14-7: Net Folder Wizard Member List

 NOTE *A Distribution List can also be added to the member list, but bear in mind the permission level assigned to this single entity applies to all its members. See Chapter 8, Contacts, for details on creating and managing Distribution Lists.*

To change a permission level, select a contact entry, then the Permissions button. The Net Folder Sharing Permissions dialog is shown in Figure 14-8.

Figure 14-8: Net Folder Sharing Permissions dialog

One of five permission levels can be selected: Reviewer, Contributor, Author, Editor, or Minimum. The dialog clearly explains these options and the permissions associated with each level.

 Minimum is a special permission level for contacts not using Outlook. Instead of the shared folder being replicated on their system, they receive folder postings as regular email messages. This permission level is available only for folders configured to contain Mail items.

Creating a Custom View for Shared Mail Folders

The default view for a Mail folder is not particularly useful for a shared folder containing item types other than messages. Creating a new icon view gives you a better visual representation of the folder's contents.

To create a custom icon view:

1. Open the shared Mail folder.

2. Select View → Current View → Define Views. From the "Define Views for *foldername*" dialog choose the New button.

3. Give the new view a name (for example, Shared Icon View) and ensure Icon is selected as the type. Under the "Can be used on" option list select either the first or third choice depending on whether you want the view available in the current folder only, or all Mail folders.

4. The "View Settings…" dialog now appears. The default setting should work well in most settings. Choose Close or Apply View.

This new view is now available from both the view list on Advanced Toolbar and the View → Current View submenu.

Note that Views—custom or otherwise—are not included in a shared folder's replication process. Each subscriber would need to complete the customization on her own system.

Using Shared Mail Folders

You can add almost any object to a shared Mail folder, with one exception. You cannot store a folder from your filesystem or from Outlook itself; files, however, are fair game.

How these items are stored in a Mail folder depends both on the item itself and the method used to add it. For sake of clarity, we list the most common items you are likely to store here, how they are added, and the limitations involved for each item-type.

Message Posts and Office Documents are the two most common items created and manipulated in a shared Mail folder.

Creating a Post in a shared mail folder

A *Post* is a type of message. Posts are not addressed to a specific user, but instead serve as a response to a subject or topic. Posts are typically used as a way of conveying information to the members of a public folder. In this regard, Posts are functionally comparable to an email message sent to an Internet newsgroup.

While their format is similar to an email message, several differences exist:

- A Post is saved in the folder where it is created. It is not sent to a specific recipient like an email message. It can be thought of as a group message that is readable by anyone with access to that folder.

- Posts follow the same structural format as an email message. They lack a To field, however, and are instead distinguished by Conversation (Subject field). The lower half of the form contains the text of the message. Font, paragraph style, background, and message format (Plain Text or HTML) can be changed from the Format menu of the form (see Figure 14-9).

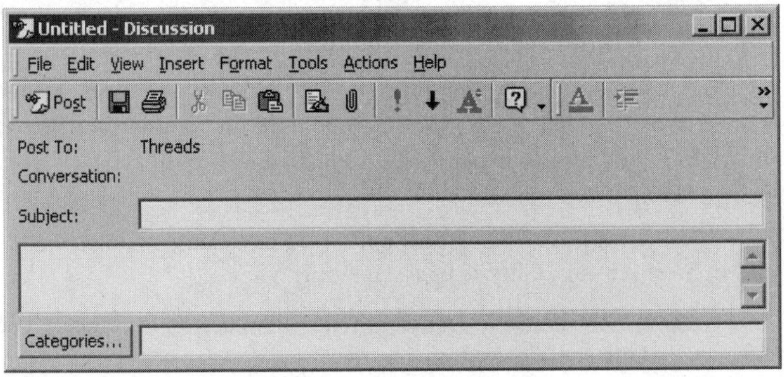

Figure 14-9: A new Post form

- When a new Post is created (File → New → Post in This Folder or Ctrl+Shift+S) the text entered in the Subject field becomes the Conversation or "Discussion Thread."

- Once a Post is saved (using either the Save command or Post toolbar icon), *both* the Conversation field and message text become read-only. You can, however, open a saved Post and apply a Category or edit the Subject field. When the changes are saved, the Subject field is copied to the read-only Conversation field.

- You can, before the Post is saved, attach a file, add a signature, or assign importance. File attachments can be opened and edited from within a Post.

To reply to a posted message, first decide which level of the discussion thread you want to respond to. Figure 14-10 shows a folder containing multiple posted messages at a variety of levels.

TIP # 155

Use By Conversation Topic View for Posts

When working in a folder that contains Posted messages, the most functional view to use is By Conversation Topic (View → Current View → By Conversation Topic). This displays folder items grouped by Conversation, then by Topic.

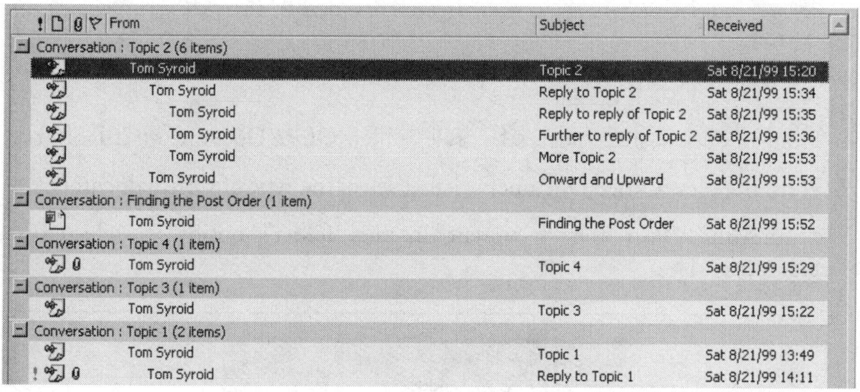

! 🗋 🖉 ▽ From	Subject	Received	▲
⊟ Conversation : Topic 2 (6 items)			
Tom Syroid	Topic 2	Sat 8/21/99 15:20	
Tom Syroid	Reply to Topic 2	Sat 8/21/99 15:34	
Tom Syroid	Reply to reply of Topic 2	Sat 8/21/99 15:35	
Tom Syroid	Further to reply of Topic 2	Sat 8/21/99 15:36	
Tom Syroid	More Topic 2	Sat 8/21/99 15:53	
Tom Syroid	Onward and Upward	Sat 8/21/99 15:53	
⊟ Conversation : Finding the Post Order (1 item)			
Tom Syroid	Finding the Post Order	Sat 8/21/99 15:52	
⊟ Conversation : Topic 4 (1 item)			
Tom Syroid	Topic 4	Sat 8/21/99 15:29	
⊟ Conversation : Topic 3 (1 item)			
Tom Syroid	Topic 3	Sat 8/21/99 15:22	
⊟ Conversation : Topic 1 (2 items)			
Tom Syroid	Topic 1	Sat 8/21/99 13:49	
! Tom Syroid	Reply to Topic 1	Sat 8/21/99 14:11	

Figure 14-10: The By Conversation Topic view showing posted messages for a shared folder

The original Conversation thread is the highest item in a group's hierarchy. Replies to this item follow at the next indented level, and replies to these replies are listed at the third level of the list (see Conversation Topic 2 in Figure 14-10).

To reply to a Post either open the message and use the Post Reply button on the form's toolbar, or right-click the message and select Post Reply to Folder from the context menu. Either action opens a new Discussion form where the message text can be entered. The Conversation field is inherited from the original Post and the Post To field shows the folder where the Discussion thread is stored.

Here are some tricks and tips when working with Posted messages:

- Existing posted messages can be dragged and dropped between Outlook folders, which moves the message. To *copy* the message, hold down the Ctrl key while you drag the item.

- You can Reply To a posted message (rather than Post Reply). This copies the item text to a new email message addressed to the creator of the selected item, but does not post the response to the shared folder. Use this option to reply privately to a post.

- Posted messages can be Forwarded to email recipients.

- Posted messages can be saved to a storage location outside Outlook's filesystem using the File → Save As command.

Creating a new Office document in a shared mail folder

Another item commonly shared with Net Folders is an Office document.

 The steps outlined here are the same regardless of the Outlook folder type and apply equally to shared and nonshared folders.

To create a new Office document:

1. From an open shared folder, select File → New Office Document (Ctrl+Shift+H).

2. From the New Office Document dialog select the type of Office document.

3. Ensure the "Post the document in this folder" option is selected (see Figure 14-11).

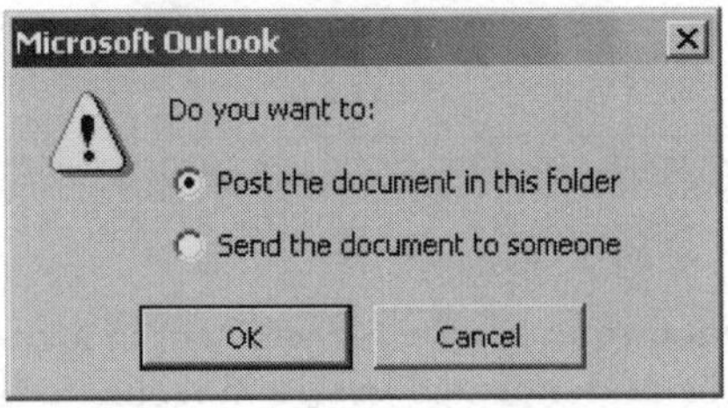

Microsoft Outlook   ☒

Do you want to:

⊙ Post the document in this folder

○ Send the document to someone

[OK]   [Cancel]

Figure 14-11: Document Post dialog

4. The Office document opens as it would normally. The only discernable difference is that you now have a Post button on the standard toolbar. Enter your text and instead of saving the document, Post it.

Office documents do not display an icon title when they are posted to a shared folder unless you use the document's File → Properties command to enter a title on the *subject* line (*not* the Title line as one would expect) as shown in Figure 14-12.

If you forget to title a document when it is first posted, you can reopen the document and supply a title on the subject line, then save the document. Once a subject is entered, you can re-edit the subject line in the properties dialog to your heart's content, but this action *does not* modify the icon title displayed in the shared folder.

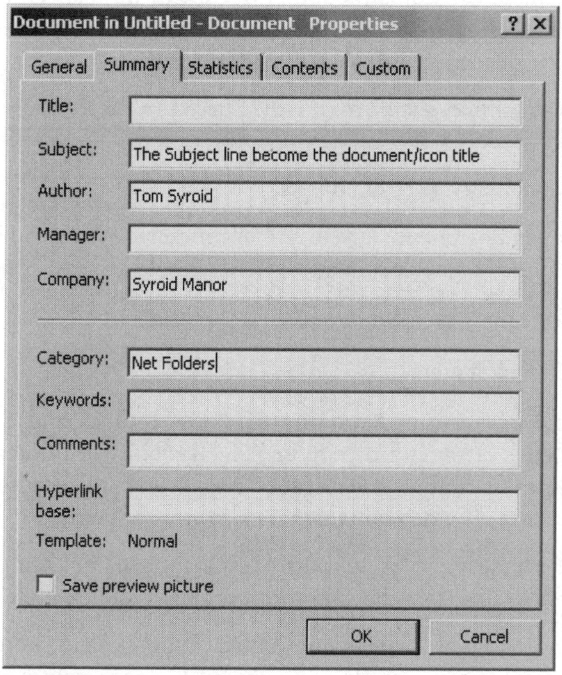

Figure 14-12: Word Document Properties dialog

Office documents display *very quirky and inconsistent* behavior when posted to an Outlook folder. In particular:

- In some cases you can edit the document—*only once*. After that the document is read-only. You can modify the document's contents, and the program asks you if you want to save changes, but no matter how you respond at this point, those changes are not saved.

- In other cases, once an Office document is posted, it becomes a read-only document immediately. No further edits to the document are possible.

For these reasons, we strongly recommend that you only post an Office document to a folder if it is a one-time addition that you do not ever anticipate requiring modification or edit. In all other cases, the best option is to create the document outside of Outlook, save it to hard disk, and then add it to the shared folder as outlined in the next section.

Adding an existing Office document to a shared mail folder

You can create a new Office document in a shared Mail folder, but there is no obvious way to post an existing document there. There is, however, a less-than-obvious workaround.

Any Office document can contain another document through Object Linking and Embedding (OLE), providing that program's data type is registered in Windows. To add an existing document to a shared mail folder:

1. Create a new Office document in the shared folder (File → New → Office Document).

2. Open the document created in Step 1.

3. Using the open document's Insert → File command, insert (embed) an existing document into this new document.

Yes, we know—it's not ideal. But it works.

Sharing other Outlook folders

As a rule, the shared Contact, Appointment, Note, Journal, and Task folder types should be used for their intended purpose. The flexibility of the shared Mail folder suits all but the most unique collaborative needs, and we recommend using this folder type when a Net Folder contains a diverse array of items.

All these folder types, however, support file attachments in their free-form Notes field (that's the Notes field on the item form, not the Outlook Note item).

We'll use the Contact item type as an example. Dragging and dropping an *.exe* file from Explorer to the open window of a shared Contacts folder creates a contact item with the EXE file displayed as a "Shortcut to `filename.exe`" in the free-form field. Now obviously a shortcut pointing to a file on your system is not going to do any member of the shared list much good. However, if you drag the same file to the Contacts folder *while holding down the right mouse button*, releasing it on the open window gives you the context menu shown in Figure 14-13.

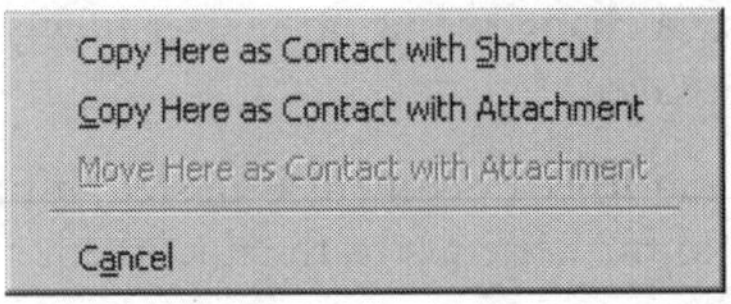

Copy Here as Contact with Shortcut
Copy Here as Contact with Attachment
Move Here as Contact with Attachment

Cancel

Figure 14-13: Right mouse context menu

Choose the second option, "Copy Here as Contact with Attachment." This embeds the file or document in a new Contact record, which can then be saved to the shared folder. The file, plus the attachment, replicates to all list members.

The third selection, "Move Here as Contact with Attachment" is only available when right-dragging between Outlook folders.

<table>
<tr><td align="center">TIP # 156</td></tr>
</table>

Think About What You Want to Post

Give some thought to the file types you add to a shared folder. While you may have the provision to open and edit a PhotoShop drawing, this may not be the case for all list members. Also have some consideration for those Outlook users with dial-up Internet connections. Multimegabyte file attachments are no big deal if you have a T1, ADSL, or cable modem connection, but they can ruin the whole day of someone who feels blessed when he can get a 44K dial-up connection. Also, remember that shared folders exchange data via email messages, and some of your participants may have mailboxes that cannot accept messages larger than 1 to 3 MB.

Maintenance and Configuration Issues

Sooner or later, the creator of a shared folder is faced with several maintenance issues pertaining to both the folder and its users. The most common tasks include:

- Changing a member's permission

- Removing a member's access to a shared folder

- Removing the shared status from a folder

- Adjusting a shared folder's configuration parameters

Changing a member's permission

This is a simple but very nonintuitive process. Select the shared folder and from the File menu, choose Share → This Folder, just as you did when you first established it as a Net Folder. This invokes the Net Folder Wizard. Proceed through the dialogs until you reach the members list. Highlight the individual you wish to modify permissions for and select the "Permissions" button. Alter the member's permission status as required, and proceed through the balance of the wizard. Changes are finalized when the Wizard completes. The list member is notified of the change and the content of the shared folder on their system is updated to reflect the new permission level.

Removing a member

To remove a participant, follow the steps just outlined. When you reach the members list, highlight the person you wish to remove and use the "Remove" button. This action is not finalized until you select Finish on the Wizard dialog, so if you remove a member in error you can back out with Cancel and no list changes are made. A removed member is sent an email notification similar to the following:

```
From: Tom Syroid [mailto:tsyroid@home.com]
Sent: Friday, August 13, 1999 8:10 PM
To: Bo Leuf
Subject: Net Folder Notification
```

> The "Shared Mail Items" Net Folder, which is administered by Tom Syroid is no longer sending you updates. If you have any questions, please contact the administrator of this Net Folder.

 Removing a participant from the member list of a shared folder does not remove the replicated folder from his system.

Revoking a folder's shared status

Two methods exist to stop sharing a folder:

- Right-click the shared folder, and choose Properties from the context menu. Display the Shared page and click the Stop Sharing This Folder button. (See Figure 14-14.)

- Highlight the shared folder and choose File → Share → This Folder. On the first screen of the Net Folder Wizard, click the Stop Sharing This Folder button.

A notification message similar to that shown in the "Removing a member" section is sent to notify all subscribed members that the folder is no longer shared.

Update settings

To access the "Update settings" options, right-click the shared folder and go to the Shared tab of the Properties dialog shown in Figure 14-14.

Using this dialog, you can change the folder description, configure "Update settings," enable Journal events for the folder, force an update, and stop sharing the folder.

Updates will be sent out every
Determines how often updates are sent out to enrolled members. Choose a value appropriate for how often the folder contents are expected to change. Too short a value causes needlessly frequent updates and increased mail traffic. Too long a value may confuse participants and cause working at cross-purposes because participants are not receiving updates in a timely manner.

Verify contents of member folders
Determines how often the items contained in the administrator's folder are verified against the folders of all subscribers. If all folder members are on a reliable connection (for example, a LAN), it is probably safe to select Never. If most subscribers use dial-up connections, it is prudent to occasionally verify that their folders are updating correctly. The number of days you want to pass between verifications depends on the importance of the folder contents. This option works independently of the normal replication process and is a safeguard to ensure that all replicated folders are exact duplicates of the original.

Update size cannot exceed
Sets a maximum size for folder updates sent to members. Shared folders containing large documents that are frequently modified necessitate a larger

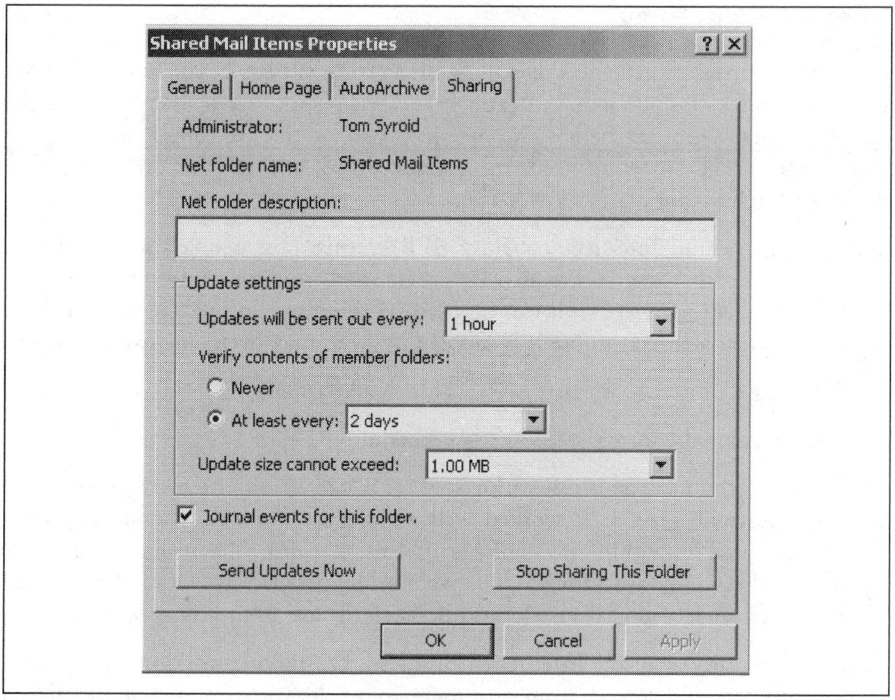

Figure 14-14: A shared folder Properties dialog

maximum update size. It is a good idea to verify the maximum acceptable message size and total mailbox capacity for each participant and to set this value to something smaller than the smallest maximum.

Journal events for this folder

Activates journaling so that additions and changes to a shared folder are added to the Activities list of the contact's record.

Send Updates Now

Immediately sends all pending updates for the folder to list members, regardless of the setting for the Update interval discussed earlier.

Stop Sharing This Folder

Immediately cancels updates to all subscribed members of the folder. Members are automatically notified of the cancellation. Outlook removes the folder's shared status, and it reverts to the functionality of a nonshared folder. Nothing contained in the folder is deleted, moved, or altered in any way. Note that this *does not* remove the replicated folders on the subscribed member systems. It simply severs the folder's shared status.

Internet Free/Busy

If you've ever tried to arrange a meeting with a group of people, you know all about the inherent frustrations involved. You invite ten people, six of them vital to the agenda topics. One day before the meeting, two of the six cancel due to prior commitments. The meeting needs to be rescheduled, and the process of trying to arrange a suitable time starts all over again.

The concept behind Internet Free/Busy (IFB) is this: post people's schedules in a central location that can be accessed by others, and make this information readily available to client software so it can be used by the program's calendaring component. It's a great idea, but to use IFB successfully you must overcome two obstacles:

- Locating a central server that is accessible to all participants

- Determining the format used to store scheduling details

The central location issue is one of logistics. IFB had its origins as a feature found on corporate mail servers. It worked well as long as you were connected to the server, and used it within the confines of this platform. Then along came the concept of the mobile workforce. Users were no longer tied to a desk; they needed access to their server from diverse locations, using diverse connectivity options.

Enter widespread use of the Internet by business. The mobile workforce could now access corporate file servers from anywhere in world with nothing more than a phone line. Adding to this complexity was the fact that users began to adopt electronic organizers, like Outlook, to schedule activities. Wouldn't it make sense to put scheduling information somewhere central, that everyone could access? Good idea, but what format do we use? It's not hard to see how complications can arise in implementing a simple idea in today's world of complex logistics and diverse "standards."

Internet Free/Busy is not ready for prime time. It's tantalizingly close, and the concept is a winner, but the implementation still has a ways to go before it's truly useable. For now, the biggest hurdle for IFB is format. A consortium of software developers created the iCalendar format and defined it as the Internet RFC standard for cross-platform exchange of scheduling information. The problem is not the standard itself, but that software developers have created products that do not fully comply with the standard. In short, there is no guarantee that a supposedly iCalendar-compliant product from Vendor A can interoperate properly with a similar product from Vendor B.

IFB works, if you can figure out how to set it up, and if you are exchanging information with a client that supports the iCalendar. It works best if you are exchanging scheduling information with clients developed by the same company, and if everyone involved uses the same message format—i.e., HTML. Beyond this, your mileage may vary.

Using IFB

Setting up IFB is the topic of the next section, but before getting embroiled in configuration details, let's look at how Outlook implements Free/Busy information. The process is remarkably simple.

User schedules are posted to an IFB server according to the options set on the Free/Busy Options dialog. These options define how much and how often updates are posted to the server. The information posted is drawn from each user's Outlook Calendar. Entries marked Private are not included.

TIP # 157

Showing Your Availability Status

When you use IFB to post your schedule, it's important to enter "Show time as" details, available on the Appointment tab of the Calendar form. This information is transferred to the graph displayed on the Attendee Availability tab as a colored bar.

Manual updates can be made at any time using the menu command Tools → Send/Receive → Free/Busy Information. This is something to keep in mind after you've entered or changed appointments that might influence others.

When you open an Appointment or Meeting form in Calendar (or Plan a Meeting), the schedules of contacts posting IFB information show as free/busy graphs on the grid displayed on the Attendee Availability tab. This schedule information only provides time and associated availability status (Free, Tentative, Busy, Out of Office). Schedule details are not shown.

Setting up IFB

Choose Tools → Options → Preferences → Calendar Options and click Free/Busy to open the Free/Busy Options dialog, shown in Figure 14-15.

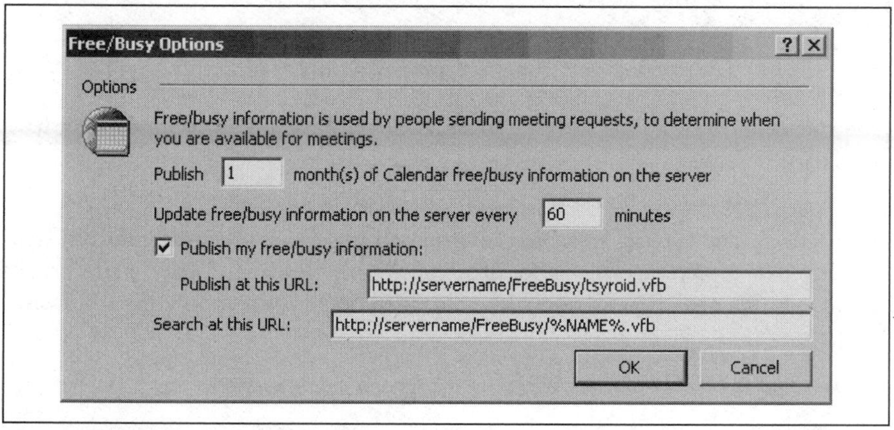

Figure 14-15: The Free/Busy Options dialog

The Free/Busy Options dialog contains the following options:

Publish x month(s)
> Determines how many months of your calendar are published.

Update free/busy information
> Determines how often Outlook sends Free/Busy information to the server. The 15-minute default is a bit too frequent for anyone making just a few calendar entries in a day; adjust this number to reflect how often you make calendar entries and how many of those entries are relevant to others.

Publish my free/busy information
> Selected this checkbox to activate the feature and enable the next two fields.

Publish at the URL
> Contains the path to the server hosting your IFB file.

> At first glance you might expect this address to be of the form *http://www...*, but in most cases such an entry fails. This is because Internet servers are—for security reasons—configured to deny direct writes (*http-post*) to their web folders, unless this is done via forms and server scripts on the site itself, or via authenticated HTTP access with special web-publishing software extensions running on the server. Path conventions for this and the Search field are detailed later in this chapter.

Search at this URL
> Specifies the default location Outlook searches for free/busy information. If a different location is entered in the Internet Free-Busy field found on the Details tab of the Contacts form (see Figure 14-16), this alternate address takes preference over the default.

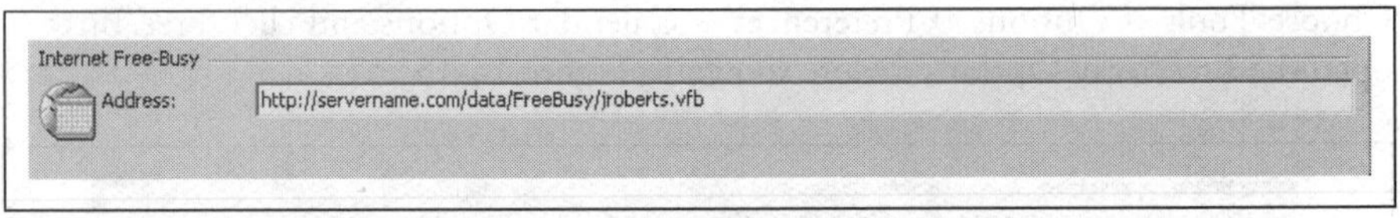

Figure 14-16: The Internet Free-Busy field from the Contacts Details tab

The entries in the Publish and Search fields of the Free/Busy Options dialog have three parts:

A transfer protocol
> Outlook can publish Free/Busy information using one of three protocols: web-server (*http-post*, *http://*), file transfer (*ftp://*), and filesystem (*file://*). Path formats and limitations of each protocol are discussed under the section "IFB protocols."

The IFB server location
> Entered in the format: *servername/full_path_to_IFB_directory*.

The IFB filename

For the Publish field, this is the user's name. The filename used should always be the same as the first portion of your email address before the "@". For example, if your email address is fredsmith@corporation.com, your free/busy filename should be fredsmith.vfb. Outlook expects to see this format when looking up a contact's scheduling information

 NOTE *Free/Busy information conforms to the iCalendar format standard. Part of this standard dictates that Free/Busy files must have the .vfb extension.*

A different convention is used under the Search field. Instead of a specific name for the *.vfb* file, this entry uses a placeholder of %NAME%. This is why the filename format discussed in the previous paragraph is so important. When Outlook searches for IFB information, it replaces the %NAME% field with the first part of a contact's email address. So, by default, Outlook looks for John Roberts Free/Busy information at *http://servername.com/ifb_directory/jroberts.vfb*. If a file by this name cannot be found at this location, then Outlook searches the Free/Busy address entered on the Details tab of the contact record for John Roberts (see Figure 14-16).

IFB protocols

Each of the three possible IFB protocols has a slightly different format, a different application, and its own peculiar quirks. In the examples given under each protocol, you would substitute username for %NAME% in the Search field.

- The *http://* protocol uses the form:

  `http://servername.com/ifb_directory/username.vfb`

  Note the warning given earlier in this chapter—most Internet servers do not support direct writes without a specific combination of server extensions and matching software (for example, FrontPage extensions and FrontPage). For this reason, entries in the Publish field of the Free/Busy dialog generally do not work with this protocol, while entries in the Search field do. The Publish field is a read/write action; the Search field is read only.

- The *ftp://* protocol uses the form:

  `ftp://username:password@ftpserver/ifb_directory/username.vfb`

  Most servers storing IFB information require the user to login so this information must be added to the path when the FTP protocol is used. The FTP protocol can be used for both the Publish field and the Search field of the Free/Busy Options dialog.

- The *file://* protocol uses the form:

  `file://fileserver/c/ifb_directory/username.vfb`

Like the FTP protocol, the file protocol can be used for both the Publish and Search entries on the Free/Busy dialog.

TIP # 158

The Strength of the File:// Protocol

If you're using Internet Free/Busy on an intranet, we recommend using the file:// protocol for pointing clients to the IFB server. It's simple, and it works without a lot of fuss and convolutions.

Web Publishing Wizards and IFB?

For some unknown reason, Outlook wants to see the Web Publishing Wizard installed on your system before publishing Free/Busy information—even if you are using FTP entries under the Publish and Search field. We have no explanation for this, except to say that our experience shows the configuration and update process seems to go a lot smoother when this component is installed.

The Web Publishing Wizard is not installed by default under anything but a full installation Internet Explorer 4 or 5. The details of installing this component "after the fact" are beyond the realm of this book, and dependent on a mix of system variables (operating system version, existing IE version, Office version, and how each of these were installed) and how Microsoft is configuring their downloads for the week.

The best advice we can offer at the time this book was written is to tell you to ensure you have the Publishing Wizard installed *before* you upgrade or install Outlook 2000.

Chapter 15

Security and Encryption

Over one hundred million messages are sent across the world's networks every single day. People use email for all the same purposes for which they use paper-based mail or the telephone—to send a greeting, ask a question, set up a meeting, or inform others of a new product. The majority of these exchanges are routine, and while they are important to the individuals who send and receive them, most are not critical.

Some of this information is critical however—very critical. With the explosive growth of the Internet, businesses have embraced email as a routine form of correspondence. It's fast, and it's almost free. In today's world of fast-paced developments and decisions, to a business fast and free are both Good Things. As a result, it is not uncommon to find business contracts, proposals, and financial information all being exchanged via email. What a lot of people do not understand is that email is transferred around the Internet in the form of clear text SMTP messages.

Since 1997 Outlook has supported the end-to-end encryption of messages using S/MIME (Secure Multipurpose Internet Mail Extensions). When was the last time you exchanged encrypted email with someone? It's ironic, but the same people who fret about using a credit card online, think nothing of sending reams of confidential information, wrapped in the guise of an email, over the Internet.

If all this technology is available, why don't more people use it? For a variety of reasons:

- Many people are simply ignorant about how email is sent and the vulnerabilities involved.

- Configuring an email client to send and receive secure messages is not as easy or seamless as it could be.

- There is a large group of people who do not see a need for secure email. Their rationale is that they don't send or receive messages important enough to warrant encryption.

This last issue is about to change, due in large part to a round of malicious computer viruses that just about brought the Internet to its knees in the fall of 1999. Receivers of the Melissa virus got email that seemed to be from people they knew. Receivers of *ExploreZip.worm*, even more insidiously, got email that seemed to be from people they knew in response to messages they had just sent to those people. In both cases, messages came from a trusted person's machine, but not from a trusted person. A digital certificate could have warned recipients of their misconceptions.

This chapter addresses the topic of sending and receiving secure email using digital certificates. Poorly implemented security, however, is almost as bad as no security at all. Using digital certificates effectively necessitates at least a passing knowledge of encryption and cryptography. So we begin there.

 Digital certificates are just one form of security available under Outlook. Check O'Reilly's web site for an online addendum to this chapter on using PGP (Pretty Good Privacy) and Outlook.

A Primer on Encryption

The goals of encryption can be summarized in four broad strokes:

- *Authentication*—proving one's identity

- *Privacy/Confidentiality*—ensuring that only the intended recipient can read the contents of a message

- *Integrity*—assuring the recipient that a received message has not been altered from the original

- *Nonrepudiation*—proving the sender sent the message

Keep these goals in the back of your mind as you read through the following material. We'll come back to these items shortly.

All forms of encryption—digital certificates, PGP, even the lowly password—comprise four distinct elements:

- *Plaintext*—the message or document you want to encrypt

- *Ciphertext*—the encrypted document

- An *algorithm*—a mathematical formula used to convert plaintext into ciphertext

- A *key* (or keys)—a word or phrase used by the algorithm to lock and unlock the ciphertext

The algorithm is an essential ingredient to encryption. Algorithms are based on a branch of mathematics called cryptography. The number of keys used by the cryptographic algorithm is often used to categorize encryption methods:

Secret key cryptography
  Uses one key, both for encryption and decryption

Public key cryptography
  Uses two keys—one for encryption, and one for decryption

Hash functions
> Use a mathematical function, rather than a key, to irreversibly encrypt plaintext into ciphertext

The key is the second ingredient. Most people equate an encryption key to a password. Enter the right combination of letters and/or digits, in the right order, and whatever it is you're trying to access opens. But whereas a password is measured in, say, ten digit or letters, the *passphrase* you enter to encrypt a document takes those same ten digits and, using a cryptographic algorithm, generates a key. The length of this key is determined by the strength of the algorithm. Current commercially available algorithms use key lengths that range from 56-bit to 4096-bit.

 There is one direct correlation between keys and passwords: the longer they are, the more secure your document is.

Secret Key Cryptography

Under secret key cryptography, the sender uses a key to encrypt a plaintext file, and then sends the ciphertext to the recipient. The recipient applies the same key to decrypt the ciphertext and recover the original message in plaintext.

In secret key encryption, both sender and receiver must know the key. And herein lies the biggest challenge of this method of cryptography—the secure distribution of the key.

Public Key Cryptography

In 1976, Stanford University professor Martin Hellman and graduate student Whitfield Diffle came up with a solution to secure key distribution. The Diffle-Hellman scheme solves secret key cryptography's key exchange problem by using two keys: one to encrypt plaintext and a second to decrypt ciphertext.

In public key cryptography, one key is called the *public key* and the other is called the *private key*. As the names imply, the first key is advertised or made public by the owner; the second is kept private. The sender uses the recipient's public key to encrypt information and the receiver uses his private key to decrypt the ciphertext. The order the keys are applied in does not matter—one key encrypts and the other decrypts. The two keys are mathematically related (using very large prime factors), but you cannot determine one key by knowing the other. This leaves the private key secure—providing the owner keeps it as such.

Hash Functions

Hash functions do not use a key, but instead use a *mathematical* function, e.g., a message digest (MD), to create a *hash value* that is a digital fingerprint of the contents of a document or message. The number is then signed with the user's private key, producing a *signature message block,* and this signature is placed at the end of the message.

TIP # 159

Digital Signatures Revealed

Digital signatures can detect a change in a message as insignificant as a space added after a comma. Unfortunately, a digital signature can only tell you that a document has changed; it can't tell you what has been changed or how much.

This message block is analogous to the old tradition of placing a document in an envelope and sealing it with a unique wax imprint. On receipt, if the wax was broken the recipient knew the envelope had been opened—they could not, however, discern how or in what form the contents had been changed. If the envelope arrived and the seal was intact, then it was safe to assume the contents were unchanged.

In the digital age, a signature message block tells the recipient two things: that the message was not altered, and the person who sent it is indeed the sender; no one else could have signed the document. Note that this does not say the sender is who they claim to be.

 Many operating systems use hash functions to encrypt user passwords.

Encryption and Cryptography Applied

So why doesn't encryption just use one cryptographic method for everything? Because each cryptographic method is best suited to a specific task:

Secret key cryptography
> Ideal for encrypting messages. The sender's software generates a *session key* (based on the passphrase supplied) to encrypt a message. The recipient uses this same session key to decrypt the message. Secret key cryptography is fast, and secure.

 Session keys remain encrypted in the message should the recipient need to decrypt it again at a later date. The software used to extract the session key—when properly written—destroys the session key from your system's memory immediately after use.

Public key encryption
> Used primarily for key exchange. These schemes are also used for Nonrepudiation—if the recipient receives the session key encrypted with the sender's public key, only the sender could have sent the message. It is possible to use public key cryptography to encrypt data, but public key encryption is slow in contrast to secret key.

Hash functions

> Best employed to ensure data integrity. If an outside source changes the content of a message, the recipient ends up with a different hash value than the sender supplied. Hash functions are simple, unique, and virtually foolproof.

Used in conjunction, these three cryptographic methods allow the use of secure, private, authenticated communication between two or more users.

It's time for an example. Matt is planning a large-scale corporate merger and wants to get advice from his friend Bob. They can talk on the phone about it, but Bob wants to see Matt's proposal on paper before he comments. Enter encryption and cryptography.

Matt uses secret key cryptography to generate a session key, which is used to encrypt the document. He then uses Bob's public key to encrypt the session key. Together, the encrypted message and the encrypted session key form a *digital envelope*, which is sent by email to Bob. On receipt, Bob uses his private key to recover the session key and decrypt the original document.

Matt's message also includes a *digital signature*. This assures Bob that the message was not altered by anyone or anything (for example, a virus) in transit. To create the digital signature, Matt's software generates a hash value for the message based on content. This hash value is then encrypted with Matt's private key. When Bob receives the digital signature, his software decrypts the hash value using Matt's public key. Bob's software then independently calculates the hash value of the message he received. If this hash value is different than the one Matt provided, Bob knows that something is amiss and the message has been altered. In addition, matching hash values proves to Bob that Matt sent the message because Matt is the only one who holds the key that encrypted the hash value.

There's just one small problem with all this. Where did Bob get Matt's public key? Matt could, of course, simply send the key to Bob in a message. But this begs the question. How does Bob know that the message containing Matt's public key was in fact sent by Matt? Anyone today can get an email address in five minutes, and with a little ingenuity, that email address can contain any name or string of characters. We've come full circle. Bob can't talk to Matt, shake his hand, or question his moral values. The only connection Bob has to Matt is an email address.

Key Distributions and Trust

Remember that one of the goals of security is authentication. And as you can see by the preceding example, almost everything to do with security hinges on authentication. The question is: how do two individuals build a trust relationship without prior contact? When you receive a public key, how do you know it belongs to the person who sent it? The solution, while not perfect, is the *public key certificate*.

A certificate is a digital document that contains a serial number, a digital signature algorithm identifier, the issuer's name, the validity period, the name of the person the certificate was issued to (usually in the form of an email address), and public key information. The role of a certificate is twofold: to establish an identity and to define what actions the holder of the certificate can take.

Certificates are obtained from a Certificate Authority (CA), which can be any organization with the necessary software to generate such documents. CAs are typically of two varieties: private and public. Private CAs take the form of universities or companies that need to authenticate users strictly within the bounds of their own organization. Public CAs, on the other hand, cater to the general public, so they have to be reputable.

 Private or public, all CAs must also have certificates, which creates a certificate chain that leads to a trusted root CA.

Acquiring a Digital Certificate

Digital certificates can be acquired from numerous Certificate Authorities. Two of the most popular are VeriSign (*http://digitalid.verisign.com*) and Thawte (*http://www. thawte.com*). Here are some considerations to keep in mind when choosing a CA:

- First and foremost, ensure the CA is reputable. Ask friends and associates who use digital certificates their opinion.

- Certificates typically come in a variety of levels, each with a different range of features targeted at a specific audience. Examine each CA's offerings carefully. Some certificates, for example, are restricted in the range of algorithms supported.

- If you plan to use digital certificates on a regular basis, make sure people can find and download your certificate. Some CAs make it easy to search for issued certificates; other have no search/download provision (for example, at the time of this writing, Thawte).

- Most certificates have a yearly fee; some are free (for example, Thawte). If you want to experiment with using certificates, most CAs offer a free trial period. Before you sign up for a free trial, however, read the fine print.

At the time of installation, some certificates allow you to select a security level:

High
Your private key is password protected. Each time you use the certificate, you'll be asked to supply a password.

Medium
Your private key is not password protected. Outlook displays a message each time you use your private key.

Low
Your private key is not password protected and no messages are displayed.

Finally, once your key is installed, make a backup copy. See Tip # 164.

Sending and Receiving Signed Messages

The following section details the process of signing and encrypting messages.

With a digital certificate installed on your system, you can sign, encrypt, or sign *and* encrypt messages. The section "Certificate and Security Options" later in the chapter explains how to set secure messaging defaults. You can also change these defaults on a per-message basis using the toolbar icons added to Outlook's message form when secure messaging is enabled.

Figure 15-1 shows message form toolbar from Outlook's default editor. Click the button depicting an envelope with a red seal on it to digitally sign a message; the envelope with the blue seal encrypts a message.

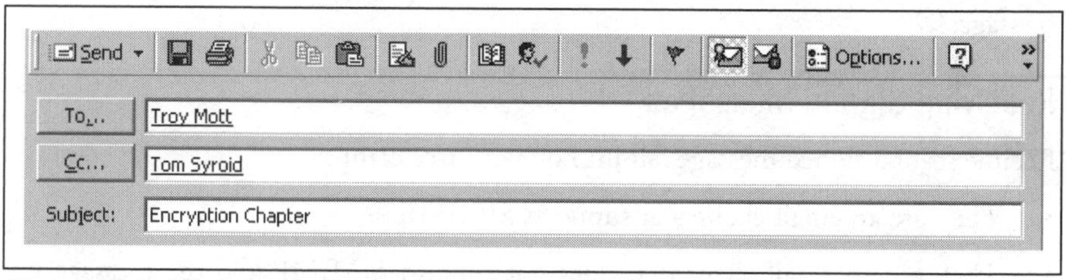

Figure 15-1: The message form toolbar showing the Sign and Encrypt buttons

Sending Signed Messages

Digitally signed messages are easy, seamless, and can be used in a multitude of scenarios. For example:

- Sign messages containing important information. This tells the recipients that you are the author, and the contents of the message have not been altered.

- Distribute a price list or catalogue containing verified information.

- Organizations and government agencies can use digital signatures to sign important announcements or press releases.

- Sign messages containing file attachments. This not only informs the recipient you are indeed the sender and they are safe in opening the attachment, but it also ensures the document has not been infected with a virus or other obnoxious predator en route (just make sure you scan files before you send them, signed or not).

- Signed documents represent an electronic form of verification. The time and date the message was signed (sent) are recorded in the signature.

The sender of a signed message must have a digital certificate installed on her system. The recipient does not require a preexisting certificate (one is sent with then signed message)—contrast this with receiving an encrypted message in the next section.

Digitally signed messages contain two messages: the original (plaintext) and an encrypted signature block. When a signed message is received by an S/MIME compliant email client (see both the "Secure email options" and "Receiving Signed Messages" sections later in this chapter), the original message is checked against the certificate key and the signature block to ensure the message is unaltered. Any differences between the two indicate the message has been altered. The recipient can also examine the attached signature to verify the sender.

Sending a signed message is no different than sending a normal message. Just make sure the Digitally Signed Message icon on the standard toolbar is showing as depressed. As an alternative, open the Message Options dialog (View → Options) and make sure the checkbox is selected for "Add digital signature to outgoing message."

Receiving Signed Messages

Recipients of a signed message fall into one of three camps:

- They use an email client that supports S/MIME.

- They use an email client that does not support S/MIME and the message was sent with the "Send Clear Text" option enabled.

- They use an email client that does not support S/MIME and the message was not sent with the "Send Clear Text" option enabled.

Configuring a certificate's Send Clear Text option is detailed under "Secure Email Options" later in this chapter.

In the example shown in Figure 15-2, the recipient's client is Outlook (so S/MIME is supported). A signed message is displayed as a closed envelope with a red ribbon affixed. The sender's digital certificate is attached, as indicated by the paper clip icon in the attachments column.

 Opening a signed or encrypted message does not change the closed envelope to an open one as it does with normal messages.

The open message is shown in Figure 15-3 (top). The message header contains the usual To-From-Subject information, as well as a Security field showing the word "Signed." In addition, there is a small red ribbon in the lower-right corner of the header.

Click the red ribbon to display a dialog containing details of the digital signature used to create the message (see Figure 15-3, bottom). The signature dialog lists the

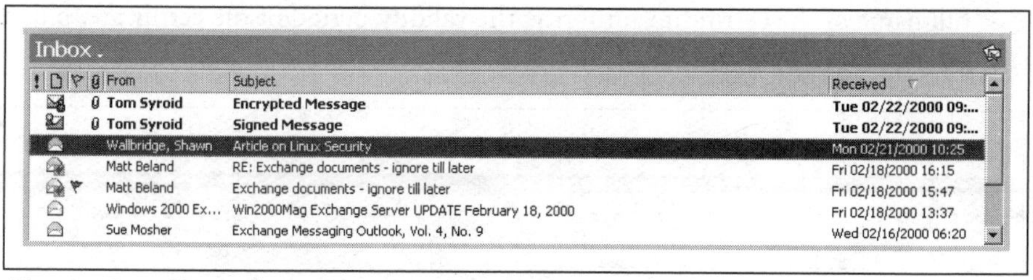

Figure 15-2: A signed message received in the Outlook Inbox

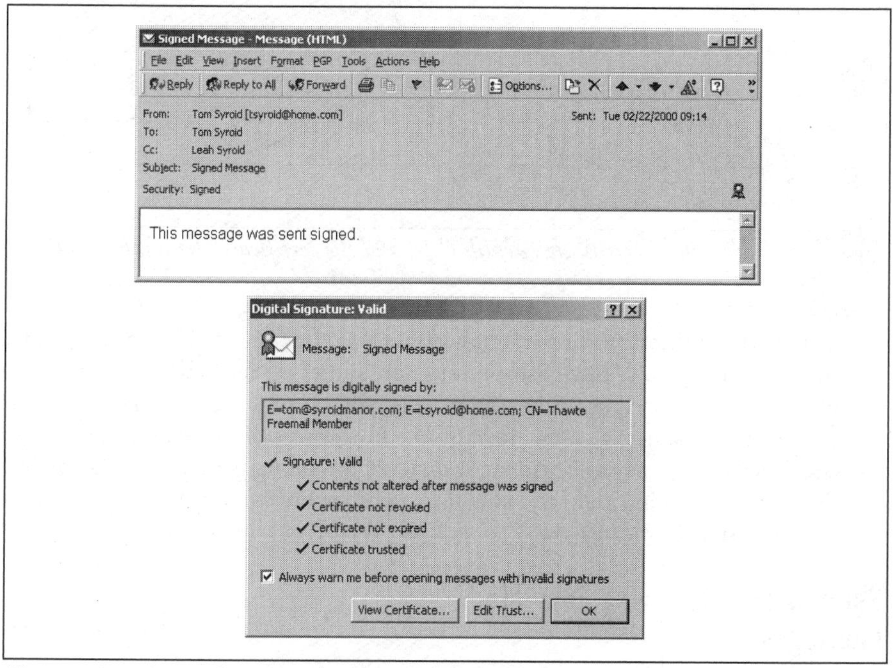

Figure 15-3: A signed message (top), and the details of the attached certificate (bottom)

sender's email address, the issuer of the certificate, and verification that the certificate is valid, not revoked, and the contents of the message have not been altered.

> **NOTE** *For a message to be fully authenticated, all five items on the Valid Digital Signature dialog should be checked.*

On the bottom of the certificate dialog are two buttons:

View Certificate

Opens a detailed view of the certificate as shown in Figure 15-4 (left). (Note that the signature dialog just discussed showed details of the *signature*, this dialog shows details of the *certificate*.) Here you can see further details, such as full name of the certificate authority, the validity period of the certificate, plus a range of other specifics.

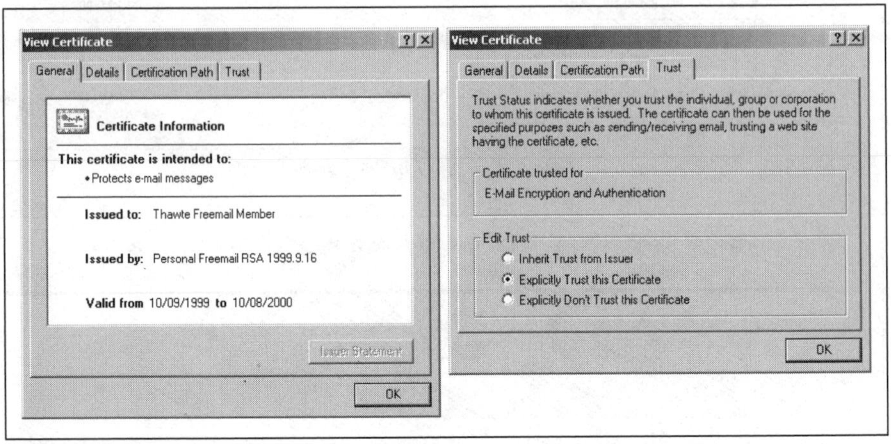

Figure 15-4: Viewing a certificate's details (left) and the certificate's trust tab (right)

Edit Trust

Opens the certificate with the Trust tab selected (see Figure 15-4, right). As we noted in the section "Key Distributions and Trust" earlier in the chapter, certificates are based on a chain or web of trust. By default, a certificate inherits its trust from the issuer. You might want to edit this trust if, for example, you have been exchanging messages with an individual for a long period and you have no doubt in your mind they are who they say they are, or you have good reason not to trust a certificate.

Sending and Receiving Encrypted Messages

Sending and receiving encrypted messages is functionally equivalent to working with signed messages, the only differences being:

- You may or may not have to provide a password before sending or receiving an encrypted message; this depends on your certificate and the options you chose when installing it.

- You must have a copy of the recipient's certificate saved in your Contacts folder. Trying to send an encrypted message to a contact that does not have a certificate attached to their record results in the dialog shown in Figure 15-5.

You have only two choices: remove the recipients without a certificate from the message, or send the message unencrypted.

Figure 15-5: The dialog displayed when you try to send an encrypted message to a contact without a certificate

How do you get someone's certificate? There are two ways:

- The best approach is to ask the individual to send you a digitally signed message (see "Sending and Receiving Signed Messages," earlier in this chapter). On receipt, open the message, right-click the sender's name in the From field, and choose Add to Contacts from the context menu. This creates a new record if one does not already exist, and updates the record with the certificate if one does exist.

TIP # 160

Certificates Are Issued to an Email Address

When you send encrypted email to someone, you must use the email address the certificate was issued under. This is the address that has the certificate you need.

- An alternative method is to download the certificate from the issuer's database as follows:

  - Using a browser, connect to the certification authority that issued the certificate.

  - Follow the instructions on the web site to query the database and download the certificate as a file to your computer.

  - If you don't have a contact record for the individual, you must create one. Then, open the contact and click the Certificates tab.

  - Click Import to import the certificate from the location you saved it to in the second step.

Certificate and Security Options

Outlook's certificate and security options are located on the Security tab of the Options dialog (Tools → Options) shown in Figure 15-6.

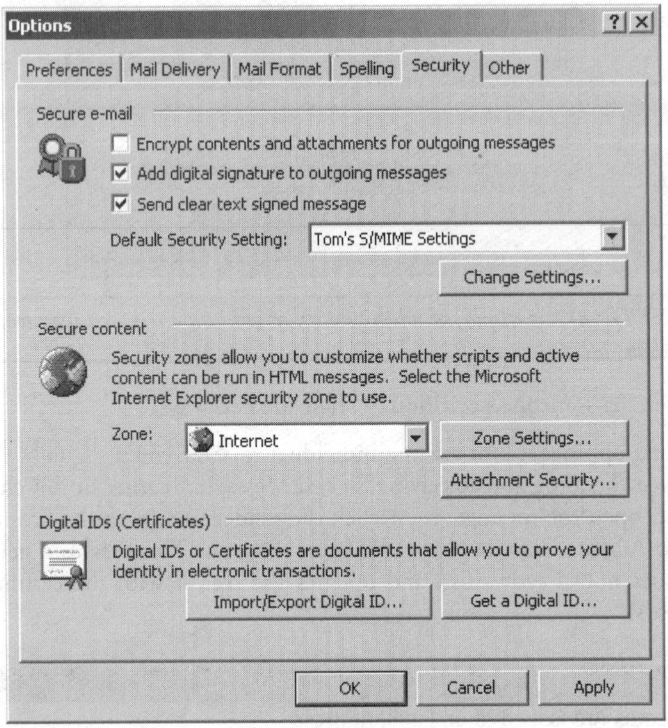

Figure 15-6: The Security tab of Outlook's Options dialog

This dialog contains the options to set defaults for how secure email is sent, create security setting profiles, a section to configure permissible content in web pages and HTML messages, an option to configure how attachments are handled, and a section pertaining to managing and acquiring digital certificates.

> **NOTE** *Digital ID is a brand name used by VeriSign for digital certificates.*

Secure email options

The first section at the top of the Security tab configures the defaults for how email is sent when a digital signature is installed on your system. If you do not have a certificate installed (or another encryption system like PGP), the options here are unavailable and the Change Settings button is labeled Setup Secure Mail:

Encrypt contents and attachments for outgoing messages
  Encrypts all outgoing messages and attachments.

Add digital signature to outgoing messages
  Signs all outgoing messages.

Send clear text signed message

Unchecked, signed messages are only readable by email clients that support S/MIME. Recipients can verify that the message was not tampered with and that it came from you (see "Sending Signed Messages" earlier in this chapter).

When this option is checked, signed messages are sent in clear text. All recipients can read the message, however clients that do not support S/MIME will not be able to verify the message came from you, nor will they know if the message has been tampered with.

The Change Setting button opens the dialog shown in Figure 15-7. Here you can create a security profile based on message format, certificate, and algorithms used for hash and encryption:

Security Settings Name

Lists all defined security profiles. You cannot change the name of a profile from this field. To create a new profile, click the New button at the bottom of the Preferences section. This clears the dialog, and allows you to specify a new group of settings based on the options chosen. The Delete button removes a profile. If you delete a profile by mistake, Cancel out of this dialog before clicking OK.

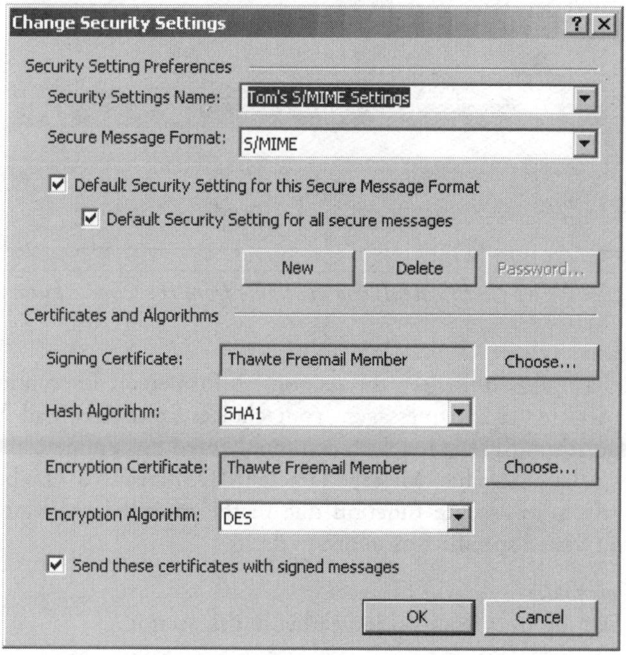

Figure 15-7: The Change Security Settings dialog

Secure Message Format
> Selects the message format to use for signed and encrypted mail. Your only two choices are S/MIME and Exchange Server Security. Use the latter only if you are using Outlook as a client to Exchange. When installed, Exchange uses Key Management Server (KMS) to create and manage keys.

Default Security Setting for this Secure Message Format
> Uses the Secure Message Format specified as the default for all security profiles.

Default Security Setting for all secure messages
> Sets the profile selected under Security Settings Name as the default for all secure message sent.

Signing Certificate
> Use the Choose button to select a certificate to use for signed messages. Different certificates support different levels of hash and encryption. This option allows you to pick a specific certificate to use for signing (and encryption). Certificates must be already installed on your system before they are available under the Select Certificate dialog shown in Figure 15-8.

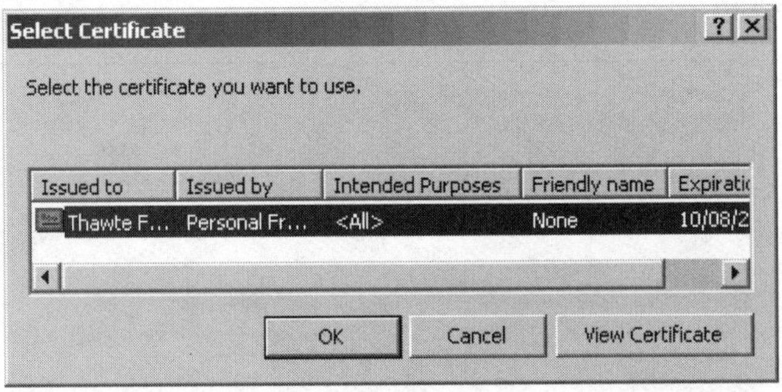

Figure 15-8: The Select Certificate dialog available from the Choose button

Hash Algorithm
> Sets the hash algorithm (see the section "A Primer on Encryption" earlier in this chapter) for signed messages. Your choices are SHA1 and MD5. Secure Hash Algorithm (SHA1) is a hash commonly used by commercial products and produces a 160-bit value. Message Digest (MD5) creates a 128-bit hash value, theoretically a less-secure function due to the shorter key length. Use SHA1 unless you have a specific reason not to do so.

Encryption Certificate
> See the Signing Certificate option earlier in this section.

Encryption Algorithm
> Sets the algorithm used for encrypted messages. As we pointed out earlier in this chapter, encryption algorithms are based on key length; the longer the key,

the stronger the encryption. There are two factors to consider when choosing an encryption algorithm: how much is enough, and whether the recipient of your message can decrypt it when it arrives. Depending on the certificate installed on your system, you will have one or more of the following choices: RC2 (40-bit), DES (56-bit), RC2 (128-bit), or 3DES (which employs three encryption steps, and can use one, two, or three 56-bit keys, making a 168-bit key length possible).

Send these certificates with signed messages

By default, Outlook attaches a copy of your certificate to all signed messages. If for some reason you do not want to do this, uncheck this option.

TIP # 161

Don't Use Signed Messages If You . . .

Routinely send messages to newsgroups, or people that do not use MIME-compliant software and text-only email tools (for example, Mutt).

Secure content options

The Secure content section of the Security options dialog is shown in Figure 15-9.

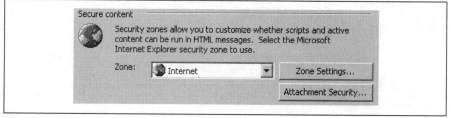

Figure 15-9: The Secure content section of the Tools → Options Security tab

Email messages and web pages can contain scripts and ActiveX controls that run on your computer. While most of these applets are useful, some may either accidentally or deliberately damage files on your hard drive. Security Zones control what happens when a script or control is received. Choices include accepting all content, warning about potentially damaging content, blocking specific content totally, and setting up Custom Zones.

TIP # 162

Security Zones Are Not Outlook Specific

Your choice of Zone setting affects both Internet Explorer and Outlook (for messages received as HTML). There is no option to set the content control separately for each program. This means that if you want to protect your incoming email from rogue scripts and badly behaved ActiveX controls, this same setting is enforced when you are browsing the Web.

The Zone Settings button opens the Security dialog shown in Figure 15-10 (left). Click an icon in the upper pane for a description of the settings attached to that zone.

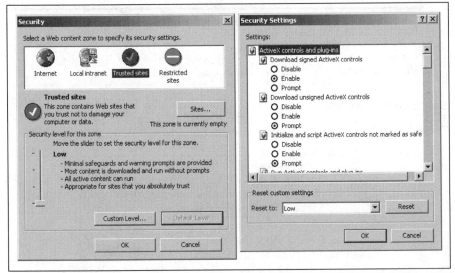

Figure 15-10: The Security dialog for configuring Security Zones (left) and the Security Settings dialog for configuring a custom security level (right)

You can also reconfigure a zone by selecting it and clicking the Custom Level button. This opens the Security Settings dialog shown in Figure 15-10 (right).

The Secure content section (see Figure 15-9) also contains an option for setting Attachment Security levels. The Attachment Security dialog is shown in Figure 15-11.

There are only two options here: High and None.

High

Displays a warning dialog whenever you open an attachment from an email message. Sometimes. Word attachments are the one notable exception. Double-click a Word file attached to a message and it opens without protest or warning. Keep this in mind if you routinely exchange Word documents with colleagues.

Figure 15-11: The Attachment Security dialog

The safest approach here is to open the message, and right-click the attachment in the lower pane of the message form. Choose Save As from the context menu, and use an anti-virus scanner on the file before opening it.

None

No warning dialogs appear, ever. Not a good option considering the number of potentially malicious attachments floating around the Internet these days.

We recommend you leave attachment security set to High, and download the Outlook 2000 patch detailed in Tip # 163.

TIP # 163

Upgrade Outlook's Attachment Dialog

Microsoft has posted a patch for Outlook that changes the dialog displayed when you open a message attachment. The new dialog contains more explicit warning language and requires you to save the attachment to the filesystem before opening it. This patch can be found at http://officeupdate.microsoft.com/2000/downloadDetails/O2Kattch. htm. Note that this patch is only for Outlook 2000.

Digital Certificate options

The Digital IDs (Certificates) section of the Security tab lets you import and export certificates and obtain a certificate from VeriSign using your web browser. Click the Import/Export Digital ID button to open the dialog shown in Figure 15-12.

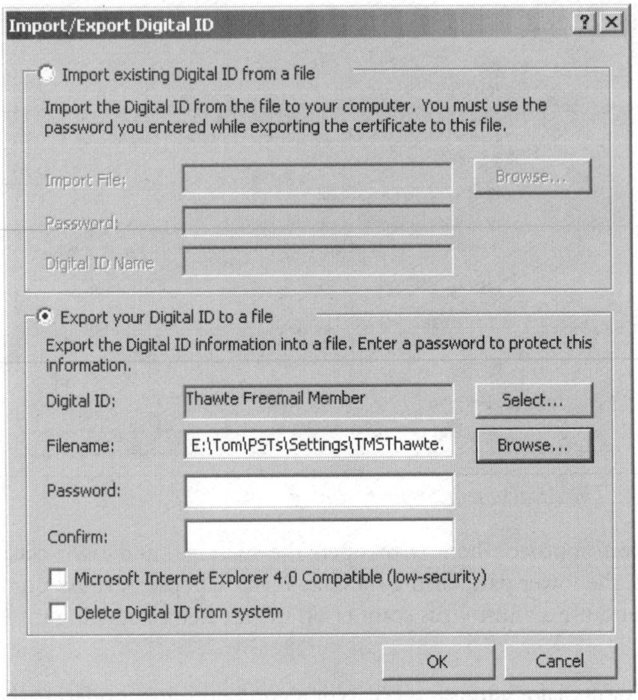

Figure 15-12: The Import/Export Digital ID dialog

We recognize that this is out of step with the dialog, but we're going to cover the Export section first because it is the most important. There are two very good reasons for exporting (read, backing up) your digital certificate:

- To restore your certificate without downloading it again if your hard drive is damaged or your operating system crashes beyond repair

- To move your certificate to another computer or hard disk

TIP # 164

Save Your Certificates to Floppy

Always save a copy of your certificates to a floppy disk and store this disk somewhere safe. Certificate information is stored in the Windows Registry, so if something happens to your system and this information is damaged or lost, you cannot send or receive encrypted messages until you download and reinstall your certificate.

To export a certificate:

1. Use Select to choose a certificate from the dialog displayed (see Figure 15-8).

2. Choose a filename and location.

3. You *must* supply a password. This does not necessarily have to be the same password supplied when you first obtained the certificate. As a security precaution, Outlook password protects the certificate before copying to your hard drive so no one but you can open, access, or install it.

At the bottom of the Export section are two further options:

Microsoft Internet Explorer 4.0 Compatible
Saves the password you supply when a certificate is exported in a low-security format (40-bit).

Delete Digital ID from system
Removes a certificate from your system. Deletes the appropriate Registry entries and any Outlook configuration files that reference the certificate, *after the file is exported.* When you save the export file to your hard drive, this does not technically remove the certificate from your system; it decouples it from Outlook.

 NOTE *The only way to remove a digital certificate from Outlook is to export it and select the "Delete Digital ID from system" checkbox. You cannot remove a certificate without exporting it.*

The import process works exactly the same, in reverse: choose a location and supply the password you entered when you exported the certificate. The Digital ID Name is optional and applies to Exchange security options. Certificates generated by Exchange allow you to specify a *keyset name*, which is typically your mailbox name.

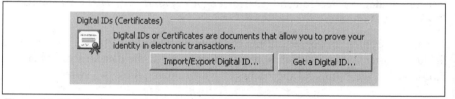

Figure 15-13: The Digital ID section of the Security Options tab

Finally, the Digital ID section of the Security tab (see Figure 15-13) has a button labeled Get a Digital ID. Clicking it opens your web browser to a page on the Office Update Site (*http://officeupdate.Microsoft.com*), which lists sources for digital certificates. At the time of this writing, the links available were:

VeriSign (*http://digitalid.verisign.com*)
GlobalSign (*http://www.globalsign.net*)
British Telecommunications (*http://www.trustwise.com*)
Thawte Certification (*http://www.thawte.com*)

Chapter 16

Outlook and the Palm

The Palm is an engineering marvel. It is roughly 5" by 3", weighs less than 6 ounces, and is powered by a Motorola 68328 processor. The Palm IIIx is based on version 3.01 of the Palm OS, which occupies a paltry 40K of the 4 MB of installed memory. That, incidentally, is roughly 100 times smaller than the base code for Windows 98. Of course, the Palm does not do everything Windows 98 does, but it was not designed as a desktop operating system—it was designed to supplement your desktop operating system. On the other hand, Windows 98 does not fit in your pocket, either.

This chapter is not about using the Palm; we assume our readers have already figured out how to turn it on, write memos in Graffiti, and make a calendar entry. If you are new to the Palm, there are a number of excellent books out there on the subject; if you are just starting out with this marvelous little tool and need a good general guide, we recommend David Pogue's *PalmPilot: The Ultimate Guide* (O'Reilly & Associates).

What this chapter does cover is using the Palm with Outlook 2000. Topics covered include setting up the HotSync software, differences in the data structures between Outlook and the Palm, and approaches to synchronizing these two systems.

Installation and Setup

Before you can use your Palm with Outlook, you need to install the Palm Desktop software. This program is supplied on the CD that comes with the Palm, and provides the software to synchronize the data on your Palm with Outlook (and visa-versa). There are three possible installation scenarios:

- You have neither Outlook nor any Palm software installed.

- Outlook is installed on your system, but not the Palm Desktop.

- The Palm software is installed on your system, and you want to use Outlook.

Let's start with the easiest first.

NOTE

At least one reader has informed us that his new Palm did not come with the appropriate software to sync it with Outlook. While we have no direct experience with this, if you're going to buy a Palm, we recommend you ask the appropriate questions before putting your money on the counter.

Starting Fresh

Begin by installing Outlook *first*. Detailed instructions can be found in Chapter 2, *Installing Outlook*. It doesn't matter which installation mode you choose (No E-mail, IMO, or CW). What does matter, however, is what you do after Outlook is installed. The Palm software needs to see Outlook both as a registered program on your system, *and* as the default mail client. For this reason, we suggest the following installation procedure:

1. Install Outlook following the guidelines given in Chapter 2.

2. Restart your system—even if the installation routine does not tell you to do so. This ensures that Outlook is properly registered with Windows.

3. Start Outlook and follow the instructions given by the Setup Wizard (again, see Chapter 2). Make sure you enable Outlook as the "default manager for Mail and News" if you see the dialog shown in Figure 16-1 (which you will if you've been using Outlook Express as a mail client).

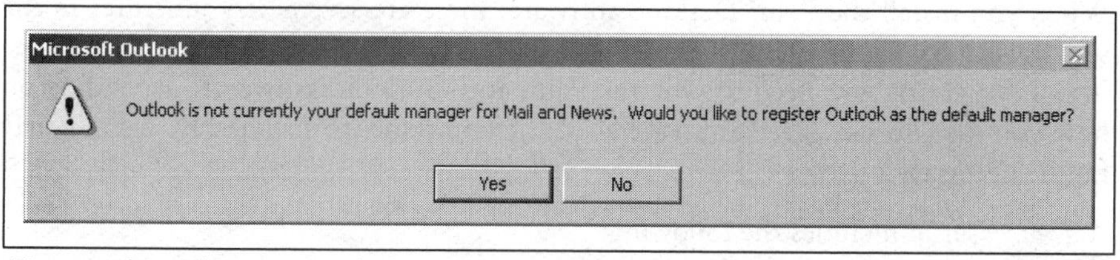

Figure 16-1: The warning dialog shown when Outlook is not the default client for Mail and News

TIP # 165

Forcing Outlook as the Default Mail Client

If Outlook is not your default Mail client, you can force Outlook to display the dialog shown in Figure 16-1 by closing the program, and typing outlook.exe /check-client in the Run dialog of the Windows Start menu.

Starting Outlook is an important step before installing the Palm software:

– It ensures that Outlook works as advertised. This keeps things simple from a troubleshooting perspective. Trying to sort out layered installation problems is not something you want to do if it can at all be avoided.

– It ensures Outlook is properly registered with the operating system.

- It creates a user database or information store for Outlook records.

- Palm software installations go a lot smoother if you ensure all these elements are in place before you begin.

4. Now install the Palm software as detailed in the next section.

Installing the Palm Software

Before you proceed, read the following preinstallation steps carefully. They are firmly grounded in experience.

1. Stop and back up your Outlook files (see Chapter 13, *File Management*, for details). If you happen to configure the synchronization defaults incorrectly, there is a possibility you could overwrite your data in Outlook with the data on the Palm.

2. Make sure your COM port is configured and working correctly. You can configure and adjust this later if problems arise; it's just a lot easier to sort any hardware issues out up front.

3. Make sure Outlook is running. If Outlook is not running at the time of installation, the setup program will not complete (you'll make it all the way to the last step), and you will have to run the setup program again.

When you install the Palm Desktop software, there are several key junctures in the setup routine to be aware of. Clicking through the setup dialogs will, in most cases, install everything you need to sync the Palm and Outlook. However, depending on how you plan to use the Palm, several of the components installed by default may not be necessary.

A *Typical* setup includes the following:

Palm Desktop
This is Palm's version of a PIM (Personal Information Manager). It includes a calendar, phone book, to-do list, and memo pad. The Palm Desktop also includes several utilities such as an import-export tool. You do not need this application installed to use Outlook with the Palm.

HotSync® Manager
These are the conduits required for syncing the Palm with the applications (the Palm Desktop, Outlook, etc.) on your PC. The HotSync Manager is a required component of the Palm software installation.

Mail Application
Includes the conduits required to sync the Mail application on the Palm with a compatible email client on your desktop. With this option installed, you can sync Outlook's Inbox with the Palm. You can then read and reply to email from the Palm, and sync any changes back to your PC.

Expense

Installs a conduit that allows you to sync data between the Palm's Expense program and MS Excel (5.0 or later).

Quick Tour

Installs a guided multimedia tour explaining how to get started using the Palm.

What should you install?

- If you do not need any file import/export capabilities, and plan to use Outlook as your PIM, skip the Palm Desktop option. Note that when you install the Palm software, you can only synchronize data with *one* application—Outlook (or another supported application) or the Palm Desktop. If you decide later that you'd prefer to use the Palm Desktop, this requires reinstalling the Palm software anyway, so omitting this option is not critical.

- You must install the HotSync Manager—no choice here.

- The mail application software is useful if you travel with a Palm, or use the Palm away from your desktop for extended periods. Unless you have a modem for your Palm (or are using one of Palms new wireless models), you still must resync changes with your desktop before they can be sent to a mail server.

- If you plan on using the Palm's Expense program, and you have at least Excel 5.0 installed on your desktop, this option allows you to transfer data from your Palm into an Excel spreadsheet for tweaking and/or printing. The Expense program exists only on the Palm itself; there is no associated component packaged with the Palm Desktop.

- If you're new to the Palm, you might find the Quick Tour entertaining. Keep in mind, however, there is no separate routine to uninstall just the Quick Tour. Once you're viewed it several times, and it is of no further use to you, the only way to scour it from your hard drive is to uninstall the Palm Desktop software and reinstall the program again without it.

To install the Palm Desktop software:

 The information in this section details the installation of the Palm Desktop version 3.0.1. If you are using an earlier or later version of this product, the dialogs and options shown may vary.

1. Begin by connecting the HotSync cradle to an available COM port. Make sure the Palm is not in the cradle at this time. We recommend closing all running programs before you begin—*except Outlook*.

2. Insert the CD and follow the prompts. After the obligatory Welcome and preinstallation dialogs, you are asked to choose a setup type and destination folder (see Figure 16-2). Choose your preferred Setup type and click OK.

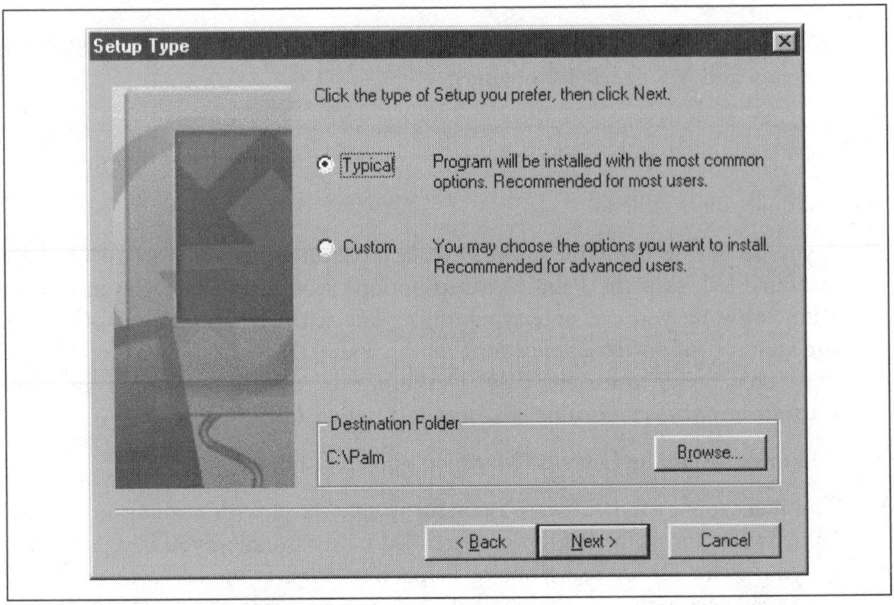

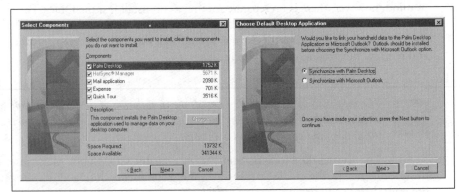

Figure 16-2: The Palm software Setup Type dialog

 The setup program does not install the Palm software in <drive>\Program Files\<application> as might be expected. We recommend changing this to the folder where the rest of your program files are located.

3. Choosing Custom displays the dialog shown in Figure 16-3 (left). Select the components you want to install and click Next.

Figure 16-3: Selecting the Palm components (left) and choosing a default Desktop application (right)

4. The Choose Default Desktop Application dialog, shown in Figure 16-3 (right) is one of the key junctures we talked about earlier in this section. This is where you decide which desktop application the Palm synchronizes with. Your choice

here cannot be reversed with software settings; to change desktop applications, you must reinstall the Palm Desktop software.

5. Next you are asked to enter a username (see Figure 16-4). This identifies your Palm, and is recorded in both the desktop software and the Palm itself. Make sure the name you choose is unique.

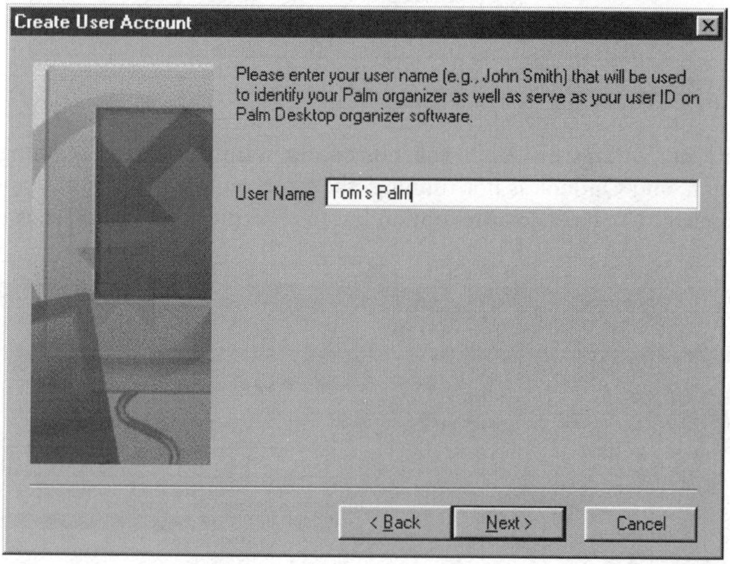

Figure 16-4: Entering a User Name

TIP # 166

Naming Your Palm

If you only sync one Palm with your PC, the username is not important. When you sync multiple Palms with a single PC, however, the username is critical; it tells HotSync which Palm it's synchronizing with. In a multiple-Palms-one-PC scenario, do not give two Palms the same name. This confuses the HotSync software and there is a very real possibility of the data on both Palms getting hopelessly scrambled.

6. After selecting a program folder for the Palm's software shortcuts, you are asked to place your Palm in the HotSync cradle so it can be detected (see Figure 16-5). Click OK to proceed. If Setup cannot find the Palm (or the cradle) for whatever reason, you can skip the warning dialog displayed and configure the COM port later. The next screens guide you through configuring an email application (if chosen in the Setup options).

7. Figure 16-6 shows the Mail Settings dialog. Choose Outlook from the dropdown list provided. This is another important juncture. You cannot back out of

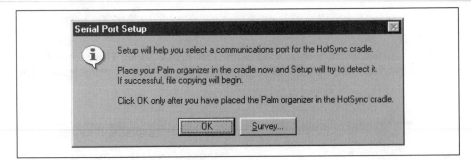

Figure 16-5: The Serial Port Setup dialog

the Mail Settings dialog. If you missed our warning at the beginning of this section, and Outlook is not running, the setup program will protest and fail to complete. You have no other option but to close the program and start over.

Figure 16-6: The Palm's Mail Setting option dialog

 NOTE *It is possible to change the Mail Settings dialog after installation by running the command available at: Start → Programs → Palm Desktop (or whatever you named it) → Palm Mail Setup.*

8. After you've chosen an email application, if this is a first time installation, you are asked if you want to create a profile for Outlook. Answer Yes. Profiles are simply the details of your email address, reply name, POP account, SMTP account, etc.

Installing Outlook After-the-Fact

If you have been using the Palm Desktop software as a PIM, and you want to switch to Outlook, there's no point-and-click way to do this. You must uninstall the Palm software, install Outlook (if it is not already), and reinstall the Palm software.

Fields, Folders, and the Palm

Before looking at how to transfer data between Outlook and the Palm, we need to address the issue of *what* gets transferred, and *where* it goes. It's always good to know things like this before you start zapping records between two platforms.

As you know from Chapter 3, *Program Insights*, Outlook stores data in information stores, which contain folders, which contain individual records. The Palm uses a similar structure. Think of the handheld as the store, and the Palm's programs as equivalent to Outlook's folders. While not as graphically depicted, records stored in the Palm are no different than items in Outlook. Table 16-1 compares program components.

The Palm software can only synchronize the data from your default information store—there is no provision for selecting an alternate source for Outlook data.

Table 16-1: Outlook and Palm Components Compared

Outlook Folder	Palm Equivalent
Mail	Mail
Calendar	Date Book
Contacts	Address
Tasks	To-Dos
Notes	Memos
Journal	N/A

 The Palm's base configuration does not support Outlook's Journal component. You can, however, add this capability with a third-party product called PocketJournal. See the sidebar "Chapura's Solutions" for more details.

The major difference between Outlook and the Palm are the fields supported, which, considering the size and capacity of the Palm, is to be expected.

Table 16-2 lists the fields available in each of the Palm's five components also supported under Outlook. Outlook's equivalent names and fields (or properties, in the case of Date Book's No time=Event) are shown in brackets.

Table 16-2: The Palm's Component Fields

Palm Component	Fields Available
Mail (Mail)	To, CC, Subj (Subject), Body, Priority, BCC, Signature, Confirm Read (Read Receipt), Confirm Delivery (Delivery Receipt)
Date Book (Calendar)	Date, Start Time, End Time, No Time (Event), Detail line (Subject), Alarm, Repeat (Recurring Appointment), Note (Notes field), Private
Address (Contacts)	Last Name, First Name, Company, Title, Work, Home, Fax, Other, E-mail, Address, City, Province or State, Postal Code or Zip, Country, Custom 1 thru 4 (no equivalent under Outlook), Note (Notes field), Show in List (no equivalent), Category (N/A), Private
To-Dos (Tasks)	Detail line (Subject), Priority, Due Date, Private
Memos (Notes)	Multiple-line entry, Category (N/A), Private

The following explanations and/or clarifications refer to Table 16-2:

Mail

Priority on the Palm is selectable as 1 to 5. Under Outlook, these translate to 1 (High), 2 to 4 (Medium), and 5 (Low). High Priority mail items are displayed in bold on the Palm.

Priority, Bcc, Signature, Confirm Read, and Confirm Delivery are available on the Message Detail dialog of the Palm. Tap Details from a new message screen.

The Palm supports email signatures, but existing signatures from Outlook are not transferred. In order to create a signature on the Palm, tap Menu → Options → Preferences.

File attachments are not transferred to the Palm. If there are attachments, the Palm displays "There are 1 file(s) attached to this message on your Desktop" in the body of the message.

The Palm has provisions for Inbox, Outbox, Deleted, Filed, and Draft. These correspond to Outlook's counterparts with the exception of Filed. Filed messages are stored on the Palm and not transferred back to Outlook during a HotSync.

Date Book

"No Time" appointments that are entered from the Palm are displayed as Events in Outlook.

Address

The Palm supports selectable field titles for phone numbers and email addresses similar to Outlook. The field titles shown in Table 16-2 are the defaults. To display field lists on the Palm, tap the down-arrow next to the field title.

The Palm Address program has four custom fields: Custom 1 through 4. Contents of these fields are not transferred to Outlook.

Memos

The Palm supports stamping a Memo as Private, Outlook does not.

TIP # 167

Limitations of a Memo

The Palm's Memo field is excellent for jotting quick notes, but it a bit inadequate for writing a book—each Memo can only hold 4K of information.

Synchronizing the Palm and Outlook

The act of synchronizing data between the Palm and another application is called a *HotSync*. In the context of Outlook, this is the process where the records in a specific folder are synchronized with a matching item type on the Palm. A comparison of the relationship on item types between the two programs is shown in Table 16-3.

When a HotSync is requested, the software compares each record on the Palm against the records on the PC. The default action is to *Synchronize the files*. When this happens, the HotSync software looks at the internal date stamp of each record to decide how to proceed. Table 16-3 shows how records are synchronized. The Actions column define an action on the part of the user, the HotSync Synchronize Command column details how this action is resolved.

Table 16-3: The Palm Synchronize Function

Action	HotSync Synchronize Command
Create new record (Palm or Outlook)	The record is added to the opposite system.
Delete record (Palm or Outlook)	The record is deleted from the opposite system.
Change a record (Palm or Outlook)	The change is updated on the opposite system.
Change the same record in the same way on both systems	No changes are made to either system.
Change the same record in different ways on both systems	The record appears twice on each machine— one is the original entry, the other is the entry made on the opposite system. An error message is logged.
Change a record on the Palm, delete the opposite record in Outlook	The record remains in its present form on both systems. An error message is logged.

TIP # 168

Curing Duplicate Records

The solution for dealing with duplicate records (see the entry in Table 16-3, "Change the same record in different ways on both systems") is to delete one duplicate on one system, and then HotSync again.

Conduits Explained

Before turning to HotSync options, a rudimentary understanding of *conduits* is in order. A conduit is a software program written to synchronize *one type* of data between a desktop application and the Palm. The Palm software installs five conduits specific to Outlook: Mail, Outlook Calendar, Outlook Contacts, Outlook Notes, and Outlook Tasks. Each individual conduit:

- Is responsible for synchronizing its corresponding Outlook item type

- Can be turned on or off independently from the rest

- Can be set for a specific action: Synchronize, Overwrite the Desktop, Overwrite the Palm, and Do Nothing

This flexibility allows you to tailor a conduit's response during a HotSync operation for either a one-time transfer or as the default. For example, you might decide to HotSync only your address book, as this is the only data changed since the last update. By limiting the records checked and transferred, you can speed up the HotSync. This selective data synchronization also allows you to restore a damaged group of records from either source, to either destination.

TIP # 169

Use the Palm to Back Up Outlook

Keeping your Palm closely synchronized with Outlook is an excellent way to keep a current backup of your working information store. It's quick, it's easy, and it's portable. What more could you want? With the current drop in price of an entry-level Palm, the cost is almost justified even if you only used it as an alternative backup for your Outlook data. Of course, you won't just use it for that...

Configuring HotSync Options

To display HotSync options, click the HotSync icon in the System Tray (the circle with two diagonal arrows joining in the middle) and select Custom from the context menu. From the Windows Start menu, choose Programs → Palm Desktop → HotSync Manager. The Custom dialog is shown in Figure 16-7.

When you synchronize the Palm with Outlook, there are three possible options:

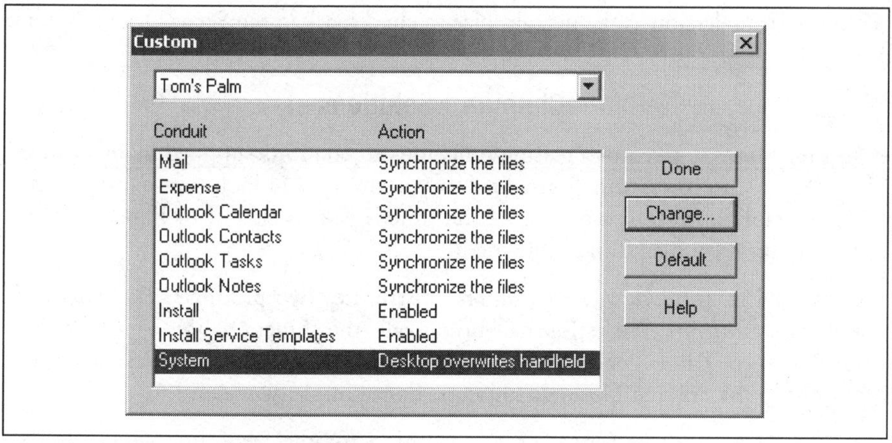

Figure 16-7: HotSync's Custom dialog

Synchronize the files
> This is the default. See Table 16-3 for the action taken based on how and where the record is changed.

Desktop overwrites handheld
> All records for the selected conduit overwrite what's stored on the Palm.

Handheld overwrites Desktop
> All records for the selected conduit overwrite what's stored in Outlook.

Do nothing
> Use this option to update another program (with an installed conduit) without updating the selected Outlook conduit.

To change a conduit's action during a HotSync, click Change to open the Change HotSync Action dialog shown in Figure 16-8.

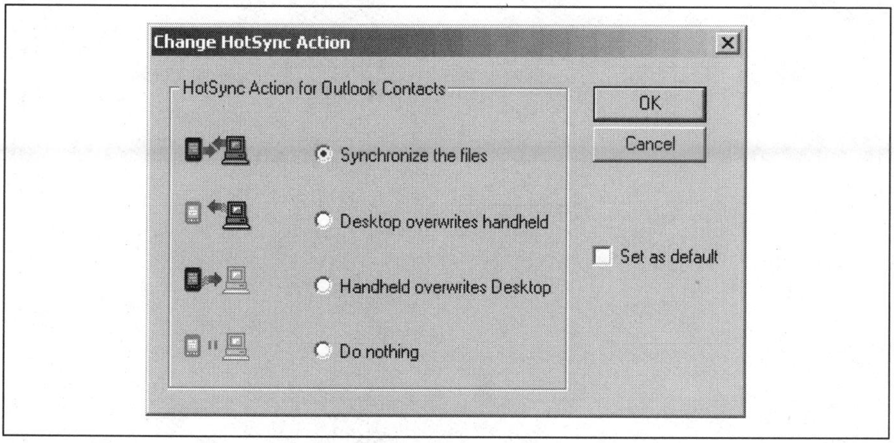

Figure 16-8: The Change HotSync Action dialog

To preserve a selection as the default, place a checkmark in the Set as Default option.

Chapura's Solutions

You may have noticed two glaring omissions to conduits supplied by 3Com for the Palm: Categories and Journaling. If you are an Outlook power user, these are probably both tools you use all the time. Luckily, thanks to Phil Chapura, you can have your cake and HotSync it too.

Chapura Inc. (*http://www.chapura.com*) distributes two products: *PocketJournal* and *PocketMirror*. PocketJournal brings all the functionality of Outlook's Journal to the Palm. PocketMirror is a Conduit Manager that adds several useful options to the existing HotSync software. For example, you can:

- Preset a one-time synchronization option for the next time your Palm is HotSynced.

- Map categories between Outlook and the Palm.

- Filter items marked Private.

- Enable Journaling for contacts added to the Palm.

- Display full SMTP addresses for a contact rather than the Display Name.

- Set the contacts File As order when a name is saved on the Palm and add the company to this field just as it's displayed in Outlook: Company (Last, First), for example.

Chapura's products work, and they work well. If you use Outlook and a Palm, you owe it to yourself to check out these products. Demos are available for 30-day trials.

Chapter 17

Outlook and Exchange

Microsoft's Exchange Server is a powerful messaging platform. Used in conjunction with Outlook, it opens up a whole new world of collaboration capabilities. It also opens a whole new way of using Outlook. Exchange information stores are server-based, which opens up a host of connectivity and storage location issues. Mail rules are now implemented on the server (at least most are) and adopt the term "Out of Office Replies." Exchange folders support multiuser access, making them ideal for sharing information. But Exchange is run on a server, so user access is dictated by permissions. In short, all these features and functionality add yet another layer of complexity to an already diverse application.

One chapter does not do justice to the topic of using Outlook as a client to Exchange—the features unique to this platform, and how to use those features, could easily fill a whole book (yes, we're thinking about it). In this chapter, we focus on using the collaboration tools available under Exchange: Public Folders, Delegate folders, and shared folders. In addition, we touch on setting up and using Offline folders, creating Out of Office Replies, and message recall. The chapter ends with a troubleshooting section that details some of the common problems Outlook users face specific to Exchange.

Keep in mind that Exchange Servers are lorded over by an administrator (some-times fervently). Every object on an Exchange Server has an associated set of permissions (read, edit, create, etc.) so the options and features available to each user vary. The best advice we can offer is to talk to your system administrator, find out what's available, and what you can access.

Storage Locations

When run as a standalone application (in either IMO or CW mode), Outlook items are stored locally on your hard drive in a PST, or Personal Folders File. Using Outlook as a client to Exchange is a whole different ballgame. You now have a choice of three locations to store data:

- In a local information store

- In a local Offline folder

- In a remote Exchange information store

When you connect to Exchange you must have a user account, which implies an Exchange mailbox and associated information store. You can also optionally store data in a local PST and/or an Offline folder. To decide which storage locations best suit your needs, consider the following:

Availability

How available is the information store? Local information stores are accessible any time the user's machine is on. Exchange necessitates a connection (either LAN or dialup). When Exchange is not available, an Offline folder can be used in its place.

Location

Where is the information store located—on the user's local hard drive, or within an Exchange database? Some system administrators stipulate that all data be stored on the server. This facilitates central data administration and backups.

Function

Each information store has a different function. PSTs are similar to an Exchange store, but lack many of the collaborative features integral to a server-based messaging platform. Offline folders are unique in that they provide a user with a way to work with data created on Exchange without a permanent connection.

Figure 17-1 shows one example of these concepts.

1. Mailbox – *user*

   This is the user's personal store and is located on the Exchange Server. It has the same characteristics as a local personal store: folders contain specific types of Outlook items; the mailbox contains a default set of system folders; the user is free to add additional folders or subfolders.

2. Outlook Today – [Personal Folders]

   This is a local personal store, separate and distinct from the Exchange store. In this example, this is the user's default information store where POP mail is delivered. The Home/Clock icon denotes the default information store used by Outlook.

3. Personal Mail

   In this example, the user has a second personal store for sorting and organizing items (see Chapter 13, *File Management*, for an explanation of using and creating multiple PSTs).

4. Public Folders

   This is a special information store, located on the Exchange Server, and used to give a group of people shared access to information.

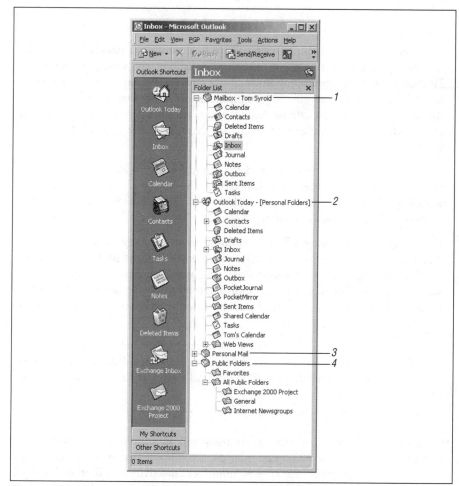

Figure 17-1: An example Folder List view of multiple information store types and locations

If Outlook was in "offline mode," the user mailbox displayed in Figure 17-1 (item #1) would be replaced by an Offline folder—if Outlook's Exchange service was configured for this feature. Nothing in the figure shown, however, would look any different.

PSTs: An Exchange Administrator's Perspective

Many Exchange administrators equate PSTs with a plague, and either have a strict policy against their use, or get a nervous twitch when they discover their existence on a user's computer. Here are some reasons why:

A Personal Who?

Microsoft has a nasty habit of using illogical or confusing names for program elements, and then gluing them to dialogs, warnings, etc. One example is the *Personal Folders file*, commonly known as a *PST* (or Personal Store). A PST is not in fact a folder at all—it's an information store that contains folders. Another example is the Offline folder; again, it's an information store, not a folder. Most people overlook the fact that these terms are appended with the word "file."

This is all well and good for the standalone Outlook user, who typically uses one information store, and the name displayed in the Folder List is not particularly significant. When you connect Outlook to Exchange however, things get interesting—and confusing—in a hurry.

If you happen to be using a PST in addition to an Exchange mailbox, accurate descriptions of the contents of these stores becomes a thorny problem. You have personal folders in your Exchange store, and you have personal folders in the store on your local hard drive. Add to this complication the fact that the system folders (Inbox, Contacts, Sent Items, etc.) cannot be renamed. So *which personal folder* are you working in?

This is precisely why we avoid the use of the term Personal Folders file in our writing. Unfortunately, we also have to refer to Outlook's dialogs with accurate descriptions. We sincerely hope you do not find all this as hard to read and decipher as it was to write.

- Local data is difficult to manage centrally and an administrative nightmare to back up on a routine basis. PST files do not support shared access. Outlook is supposed to close a PST file after 30 minutes of inactivity, but if other MAPI clients are running, scheduled backups can't access the file because it's still in use.

- Locally stored data negates the benefits of Exchange's single-instance storage, so it's much easier for users to lose their mail data.

- PSTs use at least twice as much space as an Exchange information store. PSTs store two copies of each message: one as Plain Text and one in Rich Text format (RTF).

- Server-based rules do not work on local PST data.

- Users whose calendars are stored in PST files can't share this information with server-based users. This means users lose many of the benefits of Exchange's rich calendaring options.

Paul Robichaux (author of *Managing Microsoft Exchange Server*, O'Reilly & Associates), one of the industry's leading experts on Exchange, offers the following advice regarding the use of PSTs in an Exchange environment:

> As a general rule, I recommend that Outlook users avoid using PSTs as the default mail delivery location. There is one place where PST files can be useful: for storing older, non-critical messages or archived items that no longer need to be stored on the server. Since those messages are basically archival material, they won't change terribly often, they can be backed up less frequently, and they generally won't need to be shared among multiple users.

If you choose to disregard this advice and use PST files as your primary mail storage method, here are a few things to be aware of:

- Be very careful to note what the client's Default Delivery Location field says (check the Delivery tab in the dialog that appears when you use the Tools → Services command). If you're using an Exchange mailbox you will, in almost every instance, want the default delivery location to be the mailbox in the IS [Exchange Information Store]. If you set the default location to a user's PST file, all of the mailbox's mail will be moved to the Inbox of the PST file.

- Reminders will fire only from the root folders of the default delivery location. If you have the default delivery set to the Exchange mailbox, reminders for any tasks or calendar items that user puts in the PST folder do not activate.

- It's very easy for users to get confused about which version of the Inbox or Calendar they are looking at. Caution them to be careful about not inadvertently posting or scheduling in the wrong location.

On the flip side, there are companies that *require* users to create and maintain local PSTs to store personal, noncritical, or sensitive information. This data is intentionally not backed up or archived. The reason for this is legal, rather than logistical. Companies are finding, as a result of recent court decisions, that all email that is stored as a whole can be subpoenaed, which means that if a litigant can show just one message of this group to be important, they can claim the entire Exchange data store. Local PSTs eliminate that risk, or at least minimize it by limiting the risk to one machine at a time.

Our advice is to check with your Exchange administrator and ask about your company's policy on the issue.

TIP # 170

One Local PST Advantage

If you frequently travel and find yourself out of touch with your office for long periods, it's useful to have a copy of emails with you to use for reference, particularly if your business relies on email for most communication. While an OST can serve a similar purpose, it doesn't hurt to have a backup copy of important messages and contact information on your system.

Offline Folders

Offline folders are designed for people who do not have a full-time LAN connection. Typical uses for Offline folders are notebook users and users that connect to Exchange with a dial-up connection. With an Offline folder configured, you can connect to your Exchange mailbox (or a Public Folder), synchronize the contents, disconnect, and continue working in Outlook just as you would if you were still online.

> **NOTE** *The key difference between a PST and an OST is the former contains a set of Outlook folders that are independent of any other information stores. An OST, on the other hand, contains a set of Outlook folders that mirror the structure and contents of the mailbox they were created for.*

An Offline folder is stored locally on the user's hard drive (file extension *.ost*). When Outlook is not physically connected to Exchange, the Folder List continues to display the user's mailbox and folder structure (Outlook Today – [Mailbox – *username*], see Figure 17-1). You can work with the contents of any folder, send mail, or look up a contact. As a matter of fact, the only clue available that you are not directly connected to Exchange is the presence of a small offline icon in Outlook's status bar.

Changes are synchronized between stores in two ways:

1. Manually, by using the commands available under Outlook's Tools → Synchronize menu (or by pressing F9).

2. Automatically, when Outlook reconnects with Exchange or when the File → Exit and Log Off command is used.

Offline folders are typically created when the Microsoft Exchange service is first added to a user's profile (see Chapter 2, *Installing Outlook*), and function as a subset of this service. To add an Offline folder to an existing profile:

1. Connect to the Exchange Server mailbox you want to create an Offline folder for.

2. Open the Services dialog (Tools → Services) and select Microsoft Exchange Server from the services listed. Click the Properties button, and move to the Advanced tab.

3. Select the Enable Offline Use checkbox, and click the Offline Folder File Settings button. The dialog shown in Figure 17-2 is displayed.

4. Choose a location and filename for the Offline folder. We do not recommend accepting the defaults Outlook suggests. While the location is not critical, use a name for the OST that reflects the user and/or mailbox it will serve. Click OK, and the server-based mailbox is mirrored to the file specified.

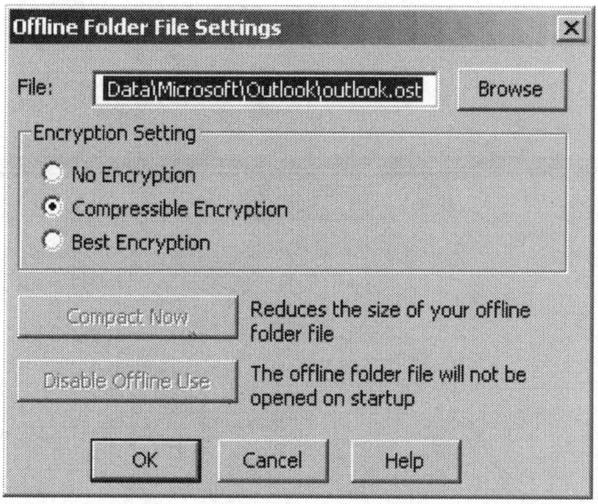

Figure 17-2: The Offline Folder File Setting dialog

TIP # 171

Changing the Filename or Path of an OST

To change the filename or path of an OST file, the existing local file must be deleted and a new OST created.

When an OST is created, all folders contained in the Exchange mailbox of the profile are replicated to this file. This includes the usual default system folders (Calendar, Contacts, Delete Items, Drafts, Inbox, Journal, Notes, Outbox, Sent Items, and Tasks), plus any folders or subfolders added by the user. This initial synchronization does not, however, include any public, delegated, or shared folder listed in your Exchange Favorites folder. These must be manually added. Instructions for adding a public folder to an OST are detailed later in this chapter under the "Setting up Delegate Access" section.

Synchronizing an OST with your Exchange mailbox can dramatically add to Outlook's logon/shutdown time. You can reduce this delay by only synchronizing required folders, or filtering the range or content of items replicated. The ten system folders are included in the Offline folder by default, and there they cannot be configured otherwise. You can, however, include/exclude any other folders or subfolders added to the store.

Offline folder settings are configured from the Synchronization tab of a folder's Properties dialog (right-click and select Properties from the context menu) as shown in Figure 17-3. To include a folder in the offline synchronization, select "When offline or online;" to exclude it, select "Only when online." The Filters button opens a dialog allowing you to specify criteria under which items are synchronized. Filtering Outlook items is discussed in Chapter 3, *Program Insights*.

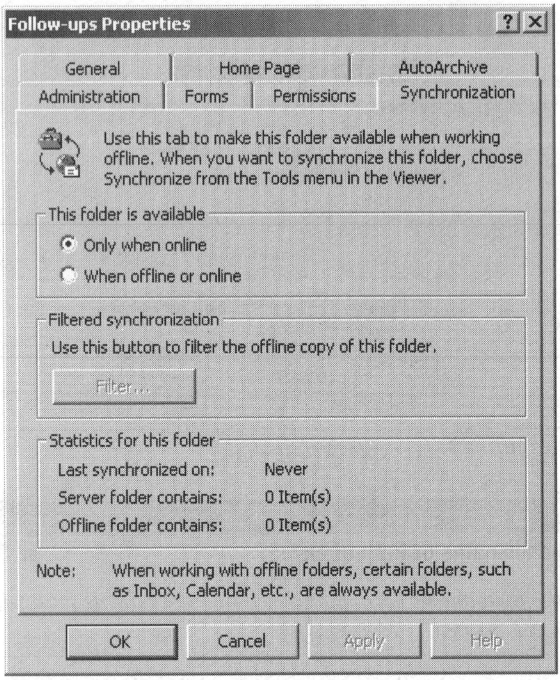

Figure 17-3: The Synchronization tab of the folder Properties dialog

> **NOTE** *Two blue arrows superimposed on a folder icon indicate an Offline folder.*

Sharing Information Under Exchange

There are three ways of sharing information under Exchange:

Public Folders
Are information stores used to distribute information to a group or throughout an organization.

Delegate Access
Allows one or more people to access your Exchange mailbox and act on your behalf.

Shared Folders
Let you share a folder with one or more people within a workgroup.

Public Folders

Public folders are a special type of information store and are located on an Exchange Server. They are created and managed, however, from the client—which in our case is Outlook. Public folders can be used for:

- Posting information of interest to a group of people. Topics are typically arranged in separate folders. Access permissions are assigned to groups and/or individuals, allowing them to either read or contribute to the folder's contents.

- Maintaining an unmoderated bulletin board. Used in this way, a public folder is very similar to an Internet newsgroup. Everyone has permission to read and post information. Normally, one person has permission to delete folder contents.

- Maintaining a moderated bulletin board. Users submit items to an assigned moderator, who then decides which material to post to the folder.

- Sharing Outlook items with other people. The owner of the item (or items) copies it to a public folder and assigns permissions that give specific people or groups access to the item.

- Sharing files created in other applications. This is where the real power of public folders is seen. Documents created in Word or Excel can be copied to a public folder. Users are assigned access permissions that vary from simply viewing the document, to editing or deleting it.

Beyond the collaborative aspects of public folders, there is a recurring theme in the preceding list: permissions. All Exchange objects are based on permissions, which determine who accesses what and how. Public folders are no different. Before you can create a public folder, you must have the appropriate permissions. The Exchange administrator is responsible for assigning these permissions.

Creating a public folder

To create a public folder, open Outlook's Folder List (see Figure 17-4) and navigate to Public Folders/All Public Folders. Right-click and choose New Folder from the context menu. Public folders are created exactly as you would any other Outlook folder—enter a name and a folder type.

Unless you intend to use the public folder to store one specific type of Outlook item (for example, a Corporate calendar), stick with the Mail folder type. This allows the most flexibility in both application and range of possible items the folder can contain.

Assigning access permissions

The creator of a public folder is the de facto owner, and has control over who can access it, and in what *role*. The only other person who can control access of a public

Figure 17-4: A Folder List view of several types of public folders

folder is the Exchange Administrator. Access permissions can be assigned in one of two ways: to an individual, or to a group.

Permissions are defined by the role assigned to an individual or group by the folder's owner. Each role has three parts: access rights, folder ownership, and who can delete what. These permission types and their associated permissions are shown in Table 17-1. Table 17-2 lists the preconfigured roles available. These same roles and permissions also apply when assigning a delegate to a folder, or sharing a folder with another user.

Table 17-1: Folder Permission Types

Permission Type	Permissions
Access	Create items; Read items; Edit own items; Edit all items; Create subfolders; Folder visible
Ownership	Folder owner; Folder contact
Delete	Delete own items; Delete all items

Table 17-2: Predefined Roles

Role	Permissions
Author	Create, read, modify, and delete own items
Contributor	Read items; Submit items and files
Custom	Any combination of permissions
Editor	Create, read, modify, and delete all items and files
Non-Editing Author	Create and read items; Delete own items
Owner	Create, read, modify, and delete all items and files; Create subfolders; Set permissions for other users
Publishing Author	Create and read items; Modify and delete own items; Create subfolders
Publishing Editor	Create, read, modify, and delete all items and files; Create subfolders
Reviewer	Read items

Public folders are created with three default permissions assigned: Default, Anonymous, and the owner's name.

Default

Defines the permission level granted to anyone with an Exchange Server account. Exchange assigns Author permissions to default users.

Anonymous

Defines the permission level assigned to someone who does not have an Exchange account, but is given access to the server (by the administrator) as an anonymous user.

`Owner name`

Defines the folder owner's permission level. This defaults to Owner.

TIP # 172

Limit User Access to a Public Folder

If the target audience of a public folder is not the general public, make sure you change the Default permission to None.

Permissions for a public folder are assigned and modified from the Permissions tab on the folder Properties dialog (see Figure 17-5).

Choose a name from the list displayed to see the permissions assigned to that group or person. Selecting permission options shifts the role assigned accordingly; if the combination of options selected is not predefined, the role changes to Custom.

The Add button opens the Add Users dialog shown in Figure 17-6. From here you can select one or more people to add to the Names field. Click OK to return to the folder Permissions tab and assign roles.

Posting information to a public folder

Public folders are designed to contain topics for discussion or review targeted at a defined group of people. For this reason, messages are *posted* to the folder. This is similar in principle to sending an email, however, the recipient is the folder, not an individual.

To post a message to a selected public folder, use the New Post in This Folder command from either the File → New menu or Outlook's standard toolbar (sorry, there is no context menu entry for this command for some reason). This opens a Discussion form similar to the one shown in Figure 17-7.

Fill in a subject (which is copied to the noneditable Conversation field when the message is posted), enter any details or comments in the text box, and click Post. All other elements on the form function the same as sending an email.

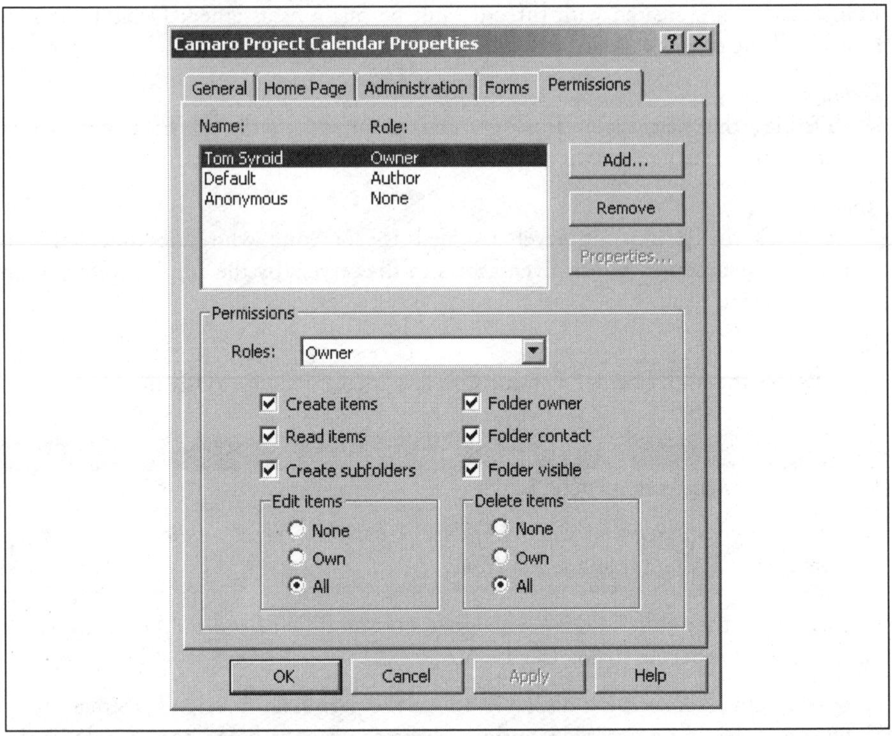

Figure 17-5: The Permissions tab of a folder's Properties dialog

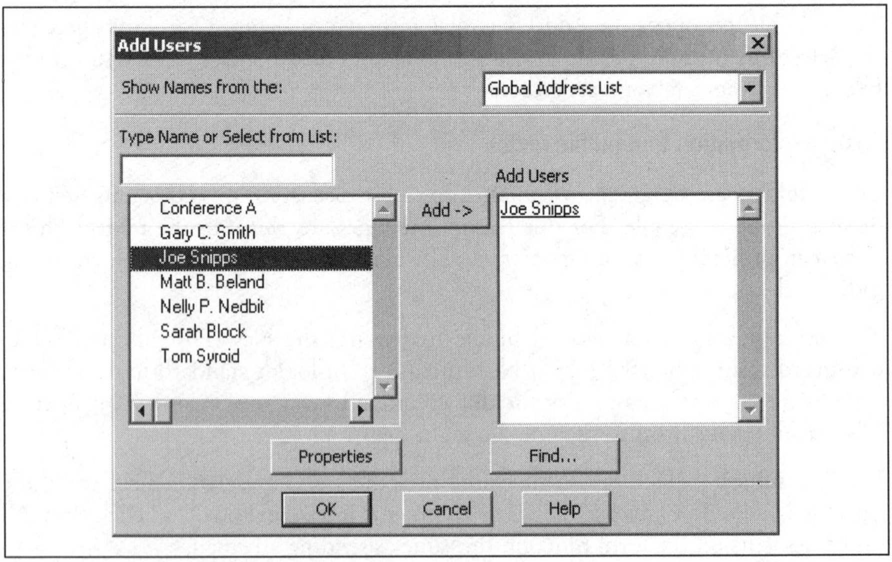

Figure 17-6: The Add User dialog

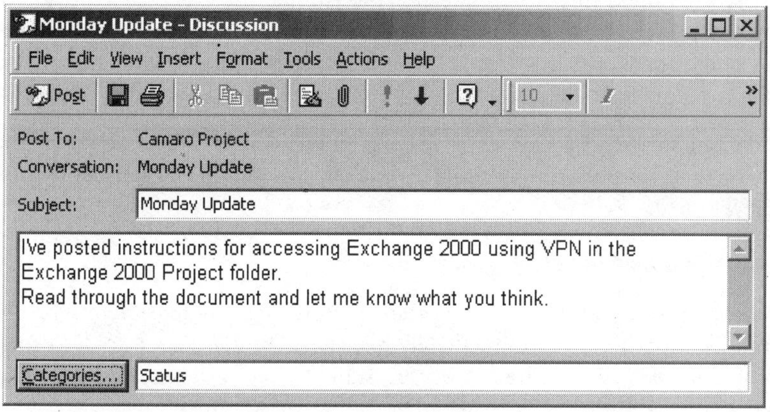

Monday Update - Discussion

File   Edit   View   Insert   Format   Tools   Actions   Help

Post To: Camaro Project
Conversation: Monday Update
Subject: Monday Update

I've posted instructions for accessing Exchange 2000 using VPN in the
Exchange 2000 Project folder.
Read through the document and let me know what you think.

Categories...   Status

Figure 17-7: Posting a message to a public folder

Here are some tips for working with public folders:

- New posts begin a new conversation thread. If you want to ask a question or add information to an existing topic, select a specific post within an existing thread and use the Post Reply to Folder command from the context menu. This adds the new post to the folder at the discussion level chosen.

- Use the Subject field of a post to briefly summarize the contents of your message. This makes it easy for users to scan a public folder for topics of interest. Remember, the Subject of a new post defines the conversation thread for all subsequent replies.

- To add a document to a public folder, drag it from Windows Explorer and drop it on the open view. If the document needs explanation or elaboration, attach it to a message post (from the post form, Insert → File).

- To add an Outlook item from a personal folder to a public folder (for example, to add a contact item to a Mail type folder), hold down the right mouse button while dragging it to the folder. On release, the context menu shown in Figure 17-8 is displayed.

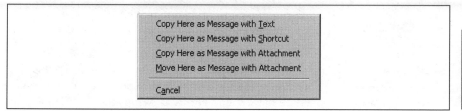

Copy Here as Message with Text
Copy Here as Message with Shortcut
Copy Here as Message with Attachment
Move Here as Message with Attachment

Cancel

Figure 17-8: The right button context menu displayed after dragging an Outlook item to a new folder

- Items contained in public folders of the Contact or Calendar type add a command to the Action menu and the standard form toolbar—Copy to Personal Calendar (or Contacts). Use it to send the open entry to your personal Calendar or Contacts folder.

- You can also send a new email from a public folder. Note, however, that this message is not posted to the folder: it is sent to only to the recipients entered in the To field.

Moderating a public folder

By default, anyone with the appropriate permissions can post items to a public folder, and those items are immediately displayed. In contrast, a folder can also be configured as *moderated*, where posts are submitted to a designated moderator for review. This person then decides whether to post the submission.

 To designate a public folder as moderated, you must be the owner of that folder.

To set up a moderated public folder:

1. Open the Folder List, select a public folder, and choose Properties from the context menu. Go to the Administrative tab and click the Moderated Folder button.

2. On the Moderated Folder dialog shown in Figure 17-9, enable the "Set Folder up as a moderated folder" option.

3. The To button opens the "Forward new items to" dialog. At the top of the dialog is the usual "Show Names from..." pick list where you can choose addresses from any source recognized by Outlook as a valid Address Book (see Chapter 3 for details on Address Books). Everyone listed in this field receives all items submitted to the folder, but are *not necessarily* the same people who accept or reject the submissions. The "decision makers" are specified in the Moderators list discussed later in this section. You might, for example, want to forward submitted items to three or four people for review, but leave the final say to one individual.

 Instead of naming a person, you can name another public or shared folder where submitted messages are forwarded for review by the moderators.

4. If you want Exchange to automatically reply to all submissions, select "Reply to New Items With." You can choose a preconfigured response, or use a template to create a custom one (see the section "Forms as Templates" in Chapter 3 for details on creating a template).

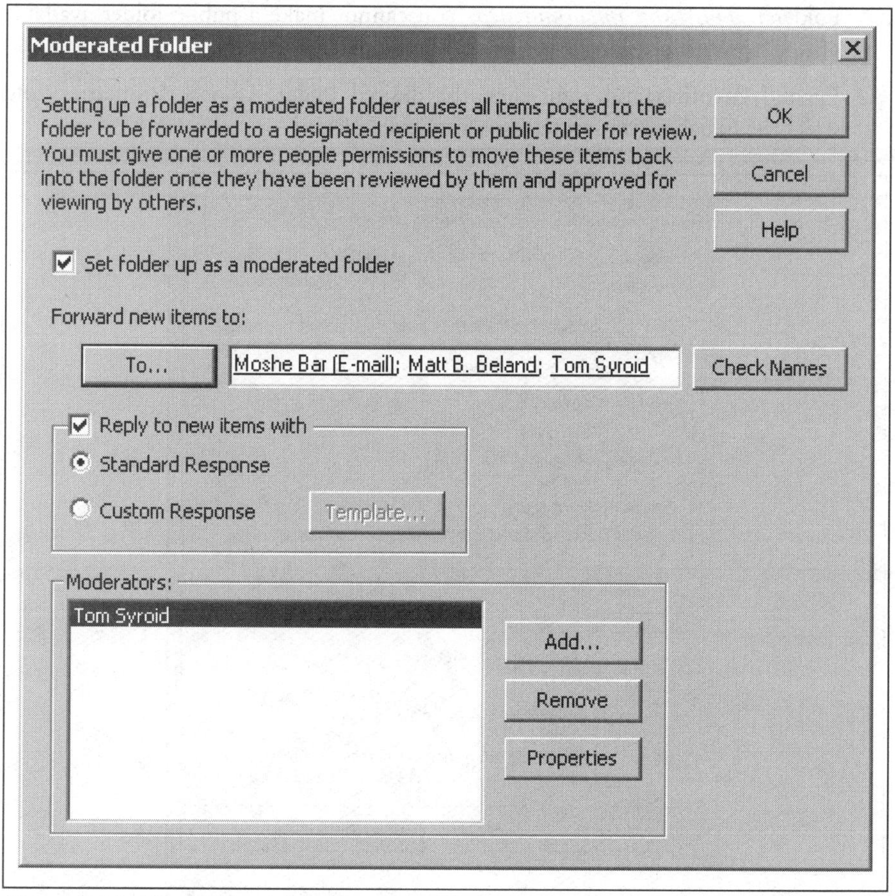

Moderated Folder ☒

Setting up a folder as a moderated folder causes all items posted to the folder to be forwarded to a designated recipient or public folder for review. You must give one or more people permissions to move these items back into the folder once they have been reviewed by them and approved for viewing by others.

[OK]

[Cancel]

[Help]

☑ Set folder up as a moderated folder

Forward new items to:

[To...] | Moshe Bar (E-mail); Matt B. Beland; Tom Syroid | [Check Names]

☑ Reply to new items with
   ⦿ Standard Response
   ○ Custom Response   [Template...]

Moderators:

| Tom Syroid |

[Add...]

[Remove]

[Properties]

Figure 17-9: The Moderated Folder option dialog

5. Under the Moderators section of the dialog, use Add to create a list of folder moderators. All moderators must have Create Item permission to the public folder so that they can post approved messages.

Making a public folder available offline

Public folders can be enabled for use offline. Choosing this option replicates the folder to the user's Offline folder file (see the section "Offline Folders" earlier in this chapter). All the same principles that apply to an offline mailbox also apply here.

 NOTE *You must be connected directly to Exchange in order for the following procedure to work. Working in offline mode does not allow you to access the subfolders under the All Public Folders branch of the Public Folders tree.*

To configure a public folder for use offline:

1. Open the Folder List, navigate to All Public Folders, and select the folder you want available offline. Drag it to the Favorites folder (a subfolder of Public

Outlook and Exchange

Folders). *This is an important step.* You cannot make a public folder available offline from its location under All Public Folders.

2. Expand Favorites and right-click the desired folder. Choose Properties, and select the Synchronization tab (see Figure 17-10).

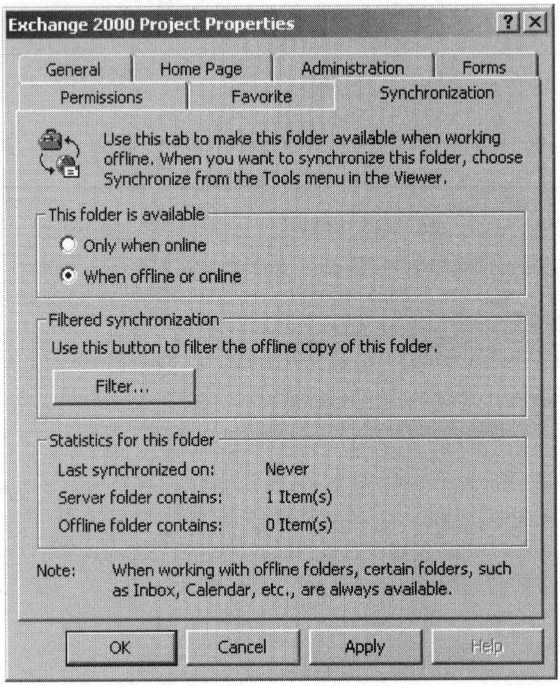

Figure 17-10: The folder Properties dialog with the Synchronization tab selected

3. Under the section "This folder is available," click "When offline or online." Use the Filter option to limit the items synchronized.

Like personal folders, any changes made to the local copy of the public folder are not replicated to the server until your offline folder is synchronized. Keep this in mind when using public folders offline, especially if they are active in the dynamic sense of the word. Responses you post offline may be out of date by the time they are copied back to the folder. For this reason, we recommend using the offline feature to catch up on the information posted to a public folder, and saving any responses until you are online again.

TIP # 173

A Caution About Offline Public Folders

Public folders can be big, depending on their contents. Synchronizing a large folder of any kind can put a serious dent into the time it takes to log on and off an Exchange Server. You might want to check this information (File → Folder → Properties, and click Folder Size) before enabling a folder for offline use.

Delegate Access

Under Exchange, delegate access can be assigned to one or more of your Outlook folders. This is a useful way to handle messages or meeting requests that do not need personal attention and can be managed by, for example, an assistant or colleague. Delegate access is also one way of handling mailboxes assigned to resources rather than a user. Requests for this resource are then routed to one or more delegates, who then make scheduling decisions or respond to questions.

TIP # 174

Delegate Your Mailbox

If you're going on a business trip or a holiday, delegate your mailbox to a trusted assistant or co-worker. This way your business contacts get a personal touch, rather than a cookie-cutter Out of Office Reply.

Setting up Delegate Access

The Delegate Access feature is implemented through the use of an add-in (file extension *.ecf*) to Outlook. To ensure the add-in is installed and activated, go to Tools → Options → Other → Advanced Options → Add-In Manager. Figure 17-11 (top) shows the Add In Manager dialog.

If there is no entry for Delegate Access displayed, click the Install button on the Add-In Manager dialog. This opens the Install Extensions selection dialog shown in Figure 17-11 (bottom). The file you want is *dlgsetup.ecf*. Select it and choose Open.

Naming and configuring a delegate

The owner of the mailbox controls delegate access. Delegates are given access to a folder (or folders), and granted permissions within each folder. Although Outlook allows you to assign more than one delegate, it's usually best to stick to one—confusions can arise otherwise.

 NOTE *The procedures outlined in this section are based on the assumption that you maintain your default information store on an Exchange Server. If this is not the case, and your default store is a local PST or Offline folder, a delegate can only send mail on your behalf, not access your folders.*

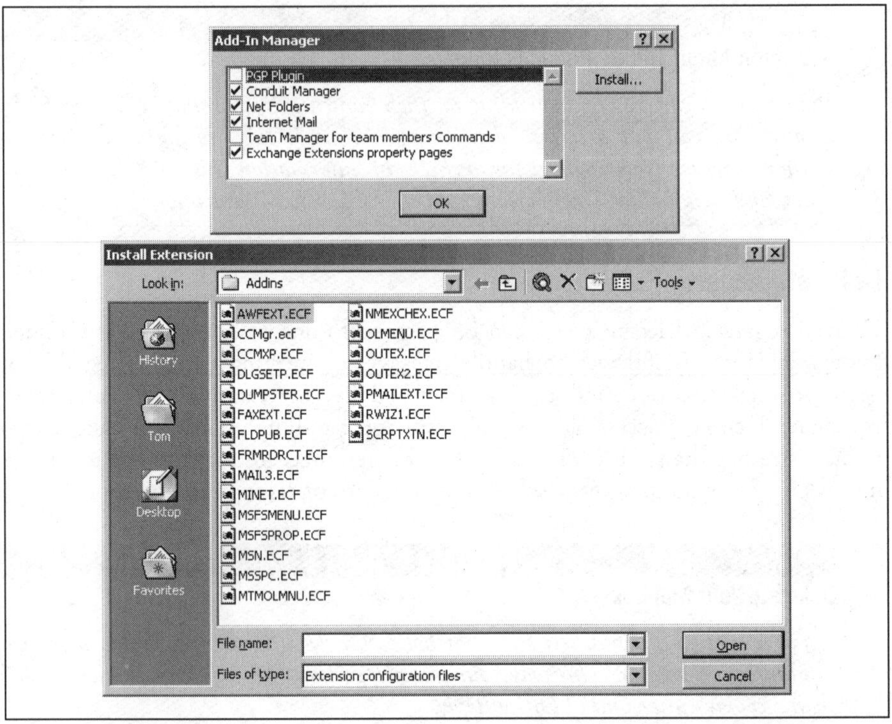

Figure 17-11: The Add In Manager dialog (top), and the Install Extensions selection dialog (bottom)

To configure a delegate, go to Tool → Options, and select the Delegates tab as shown in Figure 17-12 (this tab is only available when the Microsoft Exchange Server information service is configured).

Click Add to display the Add Users dialog and choose a delegate. Depending on your configuration, other Address Books may be available from the "Show Names …" list. The Address Book you select from should be the one that contains the names of people who have accounts on your Exchange Server. In most cases, this is the Global Address List. Click OK and the Delegate Permissions dialog opens (see Figure 17-13).

Each folder listed on the dialog has an associated drop-down list where you can choose one of the following permissions:

Editor
Author
Reviewer
None

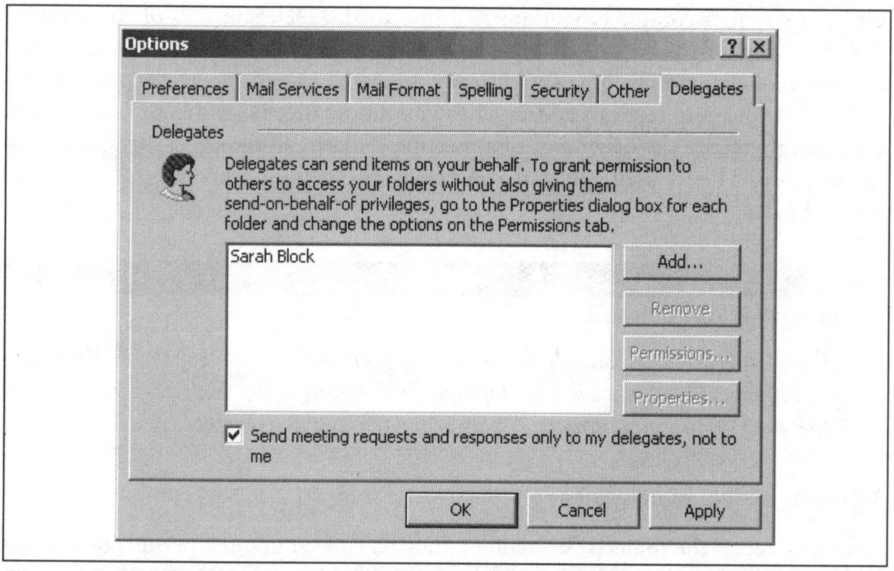

Figure 17-12: The Delegates tab of the Tools → Options dialog

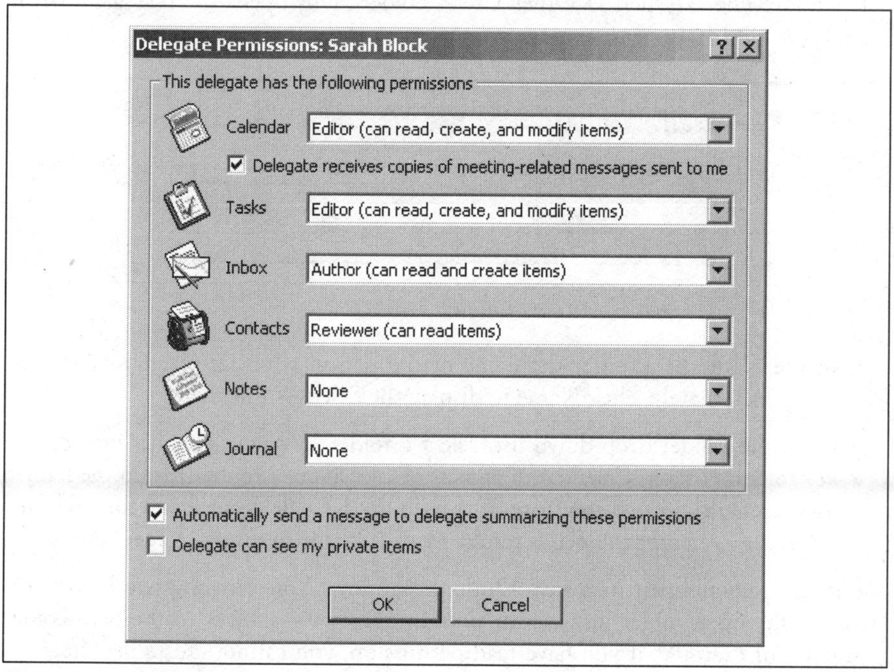

Figure 17-13: The Delegate Permissions dialog

Explanations of these permissions are displayed next to the selection. At the bottom of the dialog is an option for sending the delegate a message summarizing the access permissions you've granted them, and on what folders.

Once this step is complete, you are returned to the Delegates tab of the Options dialog. At the bottom of the dialog (see Figure 17-12) is a checkbox labeled "Send meeting requests and responses only to my delegates, not to me." Select this option to have any meeting requests addressed to you automatically sent to the delegate. In addition, if you are the originator of a meeting request, all responses are also sent to the delegate. This is useful if your delegate is an assistant who normally manages your calendar.

TIP # 175

Delegating Your Calendar

If your delegate is responsible for managing your calendar, make sure he has Editor permissions. From the Tools → Options → Delegates tab, select the delegate, and click the Permissions button to display or modify user access rights.

Accessing folders as delegates

Delegates access the folder(s) or mailbox they have been granted permissions to just as they would their own. To open a delegated folder:

1. Choose File → Open → Other User's Folder. This opens the dialog shown in Figure 17-14.

Figure 17-14: The Open Other User's dialog

2. In the Name field, enter the name of the person who has given you delegate access. Alternately, click Name to display the Select Name dialog.

3. From the Folder drop-down list, select a folder to open. This list includes six key folders (Inbox, Calendar, Contacts, Tasks, Notes, Journal) from the named user's default information store. If you do not have delegate access for a selected folder, any attempt to open it results in an "Unable to display folder" message.

Delegated folders open in a new Outlook window. You can now work with the items in the open folder just as you would your own—subject to the permissions granted. For example, if you have read permission, you cannot create new items or edit existing ones.

Sending messages on someone's behalf

If you have delegate access for a user's mailbox (this does not work if, for example, you have delegate access only on their Calendar folder), you can send a message on behalf of another person.

Open a new message form. With the Delegate Access add-in installed, there is now a From field displayed. Enter the user's name you are sending the message for in this field. Complete and send the message as you would normally. A copy of the message is saved in your Sent Items folder.

> **NOTE** *If you send a message on behalf of a user, and you do not have delegate access to that person's mailbox, Outlook dutifully dispatches the message— it doesn't know any better. Exchange does, however, and sends a message to your Inbox stating "The originator does not have permission to submit the message."*

The From line shows the message as sent From `delegate` on behalf of `mailbox owner`. Replies are sent to the mailbox owner, not the delegate.

Delegating resources

Meeting and conferencing resources (meeting rooms, audio-visual equipment, etc.) exist as a special type of user. The resource account is created based on an existing account, typically either a member of the Exchange administrator group or the person responsible for scheduling and managing these resources. The latter option can present problems. If the employee quits or changes jobs within the company, her mailbox is removed, and with it, the resource.

A better solution is to leave the ownership of the resource under the control of an administrator's group, and assign a delegate. Here's how to do that:

Create a profile for the resource and log onto Exchange using that profile. Use the steps outlined earlier in this section and configure delegate access for the employee responsible for the resource.

If you have access permissions to the resource, you can further automate requests for scheduling requests to a first-come-first-served basis. Again, log on to Outlook using the resource profile created previously. Choose Tools → Options, and select Calendar Options on the Preferences tab. On the Calendar Options dialog, click Resource Scheduling as shown in Figure 17-15.

The Resource Scheduling options here are straightforward and self-explanatory. The "Automatically decline recurring meeting requests" option works best for a resource that is in high demand by many users.

Shared Folders

Public folders are a good way to share information with a large group of individuals. To share information with a smaller group or just one or two individuals,

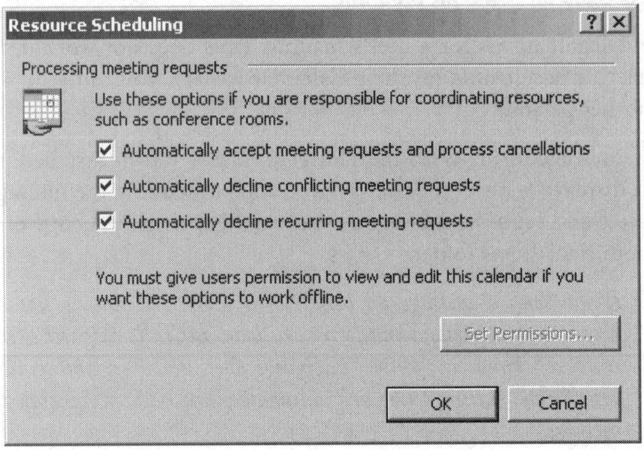

Figure 17-15: Automating resource scheduling using Calendar Options

Exchange users can share a folder within their personal Exchange store. The same concepts apply here that were discussed for Public and Delegated folder: the owner of the folder grants access to one or more people (who must also have Exchange accounts), and assigns a permission level to each individual. This permission level defines the level of access allowed.

To share an Exchange-based folder:

1. Open the Folder List and right-click the folder you want to share. From the context menu, choose Properties. Select the Permissions tab, shown in Figure 17-16.

2. Choose Add to display the Add Users dialog. Select the people you want to share the folder with from the list provided. Click OK to return to the Permissions tab.

3. The default role is None, meaning no permissions in the folder. Select each name on the list displayed and choose an appropriate access level from the list provided. The roles available here are the same as those shown in Table 17-2 under the section "Assigning access permissions" earlier in this chapter.

Out of Office Replies

Creating and using Out of Office replies is similar to creating and using Mail rules (see Chapter 6, *Mail*), with the following exceptions:

- Mail rules are applied continuously (as long as Outlook is running); Out of Office replies are turned on or off by the user.

- Mail rules can be created to handle more than just incoming messages; Out of Office replies only act on messages arriving in the user's Inbox.

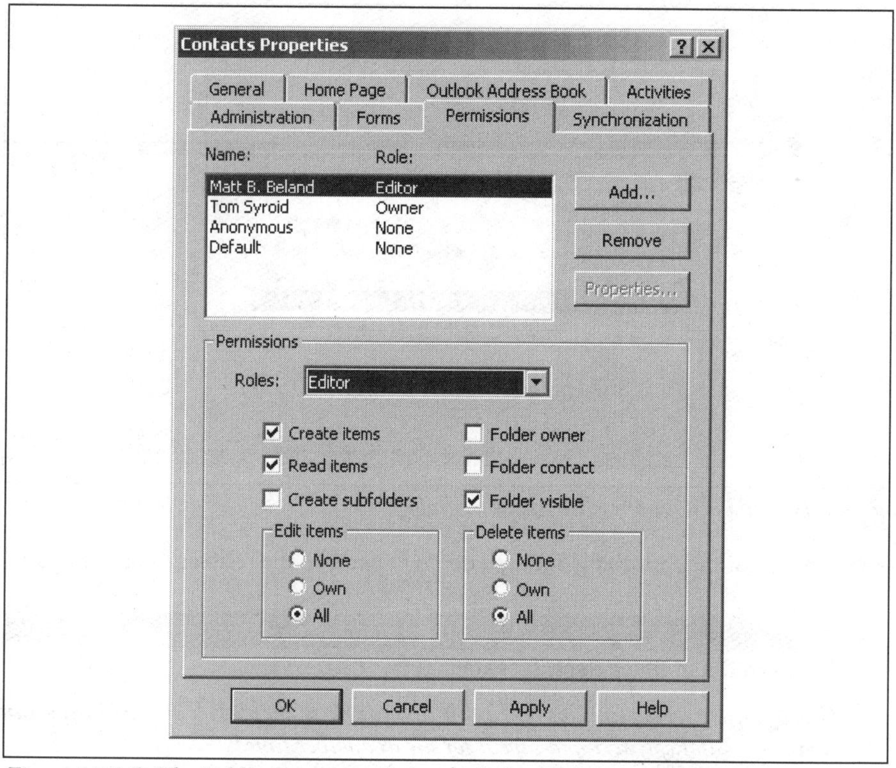

Figure 17-16: The Folder Properties dialog with the Permissions tab selected

- Mail rules are client based; Out of Office replies are server based. This means that Out of Office replies continue to function even if Outlook is closed and/or disconnected from Exchange—providing, of course, the Exchange server they are configured under is running.

Out of Office replies are created and managed using the Out of Office Assistant (Tools → Out of Office Assistant), shown in Figure 17-17, and consist of three parts:

- The "switch" to turn the reply on or off

- The AutoReply text

- The rules that govern which messages receive the AutoReply

To send the same reply to every message that arrives in your Inbox, simply enter text in the field provided and turn the feature on. The Assistant tracks the people it replies to so that each person receives a response to their first message; subsequent messages from the same person do not generate a response.

You might also want to note the following:

- The Subject field of an AutoReply message reads: Out of Office AutoReply: *original message subject*.

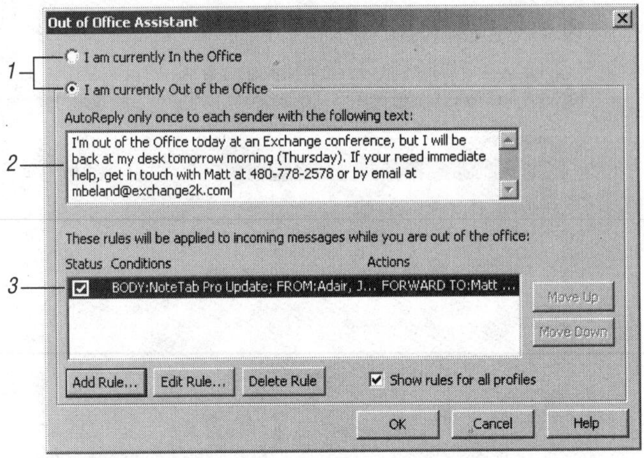

Figure 17-17: The Out of Office Assistant dialog

- The text of the AutoReply message doesn't appear in the recipient's preview pane.

TIP # 176

Create an Out of Office Reply for Later

Out of Office replies are not sent until the feature is enabled. This means you can create the AutoReply text and save it for use at another time.

You can also create rules that determine when and to whom an Out of Office reply is sent. Click Add Rule to open the dialog shown in Figure 17-18.

The top half of the dialog sets the rule conditions, and the lower half determines the actions implemented when those conditions are met. Again, we refer you to the section "Tools → Rules Wizard" in Chapter 6 for details on creating rules.

There is one important condition you can assign a rule that is specific to Out of Office replies. Selecting the Advanced button on the Edit Rule dialog open the subdialog shown in Figure 17-19.

Note the Received options located next to the OK/Cancel buttons. Here you can set a date range when a rule is in effect. This allows you to create a rule that sends Out of Office replies to all (or specific) messages received during a defined period, and stops functioning when that period passes. Use this condition if, for example, you are planning to attend a conference. Use the reply text to tell customers what booth they can find you at, during what hours.

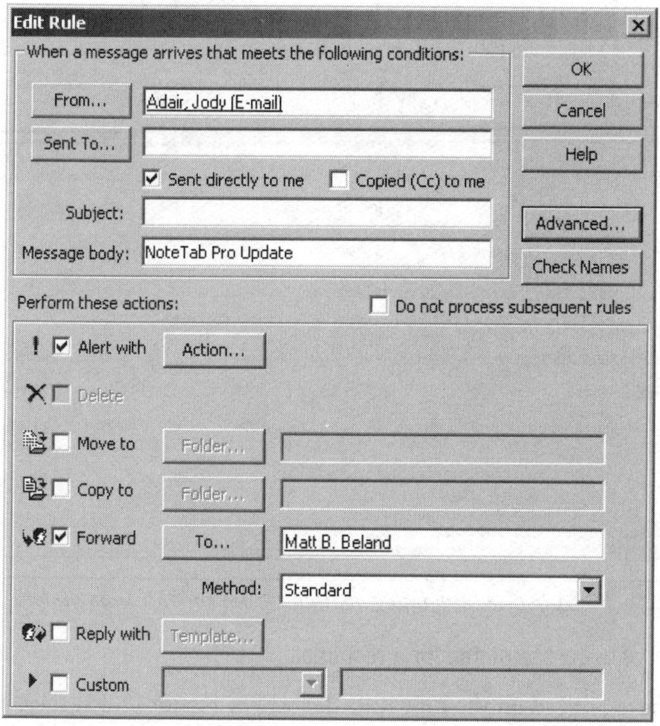

Figure 17-18: The Edit Rule dialog used for adding rules to an Out of Office reply

Out of Office Replies: Cautions and Tips

Like Mail rules, Out of Office replies with rules have a tendency to confuse users. Try to keep the following in mind when you are working with rules of any kind:

- You can have multiple conditions in a single rule.

- You can have multiple actions in a single rule.

- You can have multiple rules.

- Multiple rules are applied in the order in which they're listed on the Out of Office Assistant dialog.

Action rules that involve folders are tricky

As we noted early in this section, Out of Office replies are server-based. Server-based rules include only actions that can be performed within your private information store (mailbox). This means that if you create a rule to move messages received from a specific individual or group to, for example, a public folder, that action does not take place unless you are logged onto the server. This is important to remember for people who connect to Exchange remotely.

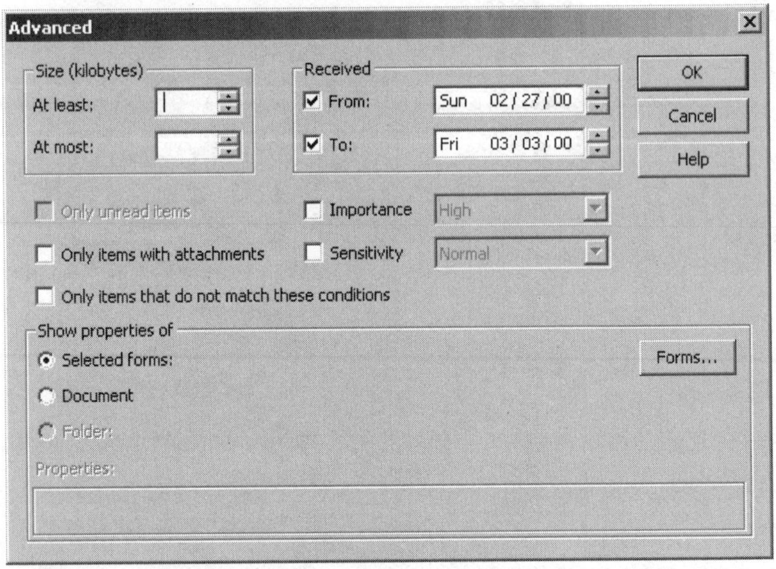

Figure 17-19: The Advanced subdialog available from the Edit rule dialog

Limitations of using templates for a response

You may have noticed on the Edit Rule dialog (see Figure 17-18) there is an option to send a response based on a template. A discussion of creating and using templates can be found in Chapter 3, and we refer you there for details. There are limitations to using a template with an Out of Office reply to be aware of:

- The Subject field of a response that is sent using a template does not include the original subject.

- A response is sent every time a message is received, instead of being sent just once to each sender.

Customized response templates

With the previously mentioned limitations out of the way, templates can be a very useful way to custom configure specific Out of Office replies for a situation or audience. When you are creating a response template, remember that any message properties you set become part and parcel of the reply. For some suggestions, simply open the Message Options dialog from the message form (View → Options) you are using to create the template (see Figure 17-20). For example, you could specify an assistant to send replies to (Have replies sent to), or set a date to defer the response (Do not deliver before).

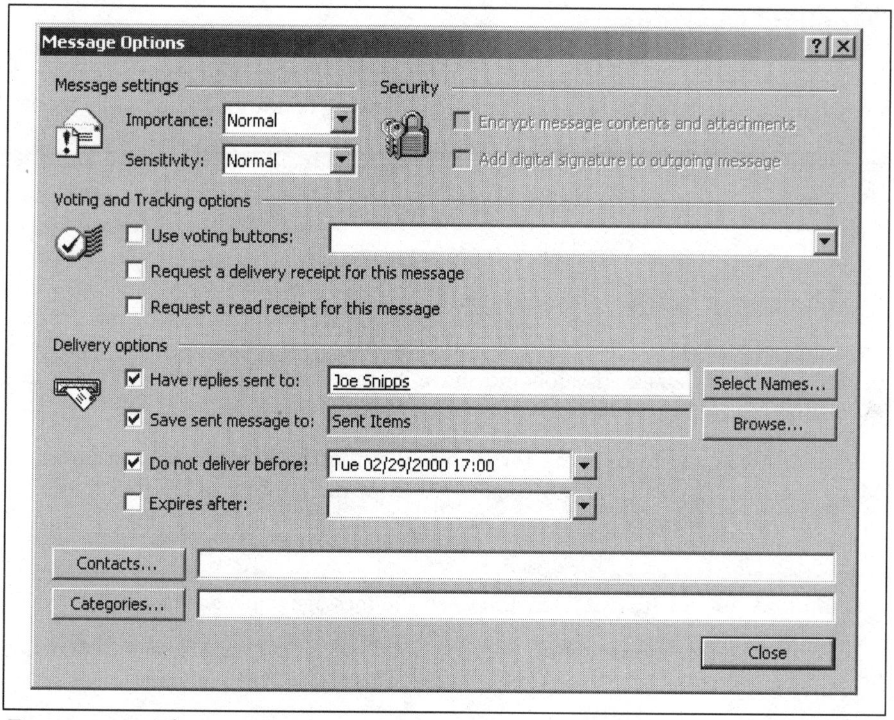

Figure 17-20: The Message Options dialog

Controlling Inbox overflow

If your absence from the office is going to be a lengthy one, there is a way to alleviate coming home to an Inbox containing 1000 unread messages. Create a rule that moves all messages received with the word URGENT in the Subject field to a subfolder of your Inbox. Now, in a counter-balancing rule (messages that do not have URGENT in the Subject line), send a response and delete the message. In the text of the response template, explain to the recipient that you are away from the office, and if they need to contact you send another message with the word URGENT in the subject line, and give them an alternative contact should the matter need immediate attention.

TIP # 177

Don't Delete Out of Office Rules

Don't delete the rules you create for Out of Office replies; simply turn off the Out of Office Assistant when you're not using it and deselect those rules that are not appropriate for a given situation.

Recalling Messages

It is possible, *under certain conditions*, to recall a message sent to another Exchange user. For message recall to be successful, the following conditions must all be met:

- The recipient must be logged into Exchange.

- The recipient has not yet opened the message.

- The recipient must have Outlook running.

- The message must be in the recipient's Inbox.

As you can see, that's a lot of "ifs." In other words, do not count on message recall to save you from a "Take this job and shove it" memo hastily sent to your boss in a momentary fit of rage.

The first three conditions speak for themselves; the last item deserves elaboration. Many users employ rules to move messages from their Inbox to another folder. In these situations, message recall fails. With these cautions in mind, here is how to recall a message:

1. Go to your Sent Items folder, and open the message you want to recall.

2. From the open message form select Actions → Recall This Message. The dialog shown in Figure 17-21 is displayed.

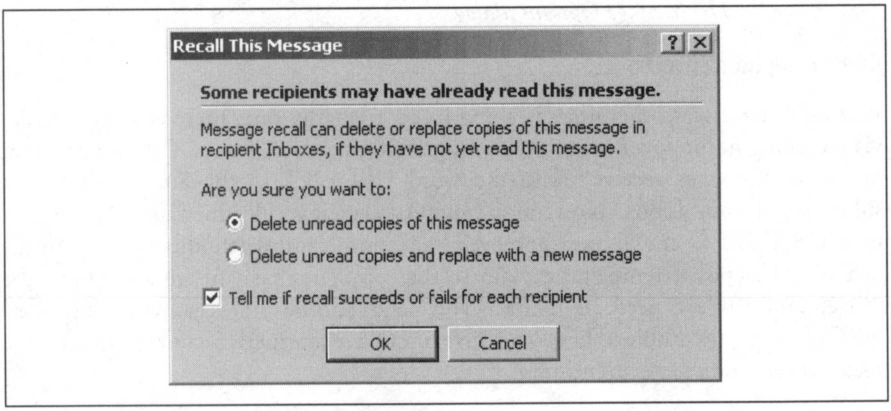

Figure 17-21: The Recall This Message dialog

3. Choose:

    - "Delete unread copies of this message" to simply delete the message.

    - "Delete unread copies and replace with a new message" to replace the sent message with an alternate. The original message opens in the default mail editor, where you can edit the contents. If the recall is successful, the revised message replaces the original.

    In either case, you can optionally select to be notified if the recall is successful.

TIP # 178

No Option Message Delivery

When Outlook is configured in CW mode and connected to an Exchange server, you have no option as to when new messages are sent. As soon as you click Send, the message is dispatched.

Troubleshooting

In this section, we are going to look briefly at some common problems you may encounter using Outlook and Exchange. Topics discussed here are client issues that can be typically resolved from Outlook.

Opening a Message in the Outbox is a Bad Idea

Opening a message in the Outbox and closing it again, marks it as "Read." Outlook, in its infinite wisdom, will not send a Read message from the Outbox. The only solution is to open the message, and click the Send button on the form's toolbar.

This problem typically rears itself with offline users—most users with an active connect usually do not have enough time to get to the Outbox and open the message before it is spooled to the server.

Corrupt PST files

Corrupt PST files exhibit all sorts of strange behaviors. One of the most common is a failure to send messages. If you've exhausted the obvious (no LAN connection, the message has been opened, etc.) try running the Inbox Repair Tool as detailed in Chapter 13. If the problem persists, you can also try:

- Creating a PST and configuring it as the default location for POP mail.

- Creating a new mail profile.

User Profiles

We've said it before; we'll say it again—user profiles are fragile beasts. If you use multiple complex configurations to more than one email account, changing an option in one profile frequently corrupts another. The obvious solution is routine backups of your Outlook configuration (see Chapter 13 for details). However sometimes restoring a backup just to get a profile back is more effort than it's worth. For this reason, we suggest the following alternative solutions:

- The easiest way to restore a corrupt profile is to simply recreate it from scratch. Make sure you keep written notes of your profiles somewhere safe. Screen shots

Outlook and Exchange

of Outlook's various configuration dialogs also work well. We use and recommend SnagIt for this task (*http://www.techsmith.com*).

- A second alternative is to create a set of base profiles, and *before* you start Outlook, back these up to floppy for safekeeping. Once you've logged on and enabled a profile, Outlook starts writing various additional configuration files to the folder where profiles are stored. As soon as this happens, it's hard to know what to include in your backup, and what to ignore.

Disappearing File Attachments

You send a message to Joe Snipps with a file attachment. Ten minutes later, Joe phones you and asks, "What's up? Where's the file?" The message arrived, it shows a file attachment, but there's no file to be found. Before you resend the message, check what format you used to send the original.

If the message was sent in MS-RTF, your encoding is set to MIME (Tools →
Options, Internet E-Mail tab), and the recipient uses a POP3 email client, chances are the attachment did not make it. Resend the attachment using either a plain text or HTML message format.

Chapter 18

Working with VBA

In previous chapters, you've seen how Outlook's look, feel, and general operations can be customized to suit your own style. This capability is a powerful, and often frustrating, aspect of using this application. But you're not limited to tweaking what you see in menus and toolbars. You have the ability to enhance and *extend* the capabilities of Outlook.

We can push back the boundaries of Outlook's features by writing custom code. This can be code that reacts to button clicks and other events (such as email being sent or received), and then performs custom actions. We can also automate tedious tasks by writing *macros*, pieces of code that act as a script for Outlook to perform.

You can extend Outlook in three ways: by writing COM (*Component Object Model*) Add-Ins, by using VBScript to react to form events, or by writing VBA (*Visual Basic for Applications*) code. Of these choices, VBA code provides the best balance of robustness and ease of use.

VBScript and COM Add-Ins

VBScript is a subset of VBA used for scripting environments such as web servers or browsers. Unlike VBA, VBScript code is tied to particular elements of an Outlook form, and that form must be open in order for that VBScript code to run. This also means that you can't use VBScript to respond to events that occur outside of a form, like Outlook being closed. VBScript does have its place, though; it's the only way to build custom forms in Outlook.

A COM Add-In is a DLL (Dynamic Link Library) that you write to extend Outlook. In order to create an Add-In, you need either the Developer edition of Office or a full-blown development environment like Visual Basic or Visual C++. COM Add-Ins provide flexibility that VBScript and vanilla Outlook VBA cannot provide, but at the cost of learning more advanced programming concepts.

This chapter provides an overview and quick introduction to VBA, illustrating how to write and execute VBA code in Outlook. It's not intended to be a full-blown reference. If what you see here whets your appetite, you can read a more complete treatment of VBA in *VB & VBA in a Nutshell* (O'Reilly & Associates).

What Is VBA?

VBA is a subset of the Visual Basic programming language. It is a hosted language component, meaning that an application provides the environment in which VBA code is written and executed. In Office 97, all Office applications except Outlook were viable hosts for VBA. With the Office 2000 release, Outlook can host it as well.

With each host application comes a different flavor of VBA. It is typically used to extend the functionality of the hosting application through the application's *object model*. An object model is a hierarchy of logical entities (objects), such as a word processing document in Word, a spreadsheet in Excel, or the preview pane in Outlook. By using an application's object model (explained later in this chapter), you can programmatically perform standard operations—like creating a new contact—and more complex logical tasks, some of which may require interaction with the user.

You can even use VBA in one Office application to control another Office application. This allows you to write programs that integrate the capabilities of several Office components. Since this is a book on Outlook, we'll be focusing on how to use VBA to control Outlook internally.

See "Microsoft Office 2000/Visual Basic Programmer's Guide" (*http://msdn.microsoft.com/library/officedev/odeopg/deovroffice2000visualbasicprogrammersguide.htm*) for more information on Visual Basic and Office 2000.

A VBA Language Primer

In this section, we'll take a look at the syntax and structure of the VBA language. Entire books have been devoted to VBA, but we'll just hit the high points here. When you're through with this section, you'll understand the basic building blocks of VBA and how to use them to create a program.

Statements

A *statement* in VBA code is like an imperative sentence in a spoken language. Each statement in a program is a command for your machine to perform. The following statement displays a message box with the text "Hello, world!":

```
MsgBox "Hello, world!"
```

Very long statements may be broken into several lines by using the line continuation character "_". You can also use indentation to make your code more readable:

```
nTotalPerimeter = CalculateRectanglePerimeter(4,6) + _
                  CalculateTrianglePerimeter(3,4,5) + _
                  CalculateCirclePerimeter(8)
```

Comments

Comments are documentation in your code. The more you comment, the better you—and anybody else—will understand your code later. You add a comment by prefacing a line of text with a single quote, or by typing a single quote and additional text after a statement. Anything following the quote is considered a comment and will not be executed. For example:

```
' This is a comment that takes up an entire line.
i = 3 ' This is a comment after a statement
```

Variables

A *variable* is a name that you define to hold a value. Variables can hold basic types of data like numbers, text values, or dates, as well as more complex, structured data. In order to use a variable, it must first be *declared*; this associates a variable name with the chunk of memory that holds the variable's value. You usually declare a variable yourself, although VBA may declare a variable for you, as you'll see. Once declared, a variable's value can be changed; this is called *assignment*.

You can give a variable any name you wish, using any combination of letters and numbers. It's best to use descriptive variable names like `personalFolder` or `newMailMessage` to make your code more readable. You may also find it useful to prefix each variable name with a few characters describing the type of data the variable is holding. You might use `fld` for a folder, `n` for a number, and `str` for a string, for instance.

You use the `Dim` keyword (short for "dimension") to declare a variable. For example, you can declare integer and string variables by typing in the following statements:

```
Dim nVariable As Integer
Dim strString As String
```

You can also declare a variable without specifying its data type:

```
Dim variable
```

Variables declared in this fashion have a default data type; they're called *variants*. A variant is a chameleon data type that can mimic any built-in VBA data type. So, one variant might contain an integer, while another contains a string.

Variables are also implicitly declared as variants when you assign a value to a variable that you haven't declared with `Dim`:

```
' nVariable has not been declared
nVariable = 10
```

While variants are flexible, their use is discouraged except when you must store two different data types in the same variable. Your code will run slower when using variants, since variant values need to be interpreted as a specific data type before they can be used. It is best to declare your variables explicitly with Dim. You can get some help from the VBA environment in this regard. Simply include the Option Explicit statement at the top of your VBA code. When this statement is present, the environment will pop up an error message if you try to use a variable before declaring it.

Assigning a value to a variable overwrites any previously stored data. An assignment statement consists of the variable name, an equal sign, and the data you wish to assign. This can be a value, a calculated value, or another variable:

```
nInteger = 2000 ' assigning an integer value of 2000
nInteger = 5 * 10 ' assigning the result of a multiplication
nThis = nThat ' assigning the contents of another variable
```

You can see that assigning numeric values is fairly intuitive. Text and date variables require a bit more explanation. Text values are called *strings*, and are surrounded by double quotes:

```
strVar = "remember this" ' assigning a string to a variable
```

You can create a string from smaller strings, or even different data types, by using an ampersand between each piece of data:

```
' concatenating strings
strMessage = "The color is " & strColor

' concatenating strings and numeric data
strMessage = "The price of " & strItem & " is " fPrice
```

NOTE *The ampersand is the string concatenation operator in VBA, a fancy term for a character that simply splices together parts of a string.*

A date is written as text surrounded by pound signs (#), and can take one of several standard forms. The interpretation of some dates, such as 9/7/99, depends on your system's locale settings. Either of the following statements will assign September 7, 1999 to the variable dtSomeday:

```
dtSomeday = #7-September-1999#
dtSomeday = #Sept 7, 1999#
```

Constants

Constants are essentially variables whose values cannot change. They have names like variables, and can contain any data type you'd use for a variable. However, you must assign a value to a constant when you declare it, and that value will remain static throughout the course of your program. Constants help document your program by replacing oft-used values with a more meaningful label. Constants are also very useful for defining values that are used in more than one location in your VBA code, enabling easier code modification later. In Outlook VBA, you'll probably end up using Outlook's predefined constants more often than defining your own.

You declare a constant by using the Const keyword:

```
Const DefaultImportance = "High"
Const NumFingers = 10
```

It's best to declare all of your constants in one spot at the top of your code, so you'll always know where to find them.

You use a constant just as you would use a variable, except that you can't assign a value:

```
MsgBox "I have " & NumFingers & " fingers."
```

Conditional Statements

Conditional statements contain the logic of your program. The If Then Else construct lets you make decisions on which code to execute next, based on the truth of a condition or combination of conditions. Take the following example:

```
If fPrice > 3.99 Then
    MsgBox "The price is too high!"
End If
```

In this case, if the variable fPrice contains a value greater than 3.99 (in other words, if the condition is true), a message box is displayed. If the condition is false, the statement that displays the message box is not executed. We can also use the optional Else clause to execute code in this case:

```
If fPrice > 3.99 Then
    MsgBox "The price is too high!"
Else
    MsgBox "The price is right!"
End If
```

Note that the If Then portion of the code is paired with an End If statement to block off the conditional code.

You can test multiple conditions by using the And or Or keywords. For multiple conditions involving both And and Or operations, you may need to group conditions together with parentheses so that the compound condition is evaluated correctly. For example, the following test for a suitable car will be true if the car is a red V6, or if it's just a sports car:

```
strEngine = "V6" and strColor = "red" or strStyle = "sports car"
```

The And operator has precedence over the Or operator. This means that And operations are evaluated first, just like math, where multiplication has precedence over addition. In our example, this groups the "red" and "V6" conditions. We could force a different precedence and look for a car that's a V6 and is either red or sporty by adding parentheses (again like in math), which explicitly group conditions:

```
strEngine = "V6" and (strColor = "red" or strStyle = "sports car")
```

Functions and Subprocedures

If statements are like sentences, then *functions* and *subprocedures* are like paragraphs. These are groups of statements that you can call (execute) by name to accomplish a task. For example, you might have a function that performs a math calculation and gives back the result. Or you might have a subprocedure that hides Outlook's preview pane if it's visible. Note that functions return values back to your program, while subprocedures do not.

> **NOTE** *The terms routine, subroutine, function, procedure, and subprocedure are sometimes interchanged loosely (as they are in the rest of this chapter). Functions and subprocedures are routines, but only functions return values.*

In order for a function to do some useful work for you, you may have to give it some information (this is called *passing* information). For instance, a routine that adds two numbers will need the numbers passed to it. In this case, the two numbers are called *parameters*. Taken as a unit, the numbers are the routine's *parameter list*. Parameters appear as declared variables, surrounded by parentheses and separated by commas, after the name of the function or subprocedure. A parameter list may be empty if the routine doesn't need information sent to it in order to do its job.

You pass some parameters with the intent that their values won't be changed (i.e., they're read-only inside a function). This is called *passing by value*, and such parameters are preceded by the ByVal keyword. You may also pass parameters to receive values from the function or subprocedure call. These parameters are preceded by the ByRef keyword and are *passed by reference*.

Functions and subprocedures are denoted by the Function and Sub keywords respectively. To begin the body of a function or subprocedure, you use one of these keywords in conjunction with the routine's name and parameter list. You end the routine with the End keyword followed by Function or Sub. For example, say you have a subprocedure that displays a message. You pass it the message as a string, and the procedure formats it and displays it in a message box:

```
Public Sub DisplayMsg(ByVal strMsg As String)
    MsgBox "Important message: " & strMsg
End Sub
```

You'll notice that the subprocedure begins with the Public keyword. This determines the *scope* of the procedure (more on this in the "Scope" section later in this chapter). The routine's name is DisplayMsg, and it is being passed a string in the variable called strMsg. Since strMsg is passed by value, we cannot modify its value in our subprocedure's body. Like all subprocedures, ours ends with End Sub.

To call a subprocedure, you type its name, followed by its parameters (separated by commas if there is more than one):

```
DisplayMsg "This is string to display."
```

As we mentioned earlier, a function returns a value (called, strangely enough, the *return value*) to the part of the program that calls it. You declare the data type of a function's return value after the function's parameter list, and you assign its value by assigning to the function's name. Take a look at a function that calculates a circle's area:

```
Const PI = 3.14

Public Function CalcCircleArea(ByVal nRadius As Double) _
            As Double
    CalcCircleArea = PI * (nRadius^2)
End Function
```

The function `CalcCircleArea` takes a decimal number (denoted by Double) as a circle radius, squares it and multiplies it by pi, and returns the result (by assigning it to the function name). We use the `Function` keyword in the first and last lines of the function body.

You call a function just as you call a subprocedure, except that you need a variable to hold the value that the function passes back to you:

```
Dim nThisArea As Double

nThisArea = CalcCircleArea(2.5) ' nThisArea = PI * (2.5^2)
```

 You can choose to ignore a function's return value. In this case, you don't need to surround its parameter list with parentheses. Any time you want to assign the return value to a variable, parentheses are required around the function's parameter list.

The return values of one or more function calls can be used in place of variables in calculations, or as parameters to other function or subprocedure calls:

```
nCylinderVolume = CalcCircleArea(2.5) * nLength

nCylinderVolume = CalcCylinderVolume(CalcCircleArea(2.5), nLength)
```

Scope

The *scope* of a variable, function, or subprocedure determines when—and from where—you can use it. In VBA, scope is determined by where a variable or routine resides and how you declare it.

VBA code lives in *code modules*. These are files containing related variables, constants, functions, and subprocedures. A variable that you declare outside of a function or subroutine has *global scope* within its code module. This means that any routine within the variable's module can access it. When you declare a variable in the body of a routine, it has *procedure scope*. The variable is not accessible from other functions in the same—or any other—module. Put another way, you give the variable life when you declare it in a routine, but it dies when the routine is exited.

```
' Display the recipient
    MsgBox objRecipient.Name
Next
```

Some things to note about this code:

- The `For...To` statement defines the range over which you want to iterate. In this case, we want to go from the first object (at index 1) to the last object.

- We use the `Set` keyword to fill our object variable with a value from the collection. We need to tell the collection *which* item we'd like back. We use the loop counter for this.

- Once we've filled our object variable, we can use it. In this case, we just display a recipient's name.

- We don't set the object variable to `Nothing` after using it. This is because the object is part of the collection, and we don't want to delete it.

- We end the body of the loop with a `Next` statement.

There is another, easier way to loop through an entire collection. The `For Each` construct does a lot of the legwork of looping for you. You don't need to declare a counter, and the `Set` operation is done under the covers for you. We could rewrite the previous example as:

```
For Each objRecipient In collRecipients
    MsgBox objRecipient.Name
Next
```

Through each iteration of the loop, subsequent `Recipient` objects are assigned to the `objRecipient` loop variable. You then just use `objRecipient` to do your work.

In our first looping example, we used the `Item` property and an index (the loop counter in this case) to indicate which recipient to grab from the collection. For collections in Outlook VBA, the `Item` property is the *default property*. This means that we can forego querying the `Item` property and just type in an index after the collection variable:

```
Set objRecipient = collRecipients(nCounter)
```

Some collections also support using a "key" string to reference an object in a collection. For instance, you can fetch a subfolder of a folder by name:

```
Set fldSubfolder = fldInbox.Folders("Important Mail")
```

Error Handling

Ideally, your code would run without any problems. But errors happen. Normally, a VBA program will stop running and a message box will be displayed when an error occurs. By using the `On Error` statement, you can replace this default behavior with your own, which is probably more useful. You can react to otherwise fatal errors and take corrective action, or you can choose to ignore the error and continue executing—at your own risk, of course.

The On Error statement has several forms, but the two of most interest are On Error Resume Next and On Error Goto. You use these statements before the piece of code in which you want to catch errors. Let's examine these options:

```
Private Sub DoLoop()
    On Error Resume Next
    For Each objRecipient in collRecipients
        MsgBox objRecipient.Name
    Next
End Sub
```

The DoLoop procedure uses the Resume Next form. If an error occurs in the loop, it is ignored, and execution continues (we keep on looping). This is the "so what?" form of error handling:

```
Private Sub DoLoopCarefully()
    On Error Goto Loop_Err

    For Each objRecipient in collRecipients
        MsgBox objRecipient.Name
    Next

    Exit Sub

Loop_Err:
    MsgBox "Error " & Err.Number & ": " & Err.Description

End Sub
```

If we encounter an error in the DoLoopCarefully procedure, execution will continue at the Loop_Err label at the end of the procedure body. This part of the procedure is called an *error handler*. The error handler in this example is retrieving properties from an object called Err. This is VBA's built-in error object. Here, we're using it to display an error number and a description of the error.

You should also note the Exit Sub statement after the loop. At this point, we've successfully done our job, and we need to exit. If we don't, we'll fall into the error handler and display a bogus error message.

The Outlook Object Model

To accomplish a task in Outlook VBA, you use the Outlook object model, a hierarchy of related objects that you use to retrieve information, create new items, and cause Outlook to perform actions. Figure 18-1 shows the object model.

The object model is obviously large and deep, and it's not our intent to cover the whole thing here. But you can get a good feeling for how to control Outlook by examining some of its major objects: Application, NameSpace, MAPIFolder, Explorer, and Inspector. (For full details on all the objects and their methods and

Working with VBA

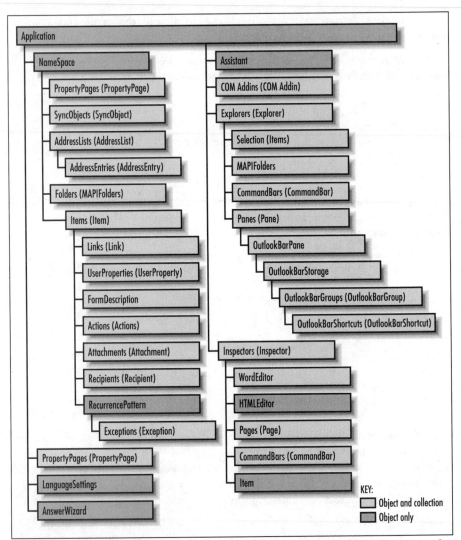

Figure 18-1: The Outlook Object Model—collections are followed by the data types of their contained objects in parentheses

properties, consult the Outlook VBA help available through the VBA editor.) Before we get into the specifics of these objects, we should take a look at a feature common to many of them—events.

Events

Certain objects in Outlook's object model can respond to *events*. Events are external actions on an object to which the object can react. For example, the Application object can react to new mail being received through the NewMail event. You react to this event by writing an *event handler*, or a routine that executes when the event occurs:

```
Private Sub Application_NewMail()
      MsgBox "You have new mail!"
End Sub
```

The name of an event handler has the form Object_Event. In this example, the event handler will display a message box when new mail is received. Note that event handlers are private subprocedures, and they may have parameters passed to them. The help file or the VBA Object Browser (see the "The VBA Editor in Outlook" section) will point you to these parameters.

The Application Object

The Application object is the root object of the Outlook object model, and represents the entire Outlook application. There is always one, and only one, Application object available for use in Outlook-hosted VBA. This makes sense, since you need Outlook to be running in order to run VBA code, and by virtue of the application running, you should be able to reference it in object form.

Using the Application object as a starting point, you can access objects further down in the model (*child objects*). From any object (except the Application object), you can also ask for the object immediately above the current object (its *parent object*) by getting its Parent property:

```
' Get the namespace called "MAPI"
Dim mapiNamespace As NameSpace
Set mapiNamespace = Application.GetNameSpace("MAPI")

' Get the MAPI folder containing an item
Dim folder As MAPIFolder
Set folder = item.Parent
```

Usually object models have their own way of creating new objects (i.e., you rarely need to use the New keyword), and Outlook's is no exception. To create a new object, you ask an existing object for a new child object. Note that the new object need not be directly below the creating object in the model, but wherever it makes sense. For example, to create a new mail item, you ask the Application object for one:

```
Dim newMailItem as MailItem
Set newMailItem = Application.CreateItem(olMailItem)
```

Writing event handlers for the Application object requires little effort. Since the Application object is always available, you can simply write up an event handler and you're done. There are a couple of additional steps if you want to handle other Outlook object events. You need to declare an object variable with the WithEvents keyword to indicate an object whose events you'll handle. This variable will need to be assigned an actual object value to use. You can do this in the Application_ Startup handler. With this done, you have an object variable that you can reference in your event handler. While Outlook objects will be deleted for you when you close the application, it would be courteous to also delete any global objects in the `Application_Quit` handler:

```
' Put up a message box when the user changes folders.
Dim objExplorer As Explorer

Private Sub Application_Startup()
    ' Get a reference to the active explorer.
    Set objExplorer = Application.ActiveExplorer
End Sub

Private Sub objExplorer_FolderSwitch()
    MsgBox "You've switched folders!"
End Sub

Private Sub Application_Quit()
    ' Clean up our object.
    Set objExplorer = Nothing
End Sub
```

 Remember when writing code for the Application object's Startup and Quit events that these events are fired (triggered) when you start and exit Outlook, respectively. If your event handler isn't behaving as expected, you may need to exit and restart Outlook to initialize object variables in Application_Start.

The Application object can also react through its events to new mail, sent items, and reminders.

One useful Application object method (mentioned earlier) is CreateItem. You call this method to create new mail messages, contacts, appointments, notes, and tasks:

```
Dim objNote As NoteItem
Set objNote = Application.CreateItem(olNoteItem)
```

 Creating an item does not display it on the screen. To do that, you call the item's Display method.

You'll probably use the `GetNameSpace` method often in Outlook VBA programming. This method returns a NameSpace object, which we describe next.

NameSpace

The NameSpace object represents generic data storage in Outlook. You get a reference to the NameSpace object by calling the Application object's `GetNameSpace` method with the type of namespace you want as the single string parameter.

```
Dim ns As NameSpace
Set ns = Application.GetNameSpace("MAPI")
```

Currently, Outlook only supports a MAPI namespace, which you obtain by specifying `"MAPI"` as the namespace type.

Folders

The MAPIFolder object represents a single folder in Outlook. The Folders collection represents a group of folders. Just as folders in Outlook are hierarchical, so is the relationship between the Folders collection and MAPIFolders. Each MAPIFolder has a Folder collection, which in turn may contain more MAPIFolders. Take a look at the hierarchy in Figure 18-2.

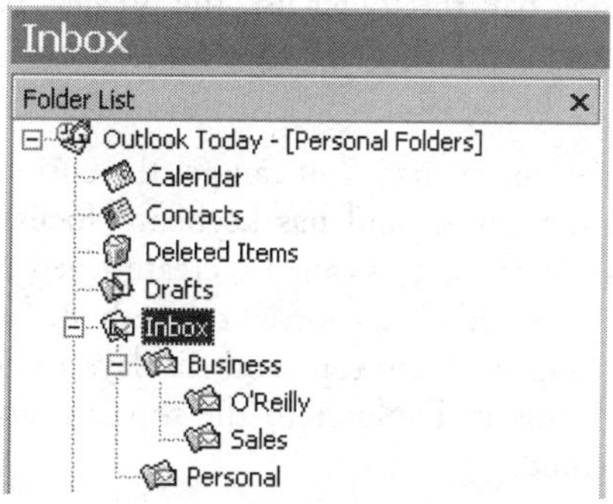

Figure 18-2: A folder hierarchy

So how would you get the Sales folder? The Inbox is a standard folder that can be retrieved by using the NameSpace object's GetDefaultFolder method. This method takes as a parameter a constant with the form olFolderName (where Name is a folder name), and returns a MAPIFolder. So to get the Inbox folder, you could write:

```
Dim fldInbox As MAPIFolder
Set fldInbox = mapiNamespace.GetDefaultFolder(olFolderInbox)
```

The MAPIFolder object has a property called Folders that returns a Folders collection containing any child MAPIFolders. You can reference a folder in the collection by index or by name. So, given the hierarchy of Figure 18-2, you could get to the O'Reilly folder by typing:

```
Set fldBooks = fldInbox.Folders("Business").Folders("O'Reilly")
```

Of course, folders don't just contain other folders. They contain items as well. The Items property will return the collection of items for a folder. The items in this collection are of the corresponding type for the folder. The Calendar folder contains AppointmentItems, the Task folder contains TaskItems, and the Inbox contains MailItems. The following sample code will get the first MailItem from the Inbox, if the folder isn't empty:

```
Set fldInbox = mapiNamespace.GetDefaultFolder(olFolderInbox)
If fldInbox.Items.Count > 0
     Set objMailItem = fldInbox.Items(1)

     ' Do something with the mail item.
End If
```

A MAPIFolder object can also move and copy itself to other folders via the MoveTo and CopyTo methods.

Explorers and Inspectors

The Explorer and Inspector objects are used to display Outlook's folders and their contents on the screen. The Explorer object represents the window containing the contents of a folder (e.g., the mail items in your Inbox) and the surrounding controls, like the Outlook bar, the folder list, the preview pane, and the command bars. The Inspector object represents the window in which an individual Outlook item (e.g., a mail item) is displayed.

Let's look at the Explorer object first. You can get the currently active Explorer (the Outlook window that is topmost and has keyboard focus) using the Application object's ActiveExplorer method. You can also create a new Explorer for any MAPI-Folder object by calling the folder's GetExplorer method. GetExplorer opens a new window (but doesn't bring it to the top) and displays the contents of the MAPI-Folder in it. You can bring an Explorer to the top and give it focus through the Explorer's Activate method.

The Explorer object gives you access to various graphical elements in Outlook. You can get to Outlook's menus and toolbars via an Explorer's CommandBars property. You can get the currently displayed folder (CurrentFolder property), or Close the Explorer. You can also control the visibility of the Outlook bar, preview pane, and folder list. For example, the following code shows the preview pane in the active Explorer if it's not already visible:

```
Dim curExplorer As Explorer
Set curExplorer = Application.ActiveExplorer

If curExplorer.IsPaneVisible(olPreview) = False Then
    curExplorer.ShowPane olPreview, True
End If
```

The Explorer object has Activate and Deactivate events (triggered by the Explorer window gaining and losing focus), as well as several folder events to which you can react.

You can obtain an Inspector object by methods similar to the Explorer object. You get the topmost Inspector through the Application object's ActiveInspector method. You can use the GetInspector method of an item object (e.g., MailItem or ContactItem) to retrieve the Inspector for that item.

 The graphical objects returned by the ActiveExplorer and ActiveInspector may not be active, since other applications besides Outlook could be running. You may also get a return value of Nothing from these methods, indicating that there is no active MAPIFolder or item.

> *There is also another situation in which you won't get an Inspector for an item. When Word is the default mail editor and a message is being edited in plain text or HTML, GetInspector and ActiveInspector will return Nothing.*

You can see which editor (HTML, RTF, text, or Word) is used in an Inspector through its `EditorType` property. The `HTMLEditor` and `WordEditor` properties give you the ability to use external Document Object Models (DOMs) to programmatically edit HTML and Word documents in an Inspector. You can also `Activate` or `Close` an Inspector, and react to the `Activate` and `Deactivate` events.

The VBA Editor in Outlook

We've seen the syntax and structure of the VBA language, and we've hit some high points in Outlook's object model. Now we can explore how you actually enter code and make Outlook do useful things for you. Like the other Office applications, Outlook uses the Visual Basic Editor as its development environment.

To launch the editor, select Tools → Macro → Visual Basic Editor, or hit Alt+F11. You should see something similar to Figure 18-3.

The Project Explorer and Properties Window

The Project Explorer (the window with the "Project - VbaProject" title in the figure) contains the modules in your project, displayed in a tree structure. The root (top-left) node of the tree is the project itself. This node has the form *ProjectName (VbaProject.OTM)*. *VbaProject.OTM* is the filename of the one and only Outlook VBA project file for a particular user. This file is stored in one of the following folders:

- In Windows 95 or 98 with no user profiles set up, the *C:\Windows\Application Data\Microsoft\Outlook* folder

- In Windows 95 or 98 *with* user profiles set up, *C:\Windows\Profiles\UserName\Application Data\Microsoft\Outlook* folder

- In Windows NT, the *C:\Winnt\Profiles\UserName\Application Data\Microsoft\Outlook* folder

- In Windows 2000, the *C:\Documents and Settings\UserName\Application Data\Microsoft\Outlook* folder

Below the project node in the Project Explorer are nodes for standard code and class modules, organized into module types by folders. In Outlook, there is a Microsoft Outlook Objects folder with a single class module called ThisOutlookSession. ThisOutlookSession represents a code module for the Outlook application. It's in this file that you write event-handling code for the Application object and any other objects for which you want to handle events.

Working with VBA

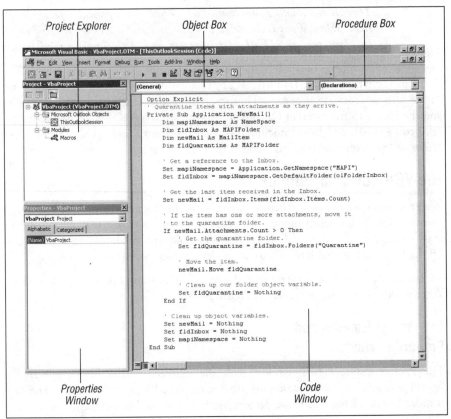

Figure 18-3: The Visual Basic Editor in Outlook

The Modules folder holds standard (non-class) code modules. Your macro code will reside here.

Another folder, Class Modules, holds code modules containing user-defined classes, which we do not cover here.

The window below the Project Explorer is the Properties window, which shows the properties of various objects and allows you to modify them. If you're just writing macros and event handlers as we are here, this window won't be all that exciting. You can use this window to change the name of your VBA project by clicking on the project node in the Project Explorer, clicking the column next to (Name), typing in a new value, and hitting Enter.

The Code Window and Object and Procedure List Boxes

The area to the right of the Project Explorer and Properties window is where the work gets done in the VB Editor. This is the code window, topped by the object

Macro Security and Digital Signatures

After you've written some macros or event handlers in your VBA project, you'll get a macro security warning when you start Outlook. This happens with other Office applications, and is a good safeguard. But sometimes being safe can be a bit annoying.

You could just set your macro security level to Low in the Tools → Macro → Security → Security Level tab, but this would open an undesirable security hole. Fortunately, there's a better way: a personal digital signature.

A digital signature allows you to sign your VBA code so that only *you* can run it. Having a digital signature lets you crank that macro security setting all way up to High, at which level only your macros can be run in your Outlook session.

To create a digital signature, you'll need Digital Signature for VBA Projects installed. This component is included on the Office 2000 CD, and can be found under the Office Tools folder. With the Digital Signature component installed, run the file *selfcert.exe* from your Office program folder (*C:\Program Files\ Microsoft Office\Office* by default), put in your name, and click OK. You've just created a digital signature.

Now you can sign your VBA project. In the VBA editor, select Tools → Digital Signature, click the Choose button, and select your signature. Your VBA project is now signed.

Close and restart Outlook. You'll be presented with a dialog full of portent telling you that you can't trust your own macros. Clicking the checkbox labeled "Always trust macros from this source" and then the Enable Macros button will dispatch this message—and that old macro security warning—permanently.

---

and procedure combo boxes. The code window is where you craft code, and the combo boxes are there to save you some typing.

As you type code in the code window, the editor formats it for you. Keywords are colored in blue, comments in green. When you hit Enter or move off of a freshly typed statement, the editor capitalizes keywords for you. When you enter a statement with an error in it, the editor displays a message box telling you what's wrong, and colors the statement red until you fix it.

As you type, you'll also notice that the editor will try to help you out. After you type the name of a defined function or subprocedure, it will show the parameters in a tool tip, bolding the one you should currently be typing in. It will show a list of data types as you type your Dim statement, and a list of methods and properties after you type an object variable and a period. By selecting an item from the list and hitting Tab, the editor will complete the code entry for you. This feature is called IntelliSense. You can type part of a variable name or constant and have the editor take its best guess at it for you by hitting Ctrl-Space. If it can't complete the name for you, it will display the closest matches to it in a list box. Figure 18-4 and Figure 18-5 show some of these features in action.

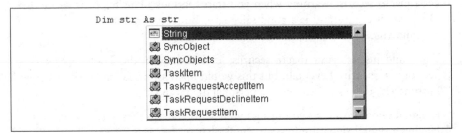

Figure 18-4: IntelliSense suggesting data types

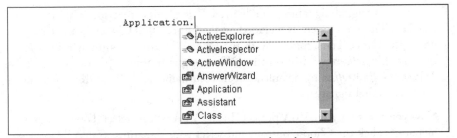

Figure 18-5: IntelliSense listing object properties and methods

As we mentioned earlier, the object and procedure combo boxes help you code more quickly. The object combo box is the leftmost of the two and contains a (General) entry and objects. The (General) entry is shown when the code window's cursor is in the module's global code, where you'd type Option Explicit or your global module variables for event handlers. When the cursor is in procedure code for an object, the object is shown in the object combo box, and the procedure (which could be an event handler) in the procedure combo box. You can have the editor fill in the beginning and end of a particular procedure by selecting the object and procedure of interest in the combo boxes. Try this: double click ThisOutlook-Session in the Project Explorer to make sure its code module is open. Select Application from the object combo box. The editor will create a skeleton for the ItemSend procedure, since it's the first event handler in the procedure combo box. Now select NewMail from the procedure combo box. Your screen should now look like Figure 18-6, with two event handlers ready for the filling.

Now let's write a little code. Let's make a message box pop up whenever you get new mail. Type in the following code in the NewMail handler:

```
Private Sub Application_NewMail
    MsgBox "Hello!"
End Sub
```

```
┌─────────────────────────────────────┬─────────────────────────────────────┐
│ Application                        ▼ │ ItemSend                          ▼ │
├─────────────────────────────────────┴─────────────────────────────────────┤
│   Private Sub Application_ItemSend(ByVal Item As Object, Cancel As Boolean)▲│
│                                                                            ││
│   End Sub                                                                  ││
│                                                                            ││
│   Private Sub Application_NewMail()                                        ││
│                                                                            ││
│   End Sub                                                                  ││
└────────────────────────────────────────────────────────────────────────────┘
```

Figure 18-6: Event handler skeletons created via the object and procedure combo boxes

---

Macros

Macros are routines that you write to perform a task or set of tasks. They are not reactive like event handlers. You purposely execute a macro because you want Outlook to do something for you.

You cannot record keystrokes or menu commands to create a macro in Outlook, as you can in other programs. It's up to you to write the VBA code for your macro by hand.

Macros are public subprocedures with empty parameter lists that reside in a standard code module; they cannot be functions or private subprocedures. To create a standard module manually, launch the VB editor and select Insert → Module from the menu or right click the project node in the Project Explorer to get a context menu and choose Insert → Module from there. This will add a code module called Module1 (which you may rename) to your VBA project and open it for you.

You can view and manage the macros you've created by selecting Tools → Macro → Macros from the Outlook window (not the editor), or by hitting Alt+F8. This brings up the dialog in Figure 18-7.

You can run a macro, debug it or edit it in the editor, create a new macro, or delete an existing one. If you don't have a code module for your macros in your project when you create a macro from this dialog, the VBA editor will create the Module1 module for you.

To get easy access to the macros you use most often, you can assign macros to toolbar buttons. Clicking the buttons will execute the macros. To do this, from the Outlook application window, select Tools → Customize. On the Commands tab, click the Macros category. You'll see your Macros listed in the Commands list box. Drag your macro "button" to its resting place on one of your toolbars. You can now execute your macro with the click of a button.

You can run this code by placing the cursor in the procedure's body and hitting F5, the Run Sub/UserForm toolbar button, or—for this particular example—by

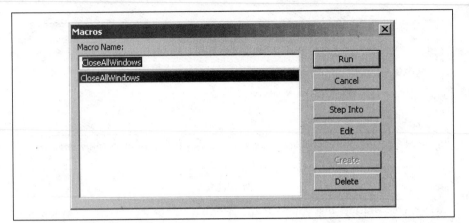

Figure 18-7: The Macros dialog

sending email to yourself. You should see a message box pop up and say "Hello!" Be sure to remove this code if you don't want Outlook greeting you whenever new mail arrives.

That's really all there is to writing code in the VBA editor. Of course, if you want to get serious about VBA customizations to Outlook, you'll want to explore debugging and other helpful features of the editor, as well as getting your hands on a more complete Outlook VBA reference, like *VB & VBA in a Nutshell.*

The Object Browser

While you can certainly use the online help (accessed by the Help menu or F1) provided in the VBA editor to explore Outlook's object model, there is an alternative. The editor has a built-in tool called the Object Browser that lets you see the Outlook VBA objects and their methods, properties, and events.

To access the object browser, select Tools → Object Browser, hit F2, or click the Object Browser button on the toolbar. The screen in Figure 18-8 will overlay the code window.

You can choose which library of objects is displayed in the browser by selecting one from the top-most combo box. Here, we've chosen just Outlook VBA objects.

You can view object properties, methods, and events in the Members pane by clicking on an object's class in the Classes pane. When you click on an entry in the Members pane, information about that entry will appear in the text area at the bottom of the browser screen. You can also bring up the help screen for a class or one of its members by hitting F1 when you have an entry in either pane highlighted.

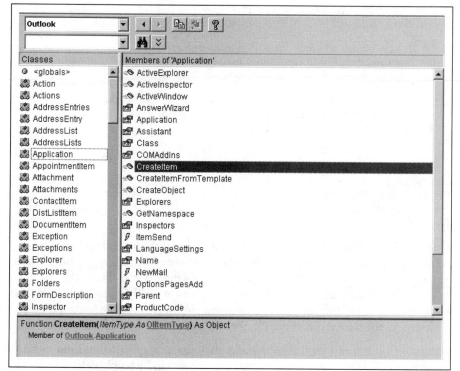

Figure 18-8: The Object Browser

Code Examples

In this section, we'll take a look at some examples that more fully illustrate some of the things you can do using VBA in Outlook.

Example 18-1 is a macro that opens all high-priority mail items in your Inbox. Notice that the macro is declared as a public subprocedure with an empty parameter list.

Example 18-1: Opening High Priority Mail Items in Your Inbox

```
Public Sub OpenHighPriorityMsgs()
    ' Declare some object variables.
    Dim mapiNamespace As NameSpace
    Dim inboxItems As Items
    Dim hiPriorityMsgs As Items

    ' Get the MAPI namespace.
    Set mapiNamespace = Application.GetNamespace("MAPI")

    ' Get all the items in the Inbox.
    Set inboxItems = _
        mapiNamespace.GetDefaultFolder(olFolderInbox).Items
```

Example 18-1: Opening High Priority Mail Items in Your Inbox (continued)

```
' Get the subset of Inbox items with high importance.
Set hiPriorityMsgs = _
        inboxItems.Restrict("[Importance] = 'High'")

' Display each high-priority mail message.
For Each msg In hiPriorityMsgs
    msg.display
Next

' Clean up our object variables.
Set hiPriorityItems = Nothing
Set inboxItems = Nothing
Set mapiNamespace = Nothing
End Sub
```

After we get the MAPI namespace, we grab all of the items in the Inbox into an Items collection (inboxItems). We then get a subset of these items (another Items collection) through the Items collection's Restrict method, which filters the collection based on given criteria. Here, we're indicating that we only want items with high importance. We use the For...Each construct to display (open in an Inspector for) each item in the filtered collection. On the way out, we clean up our object memory.

Example 18-2 is a new mail event handler that moves mail with attachments into a "quarantine" folder, whose contents you can review (and possibly delete) later. You will first need to create a folder called "quarantine" under the Inbox.

Example 18-2: The Mail Attachment Quarantine Example

```
' Quarantine items with attachments as they arrive.
Public Sub Application_NewMail()
    Dim mapiNamespace As NameSpace
    Dim fldInbox As MAPIFolder
    Dim newMail As MailItem
    Dim fldQuarantine As MAPIFolder

    ' Get a reference to the Inbox.
    Set mapiNamespace = Application.GetNamespace("MAPI")
    Set fldInbox = mapiNamespace.GetDefaultFolder(olFolderInbox)

    ' Get the last item received in the Inbox.
    Set newMail = fldInbox.Items(fldInbox.Items.Count)

    ' If the item has one or more attachments, move it
    ' to the quarantine folder.
    If newMail.Attachments.Count > 0 Then
        ' Get the quarantine folder.
        Set fldQuarantine = fldInbox.Folders("Quarantine")

        ' Move the item.
        newMail.Move fldQuarantine
```

Example 18-2: The Mail Attachment Quarantine Example (continued)

```
        ' Clean up our folder object variable.
        Set fldQuarantine = Nothing
    End If

    ' Clean up object variables.
    Set newMail = Nothing
    Set fldInbox = Nothing
    Set mapiNamespace = Nothing
End Sub
```

Again, we use the MAPI namespace to get to the Inbox folder. We get the last item that arrived in the folder (its index will be the number of items in the Inbox), and see how many attachments are in its Attachments collection. If we have one or more attachments, we fill our quarantine folder variable. Using the quarantine folder as the parameter, we call the MailItem's Move method to move the mail message. As always, we clean up any object memory we use at the end of the routine.

Example 18-3 is an event handler for the Appointments collection. This event handler will fire when you save a new appointment in the Calendar. Be sure to save the macro code, close all of Outlook, and restart the program, since this marcro is dependent on the startup of Outlook to take effect. If the new appointment is of the "Sales Meeting" category (which must be created), the handler sends email to an assistant, with a copy of the appointment attached.

Example 18-3: Event Handler for New Appointments

```
Dim WithEvents collAppointments As Items

Private Sub Application_Startup()
    Set collAppointments = _
Application.GetNamespace("MAPI").GetDefaultFolder(olFolderCalendar).Items
End Sub

Private Sub collAppointments_ItemAdd(ByVal Item As Object)
    ' See if the appointment that was just added is in
    ' the Sales Meeting category.
    If InStr(Item.Categories, "Sales Meeting") Then
        ' Declare and create a new mail message.
        Dim newMail As MailItem
        Set newMail = Application.CreateItem(olMailItem)

        ' Address the message, and give some basic info in the
        ' subject and body.
        newMail.To = "My Trusty Assistant"
        newMail.Subject = "New meeting: " & Item.Subject
        newMail.Body = "Time: " & Item.Start & vbCrLf & _
                       "Place: " & Item.Location

        ' Save off what we have so far.
```

Example 18-3: Event Handler for New Appointments (continued)

```
        newMail.Save

        ' Attach the full appointment.
        newMail.Attachments.Add Item, olByValue

        ' Send it.
        newMail.Send
    End If
End Sub

Private Sub Application_Quit()
    Set collAppointments = Nothing
End Sub
```

The first thing we need to do is declare a global variable collAppointments that can react to events. In the Application object's startup routine, we fill this object variable with the Calendar's item list (a list of appointments), using the MAPI namespace to get to the Calendar folder.

Our event handler is called collAppointments_ItemAdd. The ItemAdd handler is available for several collection objects, so its Item parameter is of the generic Object data type. Since our collection contains appointments, Item is an Appointment object as far as we're concerned.

We use the VBA Instr function to determine if the string "Sales Meeting" is in the appointment's category list (returned by querying the Categories property), since it may contain more than one category (separated by commas). If we determine that this appointment is in the sales meeting category, we declare a MailItem object variable, and ask the Application object to create a mail item for us. We fill in the mail item's To property with an assistant's address (e.g., replace "My Trusty Assistant" with a contact name of the assistant), and use the Subject and Body properties to provide some basic information about the appointment. You'll notice vbCrLf in the Body assignment. This is a VBA constant representing a carriage return and line feed combination. We use this to put the start time and location of the appointment on separate lines.

To be safe, we Save our mail item at this point. We then add the appointment to the mail item's Attachments collection, and send off the mail message. When Outlook is closed, the Application_Quit event handler is executed, and our appointments collection variable is cleared.

Part 4

Appendixes

Appendix A

Keyboard Shortcuts

With today's graphical interfaces, people tend to get fixated on using the mouse. But because many of the tasks you perform with Outlook involve keyboard entry, it's often more efficient to use a keyboard shortcut to perform a task or access a menu command. You'll be surprised at how much faster you can work by learning just a few of the more common keyboard shortcuts for the components and views you work in most frequently.

> **NOTE** *With the sheer number of keyboard shortcuts offered, you are probably going to experience a shortcut conflict between Outlook and another running program at some point in time. If this happens, note the action or dialog generated by the keys pressed, and close the offending program. If you use the Internet chat program ICQ, this product has known keyboard conflicts with Outlook that can only be resolved by closing it.*

The following tables list many of the keyboard shortcuts available in Outlook. Each table focuses on a topic area (like views, or working with Calendar); a task description is in the left column, and the associated keyboard shortcut is in the right.

Table A-1: General Program Keyboard Shortcuts

Task	Keyboard Shortcut
Cancel current operation	Esc
Display Screen Tip for selected item, dialog control, or navigation tool	Shift + F1
Expand selected group	+ (Numeric keypad)
Collapse selected group	- (Numeric keypad)
Select item	Enter
Turn on editing in a field	F2
Move from item to item	Arrow Keys
Select all	Ctrl + A
Delete item or selected text	Ctrl + D
Switch to next tab on a form	Ctrl + Tab or Ctrl + Page Down
Switch to previous tab on a form	Ctrl + Shift + Tab or Ctrl + Page Up
Display address book	Ctrl + Shift + B
Open Dialer	Ctrl + Shift + D

Table A-1: General Program Keyboard Shortcuts (continued)

Task	Keyboard Shortcut
Use Advanced Find	Ctrl + Shift + F
Flag for Follow Up	Ctrl + Shift + G
Create new Office document	Ctrl + Shift + H
Find people	Ctrl + Shift + P
Move to next item (with item open)	Ctrl + Shift + >
Move to previous item (with item open)	Ctrl + Shift + <
Switch between panes (Folder List, item view, and preview pane)	Ctrl + Shift + Tab or F6
Activate in-cell editing on selection (for those views that support it, and only when enabled)	F2

Table A-2: Keyboard Shortcuts for Creating Items

Task	Keyboard Shortcut
Create an appointment	Ctrl + Shift + A
Create a contact	Ctrl + Shift + C
Create a folder	Ctrl + Shift + E
Create a journal entry	Ctrl + Shift + J
Create a distribution list	Ctrl + Shift + L
Create a message	Ctrl + Shift + M
Create a meeting request	Ctrl + Shift + Q
Create a note	Ctrl + Shift + N
Create a task	Ctrl + Shift + K
Post to this folder	Ctrl + Shift + S
Create a task request	Ctrl + Shift + U

Table A-3: Mail Keyboard Shortcuts

Task	Keyboard Shortcut
Mark as read	Ctrl + Q
Reply	Ctrl + R
Reply to All	Ctrl + Shift + R
Forward	Ctrl + F
Switch case of selected text (MS-RFT format only)	Shift + F3
Send/Receive (check for new mail)	Ctrl + M or F5
Check names (default editor, not Word)	Ctrl + K

Table A-4: Common Menu Shortcuts

Action	Keyboard Shortcuts
Save	Ctrl + S or Shift + F12

Table A-4: Common Menu Shortcuts (continued)

Action	Keyboard Shortcuts
Save and close (Contact, Calendar, Journal, and Tasks)	Alt + S
Send (mail item)	Alt + S
Save As	F12
Go to folder	Ctrl + Y
Go to Inbox folder	Shift + Ctrl + I
Post to a folder	Ctrl + Shift + S
Print	Ctrl + P
Create a new message	Ctrl + N
Cut to the Clipboard	Ctrl + X or Shift + Delete
Copy to the Clipboard	Ctrl + C or Ctrl + Insert
Copy item	Ctrl + Shift + Y
Paste from the Clipboard	Ctrl + V or Shift + Insert
Move item	Ctrl + Shift + V
Undo	Ctrl + Z or Alt + Backspace
Delete	Ctrl + D
Select all	Ctrl + A
Display context menu	Shift + F10
Display Outlook control menu when menu bar is active	Spacebar
Display window control menu	Alt + Spacebar
Select next command on menu	Down Arrow
Select previous Command on menu	Up Arrow
Select menu to the left	Left Arrow
Select menu to the right	Right Arrow
Select first command on menu	Home
Select last command on menu	End
Activate menu bar	F10
Move between toolbars	Shift + Ctrl + Tab
Advanced Find	Ctrl + Shift + F or F3
Find text (from open item)	F4
Find next	Shift + F4
Refresh	F5
Check spelling (open message form)	F7
Display Favorites menu	Alt + O
Close print preview	Alt + C
Accept (Calendar or Task request)	Alt + C
Decline (Calendar or Task request)	Alt + D

Table A-4: Common Menu Shortcuts (continued)

Action	Keyboard Shortcuts
Close menu and submenu (if open)	Alt
Close menu and submenu	Esc

Table A-5: Toolbar Shortcuts

Action	Keyboard Shortcut
Activate menu bar	F10
Select next toolbar	Ctrl + Tab
Select previous toolbar	Ctrl + Shift + Tab
Select next button or menu	Tab
Select previous button or menu	Shift + Tab
Open selected menu	Enter
Perform action of selected button	Enter
Enter text in selected text box	Enter
Enter text in Quick Find Box	F11
Select option from drop-down list or menu	Up Arrow or Down Arrow, Enter

Table A-6: Dialog Box Shortcuts

Task	Keyboard Shortcut
Move to next option or option group	Tab
Move to previous option or option group	Shift + Tab
Move to next tab	Ctrl + Tab
Move to previous tab	Ctrl + Shift + Tab
Move to next item in drop-down list	Down Arrow
Move to previous item in drop-down list	Up Arrow
Move to first item in drop-down list	Home
Move to last item in drop-down list	End
Perform action assigned to button	Spacebar
Select or clear check box	Spacebar
Open a drop-down list	Alt + Down Arrow
Close a drop-down list	Alt + Up Arrow or Esc

Table A-7: Formatting Shortcuts

Action	Keyboard Shortcut
Make bold	Ctrl + B
Italicize	Ctrl + I
Underline	Ctrl + U
Add bullets	Ctrl + Shift + L
Left align	Ctrl + L
Center	Ctrl + E

Table A-7: Formatting Shortcuts (continued)

Action	Keyboard Shortcut
Increase indent	Ctrl + T
Decrease indent	Ctrl + Shift + T
Increase font size	Ctrl +]
Decrease font size	Ctrl + [
Clear formatting	Ctrl + Shift + Z or Ctrl + Spacebar

Table A-8: General Text Selection Shortcuts

Action	Keyboard Shortcut
Move to beginning of text box	Home
Move to end of text box	End
Move one character to left	Left Arrow
Move one character to right	Right Arrow
Select from insertion point to beginning	Shift + Home
Select from insertion point to end	Shift + End
Select or unselect one character to left	Shift + Left Arrow
Select or unselect one character to right	Shift + Right Arrow
Select or unselect one word to left	Ctrl + Shift + Left Arrow
Select or unselect one word to right	Ctrl + Shift + Right Arrow

Table A-9: Hyperlink Shortcuts

Action	Keyboard Shortcut
Edit a URL within a message	Ctrl + left mouse button
Locate Link Browser	Shift + left mouse button (specify the browser program that will open URLs)
Insert a hyperlink	Ctrl + K (Word as email editor)

Table A-10: Table Shortcuts

Action	Keyboard Shortcut
Open item	Enter
Go to next item	Down Arrow
Go to previous item	Up Arrow
Select noncontiguous items	Ctrl + Down Arrow or Up Arrow, then Spacebar to select
Go to first item	Home
Go to last item	End
Go to item at bottom of screen	Page Down
Go to item at top of screen	Page Up
Extend item selection by one	Shift + Up Arrow
Reduce item selection by one	Shift + Down Arrow

Table A-10: Table Shortcuts (continued)

Action	Keyboard Shortcut
Select all items	Ctrl + A

Table A-11: Shortcuts for Groups in a Table

Action	Keyboard Shortcut
Expand group	Enter or Right Arrow
Collapse group	Enter or Left Arrow
Select previous group	Up Arrow
Select next group	Down Arrow
Select first group	Home
Select last group	End
Select first item in expanded group	Right Arrow

Table A-12: Card View Shortcuts

Action	Keyboard Shortcut
Go to next card	Down Arrow
Go to previous card	Up Arrow
Go to first card in folder	Home
Go to last card in folder	End
Go to first card on current page	Page Up
Go to first card on next page	Page Down
Go to closest card in next column	Right Arrow
Go to closest card in previous column	Left Arrow
Select or unselect active card	Ctrl + Spacebar
Extend selection to next card	Ctrl + Shift + Down Arrow
Extend selection to next card and unselect previous card	Shift + Down Arrow
Extend selection to previous card and unselect subsequent cards	Shift + Up Arrow
Extend selection to last card	Shift + End
Extend selection to first card	Shift + Home
Extend selection to last card on previous page	Shift + Page Up
Extend selection to first card on next page	Shift + Page Down
Extend selection to previous card	Ctrl + Shift + Up Arrow

Table A-13: General Calendar Shortcuts

Action	Keyboard Shortcut
Move between Calendar, TaskPad, and Folder List	Ctrl + Tab or F6
Select next appointment	Tab

Table A-13: General Calendar Shortcuts (continued)

Action	Keyboard Shortcut
Select previous appointment	Shift + Tab
Go to next day	Right Arrow
Go to previous day	Left Arrow
Move from item to item	Tab
View 1–10 days (0 to 10 days)	Alt + $<n>$
Switch to weeks	Alt + -
Switch to months	Alt + =
Move selected appointment to next day	Alt + Right Arrow
Move selected appointment to previous day	Alt + Left Arrow
Go to same day in next week in Day and Work Week views	Alt + Down Arrow
Go to same day in previous week in Day and Work Week Views	Alt + Up Arrow
Move selected item to same day in next week (Month view)	Alt + Down Arrow
Move selected item to same day in previous week (Month view)	Alt + Up Arrow

Table A-14: Date Navigator Shortcuts

Action	Keyboard Shortcut
Go to first day of current week	Alt + Home
Go to last day of current week	Alt + End
Go to same day in previous week	Alt + Up Arrow
Go to same day in next week	Alt + Down Arrow
Go to first day of current month	Alt + Page Up
Go to last day of current month	Alt + Page Down

Table A-15: Calendar Day View Shortcuts

Action	Keyboard Shortcut
Select beginning of work day	Home
Select end of work day	End
Select previous block of time	Up Arrow
Select next block of time	Down Arrow
Select block of time at top of screen	Page Up
Select block of time at bottom of screen	Page Down
Extend selected time	Shift + Up Arrow
Reduce selected time	Shift + Down Arrow
Move selected appointment back	Alt + Up Arrow
Move selected appointment forward	Alt + Down Arrow

Table A-15: Calendar Day View Shortcuts (continued)

Action	Keyboard Shortcut
Move start of selected appointment	Alt + Shift + Up Arrow
Move end of selected appointment	Alt + Shift + Down Arrow

Table A-16: Timeline Shortcuts with Item Selected

Action	Keyboard Shortcut
Open selected item	Enter
Open previous item	Left Arrow
Open next item	Right Arrow
Select adjacent previous items	Shift + Left Arrow
Select adjacent subsequent items	Shift + Right Arrow
Select non-adjacent previous items	Ctrl + Left Arrow + Spacebar
Select non-adjacent subsequent items	Ctrl + Right Arrow + Spacebar
Display items one screen above	Page Up
Display items one screen below	Page Down
Select first item	Home
Select last item	End
Display first item without selection	Ctrl + Home
Display last item without selection	Ctrl + End

Table A-17: Timeline Shortcuts with Group Selected

Action	Keyboard Shortcut
Expand group	Enter or Right Arrow
Collapse group	Enter or Left Arrow
Select previous group	Up Arrow
Select next group	Down Arrow
Select first group	Home
Select last group	End
Select first onscreen item in expanded group	Right Arrow
Move back one increment of time	Left Arrow
Move forward one increment of time	Right Arrow
Switch from upper to lower time scale	Tab
Switch from lower to upper time scale	Shift + Tab
Select first onscreen item or first group (with lower time scale selected)	Tab

Table A-18: Print Preview Shortcuts

Action	Keyboard Shortcut
Open print preview	Ctrl + F2
Print from print preview	Alt + P

Table A-18: Print Preview Shortcuts (continued)

Action	Keyboard Shortcut
Print preview page setup	Alt + S, then Alt + U
Zoom	Alt + Z
Display next page	Page Down
Display previous page	Page Up
Display first page	Ctrl + Up Arrow or Home
Display last page	Ctrl + Down Arrow or End

Table A-19: Help Shortcuts

Action	Keyboard Shortcut
Get Help from Office Assistant	F1
Activate the Office Assistant balloon	Alt + F6
Select Help Topic <n>	Alt + <n>
See more Help topics	Alt + Down Arrow
See previous Help topics	Alt + Up Arrow
Close Office Assistant message	Esc
Context sensitive help	Shift + F1
Display next tip (when screen tips activated)	Alt + N
Display previous tip	Alt + B
Close tips	Esc

Table A-20: VBA Shortcuts

Action	Keyboard Shortcut
Open Macro Selector	Alt + F8
Open VBA Development Environment	Alt + F11

Appendix B

Registry Keys

Outlook stores many of its program settings in the Windows Registry. For the average user, the structure and data contained here is of no real interest—it's enough that the program simply works, and remembers the contact you last looked up or the position of a dialog. There are some administrative tasks, however, that can only be accomplished by working directly with the Registry. The categories stored in your personal Master Category List, for example, are saved in the Registry, and if you want to back them up or share them, this is where you'll have to come to do it (see Chapter 3, *Program Insights*, for the steps involved).

All of the keys listed in Table B-1 are found under the root entry: HKEY_CURRENT_USER\Software\Microsoft\. This list is not intended to be exhaustive. Registry keys are added according to the program components, forms, and options installed, so the entries present on any given system will likely differ from those listed.

> ### WARNING
>
> *Always make a backup copy of the Registry before making any changes here, and know how to restore this backup should the need arise. Windows depends on information stored here, and if you inadvertently delete a critical key, you could render your system unusable.*

Table B-1: Outlook's Registry Keys

Key	Description
Office\9.0\Outlook	General Outlook key
Office\9.0\Outlook\Appointment	Appointment/Calendar settings
Office\9.0\Outlook\Categories	Master Category List
Office\9.0\Outlook\Contact	Contact settings
Office\9.0\Outlook\Contact\QuickFindMRU	Recent entries from Quick Find contacts list
Office\9.0\Outlook\CustomizableAlerts	Web-based help options
Office\9.0\Outlook\DistList	Distribution List form state
Office\9.0\Outlook\Journal	Journal settings and log
Office\9.0\Outlook\Journal Entry	Journal entry form state
Office\9.0\Outlook\Message	Message entry form state

Table B-1: Outlook's Registry Keys (continued)

Key	Description
Office\9.0\Outlook\NetFolder	Net Folders log and settings
Office\9.0\Outlook\Note	Default Note properties
Office\9.0\Outlook\Office Explorer	Set up roaming or multiple users
Office\9.0\Outlook\Office Finder	Find a contact MRU list
Office\9.0\Outlook\OLFax	WinFax SE settings
Office\9.0\Outlook\OLFax\7.0	See sub key
Office\9.0\Outlook\OLFax\7.0\General	Configuration setting for Symantec Fax
Office\9.0\Outlook\Options\Calendar	First day of the week, work week, etc.
Office\9.0\Outlook\Options\General	Default editor and attachment settings
Office\9.0\Outlook\Options\Mail	Mail option settings
Office\9.0\Outlook\Options\MSHTML	International code pages for mail
Office\9.0\Outlook\Options\NewFolder	New Folder prompt
Office\9.0\Outlook\Options\Note	Default Note font and size
Office\9.0\Outlook\Options\Tasks	Unit settings (per day, per week)
Office\9.0\Outlook\Options\Spelling	Location of spelling dictionary, dialog position, and exceptions
Office\9.0\Outlook\OST	Offline folder settings
Office\9.0\Outlook\Post	Post form settings
Office\9.0\Outlook\Preferences	Other miscellaneous mail settings
Office\9.0\Outlook\Printing	Print settings (paper size, width, length)
Office\9.0\Outlook\Printing\PrintTypesDefault	Customize print styles
Office\9.0\Outlook\Security	Security options
Office\9.0\Outlook\Setup	Setup configurations and settings
Office\9.0\Outlook\Signatures	Location of Digital Signatures
Office\9.0\Outlook\Task	Task entry form state
Office\9.0\Outlook\Today	Outlook Today settings
Office\9.0\Outlook\Today\Folders	Folders included in view
Office\9.0\Outlook\OMI Account	Mail Account Information (IMO)
Office\9.0\Outlook\WAB	Location of the Windows Address Book
Office\Outlook\OMI Account Manager	Top level key: Default accounts Lower keys: Individual account configurations
Office\Common\Assistant	Office Assistant position and state
Shared Tools\Outlook\Journaling	Subkeys for applications and items to be journaled
WAB\	Account information for services such as directory lookups (LDAP)
WAB\Server Properties	Location and state of server-based address books (e.g., Exchange)

Table B-1: Outlook's Registry Keys (continued)

Key	Description
WAB\WAB Sort State	Contact display options
WAB\WAB4	Address Book subkeys
Windows Messaging Subsystem\Profiles	Personal Folders information

Appendix C

Command-Line Switches

The command-line switches listed in Table C-1 and Table C-2 start Outlook with the entry form noted or execute the task detailed in the Purpose column. Use these commands from the Start Menu → Run dialog or from a desktop shortcut using the following format:

```
outlook.exe /switch
```

Or, if Windows requires a fully qualified path, type:

```
"C:\Program Files\Microsoft Office\Office\Outlook.exe" /switch
```

If this path contains long folder names (such as "Program Files" or "Microsoft Office"), the complete path must be contained within quotes as shown in our example. The supplied switch is *not* contained within these quotes.

Table C-1: Item Entry Form Command-Line Switches

Command-Line Switch	Purpose
/c ipm.activity	Opens a Journal entry form
/c ipm.appointment	Opens an Appointment entry form
/c ipm.contact	Opens a Contact entry form
/c ipm.distlist	Creates a new Distribution List
/c ipm.note	Opens a New Message form
/c ipm.post	Opens a Post or Discussion form
/c ipm.stickynote	Opens a Note form
/c ipm.task	Opens a Task entry form
/c <messageclass>	Generic command line for opening Outlook with a specific class or type of item

Table C-2: Troubleshooting or Maintenance Command-Line Switches

Command-Line Switch	Purpose
/cleanprofile	Removes and recreate Outlook's default Registry keys
/cleanpst	Starts Outlook with a clean (empty) PST (IMO only)
/safe	Starts Outlook without any add-ins, preview pane, or toolbar customization

Table C-2: Troubleshooting or Maintenance Command-Line Switches (continued)

Command-Line Switch	Purpose
/profiles	Starts Outlook with a "Choose Profile" dialog regardless of options set
/profile <profilename>	Starts Outlook with a specified profile
/s <filename>	Loads a specified shortcuts file (*.fav*)
/p <msgfilename>	Prints a specified message
/resetfolders	Restores missing or damaged system folders to the default delivery location
/resetoutlookbar	Rebuilds the Outlook Bar (to default configuration)
/cleanviews	Restores all views to default
/checkclient	Runs the prompt to make Outlook the default client for email, news, and contacts
/cleanfreebusy	Cleans and regenerates FreeBusy information
/cleanreminders	Cleans and regenerates all reminders

Appendix D

Tip Reference

Tip Reference

Index

Journal entries
    accessing with context menus, 436
    forwarded Journal items, 431
    View Attachments command, 438
  notes field (Contacts form), adding
      to, 339
  notes, forwarding as, 407
  Outlook items (Outlook editor), 217
  pictures, inserting into message
      body, 219–220
  quarantining mail with, 588
  searching for items with/without, 118
  signatures, inserting or changing, 220
  vCards, 218, 359
  Word, lacking support for, 169
attendees (meetings)
  adding or removing, 308, 311
  availability of, 303
  selecting, 308
  status list, 306
  types, 299
attributes, 59, 572
  (see also properties)
authentication with SMTP servers, 245
AutoArchive feature, 459–462
  settings (Journal), 421
AutoArrange option (Notes, Icon
    view), 410
automatic capitalization
  contacts names and titles, 333
  organizational name fields (Contacts
    form), 343
Automatic Name Checking, 227
automatic spell checking, on/off toggle, 194
automatic telephone dialing from
    Outlook, 337
automatic tracking (Journal), 419–423
  AutoArchive option, 421
  automatic Journal entry creation,
    using, 422
  delays in manual or automatic timed
    saves, causing, 423
  Office documents, linking to
    Journal, 429
  selecting items for, 420
AutoPreview, 273
  Calendar, Day/Week/Month and table
    views, 315
  enabling for table, 91
  mail messages, 265
  Note views, toggling to display, 408

B

background colors (see colors)
background images
  choosing for stationery, 186
  messages, changing, 210
backing up Outlook, 463–468
  helpful hints, 465
backup for email via ISP Server, 29
Bcc's (Blind Carbon Copies), options for
    sending, 169
Begin a Group, inserting divider above
    selected item, 138
Best Fit command, 369, 374
binary attachments, 68
  forwarded Journal items, 432
BinHex encoding, 198
birthdays, 320
  Birthday field (Contacts form), 343
bit and binary formats, selecting for message
    encoding, 199
Booklet print styles, 99
bookmarked section of document,
    locating, 139
Boolean searches, 121
boxes (titles), grouping by, 373
browsing for material to assign
    hyperlink, 139
Business address type, 336
Button Editor, 137
button images, customizing and
    resetting, 136
By Category view
  Calendar, 322
  Contacts, 364
  groups, working with, 365
  Journal entries, 434
  Notes, 407, 412
  Tasks, 397
By Color view (Notes), 407, 413
By Company view, 365
By Contact view (Journal), 434
By Conversation Topic view (Mail), 267
By Follow-up Flag view, 366
  Mail messages, 265
By Location view (Contacts), 365
By Person Responsible view (Tasks), 398
By Sender view (Mail), 268
By Type view (Journal), 434
ByRef and ByVal keywords, 570

historical name match, 203
holidays
    adding to Calendar, 281
    Outlook, automatically adding, 320
Home address type, 336
Home Page folder, 104
Home Page views, 102–105
HotSync (Palm IIIx), 531
    configuring options, 532
hours for workdays, defining, 279
HTML
    mail editor, starting in (no
        stationery), 233
    message format
        circumstances for using, 208
        pictures, inserting into message
            body, 219–220
        support by Outlook, 170
        switching to/from Plain Text or MS-
            RTF, 209
    messages, previewing, 273
    stationery as, 188
    task requests, using for, 386
HTML page, associating with
    folder, 102–105
HTML templates (stationary), 17
HTMLEditor property, 581
http:// (Hypertext Transfer Protocol
    (HTTP)), 213
https:// (Hypertext Transfer Protocol
    (Secure)), 213
hyperlinks, 212–215
    assigning to menus, toolbars, or
        documents, 138
    Customize dialog commands, inability to
        activate, 154
    keyboard shortcuts, 597
    messages, inserting into, 214
    protocols supported, 213

I

iCalendar format, 15
    forwarding items in, 311
    meeting requests, 279, 303
Icon views, 79
    custom, 489
    Format Icon View dialog, 409
    Notes, 407, 409
        placement options, 410

icons
    displaying as Large or Small on Outlook
        Bar, 156
    Journal entry types, creating new, 439
    for menu items, selecting or
        modifying, 140
    Simple List view (tasks), 395
    Tasks, 400
IFB (see Internet Free/Busy)
If...Then...Else statements, 569
images
    buttons, customizing and resetting, 136
    mail message backgrounds, 210
    stationery backgrounds, 186
IMAP4 (Internet Message Access Protocol
    Version 4), 13
IMO (see Internet Mail Only)
Import a File dialog, 455
Import and Export Wizard, 444
    Import Wizard, 448
    selecting a file to export, 452
Importance and Sensitivity settings (Mail
    messages), 206
importance, searching for items by, 118
Importer and Exporters, 17
importing data into Outlook, 443–449
    Access database, 448, 455
    different email client configurations and
        data, 18
    field mappings, viewing and
        changing, 444–446
    options (Outlook), 447
importing Master Category List, 112
Inbox folder
    dropping note on icon, 413
    high priority mail items, automatically
        opening, 587
    item, context menu for, 143
    MailItems, 579
    retrieving with GetDefaultFolder method
        (pace), 579
Inbox Properties dialog, 62
Inbox Repair Tool, 472–475
in-cell editing
    activating for flags, 265
    Journal fields in table views, 433
incoming mail
    delivery locations, configuring for
        CW, 37
    profile, configuring for delivery, 31

Items, 58
    adding to Outlook Bar, 162
    creating another from Notes, 413–415
    creating, keyboard shortcuts, 594
    displaying individual in window, 580
    Items collection, 588
    Items property, 579
    linking to contacts, 355
    properties, 59
    Properties dialog, 64
    size, searching by, 119
    storing in root of PST, problems with, 60
iterations
    defining range of, 574
    through collections, 573

J

Journal, 419–439
    Actions menu, 423–432
        Forward, 431
        New Journal Entry, 424–431
    Activities tab as outgrowth of, 346
    context menus, use of, 436–439
    entry, creating new for contact, 353
    entry types, creating new, 439
    file, linking to contact, 355
    notes, dropping on icon, 415
    options, 419–423
        Also record files from, 421
        AutoArchive, 421
        automatic entry creation, situations for
            use, 422
        Automatic tracking for these
            contacts, 421
        Automatically record these items, 420
        Double-clicking a Journal entry, 421
    View menu, 432–439
        By Category view, 434
        By Contact view, 434
        By Type view, 434
        Entry List view, 435
        Last Seven Days view, 436
        Phone Calls view, 436
Junk E-mail command, 236
    Add to Adult Content Senders List, 239
junk email, creating Mail rule for
        handling, 122

K

keyboard shortcuts, 593–601
    Calendar, 5
    comprehensive list, accessing in online
        help, 167
    Contacts, 6
    Journal, 10
    Mail, 4
    Notes, 9
    Tasks, 7
keys, encryption, 505
keys (registry) (see registry keys)
keywords
    And or Or, testing multiple conditions
        with, 569
    ByVal and ByRef, 570
    Function and Sub (subprocedure)
        keywords, 570
    New, creating object with, 572
    Public, 570
    Public and Private, 572
    Set, 574
    VBA Editor, formatting in, 583

L

labels, changing for column titles in
        views, 375
languages
    character sets, changing for messages, 211
    options, mail editors, 200
Large icons, displaying on Outlook
        Bar, 156
Large Icons view (Notes), 407, 409
large tables, saving items in, 62
Last Seven Days view
    Journal entries, 436
    Mail messages, 267
    Notes, 407
LDAP (Lightweight Directory Access
        Protocol), 13, 228
    Microsoft Directory, adding in CW
        Outlook, 36
left-click drag-and-drop with Notes, 413
letter, sending new to contact, 350
line length, specifying in messages, 199
Link command, 354
Link File command, 355
Link Items command, 355

About the Authors

Tom Syroid lives in Saskatoon, Canada, and spends his days working as a systems consultant and freelance writer. He specializes in small business networking, NT Server administration, and training users how to avoid crashing Microsoft Office. Current topics of focus include knowledge management, collaboration platforms, and exploring the nuances of IBM's AIX operating system. In those rare moments when Tom's not writing something, you'll find him chasing his 10-month old son around the house, doing crafts with his daughter, or enjoying a quiet summer evening on the back porch with his wife Leah. You can contact Tom via email at *tom@syroidmanor.com* or through his web site: *www.syroidmanor.com*.

Bo Leuf has been an independent consultant in the computing sector for more than 20 years, responsible for several major software development and localization projects. He is currently a freelance consultant dealing extensively with software documentation, translation, and design-team training issues.

Colophon

Our look is the result of reader comments, our own experimentation, and feedback from distribution channels. Distinctive covers complement our distinctive approach to technical topics, breathing personality and life into potentially dry subjects.

The animal on the cover of *Outlook 2000 in a Nutshell* is a herring gull, whose common name is the seagull. An adult herring gull is a large bird with a white underside, a gray topside, black-tipped wings with white spots, pink legs, and a yellow beak. Adults reach a size of approximately twenty inches long, with a wing-span of up to sixty inches. Young herring gulls are a brown-gray color with black bills. They mature in color and size at around four years of age.

These birds live along the water in North America, primarily in Alaska and Canada and down the Atlantic coast. They also live in the northern part of the Pacific Ocean off the coast of Japan, as well as in several countries in western Europe.

They nest in large groups, have a typical loud gull call, are bold, and are excellent scavengers. They hunt for fish by diving into the water, though not totally submerging themselves. They also take young chicks and eggs from unguarded bird nests. Many can be found in or around garbage dumps, beaches, or parking lots, foraging for food. Though sometimes considered a pest, herring gulls help keep such places free of waste, so they are a protected species in many areas.

Colleen Gorman was the production editor and proofreader, and Clairemarie Fisher O'Leary was the copyeditor for *Outlook 2000 in a Nutshell*. Nicole Arigo and Jeff Holcomb provided quality control. Emily Quill and Ann Schirmer provided production support. Ellen Troutman-Zaig wrote the index.

Hanna Dyer designed the cover of this book, based on a series design by Edie Freedman. The cover image is a 19th-century engraving from the Dover Pictorial Archive. Emma Colby produced the cover layout with QuarkXPress 3.32 using Adobe's ITC Garamond font.

Alicia Cech designed the interior layout. Mike Sierra implemented the design in FrameMaker 5.5.6. The text and heading fonts are ITC Garamond Light and Garamond Book. The illustrations that appear in the book were produced by Robert Romano and Rhon Porter using Macromedia FreeHand 8 and Adobe Photoshop 5. This colophon was written by Nicole Arigo.

Whenever possible, our books use RepKover™, a durable and flexible lay-flat binding. If the page count exceeds RepKover's limit, perfect binding is used.

Eliminating Annoyances

Windows 98 Annoyances

By David A. Karp
1st Edition October 1998
464 pages, Includes CD-ROM
ISBN 1-56592-417-7

Based on the author's popular
Windows Annoyances Web site
(http://www.annoyances.org), this
book provides an authoritative collection
of techniques for customizing Windows
98. It allows you to quickly identify a
particular annoyance and immediately offers one or more
solutions, making it the definitive resource for customizing
Windows 98. Includes a CD with a trial version of *O'Reilly
Utilities: Quick Solutions for Windows 98 Annoyances.*

Windows Annoyances

By David A. Karp
1st Edition June 1997
300 pages, ISBN 1-56592-266-2

A comprehensive, detailed resource
for all intermediate to advanced users
of Windows 95 and NT version 4.0.
This book shows step-by-step how
to customize the Win95/NT operating
systems through an extensive collection
of tips, tricks, and workarounds. Covers
Registry, Plug and Play, networking, security, multiple-user
settings, and third-party software.

Outlook Annoyances

By Woody Leonhard,
Lee Hudspeth & T. J. Lee
1st Edition June 1998
400 pages, ISBN 1-56592-384-7

Like the other Microsoft Office-related
titles in the Annoyances series, this
book points out and conquers the
annoying features of Microsoft Outlook,
the personal information management
software included with Office. It is the
definitive guide for those who want to take full advantage
of Outlook and transform it into the useful tool that it was
intended to be.

Excel 97 Annoyances

By Woody Leonhard,
Lee Hudspeth & T.J. Lee
1st Edition September 1997
336 pages, ISBN 1-56592-309-X

This book uncovers Excel 97's
hard-to-find features and tells how
to eliminate the annoyances of data
analysis. It shows how to easily retrieve
data from the Web, details step-by-step
construction of a perfect toolbar,
includes tips for working around the most annoying gotchas
of auditing, and shows how to use VBA to control Excel in
powerful ways.

Office 97 Annoyances

By Woody Leonhard,
Lee Hudspeth & T.J. Lee
1st Edition October 1997
396 pages, ISBN 1-56592-310-3

Despite marked improvements,
much in Office 97 remains annoying.
This book illustrates step-by-step how
to get control over the chaotic settings
of Office 97 and shows how to turn the
vast array of applications into a simplified
list of customized tools ready to execute the task at hand. Also
uncovers many hidden gems tucked away on the Office 97 CD.

How to stay in touch with O'Reilly

1. Visit Our Award-Winning Site

http://www.oreilly.com/

★ "Top 100 Sites on the Web" —*PC Magazine*
★ "Top 5% Web sites" —*Point Communications*
★ "3-Star site" —*The McKinley Group*

Our web site contains a library of comprehensive product information (including book excerpts and tables of contents), downloadable software, background articles, interviews with technology leaders, links to relevant sites, book cover art, and more. File us in your Bookmarks or Hotlist!

2. Join Our Email Mailing Lists

New Product Releases

To receive automatic email with brief descriptions of all new O'Reilly products as they are released, send email to:
listproc@online.oreilly.com
Put the following information in the first line of your message (*not* in the Subject field):
subscribe oreilly-news

O'Reilly Events

If you'd also like us to send information about trade show events, special promotions, and other O'Reilly events, send email to:
listproc@online.oreilly.com
Put the following information in the first line of your message (*not* in the Subject field):
subscribe oreilly-events

3. Get Examples from Our Books via FTP

There are two ways to access an archive of example files from our books:

Regular FTP

* ftp to:
  ftp.oreilly.com
  (login: anonymous
  password: your email address)
* Point your web browser to:
  ftp://ftp.oreilly.com/

FTPMAIL

* Send an email message to:
  ftpmail@online.oreilly.com
  (Write "help" in the message body)

4. Contact Us via Email

order@oreilly.com
To place a book or software order online. Good for North American and international customers.

subscriptions@oreilly.com
To place an order for any of our newsletters or periodicals.

books@oreilly.com
General questions about any of our books.

software@oreilly.com
For general questions and product information about our software. Check out O'Reilly Software Online at **http://software.oreilly.com/** for software and technical support information. Registered O'Reilly software users send your questions to:
website-support@oreilly.com

cs@oreilly.com
For answers to problems regarding your order or our products.

booktech@oreilly.com
For book content technical questions or corrections.

proposals@oreilly.com
To submit new book or software proposals to our editors and product managers.

international@oreilly.com
For information about our international distributors or translation queries. For a list of our distributors outside of North America check out:
http://www.oreilly.com/www/order/country.html

5. Work with Us

Check out our website for current employment opportunites:
www.jobs@oreilly.com
Click on "Work with Us"

O'Reilly & Associates, Inc.
101 Morris Street, Sebastopol, CA 95472 USA
TEL   707-829-0515 or 800-998-9938
           (6am to 5pm PST)
FAX   707-829-0104

O'REILLY®

International Distributors

UK, EUROPE, MIDDLE EAST AND AFRICA (EXCEPT FRANCE, GERMANY, AUSTRIA, SWITZERLAND, LUXEMBOURG, LIECHTENSTEIN, AND EASTERN EUROPE)

INQUIRIES
O'Reilly UK Limited
4 Castle Street
Farnham
Surrey, GU9 7HS
United Kingdom
Telephone: 44-1252-711776
Fax: 44-1252-734211
Email: information@oreilly.co.uk

ORDERS
Wiley Distribution Services Ltd.
1 Oldlands Way
Bognor Regis
West Sussex PO22 9SA
United Kingdom
Telephone: 44-1243-779777
Fax: 44-1243-820250
Email: cs-books@wiley.co.uk

FRANCE

INQUIRIES
Éditions O'Reilly
18 rue Séguier
75006 Paris, France
Tel: 33-1-40-51-52-30
Fax: 33-1-40-51-52-31
Email: france@editions-oreilly.fr

ORDERS
GEODIF
61, Bd Saint-Germain
75240 Paris Cedex 05, France
Tel: 33-1-44-41-46-16 (French books)
Tel: 33-1-44-41-11-87 (English books)
Fax: 33-1-44-41-11-44
Email: distribution@eyrolles.com

GERMANY, SWITZERLAND, AUSTRIA, EASTERN EUROPE, LUXEMBOURG, AND LIECHTENSTEIN

INQUIRIES & ORDERS
O'Reilly Verlag
Balthasarstr. 81
D-50670 Köln
Germany
Telephone: 49-221-973160-91
Fax: 49-221-973160-8
Email: anfragen@oreilly.de (inquiries)
Email: order@oreilly.de (orders)

CANADA (FRENCH LANGUAGE BOOKS)

Les Éditions Flammarion ltée
375, Avenue Laurier Ouest
Montréal (Québec) H2V 2K3
Tel: 00-1-514-277-8807
Fax: 00-1-514-278-2085
Email: info@flammarion.qc.ca

HONG KONG

City Discount Subscription Service, Ltd.
Unit D, 3rd Floor, Yan's Tower
27 Wong Chuk Hang Road
Aberdeen, Hong Kong
Tel: 852-2580-3539
Fax: 852-2580-6463
Email: citydis@ppn.com.hk

KOREA

Hanbit Media, Inc.
Chungmu Bldg. 201
Yonnam-dong 568-33
Mapo-gu
Seoul, Korea
Tel: 822-325-0397
Fax: 822-325-9697
Email: hant93@chollian.dacom.co.kr

PHILIPPINES

Global Publishing
G/F Benavides Garden
1186 Benavides St.
Manila, Philippines
Tel: 632-254-8949/637-252-2582
Fax: 632-734-5060/632-252-2733
Email: globalp@pacific.net.ph

TAIWAN

O'Reilly Taiwan
No. 3, Lane 131
Hang-Chow South Road
Section 1, Taipei, Taiwan
Tel: 886-2-23968990
Fax: 886-2-23968916
Email: taiwan@oreilly.com

CHINA

O'Reilly Beijing
Room 2410
160, FuXingMenNeiDaJie
XiCheng District
Beijing
China PR 100031
Tel: 86-10-66412305
Fax: 86-10-86631007
Email: beijing@oreilly.com

INDIA

Computer Bookshop (India) Pvt. Ltd.
190 Dr. D.N. Road, Fort
Bombay 400 001 India
Tel: 91-22-207-0989
Fax: 91-22-262-3551
Email: cbsbom@giasbm01.vsnl.net.in

JAPAN

O'Reilly Japan, Inc.
Yotsuya Y's Building
7 Banch 6, Honshio-cho
Shinjuku-ku
Tokyo 160-0003 Japan
Tel: 81-3-3356-5227
Fax: 81-3-3356-5261
Email: japan@oreilly.com

ALL OTHER ASIAN COUNTRIES

O'Reilly & Associates, Inc.
101 Morris Street
Sebastopol, CA 95472 USA
Tel: 707-829-0515
Fax: 707-829-0104
Email: order@oreilly.com

AUSTRALIA

Woodslane Pty., Ltd.
7/5 Vuko Place
Warriewood NSW 2102
Australia
Tel: 61-2-9970-5111
Fax: 61-2-9970-5002
Email: info@woodslane.com.au

NEW ZEALAND

Woodslane New Zealand, Ltd.
21 Cooks Street (P.O. Box 575)
Waganui, New Zealand
Tel: 64-6-347-6543
Fax: 64-6-345-4840
Email: info@woodslane.com.au

LATIN AMERICA

McGraw-Hill Interamericana
Editores, S.A. de C.V.
Cedro No. 512
Col. Atlampa
06450, Mexico, D.F.
Tel: 52-5-547-6777
Fax: 52-5-547-3336
Email: mcgraw-hill@infosel.net.mx

O'REILLY®

O'REILLY™

O'Reilly & Associates, Inc.
101 Morris Street
Sebastopol, CA 95472-9902
1-800-998-9938

Visit us online at:
http://www.ora.com/
orders@ora.com

O'REILLY WOULD LIKE TO HEAR FROM YOU

Which book did this card come from?

_____

Where did you buy this book?
❏ Bookstore   ❏ Computer Store
❏ Direct from O'Reilly ❏ Class/seminar
❏ Bundled with hardware/software
❏ Other _____

What operating system do you use?
❏ UNIX   ❏ Macintosh
❏ Windows NT   ❏ PC(Windows/DOS)
❏ Other _____

What is your job description?
❏ System Administrator   ❏ Programmer
❏ Network Administrator   ❏ Educator/Teacher
❏ Web Developer
❏ Other _____

❏ Please send me O'Reilly's catalog, containing
   a complete listing of O'Reilly books and
   software.

Name _____   Company/Organization _____

Address _____

City _____   State _____   Zip/Postal Code _____   Country _____

Telephone _____   Internet or other email address (specify network) _____

Nineteenth century wood engraving
of a bear from the O'Reilly &
Associates Nutshell Handbook®
Using & Managing UUCP.

POST CARD

BUSINESS REPLY MAIL

FIRST CLASS MAIL   PERMIT NO. 80   SEBASTOPOL, CA

Postage will be paid by addressee

O'Reilly & Associates, Inc.
101 Morris Street
Sebastopol, CA 95472-9902